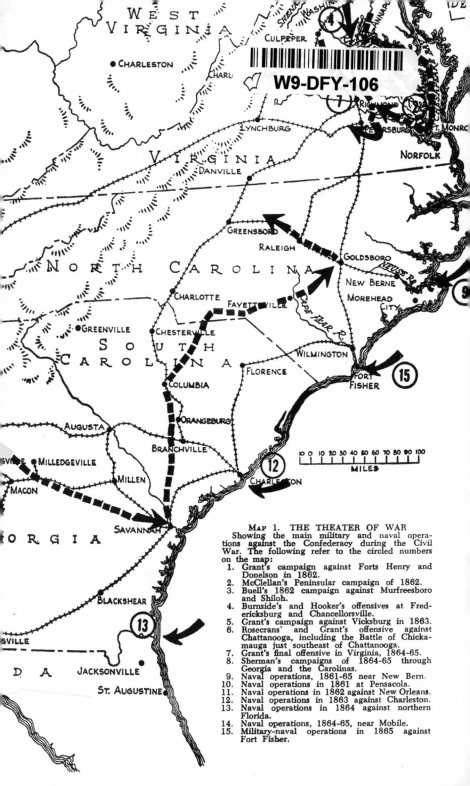

W9-DFY-106

MAP 1. THE THEATER OF WAR

Showing the main military and naval operations against the Confederacy during the Civil War. The following refer to the circled numbers on the map:

1. Grant's campaign against Forts Henry and Donelson in 1862.
2. McClellan's Peninsular campaign of 1862.
3. Buell's 1862 campaign against Murfreesboro and Shiloh.
4. Burnside's and Hooker's offensives at Fredericksburg and Chancellorsville.
5. Grant's campaign against Vicksburg in 1863.
6. Rosecrans' and Grant's offensive against Chattanooga, including the Battle of Chickamauga just southeast of Chattanooga.
7. Grant's final offensive in Virginia, 1864-65.
8. Sherman's campaigns of 1864-65 through Georgia and the Carolinas.
9. Naval operations, 1861-65 near New Bern.
10. Naval operations in 1861 at Pensacola.
11. Naval operations in 1862 against New Orleans.
12. Naval operations in 1863 against Charleston.
13. Naval operations in 1864 against northern Florida.
14. Naval operations, 1864-65, near Mobile.
15. Military-naval operations in 1865 against Fort Fisher.

THE WILDERNESS CAMPAIGN

THE WILDERNESS CAMPAIGN

The Meeting of Grant and Lee

By
EDWARD STEERE

Introduction by
Robert K. Krick

STACKPOLE
BOOKS

Published by
STACKPOLE BOOKS
5067 Ritter Road
Mechanicsburg, PA 17055

Printed in the United States of America

Second hardcover edition, Stackpole Books

Originally published in hardcover by the Stackpole Company in 1960.

10 9 8 7 6 5 4 3 2 1

Library of Congress Cataloging-in-Publication Data

Steere, Edward, 1898–1974.
    The Wilderness campaign / Edward Steere ; introduction by Robert K.
Krick. — 2nd hardcover ed.
        p.   cm.
    Includes bibliographical references (p.   ) and index.
    ISBN 0-8117-1890-5
    1. Wilderness, Battle of the, Va., 1864.   I. Title.
Armstrong, 1839–1876.   I. Title.   II. Series
E476.52.S78   1994
973.7'36—dc20
                                                                                          93-26944
                                                                                               CIP

DEDICATION

CONTENTS

LIST OF MAPS

FOREWORD

The great field of military history embraces many thousands of volumes. Even so, exact descriptions of battles are rare. Even rarer is an exact description of a battle written by an author who possesses the professional historian's respect for fact and skill in judging evidence, and who combines his knowledge of the historian's craft with the military man's grasp of the interrelationships between weapons, organization, tactics, and terrain.

The Civil War student is fortunate in the lastest offering in the Stackpole Company's CIVIL WAR CAMPAIGNS series. The author gained his theoretical military knowledge through years of study, and acquired his practical military knowledge as a Royal Canadian Horse Artilleryman in that most arduous of all schools, the First World War. In addition to his military learning he has brought to bear on his complicated subject the skilled historian's craft he has practised in the U.S. National Park Service and in the Quartermaster Corps of the U.S. Army. The battle in the Virginia wilderness was an indecisive meeting engagement in the 44-day campaign that was the bloodiest of the Civil War. The Wilderness fight is also one of the most difficult to describe, and many historians, avoiding exact descriptions, have taken refuge in generalities. Mr. Steere has spent years of painstaking research in discovering the precise location and movements of each unit, and in placing each unit's operations on the correct piece of ground. He has sought the truth among the thickets and swamps of contemporary evidence, especially the dispatches written on the field. This is not to say he has neglected the vast body of literature on the Civil War. He has exploited every piece of primary and secondary evidence available, and his detailed examination of the primary evidence has enabled him to avoid the pitfalls and traps that second-guessing writers of self-justifying memoirs and reports have set for the unwary. His text and the excellent maps that he and Colonel W. S. Nye have compiled make plain to the reader the intricacies of this frightful battle, offer some new interpretations regarding the purposes of the two opposing commanders, and correct several misconceptions of many years' standing.

All aspects and levels of the struggle in the Wilderness are treated, from the motives and decisions of the high commanders to the operations of basic tactical units. Here was the first clash between the Civil War's greatest generals, Ulysses S. Grant and Robert E. Lee, and this clash illustrates some of the fine qualities of these two splendid soldiers: Grant's cool perception and indomitable will, Lee's bold judgment and gallant leadership. Mr. Steere's careful analysis also illustrates several problems that constantly recur in warfare. Work by the unspecialized and amateur staff officers was often slipshod; information was not transmitted quickly or coherently. The fog of war lay heavily over the Wilderness. Troops were often not where they were supposed to be. Officers did not always write clear and simple messages, nor were messages always delivered to the proper persons. The dual command system in the Union Army sometimes worked at cross purposes, and high commanders interfered in the handling of lower units. While tactical units frequently collected facts about the enemy which should have alerted their superiors, superiors often disregarded those facts which did not fit their preconceived notions and, in consequence, incorrectly estimated enemy strength and dispositions.

The Wilderness battle was typical of Civil War operations; it demonstrated that the weapons of 1861-1865 gave a tremendous advantage to the defender. It is not too sweeping a generalization to state that a successful assault—"charge" in Civil War terminology—was a rarity, as was successful pursuit. The number of fingers possessed by one human being is more than sufficient to count the successful assaults delivered against trained troops during the entire war. Yet the great strength of the defense was not always appreciated by the senior commanders. "Wherever the Federal troops moved forward, the Rebels appeared to have the advantage. Whenever they advanced, the advantage was transferred to us." These shrewd words came not from Grant, Meade, or Hancock, but from a chaplain.

The explanation of the defense's advantage lies in the fact that Civil War tactical formations were based on the 18th Century musket with its poor accuracy and its range of about 100 yards. But the standard weapon of the Civil War infantryman—the single-shot, muzzle-loading rifled musket, caliber .58—fired a Minie ball with deadly effect. It could shoot accurately at ranges varying from 200 to 400 yards and it could kill at 800 to 1000 yards. It compared favorably with the Second World War rifle whose maximum effective range was about 600 yards. The Civil War infantry rifle, plus the high rate of fire of the cavalryman's breechloading carbine and the power and accuracy of the field artillery, account for the terrifying destructiveness of the 1861-1865 struggle.

The author has made these facts, dimly grasped at the time, plain to the modern reader. *The Wilderness Campaign* promises to be the definitive account of the gory and horrible two-day struggle that slashed from the muster rolls of the Confederacy many names it was to miss desperately.

JOHN MILLER, JR.

INTRODUCTION

The Wilderness Campaign, historian David Donald declared in the New York *Herald Tribune,* is "a superb piece of technical military history, characterized by thoroughness, accuracy, and insight." Donald added an analysis that the passage of more than three decades has borne out: "It is . . . an enduring contribution to our military history."

Edward Steere earned his knowledge of the Wilderness battlefield in the most efficacious manner imaginable — as a National Park Service historian responsible for the site. An aged photo in the files of the battlefield park shows Steere and four other historians, all of whom later attained distinction in writing about or preserving Civil War sites, leaning on axes and brush hooks after a day of grubbing out an historic road trace in the Wilderness. Years of such explorations and on-site endeavors gave Steere a familiarity with the ground that would prove invaluable as an adjunct to his documentary research.

Steere was born in Los Angeles on April 21, 1898, and grew up in the Philippines, where his father operated a business. After service during World War I in France with a Canadian artillery unit, Steere received bachelor's and master's degrees from the University of Texas. He wrote for the Austin *Statesman* for a time, then went to work at Fredericksburg and Spotsylvania National Military Park as an historian (officially an "Assistant Historical Technician," in the antique jargon of the era). His duties included efforts to develop the Wilderness battlefield for visitor use. Steere later transferred to Antietam National Battlefield and then to historical work in Washington for the Department of the Interior.

During World War II and thence until his retirement in 1955, Ed Steere served as an historian for the Office of the Quartermaster General of the United States Army. He specialized in the history of the development of the mournfully busy department responsible for burial of American war dead. In 1951 the Government Printing Office issued Steere's 210-page monograph, *The Graves Registration Service in World War II.* Six years later, soon after Steere retired, his former employers published a mammoth (710 heavily illustrated pages) collaborative effort by Steere and Thayer M. Boardman entitled *Final Disposition of World War II Dead, 1945–1951*. Steere wrote widely for military periodicals, but his Wilderness study was the only other published book that he produced.

While he was stationed at Fredericksburg, Steere met and married Sue Yates Embrey (1905–1982), daughter of a prominent and historically inclined local family. Sue Embrey was, her husband declared, "an unreconstructed rebel." The Steeres retired to the Northern Virginia suburbs of Washington. He died there of cancer on November 25, 1974. Both Steeres are buried in the Embrey family plot in Oak Hill Cemetery, just west of Fredericksburg on the Salem Church battlefield and not too many miles from the Wilderness. They had no children.

When he retired, Steere undertook preparation of his study of the Wilderness for publication. During the 1930s he had produced for the National Park Service a detailed manuscript of nearly one thousand typescript pages on the battle. In 1945, Park Historian Francis F. Wilshin (another Fredericksburger, destined to be associated with the Manassas battlefields for several decades) transmitted Steere's report to headquarters covered with a rash of suggestions, corrections, and editorial marks. *The Wilderness Campaign* as published is an improved — and shortened — version of that early manuscript.

As was typical of Civil War research and writing in the 1930s, Steere's work relied heavily on government documents from the *Official Records*, used other primary published accounts only sparingly, and virtually ignored manuscript sources. The absence of extensive original research in manuscript collections is the book's primary shortcoming by modern standards. The result is a work far more given to tactical explication than to human drama. Readers can draw from Steere's pages little empathy for the experiences of soldiers on either side. The Wilderness as a clash between brigades stands clear in the narrative; the individual struggles of nearly 200,000 Americans remain less distinct.

Steere's perspective in examining developments in the

National Park Service historians on an exploratory excursion through Wilderness battle-field in June 1935: Ed Steere, T. Sutton Jett, Raleigh Taylor, Ralph Happel, and Branch Spalding. Each of these men subsequently made substantial contributions to Civil War scholarship or preservation of battlefield sites.

Wilderness is somewhat inclined toward the Unionist view-point, perhaps because of the nature of his sources: the primary report volume for this campaign in the *Official Records,* on which the author placed such extensive reliance, supplies 1,021 pages of Federal material as against only 80 of Confederate! The proportion of attention to things Northern in *The Wilderness Campaign* does not approach that twelve-to-one ratio, nor does Steere's emphasis on Federal operations lead to unfair treatment of Confederates. The author's analysis of command and control of the armies does, however, conclude with a more favorable view of Grant's ability than of Lee's. Despite its title, the book covers only the Battle of the Wilderness and its immediate context, not the campaign of which the Wilderness was the opening act.

A great strength of *The Wilderness Campaign* is its numerous and detailed maps. Steere's careful study of troop dispositions provided raw material that the seasoned and skillful cartographer Colonel Wilbur S. Nye turned into twenty-seven superb maps. Those maps remain today, thirty-three years after publication, the unquestioned best graphic depiction of the action in the Wilderness.

By 1960, the Stackpole Company had published four studies of Civil War battles or campaigns, all of them written by General Edward J. Stackpole. The general subsequently would produce a fifth campaign study. Steere succeeded in placing his manuscript with the company for production in the series. It would be the only title written by anyone other than Stackpole.

The Wilderness Campaign came off the press in the fall of 1960 and apparently sold reasonably well, judging by the number of copies that remain in circulation. The book earned reviews, mostly favorable, in a wide and eclectic circle of prominent periodicals. Earl Schenck Miers gave it a brief mention in the *New York Times* on Christmas Day. The Springfield *Republican* called the book "One of the best military histories ever written." Writing in the prestigious *American Historical Review*, D. H. Hill biographer Hal Bridges applauded the "painstaking thoroughness and accuracy" of Steere's historical method. Bridges expressed his only substantive disappointment over the "relatively little fresh manuscript material" discernible in the bibliography and notes.

Most reviewers pointed out the inescapable truth that Steere's book is of a technical and tactical sort. "It is military history—pure, detailed, and painstakingly presented," *Civil War History* noted. Some commentators suggested that *The Wilderness Campaign* as a result would appeal "mainly to the battle specialist," or only to "the most enthusiastic and proficient Civil War buff." The work's enduring success has shown those narrow concerns to be ill founded.

The most interesting commentary on Steere's work came from Clifford Dowdey in *The Virginia Magazine of History and Biography*. Dowdey's own book, *Lee's Last Campaign*, appeared almost concurrently with *The Wilderness Campaign* and covered the same ground before following the armies on to Richmond. As the leading authority at the time on the Army of Northern Virginia, Dowdey could be expected to condemn Steere's dismissal of Lee's skills. The reviewer did indeed take Steere to task for being "inclined to minimize Lee's deductive powers" and "presenting Lee as fumbling his way, baffled over the enemy's movements. . . ." Even so, Dowdey hailed *The Wilderness Campaign* as a "finely detailed treatment of the battle" and "a splendid example of well organized research." Steere subsequently reciprocated with a favorable review of Dowdey's book.

After the Stackpole edition of *The Wilderness Campaign* fell out of print, a succession of discount versions appeared. Hardbound (but cheap quality) copies of the book could be had at a modest price until about 1980. This new edition from the original publisher makes Steere's classic work available again for the first time in more than a decade. Because *The Wilderness Campaign* remains to this date by far the best book ever written on the battle, its renewed availability affords a welcomed opportunity for Civil War students and book collectors interested in the Virginia theater of the Civil War.

ROBERT K. KRICK
FREDERICKSBURG, VIRGINIA
MAY 1993

CHAPTER 1

THE ADVERSARIES

Long known as the Wilderness of Virginia, a dreary waste-land fringing the south bank of the Rapidan River lends its name to a famous battle of history. Once cherished by the Indians as a bountiful hunting ground, the primeval forest of stately pine and sturdy oak was felled by white invaders to provide fuel for smelting the iron ore torn from shallow pits. In later days a second growth of scrub trees, interlaced with dense underbrush and thorny vines, rudely covered the ugly scars left by robbery of the subsoil. Casting eternal shadows over stagnant pools and marshy creek bottoms, this brooding jungle not only inspired the name but imposed the conditions of combat in its gloomy depths.

At high noon on May 5, 1864, Lieutenant General Ulysses S. Grant, supreme commander of the United States field forces and personally directing operations of the Army of the Potomac and the independent IX Corps, joined battle in the Wilderness with General Robert E. Lee, commanding the Army of Northern Virginia. They fought to a tactical impasse.

As nightfall on the 6th stilled the roaring musketry, both armies lay exhausted amid forest fires that gave a final touch of horror to the stricken battlefield. The moaning of the un-recovered wounded, many of whom perished hideously in the spreading flames, mingled discordantly with the chorus of whippoorwills and other nocturnal creatures of the forest.

Commanding Minds

The historic importance of this battle is disguised by the brutal nature of the combat. Yet the sustained brutality is in itself historically significant. The volleys in the Wilderness thundered the prologue to a tragic contest between two in-

1

domitable wills. One faithfully portrayed the ideals of a landed aristocracy, sanctioning slavery and upholding the political doctrine of local sovereignty as the means of best preserving a traditional way of life. The other reflected the spirit of a dynamic society, imbued with the vision of a democratic nation, mighty and indivisible in a vast domain reaching from ocean to ocean, and ruthlessly intolerant of local traditions and institutions that impeded the onward march to destiny. Thus inspired, the contest of wills was frightening in the attendant loss of life and awesome in the grim determination with which both pursued their conflicting aims to the bitter end.

The definition once given of an army as the armed mind of its commanding general has a unique application to the unforeseen series of events ushered in by the onset in the Wilderness. The armies led to battle by Grant and Lee never suffered defeat because of any impairment of their mental faculties. Only physical deterioration of one beyond the point of response to its commanding mind permitted the other to triumph. What manner of men were these two commanders and what are the circumstances that brought them face to face in those dismal thickets on south bank of the Rapidan?

Colonel Lee and Captain Grant

Both Lee and Grant attended the United States Military Academy at West Point on the Hudson, Lee graduating with high honors in 1829 and entering the Corps of Engineers. Grant graduated fourteen years later, and was assigned to the Infantry. In contrast to Lee's immaculate record, Grant's career as a cadet was undistinguished; he excelled only in horsemanship. An unusual aptitude for mathematics enabled him to coast through the academic course. The leisure hours thus afforded were devoted to an industrious but indiscriminate program of reading in the Academy library. Where Lee personified the ideals of the Corps of Cadets and the Army, Grant appears to have remained relatively untouched by those sentiments that are supposed to mold the character of a future officer.

Lee was the perfect soldier in every situation confronting an officer dedicated to the profession of arms. Grant was the plain, quietly martial type that flourishes only in war but deteriorates with the dull routine of peacetime. He resigned his commission as captain in 1854 under conditions that have distressed his sympathetic biographers. Lee, credited with a brilliant record as topographical engineer on the staff of General Winfield Scott during the Mexican War, later served with distinction as Superintendent of the United States Military Academy—an assignment coveted by every ambitious officer of the Regular Army. In 1861 he stood at the threshold of an even greater career in his chosen profession.

As the gathering war clouds darkened with establishment of the Confederate Government at Montgomery, Alabama, Lee was promoted to the grade of colonel in the Regular Army. In accepting the commission he renewed his oath to defend the Constitution of the United States. Then at the instigation of General Scott, President Lincoln conveyed through unofficial channels the suggestion that the appointment of Colonel Lee as commanding general of the National forces would be favorably entertained.

Consideration of the alluring offer cast Lee into the throes of a moral dilemma. Like a dutiful son confronted with an irreparable breach between his father and mother, he must decide which one had the greater claim on his loyalty and affections. While he deplored secession as an unjustifiable act of revolution, and condemned slavery as morally wrong and economically unsound, he could not regard his sworn allegiance to the Federal Union as an obligation to participate in armed suppression of the secessionist states. To this extent, at least, he sanctioned the social and political aspirations of the South.

His doubts were resolved by the secession of Virginia, his mother State. Reluctantly resigning his commission in the United States Army, he went to Richmond where he was appointed major general commanding the military forces of Virginia. In this capacity he undertook the organization and training of a miscellaneous collection of militia units, while his future adversary of the Wilderness campaign was suffering the buffets of discouragement in seeking the colonelcy of a volunteer regiment.

Victorious Generals

With the many paradoxes that are encountered in attempting to compare and contrast the personalities of Robert E. Lee and Ulysses S. Grant, the most striking one is that Grant should have been first to win widespread acclaim as a victorious general in the field.[1]

Grant had been commissioned colonel of the 21st Illinois Volunteer Infantry and then assigned with the rank of brigadier general to command of the Military District of Cairo, at the confluence of the Ohio and the Mississippi. He early perceived the military potentialities of water transportation and the gun power of the inland waters flotilla in rupturing the Confederate line that barred access to the Cumberland and Tennessee Rivers and the lower course of the Mississippi.

These navigable streams, Grant realized, offered easy avenues of invasion into the South. His reduction, during February 1862, of Forts Henry and Donelson, which dominated the lower courses of the Tennessee and Cumberland, flowing through parallel channels only twenty miles apart into the Ohio, made an irreparable breach in that line. Confederate fear of the armored gunboats, striking with their heavy batteries far beyond the reach of conventional land forces, caused the evacuation of Nashville, the rail center of central Tennessee and supply base of the original line of defense. Then the Federal advance up the Tennessee River toward Pittsburg Landing, near Shiloh Church, turned the Confederates out of Columbus, the anchor of their line on the Mississippi.

News of the first great victory of Federal arms electrified

---

[1] This bibliographical note, and all succeeding notes of this type, will be found in the APPENDIX, under *Bibliographical Notes*.

the nation. The President commissioned Grant a major general of United States Volunteers. His reply to a request of the beleaguered commander at Fort Donelson concerning conditions of capitulation help to further popularize his fame. "My terms," he stated, "are immediate and unconditional surrender." With the play upon the initials of his given names, "Unconditional Surrender Grant" became a household phrase throughout the North. Three months were to elapse before Lee was to be called to the command of a field army.

Meanwhile, Grant exhibited the implacable determination that turned the wavering tide of battle on the bloody field of Shiloh into another Federal victory.

The deep salient driven into Confederate territory persuaded Major General Henry W. Halleck, commanding general in the West, that the control of events at the front required closer supervision than could be given from his administrative desk in St. Louis. Assuming personal command in the field, he took matters in hand by slowing the pace of movement. Instead of directing a rigorous pursuit, he effected a ponderous concentration of three Federal field armies, including Grant's victorious veterans of Donelson and Shiloh, at Corinth, in the northeastern corner of Mississippi.

A junction point on the only continuous line of rail communications then traversing the Confederacy from the South Atlantic seaboard to the Mississippi River, Corinth gave access on the landward side to Memphis, the river port at the terminal of the line through Corinth which was destined to serve as Grant's supply base during his final drive on Vicksburg. For the moment, however, Grant went into eclipse, serving as deputy commander of the forces at Corinth.

As Halleck completed his occupation of Corinth, McClellan's Federal Army of the Potomac, after landing at Fortress Monroe and advancing up the Peninsula of Virginia, deployed in overwhelming force before Richmond. On the first day of June, 1862, the echoing chimes of the clocks in Richmond's spires announced the passing hours to McClellan's watchful pickets.

At this crisis Lee was called from his staff assignment as military adviser to the Confederate President and directed to assume command of the Army of Northern Virginia. Assuming the offensive, he smashed McClellan's right and hustled the disordered Federal columns back against the James River. Thus Lee delivered the Confederate capital from the sudden violence of an assault or the protracted horrors of a siege. Celebrated as the Seven Days' Battles, this feat of arms established Lee's renown as the foremost soldier of the Confederacy.

Flood Tide of Confederacy

Meanwhile, Halleck's faulty performance as a field commander in the West set the stage for a general Confederate counteroffensive. As Lee was neutralizing McClellan's threat to Richmond, Halleck deliberately dissipated his own concentration at Corinth, assigning elements of the force to missions that tended to jeopardize rather than enhance the advantages of a still favorable military situation.

Dispirited and reduced in strength, the Confederate army that had failed to destroy Grant at Shiloh slowly fell back through Corinth down the Ohio and Mobile Railroad to Tupelo, in central Mississippi, where Braxton Bragg superseded Beauregard in command. Unmolested by Halleck, Bragg refitted his depleted units and successfully performed the difficult task of shifting the army to Chattanooga—his infantry going by rail via Mobile and Atlanta, the mounted units marching overland.

The shift completed, Bragg would debouch from his sally-port on the middle reaches of the Tennessee River and, after turning the Federals out of Nashville, impose his own terms of battle in Western Kentucky on the retreating enemy. While the strategic regroupment went forward from central Mississippi to eastern Tennessee, Kirby Smith assembled a force in the upper valley of the Tennessee to push through Cumberland Gap and occupy the Bluegrass region of Kentucky. At the same time, Sterling Price and Earl Van Dorn collected troops from both sides of the lower Mississippi for a movement on Corinth, where Grant remained with a relatively small holding force.

Failing to interpret the evidence of enemy movements as indicative of offensive intentions, Halleck persisted in his course of unwittingly favoring Confederate designs. A competent administrator and justly entitled to fame as the "organizer of victory" in the West, he was accorded undue credit for the actual field victories won by armies under his nominal command. President Lincoln called him to Washington to fill the vacant post of General in Chief of the Army. With enhanced authority, he completed in the East the vast mischief contrived by his maladroit dispositions in the West. He ordered McClellan to evacuate the Peninsula and reinforce a new formation, the Army of Virginia, commanded by John Pope. Pope's army was to advance southwest on Gordonsville, with Richmond as a possible eventual objective.

Assured by the presence of the shipping assembled at Fortress Monroe that McClellan was withdrawing from the Peninsula, Lee determined to exploit the temporary advantage of interior lines. He turned northward, passed Pope's right on the Rappahannock River and, sending his army in two echelons of maneuver through Thoroughfare Gap, defeated Pope on the field of Second Bull Run. A few days later Lee crossed the Potomac into Maryland. In the West, the columns of Kirby Smith, Braxton Bragg, Sterling Price, and Van Dorn were also in motion.

There is no occasion here to narrate the events of this daring general offensive of the Confederate armies. It should be noted, however, that the hopes entertained for success were denied by the absence of a supreme command. There was no over-all authority which could impose coordination of movement. Furthermore, the bid for victory was made at a time when effective strength of the Confederate armies was approaching the limits of Southern manpower. Barring foreign intervention or war weariness in the North, failure to win a decision at this juncture spelled the eventual ruin of the Confederacy.

Lee withdrew from the shambles of Sharpsburg (Antietam) on September 19. Kirby Smith failed to reinforce Bragg at the crisis of the campaign in western Kentucky. Missing his opportunity to destroy the Federals in retreat from Nashville, Bragg followed to the Ohio River opposite Louisville, only to stand idly by while the enemy refitted and augmented his strength. After fighting an indecisive battle at Perryville, Kentucky during October, Bragg retired through the Cumberland Gap to Chattanooga. Van Dorn and Sterling Price recoiled from their headlong assault on a corps of Grant's Army of the Tennessee near Corinth on September 19, the same day that Lee recrossed the Potomac into Virginia.

Recession of the tide of Confederate military power is disguised by Lee's exhibitions of prowess on the battlefield that, however brilliant in tactical execution, were destitute of strategic consequences. Yet the fiction of victory sustained the Confederacy and appalled the North. Even failure of the first Confederate invasion of Northern territory, following Lee's triumph at Second Manassas, seems to have been redeemed by the magnificent performance of his troops at Sharpsburg—a name that stirs the same pride in Southern hearts that Dunkerque arouses in the breast of every true Briton.

Deprived of victory in Maryland, Lee established the military frontier of Virginia along the river line of the Rapidan-Rappahannock. His defensive victory over Burnside at Fredericksburg during December 1862 gave assurance that the cost of carrying this line by frontal assault would discourage the repetition of any such effort.

Hooker's attempt to turn the river line in May 1863 evoked Lee's counteroffensive operations around Chancellorsville, the decisive action of which was fought in the eastern confines of the Wilderness. A miracle of tactical genius, Chancellorsville inspired hopes again of winning a decisive victory on enemy soil. These hopes were dashed at Gettysburg on July 3, 1863, after which Lee retired to the Rapidan-Rappahannock line and posted his army on the west side of the Wilderness.

Strategy of Annihilation

While the Confederates marched from one ephemeral triumph to another in the East, the Federals were weaving a pattern of aggressive strategy, the golden threads of their victories in the West tracing a stern design on the somber background of high state policy. In challenging the secessionist states, President Lincoln stood committed from the first to waging a war in which there could be no deviation from an avowed purpose of destroying the armed power of the Confederacy as the only means of preserving the Union. Pursuit of such a policy prohibited any limitation of military objectives or parley with the enemy looking to peace by negotiation.

Just as the South discovered in the Eastern theater a leader who personified the Confederate genius that flashed so brilliantly at Second Manassas and Chancellorsville, so the North found in the West a captain who expressed in the planning and execution of his operations the remorseless determination of the National Government and a majority of its people to compel secessionist states to return to the Union. But in rising to preeminence, this captain did something more than win a succession of decisive victories; he grasped the unity of a strategic scheme of conquest. After failure in an overland advance on Vicksburg, Grant reduced the great river fortress by reliance on water transportation and employment of the rear attack. News of the surrender on July 4, 1863, the day following the repulse of Pickett's charge at Gettysburg, swept with wild acclaim through the North. While Grant was universally hailed as the foremost commander of the war in the West, Lincoln quietly amended that estimate by regarding him as the coming general of all the Union armies.

With the fall of Vicksburg an outline for the strategy of total conquest took shape in Grant's mind. He regarded control of the Mississippi from Cairo to the Gulf as only the first auspicious step in a territorial dismemberment of the Confederacy. He was careful, however, to avoid confusion between military and geographical objectives; in his strategic thinking, he knew that the occupation of a designated area could come only in consequence of the destruction of the defending force. Escape of such a force necessarily committed the formations earmarked for occupation to active operations elsewhere.

The next step in the process of dismemberment, he urged, should be the isolation of that area westward of the line Chattanooga-Atlanta-Montgomery-Mobile. This was to be accomplished by a massive rear attack through the soft underbelly of the Confederacy. Supported by water transportation based on New Orleans and protected by the Navy, Grant intended to lead his veteran Army of the Tennessee through Mobile and up the Alabama River toward Montgomery. Meanwhile, Rosecrans' Army of the Cumberland was to proceed overland across the Tennessee River into northern Georgia and push down toward Atlanta.[2]

Confronted with the crisis in Mexico precipitated by intervention of Napoleon III, Emperor of the French, President Lincoln withheld approval of the rear attack. Only a demonstration of the National power in Texas, he insisted, would restrain the imperialistic ambitions of Napoleon. But he felt constrained to confide in a personal note to Grant that the Mobile venture looked tempting. The overland thrust into Georgia, however, was put in motion during September 1863.

After bypassing Chattanooga and penetrating the mountainous region of northern Georgia, Rosecrans suffered a disastrous defeat at Chickamauga. Falling back into Chattanooga with Bragg's victorious Army of Tennessee on his heels, Rosecrans rushed preparations to withstand a siege, while issuing a flood of confused and contradictory reports. With the Tennessee River under blockade and a crippled field transport unable to support the overland haul from the railroad at Bridgeport, Alabama, the partially beleaguered garrison was reduced to starvation rations.

In this perilous situation—one that momentarily promised

Bragg a victory of greater magnitude than any won by Lee in Virginia—the Federal high command reacted with promptness and resolution. Grant was appointed commanding general of the Military Division of the Mississippi, a new jurisdiction combining the forces of several military departments under a single command.

Replacing Rosecrans with Major General George H. Thomas, the resolute Virginian who saved the army from annihilation at Chickamauga, Grant concentrated at Chattanooga the XI and XII corps, detached from the Army of the Potomac, and the bulk of his old Army of the Tennessee, now under Sherman. He then struck back at the Confederates late in November. In a brilliant series of operations extending over four days, he drove Bragg's investing force in headlong rout from Missionary Ridge and threw open the gateway into Georgia. The worsted Confederates withdrew to an entrenched camp at Dalton in northern Georgia, where Joseph E. Johnston superseded Bragg in command.

Victor of Chattanooga

Just as the fall of Vicksburg prompted Grant to survey the strategic opportunities given by control of the Mississippi, so now the open gateway at Chattanooga suggested another examination of strategic possibilities. Grant was aware that the winter rains forbade large scale operations over the unpaved wagon tracks of northern Georgia. He insisted that the carrying capacity of his lengthy rail communications from Louisville should be devoted to delivery of supplies at Chattanooga for the spring campaign, and without the added burden of supporting an army in idleness. Therefore he proposed a winter campaign on the Alabama River.

With waterborne transportation through New Orleans and Mobile, he reasoned that "this move would secure the entire States of Alabama and Mississippi and a part of Georgia or force Lee to abandon Virginia and North Carolina." He added: "Without this force the enemy have not got an army strong enough to resist the one I could take."[8]

Grant and Halleck were of one mind in regard to the Mobile project. Replying on January 8, 1864, to Grant's proposal, Halleck stated that Lincoln opposed the venture. It appeared that a military solution must be given to the long standing Mexican crisis. To this end an expedition under Major General Nathaniel P. Banks, commanding the independent Department of the Gulf, would be sent up the Red River and a reinforcing contingent must be furnished by the Military Division of the Mississippi.[4]

Military opinion inclined to the view that a victorious campaign on the Alabama River, striking toward the heart of the Confederacy, would be more impressive as a demonstration of National power to Louis Napoleon than a show of strength on the Red River. The President and his political advisors, however, were insistent that the generals must bow to the demands of diplomacy. As a matter of fact, the solution to that problem was found only after the Confederacy went down in ruin.

In conveying Lincoln's veto, Halleck suggested that Grant express his views on the general military situation, particularly with respect to preparations for the spring campaign. Complying during January, Grant proposed that the main attack should be delivered through the mountain corridor leading down from Chattanooga to central Georgia, while Banks, having completed his mission on the Red River, would assemble an expeditionary force at New Orleans and launch the rear attack through Mobile.

Grant's proposals for the Eastern theater are significant for two reasons: first, they were unacceptable to the President; second, they reveal aspects of Grant's strategic doctrine that deny the historic and widespread impression that Grant was merely a bludgeon general who could only batter his way to victory by fighting a brutal battle of attrition. Briefly, he proposed that a force of 60,000 effectives be drawn "at once" from the formations covering Washington and, transported by sea to New Bern, North Carolina, a port at the mouth of the

Neuse River in possession of Federal troops, strike inland across Lee's rail communications traversing North Carolina to Raleigh. A permanent base would be established at Wilmington, North Carolina, as soon as that port could be secured.

Possession of Raleigh, he urged, "would so threaten Lee's most interior line as to force him to use a large proportion of his army to guard it," creating a situation which must "virtually force the evacuation of Virginia and indirectly of East Tennessee."

Grant pointed out that Lee's concern for his communications should tend to allay any fears aroused by drawing Federal troops from the front of Washington (Grant specified a larger protective force than the one McClellan provided during the Peninsula campaign). He also listed other advantages, namely that the diversion of Confederate formations from dispositions of their own choice to new lines of operations for which they were not prepared would deny them liberty of action in preparing for the spring campaign; that the occupation of Wilmington would strengthen the blockade by closing the only useful port still in enemy hands; and, finally, that the attack across North Carolina "would enable operations to commence at once by removing the war to a more southern climate, instead of months of inactivity in winter quarters." [5]

Obviously, Grant offered the North Carolina movement as a substitute for the winter campaign on the Alabama River. It was an expression of his preference for water transportation over the difficulties of overland haul—a lesson he had learned in his initial attempts to advance on Vicksburg—and his appreciation of the devastating effects of the rear attack. Certainly, the direction and timing of the stroke across Lee's communications did not arise from a mentality capable of thinking only in an elementary branch of the strategic art.

The Supreme Commander

The President's objections to the North Carolina campaign did not diminish the esteem in which he held the Victor of Chattanooga. When Congress late in February, 1864 restored the grade of Lieutenant General, a rank held previously only by Washington and provisionally by Winfield Scott in a brevet status, Lincoln appointed Grant to the office, relieving Halleck of his responsibilities as general in chief.

On March 17 the lieutenant general issued General Orders No. 1, stating:

> I assume command of the Armies of the United States, headquarters in the field, and until notice will be those of the Army of the Potomac. There will be an office headquarters in Washington to which all communications will be sent except those from the army where headquarters are at the date of address.[6]

The orders of March 17 were equivalent to an announcement that the main attack would be delivered in Eastern theater, with Lee's Army of Northern Virginia as the primary objective.

After establishing his headquarters late in March at Culpeper Court House, on the Rapidan front, Grant spent the month of April in developing a master plan for the culminating effort of Federal arms against the Confederate States.

In essence, this project may be regarded as a scheme for continuation under firm coordination of Supreme Commander of those movements that, despite heartbreaking setbacks and want of concerted action, had been carried to partial success during three years of war. Indeed, it brought to fruition the pattern of strategy that arose out of chaos during the first year of hostilities and gradually assumed definite form between the early spring of 1862, when Grant opened the water roads of the Cumberland and the Tennessee, and the late autumn of 1863, when he forced the gateway into Georgia.

Impelled by the relentless policy of total subjugation of the secessionist states, these movements took the form of four major attacks that gradually gathered headway along the front of Federal deployment from the Mississippi River to Chesapeake Bay. Poorly coordinated in their incipiency and pressed without guidance of objectives stating in military terms the long range aims of political policy, these four attacks may be characterized as: first, on the right, an advance from Cairo along the western water roads to Vicksburg, the river fortress that dominated the lower course of the Mississippi; second, at the center, an overland thrust from Louisville across the Nashville basin toward Chattanooga, gateway to the mountain corridor through northern Georgia to Atlanta; third, on the left, a series of misguided drives on Richmond, the outcome of which may be described as a prolonged duel between the Army of the Potomac and the Army of Northern Virginia; fourth, an attack from the sea that, while slowly strangling the economic life of the South in the tightening grip of blockade, lent effective cooperation on the right and left.

When Lee fell back from Gettysburg to the Rapidan-Rappahannock line and posted his army in winter cantonments on the west side of the Wilderness, the Federal attack columns of the right and center had completed a grand left wheel from the Ohio River to the Appalachian mountain chain. The strategic prizes—Vicksburg, with control of the Mississippi to its mouth, and Chattanooga—were securely held. Meanwhile, the attack from the sea, cooperating on the left, secured lodgments along the South Atlantic seaboard and, reaching toward the west, occupied New Orleans, first city of the South in population, wealth, and commercial enterprise. Beyond the Mississippi, efforts of the Confederates to regain Missouri were defeated and, moving out on the flank of the right, the Federals occupied most of Arkansas, together with Indian Territory and the Territories of New Mexico and Arizona. In failing to win a battle of annihilation on the bloody dueling ground between Richmond and Washington, Lee inadvertently permitted the Army of the Potomac to serve as the pivot of the grand strategic wheel in the West.

In accordance with the plan which Grant formulated at Culpeper during April, four Federal field armies were to move in concert against the Confederacy. The Federal striking force aggregated in round numbers 300,000 effectives. The Confederates mustered some 145,000 troops for defense of threatened areas. The aggregate strength of the United States armies, as estimated on the basis of returns during April 1864, or the nearest returns prior to that month, was 745,000. A similar computation gives a Confederate total of 303,367.[7]

Constituting the principal attack column, Meade's Army of the Potomac and Burnside's independent IX Corps (a total of 120,000), were to advance under personal direction of the supreme commander against the river line and destroy Lee's Army of Northern Virginia (63,000) while it was attempting to hold that line, or wherever it might be brought to battle.

Supporting the reinforced Army of the Potomac in its movement against Lee, the Army of the James (33,000), Major General Benjamin F. Butler commanding, would advance on the south side of the James River from Fortress Monroe toward Richmond, occupying the Confederate capital, if possible, or containing enemy troops that might otherwise move toward Lee.

Commanding a field force of 23,000 in the Shenandoah Valley, Major General Franz Sigel was to act as a sort of flank guard on the right of the Army of the Potomac by advancing toward the Confederate rail center at Lynchburg.

As the principal assault column moved forward on the left, the center column under Sherman (100,000) would push from Chattanooga down the mountain corridor, destroying Joseph E. Johnston's army (64,000) and breaking up the enemy's war resources in central Georgia.

On the right, Banks would disengage his column operating on the Red River, for assembly at New Orleans and, supported by the Navy, deliver the rear attack through Mobile so insistently urged by Grant during the past year. This movement, however, was to be a somewhat abbreviated form of the massive assault Grant proposed during the summer of 1863 and again in December of that year.[8]

War Clouds on the Rapidan

Aware of the shift in Federal dispositions, Lee prevailed upon President Davis to recall all units detached from the

Army of Northern Virginia, notably Hoke's Brigade and Pickett's Division in North Carolina and the two divisions of Longstreet's Corps in East Tennessee. Owing to a report of Federal troop withdrawals from the South Atlantic seaboard to reinforce Butler's army at Fortress Monroe, Lee suggested that Beauregard move northward with every available reserve left in the Department of South Carolina, Georgia, and Florida, and increase the Richmond defense force to a total of 30,000. He also advised that, in the absence of a threat against Mobile, Maury's local defense force (8,000) and Leonidas Polk's Army of Mississippi (10,000) would be available as reinforcements to Joseph E. Johnston at Dalton.[9] The Confederate President gave heed to these suggestions.

With a free hand in northern Virginia, Lee determined to hold the river line, either by an active defense or, circumstances permitting, by bold counteroffensive measures. The odds against him were slightly less than those he faced at Chancellorsville. Then a terrain admirably adapted to defensive tactics tended to minimize his disparity in numerical strength and, moreover, deny Grant the advantage he might elsewhere derive from the full employment of his powerful cavalry force and a heavy preponderance in field artillery. Lee's estimate of the situation did not exclude the possibility of winning another miracle victory. This, indeed, he held within his grasp for a fleeting hour in the Wilderness. Nor did he abandon hopes for a third invasion of the North which, as a matter of fact, he launched on a limited scale after the stunning repulse he inflicted on Grant a month later at Cold Harbor.

Out of these conflicting purposes came the first test of strength between Grant and Lee, but under conditions that neither commander anticipated nor desired. Grant preferred to fight on open ground beyond the Wilderness, where he might use to better advantage his superiority in cavalry and artillery. Lee, eager to meet his adversary in the woodland, would have postponed engagement until completion of the deployment of all the elements of his army on a line favorable to counteroffensive action.

The circumstances that hastened the collision that both commanders sought to avoid—one as to time, the other as to place—may best be told in the detailed story of the battle. Yet it seems pertinent to observe here that the encounter Grant planned as a battle of annihilation ended in a tactical draw. At the same time, Lee's hopes of repeating his exploit at Chancellorsville were frustrated by Grant's undaunted pugnacity. In reality, the clash in the Wilderness became the meeting engagement of a 44-day battle of attrition, the storm center of which swept across the northern and eastern approaches to Richmond and over the James River to the south side of Petersburg. Finally, it is a matter of historic interest to note that the Army of the Potomac reverted during this violent movement and the ensuing nine months' stalemate at Petersburg to its traditional role, serving now as the pivot of Sherman's enveloping march through Georgia and the Carolinas.

Grant was deprived of the dislocating effects of a rear attack through Mobile by Banks' mismanagement of the Red River campaign, and was denied the assistance that should have been given by the supporting movements of Butler and Sigel, both of whom bungled their assignments within two weeks after his own crossing of the Rapidan. Grant then had no other alternative but to hammer Lee on the anvil of Richmond while Sherman's devouring host swept through the heartland of the South.

CHAPTER 2

THE FEDERAL PLAN—OPERATION WILDERNESS

Lieutenant General Grant assumed command of the armies on March 17, 1864. After tampering ineffectually with the command structure that had failed frequently during three years of war, he established general headquarters at Culpeper Court House. Then, on March 31, as already related, he dispatched the first of a series of directives that, taken together, embody his strategic plan for commencement of the movement known to history as the Grand Campaign of 1864-65.

Archaic Staff Organization

Comparison of his elementary method with the elaborately detailed procedures of the War Plans Division in the General Staff during World War II reveals the primitive nature of Grant's staff organization. Brigadier General John A. Rawlins, a lawyer by profession who had served as Grant's adjutant general during his rise from chief of brigade to supreme commander, directed a group of 15 officers that functioned somewhat in the manner of a general headquarters staff. Halleck, the deposed general in chief, was sent with the title of Chief of Staff of the Army to an office in Washington, which was intended to serve both as the central depository of reports and a medium for the transmission of orders emanating from general headquarters.[1]

Removed from personal contact with the supreme commander, Halleck performed duties having no relation to the title he bore. Such misuse of this title betrays a singular want of knowledge concerning basic organizational changes that were reshaping the military systems of Europe, notably the Prussian and French armies. By 1864 the Prussian command and staff structure rested firmly on a corps of specialists, carefully selected and trained in peace, and available upon the outbreak of war to duplicate in the field armies the general staff organization permanently associated with the high command.[2]

Total War

If the corps of experts that might have given his headquarters staff at Culpeper the quality of corporate experience was not available, Grant had many compensating advantages. In communication by telegraph at all hours with the War Department and his army commanders in the field, he possessed the physical means of exercising strategic direction and administrative control over the largest and most complex military organization then in existence.[3] Furthermore, the sovereign advantage given by instantaneous transmission of military intelligence was amplified by the employment of many of those new mechanical devices that were rapidly transforming the foremost nations of Western Europe and the United States of America from an agricultural economy to one based on industrial enterprise, with the corresponding shift from a rural to an urban society.

Adapted to military needs during the first protracted clash of arms since the discovery of steam power and other notable advancements in scientific knowledge that gave birth to the machine age, these new instrumentalities introduced changes in the conduct of military operations as revolutionary as those attending the pursuits of peace. On land, the steam-propelled train replaced animal-drawn vehicles in the longer hauls of both men and supplies. At sea and on the inland waterways, steam and sailing vessels carried a large proportion of the supply load. Various designs of power machinery were geared to the production of munitions. Artillery guns and small arms had undergone improvement in recent years both as to range and rapidity of fire. Armored battleships fought their first duel.

All such innovations endowed the field armies and sea-going fleets with a mobility and striking power hitherto unknown in warfare and, at the same time, conferred the capacity of repairing the wastage of battle on a scale that greatly increased the actual hours of fighting in relation to the total period of engagement.

A method of conscription supplementing voluntary enlistments provided in some measure for a continuous flow of replacements from the reservoirs of manpower. Again, the offshore patrol of Southern ports by ships of war constantly on station gave added force to the economic weapon of naval blockade. Finally, the mechanical press lent its power to a new phase of armed conflict. Though not unknown in former times, the techniques of psychological warfare definitely came into play.

Indeed, within the limits of manpower and material resources at their disposal, both the Federal Union and the Southern Confederacy supported a conflict which manifested the principal elements of total war. Directing these new-found forces for the first time in a major war, and profiting by a rudimentary mobilization of industry that had been gradually carried forward in the North during three years of indecisive war, Grant appears on the battlefield in 1864 as the military heir of the Industrial Revolution. Yet no real revision of the archaic command and staff structure accompanied his elevation to the supreme command.

Faulty Solution of Command Problems

While invested with the superior rank of lieutenant general —an advantage denied his predecessors in the office of general in chief—Grant possessed no statutory authority beyond that formerly enjoyed by Scott, McClellan, and Halleck. In reality, the supreme commander owed his extraordinary power to the confidence reposed in him by President Lincoln and the popular acclaim evoked by official recognition of his exploits on the battlefield. With the President's assent, he exercised many prerogatives of the constitutional Commander in Chief. In this respect, Grant may be compared to great captains of the premachine age, when attributions of high military command were associated with the personality of a victorious general rather than the military institutions of which he was a product.[4]

Grant's decision to locate general headquarters in the field with the Army of the Potomac came in consequence of the combination of a defective command system and the enormous personal influence he exerted. Throughout its history the Army of the Potomac had been a tragic victim of political interference. Hooker owed his appointment as commanding general to indorsement of the Honorable Salmon P. Chase, Secretary of the Treasury. Meade regarded his own elevation to the command as a personal misfortune. "What have I done to deserve this!" he is reported to have exclaimed. Washington, the center of political turmoil and intrigue, Grant realized, was no place for general headquarters. Even if he managed to resist its pressures more successfully than had Halleck, the effort would be distracting.

If one aspect of the problem could be solved by going to the field, just where should he go? The answer seemed obvious —to the Army of the Potomac. His principal striking force, it needed the protection only he could give against political Washington.

The decision, as we know, was taken on March 17. Yet it was fraught with unforeseen difficulties. Grant insulated Meade, the local army commander, against political meddling, but Meade soon encountered encroachments of another sort on his authority as an independent army commander. With its lack of corporate experience, the very proximity of general headquarters gave rise to a curious kind of dual command— one that was studiously ignored in all official correspondence, but frankly accepted in fact. The trend became apparent in the detailed planning for the movement against Lee a month before the Army of the Potomac crossed the Rapidan.

The strategic plan summarized in Chapter 1 was developed in a piecemeal manner, each part of the program being unfolded in a directive to a particular army commander. The directive of March 31, for instance, assigned Mobile as Banks' objective and, at the same time, delegated to that distant field commander complete liberty of action in selecting his line of operations and whatever arrangements he might make with Admiral Farragut for naval support.[5] Sherman, Butler, and Sigel enjoyed a similar latitude of action. On March 8 the supreme commander designated the Army of Northern Virginia as Meade's "objective point." But Meade was given to understand that the determination of operational lines would be a subject for personal discussion. Grant informed this nearby army commander that

> The only point upon which I am now in doubt is whether it will be better to cross the Rapidan above or below him. By crossing above, Lee is cut off from all chance of ignoring Richmond and going north on a raid; but if we take this route all we do must be done while the rations we start with hold out; we separate from Butler so that he cannot be directed how to cooperate. By the other route Brandy Station can be used as a base of supplies until another is secured on the York or James River. These advantages and disadvantages I will talk over with you more fully than I can write them.[6]

Another circumstance—and a potent one—hastened the trend toward a dual command system. Grant's principal strategic mass was composed of Meade's Army of the Potomac and the independent IX Corps under command of A. E. Burnside. A former commander of the Army of the Potomac and senior to Meade on the list of major generals, Burnside could be brought into cooperation with Meade only through the intermediary of general headquarters. Issuance of the necessary orders proceeded from Grant's authority as supreme commander. But in so doing he acted as the commanding general of an army group that had no recognized status in the existing scheme of military organization.

In spite of these anomalous circumstances, the supreme commander completed all but certain minor details of his strategic planning by the middle of April and then gave his attention to matters concerning his position as ex officio commander of an army group that had no official existence.

Meade Directs Logistical Preparations

Meanwhile Meade prepared estimates for logistical support of whatever line of operations the supreme commander might adopt. His planning was projected in accordance with specific instructions issued by Grant on April 12.

> Should Lee's right flank be our route, you will want to make arrangements for having supplies forwarded to White House on the Pamunkey. Your estimate for this contingency should be made at once. If not wanted there, there is every probability that they will be wanted on the James River or elsewhere. If Lee's left is turned, large provision will have to be made for ordnance stores. I should say that not much less than 500 rounds of infantry ammunition would do. By the other, half the amount would be sufficient.[7]

With the tactical decision still in abeyance, Meade on April 17 apprised the supreme commander of the measures he had taken for logistical support. His report described two sets of requisitions placed with five different bureaus of the War Department.[8] The first set recapitulates quantities of subsistence, forage, ordnance stores, and medical supplies for an uninterrupted advance by the left toward Richmond and a battle in that area, or the possibility of siege operations against the Confederate capital. Quantities in the second set presupposed a battle precipitated by immediate reaction on Lee's part to a movement against either his right or left flank.

In the first contingency, a supply fleet laden with tons of rations, 8,000,000 rounds of small arms ammunition, 27,000 artillery shells, forage to feed over 50,000 animals, and medical supplies for 12,000 wounded would be assembled in Hampton Roads, under the guns of Fortress Monroe. There they would await instructions to proceed to an anchorage, either on the Pamunkey River or in the estuary of the James. The Chief of Engineers was to prepare the siege train at Washington for shipment to Fortress Monroe and assemble shipping "in such manner as not to attract attention" for embarkation of the pontoon bridge equipment purposely designed for spanning the broad estuary of the James River.

In preparing for a battle on or near the south bank of the Rapidan, Meade directed that the departments concerned complete all necessary arrangements for issuance, on notice, of 16 days' marching rations (4 of salt meat and 12 of beef on the hoof), 14,000,000 rounds of small arms ammunition, 10 days' full allowance of grain for 56,000 animals (34,071 horses and 22,528 mules) and, in the case of the Medical Department, to be ready on short notice to evacuate the sick and have on hand "all necessary field hospital supplies," presumably on a basis of 12,000 wounded.

Regarding detailed aspects of the logistical program, Meade specified that 6 days' rations would be carried on the person, 3 full rations in haversacks and 3 small ones in knapsacks, with the remainder to be conveyed by wagon or "on the hoof." Of the 150 rounds of small arms ammunition, 50 rounds were to be carried on the person. Wagon space was to be provided for the remaining 100 rounds. With 85,206 effectives reported "present for duty equipped" in the infantry and cavalry, there would be 8,520,600 rounds for assignment to the trains. According to the capacity of one transport wagon, this load would require 426 vehicles.

An apparent lack of provision in Meade's report for artillery ammunition in the event of a battle near the Rapidan would indicate that stores held in Alexandria or at the Brandy Station railhead were deemed adequate for such an encounter. Furthermore, the discrepancy between Meade's requisitions and Grant's original estimate of requirements in regard to ammunition, would indicate that Meade was thinking in terms of a continuous flow of supplies rather than an accumulation at one or two points. At any rate, Brigadier General Rufus Ingalls, Chief Quartermaster of the Army of the Potomac, clarifies the question of artillery ammunition in his statement that the army carried 73,180 rounds into the Wilderness, or an average of 275 for each of Meade's 274 field guns. A total of 675 caissons and battery wagons accompanied the combat trains and carried part of the ammunition load. The balance went in 699 "ordinary army wagons" which travelled with the great trains.

Grant Ponders the Direction of Advance

In contemplating the possibilities of movement against the Army of Northern Virginia, Grant enjoyed advantages that seldom occur in combination during war. In the first place, abundance of supplies enabled him to postpone a decision as to the choice of two possible lines of advance while Meade completed logistical preparations for both routes. Again, an advance by the left around Lee's right offered Grant an opportunity to exploit the advantages of operating from a convex base line.

Assuming that Lee should elude an attempt to envelop his right, continued movement by the left on Grant's part would approach the deeply indented shore of Chesapeake Bay, with its many admirable sites for advanced supply points in the estuaries of the Rappahannock, the York,* and the James River systems. This advantage, however, was offset by the obstacles that the heavily wooded terrain of Tidewater Virginia interposed against offensive action of the combined arms.[9]

The absence of such impediments in the Piedmont region invited attention to advantages of the alternate route toward Lee's left (west). Traversing open country, movement in that direction, it appeared, would enable Grant to realize maximum employment of his superior cavalry and artillery, together with large infantry masses in pressing the offensive. Appearances, nevertheless, were deceptive; continued movement in that direction could be sustained only at the cost of maintaining a line of overland communications, the continued protection of which demanded increasingly large detachments of infantry and cavalry. Furthermore, Grant's radius of action

---

* Geographically speaking, the so-called York River forms the lower estuary of the Pamunkey River system. The tide flows through this deep inlet into the mouth of the Pamunkey up to and beyond White House, where McClellan established his base during the Peninsula campaign, and the anchorage Grant had in mind as a supply point on that river.

on the right (west) flank was limited; on the left it could be restricted only by loss of command of the sea.

Whatever the balance between offensive opportunities in one direction against logistical advantages in the other, movement by the left involved a march through the Wilderness and the possibility of an infantry fight in the woodland. Such a prospect was viewed with grave misgivings at general and army headquarters. It was thought that the difficulty of controlling large masses in those thickets would minimize the advantage of numerical superiority in all arms. Yet a safe passage of the Wilderness and continued movement leftward promised Grant the advantage of shifting his supply line from land to the water route through Chesapeake Bay, thereby reducing land haul to the relatively short distances between advanced water bases and the front of active operations. Always inclined to reliance on waterborne communications in preference to overland transportation, with its greater cost, uncertainty, and danger of interruption by enemy action, Grant seemed predisposed from the first in favor of maneuver toward Lee's right.

"You Don't Know Bobby Lee!"

Apart from tactical and logistical considerations that urged immediate adoption of one route in preference to the other, Grant was constrained by strategic factors over which he had little or no control. One was the unpredictable Lee. The fame of his astonishing victories had not been dimmed by the repulse at Gettysburg. Even in repose he was still dangerous. Given means of mobility and substantial reinforcements, the latent threat posed by Lee assumed frightening proportions. Even the imperturbable Grant sensed its menace.

The identification of Confederate formations moving toward the Rapidan was far from complete. While it seemed reasonable to conclude that two divisions—Field's and Kershaw's—of Longstreet's I Corps were in movement from East Tennessee toward Lee, and that Pickett's Division of the same corps had quit the Neuse River front in North Carolina, the ultimate destination of this unit, as well as Beauregard's large reserve formation from the Department of South Carolina, Georgia, and Florida, remained a mystery throughout April.[10] Incited by fears akin to those inspired by Hannibal among the Romans, even after his defeat at Zama, rumor bespoke a Confederate host gathering for another invasion of the North. Nor could Grant be certain that the elements would not conspire to delay or prevent the transfer by sea of 10,000 troops of General Gillmore's Department of the South, from the Carolina coast to Hampton Roads. Then, while the organization and equipment of Burnside's IX Corps appeared to be going forward at Annapolis according to plan, and it seemed that this command would march toward the Rapidan late during April, the only positive guarantee of successful culmination of this movement would be the report of his arrival at Manassas Junction on or before the due date. Nothing is certain in war.

No doubt Grant's cautious attitude assumed a somber mood on April 21, when a dispatch transmitted by telegraph from Cairo confirmed alarming rumors of a disaster that had befallen Banks' expeditionary force on the Red River. Badly defeated at Mansfield, some 20 miles east of Shreveport, Banks had fallen back in considerable disorder to Alexandria, Louisiana.[11] While indulging hopes for a week that Banks would somehow manage to extricate his army and mount the Mobile assault force, Grant was compelled to admit on April 29, just three days before issuance of the order prescribing movement across the Rapidan against Lee's right, that Sherman's advance on Atlanta would be deprived of the dislocating effects of a rear attack through Mobile and up the Alabama River toward Montgomery.

Though exasperated more than once by repetitious warnings from senior officers of the Army of the Potomac that "You don't know Bobby Lee!" Grant did not deliberately ignore the opinion of soldiers who enjoyed the advantage of an intimate battlefield acquaintance with the redoubtable Confederate commander.[12] On April 27 he informed Halleck that Burnside's corps, then in motion from Annapolis, would be available to oppose any aggressive move Longstreet might make by way of the Shenandoah corridor.

Still uncertain as to the final disposition of Confederate formations moving into Virginia, the supreme commander withheld his decision to advance by the left. A note dispatched on April 29 to Halleck indicates an intention to march in that direction unless restrained by some such circumstance as report of a hostile force sweeping down the Shenandoah toward the Potomac. After stating that he proposed to move against Lee's army on May 4, "attempting to turn him by one flank or the other," he added:

> Should Lee fall back within his fortifications at Richmond without giving battle, I will form a junction with Butler and the two forces will draw supplies from the James River. My own notions about our line of march are entirely made up. but as circumstances beyond my control may change them, I will only state that my intention will be to bring Butler's and Meade's forces together.[13]

Events now hastened to a climax. Except for Banks' army immobilized on the Red River, Grant's program of concentration proceeded according to schedule. Rumors of a Confederate army of invasion did not materialize. Lee remained quiescent. The exact time at which Grant made his decision in the choice of routes is not known. Major General Andrew A. Humphreys, Chief of Staff of the Army of the Potomac, records that "The movement by the left flank was adopted, and I was requested by General Meade to prepare a project for it."

Humphreys Prepares An Operation Plan

In developing his "project," Humphreys was primarily concerned with perfecting a plan that offered the best guarantee against an encounter battle in the Wilderness.[14] Giving the plan its present day designation, Operation Wilderness hinged on two sets of calculations, one including an estimate of the time Lee would require in shifting his three corps elements

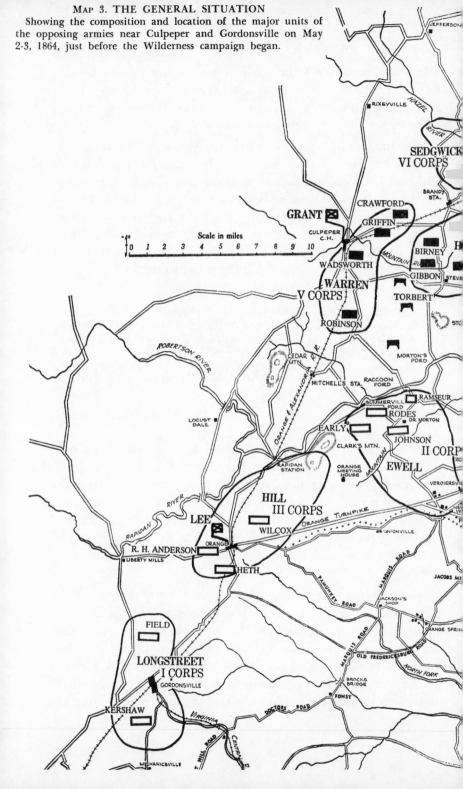

MAP 3. THE GENERAL SITUATION

Showing the composition and location of the major units of the opposing armies near Culpeper and Gordonsville on May 2-3, 1864, just before the Wilderness campaign began.

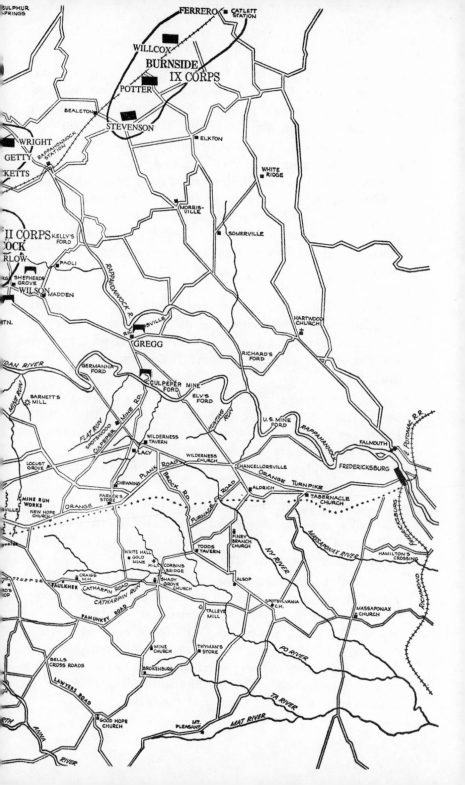

to a line of deployment in the Wilderness facing the right flank of Grant's marching columns, the other an approximation of the distance the Army of the Potomac could cover between the beginning and completion of Lee's redeployment.

Humphreys' calculations were conditioned by factors other than the marching ability of the two armies, namely the terrain to be traversed, the accessibility of roadways both as to direction and suitability in supporting the pressure of heavy wheeled traffic, and, in the case of the Army of the Potomac, the limitations of march-rate imposed by precautions for protection of the lumbering trains numbering 4,300 wagons. An exact calculation that would rule out every element of chance was impossible.

In approaching the Wilderness both armies would march on good roads through open country. But within its depths Lee had a decided advantage. Two hard-surfaced highways ran eastward from Orange Court House through the dense thickets.

One, the Orange Plank Road, traversed the low ridge between the basins of the Rapidan on the North and the Pamunkey on the South. Since over half of both Grant's and Lee's forces were drawn into the struggle for possession of the Plank Road ridge, the importance of this highway can scarcely be exaggerated.

Closely paralleling the Plank Road on the north, the Orange Turnpike cut straight across the Rapidan tributaries to Wilderness Church, where it joined the Plank Road and ran on past Chancellorsville into Fredericksburg.

A third lateral, the Catharpin Road, departed from the Plank Road near the southern extremity of Lee's return trenches along Mine Run, and, skirting the southern confines of the Wilderness, joined the Plank Road again at Aldrich's farm, a point some three miles east of Wilderness Church. Although an unpaved wagon track, the Catharpin Road was of vital importance in that its location facilitated a flanking maneuver by whichever army held the initiative.

In contrast to Lee's smooth, double-track axis of movement eastward, Grant suffered the disability of inferior roadways going south. While favorable on the whole as to direction, they were ill suited to the demands of his cumbersome, slow moving transport wagons which, aligned on a single highway, would have reached from the Rapidan to Richmond.

Two parallel roads went southward from Germanna Ford and Ely's Ford, respectively, to Wilderness Tavern and Chancellorsville. Departing from the Germanna Plank Road (the only hard-surfaced thoroughfare extending southward from the Rapidan into the Wilderness), the Brock Road ran on through the Wilderness to Spotsylvania Court House. Unpaved, this roadway cut a narrow gash through the forest, intersecting the Orange Plank Road 2½ miles south of Wilderness Tavern and the Catharpin Road at Todd's Tavern, 3½ miles farther south. Westward four miles out on the Catharpin Road from Todd's Tavern, Shady Grove Church stood at the Catharpin-Pamunkey Road intersection. Running on westerly and southwesterly courses, respectively, these two thoroughfares figured importantly in Humphrey's plan for enveloping the right of Lee's line of deployment in the Wilderness, or along Mine Run should Lee form for battle on that line.

Humphreys' problem was further complicated by the varying distances that Lee's three corps elements must traverse in arriving on a line of deployment in the Wilderness. Holding the right of the river front, Ewell's II Corps would take the turnpike into the Wilderness. Quitting the left of the line, Hill's III Corps would proceed along the Plank Road a considerable distance to the right rear of Ewell's column. Posted in the vicinity of Mechanicsville, an area to the left rear of the river line, covering Lee's rail center at Gordonsville, Longstreet's I Corps had the greater distance to go.

Experience in the Mine Run campaign of November 1863, when Meade crossed the Rapidan and pushed westward through the Wilderness to the front of Lee's Mine Run works, furnished factual data to supplement abstract speculation. Well aware that Lee had gone into the Wilderness on that occasion only for the purpose of developing Meade's advance, and had then fallen back to Mine Run, where he intended to fight, Humphreys now assumed that a firm determination on Lee's part to impose battle in the heart of the Wilderness would impel an increased rate of movement. Therefore, the factual evidence relating to Lee's previous performance was subject to correction.

Referring to the November campaign, Humphreys recalled that Meade's marching columns were detected at Culpeper shortly after dawn. Even with this early warning, Lee had required 36 hours for completion of dispositions to develop Meade's advance. Ewell had reached Locust Grove on the Turnpike at 10 a.m. the following day. Hill had arrived at Good Hope Church, a corresponding point on the Plank Road, six hours later. But if Lee improved his timetable, Meade too must find some time-saving device.

Humphreys arrived at a solution. Postponement of the warning for several hours might, he thought, be contrived by putting the Federal columns in motion toward the Rapidan at midnight. Assuming that the advance should reach the north bank without detection, it seemed safe to conclude that, although the right division of Ewell's II Corps might make its presence felt within a few hours of the crossing, his left elements could not close to complete the concentration at Locust Grove before nightfall. Nor could A. P. Hill's III Corps reach a point on the Plank Road within supporting distance of Ewell before noon of the following day. Then, unless Lee anticipated the time and direction of Grant's movement and shifted his reserve formation at Mechanicsville toward the source of Mine Run, it seemed unlikely that Longstreet's I Corps would be able to deploy on a line of battle in the Wilderness before nightfall of that day. Humphreys states the proposition as follows:

> There was every reason to believe, however, from our ex-
> perience in the movement against Lee in the preceding

November, that by setting the whole army in motion at midnight, with its reserve artillery and great trains of over four thousand wagons, it might move so far beyond the Rapidan the first day that it would be able to pass out of the Wilderness and turn, or partially turn, the right flank of Lee before a general engagement took place. There was no question of the practicability of the troops, with their fighting trains, accomplishing this, as they were equal to, and ready for, a continuous march of thirty. miles or more in twenty-four hours, by which they would have got substantially clear of the Wilderness; they had often before made such marches when called to do so; but the question was as to the practicability of moving the great trains of the army that distance simultaneously with the troops, so as to keep them under cover of the army.[15]

In reality, the necessity of covering the great trains, or second line transport, rather than natural obstacles of The Wilderness to a passage of combat troops, retarded the rate of advance. The time-period during which Grant might safely ignore Lee's efforts to bring on a general engagement was thus reduced to a narrow margin. It was expected that the rear of the great trains would cross the river late in the afternoon of the second day, or approximately the time that Longstreet might arrive within supporting distance of Ewell and Hill. Yet dispositions for the culminating phase of the movement against Lee's right flank must be completed while wagons of the second line transport were still rolling over the pontoon bridges at the Rapidan.

In frankly admitting that the Army of the Potomac would be tied to its great trains during the march toward Lee's right flank and, indeed, that even an advance pushed to the utmost limit compatible with the safety of the trains incurred the risk of inviting the battle Grant hoped to avoid, Humphreys planned the details of a maneuver which was to begin at midnight May 3-4 and end late in the afternoon on May 5.

March Order for May 4

As a matter of fact, the chief of staff drew up two "projects." Both plans, he relates, were coincident for the first day. Both were subject on the second day to material modification or complete abandonment. One proposed that the turning movement proceed "by the Catharpin and Pamunkey Roads in comparatively open country"; the other contemplated a maneuver "by roads having about the same direction as the Pamunkey but from five to eight miles eastward, passing two to four miles west of Spotsylvania Court House." Humphreys does not specify these roads.

Upon approval of the first plan, that is by the Catharpin-Pamunkey Roads, he prepared and issued, on March 2, a march order for the first day, May 4. The order for continuation of the march on May 5, the second day, was to be issued in the field upon completion of movement during May 4 and based on dispositions taken by the enemy, as reported and evaluated at Meade's headquarters.

The order for the march issued on May 2 proposed that the combat units, accompanied by their first-line transport, march in two parallel columns.[16] The right column, composed of Wilson's 3d Cavalry Division, Warren's V Corps and Sedgwick's VI Corps, was to cross the Rapidan at Germanna Ford and march to Wilderness Tavern. Moving simultaneously with the right, the left column, composed of Gregg's 2d Cavalry Division, Hancock's II Corps and the Artillery Reserve, would pass over the river at Ely's Ford and proceed to Chancellorsville.

In the event that Lee should attempt to dispute the crossing in force, the 2d and 3d Cavalry Divisions were to hold the pontoon bridges, the former at Ely's Ford, the latter at Germanna Ford, until reinforced by infantry. Anticipating such a contingency, Warren and Hancock were under instructions to throw forward half their respective commands and enlarge the bridgeheads, while reserves moved up to force the issue. Providing, however, that nothing more serious than outpost resistance was encountered, both columns were to push on into the Wilderness to their designated objectives.

The Artillery Reserve, according to the march order for May 4, was to follow Hancock's II Corps, going into bivouac along Hunting Run, near Chancellorsville. Moving as a separate element, the great trains were to be divided into two columns, one following the Artillery Reserve over Ely's Ford, the other crossing at Culpeper Mine Ford. All vehicles passing the river on the first day were to park in the vicinity of Dowdall's Tavern, which is on the turnpike between Wilderness Church and Chancellorsville. Torbert's 1st Cavalry Division was assigned the mission of covering the great trains on the north side of the Rapidan during the first day.

Much to the aggravation of military historians, Humphreys gives no detailed description of the plan he originally had in mind for execution on the second day. While it is admitted that this phase of the two-days' maneuver was subject to modification on the second day, the only indication of dispositions originally intended for completion on that day are disclosed by three precautionary instructions written into the order of march for May 4, as issued on May 2. Intended to warn one corps commander and two cavalry division commanders of the movements expected of their units on May 5, these precautionary instructions reveal enough of the original plan to permit a reasonable reconstruction of the whole.

In reference to the contemplated operation of Warren's V Corps on the second day, paragraph 3 of the order issued on May 2 states in part: "The V Corps will move the following day [May 5] past the head of Catharpin Run, crossing the Orange Plank Road at Parker's Store."

Acting in accordance with these instructions, Warren would have proceeded up the valley of Wilderness Run to Parker's Store and thence southward across the Orange Plank Road to the vicinity of Craig's Meeting House. The meeting house, it should be observed, is situated on the Catharpin Road, near the source of Catharpin Run and four miles west of Shady Grove Church, at the Pamunkey-Catharpin Road intersection.

Although no precautionary instructions were issued on May 2 to Hancock and Sedgwick, there can be no question that the march order for May 5, as issued in the field during the afternoon of May 4, curtailed movements originally intended for both the II and VI corps. Granting that the turning columns were to march by the Pamunkey and Catharpin Roads, there is no escape from the conclusion that Hancock's II Corps would have pushed beyond Shady Grove Church, his objective in the modified movement, to a point on the Pamunkey Road corresponding to Warren's position on the Catharpin Road. In accordance with the same logic, Sedgwick's VI Corps would have advanced toward Parker's Store for the purpose of covering the Plank Road and supporting Warren on the Catharpin Road.

The preparatory instructions written into the orders issued on May 2 also give a fairly clear indication of the role originally prescribed for Meade's powerful cavalry arm during the two-days' maneuver. Paragraph 2 of the march order for May 4 warned Gregg that his 2d Cavalry Division "will remain in their position to cover the passage of the army trains and will move with them [on the 5th] and cover their left flank." Paragraph 13 of the same order tentatively assigned to Torbert's 1st Cavalry Division, numerically the strongest of the mounted corps, the following mission: "On the morning of the 5th, the First Cavalry Division will cross the Rapidan at Germanna Ford and cover the right flank of the trains while crossing the Rapidan during their movement in rear of the army."

The written statement of Torbert's tentative assignment appears to have been dictated solely by fear of hostile action across the Germanna Plank Road toward the right of the great trains which would be moving from the river toward Dowdall's Tavern until late in the afternoon. Meanwhile general headquarters planned for participation of Burnside's IX Corps in the maneuver. Upon notice from Grant on May 4 that Meade's columns were crossing the river as scheduled, Burnside would abandon the Orange and Alexandria Railroad and proceed to Germanna Ford. It was expected that Burnside's leading division, awaiting orders at Brandy Station, would reach the ford early on the 5th and, followed during the day by two other divisional units, would close toward Wilderness Tavern.[17]

Relieved of its impedimenta, the Army of the Potomac could press forward. Burnside, according to Grant's plan, became responsible for the safety of Meade's rear while Meade, though powerless to regulate Burnside's dispositions, must assume responsibility for the turning movement.

Whittling Down a Good Plan

Apparently assured that the presence of Burnside's three divisions on the Germanna Plank Road afforded adequate security on the right of the trains, Meade became apprehensive during the afternoon of May 4 over the situation on the left. Disturbed by a report of a Confederate cavalry force at Hamilton's Crossing, some ten miles east from the position of Gregg's cavalry division at Aldrich's farm, Meade cancelled Torbert's tentative instructions with an order to cross the Rapidan at Ely's Ford and proceed to the Aldrich place, where Sheridan would assume command of the combined cavalry force.[18]

Never adequately explained, this modification of the role originally assigned Meade's cavalry arm marks the first significant departure from the plan as contemplated on May 2.

Although the written version of the mission tentatively assigned Torbert for May 5 appears to have been limited to protection of the trains, he would have completed this mission during the afternoon. Sheridan's angry protest over the concentration of his two strongest divisions in the rear of the army, leaving only Wilson's division to screen the front, offers convincing evidence that the cavalry commander saw a purpose in Torbert's presence on the Germanna Plank Road beyond the intent of the written order. As forseen on May 2, completion of dispositions for the culminating phase of the flank movement would have placed two cavalry divisions on the line of deployment, Torbert's on the right and Wilson's on the left. Furthermore, establishment of cavalry corps headquarters at the Omber Mine, on a side road just north of Wilderness Tavern, reveals an aggressive intent on Sheridan's part. Otherwise the chief of cavalry puts himself in the light of seeking a headquarters location far in the rear of Meade's infantry.[19]

Further discussion of this particular departure from the original plan would scarcely be profitable. Instead of the battle Grant intended to fight, he fought the one he hoped to avoid. Continued whittling at the core of a bold design compelled him to accept Lee's terms of engagement in The Wilderness. Yet it seems pertinent to observe that the timidity prompting Meade's change of assignment for Torbert not only characterized the whole whittling process but is illustrative of opportunities lost in war by want of purpose in resolutely pursuing, even at some risk, a bold course of action.

The delay imposed by a single regiment—the 5th New York Cavalry—of Wilson's division during the forenoon of May 5 on the advance of A. P. Hill's III Corps along the Plank Road offers a convincing demonstration of the damage that 3,000 dismounted troopers of Torbert's division might have inflicted on the left of the II Confederate Corps as Ewell began his deployment across Warren's front on the Orange Turnpike.

Indeed, the adaptability to forest fighting of the single-line formation of dismounted Federal cavalry, together with the vastly superior fire power of its magazine rifles, would have given a golden opportunity for effective work. As will be seen in narrating operations of the curtailed movement, Wilson's screen was torn to tatters, while the preponderance of Sheridan's powerful force stood immobile in the rear.

CHAPTER 3

LEE'S PLAN—OPERATION RAPIDAN

The suspense endured by Lee during the dreary winter of 1863-64 on the Rapidan was one that would have tested the fortitude of any great commander. Always an ardent offensive fighter, he was condemned to inactivity by want of the supplies and equipment that would have given him the means of mobility. Yet he explored every possibility for deranging the enemy's preparations by a quick offensive stab, either in East Tennessee or beyond the Rapidan.

Lee Surveys the Continental Theater

The widely accepted view that Lee deliberately restricted the scope of his strategic genius in confining his attention to the Virginia theater is controverted by the interest and intelligent appreciation he evinced in observing the tide of events that turned inexorably after the loss of Chattanooga and flowed on as Grant rose to supreme command of the Federal armies. The Army of Northern Virginia had scarcely been settled in winter quarters when, on December 3, 1863 he expressed to President Davis his apprehension that Grant's victorious force at Chattanooga could invade Georgia and seize the depots of provisions and manufactories in that region. Insisting that "more force is required in Georgia," and that the formation of any substantial reserve would be limited to troops withdrawn from Beauregard's Department of South Carolina, and Florida, together with Polk's Army of Mississippi, then posted at Meridian, and the Mobile Defense Force under Maury, he added:

> Upon the defense of the country threatened by General Grant depends the safety of the points now held by us on the Atlantic, and they are in as great danger from his suc-

41

cessful advance as to the attacks to which they are at present directly subjected.[1]

While emphasizing that every available reserve should be concentrated in central Georgia so long as that area appeared to be the primary objective of Federal arms, Lee grasped the real meaning of Grant's decision to attach his headquarters to the Army of the Potomac. On March 30, 1864, Lee reported to President Davis that there were stronger indications of vigorous operations in Virginia. "Grant," he observed, "has returned from the West. He is at present with the Army of the Potomac." [2] Nor did he miss the significance of reports that Burnside was organizing "a large army" at Annapolis and that additional forces were moving toward the Shenandoah Valley. On April 11 he informed General Breckenridge, commanding Confederate forces in the Valley, that "a combined effort of the enemy would be made to capture Richmond and that the great struggle would take place in Virginia." [3]

Lee Plans to Hold the River Line

Lee was not disposed to yield the initiative to his new adversary. Richmond, he advised, should be covered by a special defense command and, reinforced by Beauregard, disposed to meet an attack from the sea, while he held his army, augmented by the recall of detached units, in readiness on the Rapidan for any eventuality. Given an adequate reserve of supplies, he proposed to strike beyond the Rapidan while Grant was completing his preparations to take the field.

> Should God give us a crowning victory there all their plans would be dissipated, and their troops now on the Chesapeake would be called to the defense of Washington. If I am obliged to retire from this line, either by a flank movement of the enemy or the want of supplies, great injury would befall us. I have ventured to throw out these suggestions to Your Excellency in order that in surveying the whole field of operations you may consider all the circumstances bearing on the question.[4]

Meanwhile, the enemy beyond the Rapidan day by day advanced his vast preparations, mounting an offensive that would test as never before the temper of Lee's thin formations. His conflicting moods of high hope and gloomy dejection are reflected in a dispatch of April 18 to General Bragg, then acting as chief of the President's military cabinet.

> I cannot even draw to me the cavalry and artillery of the army, and the season has arrived when I may be attacked any day. If we are forced back from our present line, the Central Railroad, Charlottesville and all the upper country will be exposed and I fear great injury inflicted on us.[5]

On the same day, April 18, Lee placed the Federal force on the Rappahannock at a figure not in excess of 75,000. This calculation was approximately 20,000 under Meade's report of the strength of the Army of the Potomac. With less information at his disposal, he estimated that Burnside's command mustered some 50,000 effectives and was composed of two army corps—the IX and another made up from a consolidation of the XI and XII Corps.[6] These units, it will be recalled, had been detached from the Army of the Potomac to offset the reinforcement brought by Longstreet's I Corps to Bragg's Army of Tennessee on the eve of Chickamauga.

As a matter of fact, Burnside had only his IX Corps. While one mistake tended to compensate the other in an estimate of grand totals, Lee erred considerably in his calculation of the force he expected to engage with his own army. At the same time, his mistake in assuming that Burnside would move by Chesapeake Bay to Fortress Monroe and cooperate with Butler's advance on Richmond led to a belief that the attack from the sea would assume larger proportions than the one actually contemplated by Grant.

With 62,000 Confederates opposed to 75,000 Federals on the Rapidan, the odds against Lee were not disproportionate to those he encountered on the Rappahannock at Fredericksburg during December 1862. Again, in beating Hooker at Chancellorsville he triumphed signally against odds of over two to one. So now, after noting in a communication of April 18 to Davis that Grant would rely on a flank movement toward Richmond to draw the Army of Northern Virginia back from the Rapidan, Lee concluded with an optimistic note:

> If that movement can be successfully met and resisted, I have no uneasiness as to the result of the campaign in Virginia. I know of no better plan than that submitted in a former letter to Your Excellency.[7]

Lee's Final Preparations

During the interval between April 18 and May 4, when Grant moved into the Wilderness, Lee called insistently for the return of troops that had been detached from his army during the winter. Johnston's Brigade was still at Hanover Junction. Hoke's Brigade, with two additional regiments, together with Pickett's Division of Longstreet's I Corps, had been detained in hopes of successfully terminating operations on the Neuse River, in North Carolina. Lee's insistence, no doubt, would have been more pronounced had he known of Grant's intention to reinforce the Army of the Potomac with Burnside's IX Corps.

This eventuality was not disclosed to Lee until the IX Corps passed through Washington enroute to the Rappahannock on April 28. Stringfellow, a famous Confederate agent in his employ, joined the cheering throng as Burnside's divisions, bands blaring and colors flying, swung down 14th Street. At a convenient point near Willard's Hotel, where President Lincoln and General Burnside reviewed the parade from a second story balcony, Stringfellow made a careful estimate of Burnside's effective strength.[8]

The next day Lee knew that the odds against him had increased. But Stringfellow's count, added to his previous computation, did not give Grant more than 100,000. Thus the odds, according to Lee's final estimate, had shifted from a situation comparing favorably with that of Fredericksburg to one more nearly approaching the heavier odds with which Hooker had attempted to load the scales of fate at Chancellorsville.

While calling for the return of detached troops, Lee made

every effort within his slender means to put the Army of Northern Virginia in readiness for the field. He reduced his transportation and brought up his strongest horses. On April 18 he issued orders to send back surplus baggage and prepare for movement at any time. "There was a little stir among ordnance officers," relates Wilcox, a division commander in Hill's III Corps, and "a more than usual activity among those of the medical corps." [9] But, failing a supply of forage, Lee was quite aware that the concentration of his mounted units must await the growing grass of spring. A movement on Grant's part in the interim, he knew, meant the loss of the Rapidan line.

The anxious days of April were finally relieved by the welcome sight of green grass on the bare hillsides. Lee sensed a sudden relief from helpless inactivity. No doubt he unconsciously paraphrased in his devotions the prayers of thanksgiving offered at springtime by pastoral princes in the days of Job. On April 28, the same day that Burnside's divisions marched through Washington, Lee informed Davis that "the grass is springing now and I am drawing the cavalry and artillery to me." [10]

The next day Lee hastened to Mechanicsville and reviewed Longstreet's Corps in a broad pasture nearby. General Alexander, commanding the corps artillery, recalls that the appearance of the army commander was greeted with a great wave of sentiment. "There was no speaking, but the effect was as of a military sacrament." Dr. Boggs, Staff Chaplain of the I Corps, turned to Colonel Venable, *aide de camp* to Lee and asked: "Does it not make the General proud to see how these men love him?" Venable replied, "Not proud. It awes him." [11]

Back at Orange Court House on the 30th, Lee quietly waited for reports indicating an exodus from the great encampment beyond the Rapidan. Grant, at the same time, was perplexed by rumors that reinforcements were gathering under Longstreet for a dash down the Shenandoah. He was also worried lest Gillmore and the iron-clads convoying his reinforcements from the Carolina coast should fail to arrive in Hampton Roads by May 4.

On Monday May 2, Lee assembled his corps and division commanders at the signal station on Clark's Mountain. The view from this eminence overlooks an area embracing twenty Virginia counties. [12] To the north, the vast city of canvas that had sheltered the Army of the Potomac during the long winter months sprawled over rolling fields between the Rapidan and the Rappahannock. Far to the east, a waving sea of misty deep green marked the Wilderness. Just a year ago to the day, Lee took the desperate chance of dividing, in the presence of a vastly superior enemy, his army on the outer edge of that woodland and sending Jackson through its depths to fall on Hooker's right flank near Wilderness Church. Beyond, invisible in the distant mists, rose the spires of Fredericksburg, where Burnside's passage of the Rappahannock ended in an appalling disaster to Federal arms on December 13, 1862.

If Lee's glasses swept over the fields of his former triumphs, they returned to the rolling plain about Culpeper. After careful study of indications of movement in the enemy's cantonments, he cased his binoculars and expressed a conviction that Grant was preparing to march downstream and would cross the Rapidan, possibly at Germanna or Ely's Ford. He thereupon instructed the general officers present to have their commands in readiness to move on short notice.[13]

On May 3, the day following, records Wilcox, "an order was issued to have, in the language of the camp 'three days' cooked rations, thus putting an end to all suspense." [14]

CHAPTER 4

INTO THE WILDERNESS

At midnight May 3-4 the march began, both Federal columns moving simultaneously. Wilson's 3d Cavalry Division, escorting a section of the Cavalry Corps bridge train, left its encampment at Stevensburg and took the Plank Road toward Germanna Ford. Warren's two advanced divisions, Griffin's 1st and Crawford's 2d, with accompanying artillery, combat trains, and a section of the V Corps bridge train, entered the road from Culpeper Court House to Stevensburg. Wadsworth's and Robinson's divisions, the 4th and 3d, respectively, followed in column. Sedgwick's three VI Corps divisions quit their camps in the vicinity of Brandy Station at daylight. Getty's 2d took the advance, with Wright's 1st following and Ricketts' 3d bringing up the rear.[1]

Gregg's 2d Cavalry Division and a section of the Cavalry Corps bridge train formed in column on the Richardsville-Ely's Ford road, while Hancock's four II Corps divisions moved along by-ways to Madden, on the main road between Culpeper Court House and Richardsville. At 2 a.m. the cavalry advance started for Ely's Ford.[2]

Meade Crosses the Rapidan

Wilson's cavalry division reached the edge of the bluff overlooking Germanna Ford about 2 a.m. A squadron of the 3d Indiana Cavalry plunged into the stream and, clattering up the opposite bank, dispersed a picket of the 1st North Carolina Cavalry. Preparations for the crossing were then hurried. Pontoniers under direction of Captain Folwell launched their canvas floats and laid the decks for passage of the infantry. Wilson's mounted units splashed across the river and

47

formed in column on the south bank along the Germanna
Plank Road.[3]

At 5:50 a.m. Wilson notified Warren that his last cavalry
regiment was crossing the ford and that a canvas pontoon
bridge was nearly completed. Warren's leading division
(Griffin's) approached the river at 6 a.m. It would appear, however, that the wooden pontoon bridge, which accompanied the
advance of the V Corps, was thrown over the stream between
6 and 7 a.m. and that Wilson's horse batteries and combat
trains crossed by both bridges, thus detaining the head of Warren's column at the north bank for nearly an hour. Warren
states in his journal that he began crossing at 7 a.m., as soon as
General Wilson's cavalry division had cleared the bridges.[4]

In all probability a trooper of the 1st North Carolina
Cavalry picket hastened back to Maj. W. H. H. Cowles, the
regimental commander, and reported that enemy cavalry was
crossing the Rapidan at Germanna Ford. Confirmation of a
movement in force was not long delayed. As the rising sun dispelled the morning mists, long columns of infantry and artillery, with their accompanying combat trains, came under observation of the Confederate signal station on Clark's Mountain. A flag signal informed Lieutenant General Ewell at II
Corps headquarters that: "From present indications everything seems to be moving to the right on Germanna and Ely's
Ford roads, leaving cavalry in our front." The time of transmission was not stated.[5]

Intercepted and decoded by the Federal signal detachment
on Stony Mountain, the message originally flagged to Ewell
was relayed to Meade's headquarters at 9:30 a.m. Considerable
delay in delivery of this important dispatch may be attributed
to the circumstance that Grant and Meade, with their respective staffs, were in the saddle on the road to Germanna
Ford from sunup till noonday.*

---

* The time of delivery to Meade is unknown. According to the published
list of messages sent from Stony Mountain on May 4, three contain the text
of signals originally flagged from Clark's Mountain to Ewell. Nothing can be
deduced from the original texts of these three messages, or from the comments

Into the Wilderness

The thud of Warren's infantry on the decks of the two pontoon bridges gave Wilson his signal to begin the movement toward Wilderness Tavern. He conducted the cavalry advance on the Germanna Plank Road with extreme caution, halting at every byway while small detachments rode out to cover the right flank of the column. His main body could not have proceeded any great distance within two hours beyond the Beal place, where a wagon trail known as the Flat Run Road went westward, passing Widow Willis's farm and going on toward Barnett's Mill, near Mine Run. Observing at 9 a.m the movement from his command post on the Flat Run trail, Major Cowles reported to Ewell:

> I have discovered the enemy's pickets at this point, Mrs. Willis's house, about two miles from Germanna. I have seen some footmen, but they may be only dismounted cavalry; it is evidently a heavy cavalry picket at least, and the moving of their trains on the plank road can be plainly heard. I have sent out dismounted scouts to approach the plank road, and have taken steps to open communications with my detachment on the left.[6]

Cowles' dispatch was probably the first Confederate intelligence to the effect that Federal troops had gained the south bank of the Rapidan and were advancing into the Wilderness. Carried by courier, his message was delivered at II Corps headquarters after receipt of the Clark's Mountain signal. Lee, no doubt, was aware of the situation reported by Clark's Mountain and Cowles' cavalry pickets some time after the Federal signal officer at Stony Mountain had decoded the intercepted signal, but, in all probability, before it came to the attention of General Meade and his chief of staff.

Between 9 a.m. and noon Wilson moved leisurely on to

added by the Stony Mountain signal officer, that would indicate any movements of Lee's forces from the Rapidan River front. The fourth and final message from Stony Mountain reports at 3 p.m. the first observation from that point of a Confederate movement to the right. As discussed elsewhere in this chapter, no documentary evidence can be found to support Grant's statement that "rebel signals . . . when translated" and relayed at 1:15 p.m. disclosed Lee's intention to occupy the Mine Run entrenchments.

Wilderness Tavern and halted. Patrols went out west along the Turnpike toward Locust Grove, where shots were exchanged with a Confederate picket, and south along the Brock Road to Todd's Tavern. About noon Griffin's division, advancing on Germanna Plank Road, came within sight of the waiting horsemen. Whereupon Wilson led his troopers into the wagon track winding up the valley of Wilderness Run to Parker's Store.[7]

At 2 p.m. the cavalry of the right column reached its objective and went into bivouac near the store. Wilson detailed Lieutenant Colonel John Hammond, commanding the 5th New York Cavalry, to ride westward on the Orange Plank Road with his entire command and feel the enemy toward Mine Run. Other patrols went out from Parker's Store to the Catharpin and Pamunkey Roads.[8]

Meanwhile the cavalry advance of the left column proceeded in accordance with the orders of march. Gregg's command reached Ely's Ford before dawn and began fording the river, while pontoniers laid the canvas bridge. A galloper carried the news to Major General Fitzhugh Lee, commanding the Confederate cavalry division near Hamilton's Crossing. Upon appearance of Hancock's infantry at the bridgehead, the cavalry pushed on through Chancellorsville to Aldrich's Farm, at the Catharpin-Orange Plank Road intersection. Patrols went west, south, and east, one going well out on the Pamunkey Road beyond Shady Grove Church, another toward Spotsylvania Court House, while the third reconnoitered in the direction of Hamilton's Crossing and Fredericksburg.[9] Hancock reported the arrival of his advance at Ely's Ford in a dispatch time-dated 6:30 a.m., at which time he commenced crossing by the canvas bridge, while pontoniers, assisted by infantrymen, assembled the wooden bridge.[10]

As cavalry patrols pushed on through the Wilderness to points on a vast semicircle skirting its outer bounds, the two infantry columns continued their slow progress over the river. Griffin's division of the V Corps, leading the right column, arrived at Wilderness Tavern about noon. Turning west, Griffin went out one and one-tenth miles on the Orange Turnpike and established a strong picket line across the road.[11] Crawford's division, following Griffin in column of march, took the Parker's Store road into Major Lacy's plantation and made camp on the west bank of Wilderness Run. General Crawford established his headquarters for the night at the Lacy house. Wadsworth's division, following Crawford into the Lacy fields, made camp on the east bank of Wilderness Run. General Wadsworth detailed a detachment to picket the Turnpike toward Chancellorsville. Robinson's division, bringing up the rear of the V Corps, crossed the Rapidan at 1 p.m. and bivouacked by the side of Germanna Plank Road, near the bend of Caton Run and about a mile north of Wilderness Tavern. At 3:05 p.m. Warren reported from Wilderness Tavern that his men "were almost all in camp and washing their feet." He established his headquarters at the edge of the woods on the north side of the Turnpike and about one-half mile west of the tavern.[12]

Holding the advance of Sedgwick's VI Corps, Getty's division crossed the Rapidan in rear of the V Corps and halted on the Germanna Plank Road near Flat Run, which cuts across the highway some two and one-half miles northwest of Wilderness Tavern. Wright's division, following Getty's, camped on the roadside between Flat Run and the Rapidan. Ricketts' division, closing Sedgwick's rear, passed over the pontoons at 6 p.m. and took a position near the river bank to cover the crossing. The canvas bridge was picked up and sent to the Cavalry Corps train. The wooden bridge was left intact for Burnside's crossing on the 5th.[13]

Hancock's leading division, Barlow's 1st, reached Chancellorsville at 9:30 a.m. and went into camp on the Orange and Fredericksburg Plank Road beyond the Chancellor House. The rear of the II Corps passed over the Ely's Ford pontoons at 1:40 p.m., when the canvas bridge was picked up and sent to the Cavalry Corps train. Three divisions of the II Corps were encamped in the vicinity of the Chancellor House by 1:40 p.m. Arrival of the fourth was not reported; but in all probability the II Corps divisions were in camp by 3:05 p.m., at the time when Warren informed Humphreys that most of his men were washing their feet.[14]

Torbert, who covered the movement north of the Rapidan on the first day with his 1st Cavalry Division, withdrew all pickets along the river front west of Rapidan Station soon after dawn. During the course of the day he drew his scattered patrols toward Richardsville. While these dispositions were adequate for protection of the trains, he failed to intercept a Confederate infantry column under Brigadier General Stephen D. Ramseur, who made a reconnaissance from Raccoon Ford to Culpeper Court House and definitely established that the Army of the Potomac had moved by the left into the Wilderness.[15]

Aside from the belated march of Sedgwick's rear element and the movement of cavalry patrols along forest paths leading out from Aldrich's farm and Parker's Store, Meade's invading columns had come to rest by midafternoon. This early halt, according to Humphreys, was unavoidable. In working out the details of his two-days maneuver he had been fully aware of the desirability of pushing with all possible haste through the tangled woodland. He readily admits that both columns could easily have pushed on five miles further, the II Corps going to Todd's Tavern, at the junction of the Catharpin and Brock Roads, while the V Corps went on to Parker's Store and the VI Corps closed up near the Wilderness Tavern.

Such a disposition at dawn on the 5th would have placed the seven divisions of Warren and Sedgwick in position to cover both the Turnpike and Plank Road, with Hancock's four divisions in supporting distance at Todd's Tavern. But Humphreys had also foreseen that an advance of the two columns beyond Chancellorsville and Wilderness Tavern on the 4th would create difficulties in protecting the great trains on the morning of the 5th. Should occasion require that the right column face west and form in line of battle, the right of the line thus formed must cover the trains. With the VI Corps at Wilderness Tavern, over four miles from the river, this demand could not have been met during the early morning hours of the 5th.[16]

The danger foreseen by Humphreys might have been mitigated to a considerable extent by the presence of Torbert's 1st Cavalry Division on the Germanna Plank Road in rear of the VI Corps column. As we know, such a disposition had been tentatively assigned to Torbert's division for May 5. Furthermore, three IX Corps divisions were expected to cross the Rapidan at Germanna Ford between dawn and midafternoon and close toward Wilderness Tavern. But, like Torbert's assignment, this arrangement was tentative in nature and dependent on circumstances that could not have been foreseen on May 2. While Burnside's divisional units were to be held in readiness to move on short notice, the supreme commander realized that the signal to put them in motion could not be given until he became convinced that Meade's two columns would complete the river crossing without mishap. In brief, it would be premature to give the signal before noon on the 4th. But if Burnside's ability to cover the right flank of the trains on May 5 was contingent on circumstances that could not have been foreseen when Humphreys, on May 2, sketched his original "project," he was able at that time to make a fairly close approximation of the rate of movement of the great trains. In accordance with his calculation, it was not until 2 p.m. on the 5th that the rear of the wagon column going by Ely's Ford reached the south side of the Rapidan, and it was 5 oclock in the afternoon when the last vehicle rolled over pontoon bridge at Culpeper Mine Ford.[17]

Indications of Confederate Reaction

Since any modification of the original plan was to be written into the march orders for May 5, the preparation of these orders would be determined by the amount of information

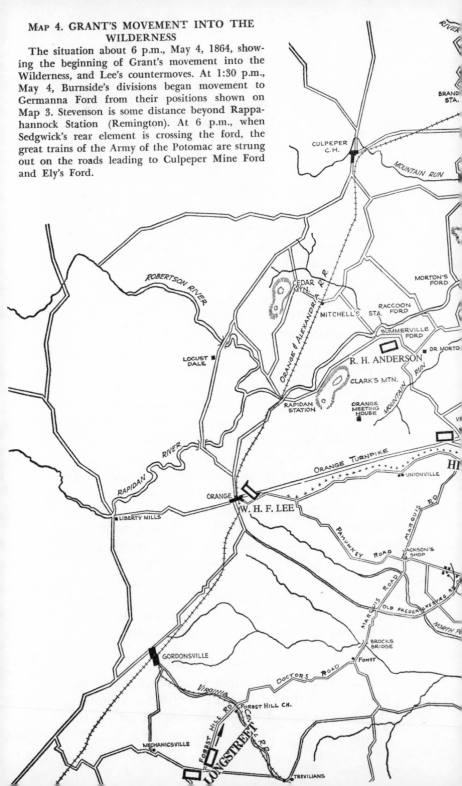

MAP 4. GRANT'S MOVEMENT INTO THE WILDERNESS

The situation about 6 p.m., May 4, 1864, showing the beginning of Grant's movement into the Wilderness, and Lee's countermoves. At 1:30 p.m., May 4, Burnside's divisions began movement to Germanna Ford from their positions shown on Map 3. Stevenson is some distance beyond Rappahannock Station (Remington). At 6 p.m., when Sedgwick's rear element is crossing the ford, the great trains of the Army of the Potomac are strung out on the roads leading to Culpeper Mine Ford and Ely's Ford.

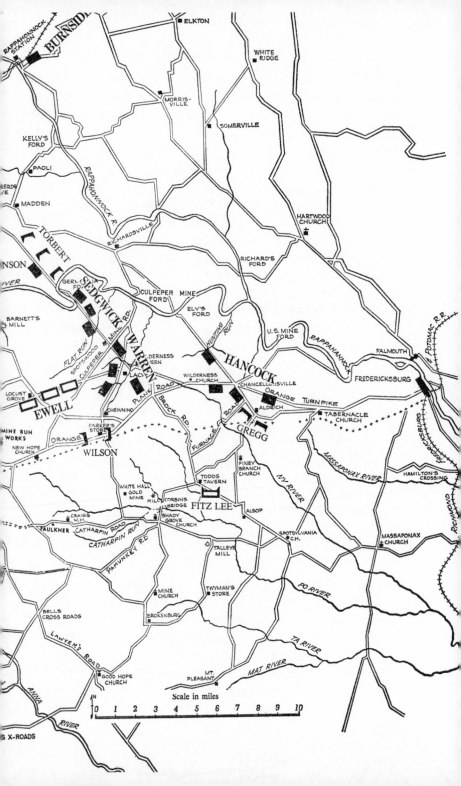

gathered in the field during May 4 and reported at army headquarters. As already indicated, some intelligence which might bear on formulation of the directive was accumulated while general and army headquarters were on the road to Germanna Ford.

Grant and his headquarters staff left Culpeper Court House about 8 a.m. and joined General Warren on the line of march. The army commander passed through Brandy Station, according to Morris Schaff, an ordnance officer of his staff, "as the sun cleared the tree tops." The supreme commander and the major generals commanding the V and VI Corps, with their respective staffs, gathered by the roadside near Germanna Ford to watch the thick, double columns file by toward the river. Lieutenant Schaff, who rode from his ammunition depot at Brandy Station with General Hunt, Chief of Artillery, joined Meade's staff near the river.[18] He recalls the spectacle:

> Under the open pines on the bluff we found Warren, Meade, and Grant, with their headquarters colors. They and their staffs spurred and in top boots, all fine-looking fellows, were dismounted and standing or lounging around in groups. Grant was a couple of hundred yards back from the ford, and except Babcock, Comstock, and Porter, he and all of his staff were strangers to the officers and the rank and file of the army. His headquarters flag was the national colors; Mead's a lilac-colored, swallow-tailed flag having in the field a wreath inclosing an eagle in gold; Warren's Fifth Corps a blue swallowtail, with a Maltese cross in a white field.
>
> Down each of the roads, to the bridges that were forty or fifty feet apart, the troops, well closed up, were pouring. The batteries, ambulances, and ammunition trains followed their respective divisions.[19]

Grant and Meade crossed the river together shortly before noon. The supreme commander rode to the top of the bluff overlooking the ford and dismounted at an old farm house with Dutch gables and a porch in front. Meade selected a site for his headquarters camp close by. While awaiting the arrival of his baggage train, Grant sat down on the steps under the gables and lapsed into one of his characteristic reveries. Finally arousing himself, he is reported by Horace Porter to have said: "Well, the movement so far has been as satisfactory as could be desired. We have succeeded in seizing the fords and crossing the river without loss or delay. Lee must by this time know upon what roads we are advancing, but he may not yet realize the full extent of the movement. We shall probably soon get some indication as to what he intends to do." [20]

Grant's expectations were soon realized. A courier from army headquarters handed him a dispatch containing the transcript of a decoded signal flagged from Clark's Mountain and relayed from Stony Mountain. After reading the text, Grant is reported by Porter to have said: "That gives me just the information I wanted. It shows that Lee is drawing out of his position and is pushing to meet us."

Unfortunately, neither Grant nor Porter identify the message either by time-date or direct quotation of text. Grant amplifies in his *Memoirs* the remark attributed to him by Porter, only to confuse the issue. After recalling that "Lee did not learn until about one o'clock by what route we would confront his army," he adds: "This I judge from the fact that at 1:15 p.m. . . . our officers took off the rebel signals which, when translated, were seen to be an order to his troops to occupy their entrenchments at Mine Run." [21]

The intercepted signal relayed at 9:30 a.m. from Stony Mt. indicated that Lee was aware long before 1:15 p.m. of the roads by which the Army of the Potomac was marching into the Wilderness. There was nothing, however, to indicate at the time of relay that Lee's forces were in motion. To the contrary, the Stony Mountain station added to its transcription of the decoded message the brief statement: "No change yet." A second intercepted message relayed at 11 a.m. contained the additional statement: "Enemy still digging." not until 3 p.m. did the Federal signal station flag a report on enemy movement from the Rapidan River line toward Verdiersville. [22]

Unless Grant read a decoded message which does not appear in the published list of signals sent from Stony Mountain during May 4, it is difficult to understand how he came by the vital intelligence which, according to Colonel Porter, he described as "just the information I wanted." If there was such a message, we have the difficult problem of reconciling incomplete source material with the dubious evidence of memoirs recorded long after the event.

Whatever the justification he may have had for believing that Lee was moving by his right toward Mine Run, Grant now felt assured that the time had come to call the IX Corps divisions forward. At 1:15 p.m., as Warren's rear division was tramping over the pontoons at Germanna Ford, the supreme commander directed Burnside by telegraph to proceed by forced marches to the Rapidan.[23]

In accordance with previous instructions from general headquarters, Burnside had concentrated his scattered units and hastened other preparations for evacuation of the Orange and Alexandria Railroad between the Rapidan and Manassas Junction. His 1st Division (Stevenson) was then at Brandy Station, the 3d (Willcox) at Rappahannock Station, the Second (Potter) at Bealeton. Ferrero's 4th Division, a unit composed of Negro troops, was already on the march from Manassas Junction, more than 40 miles distant from Germanna Ford. Stevenson's division was expected at the ford early in the morning on the 5th. It was a reasonable assumption that the two other white divisions would reach the river by midafternoon. Ferrero's division was not expected on the south side of the Rapidan before morning on the 6th.[24]

Analysis of Confederate Movement

Meanwhile, Meade and his chief of staff, together with Seth Williams, Assistant Adjutant General, Major Nathaniel Michler who, as acting Engineer Chief served somewhat in the capacity of the present-day operations officer, and other members of the army headquarters staff were thoughtfully studying reconnaissance reports with reference to large-scale maps spread out on collapsible tables that crowded the limited space of Meade's headquarters tent. There is no indication that Grant attended the staff conference or even concurred in any of its decisions. Aside from Humphreys' vague reference to changes relative to employment of the cavalry, there is no authentic account of the proceedings.[25] It therefore becomes a matter of some importance to piece together the fragments of information gathered by Sheridan's cavalry patrols deep in the Wilderness. How much did Meade learn?

Even before the supreme commander ordered Burnside forward, Meade had taken the first step in departure from the original plan for the two-days maneuver against Lee's right flank. Between noon and 1 p.m. the army commander was informed that a large force of Confederate cavalry known to have grazed their horses during the winter in the vicinity of Fredericksburg was concentrating at Hamilton's Crossing. This intelligence, together with reports from Wilson's patrols out on the Flat Run Road and the turnpike must have been delivered at army headquarters before Grant read the Stony Mountain report which is supposed to have given him just the information he wanted.[26]

At 1 p.m. Humphreys notified Hancock that some modifications of the orders for movement had been made, one of which cancelled the tentative plan for Torbert's 1st Cavalry Division to cross the river at Germanna Ford and cover the right flank of the great trains while closing from Ely's Ford toward Dowdall's Tavern. Humphreys now apprised the II Corps commander that "Torbert's division of cavalry will cross at Ely's Ford at daylight and move out to join Gregg." Hancock was also advised that "some few shots have been fired toward Robertson's Tavern (Locust Grove). Enemy moving; some force coming out toward New Verdiersville." [27]

Two messages transmitted to Gregg from Cavalry Corps headquarters at an unstated time proceeded from the decision revealed in Humphreys' dispatch of 1 p.m. to Hancock and, therefore, based upon information available at that time. These two dispatches state:

> (1) The Major General Commanding directs that in view of the large force of cavalry (rebel) reported at Fredericks-

burg, that you camp your division to-night within easy supporting distance of the infantry of the Second Corps (Hancock) that supports you.[28]

(2) General Torbert will join you in the morning with his command.

At 2:10 p.m. a dispatch from Wilson at Parker's store added some evidence to the already accepted belief that Lee was moving toward Mine Run. The dispatch stated in part:

> Troops well down toward Mine Run, on all roads, except this one (Orange Plank Road) ; none on this road nearer than 7 miles to this place . . . I have sent patrols out in all directions, but as yet hear of nothing, except a few light parties scattered through the by-roads. Plank Road in fine condition.[29]

Wilson's communication of 2:10 p.m. also reported on Lee's general dispositions on the preceding day. His information in this respect was furnished by Mr. Sime, a British subject who left his residence at Gordonsville on the afternoon of May 3 and, while traveling through the Wilderness, was apprehended by a 3d Cavalry Division patrol and escorted to General Wilson's headquarters. According to this informant, Longstreet's Corps lay between Gordonsville and Orange Court House; Ewell and Hill were near the Court House. Sime was of the opinion that the Army of Northern Virginia had received no reinforcements since the arrival of Longstreet's two divisions during April. He discounted rumors to the effect that a large formation under Beauregard was in the area.[30]

The general reliability of various reports that Lee was moving by his right received final confirmation in the message flagged from Stony Mountain at 3 p.m. Already mentioned in another connection, this dispatch reported:

> Enemy moving infantry and trains toward Verdiersville. Two brigades gone from this front. Camp at Clark's Mountain breaking up. Battery still in position behind Dr. Morton's house and infantry pickets in river.[31]

The Stony Mountain communication completed the fund of information gathered from various sources in the field previous to drafting the orders of march for May 5. Briefly summarized, the reports received between noon and 3 p.m. indicated the following situation:

1. On the left, a strong body of Confederate cavalry was in position at Hamilton's Crossing. As early as 1 p.m. it was thought advisable to alter the cavalry movements originally entertained for the next day by concentrating the divisions of Gregg and Torbert at Aldrich's Farm.

2. On the right, the Confederates appeared to be concentrating in some force toward Mine Run. All reports indicated that this movement was confined to the Orange Turnpike and other roads leading from the Rapidan toward the course of Mine Run below the turnpike crossing.

It is difficult to interpret the meaning attached by Meade and Humphreys to reports of the Confederate movement toward Mine Run. In the absence of positive intelligence concerning the actual dispositions of Hill's and Longstreet's corps on the 4th, the available evidence necessarily restricted any final estimate of the situation to an assumption that Ewell's Corps alone was taking position in the Mine Run lines, or at least was concentrating toward the right with such a purpose in mind. But until the dispositions of the other two corps were definitely established, Ewell's advance, as reported on the afternoon of the 4th, was subject to four different interpretations:

1. Ewell might occupy the Mine Run entrenchments for the purpose of covering a general retirement behind the North Anna River.

2. It was conceivable that Ewell would hold the return lines to cover a lateral shift to the left into the Shenandoah Valley, where Lee could gather supplies and start north on a raid.

3. Ewell could be holding the left of a movement *en echelon* toward Mine Run. Hill, reinforcing Ewell in the return lines, would give an adequate force for passive defense, while Longstreet, arriving on the right, would afford the possibility of

fighting a defensive battle of the Fredericksburg type, or of developing an offensive-defensive operation toward Grant's left.

4. The approach of Ewell's corps could be the partial disclosure of a movement *en echelon* beyond Mine Run into The Wilderness, with Lee seeking the opportunity of launching a battle of annihilation, such as the one attempted at Chancellorsville.

Aside from the fact that the original plan of turning Lee's right on the 5th by way of the Catharpin and Pamunkey Roads was modified during the afternoon of the 4th, there is little to indicate just what unforeseen contingency the modification was intended to meet. The change of mission assigned Torbert was, as we know, prompted by an over-zealous concern for the security of the trains. Indeed, protection of the great trains appears to have assumed greater importance at army headquarters than the turning of Lee's right. Absolute immunity against attack on the lumbering wagon columns governed the movement of every combat element of the army.

The alternative possibilities outlined in paragraphs 1 and 2 above should have strengthened confidence in the original plan. Again, if serious consideration was given to the alternative indicated in paragraph 3, even greater confidence should have been inspired. Lee was deploying on the line the turning movement by the Catharpin and Pamunkey Roads was expressly designed to outflank.

Only the fourth alternative presupposed enemy dispositions that presented the possibility of interference with the turning movement, as originally planned, by precipitating a general engagement late in the afternoon of May 5. But if momentary credence was given to this possibility—the only one that should have justified any curtailment of the flanking maneuver—it was dismissed by Meade, and Grant too for that matter, as soon as the modification was written into the march orders for May 5.*

---

* As indicated in a later section of this chapter entitled *Preview of the Fifth of May*, Meade, assuming that he faced only a detached body of Lee's main

Amended Plan

The only plausible interpretation of these obvious con-
tradictions may be found in the nature of the plan itself.
Humphreys frankly admits that his two "projects"—one boldly
contemplating a wide encirclement of Lee's right by roads
radiating from Spotsylvania Court House but rejected as the
basis of an operational plan, the other specifying envelopment
on a shorter arc by way of Shady Grove Church—"were subject to material modification or entire abandonment, dependent on the movement of Lee." [32] In other words' the plan tentatively adopted on May 2 and partially written into the orders
of march for May 4, the first day, was really based on hopes
that Lee would not succeed in forming on a line of deployment within The Wilderness before the Army of the Potomac
completed its preparatory maneuver on the 5th. Yet, while
the possibility of Lee's interference late during the afternoon
of the second day was not discounted, Meade sought to avoid
rather contest such a development by so altering the direction
of maneuver as to avert the worst consequences of interference.

No thought appears to have been given to the possibilities
of sending out large bodies of cavalry, with infantry supports,
to retard and blind the enemy's forward movement by lines
of dismounted skirmishers, causing his advanced formations
to consume valuable time in deploying against an elusive foe.
Appearance of the Federal cavalry on such a mission would
certainly have drawn Stuart's horse into action and, in consequence, have diminished the threat of attack on the great
trains to dimensions that could have been effectively handled
by infantry guards. In other words, Meade declined to appreciate the potentialities of his cavalry arm, with its preponderance in numbers and firepower, as a force capable of
strategic reconnaissance before battle.

The amended plan cancelled Warren's intended advance

---

army, ordered Warren to assembly his V Corps divisions and attack. A detailed
analysis of this situation appears in Chapter 5. It should be stated here, however, that Grant not only approved but applauded Meade's decision, urging
that "if any opportunity presents itself for pitching into a part of Lee's army,
do so without giving time for dispositions." 69 WR 403.

across the Orange Plank Road to the head of Catharpin Run, a point just south of the Catharpin Road and some four miles west of Shady Grove Church, together with whatever supporting movements may have been contemplated for the II and VI corps. In short, it again curtailed the arc of maneuver against Lee's right by prescribing a strategic deployment on the line Shady Grove Church-Parker's Store-Wilderness Tavern.

Accordingly, the right column (V and VI Corps) was to act as a moving pivot for the left column (II Corps and Artillery Reserve). As Warren's V Corps marched toward its objective at Parker's Store and Sedgwick's VI Corps closed up to Wilderness Tavern, Hancock's II Corps would swing out from Chancellorsville via Todd's Tavern into line at Shady Grove Church and extend its right toward Parker's Store. Meanwhile, Warren was to extend his right toward Wilderness Tavern. The IX Corps divisions of Stevenson, Willcox, and Potter would picket the Germanna Plank Road between Sedgwick's right and the ford.

Wilson, commanding the 3d Cavalry Division, became responsible for screening the entire front of deployment. His main body was to "move at 5 a.m. [from Parker's Store] to Craig's Meeting House, on the Catharpin Road." His orders further stated that "He will keep out parties on the Orange Court House pike and plank roads, the Catharpin-Pamunkey Road (road to Orange Springs), and in the direction of Twyman's Store and Andrews' Tavern or Good Hope Church." [33]

In striking contrast to the assignment of a single cavalry division—the weakest numerically of the corps—was the generous provision for covering the left or outer flank of the great trains in rear of the army. As Hancock's II Corps, followed by the Artillery Reserve, pushed toward Shady Grove Church, and the great trains lumbered on to a parking area near Todd's Tavern, two cavalry divisions, mustering some 10,000 sabers, were to proceed eastward away from the front of deployment. "Major General Sheridan, commanding the Cavalry Corps," stated the orders of march, "will move with Gregg's and Torbert's divisions against the enemy's cavalry in the direction of Hamilton's Crossing."

The Cavalry: Auxiliary or Combat Arm?

A just criticism of Meade's decision to employ a preponderance of his cavalry strength in a manner calculated to protect the great trains, while assigning a single division to the arduous tasks of covering the whole front of deployment, cannot be based entirely on the series of mishaps attending failure of the screening force and miscarriage of the venture toward Hamilton's Crossing.

In the first place, it must be conceded that Meade's concern for the safety of his supply trains became a dominating consideration after abandonment of the Orange and Alexandria Railroad between Rapidan Station and Manassas Junction. When the rolling stock went back, in accordance with the plan of evacuation, beyond Manassas Junction, the great trains became a moving base on which the Army of the Potomac would be entirely dependent until a new supply point was established on the indented shore line of Chesapeake Bay.

Again, the problem of achieving proper economy of force in providing the necessary protection called for a fine display of tactical judgment. Could infantry do the job without serious diminution of the army's striking power? Mounted units, admittedly, were best suited for the job. It was an established practice in the Army of the Potomac. But would Meade be justified in denying his army the benefits of far-ranging cavalry reconnaissance before battle?

In Meade's opinion, the safety of the great trains in this extraordinary situation put claims on his cavalry to the exclusion of any other venture, however promising. Furthermore, he had some justification in doubting the ability of his cavalry commander to handle large bodies of horse in battle. Sheridan's promise of performance in this respect rested on the reputation he had won in the rough and tumble school of the West as a general of infantry. His experience as a cavalry officer was limited to a brief period early in the war when he commanded the 2d Michigan Cavalry Regiment.

In making his final decision, Meade acted in accordance with the doctrine holding that recent improvements in the range and accuracy of firearms had relegated the mounted branch to a subordinate role in combined operations of the three combat arms. Then, while European military professionals were hotly debating the future role of cavalry, practical experimentation on the battlefields of America offered considerable evidence in support of the pessimistic view that the cavalry was an arm of diminishing value.

The Confederacy took the field in 1861 with a ready-made mounted force, composed of hard-riding gentry and an immediately available supply of matchless saddle horses.[34] Not until the North brought its vast resources to bear, while those of the South were approaching exhaustion, could the Federal cavalry hope to challenge its dashing adversary. But just as the Royalist cavaliers of Prince Rupert met their match in Cromwell's Ironsides, so the superb cavalry of the Confederacy was destined to feel the weight of superior organization, better equipment, greater firepower and troopers in blue who rode knee to knee in ever-increasing numbers.

Turning of the tide did not completely submerge the doctrinaires who professed to see in modern cavalry a parallel with armored knights of the late medieval period, who passed into obsolescence with the introduction of gunpowder. However, a rising school of activists disputed the pessimistic thesis that cavalry had been relegated to the role of an auxiliary of the infantry and artillery, performing special kinds of guard duty such as furnishing escorts to the supply trains and maintaining protective cordons around gun parks and cantonments of sleeping foot soldiers.

Admitting that the mounted arm had been divested of the offensive power it wielded in bygone days when the awesome rumble and flashing steel of a massed charge heralded the climax of battle, the activists contended that present-day cavalry, properly trained and armed with magazine rifles, was still a self-contained arm, capable of independent action in dismounted combat and indispensable in long-range reconnaissance before battle. They pointed to the exploits of Buford at Gettysburg and Forrest in Tennessee as shining examples.

Meade and Sheridan at Loggerheads

When Sheridan assumed command of the Cavalry Corps early in April 1864 he appeared as an exponent of the activist school. A stranger to the Army of the Potomac and a protege of the supreme commander, he expounded the tenets of his radical doctrine in a manner that excited greater resentment than the ideas he urged. In preparing at New Orleans in May 1866 his final report on operations of the Cavalry Corps from April 6 to August 4, 1864, he recalls the cold reception he received from Meade and his generals. Referring to his belief that "our cavalry ought to fight the enemy's cavalry and our infantry the enemy's infantry," Sheridan adds:

> I was strengthened in this impression still more by the consciousness of a want of appreciation on the part of infantry commanders as to the power of a well-managed body of horse, but as it was difficult to overcome the established custom of wasting cavalry for the protection of the trains and the establishment of cordons around a sleeping infantry force, we had to bide our time.[35]

The clash arising from Meade's orders for disposition of the cavalry divisions on May 5 was but an incident in this longstanding controversy. The facts of the case at hand are obscure. Humphreys states categorically that Sheridan proposed the movement toward Hamilton's Crossing and that Meade acquiesced in the proposal.

There is no reason to question Humphreys' integrity as a military historian. Furthermore, Sheridan's ardent offensive spirit and his dictum that cavalry should fight cavalry while infantry fought infantry lends credence to the supposition that he overcame Meade's reluctance to commit the greater part of his mounted force in an offensive movement that appears to have been intended to seek out and destroy Fitzhugh

Lee's cavalry division. Yet a careful analysis of Humphreys' work *The Virginia Campaign of '64 and '65* reveals that, while he shows a scrupulous regard for documentary evidence and a fine sense of impartiality in the interpretation of fact, his memory is anything but precise. And in this instance he is relying on memory alone.

Sheridan, on the other hand, submits documentary evidence that brings into question the accuracy of Humphreys' memory. While not bearing directly on the question as to whether Meade or Sheridan himself proposed the venture toward Hamilton's Crossing, the Chief of Cavalry denounced in unsparing terms the logic of the plan within 28 hours after issuance of the orders prescribing the movement. Summarizing cavalry operations on May 5 in a dispatch written at 10:10 p.m. that day, he bitterly complains that:

> I cannot do anything with the cavalry, except to act on the defensive, on account of the immense amount of material and trains here and on the road to Ely's Ford. Had I moved to Hamilton's Crossing early this morning the enemy would have ruined everything. Why cannot infantry be sent to guard the trains and let me take the offensive? [36]

Is this an honest confession of error on the part of a man who never reconsidered, never admitted to have been in the wrong? If so, we have the manifestation of a complex personality that has escaped the attention of his biographers and would have amazed his intimate associates and admirers. Moreover, General Meade was the last man on earth he would have chosen as his confessor. If it becomes impossible to believe that Sheridan could have brought himself to condemn his own proposal in writing, it follows that he took the occasion to castigate a measure he regarded as defensive in scope and intent and, despite the wording of the order to move "against the enemy's cavalry," had as its primary purpose the protecttion of the trains rather than destruction of hostile cavalry "in the direction of Hamilton's Crossing."

Preview of the Fifth of May

In the last analysis, the movement prescribed for the second

MAP 5. THE BATTLE TERRAIN

This map of the terrain on which most of the action will occur is furnished to enable the reader to refer to place names and terrain features which on subsequent maps will frequently be obscured by units and their designations.

day of the two-day maneuver abandoned the plan, as orig-inally entertained, of extending the left element of the Army of the Potomac beyond the forest zone. On May 5, therefore, Grant was not marching with the intention of clearing the Wilderness before Lee could seize the opportunity of impos-ing battle in the woodland. Quite to the contrary, Grant was maneuvering toward a line of deployment entirely within the Wilderness.

To briefly anticipate the events of May 5, Lee had no in-tention of taking the offensive against Grant until Longstreet could lend active support to Hill and Ewell in battle forma-tion. The thesis that Gen. Lee deliberately and knowingly pre-cipitated the Battle of the Wilderness by threatening Grant's marching flank has no foundation in fact. Nor is there any evidence that Lee divined Grant's intention of deploying on the line Shady Grove Church-Parker's Store-Wilderness Tavern and took steps to break up the maneuver. Evidence to the contrary is clear and convincing.

At 11 a.m., after Hancock's advance had reached a point within sight of Shady Grove Church and Warren's leading division looked down from Chewning's farm on Parker's Store, while Getty's division, in the van of Sedgwick's VI Corps, had already reached Wilderness Tavern, Lee repeated the caution given both Ewell and Hill three hours earlier to re-frain from any action that might involve their units in a general engagement. While Lee, unable to see any opportunity of engaging the enemy on advantageous terms, wisely held his forces in hand, Meade was preparing to force the issue.

Misinterpreting reports of an enemy force in front of Griffin's picket line on the Turnpike as evidence that he faced only a detached body of Lee's main army, Meade suspended the maneuver and ordered Warren to attack. The V Corps commander was forming his divisons for the assault while Ewell and Hill were held in leash by Lee's restraining order.

Meade's drastic decision, it should be noted, was taken in contravention to the assumption briefly held during the after-

noon of May 4 that Lee might advance beyond Mine Run
and create the very situation which the modified maneuver
was intended to meet. The offensive blow delivered by Warren
committed Grant to the battle he hoped to avoid and the one
Lee would have postponed.

Lieutenant Colonel Cyrus B. Comstock, confidential *aide de
camp* to the supreme commander and serving in the capacity
of liaison officer between general and army headquarters,
neatly summarizes the intent written into the orders issued
at 6 p.m. May 4 and the immediate aftermath on the 5th.
Under this date he records the following in his daily journal:

> Moving orders for A. P. (Army of the Potomac) to occupy
> line from Shady Grove Church (Hancock) to Parker's Store
> (Warren) to Wilderness Tavern (Sedgwick). Sheridan with
> Gregg's and Torbert's Cav' Div. to attack enemy's cav' at
> Hamilton Crossing to cover our trains (with 15 days' sup-
> plies) now near Chancellorsville and to be at Todd's Tavern
> tonight. Having occupied this line, A. of P. to wait for Burn-
> side to get up. About 1-2 p.m. enemy showing himself in
> force, Warren attacked on Orange C. H. turnpike.[37]

A Fireside Chat

Grant spent the night of May 4-5 at his camp overlooking
the Rapidan. While there is nothing to indicate that he col-
laborated with Meade in preparing the orders of march for
May 5, there is evidence of a meeting after dark. Meade, according to Morris Schaff, strolled over to the camp fire at
Grant's headquarters tent and talked with the supreme commander late into the night.[38]

As the two generals relaxed in the cheerful glow of their
camp fire and perhaps speculated on events of the morrow,
a lively turn to the comfortable fireside chat would have been
given by delivery of a dispatch from Wilson reporting on
developments on the Orange Turnpike, while the sun was
sinking behind the western margin of the Wilderness. No such
report arrived, however.

A former member of Grant's staff in the West and some
time chief of the Cavalry Bureau, Maj. Gen. James Harrison

Wilson assumed command of the 3d Cavalry Division at the age of 27. With practically no prior command experience, he was destined within a year to achieve enduring fame as one of the great cavalry leaders of American history. But his performance in the Wilderness was scarcely an auspicious beginning. His reconnaissance of the Orange Turnpike was singularly inept.*

Late in the afternoon he sent a patrol out on the Turnpike to scout as far as Locust Grove. The party proceeded to its destination and halted. Perhaps the red glow of the setting sun obscured the dust stirred up by a column of troops approaching from the west. Seeing nothing to attract his attention, the patrol leader turned away and, according to orders, followed a forest path to Parker's Store.

Unobserved at nightfall, Ewell's advance reached Locust Grove, less than four miles from Griffin's picket line across the Turnpike. As Grant and Meade watched the dying embers of their fire, Ewell, also enjoying the congenial warmth of a glowing bed of wood coals, was likewise speculating on events of the morrow.

---

* After waiting expectantly at Parker's Store for news from his patrol on the turnpike, Wilson deemed it superfluous to transmit a negative report when the patrol leader returned without information of enemy movements in the vicinity of Locust Grove. Wilson to Cav. Corps Hq., 7:30 p.m., May 4, 68 WR 390.

CHAPTER 5
LEE MANEUVERS FOR POSITION

The light of early dawn on May 4th presented to the Confederate signalmen on Clark's Mountain a scene that fulfilled Lee's prediction of the 2d. Country lanes on the far bank of the Rapidan were pouring endless streams of infantry into Stevensburg and Richardsville. The main roads from these two villages to Germanna and Ely's Fords were choked with dense columns of horse, foot, and guns. As the sun rose higher in a cloudless sky, the observers on Clark's Mountain noticed that two wagon trains were moving out toward the river from a vast congregation of wheeled transport near Richardsville. One crawled toward Culpeper Mine Ford; the other took the rear of the column marching in the direction of Ely's Ford. The signal detachment flagged a message to Ewell, notifying the III Corps commander that "everything was moving to the right." This message, as we know, was decoded by the Federal signalmen on Stony Mountain and transmitted to Meade at 9:30 a.m. The time of delivery to Ewell and Lee is not known.

Lee's headquarters at Orange Court House stirred in anticipation of great events. Galloping couriers came and went. Steuart's Brigade, on Ewell's extreme right toward Mine Run, received an order early in the morning of May 4th to be ready to move at an early hour. By noon the entire II Corps, less Ramseur's Brigade, together with three regiments detached from each of Ewell's three divisions, was on the march to Locust Grove. Ramseur had instructions to watch the river at Raccoon Ford and reconnoiter during the day toward Culpeper Court House.

A. P. Hill, commanding the Confederate III Corps, drew

the divisions of Heth and Wilcox from their positions on the left of the river front and formed them, Heth leading, in column of march on the Plank Road near Orange Court House. Jeb Stuart, with a force of cavalry, took the advance. Anderson's Division, of Hill's III Corps, went into position on Rapidan Heights to cover the rear. Lee quit his headquarters and rode with Hill towards New Verdiersville.

Owing to the circumstance that the III Corps had the greater distance to go in a concentration to the right, together with the fact that Anderson's Division was left behind to cover the movement, it is probable that Hill's withdrawal from the Rapidan began shortly after 9 a.m. In closing up at New Verdiersville, the rear of his column had to march a distance of twenty-eight miles.

Intelligence of Grant's movement towards the Rapidan was speedily transmitted to Longstreet's headquarters at Mechanicsville. At 9 a.m. Colonel G. Moxley Sorrel, I Corps Chief of Staff, informed General Alexander, Chief of Corps Artillery, that many of the enemy's camps had disappeared from the front and that large wagon trains were reported moving through Stevensburg. He added: "The Lieutenant General [Longstreet] desires that you will keep your artillery in such a condition as to move whenever called upon." Similar messages were sent to Field and Kershaw, generals of division.

In anticipation, perhaps, of positive orders from Orange Court House to move, Longstreet at 10:30 a.m. informed Lee of his opinion concerning Grant's intentions. He wrote:

> I fear the enemy is trying to draw us down to Fredericksburg. Can't we threaten his rear, so as to stop his move? Fredericksburg will not be a strong position, with the flank and rear exposed to a force at West Point. We should keep away from there, unless we can put out a force to hold any force at West Point in check.

Longstreet Protests the Route of March

It cannot be determined whether Longstreet's dispatch of 10:30 a.m. was sent prior or subsequent to the receipt of an order from Lee, instructing Longstreet to march in Hill's rear on the Plank Road towards Parker's Store. Longstreet states in his *Memoirs* that he received an order to this effect at 1 p.m. and that his generals of division were directed to prepare their commands for the movement. Longstreet, however, was disinclined to follow Hill into action. He immediately communicated with Lee, suggesting what he describes as "a shorter route (via Richard's Shop) that would at the same time relieve the Plank Road of the pressure of troops and trains." In the same dispatch he sought permission to go on to the Brock Road, where, he advised Lee, "we could look for and hope to intercept the enemy's march, and cause him to develop plans before he could get out of the Wilderness." [1]

Although all of the dispatches, save Longstreet's note of 10:30 a. m., have been lost, it does not appear that the exchange of view between army headquarters and Mechanicsville on May 4th reflected a serious conflict of opinion. The suggestion that Grant might be trying to draw the Confederates toward Fredericksburg, and that an effort should be made to threaten his rear, seems to have impressed Lee as a contingency which should not be overlooked. As will be presently seen, Lee considered the possibility of bringing Grant to action at an early hour on the 5th by sending Ewell against the Federal rear guard. Lee also approved Longstreet's request to march by way of Richards Shop to the Brock Road.

Considerable doubt, however, arises as to the accuracy of Longstreet's memory in asserting that the exchange of dispatches relating to his proposed changes in Lee's original order took place during the afternoon. The orders issued at I Corps headquarters by Colonel Sorrel to march by way of Richards Shop are dated at 11 a.m. It may be assumed, of course, that Sorrel transmitted these orders at the hour indicated and that Longstreet, upon receipt of the instructions at 1 p.m. from Lee to march by the Plank Road in rear of Hill, sought Lee's permission to act in accordance with the precautionary orders already issued. Identical in text, these orders were addressed to Field and Kershaw, stating:

> The Lieutenant-General Commanding directs that you get your divisions ready to move at once. Please let me know the earliest hour at which you will be able to move. The point to which you will direct your march will be Richards Shop, at the junction of the Old Fredericksburg road and the Lawyer's road, southeast of Verdiersville. The best route is probably by Forest Hill, Brock's Bridge and junction of Marcus [Marquis] and Old Fredericksburg road. I will endeavor to send you some guides. You had better, however, endeavor to get some yourself, in addition. The commanding general would like you to get off this afternoon and make five or six miles on the march. The artillery will move together under General Alexander.[2]

Military historians generally have accepted the opinion of contemporary Southern writers that Longstreet's reluctance to act upon Lee's original order was motivated by ignorance of the distances involved in the two routes under discussion, together with a temperamental disinclination to execute any direct order from Lee without question or counterproposal.

The matter is hardly susceptible to so simple an interpretation. Longstreet admittedly was wrong in his assumption that the Richard's Shop route was the shorter of the two. The actual discrepancy in distance, however, is not the real point at issue. In making his counterproposals, Longstreet had two possible situations in mind. The first is indicated in his dispatch of 10:30 a.m., suggesting that Grant might be trying to draw the Confederates down to Fredericksburg. The second is implied in his request to march by way of Richards to the Brock Road.

There is no difficulty in establishing the fact that both Lee and Longstreet were in agreement as to the danger of a Federal advance on Fredericksburg and the necessity of taking measures to prevent such a movement. The situation presupposed by Longstreet in his suggestion to strike across the Brock Road is not altogether clear. In taking the shortest route from Richards Shop to the Brock Road, Longstreet would move by the Catharpin Road toward Todd's Tavern, which stands at the Brock-Catharpin intersection. Both Lee and Longstreet were well aware that at dawn on May 4th Grant's advance elements were at Germanna Ford, a distance of not more than twelve miles from Todd's Tavern. Even admitting that Longstreet's knowledge of the meandering country roads between the North Anna and the Rapidan was somewhat vague, he certainly knew that the marching distance from Germanna Ford to Todd's Tavern was less than half the distance he must traverse in going from Gordonsville to the Tavern. As a matter of fact, the distance from Gordonsville to Todd's Tavern, by the Brock Bridge-Richard's Shop route, was approximately forty miles. Then, while the Federals were in motion at dawn, precautionary orders for the movement from Gordonsville were not issued through Longstreet's headquarters until 11 a.m. It does not seem reasonable to suppose that a general of Longstreet's sagacity really intended to beat the Federal advance in a race to Todd's Tavern. Nor is it reasonable to assume that Lee, however obdurate his great lieutenant may have been on certain occasions, would have given his assent to such a proposition. Yet Longstreet hoped to intercept the enemy's march at that point. Lee gave his assent to this plan. What, then, is the explanation?

While a certain answer cannot be given, it is reasonable to conclude that the threat of a Federal thrust southeastward through the Wilderness along the line of the Brock Road had not yet appeared as an imminent probability to either Lee or Longstreet. Therefore, their correspondence on the 4th was based on the supposition that Grant's two columns, after reaching Wilderness Tavern and Chancellorsville, would either go on downstream to Fredericksburg, or turn and push upstream towards Mine Run, as Meade had done in the autumn campaign of 1863. Given the latter contingency, Longstreet proposed that he concentrate his corps at Richards Shop, on the right of the Mine Run works. As Grant deployed before Lee's entrenched line, Longstreet would cut across Brock Road at Todd's Tavern. Such a maneuver, he thought, would anticipate an enemy advance by their own left and thus compel Grant to develop plans before he could get out of the Wilderness.

Lee Rides to New Verdiersville

It must be admitted that the want of adequate evidence withholds a definitive explanation of the matter in question. The development of a plan of action as Lee rode with Hill during the afternoon hours of May 4th is one of the enigmas of Confederate military history. Lee's report of operations in the Wilderness, together with the greater part of his military correspondence and the vast bulk of operation reports returned by general and field officers of the Army of Northern Virginia, were lost during the retreat to Appomattox. The *Official Records of the Union and Confederate Armies* contain but one order issued at Lee's headquarters on May 4th. This embodies the instructions transmitted at 8 p.m. of that day to Ewell for operations on the 5th. Of the many dispatches sent and received by Colonel Taylor, Assistant Adjutant General of the Army of Northern Virginia, only six are extant. But one of these refers to the Lee-Longstreet correspondence on May 4th.

Lee Unable to Divine Grant's Purpose

While Lee usually evinced remarkable perspicacity in anticipating his opponent's intentions, it will be found that, in any particular situation, he relied mainly upon trustworthy intelligence concerning the enemy's dispositions. In the absence of reliable evidence pointing directly to his own intentions on May 4th, such as the issuance of positive orders, or the exchange of views relating to specific developments, the extent of his knowledge concerning Grant's dispositions on that day offers a valuable clue to Lee's real intentions. How much did he know?

Lee, of course, was aware by 9 a.m. that "everything seems to be moving to the right." It will be recalled that at this time Major Cowles, of the 1st North Carolina Cavalry, sent a courier to Ewell with information that a strong force of Federal cavalry was on the Germanna Plank Road about two miles south of the Rapidan and going in the direction of Wilderness Tavern. Two hours later Cowles reported a body of the enemy's cavalry on the Orange Turnpike, about one mile from Locust Grove.

In the meantime, word was dispatched to Stuart by Fitzhugh Lee, commanding the Confederate cavalry division near Fredericksburg, that his pickets covering Germanna and Ely's Fords had been driven in at dawn and that "the enemy were crossing heavy bodies of cavalry and infantry at those points." [8] The time of delivery of this important intelligence is not known. Fitzhugh Lee then reported the enemy's occupation of Chancellorsville and, in a later communication, the appearance of a heavy column on the Orange Plank Road heading toward Fredericksburg.

Fitzhugh Lee states in his report of operations that a reconnaissance in the vicinity of Chancellorsville revealed that "the heads of the enemy's columns were all turning west from that place, marching toward Orange Court House, and that it was a general offensive move of General Grant's—their cavalry having merely moved out on the Fredericksburg road to protect such a movement."

The information furnished by Confederate cavalry patrols on both the right and left of the Federal columns offered little evidence by which Lee might judge of Grant's real intentions. Cowles' two dispatches indicated that the cavalry advance of Grant's right column was "feeling" toward Locust Grove. Fitzhugh Lee's succession of reports would tend to confirm a belief that Grant was moving directly up the Rapidan toward Mine Run, following Meade's line of advance in November of 1863. But, until the movement of the Federal columns could be more thoroughly developed, there was still reason to suspect that appearances indicating an advance up the river might, in reality, be measures taken to cover the rear in a movement down the Rapidan toward Fredericksburg.

This lingering suspicion is reflected by the fact that Ewell at 8 p.m. was instructed to follow Grant, if he went down the river, on the morning of the 5th.

However eager Lee may have been to hit at the flank of the long Federal columns as they threaded their way southward through the depths of the woodland beyond Mine Run, there was nothing as yet to justify a belief at Confederate headquarters that Grant would expose his forces to the perils of such a situation. Lee's assent to the proposal that the Confederate I Corps advance from Mechanicsville via Richards Shop to the Brock Road cannot be reconciled with a belief on his part that Grant intended to strike straight through the Wilderness to open ground in the vicinity of Spotsylvania Court House or Shady Grove Church. Nor does Longstreet's deliberation during the afternoon of the 4th suggest the auspicious beginning of a bold combination to arrest Grant's progress on such a march. Longstreet's I Corps moved from Gordonsville at 4 p.m. and marched leisurely along the Forest Hill Road toward the North Anna.

In the meantime the II and III Confederate corps were approaching their designated objectives. About sunset Ewell's advance reached Locust Grove. Early's Division bivouacked near the village. Johnson's Division and Nelson's battalion encamped two miles south of the Turnpike. Rodes' Division halted for the night in Johnson's rear, while the artillery parked along the Turnpike in rear of Early's camp. Heth's Division of Hill's III Corps marched through New Verdiersville at nightfall and encamped along the Plank Road. Wilcox's Division bivouacked to the west of the village. Stuart's cavalry covered the front toward Mine Run. Lee sought out the site of his headquarters camp during the winter campaign, which was situated opposite the Rhodes house and between the camps of Heth and Wilcox.

Early in the evening a dispatch arrived from Longstreet at Mechanicsville. The message stated that the I Corps would camp that night between Fonst and Brock's Bridge, on the

North Anna, and that the corps commander hoped to reach
Richards Shop by noon the next day.

Lee Misjudges Grant's Aim

In the event of a battle along Mine Run on the 5th, Lee
now had the assurance that Longstreet would come up within
supporting distance of Hill during the afternoon. But Lee
had not entirely abandoned the idea that Grant might move
down-river to Fredericksburg. Provision for security of the
enormous Federal trains during such a movement would require the detachment of large bodies to cover the rear. Of
necessity the pace would be slow. Longstreet should have no
difficulty in closing up. This contingency at any rate appears
to have entered into Lee's estimate of the situation at 8 p.m.,
when Colonel Taylor drafted the following order to Ewell:

> General Lee will be found in the woods opposite this house
> (Rhodes') to-night. He wishes you to be ready to move on
> early in the morning. If the enemy moves down the river, he
> wishes you to push on after him. If he comes this way, we
> will take our old line. The general's desire is to bring him to
> battle as soon now as possible.[4]

Lee's determination to engage under the conditions stated
to Ewell seems a clear indication that he was still in the dark
as to his opponent's real intentions. The dispatch of 8 p.m.
contemplates that Ewell would either engage the Federal rear
guard in a pursuit down river, or, fighting a rearguard action
himself, delay Grant's advance up-river, while the Confederates
took position in their old lines along Mine Run. In either
eventuality Ewell might engage as soon as possible. This in
effect was the interpretation Ewell put upon his instructions.
"Just the orders I like," he stated, early the next morning, to
Major Stiles of the II Corps Artillery. "Go straight down the
road and strike the enemy wherever I find him." [5]

It will be noted that no mention is made of the third
alternative open to Grant—that of pushing on southward
through the heart of the Wilderness. Consideration of this
alternative would have urged delay in bringing the enemy to

battle. Longstreet was expected to be on hand in the event of a clash along Mine Run. Lee, following Grant toward Fredericksburg, might choose his own time in developing a critical operation against the Federal rearguard. But in the event of a Federal advance through the Wilderness, Lee would encounter grave risks in a thrust against the flank of Grant's marching columns before Longstreet arrived within close supporting distance of Hill. Indeed, the instructions of 8 p.m., May 4th to Ewell offer a serious objection to any supposition that Lee threw his forces beyond Mine Run on that day with an expectation of striking the flank of Grant's columns in the Wilderness on May 5th. Furthermore, if Lee's expectations were limited to the two alternatives stated in Ewell's instructions, there is no difficulty in accounting for his acquiescence to Longstreet's suggestions. Assuming on the one hand that Ewell and Hill occupied the Mine Run lines, Longstreet would be advantageously disposed at Richards Shop for the development of a counteroffensive movement against Grant's left. If, on the other hand, Lee followed Grant in a movement down-river toward Fredericksburg, there were sound reasons for concurrence in Longstreet's objections to marching in rear of Hill on the Plank Road. Only in the event that Lee foresaw on the 4th just what actually did occur on the day following, is it difficult to offer a satisfactory explanation for the liberty of action he permitted Longstreet on the 4th.

The tendency either to ignore or to read into Taylor's dispatch of 8 p.m., May 4th a meaning that does not appear in the text leads to an impasse. If Lee really divined the Federal plan of action before putting his own forces in motion toward Mine Run on the morning of May 4th, it is difficult to deny that he committed a grave error in holding Longstreet on the southwest flank covering Gordonsville for several hours after the withdrawal of Ewell and Hill from their sectors on the Rapidan front. Admitting that Lee would have courted considerable risk in uncovering the rail center at Gordonsville before Grant was actually in motion toward the

Confederate right, he might have alerted Longstreet on May 2, when he correctly guessed the direction of Grant's advance. With preparations advanced on the 3d to move eastward on short notice, Longstreet could have put his corps in motion at 9 a.m. on the 4th, thereby gaining a start of six hours. The fact that Longstreet arrived just in the nick of time on the morning of May 6 to stay the complete rout of Hill's hard-pressed divisions cannot be ascribed to a generalship enlightened by powers of prophecy. Lee acted during the day of the 4th in the light of imperfect knowledge and with a view to meeting contingencies that were not within the scope of his opponent's intentions. Taylor's dispatch, therefore, must be accepted at face value.

Lee Revises Estimate

Sometime during the night of May 4th or early on the morning of the 5th, the tentative plans of action sketched at 8 p.m. appear to have gone into the discard. At 11:15 p.m. Stuart transmitted to Lee a dispatch from one of his patrols on the Plank Road. This late intelligence questioned the accuracy of all previous reports indicating an enemy movement up-river toward Mine Run. Furthermore it cast doubt on the alternative supposition that Grant might move down-river in the direction of Fredericksburg. According to this intelligence a body of Federal cavalry under the personal command of General James H. Wilson had been encountered on the Orange Plank Road at New Hope Church, about four miles west of Parker's Store. After a sharp skirmish the Federals had withdrawn. The dispatch added that members of the Confederate patrol overheard General Wilson while instructing his party to return within closer supporting distance of the main body near Wilderness Church.[6]

Stuart's dispatch of 11:15 p.m. seems insufficient in itself to establish beyond all doubt the fact that instead of turning either right or left Grant's columns had come to an early halt on May 4th and had bivouacked in the vicinity of Wilderness Church. Nor does this dispatch justify an assumption by Lee that the enemy would begin moving on the morrow straight through the Wilderness toward Spotsylvania Court House or Shady Grove Church.

While there is no positive evidence that Lee received additional information from Stuart during the night, there is every reason to believe that the Confederate cavalry outposts were everywhere on the alert and overlooking no opportunity to discover the enemy's dispositions. And it also may be assumed that whatever additional intelligence Stuart might have reported at army headquarters was of a quality that evoked Lee's tribute seven days later when informed of Stuart's untimely death: "He never sent me a false piece of information." At any rate it is certain that by dawn of the 5th Lee was elated over the prospects of bringing Grant to battle in the depths of the Wilderness beyond Mine Run. General Long, his former military secretary and then commanding the artillery of the II Corps, depicts Lee's pleasant surprise at this turn of events:

> The writer spent the night at Lee's headquarters and breakfasted with him the next morning . . . In the course of the conversation that attended the meal he expressed himself surprised that his new adversary had placed himself in the same predicament as "Fighting Joe" had done the previous Spring. He hoped the result would be even more disastrous to Grant than that which Hooker had experienced. He was, indeed, in the best of spirits, and expressed much confidence in the result—a confidence which was well founded, for there was reason to believe that his antagonist would be at his mercy while entangled in these pathless and entangled thickets, in whose thickets disparity of numbers lost much of its importance.[7]

The problem now confronting Lee was one of great delicacy. Ten Federal infantry divisions were massed in a comparatively small area between Wilderness Tavern and Chancellorsville. He had but five in hand. If the Federals continued their march through the Wilderness in two columns, that is, in the same formation Fitzhugh Lee had observed and reported on May 4th, it was a reasonable expectation that one column would proceed by way of Parker's Store while the other filed past Todd's Tavern on the Brock Road. Ewell's three divisions at Locust Grove were about four miles from the Federal right, or protective flank, at Wilderness Tavern. Hill's two divisions at New Verdiersville were ten miles from Parker's Store and some fourteen miles from the Plank-Brock Road intersection. Singlehanded, Ewell could not afford to engage. Hill could not support Ewell before noon. Longstreet was not expected to reach Richard's Shop, over six miles southwest of Parker's Store, before noon. There was little possibility, then, that Longstreet would be in position to support Hill before nightfall. Anderson's Division of Hill's III Corps would not be up that day. In other words Lee could not afford to develop a major offensive operation along the line Wilderness Tavern-Parker's Store-Todd's Tavern before dawn of the 6th.

Yet if Lee did not succeed in arresting the Federal advance, Grant would be in position to impose battle on his own terms by mid-afternoon of the 5th. As the unit of direction in the Federal proposed deployment on the line Shady Grove Church-Parker's Store-Wilderness Tavern, Warren's V Corps at Wilderness Tavern was only four miles from Parker's Store, its objective. In closing up to Wilderness Tavern, the elements of Sedgwick's VI Corps had an average march of less than four miles. Hancock's II Corps, which constituted the moving flank, had approximately twelve miles to go from Chancellorsville to its objective at Shady Grove Church. In view of the fact that Hancock's advance was within three miles of this objective by 9:30 a.m. on the 5th, it may be assumed that, barring suspension of the maneuver, the II Corps would have been in position at Shady Grove Church by 2 p.m., with its right extended toward Parker's Store.

If Lee was aware of the precise nature of Grant's intended deployment, then he also knew that his opportunity for delaying the Federal maneuver was narrowed down to a brief margin of about two hours during the early afternoon. Aware of this and trusting also that Longstreet would be up by nightfall, did he intend to launch his attack during the early hours of the afternoon? Or, fearful lest the five divisions of Ewell and Hill would be speedily broken in such an operation, did he contemplate the alternative of inviting an attack, thus causing the Federal columns to suspend their march?

The evidence seems clear enough to justify a negative answer to both questions. Anticipating events of the morrow for a moment, we have it on Ewell's authority that shortly after 11 a.m. Lee cautioned him against becoming involved with the enemy in his front. In addition to this caution Ewell was informed that the general commanding preferred not to bring on a general engagement until Longstreet came up. That is, Lee intended, if possible, to avoid any serious encounter with the enemy until nightfall. It is therefore difficult to avoid the conclusion that Lee was not aware of the narrow margin of time within which he must act, and that he had no intention of risking a general engagement under any conditions, until Longstreet arrived on the scene of action.

What then is the explanation of Lee's advance from Locust Grove and New Verdiersville into the Wilderness during the forenoon of May 5th?

In the light of Ewell's testimony there can be but one tenable explanation. Lee threw out the five divisions of Hill and Ewell, not for the purpose of launching an offensive stroke, or of inviting a defensive battle, but with the intention of executing a reconnaissance in force along the Turnpike and the Plank Road. While seeking every opportunity to delay the enemy's march, these detachments were to avoid battle until Longstreet could throw his weight into a swift, offensive thrust.

Here again Lee is the daring opportunist of Chancellorsville. Then, as now, the preliminary dispositions of his adversary had caught him at a serious disadvantage. In the spring of 1863 Hooker had thrown an offensive wing over the Rappahannock and across the Confederate right at Fredericksburg, where Lee faced a containing force equal in strength to his own army. Now, after crossing the Rapidan. Grant stood in overwhelming force on the south bank of the river while Lee was completing his concentration in the Wilderness. On the previous occasion Lee, after leaving a detachment to block Hooker's containing wing at Fredericksburg, sought the desperate remedy of dividing his main force in the presence of Hooker's offensive wing in order to turn the Federal right. On that occasion two Confederate divisions under Lee's personal direction succeeded in diverting Hooker's attention while the three divisions of Jackson's flanking column marched into position. Now, Lee had five divisions in hand to hold the Federals in place, while the three divisions of Longstreet and Anderson hastened forward to constitute the maneuvering element. Of the two situations, the one now facing Lee seemed the more promising. For these reasons, no doubt, Lee felt assured of his ability to outmaneuver and crush Grant in the same dreary woodland that had witnessed the ruin of Hooker's grandiose hopes the year before.

CHAPTER 6

MEADE SUSPENDS MARCH TO DEPLOYMENT

At dawn of May 5 the bugle notes of reveille aroused Meade's headquarters camp by the Rapidan. Staff tents came down one by one and were bundled into waiting wagons as his cavalry escort formed on the headquarters colors. Riding forward with the officers of his staff, General Meade led the column southward on the Germanna Plank Road.

The bivouacks of Sedgwick's divisions along the highway were noisily astir as the headquarters column clattered by, while those at Chancellorsville and around Wilderness Tavern resounded with the bustle of troops preparing to march into battle. Seven miles to the south at Parker's Store the troopers of Wilson's 3d Cavalry Division were tightening the girths of saddles that had remained overnight on the horses' backs. At 5 a.m. the unit moved from its bivouac and took a trail winding through the woods toward Craig's Meeting House. The 2d Brigade, Colonel George H. Chapman commanding, marched in advance, with Colonel Truman A. Bryan's 1st Brigade following.

Responsible for screening the front of deployment, General Wilson had been given explicit orders to keep patrols out on the Orange Turnpike and Plank Road, as well as on other specified roads leading from the west and southwest toward the sector to be occupied by Hancock's II Corps. In partial fulfillment of these instructions, Wilson left Lieutenant Colonel John Hammond's 5th New York Cavalry at Parker's Store to observe along the Plank Road and act as a connecting link between the main cavalry force and the advance of Warren's infantry. But he made no provision for keeping the Orange Turnpike toward Locust Grove under observation, an act of omission that compounded the costly consequences of his failure to watch properly the same stretch of road during the previous afternoon.

A better understanding of the maneuver toward the line Shady Grove Church-Parker's Store-Wilderness Tavern will be gained if the operations of Wilson's cavalry are briefly sketched before examining the details of the infantry advance.

A three hours' march through the woods brought Chapman's brigade over Robertson's Run to Craig's Meeting House, on the Catharpin Road and some three miles west of Shady Grove Church. At 8 a.m. a squadron of the 3d Vermont Cavalry under Colonel A. W. Preston rode out on the Catharpin Road to reconnoiter toward Mine Run. Meanwhile General Wilson posted Bryan's brigade on the north bank of Robertson's Run, at the crossing of the woods road from Parker's Store.

Pushing westward about half a mile, the Vermont squadron met an advance party of Rosser's Virginia Cavalry Brigade. The Virginians rode furiously down on the Federal horse. The Vermonters met the onset, then gave ground and fell back toward the meeting house. Bryan galloped up with reinforcements. Rosser's detachment promptly dismounted to seek cover in the dense woods bordering both sides of the road. Chapman in turn dismounted and threw a strong skirmish line at the Confederate position. Rosser's troopers recoiled before the rapid fire of Chapman's magazine carbines. The Federals pressed their pursuit a distance of nearly two miles, expending an exorbitant amount of ammunition while their wary foe avoided the dangers of close-range fighting. About noon when Warren, according to plan, should have been closing up at Parker's Store and Hancock's advance should have reached Shady Grove Church, Wilson became apprehensive on his own account. Chapman's ammunition was running low. No word had been received from army or cavalry corps headquarters since dawn. Unwilling to push the pursuit too far from Bryan's reserve position on Robertson's

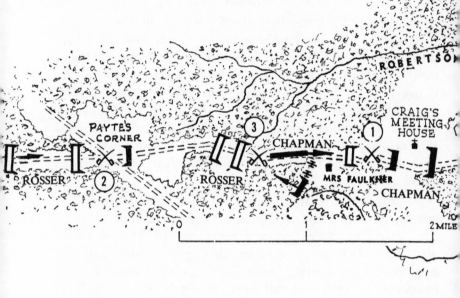

MAP 6. WILSON'S CAVALRY SCREEN IS TORN TO TATTERS

This map illustrates the cavalry action along the Catharpin Road on the morning of May 5. The sequence of events is shown by the numbers in circles, and is thus explained: 1. At about 8 a.m. Chapman's brigade of Wilson's division is just east of Craig's Meeting House, with Bryan in reserve to the north. A squadron of the 3d Vermont Cavalry, thrown out in advance, attacks and drives back a detachment of Rosser's Confederate cavalry brigade. 2. Moving out from Richards Shop, Rosser reinforces his advance party. Chapman throws forward his entire brigade. Both sides dismount and engage

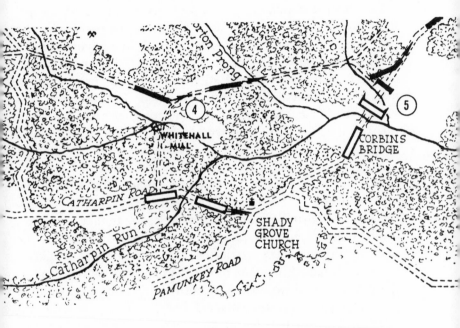

in a firefight for three hours. Reinforced about noon by Stuart, Rosser drives back Chapman in confusion. 3. Wilson slows Rosser's pursuit at his headquarters at Mrs. Faulkner's, using two horse batteries firing canister, and a mounted charge by his headquarters detachment. 4. Chapman continues the retreat past Bryan's reserve position and along a woodland path toward Todds Tavern. Bryan follows, with Brinton's 18th Pennsylvania Cavalry covering the rear. 5. Brinton holds up Rosser's advance as Bryan's column and Wilson's headquarters detachment turn from the trail into the Catharpin Road.

Run, Wilson ordered Chapman to hold his advanced line with a strong picket and assemble the rest of his brigade in an open field one-half mile to the rear.[1]

Wilson's Screen Torn

Chapman dismounted the 3d Indiana Cavalry and formed it in line of battle along a deep ravine across the road. The remaining units of the brigade formed in the open field. Wilson established his headquarters at Mrs. Faulkner's house, on the Catharpin Road and about one mile in rear of Chapman's dismounted line. Here he held Pennington's and Fitzhugh's horse batteries in reserve, together with his headquarters escort, which consisted of a detachment of fifty sabers from the 3d Indiana Cavalry, commanded by Lieutenant Long.[2]

To pursue the story of Wilson's misadventures into the afternoon ignores events of great moment that were developing on the Turnpike and the Plank Road. It may, however, avoid confusion in later picking up the tangled threads of the story if Wilson is first extricated from his unhappy plight.

About 1 p.m. Chapman received word from skirmishers in the pines beyond his advanced position that the Confederates had received reinforcements and were making preparations to advance. Realizing that he must now face heavy odds with a diminished supply of ammunition, Wilson directed Chapman to fall back rapidly past Craig's Meeting House and reform in rear of the Bryan's 1st Brigade.[3]

Developments quickly justified the wisdom of Wilson's decision. Heavily reinforced, Rosser's men swarmed out of the woods and swept across the ravine towards Chapman's advanced line of battle.[4] Chapman called on his reserve. The entire 2d Brigade came into action, but failed to stay Rosser's onrush. Step by step the dismounted Federals gave ground toward their horse lines. The led horses became unmanageable, breaking away and creating confusion along the line of retreat. The Confederates pressed their advantage with redoubled energy, driving Chapman's disorganized regiments back toward division headquarters at Mrs. Faulkner's house.[5]

Here Wilson was making strenuous efforts to stay the Confederate pursuit. Mounted, Lieutenant Long held his detachment in hand. Pennington and Fitzhugh put their six-gun batteries in position.

Shaken by the heavy attack that had broken its forward lines and overpowered the reserves as they came into action, Chapman's brigade swept by, an exhausted force now verging dangerously on complete disintegration. Wilson now took direction of the fight. Roaring salvos from the horse batteries staggered for a moment the Confederate onset. Long and his troopers rode headlong into the melee.[6]

The brief respite afforded by Wilson's strenuous measures enabled Chapman to draw off his command and turn into the road leading past Craig's Meeting House to Parker's Store. After crossing Robertson's Run, he rallied behind a line formed by a part of Bryan's 1st Brigade.

With a diminished supply of ammunition and the Confederate cavalry in command of the Catharpin Road toward Shady Grove Church, Wilson was no longer able to cover the front or left of the II Corps which, according to plan, should now be closing up to Shady Grove Church. At this critical juncture he learned from Colonel Bryan, commanding the 1st Brigade, that the enemy had seized the road to Parker's Store early during the forenoon and that none of his couriers bearing dispatches to army headquarters had succeeded in getting through.[7] Cut off now from communication with both the V and II Corps, and fearful that the avenues of escape in both directions would be speedily closed, Wilson determined to withdraw by a blind road toward Todd's Tavern, at the junction of the Brock and Catharpin Roads. The retirement is best described in Wilson's own words:

> I had scarcely taken this resolution when I perceived that the enemy were pushing rapidly down the Catharpin Road in the same direction. The march was begun at once, the 2d Brigade in advance, followed by the batteries and the 1st Brigade. The 18th Pennsylvania Cavalry, Lieutenant Colonel

W. Brinton commanding, was left to cover the rear. The main column crossed the Po near its head, and struck the Catharpin Road just beyond Corbin's Bridge. It had scarcely got upon the road when the rebels made their appearance on the hill west of the bridge. I succeeded in reaching the road with my escort just in time to prevent being cut off. The rear guard found the road occupied by the enemy, but Colonel Brinton made three brilliant and determined charges, breaking the enemy's cavalry, but finding he could not succeed in getting through without heavy loss, he struck off to the left and joined the division late in the evening.[8]

In brief, the story of Wilson's misadventures is that, instead of screening the front of deployment from Shady Grove Church to Wilderness Tavern, he occupied only a two-mile stretch of the Catharpin Road for about three hours. In giving his attention to the wrong road, he became involved in a useless fight and barely escaped disaster. As a consequence he was unable either to report his position or to furnish intelligence concerning the movements of the enemy. In the meantime Gregg's cavalry division stood inactive at Aldrich's Farm and Torbert spent the forenoon working through the press of transport wagons between Ely's Ford and Chancellorsville.[9] Then, Wilson's flight to the flank of the infantry on the Brock Road seems a complete confession that, due to the variety of objectives undertaken or forced upon Sheridan, the Federal cavalry, despite its preponderance in numbers and firepower, had been unable to cover Meade's infantry in its movement toward the proposed line of deployment.

Having witnessed the disappearance of the cavalry screen, we may now turn to developments on the Orange Turnpike. At 5 a.m. Warren notified Humphreys, Meade's chief of staff, that the V Corps was in motion. The communication also stated that Warren had decided to keep the combat trains with his column during the advance to Parker's Store. It would appear that army headquarters had suggested the advisability of sending these trains by way of the Brock Crossing and the Plank Road. Warren justified his decision to alter such an arrangement on grounds that his command had but a short march to its objective. For reasons that Warren could not foresee at 5 a.m., it was fortunate indeed that the Brock Road between Wilderness Tavern and the Brock-Plank intersection remained unobstructed by transport vehicles during the forenoon. And, as will soon be appreciated, the presence of these vehicles on the Plank Road between Parker's Store and the Brock Crossing at any time after midday would have been little short of a catastrophe.[10]

A circular issued from V Corps Headquarters at 8 p.m., May 4th, drew attention to the possibility of attack from the direction of Mine Run during the advance on Parker's Store. The batteries were to march with divisions, that is, in the order of assignment of May 4, in which division commanders were also instructed to throw flankers well out to the right. All roads passed were to be covered by detachments placed in good positions. Each detachment so placed was to remain in position until relieved by the division next in column. Vehicles of the combat trains were to move with their respective divisions on the left of the road, the infantry keeping to the right. The circular cautioned that "troops must be kept well closed and held well in hand, to meet attack at any moment. The head of the column will move slowly, to enable divisions to keep well closed up on each other. The necessity for this is paramount, and must be kept constantly in mind." [11]

At 5:30 a.m. Warren informed General Getty, who was waiting at the head of Sedgwick's column, to move off toward Wilderness Tavern, that Griffin had instructions to hold the Orange Turnpike and that at least one brigade of Griffin's division would picket that road until relieved by Getty, or the division leading the VI Corps.[12] Warren then gave his attention to Griffin's outposts. According to Morris Schaff, who served during the battle as a special *aide de camp* on the V Corps staff, Warren advised Colonel Jenkins, general officer of outposts, that his pickets, "if not already withdrawn, should remain out until the column gets well in the road on the line of march." [13]

Ewell Deploys Across Griffin's Front

Aside from the evidence given by Schaff, the time of dispatch and receipt of the communication to Colonel Jenkins is uncertain. Such a message was transmitted at an unstated time during the forenoon by Colonel Locke, Assistant Adjutant General V Corps, to Colonel Jenkins. Neglecting to note the time of receipt, Colonel Jenkins indorsed this dispatch with a statement that settled all doubts as to the advisability of any withdrawal from the Turnpike.[14] He wrote:

> Rebel Infantry on Turnpike and forming in line of battle in front of Griffin's line of battle. Skirmishers out, preparations being made to meet them. Large clouds of dust in that direction.

As the courier bearing Warren's dispatch to Jenkins travelled to the front, a message (probably Jenkins') reporting the presence of Confederate troops on the Turnpike was enroute to V Corps Headquarters. Warren, having completed the arrangements just described, was preparing to quit his headquarters camp and join the line of march. Wearing, when dressed for battle, the yellow sash of a major general, he mounted his dapple gray a few minutes before six. The divisions of Crawford and Wadsworth were in plain sight across the fields, passing the Lacy house. Just as the general's party turned into the Turnpike, a staff galloper drew rein and saluted the corps commander. General Griffin, he reported, had sent him to inform General Warren that the enemy were advancing in force on his pickets.

"I do not believe," records Schaff, "that Warren ever had a greater surprise in his life, but this thin, solemn, darkly shallow face was nowhere lightened by even a transistory glare. Hancock's open, handsome countenance would have been all ablaze. There was with Warren at this time only Colonel Locke, Dr. Winnie, the General's brother Robert, and Lieutenant Higbee. Warren first turned to me and said, 'Tell Griffin to get ready to attack at once,' then, for some reason, perhaps because of my youth and inexperience, he told Higbee to take the message."[15]

Warren immediately notified Meade of the development reported by Griffin. This dispatch was dated at 6 a.m. It read:

> General Griffin has just sent in word that a force of the enemy has been reported to him coming down the Turnpike. The foundation of the report is not given. Until it is more definitely ascertained no change will take place in the movement ordered. Such demonstrations are to be expected and show the necessity for keeping well closed and prepared to face toward Mine Run and meet an attack at a moment's notice.[16]

A postscript added: "Will remain at my old headquarters until 7 a.m."

Before the communication to Meade had been dispatched, a second courier arrived at V Corps headquarters. He bore additional information from Bartlett, commanding the 3d Brigade of Griffin's division. Warren added a second postscript to the dispatch written at 6 a.m.: "General Bartlett sends in word that the enemy has a line of infantry with skirmishers out advancing. We shall soon know more. I have arranged for General Griffin to hold the pike until the Sixth Corps comes up, at all events."

At 6:20 a.m. Warren dispatched the following order to Griffin: "The Major-General commanding [Warren] directs you to push a force out at once against the enemy and see what force he has."

Warren's order of 6:20 a.m. to Griffin was indorsed by Griffin at 7 a.m. as follows: "General Bartlett will please execute the within order."

Before following the sequence of events at Warren's headquarters, it will be helpful now to go out on Griffin's picket line with a view to understanding just what had happened between daylight and 6:20 a.m., and what further developments took place in consequence of Warren's order of 6:20.

It is evident from the report of Colonel William A. Throop, commanding the 1st Michigan Infantry, Bartlett's 3d Brigade, that Griffin barely escaped surprise in the act of forming a part of his division in column, preparatory to taking up the line of march. Colonel Throop states that he had received written orders to withdraw his pickets and rejoin the brigade on its march. "I was in the act of assembling the regiment," he records, "when the enemy was reported advancing."[17] The 1st Michigan promptly deployed along the line it had just abandoned. Colonel Throop describes this disposition as follows:

> The line was established about three-quarters of a mile in advance of the bivouac of the brigade, the right resting on and covering the Orange Court-House and Fredericksburg pike, the left swinging back and connecting with the pickets of the Second Brigade (Colonel Sweitzer). There was no connection on the right, the pickets of the First Brigade (General Ayres) that should have joined on my right, being a half mile in rear of the line of pickets of the other two brigades, and without any connection, which made it necessary for me to watch and protect my own right. When my picket-line was established there was no enemy in our front. About an hour after daylight on the morning of the 5th a strong column of the enemy's infantry, preceded by cavalry, was discovered coming down the road from the vicinity of Robertson's Tavern (Locust Grove). Upon seeing the advance of the enemy, I at once extended the right of my line to the right of the road, and reinforced it by a company to check a party of the enemy's cavalry which had been sent to turn this flank of my picket line. Upon striking my pickets the enemy immediately deployed his infantry to the right and left of the road in line of skirmishers. I at once dispatched my adjutant to General Bartlett, commanding brigade, the force and disposition of the enemy that had appeared on our front.

The intelligence received from Bartlett by Warren at 6:20 a.m. and incorporated as the second postscript in Warren's communication of 6 a.m. to Meade, probably contained the information originally furnished by Colonel Throop. If this is the case, Throop's report led to the order from V Corps headquarters to throw out a reconnaissance and develop the enemy's force. This order, as already stated, was referred by Griffin to Bartlett at 7 a.m.

Bartlett directed Colonel Hayes to take the 18th Massachusetts and 83d Pennsylvania and move up the "Stone road" and discover whether the enemy's force consisted of cavalry or infantry and what his intentions were.[18] Colonel White, commanding the 18th Massachusetts Infantry, states that orders for reconnaissance were received at about 8 o'clock. He describes the operation as follows:

> The two regiments moved up to the picket-line, and Colonel Hayes ordered two companies from each regiment to be detailed to move forward as skirmishers. The companies taken from the 18th Massachusetts Volunteers were placed under command of Captain Bent, and were moved forward by him on the right of the road, promptly engaging the enemy's skirmishers, and driving them back. It was quickly ascertained that the enemy was present with strong infantry force, and that he was busily engaged throwing up breastworks, and upon making this report to the brigade commander the skirmishers were ordered to retire. The regiment in this movement lost one man, Charles Wilson, Company I, who was the first infantryman killed in the campaign. Soon after the withdrawal of the skirmishers the regiment was placed on the left of the first line of battle of the division, which had been moved up to the picket line. The regiment on its left was joined by a brigade of the Fourth Division (Wadsworth), on its right by the 83d Pennsylvania Volunteers.

Meade Suspends March to Line of Deployment

As measures were being taken to develop the enemy in Griffin's front, Meade, accompanied by Humphreys and other officers of his staff, was hastening from Germanna Ford toward Wilderness Tavern. According to Humphreys the party met a courier from V Corps headquarters at 7:15 a.m. His dispatch, as described by Humphreys, advised Meade that the enemy's infantry was on the pike in some force about two miles from Wilderness Tavern. A few minutes later the party pulled up at Warren's headquarters. The army commander, states Humphreys, "at once directed him [Warren] to halt his column and attack the enemy with his whole force."[19]

Meade at the same time sent the following order to Hancock, then on the march between Chancellorsville and Shady Grove Church: "The enemy are on the Orange pike about 2 miles in front of Wilderness Tavern in some force. Until the matter develops, the major general commanding [Meade] desires you to halt at Todd's Tavern."[20]

This dispatch, written at 7:30 a.m., was received by Hancock near Todd's Tavern at 9 a.m. Locke, V Corps Assistant Adju-

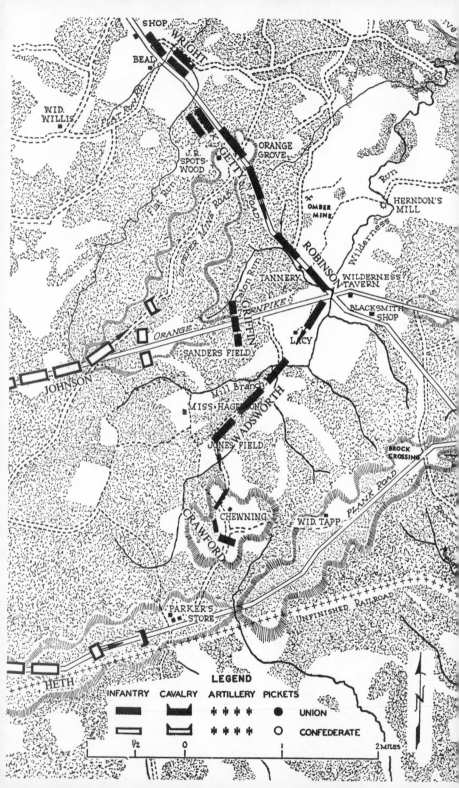

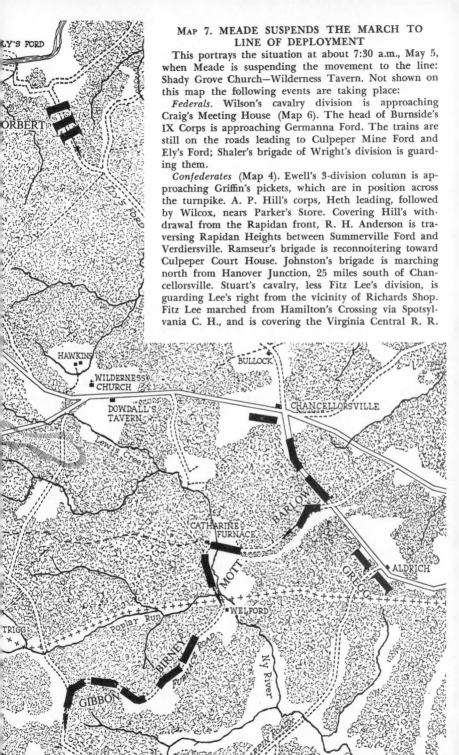

Map 7. MEADE SUSPENDS THE MARCH TO LINE OF DEPLOYMENT

This portrays the situation at about 7:30 a.m., May 5, when Meade is suspending the movement to the line: Shady Grove Church—Wilderness Tavern. Not shown on this map the following events are taking place:

Federals. Wilson's cavalry division is approaching Craig's Meeting House (Map 6). The head of Burnside's IX Corps is approaching Germanna Ford. The trains are still on the roads leading to Culpeper Mine Ford and Ely's Ford; Shaler's brigade of Wright's division is guarding them.

Confederates (Map 4). Ewell's 3-division column is approaching Griffin's pickets, which are in position across the turnpike. A. P. Hill's corps, Heth leading, followed by Wilcox, near Parker's Store. Covering Hill's withdrawal from the Rapidan front, R. H. Anderson is traversing Rapidan Heights between Summerville Ford and Verdiersville. Ramseur's brigade is reconnoitering toward Culpeper Court House. Johnston's brigade is marching north from Hanover Junction, 25 miles south of Chancellorsville. Stuart's cavalry, less Fitz Lee's division, is guarding Lee's right from the vicinity of Richards Shop. Fitz Lee marched from Hamilton's Crossing via Spotsylvania C. H., and is covering the Virginia Central R. R.

tant General, informed Wadsworth that: "The movement toward Parker's Store is suspended for the present. You will halt, face toward Mine Run, and make your connection with General Griffin on your right."

Similar instructions were issued by Locke to Crawford: "The movement toward Parker's Store is suspended. You will halt, face toward Mine Run, and connect with General Wadsworth on your right. Get your trains to rear. By command of Major General Warren."

The dispatches to Hancock, Wadsworth, and Crawford are all dated at the same time, 7:30 a.m. Crawford acknowledged Locke's communication at 8 a.m., stating that he had halted in a good position within a mile of Parker's Store and that "there is brisk skirmishing at the Store between our own and the enemy's cavalry." This acknowledgment, with its report of skirmishing on the Plank Road, did not reach Meade's headquarters until after 9 a.m.[21]

The decision to suspend the deployment on the line Shady Grove Church-Parker's Store-Wilderness Tavern was communicated to Grant at 7:30 a.m.:

> The enemy have appeared in force on the Orange pike, and are now reported forming line of battle in front of Griffin's division, Fifth Corps. I have directed General Griffin to attack them at once with his whole force. Until this movement of the enemy is developed, the march of the corps must be suspended. I have, therefore, sent word to Hancock not to advance beyond Todd's Tavern for the present. I think the enemy is trying to delay our movement, and will not give battle, but of this we shall soon see. For the present I will stop here, and have stopped our trains.[22]

Meade's Orders to Warren

At 7:50, just 20 minutes after notification to the Lieutenant General that the advance had been suspended, Warren instructed Griffin as follows: "Have your whole division prepared to move forward and attack the enemy, and await further instructions, while other troops are forming. Keep us informed of everything going on in your front."

It was probably in compliance with this order that the 1st

Division moved forward from its bivouac and formed in line of battle along the front that had been previously occupied by the pickets.[23]

No orders appear to have been given at 7:30 a.m., or immediately after, with a view to enlisting Sedgwick's support in the contemplated attack along the Turnpike. Instructions to this end, however, were certainly issued before 9 o'clock. In a dispatch of 9 a.m. to Grant, Meade remarks that "Warren is making his dispositions to attack, and Sedgwick to support him."[24]

CHAPTER 7

MEADE WITHHOLDS HIS BLOW

Although unforeseen at 7:30 a.m. on May 5, Meade's decision to suspend the advance of his columns marks the breakdown of Operation Wilderness as planned by Humphreys. There can be little doubt that at that time Meade had no intention of abandoning the attempt to turn Lee's right. Yet his dispositions and explanatory note of 7:30 to Grant betray a certain confusion of thought. He inclined to a belief that Lee was merely trying to delay his march. At the same time, he admitted the possibility that Lee might give battle. This attitude persisted for some time. He concluded the dispatch just mentioned, that of 9 a.m., in which he refers to Sedgwick's participation in the attack ordered at 7:30, with the observation that "I will, if such is the case punish him. If he is disposed to fight this side of Mine Run at once, he shall be accommodated."

Awkward Dispositions

In this confused state of mind, Meade halted his turning wing (Hancock) and, at the same time, began the concentration of troops forming the pivot of maneuver (Warren and Sedgwick). But he made no serious preparation to force the battle, or even to put his troops in position to accept a fair offer to fight a general engagement. In the event of a successful thrust of the V Corps westward along the Turnpike, as originally intended by Meade at 7:30, Warren must inevitably widen a four-mile gap between his left and the right of the II Corps near Todd's Tavern. And if the operation on the pike precipitated a general battle, Meade could not count upon Hancock's active intervention within a period of from five to six hours.[1] Meade's distribution of forces at 7:30 a.m. thus offers an interesting commentary on his uncertain course.

The 3d (Crawford), 4th (Wadsworth), and 2d (Robinson) Divisions of Warren's V Corps extended in the order named in column of march from Chewning's farm to a point on the Germanna Plank Road about one mile north of Wilderness Tavern. The distance from head to rear of the column was approximately four miles.

Meade's order suspending the advance overtook Crawford's division at 8 a.m. In acknowledging this communication, Crawford stated that he had advanced within a mile of Parker's Store and was halted in a good position. Brisk skirmishing between Federal and Confederate cavalry, he reported, could be heard at the Store.[2]

Wadsworth halted approximately midway between Chewning's farm and the Lacy house. There is no record of the fact that Wadsworth acknowledged Locke's order to halt and connect with Griffin. At 8:30 a.m., about half an hour after he should have received this order, Wadsworth describes his position in a dispatch which is thought to have been addressed to Griffin: "I find an opening and tolerable position for artillery about 1½ miles from Lacy's house. I am at the point with two batteries and one brigade. Have a brigade stretched thinly between a piece of very thick woods and one brigade near you. Crawford's troops in front, rear in sight."[3]

There is no positive evidence to establish the exact time that Robinson's division moved out in rear of Wadsworth toward Parker's Store. Since Sedgwick's advance, following Robinson's rear, got under way at 7 a.m.[4] it seems a reasonable assumption that Robinson should have cleared his camp near Caton Run and that the head of his column should have turned into the open fields around the Lacy house as his rear was filing out of camp; that is, about 7 a.m.[5]

Griffin's division, as is already known, was now under orders to form in line of battle across the Orange Plank Road. But it had not, as yet, moved out from the bivouac occupied by the main body toward the picket line, where, about 8 a.m., it began entrenching.[6]

The order to halt did not immediately affect Sedgwick's VI Corps. Getty, in the lead, moved off at 7 a.m. on the Germanna Plank Road toward Wilderness Tavern. Wright's division followed.[7] As Getty closed up slowly toward the Tavern, his objective of that day, Wright moved on from his camp near Flat Run toward the junction of the Germanna Plank Road and the Culpeper Ford or Spotswood Road. The latter route bears off southwestward along the ridge between Flat and Caton Runs to the Turnpike, joining that highway just eastward of the point from which Ewell's Confederate column was deploying on a north and south line.

Hancock Halts His Column

When the order to halt was given by Meade at 7:30 a.m., Hancock's II Corps stretched out the entire length of the Catherine Furnace Road, with the rear of the column on the Orange Plank Road, probably at or just leaving the Chancellorsville intersection. In acknowledging this order at 9, Hancock states that his advance, Gibbon's 2d Division, was about one mile out on the Catharpin Road beyond Todd's Tavern. Gibbon, then, had marched seven miles in four hours, or at the rate of approximately one and three-quarters miles an hour. One and one-half hours prior to 9 o'clock, that is, at 7:30 a.m., Gibbon would have been near the Brock-Catherine Furnace Road intersection, a mile north of Todd's Tavern, with Birney's 3d and Mott's 4th Divisions following on the Furnace Road. The rear division (Barlow's 1st) apparently had not reached Catherine Furnace, as Hancock at 9:40 informed Humphreys that "The rear division is ordered to halt at the Furnace." From front to rear, Hancock's column occupied a road space of nearly six miles. When Meade at 7:30 a.m. gave directions for suspension of the turning movement, Hancock's advance occupied a point four miles southeast of Warren's advance at Chewning farm. Upon receipt at 9 a.m. of instructions to halt at Todd's Tavern, pending developments on the Orange Turnpike, Hancock recalled Gibbon's division. Birney's division, following Gibbon's in column, was halted at the tavern. Orders were sent for Mott's 4th Division to halt at the Brock-Furnace Road intersection, while Barlow's 1st Division, as already noted, closed up in accordance with orders from II Corps headquarters, toward the Catherine Furnace, which is about two and one-half miles northeast of the Brock-Furnace Road intersection. With the possible exception of Barlow's division, these dispositions had been completed at 9:40 a.m., when Hancock informed Humphreys to this effect.[8]

Grant Approves Meade's Decision to Attack

The courier bearing intelligence to Grant of Meade's determination to suspend the march of the corps and the trains while Warren attacked on the Turnpike arrived at Grant's headquarters near Germanna Ford sometime after 8 o'clock.[9] Impatiently awaiting the arrival of General Burnside to explain to that officer the dispositions desired of his divisions as they arrived from time to time during the day, Grant replied at 8:24 a.m., approving Meade's decision to attack and urging haste in development of the operation:

Your note giving movement of the enemy and your dispositions received. Burnside's advance is now crossing the river. I will have Rickett's division relieved and advance at once, and urge Burnside's crossing. As soon as I can see Burnside I will go forward. If any opportunity presents itself for pitching into a part of Lee's army, do so without giving time for dispositions.[10]

Time was the essence of Meade's plan of attack. In default of adequate cavalry reconnaissance and supplementary detachments to hold the Confederates during the period of completion of the Federal maneuver, Meade sought to gain time by improvising a thrust against the enemy on the Turnpike. He informed Grant that the attack would be made at once. Grant, inferring that Meade intended to strike with whatever forces happened to be at hand, gave his prompt approval of "pitching into a part of Lee's army."[11] In this ready acquiescence, however, it seems doubtful if there was any distinction in Grant's mind between a rapidly prepared advance with all forces immediately available and a premature piecemeal attack with whatever troops that happened to be at hand.[12]

Problems in Moving from Column to Line

Certainly Warren took a serious view of Meade's intentions. The V Corps commander, it will be recalled, received his orders from the army commander at 7:30 by word of mouth. Warren was instructed to get all his troops in hand and then attack any force in his front.[13] Thus, while Warren was aware that circumstances required the rapid launching of an attack against an unknown force, he had every reason to believe that Meade would not grudge him the necessary time for closing up and deploying the divisions of his corps. Nevertheless Warren was caught on the horns of a cruel dilemma: he courted failure either by attacking prematurely, or by taking sufficient time to properly change his march column into line of battle for attack.

The attack involved an advance over rising ground toward the watershed running northeast and southwest between the basins of Wilderness and Flat Runs. It was known at 7:30 a.m. that the Confederates were forming their line of battle on the forward slope of the ridge, the deployment being right and left, or north and south, and being based on a point just east of the intersection of the Turnpike with the crest of the watershed.[14] Although Warren had instructed Griffin at 6:20 a.m. to develop the enemy's force in his front, it is evident that the reconnaissance did not move out until 8 o'clock, or half an hour after issuance of orders for the general attack.[15] As a consequence, the extent of the enemy's force was not apparent until Griffin formed his division in line of battle and stood fast, waiting for the supporting divisions to connect on his right and left.

Completely formed in two lines, with Robinson's division in reserve, the four divisions of Wright, Griffin, Wadsworth, and Crawford would have occupied a front extending from a point nearly three-quarters of a mile north of the Turnpike to one about a mile and a quarter south of the road. Including the the reserve division, Robinson's, the column of attack would have mustered some 30,000 bayonets which was some 4,000 more than Jackson threw against Hooker's right on the afternoon of May 2, 1863 at Chancellorsville.[16]

Flowing eastward down the slope on which the Confederates were forming, two tributaries and the main stream of Wilderness Run cut diagonally across the zone of Warren's proposed advance. The lower courses of these streams meander through stagnant, thickly wooded marshes. The northernmost of the two tributaries, Caton Run, flows through dense thickets to the north of the Turnpike. The stream bed lay about a quarter mile beyond Griffin's right flank. Mill Branch, the other tributary, follows a course through the woods roughly parallel to and about a half mile south of the Turnpike. A mile further south the main stream of Wilderness Run, after flowing in an easterly direction from its source, swings northward and receives the waters of Mill Branch nearly half a mile southwest of the Lacy house.

The peril of attacking prematurely across such a terrain is as obvious now to the military student as it must have been to the V Corps commander on the morning of May 5, 1864. Furthermore the difficulties confronting Warren in reassembling his divisions for an "immediate" attack were all but insuperable. Wadsworth must put his divisions astride Mill Branch and find Griffin's left. Crawford must reach back northward over the main stream of Wilderness Run and connect with Wadsworth's left. Wright's division (of the VI Corps), pushing southwest along the ridge between Caton and Flat Runs toward Griffin's right, had an even more difficult task. Bringing up the rear of Sedgwick's column on the Germanna Plank Road, he had the greater distance to go. After turning into the Culpeper Mine, or Spotswood Road, and pushing a mile along the ridge between Flat and Caton Runs, he must extend his line through the dense thickets bordering the latter stream to Griffin's right.

Although Ewell was unable to interfere seriously with the formation of Warren's line south of the Turnpike, the terrain was admirably suited to a passive defense. Stretching southward along relatively high ground was a chain of four clearings. Sanders' field, the northmost, lay in a shallow depression astride the Turnpike. Five-eighths of a mile east of the Turnpike-Culpeper Mine (Spotswood) Road intersection and directly in front of the Confederate line of battle, it offered a clear field of fire to Ewell's riflemen lurking in the woods to the west. This opening took the shape of an irregular ellipse, the long axis of which, paralleled by the Turnpike, measured about 400 yards. A dry watercourse, cutting through the clearing from north to south, drained into Mill Branch. In former days a wooden bridge had carried Turnpike traffic over the sharply eroded stream bed.

Half a mile south of Sanders' field is Miss Hagerson's farm, a clearing of about forty acres. This farm was situated on the south bank of Mill Branch.

Known as Jones' farm (or field), a third clearing of some 80 acres began a short distance from the south boundary of Miss Hagerson's farm and reached to the north bank of Wilderness Run.

The southmost clearing is Chewning's farm, which is situated half a mile to the south of Wilderness Run and approximately a mile and three-quarters from Sanders' field.

Referring again to Warren's distribution at 8 a.m., when the order to halt and form on Griffin's division overtook his advance division, we have the following situation: Crawford, holding the south end of the chain of clearings, was at Chewning's farm. Wadsworth's advance had reached Jones' field. Half a mile to the south, across the ravine of Wilderness Run, Wadsworth saw the rear of Crawford's column closing up on the Chewning plateau.[17] Wadsworth's column covered about a mile of roadway; therefore his rear must have been near the junction of Wilderness Run and Mill Branch. Griffin, in consequence of Warren's order of 8:50 a.m. to have his "whole division prepared to move forward and attack the enemy,"[18] advanced and formed on the line occupied during the night by his pickets. The brigades of Bartlett and Sweitzer extended in line of battle from the Turnpike toward Mill Branch. Since each brigade covered about a quarter mile of front, Sweitzer's left could not have been far from the north bank of the branch. It would follow that Wadsworth's rear must have been in the vicinity of the left of Griffin's line. If Colonel White, who participated in the reconnaissance which went forward at 8 a.m. along the Turnpike and then withdrew to the left of Griffin's line, gives an accurate account of developments in his operation report, Wadsworth's right connected with Sweitzer, on the left of Griffin's line, sometime between 8 and 9 o'clock. Then, since Getty's advance did not move out of camp at Flat Run on the Germanna Plank Road until 7 a.m., it is improbable that Wright, following Getty in line of march, could have reached the Germanna Plank-Culpeper Mine (Spotswood) Road intersection, which is a mile beyond the site of Getty's camp, as early as 8 a.m. In fact, it is most probable that Getty, who was obliged to wait until Robinson's division of the V Corps cleared the road in front of him, did not have his rear element in motion toward Wilderness Tavern before 9 o'clock, if that early. As a matter of fact, it was 11 a.m. before Wright's column closed up on Upton's brigade, his advance element at the Germanna Plank-Culpeper Mine Road intersection.[19]

Aside from difficulties incidental to the Wilderness terrain, the obstacles to a speedy deployment hinged on circumstances that were not apparent to Meade at 7:30 a.m. Ewell was in far greater strength on the Turnpike than Meade was willing to believe.

Unbeknown as yet to Meade, Ewell could seriously dispute the advance of Federal forces marching along the Culpeper Mine Road to support Warren's right flank. Also unbeknown to Meade at this time was the fact that two divisions of A. P. Hill's corps were pushing along the Plank Road toward Parker's Store and threatening Crawford's flank at Chewning's farm. These facts, however, did not become apparent until three hours later.

Crawford Tarries at Chewning's

After ordering Warren to reassemble his divisions and attack, the army commander established his headquarters at a knoll on the north side of the Turnpike and about 700 yards west of the Germanna Plank Road-Orange Turnpike intersection. Warren meanwhile moved his headquarters to the Lacy house, about 500 yards due south across the road from army headquarters. Here, at 7:50 a.m., he wrote the dispatch instrucing Griffin to push forward and prepare to attack.[20] Warren then rode out on the Parker's Store road to overtake and confer with General Wadsworth.[21]

After meeting the 4th Division commander at a point about a mile from the Lacy house and where the road, according to Schaff, swings west and follows for quite a distance the main branch of Wilderness Run, Warren held a hurried conference. The necessity for striking a quick blow was urged upon Wadsworth. Warren indicated with a sweep of his arm the deep woods to the west and added: "Find out what is in there." Colonel Roebling, V Corps Chief of Staff, was then directed to ride on to Chewning's farm and give General Crawford the details of the attack order.[22]

As the staff colonel rode off southward across Jones' field, Warren, trailed by his party, galloped back to the Lacy house. Pausing there briefly to inquire of any new developments during his absence, Warren then hastened out on the Turnpike to Griffin's front.[23]

At 9 a.m. a few minutes after the corps commander's departure, Colonel Locke, Assistant Adjutant General, received Crawford's dispatch of 8 a.m. in which the 2d Division commander acknowledged the order to halt and reported what appeared from his point of observation at Chewning's to be a lively cavalry skirmish over on the Plank Road near Parker's Store. The message was transmitted to army headquarters, with an indorsement noting the time of receipt, 9 a.m., and stating that "Warren is examining Griffin's front."[24] Ten, possibly fifteen minutes later, Meade read the message and wrote a second indorsement, stating: "Dispatch from Crawford received. I have sent to Wilson, who will himself find out the movement of the enemy."[25]

It was one of those unaccountable mischances of war that Crawford's report of Confederate troops on the Plank Road should have been virtually ignored. The army commander's apathy with reference to the Plank Road lends strength to the assumption that, while admitting the possibility of an offer of battle by the enemy, Meade, with the passage of time, became more and more dominated by a conviction that any activity on Lee's part beyond Mine Run would be limited to a delaying operation. [26] Meade appears to have attached little significance to the fact that reports of enemy troops both on the Turnpike and Plank Road should have been furnished by infantry pickets rather than by cavalry patrols. He dismissed the whole matter by ordering Wilson, who should have apprised him of the situation, to "find out the movement of the enemy." It is not surprising then that, in addition to underestimating the force Warren was preparing to attack, and failing, after significant warning, to foresee the possibility of this force being supported by a large formation on the Plank Road, Meade should have entirely overlooked the opportunities that Ewell would enjoy in delaying the advance of Wright's division along the Culpeper Mine ridge road toward Griffin's right. In truth, matters were drifting toward an impasse in which Warren, if he attacked at all, must go forward with both flanks in the air. The tragic nature of this situation was soon to be revealed—one which would bring about a savage and indecisive battle that Grant would have avoided and Lee intended to postpone.

Whatever may be the explanation of Meade's indifference to Crawford's first dispatch from Chewning's farm, Crawford himself and Major Roebling, the V Corps Chief of Staff, who had been sent by Warren to the flank of the attack column, were alert to the difficulties foreshadowed by the skirmish at

Parker's Store. Major Roebling, it will be recalled, left Warren while the latter was conferring with Wadsworth on the
Parker's Store road. Emerging from the woods on the south
bank of Wilderness Run, Roebling heard the sharp crack of
cavalry carbines off to the southwest. His quick eye took in the
importance of Crawford's position with reference to a Confederate thrust eastward along the Plank road.

In going up the basin of Wilderness Run toward Chewning's
farm, the ground rises rapidly to a tilted tableland. The plateau
skirts the headwaters of the western branches of the Run like
the rim of a great kettle[27] and falls gradually away eastward
toward the Brock-Plank Road intersection. The Parker's Store
road strikes south over the plateau at Chewning's farm and
then, bearing again to the southwest, drops into the woodland
toward the store. Another road runs east along the tapering
crest of the plateau to Widow Tapp's farm, which is located on
the Plank Road about two miles northeast of Parker's Store
and approximately one and one-quarter miles southwest of the
Brock-Plank Road intersection.

Crawford was reluctant to abandon the plateau. Although
representing the V Corps commander and therefore responsible
for an expeditious execution of the order to connect with Wadsworth, Colonel Roebling appears to have sustained General
Crawford in his hesitancy to comply with the order from corps
headquarters.[28] Five regiments were advanced and formed in
line of battle facing the Plank Road. From right to left the line
consisted of the 6th—10th—12th—13th—and 1st Pennsylvania
Reserves. The 13th covered the road to Parker's Store, with the
1st on its right refused at a sharp angle.[29] The 2d, 5th, 7th, 8th,
and 11th Regiments were held in reserve.

Cavalry Driven from Parker's Store

While these dispositions were being made, Roebling rode
down toward the store to investigate the firefight. It was now
discovered that the 5th New York Cavalry was not skirmishing
with Confederate cavalry as Crawford had reported at 8 a.m.
Roebling learned that Lieutenant Colonel John Hammond,

commanding the 5th New York, had been holding up A. P. Hill's infantry advance since dawn, and that he would be compelled to abandon the crossroads at Parker's Store unless infantry came to his assistance.[30]

Although isolated for nearly four hours, the 5th New York Cavalry had developed Hill's column on the Plank Road in time to forestall the fatal consequences that would have followed a complete surprise in that quarter. At dawn two companies under Captain Baker had gone out on the Plank Road toward New Verdiersville to reconnoiter. About two miles west of Parker's Store, Baker's detachment encountered the advance party of Kirkland's Brigade, Heth's Division.[31] Engaging fiercely, the Federal troopers compelled Kirkland to halt and begin deployment. Squads of Confederate infantry crashed through the thicket, intent on overwhelming the thin line of hostile skirmishers across their line of march. The Federals gave ground step by step, until a rumble of hoofs on the Plank Road bespoke the approach of reinforcements from Parker's Store. Galloping up to the front and hastily dismounting, Hammond threw in his entire force as skirmishers, save only the horseholders who hastened back toward the store with a cantering column of led horses. As the Spencer magazine rifles of Hammond's column came into action, the Confederate infantry recoiled. According to a prisoner taken from Kirkland's Brigade at this time of the fray, his comrades fought under the impression that they were face to face with no less than a brigade of Federal infantry.[32]

The fight developed into a furious delaying action, Hammond's troopers giving ground to avoid the envelopment of their flanks, while Kirkland's infantrymen stumbled blindly through the dense thickets, attempting time and again to overlap the elusive line of quickfiring skirmishers.

By 9 o'clock Kirkland had forced the Parker's Store crossroads and thrown out flankers toward Chewning's farm. Crawford's attempt to reconnoiter toward the Plank Road met vigorous resistance from Confederate pickets.[33]

Hill Advances on Brock Crossroads

Secured by his flankers, Kirkland pushed on after the Federal cavalry. Heth sent Cooke's Brigade forward within supporting distance of Kirkland, while Hill's main body closed up toward the store.[34]

Sometime after 9 o'clock Crawford apprised V Corps headquarters of developments on the Plank Road subsequent to 8 o'clock, the time of transmission of his first message.

If carried by courier, the second message, which was received at the Lacy house at 10:15[35] and so marked, must have been sent from Chewning farm about 9:15 a.m., the first message having been exactly an hour in transit. If transmitted by flag signals, the message in question, of course, would have been dispatched at a later time.[36] But regardless of the exact time of transmission, the fact remains that the message was read by Locke at the Lacy house at precisely 10:15 and immediately sent to army headquarters at the knoll 500 yards north of the Lacy house. Whether relayed by flag signals or courier, this important intelligence should not have been more than fifteen minutes in transit from V Corps to army headquarters. At the latest, therefore, the very information that Meade, about 9:15 a.m., had instructed Wilson to obtain was secured by infantry pickets of the V Corps and reported through Crawford's divisional headquarters an hour later.

Under the conditions—an obscure veil hanging over the enemy's forces and a growing apprehension that the Confederates in Warren's immediate front were far stronger than originally suspected—it is not difficult to imagine the perplexed anxiety with which Meade must have read and reread Crawford's second message.

This growing apprehension was in no way allayed by additional intelligence from Major Roebling at the Chewning farm. Neither the time of transmission or receipt of Roebling's message was recorded. It stands to reason, however, the message could hardly have been delivered at V Corps headquarters and relayed to army headquarters later than 10:30 a.m. As

Warren's personal representative on the left, Roebling would have taken the earliest opportunity to inform the V Corps commander of any unforeseen circumstance that tended to prevent or justify any departure from a prompt execution of the movement as ordered by Warren. It will also be noted that in the text of his message to Warren, Roebling refers to a half-mile gap between Wadsworth and Crawford. This is the approximate distance between the two units, as reported by Wadsworth himself at 10:30 a.m.[37]

We are therefore restricted to one of two alternatives: Roebling would have written his report of the situation at Chewning's farm immediately upon his arrival at that place at about 8:30, or he would have sent it by courier from Parker's Store soon after 9 a.m. From thence it would have been carried straight through by courier to the Lacy house, or perhaps transmitted from the signal station established sometime during the morning by Crawford's signal officer on the Chewning plateau. The message stated: "It is of vital importance to hold the field where General Crawford is. Our whole line of battle is turned if the enemy get possession of it. There is a gap of half a mile between Wadsworth and Crawford. He cannot hold the line against an attack." [38]

It may be confidently assumed that the first inquiry springing to Meade's mind concerned Wilson's cavalry division. Had Wilson received his message? Where was Wilson? If the Confederates first reported at Parker's Store were now working around Crawford's flank to get on the Plank Road, could it mean that the troops who were skirmishing with Wilson's cavalry at 8 a.m. had pushed northeastward up the Plank Road and were now on Crawford's left rear? Or was it possible that Confederate infantry had passed obliquely across Warren's new front and were attempting to envelop the flank at Chewning farm? In any event, the absence of news from Wilson would indicate that in moving with the main body of his division toward Craig's Meeting House he had uncovered both the front and the flank of the V Corps. It is indeed disconcerting when an army commander is apprised by his infantry pickets of the presence of the enemy in his front. And perplexity gives way to growing apprehension when it becomes apparent, upon demands for a thorough-going cavalry reconnaissance, that his cavalry screen has utterly disappeared. Such was Meade's dilemma. About 10:30 a.m., three hours after he had ordered the suspension of "Operation Wilderness" pending an attack along the Turnpike to regain the freedom of maneuver that had been lost by inept cavalry dispositions, he was compelled to admit that he had no cavalry screen and that his infantry was not ready to strike.

Chapter 8

GRANT ABANDONS MOVEMENT TOWARD LEE'S RIGHT

While news of the grave situation on Warren's left sped toward army headquarters, the Supreme Commander and his staff were pushing southward on the Germanna Plank Road. Strangely enough, the precise time of Grant's arrival at the front on May 5th has been a matter of indifference to military historians. Yet the point is one of great importance. Even before leaving his headquarters camp near Germanna Ford, Grant began interfering with Meade in the exercise of his command.

As Supreme Commander, Grant's proper sphere encroached upon functions delegated to his various army commanders whenever he issued orders on his own initiative to any of the subordinate elements of the field armies. Theoretically, his presence near Wilderness Tavern no more justified interference with details of operations of Meade's field army, than with those of the field armies in other theaters. Persistence in such practice induced the evils of a divided command. It is therefore of some consequence to establish the time at which the pernicious influence of two directing minds at the same point began confusing the preliminary dispositions for the encounter battle in the Wilderness.

Grant Rides to the Front

After describing the situation of 7:30 a.m., Humphreys states that "General Grant had been at once informed by General Meade of what was transpiring and soon joined him." After a brief conference, adds this authority, "the two rode forward a short distance and took position on a knoll in the

119

open ground around Wilderness Tavern and the Lacy Farm."
Here the two generals remained during the battle, with only
an occasional brief absence to visit the nearest troops.[1]

Humphreys' vague allusion as to the time of this all-important event has misled most students of the battle into a
tacit acceptance of a belief that Grant must have appeared on
the field within an hour of Meade's meeting with Warren.
Schaff, for instance, insists that Grant was on the Turnpike
at 9 a.m. when Meade received Crawford's dispatch of 8 a.m.,
acknowledging the order to halt and reporting the cavalry
skirmish at Parker's Store. There is no trouble, however, in
disputing this particular assertion.[2]

Grant notified Meade, in his communication of 8:24 a.m.,[3]
that he would go forward as soon as he had seen Burnside
and arranged for the relief of Ricketts' division, then posted
near Germanna Ford. He then impatiently awaited the sight
of the IX Corps commander, whom he expected to see at the
flank of his column pushing down the north bank to the
Germanna Ford pontoons. With Meade's assurance that an
attack would be made at once, Grant's patience seems to have
been unequal to the ordeal of waiting for a general (Burnside) whose fame for tardiness had not, as yet, entirely obscured the renown of his courtly manner.

As a matter of fact Grant endured the strain for exactly
sixteen minutes. At 8:40 he dashed off a note, instructing
Burnside, when he arrived, to place one division of the IX
Corps on the ridge south of the river, where it could cover
the Germanna Plank Road from the west, while his main
column crossed over and closed up as rapidly as possible in
rear of the VI Corps.[4]

Ricketts in the meantime received orders from Grant to
move forward as soon as one of Burnside's divisions had arrived.[5]

The note written by Grant to Burnside at 8:40 a.m. would
certainly indicate that, having decided not to await the IX
Corps commander's arrival, Grant did not intend to remain

longer at the ford than it would take himself and his staff to get mounted and start down the Germanna Plank Road. It is clear, then, that he could not have left his headquarters camp before 8:40 a.m. One cannot assume that he tarried much more than ten minutes after that time. That is, he must have set out about 9 a.m., just as word was received at the Lacy house to the effect that a cavalry skirmish was taking place at Parker's Store.

If Grant's departure for the front can be fixed within ten or fifteen minutes, there should be no serious difficulty in approximating the time of his meeting with Meade at the front. Four positive facts enable us to delimit the time period under consideration. We know that he could not have started before 8:40 and probably did not set out before 9 o'clock. It is also known beyond any doubt that Grant and his staff were established at their command post near Wilderness Tavern by 10:30 a.m. A message signed by Colonel Comstock of Grant's staff was dispatched from this point at 10:30 a.m.[6]

Situation Disclosed by Meade

The time of travel by horseback through the 5-mile distance involved may be reckoned variously. We may safely exclude the probability that Grant rode at a breakneck pace, with a clattering cavalcade at his heels. He did not meet Meade before 9:20 a.m., for the latter at this instant dispatched a written message to Grant, a course which would have been unnecessary had they already met and taken position on the knoll.[7] Finally, with a greater pressure of troops on the Germanna Plank Road than when the courier carried Meade's message of 7:30 to Grant, the Supreme Commander and his party, in all probability, did not travel as fast from Germanna Ford to Wilderness Tavern, after 9 a.m. as did the lone courier in the opposite direction an hour and a half earlier. Consequently, the meeting must have taken place within five or ten minutes before or after 10 a.m., and just in time for Grant to share with Meade the impact of the intelligence indicating that Wilson's cavalry division had been isolated and that the flank of the V Corps at Chewning's farm was threatened by a turning movement.

It is a safe assumption that Meade's account of the situation fell far short of Grant's expectations. Three hours had elapsed since Meade had taken the decision to halt and punish Lee for his temerity in attempting to interfere with Meade's liberty of maneuver. In this rather long time Warren had not even deployed his divisions in line. Reports from Griffin's skirmishers indicated that the Confederates were in greater force on the Turnpike than had originally been supposed. One of Wadsworth's brigades had connected with Griffin's left. The 4th Division commander, however, was having considerable difficulty in aligning his brigades. Stone's brigade apparently was astride Mill Branch. Wadsworth had found open ground at Miss Hagerson's farm for his two batteries. Robinson had been instructed at 8:45 a.m. to put one of his brigades in line between Wadsworth's right and Griffin's left. But in promptly complying with Meade's order of 7:30 a.m. Wadsworth had connected on Griffin's left, thereby leaving no room for Denison's Maryland brigade of Robinson's division in the line. Denison therefore formed on the right rear of Wadsworth's line, supporting Cutler's brigade.[8] Crawford still occupied his position on the Chewning plateau, facing south toward the Plank Road. There was nothing as yet to indicate that he had closed to the right in order to connect with Wadsworth's left. Sedgwick earlier had quit his headquarters at Spotswood's, near the Germanna Plank-Culpeper Ford Road intersection, and was conferring with Meade on the Turnpike when Grant and his staff arrived. He could offer less information concerning the dispositions of the VI Corps than Grant has seen for himself while riding to the front. Getty's division was massing at Wilderness Tavern, a fact which Grant had also seen when he rode by. Wright's division was pushing along the Germanna Plank Road. The advance brigade, Upton's, was moving out on the

Culpeper Mine Road to cover the right flank of the column while passing.[9]

Grant, as we know, had left instructions for the leading brigade of Burnside's corps to relieve Ricketts' division of the VI Corps, so that this unit, together with the other elements of the IX Corps column, could close up in rear of Sedgwick on the Germanna Plank Road. Yet, while every contingency seems to have been foreseen in the effort to effect a heavy troop concentration toward the selected point of attack, the decision of 7:30 to engage had not produced a line of battle by 10 o'clock. The apparent hesitancy to close with the enemy after having taken a decision to attack at once could only be construed by the Supreme Commander either as timidity, or a want of purpose in overcoming minor difficulties that are incidental to launching a swift, offensive stroke. Grant must have reflected with some exasperation that he had assumed full responsibility for the outcome of Meade's original decision to strike. In approving Meade's course of action, he had exhorted the army commander to lose no time in making dispositions. And now, over two hours had elapsed, yet the division commanders, instead of striking enemy, were still worrying about their flanks! Was time nothing to the high command of the Army of the Potomac? Did they demand an absolute assurance of victory before moving into action? If Lee, as Meade seemed to suspect, was merely seeking to delay the Federal movement with a detached force, he was succeeding brilliantly. And if Meade was anxious, as he had assured Grant he was, to accommodate Lee in any purpose the latter might entertain, to bring on a general engagement, there were no indications of either a lively desire, or a grim determination to come to grips. Briefly, the Victor of Chattanooga was not at all impressed by the manner in which the Army of the Potomac prepared for battle.

As Grant and Meade dismounted at the knoll which was destined to serve as their command post during the fighting in the Wilderness, the "fog of war" that hung over the battle-

field was pierced by a shaft of light. At 10:15 the second message from Crawford arrived at the Lacy house, V Corps Headquarters. This intelligence, as we already know, apprised
Warren that the Confederates were working around to get
upon the Plank Road, but that for the moment there was no
firing.[10] Relayed to Meade, from Warren's headquarters at
the Lacy house, this message indicated an aggravation of the
situation previously reported by Crawford. But Meade's em-
barassment was not limited to the situation on the Plank
Road. He and the Supreme Commander had just dismounted
at the knoll, when Major Michler, Acting Army Engineer,
reported the result of his reconnaissance on Warren's right.
Michler related that upon turning into the Culpeper Mine
Road, he heard a shot, which disclosed the presence of enemy
cavalry. He had sent this information to General Wright,
whose division was then moving on the Germanna Plank
Road towards its intersection with the road to Culpeper Mine.

In connection with the intelligence just received from
Crawford, Michler's report was susceptible to an interpretation that neither Grant nor Meade could ignore. It now appeared that the Confederates, whom Meade had determined
three hours ago to punish for their temerity in interfering
with the march of the Army of the Potomac, were now in-
solently feeling around both flanks of the forces assembling
to deliver that "punishment."

Aside from the chagrin over Warren's inability to deliver
the punitive blow and clear the way for a resumption of the
turning movement, news of hostile cavalry on the Culpeper
Mine Road was disquieting to say the least. This rude thoroughfare led straight across the Germanna Plank Road at
Orange Grove and through the forest of dwarf trees and
tangled underbrush to Culpeper Mine Ford, where the wagons
of the right column of the second line transport were rumbling
over the pontoon bridge and then disappearing southeastward
along a rough woods road toward Dowdall's Tavern. While
Wright's division was in the vicinity of the Germanna Plank-

Culpeper Mine Road intersection, and had already been warned by Michler of the presence of cavalry, the woods were full of bypaths well suited to the needs of small mounted parties and well known to many units of the Confederate cavalry that had scoured the forest country during their long service in picketing the river crossings of the Rapidan from Mine Run to the Rappahannock. Again, the possibility of an infiltration of cavalry parties along the ridge between Flat Run and Wilderness Run toward Culpeper Mine Ford, which is midway between the mouths of these two streams, was not in itself an alarming prospect to Federal headquarters. The trains were fairly well guarded with infantry detachments[11] to meet such attacks. But considered in connection with a thrust in force by the Confederates along the Plank Road ridge to the Orange Plank Road-Turnpike intersection at Dowdall's Tavern, the matter was one to be viewed with considerable apprehension. With Wilson lost, Gregg at Aldrich's, and Torbert somewhere between Ely's Ford and Chancellorsville, there was no cavalry in hand to meet such an emergency. Furthermore, Gregg and Torbert were endeavoring to combine their forces for the purpose of protecting the left of the trains against the main Confederate cavalry force, which had been reported as late as the afternoon of the day before to be in the vicinity of Hamilton's Crossing.

Grant Imposes His Will

There should be no difficulty in accounting for Grant's reaction to such a situation. When his flanks were in jeopardy, it was not his habit to solve the difficulty by retreating; if he could not threaten the enemy's communications, he threw everything at hand into a frontal assault. In this instance his directive to Meade took form in orders issued simultaneously to Griffin, Wadsworth, Wright, Getty, and Hancock, with the purpose of (1) Attacking along the Turnpike without further delay, and without regard to flanks; (2) throwing Wright's division, VI Corps, reinforced by Neill's brigade, Getty's division, VI Corps, from the Germanna Plank-Culpeper Mine

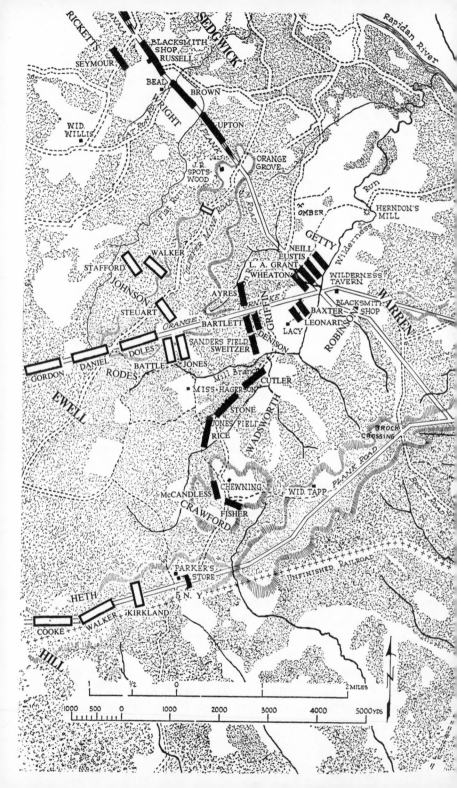

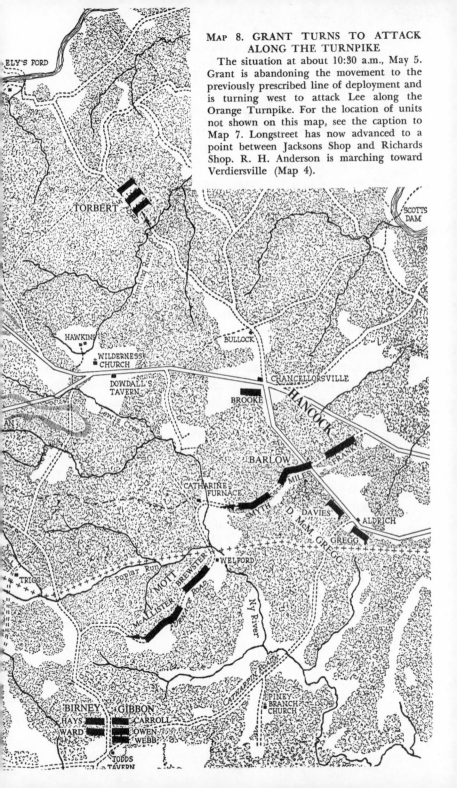

MAP 8. GRANT TURNS TO ATTACK ALONG THE TURNPIKE

The situation at about 10:30 a.m., May 5. Grant is abandoning the movement to the previously prescribed line of deployment and is turning west to attack Lee along the Orange Turnpike. For the location of units not shown on this map, see the caption to Map 7. Longstreet has now advanced to a point between Jacksons Shop and Richards Shop. R. H. Anderson is marching toward Verdiersville (Map 4).

ELY'S FORD

SCOTTS DAM

TORBERT

HAWKINS

BULLOCK

WILDERNESS CHURCH

DOWDALL'S TAVERN

CHANCELLORSVILLE

HANCOCK

BROOKE

Lewis Creek

BARLOW

FRANK

CATHARINE FURNACE

MILES

SMYTH

D. DAVIES

ALDRICH

D. McM. GREGG

TRIGG

Poplar Run

WELFORD

MOTT

McALLISTER

BREWSTER

FURNACE ROAD

Ny River

CATHARPIN ROAD

PINEY BRANCH CHURCH

BIRNEY

GIBBON

HAYS

CARROLL

WARD

OWEN

WEBB

TODDS TAVERN

Road intersection along the Culpeper Mine ridge road to connect with Griffin's advancing right flank; (3) shifting Getty's division, less Neill's brigade, from Wilderness Tavern to the Brock-Orange Plank Road intersection, with orders to attack out the Plank Road beyond Parker's Store;[12] and (4) ordering Hancock's II Corps to march by way of the Brock Crossing and support Getty's attack toward Parker's Store.

The motivation as well as the objective of these simultaneous movements is obvious. Having failed to punish Lee's detachment in its endeavor to delay the Federal movement in the Wilderness, Grant now perceived that his forces were in an awkward position, even facing a possibility that swift-moving Confederate bodies might slip through his widely scattered masses and raid the Federal trains closing up toward Dowdall's Tavern and Chancellorsville. His largest single mass, consisting of Warren's four divisions and Getty's division, VI Corps, was for the most part huddled in the basin of Wilderness Run, with a single division, Crawford's, detached and practically isolated on the Chewning plateau. Hancock's mass, the four divisions of the II Corps, were some eight miles southeast of the center of Warren's mass, with the Plank Road ridge intervening. A third mass, which may be regarded as including three divisions of Burnside's IX Corps together with Wright's and Ricketts' divisions of the VI Corps, held a front of some 4 miles along the Germanna Plank Road, with the Culpeper Mine Road ridge intervening between this mass and the one huddled in the basin of Wilderness Run. Wright's division was moving along the Culpeper Mine Road toward the central mass. One cavalry division, Wilson's, as we know, was lost; the other two were well to the rear, and so disposed to protect the trains against mounted raiders from the left, or east. The directive had a twofold purpose: (1) To push the central mass up out of the Wilderness Run basin toward the watershed along which Ewell's column was deploying, and at the same time attack out along the Plank Road toward the headwaters of the west branch of Wilderness Run at Parker's

Store, thereby establishing a continuous line on the high ground between the upper basins of Wilderness Run, on the southeast, and Flat Run on the northwest; (2) to concentrate all available forces within marching distance at the time within or near the front of attack. For the latter purpose, Hancock's four divisions were to incline northward to support Getty's movement along the Plank Road ridge; Wright's division, VI Corps, was to move out on the Culpeper Mine ridge to support the right of Warren's thrust westward out of the basin of Wilderness Run; and Ricketts' Division, VI Corps, together with Burnside's columns, less the advanced division in the march to the Rapidan, was to close up on the Germanna Plank Road toward Wilderness Tavern. The advance division, IX Corps, was instructed to cover the Germanna Ford pontoon crossing until circumstances justified its abandonment.

Proof of the purpose of the directive lies in the simultaneity of the consequent orders. There is no evidence that a directive from Grant, or from Grant and Meade in conference, incited issuance of the orders, unless it can be established that the orders in question were issued simultaneously and immediately after the conference. As a matter of fact they were, and there is no great difficulty in so proving, although reasoning to this end brings into question the accuracy of certain vague statements regarding the time of crucial decisions.[13]

Instructions affecting elements of the V and VI corps may have been given at the headquarters knoll by word of mouth to Warren and Sedgwick. At any rate there are no communications in the file of correspondence for May 5 indicating issuance of such instructions. However, a written order from V Corps headquarters to the 4th Division furnishes the real clue to the time element and the objective, as well as the conditions of the ordered attack. Addressed to General Wadsworth and signed at 10:30 a.m., the order stated: "*General*: Push forward a heavy line of skirmishers, followed by your line of battle, and attack the enemy at once and push him.

General Griffin will also attack. Do not wait for him, but look out for your own left flank."

The order instructing Getty to proceed from Wilderness Tavern to the Brock Crossing and attack out the Plank Road toward Parker's Store was issued at the same time that the dispatch ordering Hancock to the Brock Crossing was sent to Todd's Tavern.[14] We have no record of the order transmitted to Getty at Wilderness Tavern. A note, however, from Humphreys to Warren and signed at 11 a.m. informed the V Corps commander that "General Getty has been ordered to move out promptly to Orange Plank Road and drive the enemy back beyond Parker's Store." The message added that the enemy were reported one mile east of the store.[15] The fact that messages containing information of this nature are as a rule promptly transmitted by general headquarters to corps headquarters, leaves little doubt that the order to Getty mentioned by the army chief of staff at 11 a.m. had been issued not later than 10:30 a.m.

The dispatch to Hancock, which he received at 11:40 a.m., leaves no doubt as to its urgency: *Major-General Hancock, Commanding Second Corps:* The major-general commanding [Meade] directs that you move up the Brock Road to the Orange Court House-Plank Road, and report your arrival at that point and be prepared to move out the Plank Road toward Parker's Store."[16]

Wright moved off down the Culpeper Mine Road about 11 a.m., in response to orders issued a short time previously. General Getty states in his report that Neill's brigade was detached from his command at 10:30, with instructions to report to Brigadier General Wright, commanding the 1st Division, who was about to advance on the Robertson's Tavern dirt road.[17]

Colonel Daniel D. Bidwell, commanding the 3rd Brigade (Neill's) does not mention in his report the time of detachment from the 2d Division, stating only that "On the morning of the 5th May, General Sedgwick, finding that the enemy were in force on a road leading from Robertson's Tavern into the Germanna Plank Road, ordered this brigade deployed and advanced on that road."[18] Bvt. Brigadier General Emory Upton, commanding Wright's advanced brigade, states in his report of operations that shortly after moving out on a dirt road leading to Mine Run to cover the right flank of the column while passing, he moved by the left flank and formed in line of battle on the left of the corps. About 11 a.m., Upton continues, "orders were received to advance to the support of the Fifth Corps, then engaged with the enemy on the Orange Court House pike 2 miles from Wilderness Tavern." [19]

The simultaneity of these various orders leaves no doubt that a single impulse incited their issuance. And this impulse was Grant's decision, taken shortly after his arrival at the front, definitely to abandon the turning movement by way of Shady Grove Church and to attack at once, in the literal meaning of the word, and without taking additional time for making dispositions. Griffin and Wadsworth were to attack immediately, each one to move without regard to the other, Wright to march to the sound of the guns and Getty, after reaching the Plank Road, to drive the enemy back beyond Parker's Store. While these two attacks were being pushed home, by the four divisions involved—Griffin, Wadsworth, Wright and Getty—the four divisions of Hancock at Todd's Tavern and three at Germanna Ford, Ricketts of the VI Corps and two of the IX, would incline toward the front of attack.

While army headquarters was preparing the orders intended to put the V, II, and VI Corps divisions in motion, Grant gave his attention to the rectification of a muddle which his interference with interior dispositions of the Army of the Potomac had produced and the solution of which had been neatly tossed back into his lap by the army commander. This concerns Ricketts' division, which Grant without notifying Meade had ordered forward as soon as Burnside's leading division had crossed Germanna Ford and taken over Ricketts' position. Meade in the meantime had instructed Ricketts "to hold the roads leading from the enemy's line to our right flank." [20]

Hesitant to disregard Grant's instructions, and equally reluctant to disobey the last order received, Ricketts stood fast, awaiting further instructions from Grant before executing Meade's order. As already related, Meade informed Grant of this conflict of orders in a written communication dated at 9:20 a.m. Grant and his staff, as we know, set out from his headquarters camp near Germanna Ford before 9 o'clock. If he met the courier with Meade's dispatch en route to general headquarters, Grant took no action in the matter until he had seen Meade. At 10:30 a.m., after having conferred with the army commander, he instructed Lieutenant Colonel Comstock his *aide de camp,* to inform Burnside as follows:

> Lieutenant General Grant desires that you consult with General Ricketts and relieve the two brigades he has moved from the Plank Road toward Mine Run, and which were to move out about a mile toward Mine Run. You should send some cavalry out in front of your two brigades. The general desires that you should mass your command about a mile this side of Germanna Ford, on the Plank Road, and await orders.

Whoever may have been responsible for the muddle, the three-hour pause in releasing Ricketts' division was not a circumstance to mollify Grant's growing irritation over delays that had set at defiance all his time-and-space calculations. But if he was irritated over what appeared to be an inability or reluctance on the part of Meade and his corps and division commanders rapidly to concentrate and engage, he must have experienced a profound and bitter exasperation between 10:30 a.m. and noon. The abrupt shift of plan did not immediately produce the battle Grant so insistently demanded.

Out on the Turnpike, Griffin and his brigadiers were convinced that the enemy were in far greater force than army headquarters seemed disposed to believe. Warren bore the brunt of these conflicting views. He must either hasten his divisional units prematurely into an attack that his judgment condemned, or run the risk of being summarily relieved from command on the field of battle, with the implication of personal cowardice and the public disgrace of court martial. Meade's irascible temper mounted rapidly under Grant's determined insistence to hasten the pace of events. Griffin's desire to hold his entrenched line until properly supported on both flanks hardened to stubborn determination under the impact of Warren's impatient exhortations. Lieutenant Colonel Swan of Ayres' staff relates that he carried the order to attack from division to brigade headquarters. Ayres, according to Swan, sent back word urging delay. The enemy, insisted Ayres, was about to attack and the division held a strong position. Griffin thereupon left his headquarters and went to the front. Accompanied by Ayres, Bartlett, Swan, and other staff officers, he rode out to the picket line, "whence," says Swan, "the enemy could be seen leaving the road and entering the woods to the right and left." [21] Word was sent to the rear notifying Warren of this situation.

Warren, however, would not brook further delay. Reiteration of the order to attack, with a remonstrance for the hesitation, came back from V Corps headquarters. Still obdurate, Griffin sent Swan to Warren with a final protest. Warren had just left the headquarters knoll, where, according to a report that afterwards went the rounds of officers' messes and is given credence in a few memoirs of the battle, Meade had heard the bravery of his army questioned. Meeting the V Corps commander on the Turnpike, Swan drew rein and delivered his message. Warren's reply was curt. "He answered me," relates Swan, "as though fear was at the bottom of my errand. I remember my indignation." [22]

His protests unavailing, Griffin moved out from his works and advanced to the east edge of Sanders' field. Here he was compelled to halt and reform. During the half-mile advance many regiments had been compelled to work forward in column through the dwarf pine and matted underbrush, advancing usually by right of wings. Many organizations lost direction and going astray in the woods became mixed with other units. Sweitzer's brigade, either by order before the advance, or due to being crowded on its left by Cutler's brigade of Wadsworth's division, inclined to the right. It finally took position in rear of Bartlett's brigade, the right flanks of both units resting on the south side of the Turnpike. Ayres was tardy in bringing up his brigade on the north side of the Turnpike, failing to arrive, according to some reports,[23] and continue the alignment across the road before the attack. A little before one o'clock, says Swan, the lines were reformed and awaiting the order to go forward.[24]

If the irremediable slowness of developments on Warren's front was a source of exasperation at the headquarters knoll, a succession of reports from Chewning's farm contributed in no small measure to aggravate the tense situation.

It appears from the context of these reports that communication by means of flag signals established between the Chewning plateau and V Corps headquarters at the Lacy house was in operation by 11 a.m. At 11:15, just an hour after receipt of Crawford's report that the enemy were working around his position to get upon the Orange Plank Road, and which induced the decision to send Getty to the Plank Road and attack toward Parker's Store, Warren received a note from Crawford, inquiring if he should abandon his position at Chewning's and connect with Wadsworth.[25]

The reply from V Corps headquarters was that Crawford should move to the right as quickly as possible.[26] But at 11:30 came another message from the Chewning plateau reporting that except for occasional shots, firing had ceased in Crawford's front. The message added that the enemy were reported as being up the Plank Road in Crawford's rear. Warren was also apprised that the Federal cavalry had returned to the road and that Crawford had sent a patrol to the Plank Road to determine the accuracy of the report.[27]

Twenty minutes later, at 11:50 a.m., and despite Crawford's warning as to report of the Confederate pushing up the

Orange Plank Road in his rear, Warren, doubtlessly driven to distraction by the hectoring attitude of general headquarters, curtly informed Crawford that "you must connect with General Wadsworth and cover and protect his left as he advances." [28]

At noon Crawford, deferring at last to superior authority, informed Warren that the connection with Wadsworth was being made. But with a sense of justification for the fact that he had tarried on the plateau over four hours after receiving Warren's original order to withdraw and close on Wadsworth, he added cryptically: "The enemy hold the Plank Road and are passing up." [29]

Hancock Ordered to Attack

Meade's disposition to ignore Crawford's early reports of developments on the Plank Road was, to a certain extent, shared by Grant. Certainly the order issued to Getty about 10:30 to proceed to the Orange Plank-Brock Road intersection and drive the enemy out the Plank Road beyond Parker's Store, was based on an assumption, as was the order of attack issued Warren at 7:30 a.m., that only a detachment of Lee's force was in the presence of the Army of the Potomac. At 10:30, however, Grant seems to have been convinced that an immediate attack on the Confederates in Warren's front and those on the Plank Road would commit Lee to a general action. Hence his abandonment of the turning movement by ordering the II Corps from Todd's Tavern to the Brock Crossing. And now at noon comes a realization at the headquarters knoll, probably based on the information furnished by Crawford, that the Federals were confronted by a considerable part of Lee's main force, or enough, at any rate, to cast doubt on Getty's ability to drive the enemy out beyond Parker's Store. At noon Meade instructed Hancock that

> The enemy's infantry drove our regiment of cavalry from Parker's Store down the Plank Road, and are now moving down it in force. A. P. Hill's Corps is part of it. How much is not known. General Getty's division has been sent to drive them back, but he may not be able to do so. The major gen-

eral commanding [Meade] directs that you move out the
Plank Road toward Parker's Store, and, supporting Getty,
drive the enemy beyond Parker's Store, and occupy that place
and unite with Warren on the right of it.

General Warren at the present time extends from the
Orange pike within 1 mile of the Plank Road, in direction
of Parker's Store.[30]

The objective here, the high ground running between the
upper basins of Flat and Wilderness Runs, was identical to
that sought at 10:30 a.m. However, nine divisions—Wright.
Griffin, Wadsworth, Crawford, Getty, and the four of Hancock's II Corps—would participate instead of the five as
originally contemplated: Wright, Griffin, Wadsworth, Crawford, and Getty, supported by Robinson on the Turnpike.

Meade's expression of doubt at noon that Getty might not
be able unaided to reach the objective originally assigned
him on the Orange Plank Road would indicate that no grave
apprehensions were entertained at this time regarding any
possibility that A. P. Hill's Confederates might seize the
Brock Crossing before Getty's division could reach that point.

Getty himself, when the head of his division filed out in
column from its massed formation near Wilderness Tavern
about 10:50 a.m. and took the Germanna Plank Road at a
brisk pace toward the Brock Road, was probably unaware
that he was engaged in one of those dramatic tactical races
that many students like to regard as decisive factors in the
outcome of great battles. Whatever his reflections may have
been, the division commander rode briskly on ahead with his
staff to locate the crossroads where he was to turn and seek
the enemy. No doubt the tedium of holding a restive horse
to the pace of a marching infantry column had something to
do with his preference for a smart trot.

As Getty's cavalcade clattered along the Brock Road, a detachment of Federal cavalry, strung out in single file, came
down the Plank Road at a pounding gallop and, streaking
one by one across the intersection, were soon out of sight.
One of the troopers slackened pace sufficiently to shout over

his shoulder that rebel infantry was coming down the road in force.[31]

A few musket shots echoing in the woods to the west verified the trooper's warning. Getty instantly sent an aide to bring up his column at the double-quick. Then, rallying staff officers and orderlies on his headquarters flag, the division commander took post directly athwart the intersection. One of the party, Brevet Brigadier General Hazard Stevens, completes the story:

> Soon a few gray forms were discerned far up the narrow Plank Road moving cautiously forward, then a bullet went whistling overhead, and another and another, and then the leaden hail came faster and faster over and about the little group until its destruction seemed imminent and inevitable. But Getty would not budge. "We must hold this point at any risk," he exclaimed, "our men will soon be up." In a few minutes, which seemed like an age to the little squad, the leading regiment of Wheaton's brigade, the 1st, came running like greyhounds along the Brock Road until the first regiment passed the Plank Road, and then, at the command "Halt!" "Front!" "Fire!", poured a volley into the woods and threw out skirmishers in almost less time than it takes to tell it. Dead and wounded rebel skirmishers were found within thirty yards of the crossroads, so nearly had they gained it, and from these wounded prisoners it was learned that Hill's corps, Heth's Division in advance, supported by Wilcox's Division, was the opposing force.[32]

CHAPTER 9

LEE ACCEPTS GRANT'S OFFER OF BATTLE

We have indicated the nature of Lee's farflung dispositions while Meade and Grant were improvising the attack to hold off interference with their turning movement. It will be helpful at this juncture to inquire into Lee's estimate of the situation and then, in the light of his understanding of events during the forenoon of May 5th, to examine circumstances that drew him into the general engagement which he had sought to postpone.

Lee Ponders on Course of Action

During the night, as we know, intelligence concerning the position of Federal masses in the Wilderness had caused Lee to modify his plan of bringing on a battle as soon as possible on the 5th. There is no evidence that any modification was made in the instructions issued Ewell at 8 p.m. on the 4th (Chap. 5) stating that it was Lee's desire to bring the enemy to battle as soon now as possible. At dawn, quite the contrary, Ewell was under the impression that he was expected to start a fight as soon as he could find and engage the enemy. Such was his explanation to Major Styles, of the corps artillery, who shared a pot of coffee with him on the roadside near Robertson's Tavern (Locust Grove).[1]

After being helped into the saddle, Ewell rode to the head of his column and led the advance toward Wilderness Tavern. The order of march by divisions was Johnson-Rodes-Early. Jones' Brigade, with Milledge's Battery, held the advance. Kirkpatrick's and Massie's Batteries, of Nelson's Battalion, accompanied Johnson's Division. The train remained in park at Locust Grove. Overtaking the 1st North Carolina Cavalry, which had so effectively screened his front during the concentration at Locust Grove on the 4th, Ewell ordered this unit to push out northeastward on the Culpeper Mine Road. Jones covered the front of the column with skirmishers.[2]

Upon locating the enemy about 8 a.m. near Wilderness Tavern, Ewell felt constrained to report his position and seek instructions from army headquarters. He received positive orders to regulate his march on General A. P. Hill, whose progress down the Plank Road he could tell by the firing at the head of his column. He was also informed that Lee preferred not to bring on a general engagement before General Longstreet came up.

Lee obviously had abandoned any expectations of following Grant down the Rapidan toward Fredericksburg. It is also apparent that the alternative plan of concentrating at Mine Run in the event of a Federal advance up the south bank of the Rapidan had gone into the discard. Convinced now that the intentions attributed to his opponent at 8 p.m. of the 4th had been denied by subsequent intelligence, Lee determined to develop the enemy's dispositions before adopting a definite plan of offensive action. Ewell and Hill were therefore charged to avoid involvement in a general action until Longstreet arrived within supporting distance. Lee continued to ride with Hill.

The Confederates Converge in Seven Columns

The cavalry and infantry bivouacs around New Verdiersville were astir at the first light of dawn. Stuart's horse formed to the west of the village and clattered off down the Plank Road toward Parker's Store. Heth's Division, with Kirkland's Brigade and Poague's Artillery Battalion in advance, moved off in rear of the cavalry.[3] Wilcox's Division followed Heth. The remainder of the corps artillery and the train rolled along in rear of the swinging infantry column.[4]

Seven miles to the southwest, Rosser's Cavalry (Laurel) Brigade, and probably other detachments of Hampton's Division, together with some of Stuart's Horse Artillery, were streaming through the little crossroads settlement at Richards Shop.[5] The advance took the Catharpin Road out towards Shady Grove Church.

As the three Confederate columns of Ewell, Hill, and Rosser moved eastward, Fitzhugh Lee's Cavalry Division quit its bivouac near Massaponnax Church, some nineteen miles east of Rosser's starting point, and turned westward into the Massaponnax Road. By a circuitous route through Spotsylvania Court House, Fitzhugh Lee was seeking to join the main force in The Wilderness.

Meantime three additional elements were moving in from distant points to the east and southeast and south toward the general zone of concentration in the Wilderness. Having fulfilled its mission in covering Lee's rear on the 4th, Anderson's Division, A. P. Hill's III Corps, was shifting down from Rapidan Heights toward the Plank Road to reinforce Hill. Longstreet's advance had tramped across Brock's Bridge over the North Anna shortly after midnight.[6] By dawn the I Corps column was well up on the Marquis Road, moving northwestward in the slow but well-ordered deliberation that conserved the terrific striking power that Longstreet's troops invariably delivered on the battlefield. Johnston's Brigade, Early's Division, which had left Taylorsville, on the Richmond, Fredericksburg and Potomac Railroad near Hanover Junction at 11 a.m. the day before, was about midway on its forced march of 66 miles to join the main body in the Wilderness.[7]

The convergence of seven widely separated elements against a superior enemy mass within comparatively restricted bounds seems a hazardous feat. Yet under the actual conditions of forest fighting, the hazard was not so great as it might appear. Grant was attempting to turn the Confederate right rear. While his successful deployment on the line Shady Grove Church-Parker's Store-Wilderness Tavern would have forestalled Lee's plan of developing an offensive operation in the Wilderness, there was, in one sense of the term, no Confederate right or rear on the morning of May 5th to turn. Lee's rear might be determined by any direction the seven elements chose to turn. Meade, for instance, was insistent in his belief that between 7:30 and 10 a.m. he was dealing with a detachment covering Lee's rear. After 10 a.m., the evidence indicates that Grant was acting on an assumption that the main Confederate force was concentrating in his front and that Longstreet was closing up from the rear. It thereupon became Grant's purpose to destroy the enemy before they could complete their concentration.

Ewell Achieves an Unplanned Strategic Surprise

Lee, as already stated, was concerned primarily with determining Grant's plan of action. In so doing, he must avoid battle until his own concentration had been completed. It is quite evident, however, that during the period from 7:30 to 10:30 a.m., when the Federal turning movement was suspended but not as yet abandoned, Lee was in the dark as to his adversary's intentions. So far as troop movement is concerned, Hancock's turning column was not halted until 9 a.m., when his advance was within some three miles of the objective at Shady Grove Church. Yet at 8 o'clock, an hour earlier, Lee was unwilling to risk any involvement that might precipitate a general action. In other words, he had no intention of challenging his opponent's liberty of action. He took no steps with such a purpose in view. His orders, as related by Ewell, were precisely to the contrary. Yet, unbeknown to Lee, the first report of Ewell's presence on the Turnpike induced Meade, an hour and a half before the issuance of Lee's restraining order (at 7:30 a.m.) to suspend the turning movement. Thus Lee, without deliberate intention and without definite knowledge of the enemy's dispositions or intentions, reaped the benefits of a strategic surprise. As a consequence, the two armies drifted into collision. While Lee was willing and anxious to fight in the Wilderness, he could not, unless unforeseen conditions arose, afford to engage until the dawn of May 6. Grant, while eager to throw his forces into battle at the earliest possible moment, had carefully planned, with Humphrey's collaboration, a turning movement for the very purpose of avoiding the risks of an encounter in the Wilderness. In accepting the situation that each in turn had sought to avoid, the conditions of both commanders were only half fulfilled.

As Lee left his headquarters camp opposite Mrs. Rhodes near New Verdiersville to join Hill at the head of the III Corps column, his concern centered on an immediate difficulty. In addition to starting from a point some five and a half miles to the right rear of Ewell at Locust Grove, Hill's line of march diverged from that of Ewell. The Turnpike shot straight on a tangent through the woods to Wilderness Tavern.[8] At New Verdiersville, the Plank Road turned south east to go around the headwaters of Mine Run and then follow the watershed toward Parker's Store. The distance between the two highways was thereby increased from half a mile at New Verdiersville to nearly three miles, measured perpendicularly, in the vicinity of Parker's Store. After passing Mine Run the terrain between the two columns was covered by the dense thickets of the Wilderness. Under these conditions the problem of concentrating his seven scattered elements became gravely compromised by the difficulty in effecting close cooperation between the elements of Hill and Ewell, the largest of his elements and the one closest to the main body of the enemy.

A march of about two miles brought the advance on the Plank Road to Reynolds' Tan Yard. Veterans in the column became alert for a glimpse of the works they had thrown up and manned during the November Mine Run campaign. A valid report of comment along the line of files would give the historian some interesting information. As the column pushed on past the parapets that slumbered peacefully under their mantle of fresh spring grass, many of the older veterans, no doubt, began predicting another Chancellorsville. It was a year ago, on May 1, 1863, to be exact, that Lee and Jackson quit the new-made trenches along the ridge near Tabernacle Church and went on into the Wilderness to round up Joe Hooker. When Old Pete (Longstreet) came up from Gordonsville, they all now agreed, Grant would get his first taste of the Army of Northern Virginia.

About 8 o'clock the sharp crack of rifle fire was heard off to the right front. Lee, riding with Hill at the head of his main column, knew that Rosser was engaged on the Catharpin Road. Stuart immediately rode off through the woods to join the fray.[9]

Subsequent developments on the Plank Road toward Parker's Store, as understood by Lee, are uncertain. Somewhere between New Hope Church and the Store, a clash occurred between an element of Lee's advance and a detachment of the 5th New York Cavalry. This unit, it will be recalled, had been posted by Wilson at Parker's Store to serve as a connecting link between Wilson's cavalry division and Warren's V Corps. If the reports which time this affair at dawn when Hill's infantry were beginning to move out of their bivouacs at New Verdiersville, are accurate, the brush may have involved a patrol of Stuart's cavalry which had been picketing the Plank Road far out to the Confederate front during the night.[10]

After Stuart led off the main cavalry force covering Hill's advance, Kirkland's Brigade of Heth's Division moved rapidly to the front. Meantime Colonel Hammond, of the 5th New York Cavalry, moved out to reinforce the advanced detachment at a point some two miles west of Parker's Store.[11] Here Kirkland, with Richard's four-gun battery in support, struck the Federal cavalry.[12] Hammond's troopers offered vigorous resistance, falling back on Parker's Store and thence to the Brock Crossing.

Sometime after Kirkland had driven Hammond from the crossroads at the Store, and about the time Lee had been apprised of this circumstance, Major Campbell Brown of Ewell's staff reported developments on the Turnpike at army headquarters. Brown stated that the II Corps advance was within sight of the enemy near Wilderness Tavern and that Ewell had asked for instructions.[13]

Lee's reply indicates that he was aware of the situation at Parker's Store. He instructed Ewell to regulate his march by the firing at the head of Hill's column. Certainly Lee could have referred to no other firing than that of the fight engaging

Kirkland, who alone was in action. Hill closed rapidly toward Parker's Store. Cooke's Brigade went forward to relieve Kirkland and take over the advance.[14]

Meantime on the Turnpike Ewell directed Jones to prepare for action. Milledge's Battery was sent to the rear. Steuart's Brigade, following Jones in column, moved by the left to form on Jones. Walker's (Stonewall) Brigade, next in column, turned into the Culpeper Mine (Spotswood) Road and pushed out northeastward along the ridge, where he later established contact with Federal skirmishers, probably those covering Wright's advance down that road.

Stafford's Brigade closed toward Steuart to form on his left. Thus the four brigades of Edward Johnson's Division (Jones, Stafford, Steuart, Walker) began deploying in line of battle from right to left in the order mentioned.[15]

About 11 a.m. Ewell became aware of a Federal column (possibly Getty's) crossing the Turnpike from north to south. At that time being still in advance of Hill and occupying a good position, that is, just west of Sanders' field and covering the Orange Turnpike-Culpeper Mine intersection, Ewell halted and reported through Lt. Colonel Pendleton, II Corps staff, to army headquarters. Colonel Pendleton returned with substantially the same instructions delivered three hours earlier by Major Campbell Brown. Ewell brought up Rodes' Division, placing Battle's Brigade in support of Jones and Doles on Battle's right. Daniels' Brigade moved by the right, probably with a view to extending Rodes' line south of the Turnpike. Early's three brigades—Gordon, Hays, and Pegram— were held in reserve on the Turnpike behind the Orange Turnpike-Culpeper Ford Road intersection. These dispositions gave Ewell two defense lines, formed in left echelon, the left in advance and extending across the Culpeper Mine Road, the center covering the road intersection and the right reaching southward in the direction toward which the Federal column previously observed by Ewell appeared to be moving. Early's three-brigade reserve stood behind the crossroads; Gordon formed in line to the right of the Turnpike, Hays on the left and ready to close toward the center or reinforce either flank as circumstances might require. Ewell instructed his brigadiers not to allow themselves to become involved, but to fall back slowly, if pressed.

Heth Deploys Across the Plank Road

With quickened pace Hill pushed toward Parker's Store. Sometime after receipt of Ewell's second report and issuance of the second warning against any commitment to a general engagement, Cooke, now in the advance, passed Widow Tapp's farm and continued on down the Plank Road, feeling cautiously toward the Brock Crossing.[16]

His presence in the vicinity of Tapp's was causing Crawford at Chewning's farm considerable uneasiness concerning his flank and rear.

Heth's three brigades of the main column (Kirkland, Walker, and Davis) closed rapidly on the advance and began forming in line of battle across the Plank Road about one-half mile east of the Brock Crossing.[17] Pendleton directed Poague to place his guns in position at the Tapp farm. The corps artillery (less Poague's Battalion) and the train rolled up and went into park near Parker's Store.[18]

By noon Lee was able to account for a considerable portion of the enemy's force. A complete reconstruction of his intelligence, on the basis of reports which he likely had received from time to time during the morning, should have given him a general but fairly accurate picture of Grant's dispositions. Ewell had encountered and reported enemy troops in his front on the Turnpike. Walker had developed Federal skirmishers in the direction of Germanna Ford. A column was moving off by the left from Wilderness Tavern toward the Plank Road. Federal troops were known to be in position at Chewning farm. A cavalry fight was in progress on the Catharpin Road. According to report from Fitzhugh Lee, whose cavalry division had taken the Brock Road northward from Spotsylvania Court House, a great body of Federal infantry was massed in the vicinity of Todd's Tavern.[19] But nothing other than a small cavalry force had, as yet, been encountered on the Plank Road. Cooke was still "feeling" toward the Brock Crossing.

Just what conclusions Lee may have drawn from the information at hand is largely a matter of conjecture. It is certain that he had no thought of pushing by way of the Plank Road through what appeared to be a gap between the two widely separated masses of the enemy. It seems also reasonable to assume that he should have been gratified with the progress of his seven converging elements during the morning. By noon, four of these seven elements were in contact with the enemy. While the elements of Hill and Ewell, the two largest of the four in contact with the enemy, were not as yet in position to support one another, he could rest assured that Stuart would coordinate the movements of Fitzhugh Lee, Rosser, and other cavalry detachments in such a manner as to secure Hill's right. Therefore, there was no problem other than the time factor, in regard to the arrival of his converging strategic mass—Longstreet and Anderson—according to plan.

Wilcox Moves to Connect Hill and Ewell

Under these conditions a successful execution of Lee's plan to temporize pending arrival of his reserves suggested Hill's element as the pivot of maneuver. His right seemed secure. But an inviting gap lay between Hill's left and Ewell's right. According to Ewell's report of 11 a.m., Grant was moving troops toward this gap, either to effect a penetration through the opening, or to close the gap between his own two separate masses. Wilcox therefore must make the connection between Hill and Ewell.[20]

There is some doubt as to the time at which Lee ordered the deployment of Heth across the Plank Road beyond Widow Tapp's farm and the extension of Heth's flank by Wilcox toward Ewell's right.[21] Whether this decision anticipated the attack that fell about 1 p.m. upon Ewell, or came as a consequence of that movement, is also unknown. Either eventuality, however, does not detract from Lee's masterly estimate of the situation and the fine confidence he reposed in his subordinate commanders. It may be added that if Wilcox was sent off through Widow Tapp's field to establish the all-important connection after the attack on Ewell had fallen, Lee's faith in the quality of his troops was no less than the reliance he put in the judgment of their officers.

About noon Lee established his command post at the Tapp farm. Poague put his guns in battery along high ground at the west bounds of the clearing. Lee's headquarters camp was established some distance back in the woods west of Poague's guns.[22]

At 12:15 p.m. a sharp rattle of musketry broke in on the desultory firing to the front along the Plank Road. Cooke's skirmishers no doubt had stirred up some new resistance. Several volleys crashed in rapid succession. Then silence settled over the woods. If the Federals had occupied Brock Crossing with a view to attacking down the Plank Road, Heth's rifle brigades would soon proclaim the fact. At any rate, there would be a report of the affair forthwith.

Lee Resolves to Fight It Out

Lee had probably received some report on affairs at Brock Crossing when the deep mutter of distant musketry and gun fire bespoke a sudden outburst of battle on the Turnpike. The volume and extent of the rolling volleys told that if Ewell was not completely engulfed in a violent attack, he was involved to an extent that Lee had originally intended to avoid. Was the Army of Northern Virginia committed to a course its commander had not desired?

Lee had never refused an offer of battle delivered on the field by a flaming volley. It was now an hour past noon. Longstreet's advance should have reached Richards Shop. There was no great danger in permitting Grant to develop his attack. Ewell had a good position. The Army of the Potomac had never evinced any marked capacity to mount large-scale attacks in forest fighting.[23] If, however, the pressure exerted by Grant, an untried adversary in the Virginia theater, became precarious Lee could retire to the Mine Run Lines. In such an eventuality the first alternative mentioned in his instructions of 8 p.m. of the night before would still have a valid application. As a matter of fact, Ewell's withdrawal westward across the basin of Flat Run would be greatly facilitated by the presence of Hill's column on the Plank Road ridge. The circumstances under which Lee fought in his present forward position would be determined entirely by the direction and intensity of his adversary's attacks. Final justification of Lee's decision in permitting himself to become involved, between noon and 1 p.m., and contrary to his expressed determination at 11 a.m., in a general engagement can only be found in a just estimate of the situation at nightfall of that day. Additional justification rests in a careful appraisal of the deadlock in which the forces of Lee and Grant stood at the end of fighting on the night of the 6th.

Chapter 10
GRIFFIN SHAKES EWELL'S LINE

In his final effort between noon and 1 p.m. to put the divisions of Griffin and Wadsworth in readiness to strike, Warren faced difficulties that were more akin to handling lines of battle than placing units from column of march into battle formation. Between 8 and 10 a.m. the two divisions had formed a connected line. The front of deployment, however, was so far removed from Ewell's position as to require an advance of the line for delivery of the assault.[1]

An unalterable determination to attack, as ordered at 10:30 a.m., and without regard to the security of flanks, should have enjoined an immediate advance to the jumpoff line from which the assault was to be launched some two hours later. In failing to compel such an advance at that time, Grant lost the opportunity he had in mind when he advised Meade at 8:24 a.m. to attack any part of Lee's army without giving time for disposition. In permitting the two-hours' delay, Grant gave Ewell time in which to complete his defensive arrangements.

Meanwhile all efforts on Warren's part to strengthen his formation proved futile. Not until noon did Crawford begin moving to support the left of the assault column. The early attempt to reinforce the center between Wadsworth's right and Griffin's left with an element of Robinson's 2d Division had, as already stated, resulted in confusion. Denison's Maryland brigade, after failing for some unaccountable reason to execute this design, took position in support of the right brigade of Wadsworth's division.

Warren Forms Battle Line
Whatever cohesion there may have been in the six-brigade

149

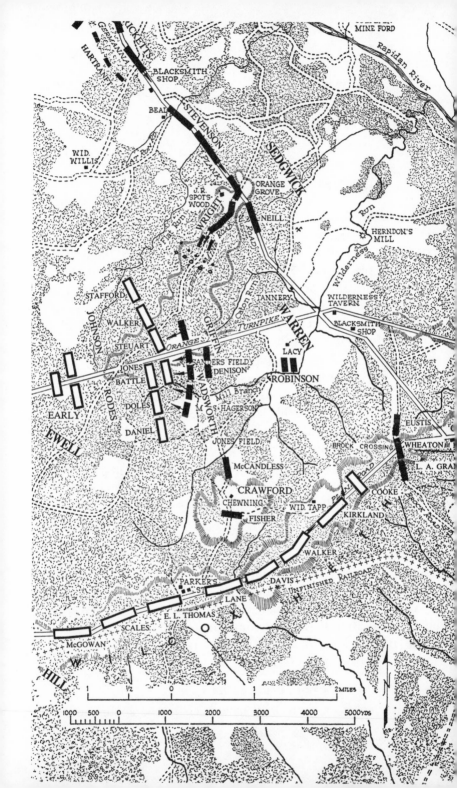

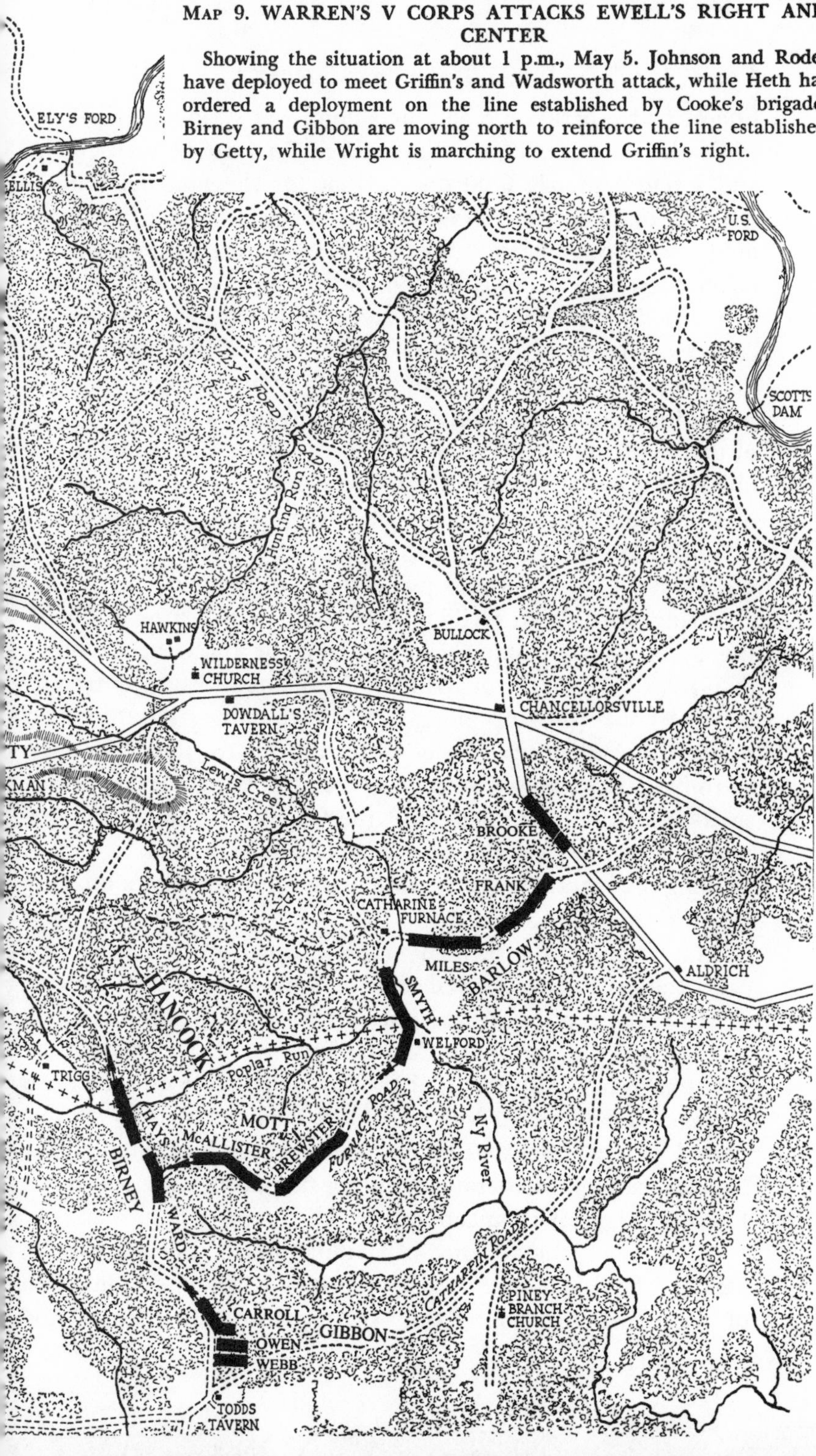

MAP 9. WARREN'S V CORPS ATTACKS EWELL'S RIGHT AND CENTER

Showing the situation at about 1 p.m., May 5. Johnson and Rodes have deployed to meet Griffin's and Wadsworth attack, while Heth has ordered a deployment on the line established by Cooke's brigade. Birney and Gibbon are moving north to reinforce the line established by Getty, while Wright is marching to extend Griffin's right.

line of battle between 8 a.m. and noon was seriously impaired when the elements of the line moved forward between noon and 1 p.m. to make final dispositions for the long-delayed assault. Griffin's forward movement to the west edge of Sanders' field has already been described. Wadsworth, conforming to Griffin's change of position, and endeavoring at the same time to maintain his connection with Griffin's left, was obliged to crowd the front of final deployment. In making his original deployment at 8, Wadsworth moved by the right from column of march to line of division. His advance at the beginning of this maneuver had reached the open ground of Jones' field, one-half mile in rear of Crawford's column on the plateau of Chewning's farm. The left of Wadsworth's division stood, according to Captain Cowdrey, Assistant Adjutant General, 4th Division, in the woods just east of Jones' field.[2]

Owing possibly to Griffin's reluctance to advance at 10:30, the order issued to attack at any time by both the divisions of Griffin and Wadsworth was not executed. Slight entrenchments were thrown up along Wadsworth's line. The historian of the 6th Wisconsin, Cutler's brigade, relates that "the men were lying at their ease in the woods, full of cheer in the warm spring morning. The officers of the 6th Wisconsin, in the second line of the Iron Brigade, laughed under a great oak tree, chaffing one another as if it were noon hour of a day's hunting expedition."[3]

This glimpse of a segment of Wadsworth's line hardly supports the generally accepted view of units floundering through the thickets in a desperate endeavor to form a connected line and join on the right with Griffin's division. It also calls attention to the fact that Ewell, at the lowest possible estimate, was allowed four hours in which to form his defense lines—a time period nearly twice that taken by Stonewall Jackson in forming the same Confederate corps for his celebrated attack on Hooker's right at Chancellorsville.

About noon the advance of Griffin toward the east edge of Sanders' field was taken up by Cutler's brigade, on the right of Wadsworth's division.[4] Both the right brigade (Cutler) and left brigade (Bartlett), respectively, of Wadsworth's and Griffin's divisions, struck the front of Jones' Confederate brigade. The connection between the inner flanks of these two divisions was maintained during the advance to the jumpoff line. Hitting the same target, both must have attacked in close unison. The withdrawal of Sweitzer's brigade from its original position on Bartlett's left suggests that this unit became crowded during the advance, thereby causing Griffin to shorten his front by one brigade.[5] Sweitzer formed in Bartlett's rear. Griffin's line, astride the Turnpike, faced almost due west. Wadsworth, forming an obtuse angle with the line of Griffin and looking northwest toward the Turnpike, could not avoid crowding Griffin, or congesting his own line, unless he changed direction. This, it will presently appear, he did not do. Preserving his original alignment, he advanced diagonally across the front of Ewell's echelon formation.[6]

In reforming for attack from a line skirting the east edge of Sanders' field, and extending to the left toward Jones' field, Sweitzer's brigade moved by the right to a position in close support to Bartlett's brigade. Bartlett formed in two lines on the south side of the Turnpike, the order being, left to right, by regiments in the first line: 18th Massachusetts-83d Pennsylvania-44th New York. The 118th Pennsylvania and 20th Maine took position in the second line, the latter on the right, with its right flank touching the road. Sweitzer's formation is not fully stated in the operation reports of his brigade. The 9th Massachusetts, 4th Michigan, and 62d Pennsylvania were apparently in the first line. The 22d and 32d Massachusetts Regiments were in Sweitzer's second line. Constituting the fourth line of the assault column in this sector, these two Massachusetts regiments were designated as an active reserve for the assault troops. Placed under command of Colonel William S. Tilton, this demi-brigade had instructions to close to the front and stand fast at the edge of the timber as soon as Sweitzer's first line of the assault column moved out across Sanders' field.[7]

General Ayres, commanding the 1st Brigade of Griffin's

division, formed his unit in two lines on the right, or north side of the Turnpike. The 140th New York held the left of the first line. Seven battalions of Regulars from the 2d, 11th, 12th, 15th, and 17th Regiments of United States Infantry extended the line to the right. Three regiments constituted the second line, the order from left to right being the 146th New York-91st Pennsylvania-155th Pennsylvania.[8]

Wadsworth's three brigades (Cutler-Stone-Rice) extended in the order mentioned the front of Warren's attack column from Bartlett's left across Mill Branch, to a point in the woods west or northwest of Jones' field. Since the precise manner in which the left of the 4th Division (Wadsworth) conformed to the movement of the 1st (Griffin) in the advance toward Sanders' field is not known, it is impossible to give an accurate description of Wadsworth's position at the moment Warren launched his assault. If his three brigades preserved the formation and direction described by Wadsworth and Cowdrey at 10 a.m.—and all the evidence indicates that they did so— it may be assumed that Wadsworth's front held an oblique alignment with respect to Griffin, its right being in close or actual contact with Griffin's left near the south edge of Sanders' field, while its left was in the air somewhere northwest of Jones' field.

As already noted, Denison's brigade took position in rear of Wadsworth's 4th Division, the four Maryland regiments supporting Cutler's right brigade. The order of deployment, left to right, was: 1st-4th-7th-8th. The balance of Robinson's 2d Division—Leonard's and Baxter's brigades—was held near the Lacy house in corps reserve.

The front of the attack column from Ayres' right to Rice's left covered a distance of approximately 2200 yards. There were six brigades aggregating 12,234 bayonets poised in attack.[9]

Under command of Col. C. S. Wainwright, Warren's supporting artillery brigade consisted of eight 6-gun batteries, of which 48 were light 12-pounders, 36 were 3-inch rifles, and 6 were 10-pounder Parrotts. Batteries C and E, Massachusetts

Light Artillery (assigned to Griffin's division), together with D, 5th United States Light, and H, 1st New York Light (assigned to Robinson's division) were held in reserve near the Lacy house. Griffin's third assigned battery—B, 1st New York Light—advanced with the assault column toward Sanders' field. Shortly after noon Wadsworth sent his two assigned batteries—B, 4th United States Light, and L, 1st New York Light —back from Jones' field to Wainwright's reserve group. Crawford's assigned battery—B, 1st Pennsylvania Light—joined the reserve soon after. Wainwright thereupon placed four batteries in position on a ridge to the right of the Lacy house to command the valley of Wilderness Run and the road to Parker's Store.[10]

A gunner by training and an ardent advocate of the Napoleonic dictum that the guns should go wherever the infantry went, Griffin instructed Capt. George B. Winslow, commanding Battery B, 1st New York Light Artillery, to put his right and left sections in position across the Turnpike. Lieutenant Shelton's left section was held in readiness to cross Sanders' field with the second line of battle and support the attack with gunfire delivered at point-blank range.[11]

Ewell Completes Defensive Formation

Opposed to Warren's six-brigade attack column was the echelon formation of Johnson's and Rodes' seven brigades, with two brigades of Early's Division held in reserve. Early's third brigade was still, according to report, in column on the Turnpike. In the Confederate left echelon stood the four brigades of Edward Johnson's Division, the order from right to left being Jones-Steuart-Walker-Stafford. Jones' left met Steuart's right some distance south of the Turnpike, Steuart having the 1st North Carolina on the right of the road, the 3d North Carolina astride the thoroughfare and his three Virginia regiments—the 10th, 23d and 37th—to the left and probably in the order mentioned. Formed in the woods along the west side of Sander's field, Jones stood immediately opposite Bartlett. His right appears to have overlapped Bartlett's left, extending a considerable distance southward across the path of Cutler's advance. Steuart's Virginia regiments, in the woods north of the Turnpike, confronted Ayres. Stafford and Walker extended the Confederate left echelon far beyond Ayres' right. Pickets covering the front of Jones and Steuart occupied the gully traversing the center of Sanders' field. Skirmishers from Stafford's and Walker's Brigades were well forward in the woods, those of Walker's having already developed Wright's advance. To the right rear of Johnson's left echelon were the three brigades of Rodes' Division—Battle, Doles, and Daniel. Battle formed in rear of Jones, with Doles on his right. Daniel held the extreme right of the right or second echelon. Ewell had the two brigades of Early's Division as an active reserve, with one, counterbalancing the two of Robinson's Federal division, as a general reserve. Gordon's and Hays' Brigades were deployed on either side of the Turnpike, Gordon's Georgians on the right, Hays' Louisianans on the left of the road.[12]

In Ewell's two echelons, 10,045 bayonets opposed the 12,254 of Warren's six-brigade attack column. Including the three Confederate reserve brigades, Ewell's available force counted a total of 14,350 bayonets. With the Maryland brigade in support of Wadsworth and two of Robinson's division in corps reserve, Warren disposed of some 18,351 bayonets.

While not affording the numerical preponderance that would justify an attack under the best of conditions, it should be realized that Meade's original plan of placing Crawford's 3d Division on the left, while four VI Corps brigades moved upon the right, was overruled by Grant's insistence that Warren attack at once and without regard to the security of his flanks. Given time for adequate preparation, Meade could have thrown some 26,000 bayonets against Ewell's 14,500.

Confederate artillery dispositions cannot be stated with any certainty. Milledge's Battery was withdrawn from Jones' front as Griffin's division advanced toward Sanders' field. According to Long, Ewell's Chief of Artillery, "a portion of Nelson's guns [3 batteries, including Milledge's, totalling 13 pieces] were posted on a commanding ridge, with a small field in front, immediately on the road 1 mile from the Lacy house." There is nothing to indicate, however, that this disposition was completed before Warren delivered his attack.[13]

Ayres Strikes Ewell's Left Center

Sometime before 1 p.m. when Ayres' brigade formed on Bartlett's right, Warren gave the orders to advance. The density of the thicket in which the elements of the assault column crouched made it impossible to transmit the order simultaneously to regimental units. Brigade staff officers had difficulty in finding regimental commanders. Many units were unaware of the movement until they saw others on their right or left breaking cover. All, however, conformed; cheers rang through the woodland; a long, swaying wave of bayonets emerged from the shadows and flashed the signal of deadly combat.[14]

Leaving its cover north of the Turnpike, Ayres' first line charged down into the gully that ran diagonally across Sanders' field, routing the Confederate skirmishers and driving them on up the opposite slope toward the woods. There the brigades of Steuart, Stafford, and Walker lurked behind felled logs. As Ayres' men crossed the draw, a furious crossfire blazed from the trees to their front and right. The 140th New York crowded to the left toward the pike. The Regulars pushed on in perfect alignment. Entangled by saplings and matted vines at the north end of the field, and decimated by the furious crossfire the right of the line struggled forward at a retarded pace. In preserving their formation, the left battalions inclined to the right. A gap opened between the 140th and the Regulars on its immediate right. Both segments of the line swept on toward the woods. The smoke of volleys, roaring at point blank, rose and drifted in fluffy white curls past the topmost branches of the swaying pines.[15]

At this critical moment Shelton's section with Captain Winslow in personal command came at a mad gallop along the Turnpike, crossed the draw and swung into action. Two-gun salvos sent a shower of solid shot, shattering tree-trunks, severing branches, and tearing into the ranks of New Yorkers and Virginians with an impartiality that excelled the accuracy of the gunnery.[16]

Ayres' second line moved up to the edge of the field as the first wave went forward. The 146th New York, an old-time volunteer regiment which still affected the Zouave manner of dress and retained its baptismal name of Garrard's Tigers, held the left. Under command of Col. David T. Jenkins, the Tigers justified their name in the shambles of Sanders' field. The 95th and 155th Pennsylvania regiments formed, in the order named, on the right.[17]

While the second line regiments were completing their formation officers and men had a brief opportunity to witness the scene on the west slope of the gully in Sanders' field. They saw the interval opening in the first line. On their left, a two-gun section of artillery rumbled along the Turnpike, drivers furiously lashing their horses, and gunners precariously riding on bouncing limbers.

Bugle notes and shouted orders brought the waiting infantrymen to their feet. With a ringing voice that carried from flank to flank of his regiment, Colonel Jenkins shouted: "Attention! Take Arms! Forward March!"[18]

The Zouaves moved out, officers in front, men in closed ranks. A clump of trees extending from the right front of the 146th into the clearing impeded progress of Jenkins' right companies, while enabling those on the left to forge ahead. At the command "Forward, Double Quick!" a broken line trotted forward through the stubble and over the plowed ground.

Jenkin's charging line entered a hail of Minié balls at the gully. Stricken men threw their arms in the air and pitched forward. Others collapsed and staggered to the rear. The rest pushed on. "The rattle of musketry," relates an eyewitness, "was interspersed with the cannon booming on the road, the fire from which obliqued across the front of the 146th. Some of us were so close that we could feel the strong wind of the discharges."[19]

The line pushed on up the slope from the gully to the edge of the forest. Instead of crowding to the left as the 140th New York of the first line had done, Jenkins led his 146th New York toward the interval in the first line. At the same time, the right regiments, the 195th and 155th Pennsylvania continued their inclination to the right, as had the Regulars and doubtlessly for the same reason. Thus Jenkins plunged into a widening gap, with his right flank dangerously exposed.

The Regular battalions, meantime, had been unable to sustain the unequal combat with the three Virginia regiments holding Steuart's left, together with those of Stafford and Walker, which extended Ewell's line north of the Turnpike by something more than a two-brigade front. Charging toward the woods, the two Pennsylvania regiments passed over the Regulars and drove in on the enemy. A withering fire shattered their line; the right flank collapsed, the left crumpled; volley after volley was poured into the wavering ranks. Lieutenant Colonel William S. Powell, 11th United States Infantry, states that the tremendous roll of the firing excluded all other sounds. "Men's faces," adds the Regular, "were sweaty black from biting cartridges ... occasional glimpses of gray phantomlike forms crouched under the bank of (smoke) clouds were obtained." [20]

Harried by the furious crossfire that blazed again from the semi-circular forest fringe, Ayres' entire attack column, less the 140th and 146th New York, streamed in broken fragments back across the gully and up the far slope toward the east edge of the woods. There Tilton's demi-brigade offered a rallying point for the shattered units. [21]

Unmindful, or unconscious, perhaps, of the impending disaster on their right, the 146th New York charged into the woods, firing on the run and holding their weapons in readiness for combat at close quarters. The left companies broke into the woods somewhat in advance of those on their right. But as each successive company to the right reached the tree line, they plunged into the thick underbrush. Steuart's three

Virginia regiments the 10th, 23rd and 37th, received the charge with terrible volleys from behind trees and breastworks. Captain W. H. S. Sweet, a company commander of the 146th, relates that: "Closing with the enemy, we fought them fiercely with bayonet, as well as bullet. Up through the trees rolled dense clouds of battle smoke, circling about the green of the pines and mingling its fleecy billows with the white of the flowering dogwoods. Underneath, men ran to and fro, firing, shouting, stabbing with bayonets, beating on his resources, grimly and desperately." [22]

A version of the fight, as seen from the extreme right, is given by Private Carrol S. Waldron, Company C, 146th New York, who was taken prisoner in the woods and recorded the experience in a memoir written shortly after his release from Andersonville Prison.

> We charged across an open field under fire to [the] edge of woods and there lay down and loaded and fired as we had been drilled. We had to load on our backs and then roll over and fire and in that manner were not much exposed to the enemy's fire. After a while the firing in front of us ceased and we lay still waiting orders.
>
> At 1 P.M. troops were passing in our rear from right to left, as I supposed our troops; but suddenly it dawned upon me that they were rebels and I raised my gun to fire at them, but my captain who lay at my elbow put my gun down and said don't fire, and 15 of our Co. C and 130 of the Regt. were captured. The other end of the Regt. fell back and escaped.
>
> The Colonel of our regiment [Jenkins] and [the] Major were killed, Lieutenant Colonel wounded and the regiment was really in command of our Capt., he being Senior Captain, but was entirely ignorant of the fact, hence the reason we got no orders.
>
> About 150 of the regiment were killed or wounded, mostly from the other end of line, where they fell back across the open field.
>
> We were marched to the rear. Their guard was mostly composed of boys from 12 to 16. They marched us all [the] rest of the afternoon and night till 3 when we reached Orange Court House.[23]

The evidence at hand does not permit a certain determination of the time that the two New York regiments, the 140th and 146th, stood at bay in the woods. Captain Sweet relates that his men completely lost their heads in the blinding smoke and raging tumult. "Many dashed directly into the enemy's fire in a belief that they were going to the rear. Officers lost control of their companies and utterly bewildered, rushed hither and thither, looking for their men." Then according to this eyewitness, "We ceased fire when not a rebel opposed us and we seemed successful." [24]

The lull mentioned by Captain Sweet in his narration may be attributed to the violence temporarily visited on opposing Confederate formations by the swift advance of Bartlett's 3d Brigade on the south side of the Turnpike.

Bartlett Ruptures Ewell's Center

As Ayres' brigade struck across Sanders field, Bartlett sent the 1st Michigan Infantry in skirmish order across the clearing on the south of the Turnpike. Driving Jones' skirmishers from the gully and pursuing them to the edge of the woods beyond, the Michigan regiment cleared Bartlett's path of advance.[25]

Supported on both flanks by moving formations, Bartlett sent the three regiments of his first line (left to right: 18th Massachusetts—83d Pennsylvania—44th New York) forward. With Cutler's brigade of Wadsworth's division pacing his left, Bartlett struck the six Virginia regiments of Jones' Brigade. Pushing forward, Bartlett's second line (left to right: 115th Pennsylvania—20th Maine) added its impetus to the assault.

The struggle was brief and violent. Striving to stay the rout, Brigadier General Jones was killed. His *aide de camp,* Capt. Robert D. Early, son of General Jubal Early, fell at the side of the heroic brigadier.

As the melee raged, Sweitzer's first line, the third of the assault column, and consisting of the 9th Massachusetts, 4th Michigan, and the 62d Pennsylvania Infantry, advanced across Sanders' field and pushed through the thickets toward the battle front. At the same time Sweitzer's second line, the fourth in the assault column, moved up to the edge of the field and formed in reserve. Owing, no doubt, to the collapse of Ayres' formation and the consequent danger of a counterattack, Colonel Tilton, commanding the force, moved both regiments, his own—the 22d Massachusetts—and the 32d Massachusetts, to the north side of the Turnpike. The 22d formed on a line described as "nearly parallel to the road; the 32d on the right, refused." [26] While crossing the Turnpike, the 32d came under severe fire. With Shelton's artillery section covering the left, Colonel Tilton's demi-brigade was advantageously placed to serve as a rallying point in the event of a retrograde movement.

At the front, Bartlett's brigade drove on, scattering the wreck of Jones' Virginians. But the shock of encounter and stress of pursuit through the tangled thickets disarrayed the attackers' alignment. Bartlett brought up his reserve regiments to fill the intervals in his first line.[27]

Holding the left of Ewell's second echelon, and standing in direct support of Jones, Battle's Brigade was thrown into disorder by the rout of the Virginia regiments. Doles' Brigade, on Battle's right, was included in the disorder. With Cutler still pacing his left, Bartlett pressed the attack.

Little is known concerning details of the clash—yet a single fact stands out. The supreme military virtue of the Army of Northern Virginia survived the crisis. The superb leadership of company and regimental units came into play. Battle's five Alabama regiments—the 3d, 5th, 6th, 12th and 61st—fought with their native ferocity, giving ground but contesting every foot of the enemy's advance. Doles' four Georgia regiments—the 4th, 12th, 21st, and 44th—offered the stubborn resistance that Lee ordinarily expected of any unit of his army engaged in defensive combat. With their traditional gallantry, the Virginians rallied and returned to the conflict. The battle raged westward, thundering half a mile through the forest.[28]

Rodes' Rally Halts Bartlett

Flushed with victory, Bartlett pushed beyond the formations that had heretofore supported his flanks. He soon realized that Ayres' brigade had lost connection on the right. Responsible

MAP 10. GRIFFIN'S BREAKTHROUGH

The situation at about 1:45 p.m., May 5. Griffin and Wadsworth assail Ewell's front. Ayres and Bartlett attack along the turnpike, Ayres on the north side, Bartlett on the south. Ayres falters in the deadly crossfire from Johnson's overlapping line. Bartlett, supported by Sweitzer and paced on his left by Wadsworth's right brigade (Cutler), shears the inner flanks of Ewell's left and right echelons of defense. The victors dash through the gap, but Ayres falls back in disorder while Wadsworth's center sags during movement over swampy ground. Then Rice, on the extreme Federal left, obliques across Daniel's front. Meanwhile Rodes, commanding Ewell's second (right) echelon, rallies his scattered regiments; and Gordon, called from reserve, breaks Wadsworth's sagging line. Warren's attack collapses.

The small units labelled "Rodes" on this map are Battle's and Doles' temporarily broken brigades plus Jones' brigade and part of Steuart's from Johnson's division.

for this flank, the 44th New York obliqued across the Turn-pike and continued the advance on the north side of the road. Then the brigade commander became aware that his left was in the air and that the scattered elements of Jones', Battle's, and Doles' commands had been rallied and were threatening his open flanks. Only one regimental officer, Colonel Throop, commanding the 1st Michigan, mentions serious resistance in the front. But all are in agreement that the decision was taken to retreat at once and that the retrograde movement, though hurried, was conducted in good order through the woods on the south side of the Turnpike. Two candid regimental historians confess that their outfits ran almost every step of the way back to the breastworks they had thrown up during the forenoon.[29]

Scenes in the rear area were now symptomatic of the demoralization that was spreading like an insidious epidemic at the front. Ambulances evacuating the wounded choked the Turnpike. Droves of walking wounded crowded along the tree-lined thoroughfare, wearily asking again and again the same question: "Which way to the V Corps Hospital?" Skulkers straggling among the wounded were challenged with opprobrious expletives appropriate to the occasion by Zouaves of the headquarters guard and turned back at the point of the bayonet.[30] Yet a watchful observer might find indications of the spirit that survives defeat. Lieutenant Colonel Lyman, *aide de camp* to the army commander, described an episode:

> I saw coming toward me a mounted officer—his face covered with blood—as he was kept in the saddle only by an officer who rode beside him and his servant who walked on the other side. "Hello, Lyman!" he cried, in a wild way, a way that showed he was wandering; "here I am; hurt a little; not much; I am going to lie down a few minutes, and then I am going back again! Oh, you ought to have seen how we drove 'em— I had the first line!" It was my classmate, Colonel Hays* of the 18th Massachusetts, as fearless a soldier as ever went into action. There we were, three of us together, for the officer who supported him was Dr. Dalton. Three classmates together, down in the Virginia Wilderness, and a great fight going on

at the front. I was afraid Hays was mortally wounded, but I am told since, he will recover. I hope so.[31]

The bloody repulse of Ayres' brigade and the hasty withdrawal of Bartlett's and Sweitzer's regiments to their reserve positions eliminated Griffin's 1st Division from further participation in the V Corps offensive. Yet the pressure exerted by this division in its forward movement, particularly the temporary breakthrough achieved by Bartlett at the center of Ewell's line, created a situation which put the Confederate formations facing Wadsworth's 4th Division in peril until the ominous threat to the center was removed. Attention must now be turned to Wadsworth's advance on the left of the V Corps assault column.[32]

---

* Col. Joseph Hays commanded Bartlett's first line during the break-through. Lt. Col. W. B. White assumed command of the 18th Mass. upon Hays' injury, and reported on operations of the regiment.

CHAPTER 11

THE V CORPS ATTACK—WADSWORTH
IS AMBUSHED

Deploying from column of march, the three brigades of Wadsworth's 4th Division took positions in accordance with their order in the marching column. Rice held the left of the front of deployment. Stone moved into the center. Cutler formed on the right, his six regiments disposed in two lines of battle and connecting on the right with Bartlett's brigade. If Cutler's formation was typical, the number of regiments in Wadsworth's first line exceeded by two to one the number in the second line.

Cutler Goes In

Famed as the Iron Brigade, Cutler's command was composed of Western regiments—three from Wisconsin, one from Michigan, and two from Indiana. Schooled in woodcraft and accustomed from boyhood to the use of the rifle, the men of this brigade were quite the equal in forest fighting to the best of Lee's infantry. Cutler placed four regiments in his first line, the order, left to right, being the 24th Michigan—19th Indiana —2d Wisconsin—7th Wisconsin. In the second line the 7th Indiana supported the 7th Wisconsin, while the 6th Wisconsin stood in support to the 2d Wisconsin.[1] After being crowded from his assigned position between the 2d and 4th Divisions, Denison, as already related, formed his four Maryland regiments in rear of the Iron Brigade. Supporting Cutler, Denison occupied a position similar to that of Sweitzer with respect to Cutler.

Wadsworth moved in unison with Griffin against the first or left echelon of Ewell's defensive formation. Cutler's 7th Wisconsin struck the right of the front occupied by Jones' six

Virginia regiments, while Bartlett's three front-line regiments hit the left of the Virginia line and that portion of the sector on the south side of the Turnpike held by two regiments of Steuart's Brigade—the 1st and 3d North Carolina. In the initial clash eight Confederate regiments met the onset of four Federal regiments. In terms of bayonets some 1,500 attackers clashed with 2,400 defenders. This imbalance was quickly redressed by the advance of Federal units from the second line. During the furious melee the 7th Indiana pushed into Cutler's first line and took a hand. Private J. N. Opel, Company C, captured the colors of the 50th Virginia.[2]

After shearing the right of Jones' line, the Iron Brigade charged down with Bartlett on Ewell's right or second echelon, which was composed, left to right, of the brigades of Battle-Doles-Daniel. His left touching the Turnpike, Battle stood in direct support to Jones; Doles blocked the path of Cutler's advance. While fiercely engaged with Doles' four Georgia regiments, Cutler lost connection on his right with Bartlett who, reinforced by Sweitzer's first-line units, overwhelmed Battle's Alabama brigade and, as related in Chapter 10, swept on half a mile through the woods.

Denison's failure at this critical juncture to reinforce the Iron Brigade with his four Maryland regiments may be attributed to want of effective liaison between 2d and 4th Division headquarters. At any rate Denison stood fast. So did the two brigades of Robinson's 2d Division, which were held in corps reserve throughout the attack.[3]

Stone and Rice Advance

Meanwhile Stone and Rice were endeavoring to carry forward the advance on the left of Wadsworth's line. Unable to keep pace with Cutler, Stone's five Pennsylvania regiments floundered in a morass bordering Mill Branch. The right inclination given Cutler's force by the circumstances of the advance imparted a similar tendency to Stone. The pull to the right was felt by Rice, on the left of the line. While Stone's men toiled over marshy ground, Rice advanced northwestward, swinging his left obliquely across Daniel's Confederate brigade, which held the right of Ewell's second echelon.[4]

Here, on the left of the V Corps assault force, Rice faced the same fatal situation that Ayres encountered on the right. Both ran into an overlapping Confederate line—the penalty of ignoring the safety of flanks while attacking in force. If the flanks were to be ignored, the assault might better have been launched at 10:30 a.m., when Ewell's deployment was but half completed. Failing immediate action at that time, Warren should have been allowed the time he required to mount an assault column that guaranteed the security of both flanks.

Gordon Restores Ewell's Right

Unaware of developments that were destined shortly to take an ominous turn for the attackers on both right and left, Ewell sensed the danger to his center. Bartlett's deep thrust through that sector had shattered the inner flanks of his two echelons. A mass of fresh reserves pouring through the breach might isolate and overwhelm his own reserve, while the two echelons were destroyed in detail. At all hazards the line must be restored before the fatal infiltration.

Ewell acted with a celerity and resolution worthy of Stonewall Jackson, his predecessor in command of the II Corps. Wheeling his horse he rode at a reckless gallop down the Turnpike toward Early's reserve division. Recognizing Brigadier General John B. Gordon at the head of his Georgia brigade, Ewell reined in. According to Gordon, the corps commander slid to a halt, his wooden leg missing by the fraction of an inch Gordon's own knee.[5] While bracing himself against the expected pain, the brigadier became aware that his Georgians were expected to redeem a desperate situation. He was instructed, he relates, "to form at once on the right of the Turnpike, for the purpose of checking the enemy's advance and saving the artillery, which at that time was moving back along the pike under the enemy's fire." Gordon continues the narrative in his official report:

I moved my brigade by the right flank and formed at right

angles to the road with as much expedition as the nature of
the ground and the fire from the enemy's artillery and advancing infantry would admit. Some of my men were killed
and wounded before the first regiment was placed in position.
As soon as the formation was completed I ordered the brigade
forward. The advance was made with such spirit that the
enemy was broken and scattered along the front of my brigade,
but still held his ground or continued his advance on my right
and left. For the protection and relief of my flanks I left a
thin line (Thirty-first and Thirty-eighth Georgia Regiments)
to protect my front, and changed front to right with three
regiments (Thirteenth, Sixtieth, and Sixty-first Georgia), and
moved directly upon the flank of the line on my right, capturing several hundred prisoners, among them one entire regiment, with its officers and colors. At the same time I caused
the regiment on the left, (Twenty-sixth Georgia) to make a
similar movement to the left, which was also successful. By
this time portions of Battle's brigade rallied, and with other
troops of Rodes' division came forward and assisted in driving
the enemy back and establishing the line, which was afterwards held.[6]

While circumstantial in the account of his maneuver, Gordon
does not tell whom he hit. If he actually struck in three directions, he must have first thrust his brigade into a gap or bay
in the enemy's line and then wheeled his flanks right and left.
The Federal line was exposed to just such an attack. Before
making dispositions to attack, Gordon states that the enemy
was broken and scattered along his front, *"but still held his
ground or continued his advance on my right and left."* *
Then, while advancing in three directions, Gordon makes clear
that the maneuver largely constituted a change of front to the
right, involving half his command—the 13th, 60th, and 61st
Georgia—while two regiments held the original direction and
one wheeled left.

In the light of Gordon's evidence, it becomes difficult to
agree with the generally accepted belief that he struck and
turned the extreme left of Wadworth's advancing line. Admitting that Ewell's center had been ruptured before Gordon
started moving by his right from the Turnpike, one has only
to consult Map 9 to appreciate that such a maneuver could not

---

* Italics supplied by writer.

possibly have been executed within less than two hours. At the expiration of this minimum time limit, there would have been no Confederate line to restore.[7]

Applying the limitations of time within which Gordon acted, together with the facts of the situation as vaguely reported by fragmentary sources, it seems more logical to conclude that Gordon found a deep bay in the Federal line, rushed into the re-entrant angle, and threw half his force to the right, that is, southward and away from the Turnpike. Stone's failure to cross the swampy ground northwest of Hagerson's farm had created just such a dent in the center of Wadsworth's line. Cutler, fiercely engaged with Doles, was north of the bay. Rice, swinging his outer flank across Daniel's front, was suddenly threatened by a double envelopment.

Advancing on the left of the V Corps assault column, Rice's brigade was rent by the blast of a volley from an unseen foe. Word came immediately from Major Young, commanding a three-company detachment of flankers from the 76th New York, that the enemy was advancing in a line of battle that extended far beyond the Federal left. Simultaneously with this ominous warning, Stone's brigade gave way, leaving Rice's right in air. The right regiments of the half-encircled brigade attempted to elude the trap by conforming to Stone's retrograde movement. At least one regiment fell into Gordon's hands. Daniel's Confederates closed in on the left, capturing Major Young's skirmishers and enfilading with close-range musketry fire the huddled ranks of Rice's battle line.[8]

The retirement quickly became a rout. Half a mile to the rear, Colonel J. W. Hoffman, commanding the 56th Pennsylvania, rallied 350 men on the crest of a slight elevation and made preparations to delay the enemy's pursuit. General Wadsworth galloped up to the position and, after briefly conferring with Hoffman, ordered him to withdraw his force. The division commander wisely preferred complete disengagement to the risk of establishing broken troops on a line within easy reach of an enemy who evinced no serious intent of strong counteroffensive action. Hoffman led his Pennsylvanians back to the open ground near Major Lacy's house, where the work of reorganization began.[9]

Gordon's swift movement into the bay on Cutler's left, and the consequent rout of Stone's brigade, exposed the left of the Iron Brigade. At the same time Cutler lost contact on the right with Bartlett. Assailed in front and on both flanks by reformed regiments of Battle's and Doles' brigades, with Gordon's 26th Georgia joining in the attack on the left, the Iron Brigade gave way. Pursued by Confederates eager to avenge their recent humiliation, Cutler's regiments broke and fled to the rear.[10]

Wadsworth's Line Disintegrates

The rout tore through Denison's line of battle, still standing fast. The four Maryland regiments managed to survive the confusion and met the first shock of pursuing Confederates. Dispositions were being made to refuse the left, when a hostile force was discovered on the right rear. The 4th, under Colonel R. N. Bowerman, reformed to counter this dangerous menace. Engaging heavily, Bowerman lost connection with Denison's main body. The 4th fell back in good order a distance of some twenty yards and opened fire. It now appeared that the Confederates were massing in force on the right of the Maryland brigade. Observing the main body in full retreat, Bowerman fell back another thirty yards and reported the situation to Denison. By order of the brigade commander, the 4th retired, preserving its alignment through the woods and joining the brigade at the reserve line of breastworks.[11]

Lee's instructions of 11 a.m. adjuring the II Corps commander against commitment in a general action until Longstreet's Corps arrived within supporting distance, probably restrained Ewell from launching a counterattack in force. Moreover, the disordered alignment of his two echelons, together with the vague knowledge at Confederate II Corps headquarters concerning the state of affairs at any particular moment, would have precluded any such effort. But Ewell's brigadiers were not denied the satisfaction of local retaliation.[12]

Little is known concerning the pursuit pressed by Danie
and Gordon after the collapse of Wadsworth's line. One o
Daniel's regiments ran into resistance, possibly on the line
temporarily established by Hoffman, while attempting to cover
Rice's retreat. A Confederate source admits that the 53d Nortl
Carolina was repulsed by infantry supported by artillery fire
Mention of artillery fire, however, suggests that this venture
some North Carolina unit may have advanced to a position
within range of Wainwright's batteries emplaced on the cres
near the Lacy house. Aside from three 2-gun sections placec
in position on north side of the Turnpike, there were no V
Corps batteries in action elsewhere.[13]

Attacking in three directions, Gordon had little opportunit
of organizing a strong pursuit. The 61st Georgia, one of the
three regiments which moved against Rice's right flank, ap
pears to have lost contact with the other two of the mair
attacking force and pushed northeastward through the dens
thickets. Advancing cautiously, the 61st ran into the 7th Penn
sylvania Reserves, which had been separated from McCand
less's brigade during the march from Chewning's farm towar
Wadsworth's left. Alert to the dread surprises of forest fighting
the Georgians became aware of the approaching foe in time
to form an ambuscade. A single flashing volley ended the fra
Utterly surprised and caught at point-blank range, 271 sur
vivors surrendered; only 40 escaped. The main body of Me
Candless reached the open ground near the Lacy house witl
out further mishap.[14]

Tragedy and Comedy in Sanders' Field

The rally of Rodes's two brigades, Battle's and Doles', from
the disorder imposed by Bartlett's breakthrough and Cutler
supporting attack brought an end to the reprieve given th
140th and 146th New York in their precarious position at th
edge of the woods just north of the Turnpike. Swept awa
with Jones' Brigade by Bartlett's initial attack, Steuart's tw
right regiments, the 1st and 3d North Carolina which origi
ally stood between Jones and the south side of the Turnpik

were now able to return to their first position. Then, as Steuart's left regiments—the 10th, 23d, and 37th Virginia—folded around the right of the 146th New York, the 1st and 3d North Carolina struck the left of the 140th. Captain W. H. S. Sweet of the 146th, who described the desperate fighting at the edge of the woods up to the moment when the Confederate suddenly ceased firing, continues his narrative:

> I knew the danger of being flanked, as by charging over the field we broke the continuity of our general line of battle, and the rebels were adepts in finding gaps. Twenty paces to the rear enabled me to look out over the open field we had just crossed. We were not only flanked but doubly flanked. Rebel troops covered the field we had just crossed. We were in a bag and the strings were tied. Those of our regiment who escaped were principally from the right, where the movement of the rebels seems to have been discovered just in time to make escape possible.[15]

Their gallant commander, Colonel Jenkins, slain, the Tiger Zouaves quit the wooded shelter in which they had found temporary refuge, to run the murderous gantlet of Confederate fire across Sanders' field. Many held canteens to their heads to secure the slight protection thus afforded. Some stumbled and fell and were made prisoners before they could arise. Others took shelter in the gully, only to delay capture. A few ran down the Turnpike and threw themselves behind dead artillery horses to avoid the hail of musketry while regaining breath and strength to continue flight. The wounded limped or crawled. "The bright red of our Zouave uniforms," relates a survivor of the flight, "mingled with the sober gray and butternut of the Confederates, creating a fantastic spectacle as the wearers ran to and fro on the field firing and shouting." [16]

Spectacular confusion and fantasy now gave way to appalling tragedy. Continous volleys bursting in the trees had ignited dead leaves and withered foliage. These smoldering fires were fanned by a brisk afternoon breeze and driven to the edge of Sanders' field. There the dry grass and stubble burst into flame and swept like a prairie fire across the clearing. Friend and foe alike joined in fighting the common enemy. Soldier in blue and gray ran through blinding smoke to succor the wounded.[17] As the roaring blaze advanced it ignited cartridge boxes of the fallen, hideously dismembering bodies of the dead and the helpless wounded. Our veteran pictures the final scene:

> The almost cheerful 'Pop! Pop!' of cartridges gave no hint of the dreadful horror their noise bespoke. Swept by the flames the trees, bushes, and logs which Confederates had thrown up as breastworks now took fire and dense clouds of smoke rolled across the clearing, choking unfortunates who were exposed to it and greatly hindering the work of rescuers. The clearing now became a raging inferno in which many of the wounded perished. The bodies of the dead were blackened and burned beyond all possibility of recognition, a tragic conclusion to this day of horror.[18]

Unfortunately this frightful episode did not conclude the inexorable march of events in Sanders' field. The fire that swept the clearing vanished as quickly as it had appeared. The alliance of expediency was dissolved and both sides returned to the grim business of war. As remnants of the 146th fled over the open ground, with Steuart's regiments in hot pursuit, a detachment of the 1st North Carolina led by Lieutenant C. R. Scott charged straight at Winslow's guns.[19]

One of the fiercest hand-to-hand grapples of the Wilderness battle flared around the battery position. A number of stout-hearted Zouaves paused in flight to lend a hand. Bayonets crossed over dead horses. Artillery sabers clashed on rifle barrels. Some went home in deadly stabs; others slashed into red gaping wounds. The roaring detonation of revolvers, hoarse imprecations, and sharp outcries of agonized pain all mingled in a frightful uproar. "It was claw for claw and the Devil for us all," wrote a Confederate participant. Gunners and Zouaves were overborne by the weight and fury of Confederate steel. Lieutenant Shelton fell with a wound and was taken prisoner. Severely wounded, Captain Winslow surrendered the guns.

The subsequent rush of events in Sander's field give something of a clue regarding the time element and sequence of action in the battle as a whole. While Lieutenant Scott's party was slaughtering Winslow's gunners, another detachment of the 1st, with the 3d North Carolina on their right, advanced on the south side of the Turnpike into the gully. Confederate troops had already passed to the right of the guns, that is, on north of the pike. Both wings of the counter-advance were thus advantageously placed for an attack on Tilton's reserve line at the east edge of the clearing. Having quelled resistance at the guns, Lieutenant Scott's detachment advanced to the shelter of the draw.[21]

A surprising development, however, deranged any aggressive move the Confederates may have intended. The wreck of Bartlett's brigade and fragments of Cutler's provisional command swept down in hasty retreat on the rear of the Carolinians. The sudden eruption of fleeing Federals seems to have taken the advancing Confederates completely by surprise. With one accord they took shelter in the gully. And there they stopped while the routed units rushed by.[22] Rodes' pursuing line of battle, with Battle's Alabama regiments on the left, came up before the North Carolina troops emerged from their hastily taken shelter. Seeing Winslow's abandoned guns, Colonel J. N. Lightfoot, commanding the 6th Alabama, hastened forward, mounted the guns and, with flag in hand, claimed the capture.[23]

Men of Lieutenant Scott's North Carolina detachment, who spilled their blood in taking the guns and capturing both section officer and battery commander, emerged from hiding to establish their prior claim. Alabama was reluctant to yield the point of honor to North Carolina. During the debate, a complete report of which would be unique in the annals of military history, the main body of the 1st North Carolina and other elements of Steuart's brigade came up to participate in the argument.

If force of logic had been without avail, intensity of feeling plus weight of numbers precipitated a parliamentary crisis. The decision had just inclined in favor of North Carolina when the Federals launched a violent counterattack. Alabamans and North Carolinians alike hastily adjourned, leaving the guns to their dead gunners.[24] The pieces remained between the lines until nightfall of the following day when, during the turmoil of Gordon's partially successful attack against the Federal right flank, a thoughtful officer of the 1st North Carolina—a participant, no doubt, of the parliamentary battle—slipped with a detachment into Sanders' field and hauled the guns to safety behind his regimental lines. With possession in this case being ten points of the law, the triumph of North Carolina over Alabama was complete.[25]

Warren Regroups

While the threat of a Confederate counterattack in force still impended, Robinson's two reserve brigades—Baxter's and Leonard's (Lyle commanding) were sent up to relieve Tilton's demi-brigade. The relief must have taken place while Scott's detachment was engaged with Winslow's gunners. The attack that cleared the field and brought an abrupt adjournment of the debate concerning title to the guns likely was launched by an element of the relieving force.[26]

Tilton's command, together with such fragments of Ayres' brigade and other units that had rallied on his line, fell back to the reserve trenches. There they joined Bartlett's brigade and the first line regiments of Sweitzer, who had crossed Sanders' field with the attack column. Colonel Bowerman's report would indicate that Denison's brigade took position in the trenches, connecting with Griffin's left and extending the line southward toward Mill Branch.[27]

Wadsworth's three brigades assembled on open ground near the Lacy house to reorganize. Crawford's two brigades (McCandless and Fisher) took position sometime later on the extreme left, extending the line southward across the Wilderness Tavern-Parker's Store Road. Fisher's brigade appears to have held its position on the Chewning plateau after the withdrawal of McCandless. At any rate, army headquarters was under the impression that Crawford's 2d Division was in the vicinity of Chewning's farm as late as 2 p.m.[28]

Assured by the withdrawal of Confederate troops across

Sanders' field that the threat of a general counterattack had passed, Lyle made dispositions to consolidate the front line at the east edge of the clearing. Convinced by the growing intensity of fire along Caton Run that Wright's long expected column would soon be at hand and remove all danger to his right, Lyle made dispositions to improve the security of his left. Refusing his right, with the 39th Massachusetts across the Turnpike, he formed his remaining regiments on a line south of the pike and running parallel to it, the front looking south toward the Chewning plateau. Baxter's brigade carried the line eastward, meeting Griffin's reserve trenches about 200 yards south of the Turnpike.[29]

The formation taken by Robinson's two brigades really amounted to a local change of front, with Lyle's right refused across the road. Wright's arrival on the right of the 39th Massachusetts, and the connection established by the left of Baxter's brigade with Griffin, produced an echelon formation somewhat similar in structure to the one originally adopted by Ewell. Wright's four brigades (Upton-Brown-Russell-Neill), together with the 39th Massachusetts, held the right, facing west. Griffin's three brigades (Ayres-Bartlett-Sweitzer), with Denison's brigade and subsequently those of McCandless and Fisher, facing west, occupied the left. Facing south, the brigades of Leonard and Baxter (Robinson's division) less the 39th Massachusetts, formed a connecting link between the two echelons. This description presupposes the deployment of Wright's elements on the right of the V Corps and the arrival of McCandless, followed by Fisher's brigade from the Chewning plateau.

The fact that Griffin's three brigades manned what now constituted a retired sector of the front line, while those of Wadsworth were sent to a rear position to refit, would indicate that the latter formations had suffered greater damage during the repulse than the former.[30] Such an assumption, however, must be qualified by two other considerations, namely, the proximity of the divisional trains and the sequence of arrival in the retrograde movement. The first troops

to arrive would, of necessity, have been placed in the unoccupied line of trenches. Again, Griffin's wagons were conveniently located with respect to refitting his troops in the
trenches they had constructed during the forenoon. Assuming that Wadsworth's combat train returned to its original
park near the encampment of the preceding night, the 4th
Division brigades were most conveniently situated for the
refitting process as it was actually conducted.

The disposition of Wainwright's supporting artillery brigade
had undergone little change since the emplacement of four
6-gun batteries on the crest near the Lacy house.

Upon withdrawal of Warren's infantry to the reserve
trenches, two sections of Winslow's Napoleons were placed in
position on the north side of the Turnpike, on a crest where
a little timber had been felled. At the same time, a section of
3-inch rifles from Philipps' Battery E, Massachusetts Light,
went into position on the pike "where," according to Wainwright, "it replied to and several times silenced, the enemy's
guns similarly posted at a distance of about 1,400 yards." [31]

Ewell Redeploys His Brigades

The Confederates meantime were completing dispositions,
both to meet the gathering threat against their left and to
reestablish the line that had been dislocated by Warren's attack. Steuart returned to his original line along the west edge
of Sanders' field. Walker and Stafford were drawn back to
extend the line northwestward across the Culpeper Mine Road.
Upon Wright's approach to the battle front Hays' and Pegram's
brigades of Early's Division, which had not yet been engaged,
were ordered to form on the left of Johnson's Division, Hays'
right touching Walker's left, with the left of Pegram extending toward Flat Run. Rodes' Division was posted south of the
Turnpike, the order from left to right being Battle-Doles-
Daniel. Battle occupied a part of Jones' old front and joined
Steuart's right at the Turnpike. Doles and Daniels continued
the line across Mill Branch and along the woods at the east
edge of Hagerson's farm. Gordon's scattered regiments were

assembled and placed on the extreme right of the corps front, the line being refused through the thickets south of Hagerson's clearing. Jones' brigade, according to Ewell, was withdrawn to reform. It entrenched along a line drawn diagonally across the Turnpike and about one-half mile to the rear.[32]

The Confederate II Corps occupied a total front of approximately 2,700 yards. While the left was withdrawn to meet the impending attack of Wright's VI Corps column, the right of the line was advanced in a manner roughly corresponding to the Federal withdrawal south of the Turnpike. Ewell, in fact, threw forward his right center in a flat salient, the center of which occupied a point somewhat in advance of the position originally occupied by Jones' right. The order of brigades from right to left was Gordon (Early's Division); Daniel-Doles-Battle (Rodes' Division); Steuart-Stafford-Walker (Johnson's Division); Hays-Pegram (Early's Division). Jones' badly-mauled brigade furnished the sole reserve of Ewell's extensive line. Orders were issued to entrench.[33]

Some of the guns of Nelson's artillery battalion, as already noted, were moving into position as Warren launched his attack. This is described as "a commanding ridge, with a small field in front, about 1 mile from the Lacy house." Gordon's statement that Confederate batteries were withdrawing under fire as he advanced would indicate that Nelson could not have completed his disposition in time to have rendered effective aid in the repulse. A position for two guns of the same artillery unit was found on the Culpeper Mine Road to support the left.[34]

In all, disregarding casualties and estimating the average strength of brigades, Ewell had approximately 13,500 bayonets in line and reserve, together with 76 guns, an unstated number of which were actually in position. In opposition, Warren and Sedgwick together (not counting Getty's 3 brigades with Hancock) had a total force of 38,800 bayonets and 96 available guns.

Wright, with 4 brigades approximating 8,900 bayonets, was

approaching Ewell's left front. Seven V Corps brigades were entrenched facing Ewell's center and right. Fisher's brigade was still on the Chewning plateau. Wadsworth's three brigades more than counter-balanced Ewell's slender reserve of one brigade—Jones'. In addition, Ricketts' two-brigade division, VI Corps, was on the march to the front. The number of V and VI Corps bayonets disposable for attack is, however, in no way indicated by such a computation. While all but two of Ewell's II brigades* had been heavily engaged, only one—Jones'—was temporarily *hors de combat*. Ewell therefore had ten brigades (13,535 bayonets) fit for defensive action. Excluding on the Federal side the six of Griffin and Wadsworth, along with Denison's Maryland brigade, all of which had been badly mauled, Warren disposed of only four brigades counting about 8,400 bayonets capable of immediate offensive action. Including Fisher's brigade, these four, together with the four VI Corps brigades in Wright's approaching column, gave 17,365 bayonets for renewal of the offensive against Ewell's 13,500. Thus the Federal preponderance did not greatly differ from the one that applied at noon.

In the event of meeting a second attack, Ewell enjoyed two distinct advantages. His smashing repulse of Warren's assault had enabled him to improve the position he had successfully defended. Again, while Wright's column constituted a strong reinforcement, the victorious Confederate brigades had little to fear in a renewal of the offensive by the formations they had handily repulsed. Then the stimulus of victory was equivalent to a large reinforcement, counter-balancing in its effect the one offered by Wright.

Griffin Speaks His Piece

Although history affords more than one example of beaten troops returning to the attack and rescuing victory from the jaws of defeat, the performance of such a deed requires some-

---

* Ramseur's Brigade, Rodes' Division, plus three regiments from other II Corps formations had not as yet returned from the reconnaissance toward Culpeper Court House. Hoke's Brigade, Early's Division, was still in detachment from the Army of Northern Virginia.

MAP 11. SEDGWICK CARRIES THE ATTACK TO EWELL'S LEFT

This shows Wright's advance to the attack at about 3 p.m., May 5. Warren's division
been pulled back, and Ricketts is marching down the Germanna Plank Road, off the
p to the north.

thing of the ardor called forth by Henry V at Harfleur:

"Once more unto the breach, dear friends, once more;
Or close the wall up with our English dead."

The drama of Harfleur and Agincourt was not to be re-enacted in the Wilderness. The confidence of V Corps troop leaders in the high command had been seriously impaired. Griffin's angry outburst at army headquarters that afternoon portrays the temper of many of his fellow officers. It offers a fitting conclusion to the abortive offensive of Warren's V Corps.

After placing his broken brigades in the reserve trenches, Griffin called for his horse and, accompanied by George Bernard, V Corps mustering officer, rode back to army headquarters. Dismounting, he strode unceremoniously into Meade's tent, where U. S. Grant, Rawlins, his adjutant general, and other staff officers were assembled.

Eyes darkly bloodshot and his stern features burning with an angry flush, Griffin demanded to know why his division had been left in the lurch.[35]

Given no answer by the startled assemblage, he charged in harsh tones that after he had driven Ewell three-quarters of a mile, Wadsworth broke on his left and Wright failed to come up with his VI Corps troops on the right. Both flanks in the air, he added bitterly, his Regulars cut to pieces, he had been completed to retreat. The censure implied criticism of Warren and Sedgwick, to say nothing of the army commander.

Incensed at Griffin's disrespect to the Supreme Commander, Rawlins wrathfully denounced the general's language as mutinous and demanded that he be put under arrest. Grant, although indifferent to the niceties of military etiquette, was not disposed to tolerate an act of insubordination. Rising and turning to Meade, he asked: "Who is this General Gregg? Why don't you arrest him?"

Resentful, perhaps of the suggestion as another of the many infringements he had suffered during the day on his command prerogative, Meade quietly intervened on behalf of the irate division commander.

In gaining his feet, Grant began fastening the buttons of his blouse the better to support his dignity. Meade arose from his camp chair and, seeking as it were to placate an angry child with soothing words, replied: "It's not Gregg but Griffin." Then, assisting the Supreme Commander with his buttons, he added: "And it's only his way of talking:"[36]

Grant fastened the middle button without further comment. Resuming his seat, he lit a fresh cigar and lapsed into meditation. Silence settled over the group of distinguished officers. The manner of General Griffin's exit is not recorded.

CHAPTER 12

GRANT STRIVES TO MOUNT A GENERAL ATTACK

Driven to exasperation by Warren's delay in assembling his attack force astride the turnpike, Grant resolved to hasten the regroupment ordered at 10:30 a.m. and transform the V Corps movement into a general assault. The objective was Lee's partially formed line of deployment. Hancock would carry the attack against the Confederate left, while Sedgwick pushed Wright's four-brigade column forward, connecting on Warren's right and engaging the extreme left of Lee's line.

It was evident by 10:30 that Lee had penetrated the Wilderness in greater force than Meade had suspected at 7:30, when he suspended his march to the designated line of deployment and ordered Warren to attack on the Turnpike. The series of orders issued at 10:30 through army headquarters indicate an intent to push back enemy forces on both the Orange Turnpike and the Orange Plank Road, while Sedgwick's VI and Hancock's II Corps converged on the right and left, respectively, of the V Corps attack column.

Changed Orders to Hancock Go Astray

At noon it became apparent that Getty's division (less Neill's brigade), which had been detached from the VI Corps column and sent to clear the Plank Road toward Parker's Store, lacked sufficient strength to carry out its mission. Army headquarters thereupon instructed Hancock to support Getty's advance from the Brock-Orange Plank Road crossing and connect with Warren's left on the Chewning plateau. Issued an hour and a half after Hancock had been ordered to the Brock Crossing, the order to attack with Getty out the Plank Road marks Grant's final abandonment of his turning movement on the Catharpin Road. But in electing to fight the battle he hoped to avoid, the Supreme Commander had no intention of surrendering the initiative to his adversary. He turned fiercely on Lee, determined to destroy the Army of Northern Virginia while it was completing its deployment.

Couched in these terms, the revised instruction given Hancock at noon reveal a determination to time the advance on Parker's Store with Warren's thrust on the Turnpike. The issuance, 45 minutes later, of orders to Sedgwick disclose a purpose to intensify the attack against Ewell. At 12:45 p.m. Sedgwick received instructions to hold Ricketts' division, VI Corps, in readiness on the Germanna Plank Road to move either toward Warren or Wright.[1]

The prospects of launching a general offensive in conjunction with Warren's attack depended upon rapidity of movement in the process of regroupment on the right and left, as ordered at 10:30 a.m., and a smashing climax to Warren's attack in the center. Grant's hopes were doomed to disappointment, both as to the celerity of movement he expected and the success of Warren's movement which, he thought, should have resulted from so much meticulous and time-consuming preparations.

On the right, Hancock at 11:40 a.m. received Meade's directive of 10:30 to proceed to the Brock Crossing. That is, the courier was an hour and ten minutes on the road between army headquarters and Todd's Tavern. The II Corps commander promptly acknowledged receipt of the message and stated that he would move as ordered and report his arrival at the Crossing.[2]

After giving the necessary instructions to put his troops in motion, Hancock, accompanied by Lieutenant Colonel C. H. Morgan, his chief of staff, and a cavalcade of aides and mounted orderlies, set out at a smart pace on the Brock Road. Upon arrival at the Crossing, Hancock conferred with General Getty, while Colonel Morgan rode on to report at army headquarters. It is not known whether Hancock sent his message time-dated at 11:40 from Todd's Tavern by a staff galloper or gave it to Morgan for delivery. The message was marked

"Received 1:30 p.m." At any rate, Morgan soon appeared and gave his verbal report.

The substance of Morgan's report to the army commander is largely conjectural. Two important items, however, are revealed by subsequent developments. It appeared that the courier bearing Meade's dispatch sent at noon and instructing Hancock to support Getty's attack toward Parker's Store, had gone astray. Therefore Hancock was still acting under the instructions issued at 10:30 a.m. and would continue to do so for the better part of another hour. Meade's chagrin was in no way mollified at this juncture by delivery of a report from V Corps headquarters that Griffin's division had been repulsed. The irate army commander dashed off a message to Hancock time-dated at 1:30 p.m., explaining that Getty had been sent to the Crossing with orders to drive back a force of Confederate infantry reported on the Orange Plank Road but that he lacked sufficient force to justify an attack.[3] Therefore Hancock must carry out the order sent at noon. Immediate action was urged in view of the situation on the Orange Turnpike: Griffin had been driven back; Crawford might be recalled, or driven from his position on the Chewning plateau.

Meade's prompt action in attempting to overcome the consequence of faulty communications fell short of resolving the situation. Unless it is assumed that Meade, like Warren, had been goaded to distraction by Grant's inexorable determination to force the pace of events, the decisions taken at army headquarters during the next two hours seem incomprehensible.

Whatever the nature of Morgan's report, Meade as well as Grant should have been aware that the II Corps divisions were disposed at 11:40 a.m. in the manner described by Hancock in his message acknowledging Meade's order to suspend the advance on Shady Grove Church while awaiting subsequent developments. In drafting this acknowledgment at 9:40 a.m. Hancock stated that Gibbon's and Birney's divisions were at Todd's Tavern. Mott was to halt in column on the Furnace Road, with his advance at the Brock-Furnace Road intersection, while Barlow would close up in column to Catharine

Furnace. The order of march, front to rear in proceeding to the Brock Crossing, would be Birney-Mott-Gibbon-Barlow.

Whether or not Meade was aware of the proposed order of march, he knew the distribution of Hancock's four divisional elements at the precise moment of the turnabout. These data alone should have enabled him to establish a fairly reliable estimate of the time Hancock would require in completing his concentration at the Crossing and forming his four divisions in battle lines. While the leading division would reach the Crossing about one hour after commencement of the movement, it would be unreasonable to expect that Barlow's rear division, the strongest numerically in the corps, could close up and form in battle order much before 6 o'clock.

Meade Miscalculates

It therefore seems incredible that a tactician of Meade's ability—one described by Lee on the eve of Gettysburg as a general who would make few mistakes—should have construed the reported presence of Hancock's headquarters party at Brock Crossing as equivalent to a heavy attack column standing in readiness to attack. Yet just such a miscalculation was made. The extent of Grant's participation in this blunder cannot be determined. But it should be realized in this connection that since 10:30 a.m. the terms "army" and "general headquarters" were synonymous if not interchangeable.

At 2:15 p.m., just 15 minutes after the time that a reasonable calculation would have established the appearance of Hancock's leading division at the Crossing, Meade informed Warren that: "General Ricketts has been ordered to report to you and will be up immediately. Hancock is up at the Orange Plank road and will attack immediately. Getty will be brought to your support, if necessary, as soon as Hancock is ready. Hancock will endeavor to connect with your left. Regiment of cavalry is sent." [4]

Then assuming that Hancock was about to attack in accordance with his orders of noon and 1:30 p.m., Meade again took occasion to prod the II Corps commander. Without mentioning the conditional promise of Getty's three brigades to Warren, "if necessary," he recounted developments in the V Corps sector that gave greater urgency to the need of striking a heavy blow against the Confederate left. The army commander related that: "Wadsworth's division, on Griffin's left, has been driven in, and Crawford's division has been called in so that his line is thrown back considerably. His left must be more than a mile in rear of where it was before. Its exact position is not reported yet; will send you as soon as it is known." [5]

Faulty Communications

Faulty communications continued to vex both Meade and Hancock. Arriving at the Brock Crossing without knowledge of developments on the Turnpike and unaware that he was expected to support the attack toward Parker's Store, Hancock found General Getty his only source of information. Unfortunately Getty could contribute little, his knowledge being restricted to the local situation. Furthermore his evaluation of this situation left much to be desired. He was convinced that two divisions of A. P. Hill's Confederate III Corps were in his immediate front. Opposed by such a force, he had entrenched instead of attacking as originally ordered to do. All efforts to open communication with Warren's left had failed. Unless given powerful support Getty advised against moving on Hill's riflemen lurking in the thickets. He impressed on Hancock that he momentarily expected an attack.[6]

Judging by Hancock's dispositions the II Corps commander seemed inclined to accept Getty's estimate of the situation. At 2 p.m. a heavy dust cloud arose above the tree tops to the south. Then a thick column of sweltering infantry came in view in the narrow lane between the opposing forest walls. Spurring forward, General Birney reported to his corps commander. Birney received instructions to form in line on Getty's left and start entrenching. An hour passed as Birney's breastworks rose like magic. Another dust column heralded the approach of Mott's division. Upon reporting, Mott was ordered to form on Birney's left and continue the line of breastworks leftward.

Hancock Finally Gets Meade's Changed Orders

At 2:40 p.m. a galloper from army headquarters delivered Meade's dispatch of 1:30. It is interesting to note that this message was one hour and ten minutes in transit and that the time between dispatch and delivery was identical to that of the message sent by Meade at 10:30 a.m. to Hancock at Todd's Tavern. The distance between army headquarters and Todd's Tavern was over twice the distance that Meade's galloper covered in carrying the dispatch of 1:30 to Hancock at the Crossing. As Hancock was digesting the message, a weary dust-covered rider appeared with another dispatch. Hancock broke the seal and read Meade's message of noon. He immediately acknowledged both communications, stating:

> Your dispatches of 12 p.m. and 1:30 p.m. received. I am forming my corps on Getty's left, and will order an advance as soon as prepared. The ground over which I must pass is very bad—a perfect thicket. I shall [form] two divisions with brigade front. General Getty says he has not heard of Warren's left, probably because he has not advanced far enough.[7]

The formation proposed by Hancock at 2:40 p.m. clearly indicates that Getty and Birney were to attack in column of brigades, Getty on the right, Birney on the left, with Mott in reserve. That is, the two assault divisions were to advance on a two-brigade front, both divisional elements having uniform columns of three brigades in depth. Mott's two-brigade division would stand in reserve.

Twenty minutes later Hancock received intelligence from army headquarters. This was conveyed in Meade's dispatch of 2:15 p.m., the contents of which have already been quoted. It will be recalled that Meade apprised Hancock of the disaster that had befallen Warren. Griffin's division had met a bloody repulse. Wadsworth's division had been broken and thrown back. Crawford's division had been recalled. While it was admitted that the left of the V Corps could not be definitely located, army headquarters thought that the precise position would soon be determined. There was no reference to the dispatch transmitted at the same time, 2:15 p.m., to V Corps headquarters, informing Warren that the II Corps would attack "immediately" and that Getty's three brigades would, if required, be sent to him.

Replying at 3 p.m. to Meade's dispatch of 2:15, Hancock informed army headquarters that General Getty, in conjunction with two II Corps divisions would attack as soon as the troops can get into position. He added: "I shall keep one division on their [Getty's] left and keep one division in reserve in rear of the advancing divisions. The objective point is Parker's Store." [8] The formation here is identical to the one described at 2:40 p.m.

The courier carrying Hancock's dispatch of 3 p.m. was cantering northward on the Brock Road when Lieutenant Colonel Lyman left army headquarters with orders from Meade requiring that Hancock and Getty attack at once. In addition to hustling Hancock into action without regard to the state of his preparations (one suspects the influence of Grant in this demand), Meade specified the attack formation— one II Corps division on Getty's right, another on his left, and two divisions in reserve, "or such other dispositions as you may think proper." [9]

Hancock so construed Meade's directive as to limit his latitude of discretion to formation of the reserve force. Since the two divisions that were to constitute this reserve were still in column of march, the employment of these elements would be governed by the situation on the battle front as they successively arrived at the scene of action. Therefore, the II Corps commander had no discretionary authority. His subsequent dispositions for the action clearly establishes that he regarded Meade's direction to attack on a front of three divisions as mandatory.

Troops Available for Attack

While general headquarters labored under the delusion

that Hancock could deliver a powerful assault against the Confederate right at or shortly after 2:15, Warren was planning with the assumption that an attack force of nine fresh brigades would be placed at his disposal for renewal of the operation against Lee's left. The promise of Getty's three brigades, together with the two from Ricketts' division, gave the V Corps commander five brigades as replacements for the seven mauled by Ewell. After assigning these seven units— Denison's Maryland brigade, Robinson's division, and the 6 of Griffin's and Wadsworth's divisions—Warren had, in addition to the five promised replacements, four V Corps brigades that had not yet been engaged, namely Leonard's and Baxter's brigades of Robinson's division and the two of Crawford's division. In all, Warren tentatively had 9 fresh brigade units for renewal of the assault against Ewell's front.

All but two of Ewell's brigades had been heavily engaged. Furthermore, the junction with Sedgwick's four-brigade column on Warren's right was now an imminent probability instead of a remote possibility, as was the case when Warren struck at 1 p.m. Finally, when Upton, on the left of Wright's advancing column, made the connection at 3 o'clock on the north side of Sanders' field, and Meade so informed Warren, Grant directed Burnside to place one of his IX Corps divisions at Sedgwick's disposal. Burnside immediately instructed General Potter, commanding the 2d Division, to hold his two brigades subject to orders of the VI Corps commander. Thus, according to the plan momentarily entertained at general headquarters for the operation against Lee's left, 15 fresh Federal brigades were opposed to the 11 available to Ewell, some of which showed symptoms of battle fatigue.

The decision taken by Grant at 3 p.m. to employ a IX Corps division in the movement against the right of Ewell's line reveals a conviction that the junction of the V and VI Corps lines was of decisive importance in development of the general offensive and should be exploited with vigor and determination. A show, at least, of determination was not long in coming.

Meade Sends Peremptory Orders

At 4:05 p.m. Lyman reached II Corps headquarters with Meade's attack orders. The orders he delivered held both Hancock and Getty individually responsible for delivering the attack at once.

The relationship between events on the Federal right and dispatch of peremptory orders demanding offensive action on the left can be understood only in terms of the persistent misunderstanding that pervaded general and army headquarters in regard to the disposition of Hancock's divisional units between 11:40 a.m. and 3:15 p.m. It will be recalled that Meade assured Warren at 2:15 that Hancock was "up at the Orange Plank Road and will attack immediately." As already noted, the leading division, Birney's, was "up" at the time of the promised attack. It was not until 2:40 that Hancock received the two dispatches sent from army headquarters, instructing the II Corps commander to support Getty's attack and connect with Warren's left. Thus during the three hours between 11:40 a.m. and 2:40 p.m. Hancock had no instructions other than those conveyed to him at Todd's Tavern in Meade's dispatch of 10:30 a.m.

Although Meade's knowledge of the positions taken by Hancock's four divisions in consequence of the order to suspend the advance on Shady Grove Church should have ruled out the false assumption he so rashly adopted at 2:15, namely that Hancock would "attack immediately" on the Orange Plank Road, Meade was obsessed until 3:15 by his fatal miscalculation. No doubt Grant shared the mood if, indeed, he was not responsible for its instigation.

Between 2:15 and 3:15 Hancock, as already related, sent two dispatches to army headquarters, reporting on his situation at the crossing and describing the preparations he had in mind for the attack. In view of the fact that the time for transmission of messages by courier between army and II Corps headquarters ranged from 45 to 70 minutes, it is doubtful if either of Hancock's dispatches reached army headquar-

ters before issuance of the peremptory order at 3:15 to attack on the Plank Road. Then the element of doubt is removed by the fact that Meade prescribed an attack formation
which disregarded the one described by Hancock in his second
dispatch. Meade therefore was still dominated by the false
assumption that prompted his message of 2:15 to Warren.
While Hancock stated that two II Corps divisions would advance with Getty, one on the right, the other following in
support, Meade directed that one of his divisions form on
Getty's right, another on the left, with the remaining divisions
in reserve.

The manner in which Lyman delivered Meade's directive
of 3:15 p.m. was most unusual. In accordance with instruction
given at army headquarters, Lyman conveyed to Getty an
order to attack at once and at the same time informed the
general in confidence that the II Corps would move in his
support. Then, after delivering the confidential message to
Getty, the *aide de camp* presented a written order [the partial
contents of which have been mentioned] to the II Corps commander. Hancock read the message:

> The commanding general directs that Getty attack at once
> and that you support him with your whole corps, one division
> on his right and one division on his left, the others in reserve;
> or such other dispositions as you may think proper, but the
> attack up the plank road must be made at once.

Three aspects of this amazing procedure reveal an attitude
at superior headquarters that tends to dissipate the confidence
of subordinate field commanders in the quality of leadership
essential to victory. In the first place, Meade issued the order
in ignorance of the fact that two of the four divisions which
were to attack "at once" were still in column of march. Again,
unless Hancock had by some occult process managed to anticipate the attack formation prescribed by Meade, he faced the
dangerous alternative of redeploying his units under fire.
Finally, it complicated the relationship between two general
officers pursuing the same objective but commanding troops
of separate organizations. Instead of assigning Getty's VI Corps

division to the II Corps command, army headquarters gave Getty to understand that his compliance with orders would determine Hancock's course of action. In other words, the conduct of the junior general officer would largely determine that of the senior general. Fortunately for Hancock, Getty was not the sort of soldier who would seek personal advantage in such a situation. His bearing both before and after his assignment to Hancock's command for the attack on the 6th was that of a loyal subordinate.

Warren Denied Promised Reinforcements

Dispatch of the orders that sent Getty and Hancock forward on the left cancelled three of the five brigades promised Warren. This reduction left Warren with six fresh brigades, two of which were still in the category of promised reinforcements.

Whatever reasons the high command may have had for committing Getty to the Plank Road operation, they do not appear in any of the dispatches emanating from general or army headquarters between 3 and 4 p.m. It is apparent, however, that the motive for this commitment, together with the stubborn resistance encountered by Sedgwick's attack force after connecting on Warren's right caused a change of mood at general headquarters that gradually receded from the optimism prevailing at 3 p.m.

Delivery of Hancock's dispatches of 2:40 and 3 p.m. did not improve the situation. The second message was particularly disconcerting. The text clearly established that only two of Hancock's divisions were in position for the attack. Instead of a power drive of five divisions, three would move against the two Confederate divisions of A. P. Hill's III Corps, both of which were thought to be available for defense of the Plank Road ridge. Then want of progress in the attack of VI Corps troops on Warren's right called for reinforcements. Seymour's brigade of Ricketts' division was sent to Sedgwick. Of the five promised brigades only one, Morris' of Ricketts' division, went to Warren.

With Hancock's advance impending, the Supreme Commander made his final effort to throw the Army of the Potomac forward in a coordinated assault. At 4 p.m. Warren was alerted by an order from Meade stating:

> General Getty is ordered to attack up the Orange Plank Road. General Hancock to attack with him, one division on his right, the other on his left. The major-general commanding directs that you make dispositions to renew the attack, if practicable. General Hancock has just been heard from and will soon attack. You will have one brigade of Ricketts' besides Robinson and Crawford, who have not been engaged.[10]

Meade's enumeration of the units available to Warren totaled five fresh brigades. That is, he had four less than the number originally allotted. His attack force was smaller by two brigades than the one he threw in at 1 p.m. A grant of discretionary power to a general whose command had been so drastically reduced was hardly an effective method of enlisting his cooperation.

General Offensive Bogs Down

The latitude of discretion given the V Corps commander marks the breakdown of Grant's effort to mount a general offensive during the afternoon of May 5. The nature of any dispositions that may have been made in anticipation of the attack foreshadowed by Meade's instructions are not known. Warren makes no mention of such dispositions in his Journal. Nor did army headquarters send directions for an attack before 6 p.m. This order, however, was issued in reference to a situation that had no connection with the one Grant was endeavoring to exploit between 1:30 and 4 p.m.

Failure to throw forward the center in accordance with the plan entertained at 4 p.m. for a general attack must be shared by general and army headquarters. It seems unreasonable to saddle any considerable part of the blame on Warren. Had there been any reason to believe that success was dependent on the participation of Warren's troops, the order to V Corps headquarters should have been mandatory, leaving no discretion to the V Corps commander. Both Grant and Meade were on the scene. A determination to overrule any apathy at V Corps headquarters could have been speedily accomplished by Grant's appearance at the Lacy house. If apathy existed, then Grant himself had become a party to the mood.

With Warren quiescent, and Wright making little or no headway after his initial contact with the left of Ewell's line, the storm center of battle shifted to the left of the Federal line, where Hancock and Getty were moving out to crush Lee's right astride the Plank Road ridge.

CHAPTER 13

HANCOCK ASSAULTS THE PLANK ROAD RIDGE

The order delivered by Lieutenant Colonel Lyman to General Getty brooked no delay. The II Corps commander was instructed that "the attack up the Plank Road must be made at once." These two orders, therefore, were positive and final, putting responsibility for compliance separately upon each general officer.[1]

A cool man, General Getty pondered the order and heard the confidential explanation that Hancock would support him. Turning to his aides he said: "Go to General Eustis and General Wheaton and tell them to prepare to advance at once." [2]

Getty Forms For Attack

Getty's attack column was quickly formed in two lines of battle. Colonel Lewis A. Grant's 2d Brigade, composed of five Vermont regiments, went into position on the left; Wheaton's 1st Brigade held the center; and Eustis' 4th Brigade occupied the right. Wheaton's left and Grant's right connected at the Plank Road.[3] The order of regiments, right to left, in the first line of Eustis' brigade was the 2d Rhode Island-10th Massachusetts; in the second line, the order was 37th Massachusetts-7th Massachusetts. Continuing from right to left there were, in Wheaton's first line, the 62d New York-139th Pennsylvania-102d Pennsylvania; in his second line the 93d Pennsylvania-98th Pennsylvania; in Grant's first line, the 4th-3d, in the second line the 2d-6th, with the 5th Vermont regiment in brigade reserve.[4]

Having no artillery with his three-brigade column Getty was reinforced by Ricketts' Battery F, 1st Pennsylvania Light Artillery, II Corps. Brockway's and Snider's sections went into

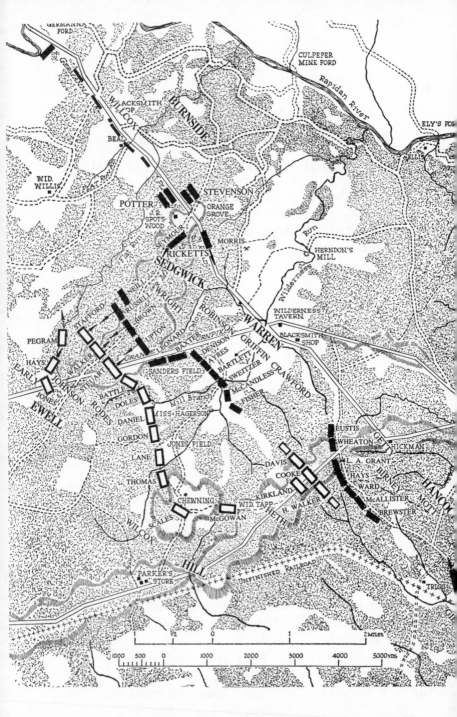

MAP 12. HANCOCK FORMS FOR THE PLANK ROAD ATTACK

The situation at about 4 p.m., May 5. Wright is making no progress in his attack again Johnson. Hancock, under orders to move against the Confederate right flank, is formi Getty, Birney, and Mott for an advance astride the Plank Road.

The position of Wadsworth's division is not plotted on this map, but it is mass position at the Brock-Plank Road intersection to support Getty's advance.[5]

The attack formation of Birney's 3d and Mott's 4th Divisions of the II Corps cannot be reconstructed on a basis of any authoritative evidence. Hancock, as we know, had originally intended to form two divisions with brigade front. This was at 2:40 p.m., as Birney was taking position on Getty's left and beginning to entrench. Mott came up on Birney's left and also began to entrench.[6] Since both the 3d and 4th Divisions numbered only two brigades each, it seems reasonable to conclude that Hancock had in mind a formation of two divisions in line, that is, abreast of one another, with each division in column of brigades, or one brigade in rear of the other. Then, replying at 3 p.m. to Meade's order to push on out the Plank Road and connect with Warren, the II Corps commander states that he intended, when ready, to attack in conjunction with Getty, keeping one of these divisions on Getty's left and "one division in reserve in rear of advancing divisions." [7]

The execution of such a maneuver would have required Mott to form by obliquing or moving directly by his right through the woods to a line in front of Birney; or Birney to move out to the front from his trenches, thereby making room for Mott to shift by his right into Birney's original position. But there is nothing in Hancock's dispatches or reports to indicate how he intended to execute the manuever in question.

Upon receipt at 4:05 p.m. of the final peremptory order to attack, with one II Corps division on Getty's left, another on his right, and to hold the others in reserve, Hancock was confronted with the problem of executing a difficult maneuver on short notice. Although two of his divisions were still in march column, he considered that Meade's order left him no discretion but that he must attack with the two divisions in hand. He instructed Birney to move by the right from his position between Getty and Mott, and then connect on the right of Getty's moving line of battle. Mott in turn received instructions to leave his trenches and rush through the woods at a right oblique until he joined Getty's left. With Getty in motion toward the enemy, the maneuver was a dangerous one. A double shift by the two II Corps divisions not only uncovered Getty's left at the jumpoff but involved the risk of bringing up the supporting formations on both flanks in broken lines, thus diminishing the impetus they might otherwise have lent the final shock, or so reducing their firepower, in the event of an enemy counterattack, as to become ineffective or even harmful.

Heth Disposed for Defense

After developing Getty's position at the Brock-Plank crossroads shortly after noon, Heth's four-brigade division had taken up a defensive position astride the Plank Road and about one-half mile from the Crossing. The order by brigades, left to right, was Davis-Cooke-Walker. Kirkland's Brigade formed in reserve. Falling back on the main body of Heth's Division after his brush with Getty at noon, Cooke occupied the center of the divisional line, with his right center on the Plank Road. The order, left to right, of Cooke's four North Carolina regiments was the 48th-27th-46th-15th. Company B of the 46th stood in the road; Company A held the right of the regimental line, on the south side of the road, the left of the brigade line extending northward towards Davis, the right southward toward Walker. The order of Walker's four Virginia units, the 40th, 47th, 55th regiments and the 22d Virginia Battalion, is not stated. Little is known concerning Davis' formation. The 55th North Carolina occupied the right center of the brigade line. Of the three remaining regiments, the 2d, 11th, and 42d Mississippi, two were formed on the left of the 55th North Carolina, one on the right and connecting with the left regiment of Cooke's Brigade—the 48th North Carolina.[8]

Occupying a front of 12 regiments, as opposed to Getty's front of 7 regiments, and overlapping Getty's line on both flanks at the initial collision, the three brigades of Davis,

Cooke, and Walker were formed in a single line. Supporting this first-line formation were four North Carolina regiments of Kirkland's Brigade.[9] These units (11th-26th-44th-47th) were placed in line of battle astride the Plank Road. The left of the 44th touched the road. The 52d North Carolina, of Kirkland's Brigade, was detached to guard the trains at Parker's Store. A single field gun from Poague's Battalion constituted Heth's artillery support. This piece was put in position along the Plank Road, immediately in rear of Kirkland's Brigade; probably it was subsequently reinforced by two additional pieces. Major C. M. Stedman, official historian of the 44th North Carolina, Kirkland's brigade, states that a detail of forty men of the 44th hauled these three pieces to a point of safety after the gun teams had been killed and that the officer commanding the detail, Lieutenant R. W. Stedman, was mentioned in an official order issued by Headquarters, Heth's Division.[10]

Heth mustered some 6,700 effectives, as opposed to Getty's three-brigade attack column of about 7,200. With the added weight of the two II Corps divisions (4 brigades of about 9,700 bayonets), the total available striking force on the Federal left aggregated about 17,000.[11] Although outnumbered slightly by Getty alone and overbalanced numerically by more than 2 to 1 after the arrival of Hancock's two leading divisions, Heth had succeeded in imposing upon Getty and Hancock to an extent that both Federal generals continued to labor under a conviction that they faced an imminent and overwhelming Confederate attack. Even after the battle joined on the Plank Road, Hancock carried on the defensive precaution of extending his field works to the left; with musketry thundering far away in the woods to their right front, various units of Gibbon's and Barlow's divisions went to work with pick, ax, and shovel as they successively came up on the line.[12]

The deception betrayed here would argue that Heth's skirmishers had been exceedingly active during the mid-afternoon, advancing across the narrow swales that furrowed the forest between the opposing lines and creating an impression that Lee was mounting a formidable force of attack in the depths of the woodland.

Difficult Terrain

Despite a decided preponderance of the 7 Federal brigades over the 4 of Heth, Hancock had good reasons to be apprehensive of the difficult terrain over which his troops must move. The density of the thickets, to which he calls attention in his dispatch of 2:40 p.m., was not the only obstacle. The Brock-Plank road intersection stands on a flat summit (see Map 11). This slight elevation, in fact, marks the intersection of the two ridges traversed by the Plank and Brock Roads. Going southwestward from the Brock Crossing, the Plank Road traverses a low ridge dividing the basin of Wilderness Run from the upper tributaries of the Pamunkey River system.

In centering attention on the topography of the immediate area traversed by the Plank Road and lying between the main opposing lines of Hancock and Heth, it will be observed that the Plank Road extends across a shallow saddle, some quarter of a mile in length. The headwaters of the east branches of Wilderness Run originate along the narrowing rim of the saddle to the north of the road; these little streams cut furrows, or swales running diagonally across the left front of Heth's line. The headwaters of Poplar Run, originating along the rim of the saddle to the south of the road give a similar topographical conformation with respect to Heth's right front.

Although there is no positive evidence to indicate the exact location of Heth's main line, it is probable, in view of the length of time he had been allowed to form his battle line, that he should have selected the best possible defensive position. This would be the low transverse ridge, northwest and southeast in its general direction, and lying south of the Plank Road between the two main upper prongs of Poplar Run and extending north of the road between the two main north-flowing tributaries of Wilderness Run. An assumption that Heth did form his main line of battle on this ridge, with a system of rifle pits and skirmish detachments well to the front, may claim a shred of substantiating evidence, however indirect. It reconciles estimates as to the distance of Heth's position from the Brock Road jumpoff trenches, from an eighth to three-quarters of a mile.

Attack is Launched

About 4 p.m. Getty's skirmishers disappeared into the woods and aroused sharp fire from Heth's restless pickets.[13] From the right of the divisional front the 2d Rhode Island and 10th Massachusetts of Eustis' first line moved out by right of companies. The short, parallel columns pushed slowly through the thicket a distance of about half a mile, when the swelling roar of musketry to the front indicated that their skirmishers had struck the enemy's main line. Squads rushed forward, filling the intervals between the columns and dressing their line on the right. Colors and officers passed the front; with closed ranks, the line of battle charged into the fire of Heth's riflemen.

"At this juncture," relates Lieutenant Colonel J. B. Parsons, commanding the 10th Massachusetts, "the regiment on our right (2d Rhode Island) gave way, and we received a destructive fire on the right flank, in addition to the fire in front." The 10th stood firm, holding its ground until ammunition ran low. As the situation became desperate, the 37th Massachusetts came up, relieved the hard-pressed regiment, and took up its fight on the firing line. Though broken, according to Lieutenant Colonel Parsons, the 2d Rhode Island appears to have rallied and held. Its supporting regiment, the 37th Massachusetts, did not become engaged.[14]

Wheaton's brigade, at the center, went forward in two lines of battle. The left flank, on the Plank Road, was supported by a section of Ricketts' battery. An eighth of a mile out in the woods, according to General Wheaton, his skirmishers became warmly engaged. The first line of battle pushed on, absorbing its scattered skirmish units and advancing over a series of low parallel ridges, separated by marshy swales.[15] Reaching the crest of one of these flat ridges, the Federal line was riven by a volley. The impact was terrific; the three regiments were staggered, company units sprawling in disorder. But battle flags pressed to the front, and officers exhorted their men to dress on the colors and reform the line. "The position," says Wheaton, "was held, the men keeping up a steady fire on the enemy, who occupied a crest not 50 yards in front." A desperate fire-fight raged on through the afternoon. The resolute brigadier adds:

> For nearly an hour the fighting was incessant, and the loss proportionately great, but the enemy was too strongly posted, and could not be dislodged. When the ammunition was exhausted by the troops in front, the first line was relieved by the second, which retained the advanced position until nearly 6 o'clock, when it was relieved by a portion of the Second Corps. Each regiment had suffered terribly, almost altogether from musketry, and we learned from prisoners that our division had been fighting the whole of A. P. Hill's Corps.[16]

General Wheaton's report of the operation is amplified, in regard to certain important details of the action, by that of Major Thomas McLaughlin, 102d Pennsylvania, who advanced on the left of the first line of battle. Major McLaughlin records that:

> About 3 p.m. the One Hundred and Second Pennsylvania Volunteers relieved the One Hundred and Thirty-ninth Pennsylvania Volunteers in the front line of battle. Shortly after the line was advanced the skirmishers, under Lieutenant Cooper, became engaged and lost heavily. The line pressed steadily forward for about three-quarters of a mile, crossing a swamp under a destructive fire. On reaching the crest of a hill, the regiment halted and continued firing, losing very heavily until about 6 p.m., when the ammunition being exhausted the regiment was relieved and retired to the second line and were supplied with ammunition. Loss in killed and wounded, 119.[17]

As the right and center of the division moved out on the north side of the Plank Road, with a section of Ricketts' battery in support, Colonel Grant's Vermont brigade went forward on the left, with its right flank at the Plank Road.

The Vermonters were massed for a quick, smashing blow, two regiments in the front line, two in the second, and one held in reserve. Colonel Grant's formation was well adapted to the requirements of the situation—a flexible column with a narrow front and a reserve in hand to meet the unforeseen contingencies of forest fighting. Here Grant anticipated the tactical masterpiece that Longstreet improvised the next day and that enabled the I Confederate Corps to turn the tide on a stricken field and throw back in utter confusion a force two-fold stronger than its own. But a grave misunderstanding of orders—one almost inseparable from the difficulties of forest warfare—marred the operation. The skirmish line on the left front of the brigade held fast as the skirmishers covering the right went forward with those in advance of Wheaton's and Eustis' brigades. Grant explains that it was doubtless owing to the want of a prompt communication of the order along the skirmish line. "Captain Ormsbee," he points out, "was at the time attending to his duties near the right of the line. The ground was covered with brush and small timber, so dense that it was impossible for an officer at any point of the line to see any other point several yards distant.[18]

The clash of hostile skirmish lines was brief and spasmodic, the Confederates giving ground rapidly before Grant's advance. The 4th, on the right, pushed out rapidly, keeping its flank to the road. The 3d, after running over its skirmishers, lost direction and obliqued off to the left, leaving a dangerous gap in the front line. Advancing straight across the saddle, with Wheaton's first line on the north side of the road and the artillery section following along the highway, the 4th Vermont joined battle with the main line of the division. The artillery came into action and firing became general along the front of the three brigades. As the front line engaged, Grant's 2d and 6th Regiments moved up to support the 4th and 3d, respectively. Grant describes a fire-fight almost identical to the one raging on the north side of the road.

> As soon as the first volleys were over, our men hugged the ground as closely as possible, and kept up a rapid fire; the enemy did the same. The rebels had the advantage of position, inasmuch as the line was partially protected by a slight swell

of ground, while ours was on nearly level ground. The attempt was made to dislodge them from that position, but the moment our men rose to advance, the rapid and constant fire of musketry cut them down with such slaughter that it was found impracticable to do more than maintain our then present position.[19]

The 3d Vermont, now isolated on the extreme left of Getty's battle front, either struck the right of Heth's main line, or became heavily engaged with forward elements of his defense system. Grant faced a precarious situation. The enemy's line overlapped his front. His left regiment was threatened with capture or annihilation. If his second line moved up to close the gap in his first, the 6th Regiment, holding the left of the second line, must advance in the face of a withering fire, and, at the same time, incur the additional risk of moving its left companies into the storm that engulfed the 3d Vermont. In such an eventuality, Grant's reserve regiment, the 5th, would be unable to avert a wholesale catastrophe, one which might involve Getty's entire division before Hancock's unready units could interfere and stem the rout.

With a skill and promptitude that equals the finest feats of troop leadership on the Wilderness field, Grant pivoted his maneuver on the left element of the second line. The 6th held fast. The 2d, on the right of the second line, obliqued to the left front and filled the interval between the 6th and the 4th, the 4th holding its original position at the south side of the Plank Road. Meantime, the isolated regiment, the 3d, fell back on the 6th, connected with its left, while the 5th moved out from reserve and connected on the left of the 3d. The line thus formed extended in a semicircle from the 4th, at the Plank Road, to the retired flank held by the 5th, the order from right to left being the 4th-2d-6th-3d-5th.

Establishment of a connected line, however, did not ensure the safety of Getty's left flank. The oblique movement of the 2d Regiment to the right of the 4th was a perilous venture—the most dangerous, perhaps, of the entire combination. According to L. A. Grant, the men of the 2d were compelled, owing to the fury of the Confederate fire, to crawl into position. And while we have no details of the movements of the other regiments, it may be inferred from the nature of the situation that all the units involved must have suffered heavily. Colonel Lewis, commanding the 5th, was wounded. Moreover, L. A. Grant's five regiments were opposed by five of Cooke and Walker, on the south side of the Plank Road—the 46th and 15th North Carolina, the 40th, 47th, and 55th Virginia Regiments, together with the 22d Virginia Battalion. Though lacking a preponderance of force for a strong counter-action, the Confederates had been securely posted, while the Vermonters, owing to their faulty start, had approached Heth's position in a scattered formation, thereby inviting severe retaliation. Furthermore both Getty and Grant fought with the conviction that they were confronted by Hill's entire Confederate corps of three divisions. Offered as a sacrifice, according to their belief, to delay an impending enemy offensive until Hancock's corps could get into position, both expected a violent blow at the weakened and retired left.

Birney Called on for Aid

L. A. Grant, after establishing his new line, called on Getty for aid. Getty, having no reserves in hand, appealed to General Birney, who had just been delegated the responsibility of directing the operations of the two II Corps divisions, his own and Mott's.

In assuming direction of the right wing and coordinating its elements with Getty's premature attack, Birney inherited a difficult situation. It will be recalled that Hancock had intended at 4:05 p.m.[20] to execute a double shift, Birney moving from the immediate left to the right of Getty's column, with Mott closing across the interval left by Birney and advancing on Getty's left. Getty's appeal for help came while the double shift of the two II Corps divisions was in progress. Birney, aware that Mott was moving toward Getty's left, would have been inclined to modify the II Corps commander's plan of throwing both brigades of Birney's division on Getty's right—

a plan which Hancock himself had regarded as mandatory. Birney, nevertheless, responded immediately to Getty's plea; Hays' 2d Brigade went on alone to connect with Getty's right; Ward's large brigade, the 1st, mustering 3,381 riffes[21] and consisting of eight regiments and the 2d Battalion, United States Sharpshooters, was retained by the attacking wing commander as a general reserve. To Grant's support Birney sent three regiments, the 40th New York, 141st Pennsylvania, and the 20th Indiana.[22]

These three regiments pushed straight out to the relief of Grant's thin, semicircular line.[23] The 141st Pennsylvania moved into the sector held by the 2d and 4th Vermont regiments, on the right of Grant's line. The 40th New York and 20th Indiana moved up within supporting distance of the 5th, precariously holding the extreme left of the Vermont line. The result is best described in Colonel Grant's own words:

> I went to Major Dudley, commanding the 5th Vermont (Colonel Lewis having been previously wounded) and called his attention to the fact that the position of the enemy in his front was less protected than it was in front of the rest of the brigade and asked him if he could, with the support of the two regiments in his rear, break the enemy's line. "I think we can," was the reply of the gallant major. I went to the commanders of these two regiments, and asked them to support the Fifth in its advance. The men rose with a cheer and answered, "We will." The order for the charge was given, and all advanced in good style, and the enemy partially gave way. The two near regiments were thrown into some confusion and soon halted and laid down, and Major Dudley, finding his regiment far in advance, and exposed to a flank fire, wisely did the same.[24]

Vermont Brigade Commended

To Grant's Vermont Brigade the Supreme Commander accorded the distinction of advancing a greater distance, consolidating and holding more ground during the violent two-day combat for possession of the Plank Road ridge than any other single brigade of the Army of the Potomac; but notwithstanding this indisputable honor, the fact remains that the 20th Indiana, one of the II Corps regiments of Ward's

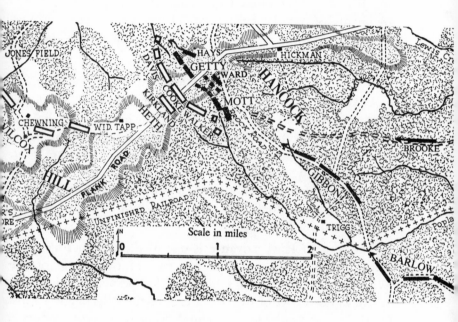

MAP 13. HANCOCK LAUNCHES THE PLANK ROAD ATTACK

Showing the situation at about 4:45 p.m., May 5. Getty goes forward
while Hancock attempts to form Birney on the right and Mott on the
left of the moving assault force. Extension of Hill's right compels
L. A. Grant to throw his five Vermont regiments out in a thin semi-
circular line. Ward is halted and faced to support Grant; Hays continues his movement to the right. Obliquing right in the dense thicket
to connect with Getty's left, Mott's units lose direction and then disintegrate while attempting to deploy under fire.

brigade that rushed to Grant's rescue, advanced sufficiently far to the front to smash into Walker's sector on the right of Heth's line, and bring back the colors of the 55th Virginia, as a memento of its brief but violent visitation. Since Cooke's two right regiments, the 46th and 15th North Carolina, extended southward from the Plank Road across the front of the 4th and 3d Vermont Regiments, one of the two II Corps regiments of Ward's brigade which reinforced the 5th Vermont in the counterattack must, therefore, have been the 20th Indiana.[25]

Hays' Attack

As Ward's three regiments were stabilizing Getty's left flank, Brigadier General Alexander Hays led his brigade by the right along the Brock Road. After forming in line of battle beyond the Plank Road intersection, he moved to the front. The 1st United States Sharpshooters, under command of Major Charles P. Mattocks, advanced rapidly through the woods, driving in the Confederate skirmishers and advanced detachments from their rifle pits.[26]

The zone of Hays' advance is one of those numerous questions that have been left as a legacy of the Battle of the Wilderness to the military historian for perpetual discussion. We have no report of the operations of the brigade, as a unit. Of the three available regimental reports, only one offers a clue. Lieut. Col. W. B. Neeper, commanding the 57th Pennsylvania, states that his regiment advanced from the Brock Crossing with "the Sixty-Third on our right and the Fourth Maine on our left, across the Plank Road." While moving forward, Neeper adds, we "had a severe engagement with the enemy."[27]

This statement would imply that Hays advanced toward Wheaton's sector in the center of Getty's divisional line. But in view of the fact that Carroll's brigade (Gibbon's division) subsequently moved over the same route to relieve Wheaton, Hays must have inclined to the right in order to connect with

Eustis, holding the right of Getty's line. Since neither Wheaton nor Carroll mention Hays' brigade in this connection, the severe engagement to which Neeper refers could scarcely have occurred betwen Wheaton's rear and Carroll's front.[28]

While supporting Neeper's evidence, the account given by James M. Martin, official historian of the 57th Pennsylvania, may be reconciled with other versions which place the clash in the thickets on the right rear of Eustis' position. Hays, attempting to execute the plan of forming on the right of Getty's divisional line, went blindly over the low parallel ridges and across intervening swales, with only the roll of musketry through the trees to guide him toward his objective. With battle lines broken, or badly disordered, the units pushed on, all inspired by a determination to march to the aid of men who had attacked in the faith that their II Corps comrades would speedily bring them support. One by one Hay's disjointed elements went into the merciless ambuscade of Davis' Mississippi riflemen. Here, in a few frightful minutes, was the bloodiest shambles of the Wilderness. The blinding flash of a volley, fired at forty yards range, proclaimed the presence of a lurking foe. A counter-volley, in which many of the roaring rifles fell from hands of desperately wounded men, told the Mississippians that they were being attacked by numerous foe, determined to stand and shoot it out. While Davis' men enjoyed the initial advantage of surprise, this was offset by the splendid discipline of Hays' regiments; surviving the first blast of Davis' fire, Hays returned to the thundering fray with a decided preponderance of rifles. As the answering roar of Confederate volleys diminished in intensity, the Federal brigadier attempted to straighten his lines. Indifferent to the hail of Minie balls tearing through the foliage of the trees, Alexander Hays went about the work as coolly as though forming his brigade for a general review. While riding along the half-completed line, a whizzing projectile struck his forehead and entered the brain. The general reeled and fell from his saddle; nearby troops recovered the body and carried it to the rear. The senior regimental officer assumed command, completed the formation, and held the field until nightfall.[29]

Conditions on the left, meantime, had gone from desperate remedies to all but utter collapse. A short time before Ward's three regiments had advanced to support the Vermont brigade, Mott's two-brigade division prepared to move out and connect with the left of Getty's battle line.

Mott's Two Brigades Move in on the Left

Formed in the line of trenches which had been thrown up along the Brock Road, McAllister's 1st Brigade on the right, Brewster's 2d (Excelsior) Brigade on the left, with a skirmish line under Colonel Sewell established well to the front, Mott received orders to attack. Instructions were sent to Sewell to drive in the enemy skirmishers and develop his position. The advance was ordered "by the right of companies to the front." [30] When formed in two lines of battle, the assault column would pass over its skirmishers and move upon the enemy's main line.

The internal structure of Mott's attack formation can only be partially stated. Six regiments are identified in McAllister's first line. The 8th New Jersey held the right, with the 5th New Jersey on its left. The 1st Massachusetts held the left of the brigade line, connecting with the right of the Excelsior Brigade. The 16th Massachusetts formed on the right of the 1st Massachusetts. The 7th and 11th New Jersey regiments were in the center of the front line. The 6th New Jersey and the 26th and 115th Pennsylvania Regiments apparently constituted the second line. There is no information concerning the formation of the Excelsior Brigade, other than the fact that it formed in two lines on the left of McAllister.[31]

The advance began sometime after Getty's assault column had gone forward. "Over the breastworks we went," relates Colonel McAllister, "but the dense thicket of underbrush made it impossible for the troops to keep their proper distance, so that, when coming into line of battle, owing to pressure from the Sixth Corps on my right and the Excelsior Brigade on my left, there was not room to form line of battle in two ranks." [32]

Owing to the wide leftward extension given Getty's front by putting all five of L. A. Grant's Vermont regiments into the first line, Grant's left was thrown across the path of Mott's advance. The account given by Colonel McAllister of this situation not only explains one of the causes that contributed to the collapse of his division, but definitely establishes the time sequence in the advance of Getty, Mott, and the reinforcing regiments from Ward's brigade of Birney's division. McAllister recalls that:

> In the advance the Eighth New Jersey Volunteers was on my right, and in coming up they found themselves in rear of the left regiment of the Sixth Corps [the 5th Vermont], who were engaging the enemy. The Eighth New Jersey laid down, but soon the troops in front gave way and the Eighth received the fire from the enemy. The Fifth [New Jersey] on its left, gave way and carried back with it a portion of the Eighth, leaving Captain Stelle with a small portion of the regiment and the colors. He was afterward relieved by Brigadier General Ward, and should be noticed for gallantry. [33]

The crowding from both flanks was soon felt at the center of the brigade line. Lieutenant Colonel John Schoonover, commanding the 11th New Jersey, reports that after proceeding some distance through the dense underbrush, he received instruction from the brigade commander to form line of battle. With crowding from both left and right, and in the midst of an almost impassible thicket, Schoonover found it impossible to form his line in the space he had originally occupied on the road. Only by sending the three left companies to the rear did he succeed in forming the remainder of his regiment in a proper line. [34] Leading the 7th New Jersey, Captain Thomas C. Thompson encountered the same fatal crowding toward the center of the line of deployment—a result, no doubt, of an inevitable tendency of parallel company columns, advancing in a general right oblique, to converge on the direction held by the right element of the formation. Captain Thompson states that after forming line and pushing on some 300 yards through dense jungle of scrub oak, it became necessary to halt and reform his line. "This," he points out, "was found to be almost impossible, as nearly the whole regiment had become overlapped by other regiments on right and left."[35] Confusion, in this instance, was avoided by withdrawing the entire command a few paces to the rear. The 7th, however, was denied the necessary time for completion of its maneuver. The other regiments seemed to have solved the difficulty by similar methods for, according to McAllister, "After moving a short distance the line of battle passed over the skirmish line and commenced firing. On receiving the enemy's fire, to my great astonishment, the line began to give way on the left." [36]

Both Brigades Meet Disaster

Some inkling of the storm that broke on the left of the divisional line is given by the historian of the 1st Massachusetts, which held the left of the 1st Brigade.

> The woods seemed impenetrable. . . . The men went forward, however, in very irregular lines, and keeping as closely together as they were able. They had advanced thus only 500 or 600 yards from the road when, directly in front, the unseen enemy opened a double volley, which sent thousands of bullets crashing through the woods into their faces. This fire, so sudden, so unexpected, and so deadly, was returned in but a feeble and scattering manner, because the men were so generally separated from their officers and so far apart from each other, besides being perplexed in forcing their way through the tangled forest, that they were comparatively without organization. The enemy answered with another terrific volley, which told with deadly effect upon the foremost groups struggling along to get into some sort of fighting array, killing and wounding a large number and straightway forcing the rest to fall back. Along the whole division the movement became at once and rapidly retrograde.[37]

While the burden of evidence, which is furnished almost entirely by 1st Brigade sources, puts the onus of failure on the Excelsior Brigade, the straightforward account given by Colonel M. W. Burns, commanding the 73d New York, of the

2d or Excelsior Brigade, contends that the second line came to the rescue of the first, passed over its stricken ranks and sustained the shock of the enemy's attack for 15 or 20 minutes. Only when threatened with overwhelming numbers on their left did the line give way and fall back in good order to the breastworks. The front line of the 1st Brigade, according to Captain Thomas C. Thompson, 7th New Jersey, passed over the second line in its precipitate movement back to the breastworks.[38] Colonel McAllister relates that, after the Excelsior Brigade gave way, "then my left regiment—1st Massachusetts Volunteers—and regiment after regiment, like a rolling wave, fell back, and all efforts to rally them short of the breastworks were in vain." [39]

The remaining regiments of Ward's 1st Brigade (Birney's division), which had been held in reserve on the Brock Road, now went forward to fill the gap opening between Getty's heavily engaged left and Mott's stricken right. These units appear to have formed in line along the Brock Road, their right extending toward the Orange Plank-Brock Road crossing. The 144th New York appears to have held the left. In keeping with practice, they were probably formed in two lines of battle.

The emergency was critical; but Ward's reserve proved equal to the occasion. Its line moved off by the left flank to get into position. It was a difficult maneuver, similar to the one which Mott had attempted and failed to accomplish. Scores of Mott's men hastening back through the woods broke through the line of the 124th New York. The regimental historian relates that

A wild storm of bullets, which rattled through the brush, patted against the trees, and hissed and whistled through the air. [We] halted to rectify our line . . . Strengthened by many of Mott's men [we] moved forward . . . and opened a counterfire, which turned the tide of battle here. The Confederates slowly and steadily retired. [We] passed over Confederate dead and wounded, then began to take prisoners, singly and in twos and threes. We could seldom see the enemy's battle-line because of the denseness of the foliage; but powder flashes from the opposing lines often told that they

were but a few yards apart . . . [We] halted on the east edge
of a swale, or low piece of ground, which was covered with
the most dense growth of saplings I ever saw.[40]

Repercussions of the difficult plight confronting many units
on the battle front induced strong reactions at II Corps headquarters, near the Brock Crossing. The body of Brigadier
General Alexander Hays was carried by on a stretcher. The
corner of a blanket covered the warrior's face. A classmate
of U. S. Grant at West Point, honored and respected by the
senior officers of the Army and loved by the men of his
command, Hays was a leader whose loss in action was a real
calamity. The silent funeral cortege, moving slowly back from
the roar of battle, was one to stir the hearts of the soldiers.
With the impression of the scene still vivid in his mind nine
days later, Lieutenant Colonel Lyman wrote amid the tumult
of Spotsylvania Court House to a friend: "He was a strong-
built, rough sort of man, with red hair, and a tawny, full
beard; a braver man never went into action, and the wonder
only is that he was not killed before, as he always rode at
the very head of his men, shouting to them and waving his
sword." [41]

Reporting about 5 p.m. at II Corps headquarters, under
instructions from Meade, with a string of mounted orderlies,
to act as an army headquarters liaison officer with the left
wing of the army, Lieutenant Colonel Lyman arrived just in
time to witness the route of Mott's brigades.

Hancock's first report to the *aide de camp* from army headquarters was hopeful: "Report to General Meade," instructed
the II Corps commander, "that it is very hard to bring up
troops in this wood, and that only a part of my corps is up,
but I will do what I can."

Lyman's transcript of the verbal report given by Hancock
had scarcely been dispatched when an officer of Getty's staff
galloped up. Reining in, he reported: "Sir! General Getty is
hard pressed and nearly out of ammunition!"

"Tell him to hold on," ordered the II Corps commander,
"General Gibbon will be up and help him."

Another officer, galloping from the south, drew rein. His face bespoke the ominous tiding he bore: "General Mott's division has broken, sir, and is coming back."

Lyman's pithy account is the only contemporary narrative of the dramatic scene at II Corps headquarters.

"Tell him to stop them, sir!" roared Hancock in a voice like a trumpet. As he spoke, a crowd of troops came from the woods and fell back into the Brock Road. Hancock dashed among them "Halt here! Halt here. Form behind this rifle pit. Major Mitchell, go to Gibbon and tell him to come up on the double-quick!" It was a welcome sight to see Carroll's brigade coming along that Brock Road, he riding at their head as calm as a May morning. "Left face-prime-forward," and the line disappeared in the woods to waken the musketry with double violence. Carroll was soon brought back wounded.[42]

Carroll and Webb Committed

Gibbon's column of three brigades reversed and marched "left in front" (Carroll's 3d Brigade leading and followed by Webb's 1st and Owen's 2d). Gibbon instructed Carroll to report to Birney.[43] Carroll formed on the right of the Plank Road, then advanced with his left on the highway; Webb, following Carroll in column, received orders to stay the rout of Mott's troops. There was no time to change formation; the pursuing Confederates were firing into Mott's disordered units. Webb shifted his file closers to the right, closed up the column and, facing his regiments left, opened fire on the enemy. Owen, bringing up the rear of the division, marched on to the Crossing, formed with his right on the Plank Road, and pushed out to the battle front.[44]

These dispositions were made shortly after 5 p.m. Gibbon states that he reached the scene of battle at this time. At 5:05 p.m. Meade's *aide de camp* reported to army headquarters on the situation at the Brock Crossing. Judging by its context, this dispatch was written immediately after report of Mott's collapse and before the dispositions made by Gibbon's brigades has been completed. It reads:

General: There is a general attack as per diagram. It holds in some places, but is forced back to the Brock Road on the left. Gibbon is just coming up to go in, and Barlow is to try a diversion on the left. A prisoner of Archer's (Tennessee) division says he was told that Longstreet was today on their right.[45]

Lyman's dispatch, as a matter of fact, reports the breakdown, rather than the progress of the offensive launched an hour before.

The consequences of the disastrous repulse sustained by Mott's two brigades are difficult to exaggerate. Aimed obliquely and pushed with resolution against the sector held by Walker's Virginia regiments, on the Confederate right, it might have dealt a staggering blow to Heth's defense. Just how Heth parried the blow, where he found the scant reserves for this emergency, and to whom is entitled credit for the superb leadership in smashing with a mere handful a veteran division of the Army of the Potomac during its critical stage of deployment are questions that cannot be answered with assurance. It is known, however, that Kirkland's reserve brigade was sent to the relief of Cooke, in the center of the first line, and probably after Carroll and Owen had brought their reinforcing regiments to the center of the Federal line.[46] Lacking specific evidence to the contrary, it is probable that Mott was broken by the troops already in position on Heth's right, and that the credit, therefore, goes to Walker's Virginia Brigade. Whoever met and parried the blow may claim a high distinction: Had Mott been permitted to develop his operation even to the actual degree of success attained by Getty and Birney, there can be no doubt that the situation thus created would have required the presence of Kirkland's North Carolina regiments on the right of the line. Such a demand would have left Heth destitute of reserves until elements of Wilcox's distant division came to his rescue. Thus Hancock's effort to restore his battered line and then resume the offensive before A. P. Hill could bring Wilcox's four brigades into action constitutes the second phase of the struggle for possession of the Plank Road ridge.

CHAPTER 14

HANCOCK CONTINUES THE ATTACK

The thunderous outburst of musketry that heralded Hancock's attack on the Plank Road interrupted Lee's plan of completing the deployment of his converging masses. Granted completion of the deployment on a line tracing high ground that looked eastward across the basin of Wilderness Run, Lee would hold a strong defensive position until the arrival of Longstreet and Anderson enabled him to pass over to the offensive.

Lee Takes Defensive Position

In pursuance of the plan to form a connected line across the Chewning plateau, Wilcox received orders to lead his column off by the left and open communication with Ewell. The movement began about 2:30 p.m., shortly after the head of Hancock's column began reinforcing Getty at the Brock Crossing. Wilcox's division was marched in the order of brigades, front to rear, Lane-Thomas-Scales-McGowan.[1]

Filing off through Widow Tapp's field under the eye of Lee, the column pushed slowly through the woods for one-half mile and emerged on the Chewning plateau. McGowan, bringing up the rear, passed Poague's batteries and marched by Lee and his staff about 4 p.m. Wilcox posted Scales and McGowan on the plateau, which he describes as a field half a mile in width about a house. He adds that the site of the farmstead commanded a good view across the basin of Wilderness Run and that "the enemy, who was drawn up on Wilderness Tavern ridge, is all moving toward our right," that is, toward the Plank Road.[2]

After reporting these dispositions to Lee, Wilcox went on with the brigades of Lane and Thomas across the main branch of Wilderness Run and up over Jones' field into the woods on the north side of the clearing. The two brigades were posted in the thicket where Wadsworth had formed the left of his line during the early forenoon. Going on northward to Hagerson's farm, Wilcox found Brigadier General J. B. Gordon, whose brigade was posted on the right of Ewell's line.

By all previous experience in concentrating his forces in the presence of the Army of the Potomac, Lee now had reason to believe that he had successfully completed his preliminary dispositions and that the arrival of the strategic reserve would endow him with the initiative. These calculations, however, were overruled by a driving power that was as alien to the Army of the Potomac as it was to Lee's experience in maneuvering against that army.

A tearing volley of musketry on the Plank Road ended the conference at Hagerson's farm. Wilcox hastened southward across Jones' field to join his troops. Near the edge of the woods he met a courier from Lee, instructing him to return with all speed to the Plank Road; Heth had been attacked with great violence and must be reinforced at once; McGowan and Scales had already been recalled from the Chewning plateau.

Orders were immediately dispatched to Thomas and Lane, giving effect to Lee's instructions. Wilcox spurred on to overtake the brigades—McGowan and Scales—already marching to the sound of the guns.[3]

Thomas and Lane, upon receipt of the orders to countermarch, pushed southward without delay across Wilderness Run and over the Chewning plateau. While hastening past the farmstead, and probably without regard to the precautions that should have been taken against hostile observation, the column was seen and reported by the V Corps signal station near Warren's headquarters at the Lacy house. The report transmitted at 5:30 p.m. to Meade from V Corps stated: "Our signal officers report a heavy column of the enemy's infantry moving in a field this side of the Plank Road and going toward General Hancock."[4]

Intelligence to the effect that a large Federal mass was moving from Wilderness Tavern ridge southward impressed Lee as evidence of an intention on Grant's part to throw heavy reinforcements from his right into Hancock's offensive on the left.[5] Going northward over the Chewning plateau, Wilcox no doubt saw Wadsworth's division in the clearing of Major Lacy's plantation. Artillery of the VI Corps parked at the Wilderness Tavern crossroads, together with the presence of numerous slightly wounded soldiers around the V Corps hospital near the tavern,[6] and the movement of Baxter's 2d Brigade (Robinson's division), which was withdrawn from the front line during the late afternoon [7] to reinforce Wadsworth's three brigades in general reserve, might well have appeared from Wilcox's distant point of observation as a strong troop concentration moving off toward the right of the Confederate line. Such, at any rate, appears to have been Lee's interpretation of the report sent by Wilcox from Chewning's farm. But Lee, informing Ewell of the circumstance in a communication received at Confederate II Corps headquarters at 6 p.m.,[8] expressed no great concern as to A. P. Hill's ability to hold on the Plank Road. This expression of confidence, however, reflects Lee's state of mind at the time of the dispatch of the communication to Ewell which was, at the closest possible reckoning, an hour before delivery of the message to Ewell. More to the point, at 5 p.m., just as the brigades of Carroll and Owen (3d and 1st, Gibbon's division) turned left at the Brock Crossing and advanced to support Getty's battle front, and Webb's 2d Brigade formed in line to stop the Confederate pursuit of Mott's routed troops, Lee was confident that the Plank Road ridge was secure. Although the unexpected intensity of the Federal attack on his right had compelled him to abandon his plan of filling the gap between his right and left wings, he reasoned that Heth, with the support of Wilcox's four brigades, would secure the decision tentatively won on the Turnpike, and that his inability to close the gap was partially compensated by the diversion of

Federal forces from Wilderness Tavern to the Plank Road ridge.

Lee's reasoning was put to a vigorous test by the renewed violence of Hancock's offensive between 5 p.m. and nightfall. Nor did Lee, it seems, fully appreciate every implication of the remorseless driving power which was the outstanding characteristic of his new antagonist.

For his part, Grant, having failed in his realization of developing a general offensive all along the line between 4 and 5 p.m., was now actually contemplating the scheme which Lee foresaw at 5 o'clock. About the time Wilcox was conferring with Gordon at Hagerson's farm relative to closing the gap between Ewell and Hill, Grant and Meade rode over to V Corps headquarters, with a view to ascertaining possibilities of finding a reserve from the inactive right center to reinforce the attacking left.[9] As Grant approached Warren's signal station he learned that a heavy Confederate column was moving from the V Corps front toward Hancock's right flank.

This intelligence incited the desire to reinforce Hancock. Selection of a suitable column for the mission appears to have been a matter of some doubt. General Wadsworth, whose 4th Division brigades had refitted in the field fronting Warren's headquarters, offered a solution. An earnest plea urged by the silver-haired veteran that his division be employed, not only overcame Grant's reluctance to entrust an arduous mission to troops that had given way under fire that same day, but caused the Supreme Commander to amend his opinion concerning the slowness of Meade's generals. Baxter's 2d Brigade of Robinson's division was included in the column; Robinson, the division commander, pleaded and obtained permission to accompany it.[10]

The advantage of prompt movement was again lost. Although the decision for this diversion of force was taken shortly after 5 p.m. and the troops were in readiness to move at short notice, the order to advance was delayed for nearly an hour.[11]

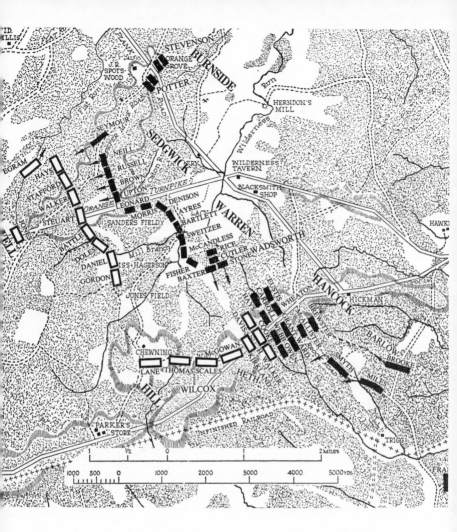

MAP 14. HANCOCK RENEWS HIS ASSAULT

The situation at about 6:30 p.m., May 5. With Hays' brigade on his right, Gibbon relieves Getty at the front. Mott reforms in the rear. Hill is heavily pressed as Barlow from the south and Wadsworth from the north move toward his flanks. Recalled from the center, Wilcox hastens to Hill's support. On the north flank, H. T. Hays and Pegram are extending Ewell's left as Seymour moves toward the right of Sedgwick's line. At this time three IX Corps divisions lie between Germanna Ford and Spotswood's. R. H. Anderson's division has reached Verdiersville; Longstreet's two divisions are at Richards Shop, where they bivouac for the night. The outcome of the day's fighting depends on the race of local reserves. Tomorrow's battle will be determined largely by the race of strategic reserves.

Hancock Renews Pressure

While plans looking to a redirection of the battle were being entertained at both Federal and Confederate headquarters, Hancock's infantry on the Plank Road continued to dominate the situation. The rim of the red, smoke-dimmed sun was sinking into the western Wilderness as Carroll and Owen led their Federal brigades forward along the north and south sides, respectively, of the road. Word went up to Wheaton's and L. A. Grant's brigades at the front that reinforcements were marching to their relief. The wearied troops expended in a sudden burst of fire the ammunition they had been carefully husbanding during the prolonged combat.

Heth, anticipating a renewal of pressure on Cooke's front, moved the North Carolina regiments of Kirkland's brigade up into close supporting distance.[12]

Carroll passed over Wheaton's lines and struck with the vigor that fresh troops usually bring to an exhausted battle front.[13] Coming up on the left, Owen was unable to hit with the power exhibited by Carroll. Mott's collapse may have induced an unfavorable situation on the south side of the road; Owen, at any rate, was stopped short by a fierce counterattack. So swiftly was the Confederate thrust delivered, perhaps by a part of Kirkland's command, that the staff officer who had carried instructions for the withdrawal of the Vermont brigade was captured while going to the rear.[14]

Ward's reserve line (five volunteer regiments and the 2d U.S. Sharpshooters), which had moved into the gap between Mott and Getty,[15] probably lent material support to Owen's left, while those regiments of Ward's first line (141st Pennsylvania—20th Indiana—40th New York), which went to Grant's assistance earlier in the battle, remained in the sector and probably reinforced Owen's regiments in throwing back the sudden attack that fell as the Vermonters were being relieved.

Federal and Confederate sources agree as to the terrific pace of the fight, its prolonged intensity of fire, and the shock and countershock of advancing regiments. "The lines of battle," reports Hancock, "were exceedingly close, the musketry continuous and deadly along the entire line." [16] A close-up view of the tumult is given by an officer of the 11th North Carolina, Kirkland's Brigade:

> In one of these charges our brigade formed part of a second line of battle, Cooke's Brigade, commanded by Colonel MacRae, afterwards our Brigadier-General, being on the first line. In advancing over him with a yell, he *sneered* sardonically: "Go ahead; you'll soon come back." And sure enough we did. We struck as he had done the Federal line behind intrenchments, from which in vain we tried to dislodge it, and recoiled, lying down in turn behind MacRae's line. I fancy he *smiled* sardonically then.[17]

Unsupported by a forward movement all along the line, Carroll's drive was deprived of the *elan* it otherwise might have retained. The havoc of his blow, however, was considerable; Cooke and Walker were dangerously pressed. Carroll himself was wounded but refused to quit the field during the heat of action. Later he went to the rear for medical attention, and resumed command the following morning.[18] Ricketts' section supported the Federal advance; hauled by drag ropes, the two guns kept pace with the second line.[19] The Confederate artillery detachment supporting Walker became isolated; the gun teams were slaughtered and the gunners, powerless to manhandle their pieces in the murderous fire, called on the infantry for aid. Lieutenant R. W. Stedman, A Company, 44th North Carolina, volunteered with a party of forty men for the perilous task. The guns were dragged to safety. Only three of the detail were unhurt, according to Major C. M. Stedman, the regimental commander. The gallant lieutenant was mentioned in divisional orders.[20]

While the battle flamed with renewed violence at sunset along the Plank Road, Gibbon's remaining brigade, the 1st, commanded by Webb, consolidated its position on the left of Mott's broken force.[21] Webb and the steadier elements of the 4th Division had no great difficulty in driving off the Confederate units that approached the Brock Road. But no advantage was won by repeated attempts to advance in force. "Wherever the Federal troops moved forward," observes the chaplain of the 1st Massachusetts, McAllister's 1st Brigade, Mott's division, "the Rebels appeared to have the advantage. Whenever they advanced, the advantage was transferred to us."[22]

Pressure on the sector held by Webb and Mott was eased by development of a new movement against A. P. Hill's right. Foreshadowed in Lieutenant Colonel Lyman's dispatch of 5:05 p.m. to army headquarters, this movement is one of the least known of the important and near-decisive operations of the battle. Fleeting glimpses of the troops involved in this action indicate that its execution was left to three brigades of Barlow's 1st Division and that Smyth's 2d (Irish) Brigade, which held the advance of the 1st Division, was intended to pivot on Webb's left, while Miles' 1st Brigade, supported by whatever reinforcements appeared to be necessary, would swing out and envelop the Confederate right.[23]

Webb, as soon as the pressure was relieved on his front, extended the line of breastworks southward along the Brock Road. Smyth's Irish regiments closed up, connected on Webb's left flank and, after forming battle lines, began entrenching the front.[24] The brigades of Miles and Frank, coming up in column along the Brock Road, arrived on the line. Each in succession turned to the apparently indispensable work of fortifying a defensive front along the road before advancing into the woods against the enemy's flank. Brooke's brigade was threading its way westward along an obscure forest track from the Furnace to a point about one mile south of the Brock Crossing.[25]

Lee Orders Wilcox to Reinforce Heth

Lee must certainly have been aware of the impending storm. The woods to the west of the Brock Road swarmed with Confederate cavalry patrols;[26] and advanced points lurked on the flank of Hancock's marching column. But pressure across the saddle from the Brock Crossing was intense; here was the imminent danger and here, on Heth's sector astride the Plank Road, was a critical need for the first available reinforcement. The decision taken by Lee about 4:30 p.m. to reinforce the Plank Road front with troops designated to fill the gap between Hill and Ewell, made provision for this need.

As previously related, Lee's order for the recall of Wilcox's Division reached Chewning's farm about 5 p.m. McGowan, after forming his troops in column, must march a mile and three-quarters eastward and then deploy before going into action on Heth's front. Scales, following McGowan, would arrive on the line later. Carroll, at this very time, was advancing along the north side of the Plank Road, with Owen on his left, toward the Federal firing line, only half a mile to the west. Could McGowan and Scales arrive in time to redress the situation created by the impact of Hancock's reinforcements?

The courier from army headquarters found the Reverend Mullaly, Chaplain of Orr's Rifles, leading the men of Mc-Gowan's Brigade in prayer. "It was one of the most impressive scenes I ever witnessed," relates the brigade historian. "On the left thundered a dull battle; on the right the sharp crack of rifles gradually swelled to equal importance; above was the blue, placid heavens; around us a varied landscape of forest and green fields, green with the earliest foliage of spring; and here knelt hirsute and browned veterans shriving for another battle."[27]

The South Carolina veterans were well shrived. The Reverend Mullaly's solemn supplication to the Lord of Hosts was promptly reinforced by the opprobrious exhortations of noncommissioned officers to form in column for a rapid march to the firing line. It may be a matter of speculation as to whether the incitement of prayer or the roll of Heth's musketry furnished the main inspiration. McGowan's South Carolina brigade, followed by Scales' five North Carolina regiments, rushed down from the plateau like an avalanche.

The column streamed across Widow Tapp's field. Here was

enacted another memorable scene. The road led directly across the front of Poague's guns. One may imagine the tumultuous enthusiasm of the gunners, who had as yet been denied the opportunity of loosing a single round of fire. Caps flew high; bared sabers flashed in the setting sun; gun rammers waved, some heaved upward, describing erratic arcs.

Along their route of march the infantry column answered in thundering cheers the salute of Lee and his staff. It was not the formal salutation prescribed by custom to a column marching under arms. This was rather a tribute, hopefully given by the army commander and his staff to the troops who carried the fate of the battle on their bayonets.

McGowan's advance turned left at the double-quick and entered the Plank Road. A mile down the straight, tree-lined lane the battle raged with increasing violence. Ambulances bearing wounded from the front crowded into the trees to give free passage to the reinforcements. Exploding shells from Ricketts' guns pounded the road. The column swept on, ignoring ugly bursts which caused occasional eddies in the onflowing stream of infantry. A few wounded left the column and joined knots of slightly injured soldiers, who were plodding toward the III Corps hospital.

Wilcox Throws in McGowan and Scales

Galloping back from Jones' field to overtake Scales' and McGowan's brigades, Wilcox reached the Plank Road and spurred on toward the firing. "The troops engaged could not be seen," he relates, "the rattle of musketry alone indicating where the struggle was severest and the points to which the reinforcing brigades should be sent." The firing was heaviest at this time on the right. Thither went Scales' North Carolina regiments, disappearing into the woods south of the Plank Road. McGowan slackened his rapid pace to deploy toward the front.[28]

The 1st South Carolina, followed by Orr's Rifles, filed right and faced front; the 14th, 13th, and 12th Regiments filed left in the order named and came into line on the north side of the road.[29] Passing rapidly over Heth's first line, which had been thinned and exhausted by the raging fire-fight, McGowan's regiments "swept like a gale through the woods." [30] An imprudent Rebel yell was answered by a staggering volley.

The advance so auspiciously launched now encountered the usual difficulties of forest fighting. A dense thicket of saplings interlaced with thorny vines and stiff bushes, broke the alignment. Many of the troops over whom McGowan's line had passed seem to have been unaware of the circumstances and answered the enemy's volley with a fire that tore through the rear ranks of their own comrades in advance. Unable to endure the fury of Federal musketry that swept the slight elevation over which his Rifles, on the right of the line, were passing, Orr halted to reply. His return fire brought down a blast from Ricketts' guns. Under the tempest of shot and shell, the Rifles withdrew. Less exposed on Orr's left, the 1st South Carolina, under Colonel Washington Shooter, held its ground. The 13th, 14th, and 15th Regiments, on the north side of the road, reformed their lines and continued the advance.

Pressing on, the South Carolinians struck Carroll's first line. The 12th broke through, captured many prisoners, and drove Ricketts' gunners from their pieces. In battering against fierce resistance to its progress, the 12th lost connection with the 13th and 14th on its left. The Federal counterattack was fierce and strong. Isolated and virtually surrounded, the 12th changed front to rear and, driving its prisoners along the new direction of attack, succeeded in reestablishing the lost connection. The 13th and 14th, meantime, had advanced slowly on the left. Reformed, the three South Carolina regiments beat off repeated Federal assaults until overpowering pressure on the left compelled McGowan to order a general retirement.[31]

It was probably during the retrograde movement of McGowan's left regiments that Carroll succeeded in recovering the abandoned guns of Ricketts' section. The 8th Ohio and 14th Indiana pushed forward behind an aggressive line of skirmishers, while a detachment of picked men from the 14th was led by Captain Francis Butterfield, of Colonel Carroll's staff, down the Plank Road to the abandoned pieces.[32] The rescue, according to Captain Ricketts, was effected without great difficulty, only three casualties being sustained by the party. Comparison of this easy adventure, with the costly sacrifice made by Lieutenant Stedman and his detachment from the 44th North Carolina in saving the guns behind Kirkland's hard-pressed line would indicate that in the ebb and flow of the battle's tide, the flood surging against the Confederate line beat with greater power and violence than did the one that washed back toward the Federal defense.

South of the Plank Road the Confederates sustained their battle line with the same precarious fortune that marked the swaying conflict to the north of the highway. Moving out on the right of McGowan's line, Scales' four North Carolina regiments drove off the Federal troops that had been threatening Heth's flank and then penetrated deep into the woods. "It was like fighting a forest fire," says Captain R. S. Williams, of the 13th North Carolina. Little, however, is known concerning this phase of the action. Captain Williams' statement that his regiment drove the enemy in repeated charges some two miles is obviously impossible; such an advance would have carried Scales' formations to the east side of the Brock Road.

Whatever may have been accomplished in averting an envelopment of Heth's line, Scales' left regiment failed for some time to connect with Orr's Rifles, on the right of McGowan's line. The Rifles, after their first withdrawal, had returned to the attack. The 1st South Carolina, on Orr's left, now fell back, leaving the Rifles in a dangerously exposed position. Both the 1st and Orr's Rifles were enfiladed from the right front. Word was sent to Scales asking support. A retrograde movement north of the Plank Road, similar to that of the 1st on the south side, opened two perilous reentrant angles in the brigade line. A withering crossfire swept the Confederates astride the road. An eyewitness describes the brigade front as "the shortest, most huddled, most ineffective line-of-battle ever seen." [33]

As glimmering twilight brought the darkened treeline into clear relief against the western sky, the thundering combat on the Plank Road reached a new pitch of intensity. Scales' North Carolina brigade fell back through the woods, yielding step by step before an irresistible drive that pressed on both its front and right. In response to the call from McGowan, Scales' left regiment made heroic efforts to extend toward Orr's Rifles without jeopardizing the brigade line.[34]

McGowan's huddled formations stood at bay; the right of the brigade line was enfiladed; the center, astride the Plank Road, was torn by crossfire, the left bore up under almost intolerable pressure. Yet the South Carolina regiments struggled grimly, holding with the valor of soldiers who, though pressed to the breaking point, fight on in fealty to the martial tradition of a great army.

Stone, commanding Davis' Brigade of three Mississippi regiments and one North Carolina regiment, had maintained his position since the beginning of the action. Aside from the terrible loss inflicted on Hays' brigade, we have no record of the feats of his Mississippi riflemen. Only the account left by Adjutant C. M. Cooke, of the 55th North Carolina, gives an inkling of the fortunes of battle, as met by Confederate troops in this sector. Cooke recalls that

> Our regiment was the center of the brigade and on the crest of a small hill or ridge. It was in a dense forest of small trees; the hill in our front sloped gradually to a depression or valley which was a few yards wide, and then there was a gradual incline on the opposite side until it reached a point of about the same altitude as that occupied by us, about 100 yards from our line. We had 340 men, including noncommissioned officers in our regiment . . . The Federal forces charged, but they got no further than the crest of the hill in front of us, and were repulsed with great loss; . . . They charged us with seven successive lines of battle, but we repulsed every one of them. Our lines never wavered. The officers and men of the regiment realized that the safety of the army depended upon our holding the enemy in check until the forces left behind could come up, and there was a fixed determination to do it, or to die. About 6 o'clock the enemy was pressing us so heavily with their successive lines of fresh troops it was thought that

they would annihilate us before nightfall, and a conference of the general officers on the field determined that it would probably become necessary, as a last resort, to make a vigorous and impetuous charge upon them with the hope that we might be able to drive them back. Colonel Belo, who was sitting just in rear of the regiment by the side of a little poplar tree, sent his orderly to the line to the writer of this sketch [C. M. Cooke], instructing him to report to him immediately. I went at once. He then stated to me that the necessity of a charge seemed apparent and that the order for making it would probably be given, and he desired that I return to the line and notify the men that they might be prepared for it, and take the command of my own company and also C, which was the flag company, the commanding officer of which had a few moments before been severely wounded, and to see that the flag was kept well to the front, and to make the charge with all the dash that was possible. I went back to the line and gave the men the information. They expressed hope that it might not be necessary to make the charge, but there was no disposition to shirk the duty if it had been imposed.[35]

Federals Converge on Hill's Flanks

The bloody drama now moved relentlessly to its appalling climax—a welter of dead and wounded, with no military decision to compensate either side for the frightful destruction of life and limb. Six brigades of the Confederate III Corps, four of Heth's Division and two of Wilcox's, were in their last gasp of resistance. Heth's four brigades (Davis, Cooke, Walker, and Kirkland) had been thinned and exhausted by the piecemeal attacks of seven Federal brigades—Hays, Eustis, Wheaton, Grant, Ward, McAllister, and Brewster. In throwing back Mott's two brigades (McAllister and Brewster), Walker's Virginia regiments had averted a wholesale catastrophe—one which probably would have compelled Lee's retirement from the battlefield under exceedingly difficult conditions. A second ominous threat, that brought by the added pressure of Carroll, Webb, Owen against Heth's front, was held in abeyance by the timely arrival of Wilcox's two leading brigades—McGowans' and Scales'. But these reinforcements were unable fully to restore the shaken battle front.

The troops of Barlow's impending flank attack were gathering like a thunderhead on A. P. Hill's right front. The pivot brigade, Smyth's, was ready to go forward. Miles' brigade was moving out through the thicket to strike the flank. At 6:45 p.m. Brooke, whose sweating brigade column had turned into the Brock Road over an hour before and was throwing up entrenchments on the extreme left of Hancock's defensive line, received instructions to move rapidly by the right flank. A subsequent order, delivered in person by General Barlow, instructed Brooke to support Smyth with two regiments and repair immediately with the remaining four to the support of Miles.[36]

Another storm cloud, distant and more remote in point of immediate threat, was gathering on A. P. Hill's left. At about 6 p.m. Wadsworth's four-brigade column moved out from the open fields around V Corps headquarters. Moving south, the heavy column disappeared into the dense belt of forest between Lacy's plantation and the Plank Road ridge.[37]

Meantime, General Hill, Colonel Palmer, his chief of staff, and Colonel Venable, Lee's *aide de camp*, spent anxious moments at III Corps headquarters, near the Plank Road. The swelling din of Federal musketry prolonged each moment into an hour of agonized suspense. Each officer asked himself the same question over and over again: Will Thomas and Lane come up in time?

The fate of the battle now resolved itself in the outcome of two separate races. The immediate salvation of Hill's front and right depended upon the race between Thomas and Lane, on the one hand, and the three enveloping brigades, Smyth, Miles, and Brooke, on the other. Yet even if the Confederates won here, there still remained the menace of Wadsworth's powerful column moving down through the woods to the north. With Lane and Thomas engaged, Hill would have no reserve to create another front. But dusk was settling over the battlefield; soon the forest walls, which were impenetrable during midday to vision at more than fifty yards, would contract, leaving the armies in Stygian darkness. The second race, then, was one which Wadsworth's bayonets would run against the wings of departing day.

Thomas and Lane Go In

The clatter of a column hurrying at double-quick along the Plank Road brought sudden elation to the despair that was gripping hearts at Hill's headquarters. Thomas' Brigade hurried by. An officer was dispatched to conduct the four Georgia regiments (14th, 35th, 45th, 49th) off through the woods on the left to relieve Davis' Mississippians. Then, in a long, rushing column came Lane's five North Carolina regiments—the 7th, 18th, 28th, 33d and 37th. These regiments constituted the most powerful of Lee's brigades in point of numerical strength.[38] In other respects the unit was the equal of any.

Thomas' Georgians lost no time in relieving Davis. Arrival of the reinforcements was most opportune. Orders calling for the suicidal charge of the 55th North Carolina were cancelled. Although the firing had lulled temporarily, the Federals had not yet spent their power in this sector. Commenting on the withdrawal of the 55th, Adjutant Cooke says:

> About sunset the firing had nearly ceased in our front, and Thomas' Georgia Brigade of Wilcox's Division came in and relieved us, and we were sent to the right of the road where we rested for the night. We had held the enemy in check. Not one yard of our line had given one foot during the three hours the fearful onslaughts had been made upon us, but of the 340 of the regiment, 34 lay dead on the line where we fought and 167 were wounded. The sergeant of the ambulance corps counted the next day 157 dead Federal soldiers in front of our regiment.[39]

Lane, under instructions from Wilcox, filed off to the right of the road. A stinging fire from Federal sharpshooters, who evidently had filtered through the gap between McGowan's 1st South Carolina and Orr's Rifles, caused Lane to deploy the 37th in line of battle parallel to the Plank Road. Colonel Barbour, commanding, was instructed to protect the left of the brigade column while filing across the rear of Scales' line.[40]

As the North Carolina brigade moved out by its right into

the thicket, Colonel Palmer galloped up with intelligence that a part of Scales' line had been shaken and that Lane was required to reestablish the front, connecting his left with McGowan's right.

Lane issued orders for the difficult maneuver. The regiments quickly swung into line, the formation from left to right being the 7th-33d-28th-18th.[41] After cautioning Colonel Davidson, commanding the 7th, against firing into McGowan, Lane ordered the advance.

The forward movement was slow; the line toiled across swampy ground and a dense growth of trees littered with fallen timber. Covered by a party of sharpshooters on the extreme right the 18th cleared the swamp then inclined outward to make room for the 38th North Carolina, of Scales' Brigade, between its left and the right of the 28th. As Lane's rifles came up on the line, the whole Wilderness roared like fire in a canebreak.[42]

Holding its fire on the left, the 7th pushed through the swamp. Unknown to Colonel Davidson, McGowan's right had been withdrawn; the 7th worked cautiously forward to a position within seventy-five yards of the enemy's main line, which occupied a low ridge looking down into the swale.

A furious fire burst from the ridge. Then, under cover of the smoke and growing darkness, a Federal detachment swept past Davidson's left, and coming into line, enforced its demand for surrender with a devastating volley. The 7th broke and fell back in disorder across the swamp. As the left of the line wavered, Colonel Barry's 18th Regiment, on the right of the line, was threatened by an enveloping movement. Barry broke back his two right companies and held off the flanking attack until orders came to abandon the advanced position.[43]

The habit of telling time by the sun seems to have been universal. With the indefinite horizon of a dense forest, shadowed by the pall of smoke drifting up from hidden battle lines, such a method was prone to considerable error.[44] With regard to the particular problem in hand, we know that Hancock contemplated the flank movement as early as 5:05 p.m., at which time Colonel Lyman reported to army headquarters that "Barlow is to try a diversion on the left" (Confederate right).[45]

Lane Stops Barlow

While the Confederates, according to their own testimony, were fighting in desperation to hold fast, a pessimistic view of the situation pervaded Hancock's headquarters. Lyman, at 5:50 p.m., reported: "We barely hold our own." Hancock was beginning to sense the danger of a smashing blow by Longstreet's corps on his left—one which would dog his operations on the morrow and would have much to do with Longstreet's successful exploitation of this very fear.[46] In the dispatch just cited Lyman also reported that a Confederate prisoner from Heth's Division had divulged information to the effect that "Longstreet was today on their [Confederate] right." [47] At 6:14 p.m. Hancock betrays in a communication to Humphreys a dubious state of mind as to the advisability of pushing with the utmost possible vigor his intended diversion against A. P. Hill's right. He notified the chief of staff that "A new line of fire farther to the left had been heard (skirmish fire); an advance of cavalry coming down the Brock Road has been seen. Nothing but skirmishing as yet; yet Gibbon had better be prepared to come up if other firing is heard."

A postscript to this communication adds: "The signal officer reports that where line of fire was seen first to the left he can observe cavalry, but nothing more." [48]

While the pessimism reflected in Lyman's communication of 5:50 and Hancock's of 6:14 p.m. impeded the vigor of action that might have swept the field before nightfall, we know that Scales' Confederate brigade advanced on the right (south) of the Plank Road and made some progress until shortly before dark, when his line was badly shaken. Also that Lane had advanced to reestablish the front. Lane, as already related,[49] was partially enveloped on both flanks and forced to withdraw. The retirement, according to Lane's report, was executed with great difficulty, owing to darkness and the rough ground.[50]

On the Federal side there is but one circumstantial report of operations relating to events in this area at the time darkness was settling over the battlefield. Already cited, this is the report of Colonel (later Brigadier-General) John R. Brooke, commanding Barlow's 4th Brigade. After receiving instructions at 6:45 p.m. to discontinue entrenching on the extreme left of the line and move to his right, Brooke was ordered by General Barlow in person to support both Smyth and Miles.[51] The nature of these instructions would imply that Miles and Smyth were either actively engaged, or in the final development of preparations preceding engagement. Having marched by his right a distance of half a mile since 6:45 p.m., it is apparent that Barlow's personal order should have been given to Brooke between 7 and 7:15 p.m.[52] Brooke's narration of subsequent events offers considerable evidence, though admittedly inconclusive in a final analysis, that the elements of his command, which acted as a connecting link between Smyth's left and Miles' right, formed a part of the attack column that, striking Lane and partially enveloping both his flanks just before dark, compelled the North Carolina brigade to retire as darkness was falling and take up a second line of defense. Brooke reports:

> General Barlow directed me to send two regiments to support the Second Brigade [Smyth's] then engaged in my immediate front. I sent the Sixty-fourth and Sixty-sixth New York Volunteers, under command of Lieutenant Colonel Hammel of the Sixty-sixth New York. These regiments moved up and formed on the left of Smyth's line, and at nearly right angles to it. I was then ordered in with the rest of my brigade, four regiments, to support the First Brigade [Miles'], which was then formed on the left of Colonel Hammel's command. It was by this time quite dark, and very difficult to pass through the dense thicket of the Wilderness. At about 9 p.m. I found Miles' brigade and formed my troops in support, leaving Colonel Beaver's regiment, One hundred and forty-eighth Pennsylvania Volunteers, on the extreme left, where I had sent it when the movement began. The loss of the Sixty-fourth and Sixty-sixth New York was considerable in this part of the fight.

I remained in this position until about 3 a.m. of the 6th
instant.[53]

Lane, after having established a new line along high ground
in rear of the swamp he had crossed and recrossed, received
orders to place his troops behind Scales' Brigade, which now
occupied a line of breastworks running diagonally toward the
Plank Road. Falling back over the works, Lane found the
37th Regiment, which had originally been deployed parallel
to the Plank Road in order to protect the left flank of the
brigade while filing by the right toward its line of deployment.
Colonel Barbour, the regimental commander, explained, not
altogether to Lane's satisfaction, that he had been ordered to
occupy the entrenchments.[54]

His regiments finally disposed in reserve, General Lane
rode off to give a personal report to the divisional commander.
The sense of this report was probably similar to the summary
of events in Lane's official report. He remarks that his brigade
was the last to become engaged; that without hope of support
he had fought on until 9 p.m., when the threatened envelopment of his whole command induced a withdrawal. General
Wilcox instructed Lane to remain in position, promising that
Anderson's Division would arrive on the field before daylight
and take over the front.

The evidence of both Lane and Brooke supports a conclusion that Hancock's long deferred flank attack broke with
great violence about 7 p.m. and that at dark, which both
Lane and Brooke place around 9 p.m.,[55] Lane was compelled
to give ground before the mounting intensity of Hancock's
attack. Moreover, Lee offers weighty evidence as to the gravity
of the situation of A. P. Hill's right at 7 o'clock.

After receiving Palmer's report at III Corps headquarters
that he had put Lane's Brigade in action, Colonel Venable,
aide de camp to Lee, hastily mounted and, gathering up his
reins, said to the III Corps chief-of-staff: "Thank God! I will
go back and tell General Lee that Lane has just gone in and
will hold his ground until other troops arrive tonight." [56]

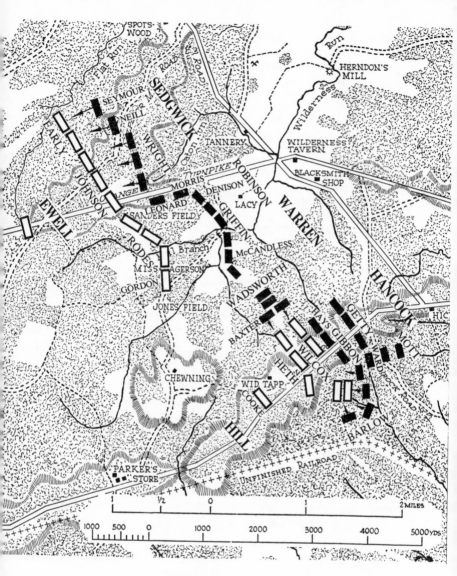

MAP 15. HANCOCK'S DOUBLE ENVELOPMENT CLOSES ON HILL'S CORPS

Showing the situation at about 7:30 p.m., May 5. The two flank attacks close on Heth as Wilcox goes to the latter's relief. On the north the fighting continues. Seymour's attempted envelopment of Ewell's left flank is frustrated by the arrival of Hays and Pegram. Thus Lee wins the race of local reserves. The fighting between Sedgwick and Ewell continues until dark.

The trains of the Army of the Potomac have closed up at Dowdalls Tavern. Johnston's brigade of Rodes' division is still enroute from Hanover Junction; it arrives on the battlefield the morning of May 6.

At 7 p.m., after Venable had reported at army headquarters, Lieutenant Colonel Marshall drafted the following instructions to Ewell:

> The commanding general directs me to repeat a message sent to you at 6 p.m. The enemy persist in their attack on General Hill's right. Several efforts have been repulsed, and we hold our own as yet. The general wishes you to hurry up Ramseur, send back and care for your wounded, fill up your ammunition and be ready to act by light in the morning. General Longstreet and General Anderson are expected up early, and unless you see some means of operating against their right, the general wishes you to be ready to support our right. It is reported that the enemy is massing against General Hill, and if an opportunity presents itself and you can get Wilderness Tavern ridge and cut the enemy off from the river, the general wishes it done. The attack on General Hill is still raging. Be ready to act as early as possible in the morning.[57]

Lane had more than justified Venable's expectations. His swift intervention on the right had delayed the development of Barlow's flank maneuver to an extent that denied Hancock the opportunity of throwing his full power into a culminating blow before dark. But Scales' North Carolina regiments should share with Lane's a measure of credit for this feat of arms.

While Lane was heavily engaged in the advance, Scales succeeded in extending his left and taking over all of McGowan's front on the right (south) of the Plank Road. With a shortened line, McGowan strengthened his connection on the left with Thomas, which had been precariously held by a thin skirmish line, and sent his most battered units back in reserve.

Consolidation of the Confederate lines tended only to deepen the din of musketry; its reverberating thunder continued to roll through the woods. Hill had won the race of reserves. His lines were holding.

Skirmishers Halt Wadsworth

At 7 o'clock Lee appears to have had no apprehension on this score. While he had informed Ewell that the enemy was massing against Hill and that Ewell was to be prepared at daylight either to strike Grant's right on the Wilderness Tavern ridge, or be prepared to support Hill on the Confederate right, no urgent appeal was made for immediate assistance. Venable, upon learning that Lane had gone in, appears to have been satisfied that the battle would be stabilized until Longstreet and Anderson came up. And such was undoubtedly the view at army headquarters. Yet this momentary relief was dissipated by an ominous threat from the north. Certainly Lee must have experienced anxious moments upon learning that a powerful force was moving down across the gap he had been unable to fill during the afternoon. Hill's reserves were exhausted.

After moving off at about 6 p.m., Wadsworth's column penetrated the dense thickets stretching south of the Lacy plantation. Fearful, no doubt, of again encountering an enemy lurking at point-blank range on front and flanks, the force advanced slowly in two lines of battle, followed by a strong reserve. Two brigades, Baxter's and Stone's, formed the first line, Baxter on the right. Baxter supplied the skirmish line covering the advance. Cutler, in battle formation, supported the two-brigade front line. Rice, who had suffered heavily during the fighting of the early afternoon, constituted the reserve.

By what means and at what time intelligence of this threat came to army or III Confederate Corps headquarters we do not know. There can be little doubt, however, that the gap which had been a matter of grave concern to Lee throughout the afternoon, was picketted toward nightfall. Captain E. B. Cope, Warren's *aide de camp* accompanying the column informed V Corps headquarters at 6:20 p.m. that resistance was being encountered.[58] Thomas probably had flankers out on his exposed flank. But report of the movement, as a direct threat to Hill's left rear, did not come until sometime after 7 p.m.

Destitute of reserves, Hill could not withdraw a single formation from his extended front. The only available force for immediate use was a small detachment, 125 men in all, of the 5th Alabama Battalion, which had been detailed to guard prisoners. These Alabamians were hurriedly sent to develop the menacing Federal advance.

Wisely employing the most effective tactic of forest warfare, surprise, the small detachment deployed on a wide front and crept stealthily forward. At a given signal, the Alabamians let forth a demoniacal yell and opened fire. The shout and the volley were magnified tenfold in the weird, woodland twilight. Baxter's skirmishers returned the fire. Unnerved by the flashing burst of musketry in their front, Stone's men, who had been first to quit the line in the fight with Ewell's Corps, now broke and ran in disgraceful panic. The brigadier's horse reared in fright; Stone fell to the ground and was carried from the field, never to return to the Army of the Potomac.[59] Cutler's men, in support, lowered their bayonets to the charge and stopped the panic-stricken mass.

The arrest caused by the daring Alabama detachment was fatal to Federal hopes of dealing an effective blow at Hill's flank. Delay followed in reforming the column. Stone's officers are credited with energy and resolution in restoring order and inspiring their men. The advance was eventually resumed; the hostile skirmishers were pushed steadily back through the woods until darkness overtook the column. At 9 p.m., as Lane was retiring to form in reserve behind Scales, and Brooke was disposing the four regiments under his personal command in support to Miles, Wadsworth halted in the thickets about half a mile north of the Plank Road.[60] He had lost the race against time.

Line was formed in the darkness. Rice moved up from reserve and deployed on the right of Baxter; Cutler took position on Baxter's left. Rice's right, extending toward Widow Tapp's field, was refused. Stone's brigade was held in reserve. The left of the line is reported to have rested at a point some 900 yards west of the Brock Road.

As Wadsworth halted and formed facing the Plank Road the musketry died away to the spasmodic firing of nervous skirmishers. And this, in turn, gave way to the silence of the Wilderness, disturbed only by whippoorwills and the moaning of the wounded who lay between the lines.

CHAPTER 15
SEDGWICK'S ATTACK

While Hancock's attack waves stormed along the Plank Road ridge and attained a tempest fury at nightfall that was calmed only by ebon darkness of the deep forest, general headquarters continued efforts to renew the offensive on the right and extend it around Lee's left. Wright, with his column of four VI Corps brigades, had failed to make a connection with Warren and participate in the meeting engagement on the Turnpike. The continuation of his movement became invested with a new purpose. Now, instead of converging on a detachment of Lee's main force, Wright was joining battle with the principal body of the enemy in position. His mission was to turn or cripple the Confederate left flank and thus facilitate the development of a situation in which a general offensive, or even a strategic pursuit, might be launched.[1]

The advance was made in battle order; Wright's 1st Division moved in line, the order by brigades from left to right being Upton-Brown-Russell; Neill's brigade of Getty's division marched in a deployed formation, proceeding as a second line and supporting Russell.[2] No artillery accompanied the column; nine batteries of corps artillery were parked in the vicinity of Wilderness Tavern.[3]

The rate of movement from Spotswood's farm to the battle front ultimately established in the woods north of Sanders' field should be regarded as a significant piece of evidence, rather than an insoluble mystery. Wright's progress was so slow that, paradoxically, difficulties arise in condemning the movement on grounds of slowness. The distance traversed was about one and one half miles. It took over three hours—from 11:30 a.m., when Wright's deployed column started, until about 3 p.m., when he developed Ewell's main line of battle. One may walk the distance at a leisurely pace in thirty-five minutes.[4] It is idle, however, to speculate on reasons that might have re-tarded Wright, unless one considers the difficult terrain and the nature of the resistance encountered along the heavily wooded watershed.

Three significant facts are immediately apparent. In the first place, Cowles' 1st North Carolina Cavalry, which had been screening Ewell's concentration during May 4th, pushed out sometime before 8 o'clock on the Culpeper Mine Road to re-connoiter toward Germanna Ford.[5] Confederate cavalry was reported at an early hour in the woods north of the Turnpike by Griffin's pickets.[6] Major Michler, Meade's Engineer, confirms this report by his own reconnaissance along the Culpeper Mine Road between 8 and 9 o'clock.[7] In the second place, Ewell, after ordering the deployment of Jones' and Steuart's brigades on the right and left, respectively, of the Turnpike, instructed Walker to advance on the Culpeper Mine Road and establish contact with the enemy's skirmishers. This was accomplished between 10 and 11 a.m., while Wright was preparing to move forward and connect with Warren's flank.[8] In the third place, there is strong evidence to the effect that, during the mile and a half advance toward Warren's flank, Wright's deployed col-umn, in the order, left to right, Upton-Brown-Russell, met sharp skirmish resistance; Cowles' dismounted troopers and Walker's Virginia riflemen employed every tactic known to forest warfare from 11 a.m. until 3 p.m., when Federal army headquarters informed Warren that Wright had connected with Robinson's right and that Ricketts would be put in po-sition to support both.[9]

Resistance appears to have been most stubborn at the center and right of the line. Upton, on the left, states that the advance of his brigade was made by right of wings, it being impossible to march in line of battle on account of the dense pine and im-penetrable thicket.[10] Skirmishing in front of Brown's 1st Brig-ade, in the center, was continuous.[11] Supporting Russell, Neill's

1st Brigade, Getty's division, according to the report of the officer commanding, "drove the enemy for about 2 miles when we came upon an entrenched line supported by artillery." In the lead, Brigadier General D. A. Russell seems to have been unaware of any such sweep!

Intimate narratives in various regimental histories elaborate the factual statements of official reports. Sergeant Robert S. Westbrook, 49th Pennsylvania (Russell's brigade) records that his regiment "advanced in line of battle, pushing the enemy. We drove the Confederates like sheep." The historian of this unit gives a more restrained account: The Federal skirmish line, he relates, engaged Confederates who invariably fell back. Our line, he adds, would suddenly encounter a line of Rebels lying on the ground and hidden by brush and leaves. Then the Confederates would spring to their feet, fire a deadly volley and pull back.[12]

Ewell Extends His Left

Ewell's dispositions for the defense of his left have already been described.[18] To recapitulate in part, Edward Johnson's Division, less Jones' Brigade, immediately reformed along the line it had defended against Warren's attack. Hays' and Pegram's Brigades of Early's Division, which had been held in reserve on the Turnpike during the fighting of the early afternoon, were sent to left of the line. Gordon's Brigade, Early's Division, it will be recalled, was drawn from the reserve to reinforce Rodes' Division during the fighting on the right, or south side of the Turnpike.

With no immediate threat on the left, it may be deduced that Hays and Pegram would not have been sent to extend Johnson's line until the outcome of the battle on the right, where Gordon had intervened, was assured. Knowing that the menace of Wright's column was remote and that, after the repulse of Ayres' attack across Sanders' field, there was no immediate danger to his left, Ewell would have held his reserve in hand until the situation was stabilized on the right, beyond which lay the dangerous gap between his corps and A. P. Hill's.

Ewell would not have been aware of the collapse of Wadsworth's movement much before the reports of this event came to Federal army headquarters. Meade's chief of staff was apprised of the circumstance sometime between 1:30 p.m. and 2:15.[14]

If the pace of Wright's progress along the ridge toward Ewell's left was uniform, his column was more than half way to its objective by 1:30 p.m. Shortly after this hour, Ewell should have been at ease concerning his right. Yet the threat of Wright's approaching column became imminent. Granting this obvious situation, Ewell faced a grave crisis: His line must be extended at once beyond the left of Johnson's flank; Hays and Pegram must hasten thither in order to block an envelopment of the exposed flank; and these two units must march and deploy with speed, for at 1:30 p.m. Johnson's flank was about equidistant from the position occupied by Ewell's reserve and Wright's oncoming column.

The Attack Is Launched

The Federals pushed on, their covering cloud of skirmishers swarming through the trees toward Johnson's main line. Steuart's composite Virginia-North Carolina brigade withdrew from its cover and charged into Upton's force. The woods around Sanders' field awoke with the roar of musketry. A savage encounter followed. Steuart strove for half an hour to force back Wright's left, hoping no doubt to arrest the advance while Early came into position opposite the Federal right. The effort seems indicative of a critical state of affairs on the Confederate flank. Steuart, in extending his right across the interval vacated by Jones, had created what Colonel Thurston, commanding the 3rd North Carolina, describes as "a long brigade distance between the flanks of hitherto closed lines of the two brigades." [15] An advance under such conditions must have been perilous indeed.

Upton in the meantime had connected with the right of the V Corps. Lieutenant Colonel Edward Carroll, commanding the 95th Pennsylvania, fell in the raging fire-fight at the head of his regiment. Three companies of the 95th went forward and carried "a hill" on which the enemy was strongly posted. Thirty prisoners were taken. "The position," states Upton, "although 200 yards in advance of the Fifth Corps line was important to hold and the line was established there." Upton also notes that the woods in front and around his position were burning and that the ground was strewn with dead and wounded, both Federal and Confederate, of the previous fighting, many of whom must have perished in the flames, as corpses were found partly consumed.[16]

Brown and Russell, with Neill in support, came up on the line established by Upton. The four brigades swept forward, driving Johnson's advanced elements back on the main position, which lay along a low, flat ridge extending northwestward from the northwest corner of Sanders' field toward Flat Run.

Steuart fell back into the interval between Battle and Stafford. Walker's (Stonewall) Brigade of five Virginia regiments, withdrew before the concentrated power of Wright's four-brigade assault column. The Virginians, covered on their right by Steuart, retired on Stafford's Brigade. Stafford moved by his left to create an interval for Walker.

Wright launched his attack all along the line. The right of the assault column struck Johnson's entrenched line and recoiled; Upton's regiments became intermixed with those of Brown's New Jersey brigade; a counterattacking force of Confederates secured a lodgement on the slight eminence gained by Carroll's 95th New York. General Sedgwick rode into the turmoil and ordered Colonel W. H. Penrose, commanding the 15th New Jersey, to storm the heights.[17] The 15th went gallantly forward; the 125th New York, supporting Penrose, closed the gap in Upton's line. Alanson A. Haines, chaplain of the 15th New Jersey, records in his history of the regiment the fierce fighting at this juncture.

> Here we were established, while at times the conflict raged around us and on our front, the remainder of that day and the day following. Being by the emergency detached from our brigade, we were temporarily united with the second

brigade, under Colonel Upton. It was impossible to see the enemy; and though we peered through the thick woods, we were fighting invisible foemen. We soon began intrenching. Our men scraped the stones and earth before them as best they could, until spades were brought. All the time the enemy were sending a shower of bullets over and past us. It would at times lessen, then start again afresh. We lay on the crest of the hill, stooping low as every fusillade swept over. It was wonderful that our casualties were not greater in that leaden storm. We replied by occasional volleys, but could not see what damage we inflicted. We were screened by bushes on our front. The enemy before us was screened in the same manner. Between the two lay an open, cleared flat [Sanders' field] of small extent, through which passed the Orange pike.[18]

The five New Jersey regiments remaining under Brown's command charged and grappled with the five Louisiana regiments of Stafford's Brigade. The struggle was violent and sanguinary. General Stafford fell, mortally wounded.[19] He was borne to the rear; his men closed ranks and drove the Jerseymen from their front.

Indecisive Results

While the fighting on the left settled into an indecisive fire fight, Russell's and Neill's brigades clashed with Harry Hays' Louisiana brigade. It would appear that Hays, upon coming into position on Stafford's left, went forward, either with the intention of holding up the Federal advance until Pegram could form on the extreme left of the Confederate line, or, perhaps, with a view to turning the flank of the Federal force while it developed its attack on Johnson's front. According to Early, Hays advanced until stiffening Federal resistance brought him to a standstill. Then, excepting only the 25th Virginia of Jones' Brigade, the supports who should have joined Hays failed to appear.[20]

Before giving his order to attack, Russell, on the right of Wright's line, detached five companies of the 5th Wisconsin under Major Totten, with orders to deploy as skirmishers on the extreme right of the line.[21] Then Russell, with Neill in support, advanced to the attack. Moving swiftly through the woods, Hays' Louisianans met the oncoming column. The 25th

Virginia swung in on the left of the Louisiana line and joined an attack on the right of Neill's brigade. The 49th New York and 7th Maine fought off the assailants until Totten's Wisconsin detachment slipped through the woods and, dividing into two parties, surrounded the Virginia regiment.

Facing heavy odds and denied the support he had expected, Hays fell back. The 25th Virginia left 300 prisoners and a stand of colors with Totten's command.[22] Russell pushed forward; Neill came up on his right and, advancing to develop the enemy's position, struck an entrenched line supported by artillery.[23]

Comments

Just as the initial power of Hancock's offensive thrust on the Plank Road ridge was unequal to the task of dislodging the Confederate right, so Wright's attack column failed in its original mission against Lee's left on the Culpeper Mine Road ridge.

The conditions of failure were strikingly similar. Both involved piecemeal attacks against partially prepared defensive positions. Federal and Confederate reserves were marching to the sound of the guns. While Gibbon and Barlow hastened to Hancock's front, Wilcox rushed to Heth's assistance; Ricketts moved toward Wright's attacking column, as Early tore through the thickets toward Edward Johnson's threatened flank. In each case the Confederates completed their dispositions for defense before the attackers could develop sufficient power to shatter the defense and sweep it from the field. There were minor differences. Hancock enjoyed a limited artillery support; the center of his column was aided by a mobile section; his flanking movement against A. P. Hill's right was, in some measure, prepared by long range fire from the corps artillery massed at the extreme left of his line.[24] Wright, on the other hand, had no artillery support; on the contrary, he attacked a partially entrenched line supported by Confederate guns in carefully chosen positions. His left lay within range of Nelson's artillery mass emplaced beyond Sanders' field on the south side of the Turnpike.[25] His center and right were intermittently swept by the enfilading fire of guns that Colonel Carter, commanding Ewell's left artillery group, had placed in position north of the Turnpike.

The moral effect of crashing shot and bursting shells was probably greater than that of the actual loss sustained by direct hits. Wright's men were denied the comforting music of their own artillery.[26] Good infantry the world over will take terrific punishment from the enemy's guns, whenever afforded the guarantee that their own supporting artillery will give measure for measure.

Battle Scenes

Particular battle scenes may be horrifying to inexperienced witnesses, but such intermittent occurrences seldom demoralize large bodies of seasoned troops. A remarkable case in point is given. Reporting back to Sedgwick after detachment at army headquarters during the forenoon, Brevet Brigadier General Thomas W. Hyde, of the VI Corps staff, encountered hostile shell fire within a few yards of the corps commander. An explosion decapitated a New Jersey private nearby. The gory head struck Hyde full in the face, filling his mouth with bloody mucous and knocking him to the ground. Splattered with blood and brains, he regained his feet. General Sedgwick looked on in helpless horror as Hyde spewed out an unsightly mess. Only when the corps commander realized the true nature of Hyde's mishap did he again turn his attention to the battle. "I was dazed for ten minutes," admits Hyde.[27]

Despite the horror wrought by an occasional shell, the volume of Confederate rifle fire and the confident spirit of Johnson's and Early's infantry, who missed no opportunity to strike with a savage counter-charge, caused far greater discouragement to the Federal offense than the sniping fire of individual Confederate cannon.

The opposing lines, according to Surgeon George T. Stevens, 77th New York, Neill's brigade, ran along slight ridges on opposite sides of a wooded marsh about 300 yards in width. The dense growth extended up from the marshland, covering both crests and completely masking the opposing lines of trenches to hostile observation. Stevens describes the fighting between 3 and 4 o'clock, as follows:

> The rattle of musketry would swell into a continuous roar as the simultaneous discharge of 10,000 guns mingled in one grand concert, and then after a few minutes, became more interrupted, resembling the crash of some huge king of the forest when felled by the stroke of the woodsman's ax. Then would be heard the wild yells which always told of a rebel charge, and again the volleys would become more terrible and the broken crashing tones would swell into one continuous roll of sound, which would presently be interrupted by the vigorous manly cheers of the northern soldiers, so different from the shrill yell of the rebels, and which indicated a repulse of their enemies.[28]

During this hour, 3-4 p.m., general headquarters, as has been related in Chapter 12, was hopeful of developing an advance all along the line. It will be recalled that at 3 p.m. Warren was informed that Ricketts would be put in position to support both the V and VI corps and that Burnside had received instructions to give General Sedgwick one of the three IX Corps divisions, if called upon by Sedgwick to do so.[29] Fifteen minutes later, and after army headquarters had informed Warren that Sedgwick had connected with the right of the V Corps, orders were issued for the attack of Getty's division and Hancock's II Corps along the Plank Road.[30] Then, at 4 o'clock, upon hearing that Getty and Hancock would attack in accordance with the orders of 3:15 p.m., army headquarters informed Warren of this development and instructed the V Corps commander to prepare to attack, if practicable, with the divisions of Robinson and Crawford and one brigade of Ricketts, whenever directed by the army commander.[31]

Success of the general movement depended upon a variety of separate developments; The attacks of Sedgwick and Hancock must attain, or give promise of attaining, their local objectives. Warren, given discretionary powers in the decision to attack, must be convinced in his own mind that progress against both the Confederate right and left was such as to justify an attack on the Confederate left center, while his own left effected a junction with Hancock's right opposite the gap in the Confederate line. Finally, Ricketts' two brigades and one of Burnside's must be available as reinforcements to the V and VI Corps whenever their presence might be required to develop or to exploit the desired situation.

Seymour's Brigade Arrives

By 5 p.m., when Mott's division staggered back to the Brock Road, imposing a delay on the subsequent development of Hancock's offensive that could not be overcome before nightfall, Sedgwick's advance had been stopped and the fire-fight following his repulse had died down.[32] The promised brigade from Ricketts' division now arrived at the front; Seymour, leading the 2d Brigade, changed direction to deploy on the right of Neill's brigade.[33]

The Federals had lost another race between reserves in the march toward a swaying battle front. The appearance of Seymour's unit an hour earlier would have given Sedgwick a preponderance of force that Ewell could scarcely have met. With an additional division from the IX Corps in close supporting distance, Sedgwick's striking power would have been irresistible. At 5 o'clock the belated arrival of Seymour's force was neutralized by the appearance of Pegram's 5-regiment brigade, which had followed Hays' Louisianans toward the imperilled flank. The prospects of turning Ewell's left were greatly diminished.[34]

Seymour's tardy arrival cannot justly be attributed to the brigade commander; the fault lay with the uncertain workings of a divided command. As hitherto related, General Ricketts had been perplexed by a series of contradictory orders from general and army headquarters, each issuing its own instructions without regard to the other.[35]

Grant's deference to Meade at 10:30 a.m. in the matter concerning Ricketts' division was most unfortunate. Insistence on his part that the original order given Ricketts must be executed without further delay would have put the brigades of

Morris and Seymour in motion toward the front by noon. As matters eventuated, Burnside did not relieve Ricketts until 1:30 p.m.[36] With an hour and a half to the good, Seymour could have reinforced Sedgwick at the crisis of his thrust along the Culpeper Mine Road ridge.

Between 5 and 6 o'clock the situation on both active fronts was almost identical. Both right and left Confederate flanks had been severely shaken; but reserves had arrived in time to prevent the attackers from overwhelming them. The failure of Mott's division on the Federal left had delayed Hancock's final effort by at least an hour. A misunderstanding in regard to Ricketts' division imposed a similar delay in effecting dispositions for another blow by VI Corps troops on the right.

About 5:50 p.m. army headquarters received Lyman's dispatch of 5:05, stating that Gibbon's division was going in and that Barlow would try a diversion on the left.[37] At 6 p.m. orders issued by Meade reflect a final attempt to develop the general offensive that Grant had planned as early as 2:15 p.m. and had attempted to launch by 4 o'clock. Meade directed Warren renew the attack on the pike immediately. The V Corps commander was informed that "Sedgwick is ordered to renew Wright's attack at once." [38] At the same time, Wadsworth, after waiting an hour, received the order to advance southward through the thickets opposite the gap in Lee's line toward A. P. Hill's left.[39]

Seymour Ordered to Turn Ewell's Left

The phases of the general movement as executed by Barlow and Wadsworth have been narrated. There remains to tell the story of Sedgwick's second encounter, in which Upton-Brown-Russell-Neill were expected to fix Ewell's left front while Warren's V Corps struck his right front and Seymour enveloped his left flank.

The selection of Seymour's brigade for such a mission was unfortunate indeed. Originally incorporated in the Army of the Potomac as a unit of the III Corps on July 9, 1863, and then transferred to the VI Corps in the reorganization of

March, 1864,[40] this unit was still regarded as a stranger by its companion brigades. Seymour's brigade was regarded as an outfit of insufferable recruits. Its commander, also a stranger to the Army of the Potomac, had been disastrously defeated at Oluste, Florida, during February, 1864, while leading a force inland from Jacksonville toward Tallahassee. An unsuccessful general, assigned to the command of a reconstituted brigade on the very morning of a great battle, he was given a mission which should have been entrusted only to seasoned troops, with a successful leader who enjoyed the absolute confidence of his men. In justice, however, to the officers and men of Ricketts' division, it must be stated in this connection that their subsequent achievments won full admission to the proud brotherhood-in-arms of the old VI Corps divisions.

Seymour formed his five regiments for attack in two lines. In the first were the 6th Maryland-110th Pennsylvania, the latter on the right; in the second, the 122d Ohio-138th Pennsylvania-126th Pennsylvania formed from left to right, in the order given. His position was on gently rolling ground, thickly covered with trees.[41]

Having reconnoitered to the front, Seymour was satisfied that his right overlapped the enemy's line a considerable distance. With Neill supporting on his left, he determined to develop the main Confederate line and then swing his right against the exposed flank. The reconnaissance, however, was incomplete, either in regard to distance covered or the length of time the skirmishers were out. At any rate they failed to establish the significant fact that Pegram's Virginians were extending the Confederate line beyond Seymour's right.[42]

When all was ready General Seymour instructed Colonel J. Warren Keifer, commanding the 110th Ohio, to lead the first line. The advance is described by Keifer, who in later years was Speaker of the House of Representatives:

> The troops charged forward in gallant style, pressing the enemy back about one-half mile, when we came upon the slope of a hill, entrenched behind logs, which had been hurriedly thrown together. During the advance the troops were twice

halted, and a fire opened, killing and wounding a considerable number of the enemy. The front line was upon the extreme right of the army, and the troops upon its left were said to have been commanded by Brigadier-General Neill. Failing to move forward in conjunction with it, I deemed it prudent to halt, without making an attack upon the enemy's line. After a short consultation with Colonel John W. Horn [6th Maryland], I sent word to Brigadier-General Seymour that the advance line of the brigade was unsupported upon either flank, and that the enemy overlapped the right and left of the line, and was apparently in heavy force, rendering it impossible for the troops to attain success in a further attack. This word was sent to Lieutenant Gump, of General Seymour's staff. I soon after received an order to attack at once. Feeling sure that the word I sent had not been received, I delayed until a second order was received to attack. I accordingly made the attack without further delay. The attack was made about 7 p.m. The troops were in a thick and dense Wilderness. The line was advanced to within 150 yards of the enemy's works, under a most terrible fire from the front and flanks. It was impossible to succeed; but the two regiments, notwithstanding, maintained their ground, and kept up a rapid fire for nearly three hours, and then retired under orders for a short distance only. I was wounded about 8:30 p.m., by a rifle ball passing through both bones of the left forearm, but did not relinquish command until 9 p.m.[43]

There is little or no evidence to rebut Colonel Keifer's implication that the turning movement was ill-considered and that Seymour's insistence upon a vigorous prosecution of the attack after all possibility of a flank operation had vanished, led only to useless sacrifice of life. The 110th Ohio suffered 113 casualties in the action. The 7th Maryland lost heavily; the commanding officer, Colonel John W. Horn, states that he held the position gained in the final advance until 10 o'clock, "having no orders to fall back, although I had repeatedly reported that I had no support upon my left, the regiment on my left having fallen back as soon as checked by the enemy."

Although Neill is accused of having failed to maintain his connection with the left of Seymour's brigade, Neill's regiments nevertheless maintained the fight with an obstinacy that was true to the tradition of the VI Corps.[44] Major A. F. Brewer, historian of the 61st Pennsylvania, records that Seymour and Neill attacked the Confederate works with little or no advantage and sustained heavy losses. The Federals returned to the attack after 6 p.m., the 61st expending about 100 rounds of rifle ammunition per man. Their Springfields became too hot to hold. About 7 p.m. Neill was obliged to relieve his front line, an expediency which Seymour either ignored or felt no need of adopting. The regimental historian says that Colonel George T. Smith performed valiantly here, refuting the charge of cowardice unjustly made on a previous occasion. He sent his horse to the rear, then stayed on the firing line during the entire remainder of the day. The Confederate infantry could not be seen; the enemy's batteries, hidden to view, enfiladed Neill's line. The thick underbrush was matted together with vines, through which hostile bullets came in showers. The woods were afire all along the line.[45]

Brown's New Jersey brigade, with Russell's and Upton's brigades on the left, supported the attack with vigorous fire. So far as is known, no advance in force was attempted.[46] Warren failed to renew his attack on the Turnpike. Morris' brigade closed up and replaced Wadsworth in reserve.[47] Crawford and Robinson, each with two brigades, remained in their trenches. Colonel Wainwright, V Corps chief of artillery, reports some satisfactory artillery practice:

> At times during the afternoon the rifled batteries opened on bodies of the enemy seen passing the open ground [Chewning's farm] to which Crawford at first advanced. The distance was about 2,700 yards; practice good. I had here an opportunity of judging of the relative merits of the Parrotts and 3-inch guns at this range. The elevation required was the same for each nor could I see any difference in the accuracy of the fire. I should judge the proportion of shells which burst about 5 to 4 in favor of the 3-inch (Hotchkiss), while five Parrotts and three 3-inch burst within a few yards of the muzzle . . . the remaining four guns of Winslow's battery and a section of Philipps' battery posted on the pike replied to and several times silenced, the enemy's guns (Nelson's), similarly posted at a distance of about 1,400 yards.[48]

Just what might have been the effect of a thrust by Warren's available force, five brigades, at the four-brigade line (Battle-

Doles-Daniel-Gordon), on south of the Turnpike was probably decided on the ground by Grant himself. Unless it was certain that Ewell's left was crumbling, it would not have seemed advisable to risk four Federal brigades in frontal assault against the south (right) flank, which was entrenched to a line of far greater natural strength than that held by the left. Only in the event of a complete rout of the left could Grant afford to throw in Morris' brigade, his sole reserve, and Griffin's decimated division. These conditions did not exist; Warren remained quiescent, probably with Grant's approval.

Grant Still Holds Initiative

Decisive fighting on the Federal right came to an end about 9 p.m., when Colonel Keifer, his broken arm in a rough, blood-soaked dressing, went to the rear. Darkness had halted Wadsworth, with only a thin line of sniping skirmishers between him and A. P. Hill's helpless left. The troops on Birney's front sank down in exhaustion when dark called an end to the futile roar of musketry. Barlow's turning column stood face to face with the Confederates covering Hill's left.

Grant had fallen short in the realization of his endeavor to mount a general offensive all along the line. The collapse of Mott's division on the left, the muddle that withheld Ricketts' troops from an opportune intervention on the right, and Warren's reluctance or inability to take the offensive either at 4 p.m. or 6 p.m., marred the program and, in their accumulative effect, ruined Grant's hopes of a decision before dark.

Lee, however, had not created the situation in the fighting of the 5th that promised a rapid transition to the offensive on the morrow. He had failed to close the gap at his center. While Ewell had held his own, A. P. Hill lay badly beaten on the field. Only darkness had averted an overwhelming defeat.[48] Hill's Corps was virtually surrounded. His forces "were huddled together in the utmost confusion, 'cross and pile', with no line formed," observed a private soldier of the 18th North Carolina.[49] Colonel Palmer, Hill's chief-of-staff—a more eminent authority—wrote to a comrade after the war that "they were like a worm fence, at every angle." [50]

Here, surely, was no springboard for a Confederate counter-offensive operation at dawn. To the contrary, there was nothing to indicate at nightfall that the offensive power of Grant's troops had waned. The gap in the Confederate line invited attack. The three reserve divisions of Longstreet and Anderson were counterbalanced by an equal number of the Federal IX Corps. Having crossed over the Germanna Ford pontoon bridge at intervals during the day and taken position along the Germanna Plank Road about a mile and a half south of the Rapidan, Grant's reserve was closer to the center of his line than was Longstreet at Richard's Shop or Anderson at New Verdiersville with respect to Lee's center. In the Germanna Plank and Brock Roads Grant had a good lateral highway for movement behind his front. In other words, Grant had more nearly completed his concentration for a general offensive than had Lee; his command of means of lateral communication conferred greater possibilities for maneuver during battle. Furthermore, while Grant's piecemeal attacks of the 5th had failed to culminate in a general offensive, his inability to carry Lee's lines should not be regarded as a defeat. He had prevented Lee from completing his defensive dispositions. He still held the initiative.[51]

CHAPTER 16

MISADVENTURES OF SHERIDAN'S CAVALRY

Before drawing night's dark curtain over the historic May 5, 1864, it is necessary to recount briefly the operations of Sheridan's cavalry in the rear and on the left flank of the army. In an attempt to execute its strategic role as the "eyes and ears of the army," the Federal cavalry saw little and heard scarcely anything. An analysis of this debacle is closely identified with developments that shaped the main course of operations during the day.

Defective Planning and Faulty Execution

The circumstances and events attending the destruction of Sheridan's cavalry screen on the left front, while Meade was making dispositions to fight an infantry action on the right, have already been recounted. To recapitulate, Meade at 7:30 a.m. on May 5 had suspended the flanking movement, as modified in the orders of 6 p.m., May 4. Three significant circumstances will also be recalled: (1) General Wilson, who was to form the screen with his 3d Cavalry Division, ignored that part of his instructions specifying that he should keep out parties on the Orange Court House Pike and Plank Road; (2) Hammond's 5th New York Cavalry, which was left at Parker's Store as a connecting link between Wilson's main body and the advance of Warren's V Corps, rose gallantly to the requirement of picketing the Plank Road but was unable to maintain its connection with the 3d Cavalry Division; (3) Wilson, when required by Meade to develop the Confederate force reported at 7:30 a.m. by Crawford on the Plank Road, was cut off from communication with army headquarters, thereby denying Meade the use of his "eyes and ears." Deaf and blind, as it were, and in an uncertain state of mind as to whether Lee was merely attempting to impose upon his freedom of maneuver, or was actually offering battle in the Wilderness, Meade made dispositions which were too slow for the first contingency and entirely inadequate for the second one. Such was the impasse which confronted Grant when he arrived at the front shortly before 10 a.m.

It goes without saying that Sheridan's strong, mobile cavalry force, endowed, for the most part,[1] with the high firepower of magazine rifles, could and should have averted such an impasse. Much might be made of the fact that, although Sheridan had established a reputation in the West as a resolute and dashing general of infantry, he had never commanded a large body of horse. A similar indictment may be brought against Wilson— a brilliant young staff officer who, up to the time of his assignment to the 3d Cavalry Division, had never commanded troops in the field.

Wilson was remiss in his failure to properly patrol and picket the Orange Turnpike, both during the late afternoon of the 4th and early on the morning of the 5th. The consequences of this failure were far reaching. It was the immediate cause for suspension of the flanking maneuver at 7:30 a.m.

The degree of Sheridan's complicity in the failure of his division commander is difficult to determine. Any evaluation of Sheridan's share of the blame encounters the military maxim that a commander cannot hide behind the lapse of a subordinate. There are, however, limitations and obvious exceptions to this maxim. Certainly, whenever the commander confers discretionary powers on the subordinate, as was done by Grant to Warren at 4 p.m. on this day, then the decision of the subordinate, right or wrong, is the decision of the commander. Again, whenever an order is vague or contradictory, requiring a latitude of interpretation on the part of the subordinate, together with an adaptation of means unforeseen at the time of issuance of the order, the degree of responsibility thus conferred becomes tantamount to a grant of discretionary powers. Failure of the subordinate in such circumstances is the failure of the commander. When, however, the order is clear, precise, and beyond any possibility of alternative construction, and the means of strict compliance on the part of the subordinate are well within the margin of his capabilities, then, certainly, the commander is not required to share responsibility for the lapse of his subordinate.

The "order of march" issued from army headquarters at 6 p.m. May 4, constituted a directive, or general statement of policy for the information of the various corps commanders. These authorities in turn issued orders for the purpose of carrying out the army commander's directive. Their subsequent orders may be regarded as modified directives for the guidance of division commanders in making dispositions best calculated to implement the original directive. In what manner did Sheridan articulate Meade's directive, insofar as concerned the required dispositions on the part of Wilson's 3d Cavalry Division?

The evidence here is scant. We cannot produce such an order. Nevertheless there is ample support for the statement that Sheridan was keenly alert to his responsibility in this respect. His anxiety to instruct his division commanders was such that even before issuance, at 6 p.m. on the 4th, of march orders for the 5th, he informed Humphreys of the location of cavalry corps headquarters. After giving precise instructions for the guidance of couriers seeking that place, he added the postscript: "I should like to be informed to-night of the probable movement of troops tomorrow, and the points at which the different headquarters of the army and corps will be." [2]

Wilson was equally conscientious. At 7:40 p.m. on the 4th May he addressed cavalry corps headquarters stating that he had executed all orders, and requesting instructions for the morrow.

Now comes the crux of the question: Did Wilson receive instructions? If so, what did they say?

A qualified affirmative answer to the first question can be

given. Describing operations of the 5th in his official report, Wilson states: "Having received no counter instructions during the night, and the enemy having made no demonstration, in compliance *with my original order* (Italics added by editor), at 5 a.m. of the 5th, leaving Colonel Hammond with his regiment on the road before Parker's Store, I pushed on toward Craig's Meeting House on the Catharpin Road." [3]

This was equivalent to saying that any orders received had not been countermanded. Since such orders cannot be identified, it cannot be established that Sheridan answered his request of 7:40 p.m. for detailed instructions.

Blame is Shared

An obscure reference in Wilson's communication of 7:20 p.m. to cavalry corps headquarters furnishes grounds for even more serious charges than those heretofore reviewed. These involve three principals—Meade, Sheridan, and Wilson himself.

Reports of Wilson's various reconnaissances on the 4th had disclosed information indicating that all roads leading eastward toward the Mine Run lines were, with the exception of the Orange Plank Road, filled with Confederate troops. One of Wilson's cavalry patrols had clashed about 11 a.m. with a party of Confederate horse on the Turnpike near Robertson's Tavern.[4] At 7:20 p.m. while writing to Sheridan for instructions, Wilson mentioned the fact that the patrol he had ordered during the afternoon to push out on the Turnpike as far as Robertson's Tavern and drive the enemy away from that place had not as yet joined the main body at Parker's Store.

The patrol mentioned in Wilson's report performed its mission in a perfunctory compliance with order, but in gross violation of the real requirements of its assignment. Upon reaching Robertson's Tavern the party then turned off through the woods toward Parker's Store, just in time to miss the appearance of Ewell's advance, pushing along the pike toward the tavern.[5]

Whatever may have been the report of the patrol leader,

Wilson appears to have been satisfied with a negative account of the affair. Furthermore, he appears to have reasoned toward the surprising conclusion that the brief visit of his patrol to Robertson's Tavern established beyond any reasonable doubt that, although Confederate troops were pouring down throughout the day by all routes excepting the Plank Road, toward Mine Run, none of these formations could have pushed out eastward from the works along that stream. Nor does Wilson's intention of withdrawing the patrol from the Turnpike, which is made perfectly clear in the dispatch, seem to have impressed either Sheridan, Meade, or Grant as ill advised.

Meade, who had already issued his directive for the 5th, stating that "Wilson will move at 5 a.m. [and] will keep out parties on the Orange Court-House pike and plank roads." [6] does not appear to have been concerned as to provisions for holding those roads with sufficiently large bodies of cavalry to develop any hostile movement in force on either of the roads in question. Given Wilson's assignment for the 5th, he could not, with the force at his disposal, have pursued his objective on the Catharpin Road with any hope of success and at the same time have spared detachments in sufficient strength to have conducted a reconnaissance on a strategic scale on either the pike or Plank Road. Meade's directive was inadequate.

A party of cavalry on the Turnpike in no greater strength than the force with which Hammond attempted to delay Hill's advance along the Plank Road could not have exercised any decided difference on the development of events. Despite Hammond's gallant efforts in holding up the advance element of A. P. Hill's corps, the march of the main column suffered little or no delay.[7] At no time between dawn and 7:30 a.m. when Crawford's infantry outposts at Chewning's farm reported skirmishing on the Plank Road near Parker's Store, did Hammond's slender skirmish line succeed in pinning down Kirkland's Brigade long enough to create a situation in which Hill was obliged to close up and thus reveal his strength. In other words, Hammond's regiment discovered the head of a strong infantry column and gave warning of its approach. He did not develop the enemy's column, nor impose sufficient delay to disclose both the hostile strength and intentions. The splendid conduct of the 5th New York Cavalry does, nevertheless, indicate what might have been accomplished by a cavalry brigade, with its supporting horse batteries, at dawn in a position well advanced on the Plank Road toward New Verdiersville. A similar force at a corresponding point on the Turnpike with regard to Ewell's column might well have so reduced the enemy's capabilities for movement that Grant's flanking operation by way of Shady Grove Church could have continued without interruption and the collision of the two armies in the Wilderness safely averted.

No less distinguished a witness than Meade himself appears as a damaging witness against his own faulty provision for strategic reconnaissance before battle. Shortly after 9 a.m., when he instructed Wilson to develop the Confederate movement reported by Crawford, Meade had pressing need for a powerful cavalry force at his immediate disposal. Wilson was off to the left, pushing out beyond Craig's Meeting House and establishing contact with the Confederate horse that promptly threw him back to the Brock Road.[8] Gregg with the 2d Cavalry Division was fretting at Aldrich. Intent on joining Gregg and riding with Sheridan in the direction of Hamilton's Crossing, Torbert's 1st Cavalry Division moved at a snail's pace in and out and around the interminable procession of bumping canvas-topped transport wagons on the Ely's Ford road. Over by Hamilton's Crossing, a patrol of the 1st Maine Cavalry cantered along the Old Mine Road and espied two brigades of Fitzhugh Lee's Cavalry Division in rapid march toward Massaponax Church.[9] With two-thirds of the mounted arm inactive behind his slowly forming battle front, Meade came to the bitter realization that he had no cavalry screen in his front.

The failure to send a mounted party out on the Turnpike

at dawn is but an item in a cavalry program that had no primary objective. More accurately stated, perhaps, the want of a primary objective was due to a divided purpose—that of employing the cavalry as the strategic arm before battle and, at the same time, keeping large mounted formations in hand for the protection of the great trains. Meade's directive of 6 p.m. May 4th betrays a confused state of mind in drawing a clear distinction between the main function of the cavalry during May 5 and those secondary duties that the exigencies of the situation might require. The army commander, to be sure, must assume full responsibility for the directive, whether or not it was framed in accordance with the views of his cavalry chief. In this instance the army commander, after consulting his subordinate, or heeding his opinion of the situation—as Meade did, according to Humphreys' statement of the case—cannot hide behind the lapse of the subordinate in formulating a faulty plan of action.

Discussion of the entire issue, which has been partially examined in its connection with the modification of Humphreys' original turning movement through the Wilderness, now resolves itself to a single question. This question, it must be insisted, has nothing to do with identifying the intellectual parentage of Meade's directive. Whether or not the plan was Meade's he assumed full responsibility for the brainchild at the time of its confirmation as a written directive. The measure of responsibility thus assumed is wholly determined by the nature of the plan—its suitability to the requirements of the army and the relationship of secondary duties with respect to the major function of the cavalry mass.

What were the requirements of the army in this situation, and just what did these requirements prescribe as a requisite course of action for the cavalry mass?

In justice to Meade the question should be answered with great care. The requirements of his army in crossing the Rapidan and penetrating the forest zone were extraordinary. The demands put upon the cavalry were extraordinary in the same degree. As the army marched southward from its advanced base at Brandy Station, the rolling stock of the Orange and Alexandria Railroad was moved back beyond Manassas Junction. While the railway was not abandoned, it ceased to serve as a line of supply for the advancing forces. During the transit of the Wilderness and development of the turning movement against Lee's right rear, the Army of the Potomac had no fixed depot of supplies; it subsisted during this critical interim on the fifteen-day allowance of rations and forage carried by the field transport.

In the Wilderness, therefore, the requirements put upon the Federal cavalry were of a specialized and exceptional nature. Whatever may have been the demands for strategic reconnaissance by the mounted arm, these requirements could only be met *after* adequate provision had been made for the protection of the trains. Furthermore, Meade's problem of protection was aggravated by the known fact that a large body of Confederate cavalry had wintered at Hamilton's Crossing, on the left flank of his proposed route of march through the Wilderness.

Sheridan's dictum that cavalry should fight cavalry, leaving the infantry to look after itself and guard its own trains, might have been perfectly sound under normal circumstances. Given an army operating on a front perpendicular to its line of communications, there would be no reason for diminishing the cavalry mass by large detachments to guard the trains. But under the exceptional conditions pertaining in the Wilderness, Meade had good reason to adopt a more cautious policy than the one advocated by his bold cavalry chieftain. Unfortunately, in tempering boldness with caution, Meade appears to have erred in the direction of overcautiousness.

His directive for operations of the cavalry on May 4 was a compromise. Two cavalry divisions were detailed to cover the river crossing and screen the initial penetration into the Wilderness; the third one, Torbert's, protected the rear of the trains on the north side of the Rapidan.

On the 5th of May the problem became exceedingly complex. The front of the army and the left of the turning movement required an impenetrable cavalry screen. As the endless double line of transport wagons rolled over the pontoon bridges at the Rapidan and closed up toward Chancellorsville, demands for the security of the trains increased. Then there was the additional threat of attack on the left.

Owing to reports of Confederate movements toward Mine Run and the probability of a collision during the 5th with the enemy, Meade, as heretofore described, curtailed the scope of his flanking maneuver by shortening the arc of movement. At the same time, greater emphasis was put upon protection of the trains against attack from the left than had originally been contemplated. Torbert, who had originally been directed to cross the Rapidan at Germanna Ford and cover the right flank of the trains during the movement in rear of the army on May 5th, was now instructed to proceed by way of the Ely's Ford crossing to join Gregg at Aldrich for a movement against the Confederate cavalry near Hamilton's Crossing.

It is not clear whether the so-called Hamilton's Crossing operation was offensive or defensive in character, whether it proceeded from Sheridan's offensive attitude and was adopted at his behest (as Humphreys claims), or whether Meade originated the movement as a measure of protection to the left of trains—as Sheridan's bitter condemnation of the scheme on that very day would indicate.[10] One thing, however, is certain: Adoption of the plan, together with the dispositions that were made for its execution, was nothing short of a catastrophe.

The rumble of Torbert's division on the Germanna Ford bridge at dawn of the 5th would have had an ominous sound to Confederate ears. It would be idle to speculate on developments that might have been precipitated by the appearance of this powerful Federal cavalry division on the flank of Ewell's column at about 7 a.m. Mention of the least of these possibilities is sufficient to indicate the magnitude of the opportunity thrown away. At any rate, instead of being lost in a traffic jam on the Ely's Ford road during the entire forenoon, Torbert's troopers might well have found useful employment in clearing the Culpeper Mine Road for a rapid march of Sedgwick's leading division to the right of Warren's line of battle.

Sheridan Reorients Effort

By noon Sheridan was aware that the immobilization of Torbert's cavalry on the Ely's Ford road had defeated every possibility of the movement toward Hamilton's Crossing. Furthermore, the quick shift of Fitzhugh Lee's cavalry force toward Massaponax Church had removed the purpose of the movement. If the Hamilton's Crossing operation had been motivated by an offensive purpose, the enemy had escaped; if the motive had been defensive, having in mind the security of the trains, Fitzhugh Lee had given a negative solution to his problem.

The situation now called for a redirection of cavalry effort. The position of Wilson's division was a matter of speculation: his connecting link with the V Corps had been driven from Parker's Store. All communication had been severed between Wilson and army headquarters.[11] Gregg's division was massed at Aldrich. Torbert's advance had finally reached the crowded crossroads at Chancellorsville.[12] Sometime before noon, after having waited in vain at Aldrich for Torbert, Sheridan had established cavalry headquarters near Piney Branch Church, a point on the Catharpin Road about two and a half miles southwest from Aldrich.[13]

Sheridan's shift of headquarters indicates a complete reorientation of objectives. Just before noon he received important intelligence from army headquarters in a dispatch which has since been lost. The nature of Sheridan's reply suggests that the message conveyed information of a general nature, with a suggestion, or perhaps a definite order.[14] Sheridan, however, had already anticipated the necessity for a more aggressive cavalry program. No news, as yet, had come from Wilson; his advanced brigade, Chapman's, was still in position on the Catharpin Road beyond Mrs. Faulkner's place,

Torbert, closing up at Chancellorsville, had adequate strength to cover the left of the trains. Gregg, Sheridan determined, must be pushed out on the Catharpin Road to Shady Grove Church and open communication with Wilson. At noon, upon reading Humphreys' dispatch, Sheridan informed army headquarters to this effect. His reference to the 3d Cavalry Division offers complete proof that Meade had heard nothing from Wilson. Sheridan wrote:

> Your dispatch received. I have ordered General Gregg's division via Catharpin road and Todd's Tavern, to [Shady] Grove Church, and directed him to open communication with General Wilson, who was ordered to Craig's Church in your order of last night. I will hold Torbert's division in front of Chancellorsville to cover our trains and support Gregg. General Torbert has just come up; he was delayed by the trains.[15]

Gregg Rides to Rescue Wilson

Gregg's division clattered off in column along the Catharpin Road toward Todd's Tavern. The degree of aggression implied in the forward movement does not, however, presuppose a general cavalry offensive. At 1:10 p.m. Sheridan ordered Custer's brigade of Torbert's 1st Division to proceed by the Catharine Furnace Road, take position at the Furnace-Brock Road intersection, and report to General Gregg. Instructions were sent to Gregg, informing the 2d Division commander that Custer would relieve Frank's infantry brigade, Barlow's division, II Corps, at the road intersection and that Wilson's 3d Division would be drawn back to Chancellorsville early in the morning to refit and to relieve the brigades of Torbert's 1st Division at that point. In the meantime, Gregg was given to understand that the 1st Division brigades would be made available "should you be attacked."[16]

At 2:45 p.m. Gregg reported his arrival at Todd's Tavern. "I find everything;" he said, "infantry and Chapman's brigade (Wilson's division) on the rear of the infantry. General Wilson is falling back to this point."[17]

The infantry mentioned by Gregg must have been an element of Gibbon's division, which had not as yet formed in the rear of the II Corps column. The reference here, together with the fact that Birney's advance connected with the left of Getty's division at 2 p.m. would indicate that the greater part, if not all of Gibbon's division, the third in the column of march, was still massed near Todd's Tavern. In concluding his dispatch Gregg stated: "General Wilson has not yet arrived and I can't say what I will do. The infantry (Second Corps) are moving on the Brock Road. I have my command here and will receive the enemy."

A hurried exchange of views with Chapman suggested Gregg's course of action. As related in Chapter 6, Wilson had attempted to form Chapman's broken regiments in rear of Bryan's brigade, which stood in reserve on the right bank of Robertson's Run, near Craig's Meeting House and some distance north of Catharpin Road. This disposition, it will be recalled, had been made with a view to commanding the road from the meeting house to Parker's Store.

A brief consultation with Colonel Bryan caused Wilson to change his plan of action. Confederate infantry, he learned, was in possession of the crossroads at Parker's Store. Then he observed that Rosser's cavalry had quit the hot pursuit of Chapman's brigade and was pushing along the Catharpin Road toward Shady Grove Church and Corbin's Bridge, spanning the Po River.[18]

With hostile infantry astride his communications with the V Corps, and denied the opportunity of throwing his division across the Catharpin Road between Hancock's II Corps and a victorious Confederate cavalry force, Wilson realized that he had no alternative other than extricating his command. He ordered Chapman while still in motion toward Bryan's position to continue his movement and turn right on a "blind road" that detoured across the headquarters of the Po River and then converged on the Catharpin Road just east of Corbin's Bridge. At the same time Bryan received instructions to mount his regiments as quickly as possible and follow Chapman in column. He then detailed Colonel W. H. Brinton, commanding the 18th Pennsylvania Cavalry, to cover the rear. Wilson and his headquarters party rode with Brinton.

Pressing along his circuitous route as rapidly as the worn condition of his horses would permit, Chapman turned into the Catharpin Road and went on to Todd's Tavern. Upon arrival at the tavern with his 2d Cavalry Division, General Gregg learned the particulars of Wilson's predicament from Colonel Chapman.

Following Chapman at some distance, Bryan's brigade reached the road junction just beyond Corbin's Bridge and entered on the last lap of its ride to Todd's Tavern. Meanwhile the Confederate cavalry had clattered through Shady Grove Church and went on, probably at a cautious pace, toward the Po River crossing.

As General Wilson and his headquarters party approached the road junction, a squadron of Confederate cavalry topped the ridge looking eastward across the river valley. Galloping down from the crest, Rosser's horse hit the deck of Corbin's Bridge with a clap of thunder and raced up the opposite slope.

Following Wilson's party, the 18th Pennsylvania Cavalry smashed into the head of the pursuing Confederates. A lively mélee ensued. Three times the Pennsylvanians gave ground, only to rally and return to the fray. Having gained sufficient time to insure of Wilson's safe withdrawal, Brinton broke off the fight and led his regiment through the woods to Todd's Tavern. After reforming his shattered advance, Rosser continued the pursuit on the Catharpin Road.

Another Fight on Catharpin Road

The problem confronting Gregg was not one of simply reinforcing an active rearguard in position. Wilson's rear was trying to catch the advance. Circumstances required a bolder expedient: Gregg must hit the head of the pursuit a sharp blow, causing delay while his reinforcements gathered to offer battle.

Gregg's dispositions for this purpose were prompt and adequate. Gregg moved out along the Catharpin Road about a

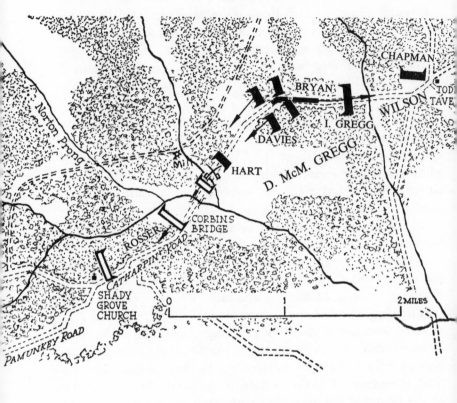

MAP 16. ANOTHER CAVALRY FIGHT ON THE CATHARPIN ROAD

This portrays the opening stages of the cavalry engagement on the Catharpin Road near Corbin's Bridge, which took place between 2:45 p.m. and 6 p.m., May 5. Wilson's two brigades, Bryan and Chapman, withdraw to Todds Tavern. They are passed through by D. McM. Gregg's two brigades, sent by Sheridan to rescue Wilson. Davies' brigade, in the lead, attacks Rosser as the latter approaches on the Catharpin Road. After a series of charges and countercharges Gregg drives Rosser west for two or three miles.

mile beyond the Tavern and threw two regiments, the 1st New Jersey and the 1st Massachusetts, of Davies' brigade, out toward the oncoming Confederates. Davies formed in support. Colonel Irvin Gregg's 2d Brigade was held as the divisional reserve. The 1st New Jersey, under command of Colonel J. W. Kester, took position on the right of the road; Major Lucius M. Sargent's 1st Massachusetts wheeled out on the left.[19]

While these evolutions were in progress, Wilson's disordered units passed through along the road to the Tavern. Under compulsion of clearing a way for the rear of the column, troopers cruelly spurred their jaded, foam-lathered horses to greater speed. The spectacle gave a semblance of panic which was alien to the situation.

Captain Hart's squadron of Kester's New Jersey regiment trotted forward as the rear element of Wilson's column appoached the protecting front. At Davies' command the squadron trumpeter sounded the charge. Cheers answered the bugle blast; sabers flashed from their scabbards; Hart's squadron rode straight at the Confederate van, broke its formation and drove the scattered unit back on its support.[20]

The Confederates were quick with the counter-stroke. A horse artillery battery rushed to the front and unlimbered, action front. A charging force hit Hart in full career; his squadron recoiled, then turned and galloped back to its own support.

As Hart went forward, Colonel Kester deployed three of his squadrons in line of battle on the right of the road, with a supporting squadron on the right. Major Sargent placed the 1st Massachusetts in a similar formation on the left of the road. The Confederate guns opened on Sargent's line; shells crashed through the trees with alarming effect until the line of fire was suddenly switched to another target. Hart's squadron came back at a furious pace, with the Confederate cavalry in hot pursuit. The New Jersey line opened to let the galloping troopers through, then closed its ranks and delivered a volley.[21]

The Confederate counter-charge ended in a mass of pitching horses, some stumbling over those that had fallen, others rear-ing in instinctive hesitancy to trample bodies on the ground. Unable to endure the hail of lead that came with an increasing intensity of "fire at will" from Kester's line, the Confederates turned and galloped away.

Davies sent the New Jersey squadrons in pursuit. Without waiting for orders, Captain Gleason, commanding A Squadron, 1st Massachusetts, joined the charge, crossing the Catharpin Road and riding on the right of Kester's line. Colonel Kester's official report gives the best narrative of this phase of the action:

> Forward we moved, as steadily as on parade, the rebels endeavoring to check us by showers of canister, but with no avail; and they hastily limbered their guns and fell back, just in time to prevent their capture. In this manner we drove the enemy 2 miles through the thick forests of the Wilderness, and halted only when we received positive orders from General Davies, we then being far on the flank of the rebel infantry. We held the position until dark, when we were relieved by another regiment, who picketed the ground we had won. In this little affair the regiment lost 6 men killed and 2 officers and 41 wounded.[22]

The stinging blows dealt by Gregg's squadrons appear to have taken the Confederate cavalry by surprise. Unwilling, perhaps, to risk an engagement with his back to the Po River, the officer in comand made no serious effort to hold the footing temporarily won on the east bank of the stream. Kester's charge decided the issue. A rapid withdrawal was made over Corbin's Bridge toward Shady Grove Church. Gregg, according to his own statement, pushed the pursuit three miles beyond Corbin's Bridge. Sheridan states in his official report that the enemy's cavalry "was attacked . . . and driven to Shady Grove Church, a distance of 3 or 4 miles." [23]

Sheridan Covers the Trains

While Federal cavalry patrols may possibly have advanced to the points indicated by Gregg and Sheridan, it is more likely that Gregg established a strong picket line along the high ground on the east bank of the Po, with an appropriate supporting force well to the front and the main reserve near

Todd's Tavern. Such a disposition, at least, would have been consistent with Sheridan's instructions of 1:10 p.m. These instructions clearly indicate that Gregg's original order to advance on the Catharpin Road to Shady Grove Church, as issued just before noon, had been modified. Custer's brigade, according to the later order, was to take position at the Catharine Furnace-Brock Road intersection and report to 2d Division headquarters, while Torbert's two remaining brigades, after being relieved by Wilson, would be available to support the 2d Division, if Gregg were attacked.[24]

After withdrawing through Gregg's force at Todd's Tavern, Wilson reformed his two brigades and put them in position to support the 2d Division. The two divisions, according to Wilson, encamped that night so as to cover the roads meeting at Todd's Tavern. Wilson's two horse batteries went into position on the left, assumedly south of the tavern, on the Brock Road. About midnight Wilson ordered Chapman to move his brigade a mile out on the Brock Road to connect with the infantry, and prevent the enemy from pushing through that interval.[25]

It cannot be definitely established that Custer's brigade took position, as ordered about 1 p.m. at the Catharine Furnace-Brock Road intersection.[26] The belated order given Chapman to cover the interval toward the left flank of the infantry may have been intended to extend the right of the cavalry at Todd's Tavern across the entire interval on the Brock Road to Hancock's left. Custer apears to have bivouacked near the Furnaces; the other two brigades of Torbert's division encamped at or near Aldrich, covering the front of Chancellorsville. At 3 a.m. of the 6th, however, Chapman marched to Piney Branch Church, either being relieved by Custer, or abandoning the interval altogether. [27]

Cavalry Fails to Avert Surprise

The main cavalry masses of both armies came to rest about 6 p.m., facing one another on the left of the Army of the Potomac. The Federal horse had failed signally in its function of strategic reconnaissance. The fact that Grant, contrary to his intentions, felt obliged to join battle in the Wilderness may be urged as strong proof of such an assertion. Stuart, on the other hand, seems to have satisfactorily met the requirements imposed upon his arm. Yet there are good reasons for suspecting that the Confederate cavalry, as did the Federal, failed to seize upon opportunities that would have had far-reaching effects on the operations of May 5th.

Stuart Loses Opportunity

Reference has been made to the blunder of sending Torbert's division downstream to Ely's Ford, when he might have crossed at the Germanna bridge and appeared on Ewell's left front within three hours after dawn. The question has also been raised as to the soundness of Stuart's judgement in drawing off the cavalry screening A. P. Hill's advance toward Parker's Store and riding to Rosser's aid on the Catharpin Road. The effect of a large body of Confederate horse at the Brock Crossing as early as 10 a.m. would have been little short of a catastrophe to Grant. The paralysis that such a stroke could have induced on Grant's freedom of movement would have given Lee the very advantage he sought in his cautious penetration of the Wilderness.

The probable results of a maneuver that for one reason or another was not undertaken do not, in themselves, offer a logical condemnation of the movement actually made. In operating parallel to his line of railway communications—the Virginia Central— Lee's army put extraordinary demands upon its mounted arm. The main cavalry mass was properly centered upon Richards Shop, on the right flank of the army, and toward the railway. Stuart rushed to the assistance of this force at the first intimation of danger. His action suggests something of the solicitude shown by Meade in taking special precautions to insure the protection of his moving supply base against attack from the left. Given the situation, Meade had good reasons for suspecting that an enterprising enemy would try a shrewd blow at his vulnerable flank. But with his preponderance of sabers—roughly 13 to 7, was it not possible that a bold offensive against Lee's weakest point might have been the best defense for the Federals trains? Stuart, on his part, had every reason to believe that an attack on Rosser would be developed with power and intensity, as, undoubtedly, it should have been.

With due regard to the extraordinary demands which each army put upon its mounted arm, it may be contended that both cavalry leaders were as aggressive as the situation permitted. Sheridan had a moving base to cover; Stuart was faced with the problem of protecting communications lying parallel to Lee's line of operations. In view, however, of the extreme caution evinced by Meade's cavalry dispositions—a feature which should have been obvious to Stuart by sundown of the 4th—it is not unreasonable to maintain that Stuart should have supported a more aggressive policy. Moreover, as usual, Stuart had a free hand.

In view of Meade's caution, manifested by the early halt of the army on the 4th and the lack of enterprise shown by its covering cavalry, together with the bold spirit of opportunism motivating Lee's plans, the utmost of daring consistent with proper protection for the Confederate right doubtlessly offered the best solution to Stuart's problem. The belated concentration of his cavalry on Lee's right appears in this light to have been as serious a mistake as the one which resulted in the immobilization of Torbert's Federal cavalry division on the morning of the 5th. At the very time Torbert was caught in a traffic jam Fitzhugh Lee, riding on his circuitous march to the right of the army, was not available for service in a crisis demanding every available Confederate saber. Stuart might have effected an earlier junction between Fitzhugh Lee's Division and the mounted mass based on Richards Shop, while a skeleton force covered the withdrawal from Hamilton's Crossing by bold demonstrations against the left of the Federal trains. Such a course might have afforded an ample body of horse for the aggressive type of cavalry action on the Catharpin and Plank Roads that was consistent with both the nature of

Lee's strategic purpose and his adversary's conservative disposition.

Sheridan Lacked Free Hand

With Sheridan the case was different. His relations with Meade were far from cordial. He was a comparative stranger to the Army of the Potomac. Like Grant, he had little sympathy with the attitude of excessive caution that seemed to characterize the army commander and many of his generals when in the presence of Lee; and just as the experience of May 5 in no way diminished Grant's offensive determination, so Sheridan was all the more restive under the restraints of army headquarters.

A striking example of the attitude that pervaded the minds of Meade and his staff is voiced in the general instructions transmitted at 6 p.m. by Colonel Seth Williams, Assistant Adjutant General, to Sheridan. In view of the fact that no difficulty had been experienced in driving Stuart's cavalry back across the Po, and that during the day Lee had nowhere taken the offensive, or had even pressed a counter-stroke beyond the bounds of local retaliation, the expression seems one of over-cautiousness, bordering on a state of nervous self-depreciation. Williams wrote:

> I am directed by the major-general commanding to acknowledge receipt of dispatch of General Gregg of 2:45 p.m. If Gregg and Wilson's divisions are compelled to fall back, the commanding general directs that you cover our left flank and protect the trains as much as possible. The left flank at present rests at the intersection of the Brock Road with the Orange Plank Road, the line extending to Germanna Ford. The infantry has been heavily pressed to-day along the whole line. If you gain any information that leads you to conclude that you can take the offensive and harrass the enemy without endangering the trains, you are at liberty to do so.[28]

Two O'Clock Courage

Sheridan, after having made dispositions in accordance with these instructions and having gathered sufficient knowledge of the operations of his divisions to forward a reliable report to army headquarters, communicated with Meade at 11:10

p.m. His angry protest over the defensive role to which he was condemned, and his unqualified denunction of the Hamilton's Crossing venture, imply in the strongest terms that the latter was part and parcel of the former and that both had aroused his bitter resentment: He replied:

> I have the honor to report that General Wilson was attacked to-day at Craig's Meeting-House. At first he drove the enemy on the Catharpin Road for some distance, then they drove him back some distance to Todd's Tavern, where he was joined by General Gregg's command. General Gregg attacked the enemy and drove them back to Beach [Shady?] Grove, distance about 4 miles. I cannot do anything with the cavalry, except to act on the defensive on account of the immense amount of material and trains here and on the road to Ely's Ford. Had I moved to Hamilton's Crossing early this morning the enemy would have ruined everything. Why cannot infantry be sent to guard the trains and let me take the offensive? The casualties of the Second and Third Divisions are between 50 and 60.[29]

Sheridan's retort to the deprecatory attitude of army headquarters cannot be viewed as a diplomatic overture to gain his desired end. Yet even before the chief of cavalry's dispatch had come to his notice, Meade had received a rebuke from Grant that rang with the same offensive spirit that motivated Sheridan.

At sometime before 8 p.m. Grant ordered that the general offensive he had striven to mount during the afternoon be launched at 4:30 a.m. on the morrow. Orders were transmitted to this effect between 9 and 11 p.m. to the various army corps headquarters. Meantime the corps commanders, in conference at army headquarters, made representations to the effect that the hour of attack be retarded by an hour and a half, "owing to the dense thicket in which their commands are located, the fatigued condition of the men rendering it difficult to rouse them early enough and the necessity of some daylight to properly put in re-enforcements." These representations were transmitted at 10:30 p.m. by Meade to Grant, who had retired to his tent and gone to sleep.[30]

Awakened to hear the import of a message from the army

commander, Grant briefly considered the matter and dictated to Lieutenant Colonel W. R. Rowley, his military secretary, a terse reply. Rowley's transcription of Grant's message brings the first day of the Battle of the Wilderness to its conclusion: *"General:* I am directed by the lieutenant-general commanding to say that you may change the hour of attack to 5 o'clock, as he is afraid that if delayed until 6 o'clock the enemy will take the initiative, which he desires specially to avoid." [31]

The Victor of Chattanooga placed greater reliance than did Meade in a belief that the rank and file of the Army of the Potomac possessed a measure of the sterling military virtue which has been described by Napoleon as "two o'clock courage."

CHAPTER 17
GRANT ATTEMPTS A GRAND ASSAULT

The grand assault delivered by Grant's army group in the Wilderness at 5 a.m. is one of the significant operations of modern military history. Briefly, the Federal Supreme Commander intended that a holding attack should fix the Confederate left while a frontal assault, supported by a local flank movement, shook the right. At the same time, a mass of maneuver, moving out from the Federal center and sweeping through the gap that Lee had been able to close in his line of deployment, would complete the destruction of the Confederate right wing.

Conditioned by the dominant role of fire action in combat, this action exemplifies some of the aspects of the battle of annihilation that German military theorists had derived from the teachings of Clauswitz and that, after appearing to have found a complete justification in the dramatic overthrow of the Second French Empire during the Franco-Prussian War, encountered the gloomy deadlock of entrenched armies in World War I. While there is no evidence that Grant was a student of German military theory, or even interested in its doctrines, he had an intuitive grasp of the concept of total war.

With many of the tactical methods of contemporary warfare appearing in rudimentary form on the battlefields of Virginia, Georgia, and Tennessee in 1864, the temptation arises to reinterpret events of May and June of that year and seek to invest them with a meaning that historians have somehow overlooked. Certainly the elements are present for one of those glittering historical analogies that strains the evidence and yet compels a re-evaluation of accepted interpretation. There are, moreover, good grounds for suggesting a thesis that the Federal march from Culpeper Court House through the Wilderness and across the James to the trench lines of Petersburg, entitles Grant to fame as one of the founders of modern war, and that the organization of supply which sustained a hitherto unparalled freedom of movement and undiminished fury of striking power, characterizes this movement as an authentic forerunner of the so-called blitz strategy.

Whatever may be the pitfalls in attempting to reinterpret past events in the light of contemporary developments, it is germane to the subject under discussion to recall that the application of steam power to the production and transportation of the munitions of war had greatly enhanced the mobility and striking power of field armies. At the same time, the rifled musket and cannon, with increased range, greater accuracy of fire, and flattened trajectory had measurably enhanced the defensive capabilities of these field armies. Attacking formations were now subjected to longer time-periods of deadly fire, while defensive works of slight proportions and low elevation sufficed to deflect high velocity missles flying on flat trajectories. In contrast to the massive field works designed (mostly in Europe) for the defense of fixed positions, the light, hastily constructed entrenchments of the latter period of the American war literally maneuvered with deployed lines on the battlefield. This practical application of new tools to old methods gave birth during the first world struggle to the system of trench warfare in which strategic direction was limited to selecting the time and place for bloody battles of position.

Despite innovations in the tactics of defense and remarkable ingenuity in adapting to military requirements such new instrumentalities as the railroad and electric telegraph, together with notable advancements in the employment of artillery and cavalry, the American school of war was singularly inept in creating a sound tactical doctrine for infantry in attack. Both Federals and Confederates seemed wedded to the close-order, double-rank formation, usually formed in two lines of battle and meticulously dressed on regimental colors in order to give maximum effect to fire by volley. Only in exceptional situations are there instances of the employment of unusually large skirmish formations as the first attacking wave of an assault force. Although anticipating the open-order system of infantry attack, this occasional practice never passed beyond the experimental stage.

There were other shortcomings. The want of an over-all general staff capable of coordinating the movements of strategic masses in a theater of continental proportions has been discussed in Chapter 2. Then the enhanced volume of firepower, with the related problem of supply, complicated the problem of directing grand tactical maneuvers to an extent that could have best been solved by duplication of the general staff system in the various field armies. Yet failure or inability to provide a general staff corps compelled Grant and Lee to direct their operations through the agency of those primitive staff organs with which they were familiar as junior officers in the Mexican War.

Lee in large measure avoided the worst consequences of defective staff organization by delegating almost complete liberty of action to his corps commanders. Denying a similar scope of independence to his corps commanders, Grant was dependent on a higher quality of performance than the staffs at army and general headquarters were capable of attaining. The manner in which Hancock was hustled into action at 4:05 p.m. on May 6, and, moreover, compelled to shift his attack formation under fire, offers a glaring example of faulty staff direction. Indeed, it seems doubtful that either Grant or Lee fully understood the revolutionary situation which had taken place in the conduct of military operations during the first three years of the war in America. Where Grant thought in terms of a battle of annihilation, Lee still indulged hopes of redressing his material deficiencies by another miracle victory. Neither foresaw in their planning for the Virginia campaign the brutal battle of attrition that brought the North to the verge of defeatism, while the hammer blows of Grant, the devastations of Sherman, and the strangle hold of blockade were crushing the lifeblood from the body of the Confederacy.

In attempting to understand Grant's first grand maneuver as Supreme Commander, it is all important to understand that his personal staff in the field had little or nothing to do with the formulation of general strategy in the Continental Theater, or with grand tactical combination of the army group in Northern Virginia. The lieutenant general usually issued directons to his army commanders by direct personal communication. His famous directive of April 10, 1864 to Sherman was sent as ordinary first-class mail. He communicated with Meade sometimes in writing, but more frequently by word of mouth, issuing what amounted to a directive after informal discussion. Such a directive would then be transmitted through staff channels to the elements of the army group. Orders affecting Burnside's independent IX Corps emerged from the personal staff of the Commander-in-Chief. The staff of the Army of the Potomac transmitted instructions to the four army corps under Meade's immediate command. This procedure was marred by two serious defects—duplication of effort and lack of proper liaison.[1]

The informal relationship existing between Meade, as an independent army commander, and Grant, as commander-in-chief of the Federal army group, together with the duplication of labor falling to their respective staffs—the army commander being coequal, rather than subordinate, to that of the army group commander in formulating operation orders—tended toward the establishment of a curious form of dual command.

Nowhere in the history of the Virginia Campaign of 1864-65 do these anomalous relationships appear in a more baffling form than during the Battle of the Wilderness. They all but prevent a critical understanding of Grant's plan of action for the general offensive of May 6. It is impossible to fix the time at which Grant determined to attack with his entire force and gave to Meade by word of mouth a directive to this effect.[2] It is, therefore, uncertain whether the general offensive of May 6 was intended to exploit any situation that might be produced by the simultaneous operations of Hancock and Sedgwick against the right and left wings of Lee's army beween 6 p.m. and dark of the 5th, or whether the decision to attack all along the line at dawn of the 6th was taken before it became evident that Warren's inability to support Hancock and Sedgwick must deprive these operations of the decisive results that had originally been entertained. In other words, the evidence does not clearly establish whether the grand assault was first conceived as an attempt to develop the attack of the II, V, and VI Corps, as planned at 6 p.m. of the 5th, or whether the offensive program of the 6th is to be regarded as an effort to redeem an incomplete realization of that plan.

Meade Issues Orders for the Assault

A series of fragmentary orders emanating from general and army headquarters in consequence of an unrecorded directive offers something of an answer to the question. It is difficult, however, to detect the first authentic order of the series and determine whether it relates to operations in progress during the late afternoon of the 5th, or to the one intended for dawn of the 6th.

The logic of events seems to identify the first communication of the series in question as one dated at 5:20 p.m., some 40 minutes before the attack columns of Hancock and Sedgwick pressed their final assault of May 5. Issued by general headquarters to Burnside, this order required that the IX Corps commander place Stevenson's division in reserve at Wilderness Tavern.[3] It is uncertain whether the disposition thus ordered proceeded from a decision to launch the general offensive at dawn of May 6, or should be regarded as an attempt to improvise a reserve in the expectation that Warren would attack in conjunction with Hancock and Sedgwick at 6 p.m. on May 5. Nevertheless, it marks a turning point of the battle, constituting the first step in creating a strategic reserve from Burnside's independent command.

It will be recalled that hitherto Burnside's IX Corps had performed a relatively minor role in conjunction with operations of the Army of the Potomac. As three of his divisions—Stevenson, Potter, and Willcox—had crossed the Rapidan from time to time during May 5, they had released VI Corps troops from guarding the Germanna Ford pontoon bridge and covering the right flank of Meade's army, as well as the right of the great trains closing up from the Rapidan toward Chancellorsville. It will also be recalled that at 3 p.m. Burnside had been instructed to put one of these divisions (Potter's) at the disposal of General Sedgwick.[4] Now at 5:20 p.m. another IX Corps division (Stevenson's) is earmarked as the nucleus of a reserve formation for the Army of the Potomac. The order of 5:20 p.m. thus marks a transition from that phase of the battle during which Meade's three infantry corps were thrown forward in premature assaults, with Burnside's independent command lending limited support on the right, to the phase in which Grant's entire army group was disposed for a combined offensive, with the IX Corps placed as a mass of maneuver between the II and V Corps and aimed at the gap in Lee's line.

At 6 p.m. a communication emanating from Meade's staff indicates in its context that the army commander had received an order to make the necessary dispositions for a general assault early on the morrow. Already discussed in another connection, this is the dispatch transmitted by Colonel Seth Williams, Assistant Adjutant General of the army, to Sheridan.[5] In general terms it prescribed the role of the cavalry. Sheridan's protest at a later hour, when preparations were well advanced for the offensive at dawn, together with references in the text to dispositions which were intended for the train guards, and which were ordered at 8 p.m., leaves no doubt that Colonel Williams' dispatch of 6 p.m. relates to the attack at dawn of the 6th, rather than to the operations conducted during the late hours of May 5.[6]

The Chief of Cavalry was directed to cover the left flank

and protect the trains as much as possible. It was also suggested that Sheridan might take the offensive and harass the enemy if any intelligence coming to hand led him to believe that he might do so without endangering the trains. This latitude of discretion, however, was qualified by the warning that "our infantry has been heavily pressed all along the line." In short, Sheridan's principal mission in the grand offensive required the adoption of dispositions that would guarantee the security of the great trains and, as a consequence, of the dispersion of force to this end, there could be no real offensive possibilities. Sheridan so interpreted his instructions when, at 11:10 p.m., he replied: "Why cannot infantry be sent to guard the trains and let me take the offensive?" [7]

Three communications released simultaneously from general and army headquarters at 8 o'clock reveal Grant's determination to throw every available bayonet into the assault. A circular directed by Seth Williams to all corps commanders of the Army of the Potomac instructed these officers to order all train guards, as well as every man capable of bearing arms to join their respective commands at the front before daylight. The circular specified that:

> For the present the trains must be protected by the cavalry, and every man who can shoulder a musket must be in the ranks. You will at once send a staff officer to the chief quartermaster at these headquaters to learn the location of your trains and conduct the train guard to the front.[8]

At the same time (8 p.m.), the following note was delivered to General Hancock:

> As soon after dark as all is quiet with you, the Major General commanding wishes to see you. The aide will wait and show you the way.[9]

A directive drafted at 8 o'clock by Lieutenant Colonel Comstock, Grant's confidential aide, instructed Burnside as to the role of the IX Corps in the operation. It stated:

> Lieutenant-General Grant desires that you start your two divisions (Stevenson and Potter) at 2 a.m. tomorrow punctually for this place. You will put them in position between the Germanna plank road and the road leading from this place to

Parker's Store, so as to close the gap between Warren and Hancock, connecting both. You will move from this position on the enemy beyond at 4:30 a.m., the time at which the Army of the Potomac moves . . . If you think there is no enemy in Willcox's front bring him also.[10]

At 8:45 p.m., as the steady roar of Lee's musketry on both his right and left indicated that the fighting of May 5 must die down without decisive results, directions went from army headquarters to Brigadier General Henry J. Hunt, Chief of Artillery, stating:

The commanding general directs that you order all the regiments and detachments of heavy [foot] artillery, as well as all train guards of your command, to report at these headquarters to yourself before daylight.[11]

Fifteen minutes later, that is, at 9 o'clock, as the musketry was dying away along the entire front of battle, Meade instructed Hancock that:

You are required to renew the attack at 4:30 tomorrow morning, keeping a sharp lookout on your left. Your right will be relieved by an attack made at the same time by General Wadsworth's division and by two divisions of General Burnside's corps . . . General Getty is under your command.[12]

An hour later, at 10 p.m., a communication from army headquarters apprised Warren of his role, stating that:

You will be reinforced during the night by the four battalions of heavy artillery serving with the Artillery Reserve, and a battalion of engineer troops. You are authorized to withdraw General Robinson with his brigade accompanying Wadsworth's column as soon as General Burnside's troops are in position or nearly so. With this force you will tomorrow at 4:30 a.m. renew the attack on the Orange Court House pike where you attacked today.[13]

Similar instructions were undoubtedly issued to Sedgwick about the same time. Although no dispatch to this effect appears in the *Official Records,* the Assistant Adjutant General of Wright's division issued the following orders at 11:30 p.m.:

This division will move forward and attack the enemy promptly at 4.30 a.m. tomorrow. The signal for advance will be given by the bugle; but should the signal not be heard, brigade commanders will move forward when troops on their right and left move. Brigade commanders will see that their commands have a full supply of ammunition tonight. Shaler's brigade will act as reserve for the division.[14]

Little is known concerning developments at the council of corps commanders, excepting an expression of opinion that the hour at attack originally set by Grant (4:30 a.m.) would not allow sufficient daylight for getting into proper formation, and the appearance of some dissatisfaction over Burnside's apparent want of understanding as to just what his mass of maneuver was expected to accomplish in conjunction with the II and V Corps. Both matters were referred to general headquarters.

Objections as to the early hour of attack were summarized by Meade in his note of 10:30 p.m. to the Lieutenant General, with a suggestion that the time be changed to 6:30 a.m. This plea, as we know, was rejected, Grant giving but a half hour's grace to the army commander and his hesitant lieutenants.[15]

Burnside Confers with Grant and Meade

Adjustment of the difficulty regarding cooperation of the IX Corps is difficult to trace. Burnside, it appears, had called at general headquarters on his way to the conference. Senior major general on the field, and serving directly under orders of Grant, Burnside probably turned aside to pay his respects to the Supreme Commander.[16] Such a course, no doubt, was dictated by considerations of military etiquette. At any rate, there is no evidence to indicate that conversation at general headquarters passed beyond the formal exchange of courtesies or entered into a serious discussion of grand tactics. During the conference at Meade's headquarters, Burnside seems to have given an impression that his grasp of the whole situation was somewhat loose. With V Corps troops on both flanks of the gap through which Burnside's force would pass, the exacting Warren would leave nothing to chance. He sent Colonel Roebling, his chief of staff, to confer with Comstock as to the direction and objective of Burnside's attack.

Roebling appeared at general headquarters about 11:30 p.m. His arrival must have been practically coincident with that of the aide bearing Meade's note requesting postponement of the attack until 6 a.m.[17]

Roebling's narration of the incident in his diary carries the suggestion that he may have conferred directly with Grant. The absence, however, of a positive statement to this effect in his account would strengthen a belief that business at general headquarters was restricted to conversation with Colonel Comstock, who had drafted the original order to Burnside and assumedly was familiar with Grant's views. It is also to be noted that Roebling returned to V Corps Headquarters about midnight without having learned that Grant had changed the hour of attack. Roebling's allusion to Grant's decision may have had reference to intentions previously disclosed to Comstock and therefore attributed to the Lieutenant General. Roebling records in his diary that:

> Two opinions presented themselves, either to go and join Wadsworth by daylight, or else obtain possession of the heights at Chewning's and fall upon the enemy's rear by that route. If successful in carrying the heights, the latter plan promised the greatest results; if not, it would fail altogether. Then again it was thought that when Wadsworth joined the Second Corps, the two together would be sufficient to drive the enemy. General Grant then decided that the Ninth Corps should go to Chewning's and I prepared to accompany them at four o'clock in the morning.[18]

Considering the fact that Roebling went to general headquarters for the express purpose of securing detailed information in regard to Burnside's operation, Warren would certainly have awaited the return of his chief of staff before drafting orders for Wadsworth's advance. These were written at 12:15.[19] Wadsworth was instructed that an advance would be made everywhere along the line at 4:30 a.m., and that he should set his line of battle "on a line northeast and southwest and march directly southeast on the flank of the enemy in front of General Hancock." [20]

Wadsworth, it will be noted, was given the original hour of attack. This fact would indicate that the question discussed by Roebling and Comstock at general headquarters was not re-

ferred to Grant and that Roebling returned to V Corps headquarters without knowledge of the change of the hour to
5 a.m.[21] At 12:30 a.m., however, 15 minutes later and after
Roebling's return to V Corps headquarters, Warren informed
Griffin of the half-hour postponement.[22]

It now becomes evident that intelligence concerning the
change of time for the attack did not reach V Corps headquarters until almost an hour had elapsed since Grant's reply
(at 11:30 p.m.) to Meade, permitting a half-hour delay. This
tardy transmission may be explained by the fact that the
Lieutenant General's decision passed through the army headquarters staff before distribution to the various corps. Meanwhile, the V Corps commander had found it necessary to in-
terrupt the work of his own chief of staff and send him to
general headquarters for information that was essential to the
issuance of intelligible orders regarding a vital phase of the
operation. The want of staff liaison revealed in this devious
expedient offered little promise of effective coordination in
execution of the maneuver during battle.

Meade Regroups for Attack

While orders prescribing the various missions of corps elements were emanating from general and army headquarters,
the regroupment of forces proceeded along the battle line.
Units floundered during the dark hours of the night through
thicket and underbrush to their posts in the forming columns
of attack.

Sheridan took the necessary measures to cover the left flank
of the army and protect the great trains, now congregated in a
vast wagon park at Dowdall's Tavern, west of Chancellorsville.
As previously stated, Gregg's two-brigade division, with Mc-
Intosh's brigade of Wilson's division, remained at Todds'
Tavern, holding the center of the cavalry front. Chapman's
brigade of Wilson's division moved off a 2 a.m. from the
Catharine Furnace-Brock Road intersection to Piney Branch
Church. Custer's brigade (Torbert's 1st Division) pushed out
from the Furnace toward the road intersection vacated by

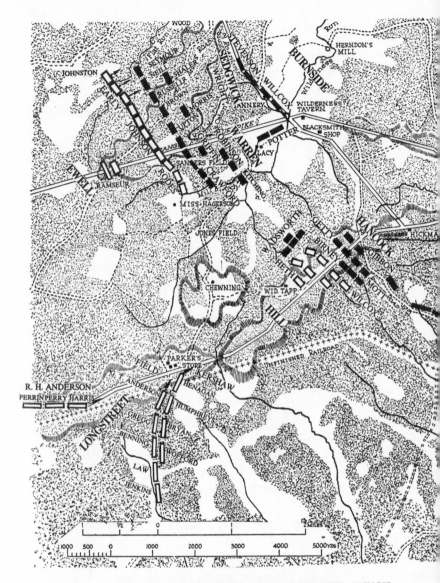

MAP 17. EWELL BEATS MEADE TO THE PUNCH

Hancock, Warren, and Sedgwick attack simultaneously at 5 a.m., May 6. However, Ewell anticipates this by attacking on his extreme left a half hour earlier. Burnside's corps is moving toward the gap between Hill and Ewell. Gibbon has been assigned to the command of a provisional corps of five brigades, posted to cover the Federal left flank.

Longstreet's corps and R. H. Anderson's division are arriving on the field. Johnston's brigade of Rodes' division has just arrived after its long march from Hanover Junction.

The Federal cavalry is on the line: Brock-Furnace Road intersection—Todds Tavern—Piney Branch Church.

Of the Confederate cavalry, Rosser, reinforced, is moving from the Confederate right toward the Brock Road. Fitz Lee, on the extreme right, is covering the Virginia Central R. R.

Chapman. Devin's brigade (Torbert's division) was put in readiness near Aldrich to support Custer. Merritt's reserve brigade (Torbert's division) was held as the general cavalry reserve at Aldrich. These dispositions, according to Sheridan, were taken to hold the line of the Brock Road beyond the Furnaces, and thence around to Todd's Tavern and Piney Branch Church.[23] It might be added that all roads leading east from Shady Grove Church and north from Spotsylvania Court House to Chancellorsville and the area of concentration of both the great trains and reserve artillery were effectively blocked. While it would be difficult to launch a mounted offensive with such a dispersion of force, there was little apprehension that Stuart could succeed in breaking through the outer cordon and then dispersing the reserve at Aldrich, before riding down on the wagon parks around Chancellorsville.

Preparations for the frontal attack against Lee's right wing were made with the meticulous care that always characterized Hancock's formations. The assignment to renew his attack in the morning, "keeping a sharp lookout on . . . [the] left," required an extensive reorganization and redistribution of the five-division force (Barlow, Gibbon, Mott, Birney, Getty). Barlow's brigades were withdrawn during the night from their advanced position toward Hill's right flank and disposed along the line of breastworks which had been partially constructed prior to the advance during the afternoon of the 5th. These troops, less Webb's brigade (Gibbon's division), together with all of the corps artillery, less Dow's battery, were assigned as a provisional corps under the command of General Gibbon.[24] The divisions of Getty, Birney, and Mott, together with Carroll's and Owen's brigades of Gibbon's division, and Dow's battery, were placed under the command of General Birney. Webb's brigade (Gibbon's division) remained in position between the two commands as a general reserve.

Gibbon undertook the mission of covering the left, where Longstreet might attack by way of the Brock Road or along a farm road running northeastward from the Catharpin Road, past Stevenson's and Trigg's farms, to the Brock Road. Miles' brigade, on the extreme left, was refused across the Brock Road, looking southward toward Todd's Tavern. The brigades of Frank, Brooke, and Smyth, probably in the order named, continued the line westward and northward along the forward slope of the *massif* on which Hancock had buttressed the left of his line. A grand battery of 69 guns under Colonel John C. Tidball, Chief of II Corps Artillery, crowned the plateau and was prepared to swing its tremendous volume of fire on any avenue of approach toward the *massif*.

Birney was to make the assault. He formed his column of attack *en echelon* (with four lines on the left, six at the center, and four on the right). In anticipation, probably, of Wadsworth's advance to the Plank Road on a line perpendicular to that of his own direction of attack, Birney threw forward his left echelon on the south side of the Plank Road and withheld his right. Left to right and formed in two lines were the brigades of McAllister-Hays-Ward, the right of Ward's brigade under command of De Trobriand resting on the south side of the Plank Road. The second element of the column, each unit of the element being in two lines, was composed, left to right, of the brigades of Brewster-Grant-Wheaton-Eustis. Wheaton, of Getty's division, formed astride the road, with L. A. Grant on the left, and Eustis on the right. Grant, on the left of Wheaton and south of the Plank Road, covered Ward and Hays, of Birney's division; Brewster's brigade covered its sister brigade, McAllister's of Mott's division, on the extreme left of the first echelon. The brigades of Owen and Carroll, Gibbon's division, constituted the third echelon, Owen being on the left of the road, Carroll on the right.

Aggregating some 20,000 effectives these nine brigades had completed their formation before dawn and stood massed awaiting the signal to go forward.

Off through the dense woods about one-half mile west of Birney's right lay the flank of Wadsworth's line of battle. There is no evidence concerning a change of formation during the night; at dawn Wadsworth's brigades probably reformed in the order of the night before. Left to right in the advance were the brigades of Cutler-Baxter-Rice, each in two lines of battle. Stone formed in reserve, probably in two lines.[25] Wadsworth's 5,000 brought the total of the attacking force to some 25,000.

Opposed to the nine brigades of Birney's assault column and the four of Wadsworth's flanking force were the eight Confederate brigades of Hill's Corps. Saved only from destruction in the closing vice of a powerful double envelopment by the fall of night, these units lay "cross and pile" over the battlefield. Perhaps two-thirds of the 14,000 bayonets they had mustered the day before could be brought into action.

Warren, betimes, had been hastening preparations for his attack against the Confederate left wing. Orders issued simultaneously from V Corps headquarters at 12:30 a.m. instructed Griffin and Crawford to dispose their divisions for attack at 5 o'clock. Griffin, reinforced by 1,042 engineers of the pontoon train, was to form on the right, relieving Lyle's brigade (Robinson's division); Crawford, moving by his right from the reserve trenches on the left of the V Corps line, and relieving the Maryland brigade of Robinson's division, was to close up and connect with Griffin's left. Warren advised Griffin that Robinson's two brigades, upon being relieved were to be formed, if possible, in reserve with the heavy artillery units and that

> Everything in the army is to be put in. General Burnside is to come up tonight and take part in the affair tomorrow morning. I have seen General Wright. He says he will fight up to sustain you. General Ricketts' brigade [Morris] has been withdrawn and sent around to General Sedgwick. Don't fail to move out, all prepared, at 5 a.m. I am at the Lacy House and can be seen at any time.[26]

Crawford, after being cautioned to replenish his ammunition supply, was specifically directed as follows:

> When you march forward let your line of march be due west and your line of battle perpendicular. Keep closed in toward General Griffin on your right, and double back your

left, so as to prevent a flank fire from any force you may drive back.[27]

The forward movement of Griffin's division toward the east edge of Sanders' field began shortly after issuance of the order from V Corps Headquarters. Sweitzer marched noiselessly up the Turnpike to the scene of his action the day before. Turning left at about 2:30 a.m., the brigade formed in line of battle.[28] Ayres took position in rear of Sweitzer.[29] Bartlett's brigade, "marching in as quiet a manner as possible," turned to the right of the pike and formed a three-line attack column in Ayres' former position. His right connected with the left of the VI Corps.

About daylight Colonel Ira Spaulding, commanding the 50th New York Engineers, led his unit up the pike and reported to Griffin. "Ammunition was distributed as speedily as possible," relates Colonel Spaulding in his official report, "and we marched into the rifle pits with ten companies, in all 32 officers and 1,010 enlisted men." [30]

The four battalions of heavy artillery, under Colonel J. Howard Kitching, and aggregating some 2,400 effectives, set out from Chancellorsville at 1 a.m. Preceding the column, an officer reported its approach to General Hunt, Chief of Artillery, at 3:15 a.m.[31] The four battalions formed in reserve near the Lacy house. Here they were joined by the two brigades of Robinson's division, Lyle's 1st and the Maryland brigade.[32]

While the V Corps reserve was forming, Crawford's division moved by the right and formed on the left of Griffin's division.[33] Most of the regiments recalled from the train guards had rejoined their commands by dawn.[34]

Sedgwick had made similar preparations to renew the attack. The units of his five-brigade line (Upton-Brown-Russell-Neill-Seymour) were refitted in position. Morris' brigade was shifted from reserve to the V Corps to that of the VI, forming in close support to Upton[35] on the left of Wright's line. General Shaler, reporting from the train guards early in the morning with his small brigade, was assigned to a reserve position in rear of the center of the VI Corps line.[36]

Burnside Moves into Position

Long before the break of dawn, three IX Corps divisions—Stevenson's, Potter's, and Willcox's—were astir in their bivouacs on the right flank of the army and began forming to march southward in rear of Sedgwick and Warren toward the gap in Lee's battle front. Marshall's Provisional Brigade, IX Corps, consisting of a dismounted cavalry regiment and two regiments of heavy artillery, was left to picket the roads leading westward past Sedgwick's right toward Mine Run.[37] At 4 a.m. the 4th Division broke camp at Mountain Run and set out on the last lap of its forced march from Manassas Junction to Germanna Ford. Composed of colored units and led by General Edward Ferrero, ex-dancing master of the United States Military Academy, the Negroes performed a feat that compares not unfavorably in distance, pace, and endurance with that of R. D. Johnston's Confederate Brigade, Rodes' Division, which left Hanover Junction on the morning of the 5th and took position 24 hours later on the left rear of Ewell's line. As the sweltering column of Negro troops pushed on through the dawn toward Germanna Ford, Ferrero received orders to hasten across the river, put his batteries in position, "and hold the bridge and situation at all hazard." [38]

Summary of Grant's Plan

The extent of Grant's plan of attack, as disclosed in the various orders issued from general and army headquarters and by disposition taken in field may now be summarized:

1. The cavalry was to be relegated to a defensive role, covering the left flank of the army group and guarding the trains.

2. The II Corps would renew its offensive along the Plank Road ridge. The danger of a movement against Hancock's left by Longstreet's Confederate Corps, or by an element of that force, required that Hancock abandon the partially developed turning operation against A. P. Hill's right flank and dispose Barlow's division, with the greater part of the corps artillery for the protection of his own left.

3. Wadsworth's four-brigade column would continue its partially developed movement against A. P. Hill's left by striking at that flank in conjunction with Hancock's frontal attack.

4. Burnside's two IX Corps divisions—Potter and Willcox —would support the combined attacks of Wadsworth and Hancock by moving out from the interval between the II and V Corps, and swinging left, endeavor to envelop Lee's right wing. In all, nine of the fifteen divisions of Grant's army group were to be aimed at the Confederate right, with one, Barlow, covering the left of the attack, and another, Stevenson, held in reserve to Burnside's mass of maneuver. Opposed to these seven attacking and two supporting divisions were the two Confederate divisions (Heth's and Wilcox's) of A. P. Hill's III Corps, in position across the Plank Road ridge, with the two divisions of Longstreet's corps (Field and Kershaw) and one (R. H. Anderson) of Hill's corps, either on the battle-field or within sufficiently close supporting distance to intervene if Hill's two forward divisions needed help. Even allowing for this contingency, Grant provided a nine-to-five preponderance of force on his left.[39]

5. Strengthened by Kitching's heavy artillery brigade and Spaulding's engineer command, the five divisions of the V and VI Corps, on the right of the army group, would oppose the three of Ewell's Confederate Corps. It is not definitely stated in orders issued prior or subsequently to 9 p.m. whether or not the V and VI Corps elements would attack in force, or limit their efforts to holding Ewell in their front, thus neutralizing three of Lee's eight available divisions.

6. It was recognized that the direction and rate of movement of Longstreet's Corps would determine the character of the impending battle. The possibility that he had not as yet arrived within supporting distance to Hill was provided for by the order to attack at 4:30 a.m. If Longstreet should attempt to support Hill by attacking the extreme Federal left, it would only be necessary to hold him off. This contingency was called

to Hancock's attention in Meade's instructions of 8 p.m. Again, Longstreet might give his support directly and, perhaps, more effectively from the rear by the Plank Road. Such a movement would impose greater difficulties on Hancock's frontal attack; it would, on the other hand, release for offensive purposes Gibbon's strong force covering his left. This, added to the three divisions of the front attack and Wadsworth's turning force, would give Hancock a considerable local preponderance over the five divisions of Longstreet and Hill, while Burnside had two divisions with a third in reserve for the envelopment of the mass resisting Hancock. Finally, there was the possibility that Longstreet, supported by Anderson, might fill the gap on Hill's left, so as to protect the III Confederate Corps from envelopment. The orders to Wadsworth[40] and Burnside provided against this contingency: Wadsworth was to hit Hill's flank in conjunction with Hancock. Burnside, although not specifically instructed to do so in his written orders, was subsequently informed that his mass of maneuver would either pass through the unoccupied gap between Hill and Ewell, or fight its way through any troops holding that interval. Then it would pivot on its left and envelop the whole right wing of Lee's army—Hill alone or Hill and Longstreet together.[41]

Barring the obvious error as to the time of issuance of many important orders relating to the operation, Grant's description of the plan in his *Memoirs* appears to be a clear and faithful expression of the purpose he had in mind while directing dispositions for the grand assault. He writes:

> After the close of the battle of 5th of May, my orders were given for the following morning. We knew Longstreet with 12,000 men was on his way to join Hill's right near the Brock Road, and might arrive during the night. I was anxious that the rebels should not take the initiative in the morning, and therefore ordered Hancock to make an assault at 4:30 o'clock. Meade asked to have the hour changed to six. Deferring to his wishes as far as I was willing the order was modified and five was fixed as the hour to move.
>
> Wadsworth, with his division . . . lay in a line perpendicular to that held by Hill, and to the right of Hancock. He was

directed to move at the same time and to attack Hill's left. Burnside, who was coming up with two divisions, was directed to get in between Warren and Wadsworth and attack as soon as he could get into position to do so. Sedgwick and Warren were to make attacks on their front, to detain as many of the enemy as they could, and to take advantage of any attempt to reinforce Hill from that quarter.

Burnside was ordered, if he should succeed in breaking the enemy's center, to swing around and envelop the right of Lee's army.[42]

A penetrating analysis of the general plan, as disclosed by the various orders issued in preparation for the operation and Grant's subsequent discussion of his intentions is presented by Atkinson. Commenting on the spirit in which the battle of the 6th was pre-arranged, this authority states that:

Hancock, Burnside, and Longstreet are the principal factors. All three, Union and Confederate, are practically predestined, by their positions and by the general military situation, to fight on the side of the Plank Road. Hancock, with six (including Wadsworth) out of the eleven divisions of the Army of the Potomac, was already on the ground, and Longstreet was known with tolerable certainty to be aiming in the same direction. Burnside, whose corps was now the only force in Grant's hand that was free to maneuver, was, as a matter of course, to be brought into the contest at the point where the director of operations desired to force the decision . . .

If the scheme were carried out on these lines, the lieutenant-general would have under his hand nine of fourteen (omitting Ferrero's) available divisions on the whole field. The other five were by vigorous action to neutralize one-third of the enemy's forces, and give the initial disproportion between the opposing armies; the plan afforded good prospects of obtaining a five-to-three superiority in Grant's favor at the decisive point. If, in addition, Hill could be routed before Longstreet made his presence felt, and Longstreet, along with the remnants of Hill's Corps, could be caught in the net by Hancock and Burnside, the victory might be of such magnitude as to end the war in Virginia altogether . . . The preparations for the frontal and local flank attack on Hill, for the defence of the extreme left, and for the holding attacks on Ewell were made, of course, by the commander of the Army of the Potomac, those for the "mass of maneuver" by the lieutenant general.[43]

In view of its complicated antecedents, together with the fact that no formally stated directive was issued through the medium of general headquarters, and that Meade's staff, in concurrence with Grant's staff, did not develop the terms of such a directive into an appreciation of the situation, the plan under review cannot be fully understood by a complete statement of dispositions and objectives, as indicated in various orders issued over a period of at least six hours. Concurrent operations, it must be realized, exerted a strong influence on these processes. Again, the divergent reactions at general and army headquarters to events lent a double meaning to decisions of major importance.

Meade's powerful cavalry, which was more numerous, better mounted, and armed with finer fire weapons than was the cavalry force at Lee's disposal, was assigned a passive role in the general offensive.[44] As has been brought out, the army commander pleaded the necessity of protecting the great trains, together with the fact his infantry had been heavily pressed all along the line. This, of course, overlooks the condition that Lee's infantry which had fought a defensive battle throughout the day of May 5th, and had been much more heavily pressed. It also disregards the fact that the long columns of Federal transport were now closed up in rear of the army, where guards composed of infantry detachments and heavy artillery regiments could, in the event of attack, offer a greater measure of protection than would have been the case during the movement of the preceding day.

Orders recalling all infantry detachments to their units at the front and assigning heavy artillery regiments, to say nothing of technical troops, to duty with the infantry of the line, are subject to different interpretations. In Meade's mind, at least, this decision indicates an attitude demanding the extraordinary sort of measures that are taken when the offensive spirit has waned and, although circumstances dictated the continuation of an offensive program, concern for the safety of the army overbalances a determination to energize the attack. Grant, on his part, seems to have been impelled by a determination to throw everything into the assault at the earliest possible moment. His inflexible will in this respect is evinced by his refusal to jeopardize his hold on the offensive by permitting Meade's infantry an hour and a half after the dawn to complete their attack formations.[45]

With Grant attempting by means of an inadequate staff organization to coordinate the operations of the army group, and Meade still exercising a large measure of command over his own army, these divergent attitudes conditioned both the development of the plan and its execution on the battlefield. While the plan was sound, its method of development through the course of the night betrays an uncertain working of the curious form of dual command imposed by the presence of the Supreme Commander. The execution on the morning of May 6 was destined to disclose all the deficiencies that appeared in the development of the plan.

CHAPTER 18

LEE AT BAY

Lee's plans for May 6 are shrouded in even greater mystery than those of the 4th and 5th. Contrary to a generally accepted belief that the Confederates succeeded, after some difficulty during the late afternoon of May 5, in beating off all assaults thrown against them, and thereby winning a hard-earned advantage, Lee, as a matter of fact, suffered one of the most serious setbacks of his military career.

Reversing his original intention to avoid any action that would commit Ewell and Hill to a general engagement before Longstreet arrived on the scene, Lee had permitted Ewell, upon assurances that he held a good position, to engage defensively. At the same time he attempted to establish a secure defensive line along high ground looking down into the basin of Wilderness Run. Given such a line, with the right on the Plank Road ridge, which ran as a long, narrow land-bridge straight toward the Federal left, the center anchored on the bastion of Chewning's plateau, and the left securely entrenched across the water shed between Wilderness and Flat runs, there were good reasons for hoping that he might seize the initiative upon Longstreet's arrival and force a decision during the 6th.

Lee Revises His Plan of Battle

Although the evidence is scant indeed regarding Lee's offensive program for the 6th, we know that Grant's relentless exercise of the initiative which he held throughout May 5 had compelled Lee to conform to the movements of the attacker, thus preventing the completion of dispositions that were essential to a Confederate offensive on May 6. While unable to preserve his freedom of maneuver in the presence of the enemy, Lee was also forced to relinquish his original plan of swinging Longstreet in on the Federal left by circumstances that required the presence of his strategic reserve on the Plank Road. Since this requirement conditioned Lee's whole course of action, compelling him to fight out the battle on terms dictated by his adversary, rather than those imposed by himself, it becomes highly pertinent to the plan under consideration. What was this requirement?

With a careless disregard for the time element pertaining to orders and movements of the Wilderness campaign, it has been accepted without serious question that Longstreet was diverted from his original route by reason of Hill's stricken condition on the Plank Road at nightfall.[1] The wide-swinging movement against Grant's left flank, it is generally believed, was abandoned in order that Hill's battered brigades might be taken out of the line before dawn. A close analysis of the available evidence will not entirely justify this conclusion.

Orders, to be sure, were sent by Lee to Longstreet, requiring that his I Corps march from its bivouac at Richards Shop to the battlefront by way of Parker's Store and the Plank Road. Colonel Venable carried the dispatch. According to Longstreet, "we [presumably the Corps commander, with the head of his column] reached Richards Shop at five p.m. . . . Soon after my arrival . . . Colonel Venable, of general headquarters staff, came with orders for a change of direction of the column through the wood to unite with the troops of the Third Corps on the Plank Road." Longstreet adds that the rear of his column closed up at dark and orders were sent to be prepared by midnight to move off. His remark in this same connection seems highly significant: "The accounts we had of the day's work were favorable to the Confederates; but the change of direction of our march was not reassuring."[2] That is, the reports were not unfavorable, which would hardly have been the case had they referred to Lee's crippled right flank on the Plank Road at nightfall.

The dispatch instructing Longstreet as to the change of

route was supplemented by a second order. Delivered orally to General Charles W. Field by Major McClellan, Chief of Staff of the Confederate Cavalry Corps, about 9 o'clock, this order stated that Lee desired the I Corps to move up at once and relieve Hill, whose disordered and decimated units must be taken out of the line before dawn.[3] Already under instructions to march at 1 a.m. Field bluntly declined to recognize the authority of a cavalry officer to countermand the orders of his corps commander. Instead of going on and presenting the matter to Longstreet, who had established his headquarters camp some distance to the rear, McClellan galloped back to army headquarters in a high state of indignation and reported Field's unseemly conduct to Lee. The incensed cavalryman suggested that he be supplied with a written order. Although gravely disturbed over the delay, Lee declined to act on the suggestion, stating that it was already after 10 o'clock and since Longstreet intended to move at 1 a.m., preparations would be in progress for the march by the time McClellan delivered the written order.

It may be inferred from Lee's reasoning that it required a well-mounted horseman at least an hour or, perhaps, an hour and a half, to cover the distance from his headquarters at Widow Tapp's farm to Richards Shop. This calculation suggests a question in reference to the first order: At what time did Lee dispatch Colonel Venable with this order? Was the rate of travel of both couriers the same and is Longstreet's reference to Venable's arrival at Richards Shop sufficiently precise to serve as a basis of calculation?

Riding by daylight, it is probable that Venable would have covered the distance in less time than McClellan, who rode in the dark. It is unlikely, however, that Venable could have covered the total distance back and forth—about 20 miles— in much less than two hours. Longstreet's reference to the time of arrival at Richards Shop could be construed to mean any time between 5 and 6 o'clock p.m. This by itself is wanting in the precision that would be required for the desired calculation.

Fortunately there is another basis, scarcely more precise than the one offered by Longstreet, but which confirms Longstreet to the extent that the order was delivered sometime between 5 and 6 o'clock. We know that Colonel Venable was back on the Plank Road as darkness was gathering. It will be recalled that Colonel Palmer, Hill's chief of staff, reported to Lee's aide de camp when Lane's Brigade went in on the right, stating that the flank would hold.[4] While the time cannot be accurately determined, this event occurred sometime between 7 and 8 p.m. Since Colonel Venable could not have been less than two hours on the road from Widow Tapp's farm to Richards Shop and back again, it is quite obvious that if, at latest, he returned by 8 p.m., he must have started at or before 6 p.m.; and if he actually reported back as early as 7 o'clock, he must have set out with the original order at or shortly before 5. That is, Lee ordered the change of direction in Longstreet's march at sometime between 4:45 and 6 p.m.

Yet why should Lee have made such an important departure from his original program at any time before 6 o'clock? At this hour, according to his own report of the situation on the Plank Road to Ewell, Heth single-handed had prevented the enemy from making any headway. Cancellation of the intended movement against Grant's left is comparable to his opponent's decision of 10:30 a.m. to abandon the turning movement against Lee's right rear.

Grant, as we know, was constrained to adopt this course by reason of the increasing show of Confederate strength on his right and the unexpected appearance of another Confederate column in motion on the Plank Road toward the wide gap separating his right and left. While endeavoring to establish a connected front of battle, Grant had launched a series of piecemeal attacks, each in turn failing to accomplish its tactical purpose but together exerting a powerful influence, in a strategic sense, on Lee's counter-movements. About 5 p.m.

Lee recognized his inability to close the gap between his own right and left. This view of the situation was induced by two developments: Hancock's first assault along the Plank Road at 4:05, which was pressed with increasing violence, and Wilcox's report from Chewning farm that Federal masses on Wilderness Tavern ridge were moving to the left. Lee therefore abandoned the plan of throwing his strategic reserve on a circuitous route by way of the Catharpin Road against Grant's left.

Lee's decision to call Longstreet up by way of Parker's Store to reinforce Hill on the Plank Road was the inevitable consequence of his inability to fill the gap between Hill and Ewell. The dispatch drafted by Colonel Marshall to inform Ewell of the situation at 6 p.m. and to govern the operations of his corps, complements the orders carried by Venable to Longstreet.

There are suggestions here of a complete change of purpose on Lee's part—the promise of another of those celebrated shifts in the direction of attack to offset a menacing disposition of his adversary. Lee's inability to turn Pope's left on the Rappahannock during the summer of 1862 was, to give a single illustration, compensated by Jackson's circuitous movement through Thoroughfare Gap on the Federal right rear and the culminating victory of Second Manassas, which was clinched by the arrival of Longstreet's wing at Groveton. In the present instance, Grant's determined pugnacity had frustrated Lee's design of turning the Federal left. The consequent threat of an overwhelming concentration against his own right was to be anticipated by a lightning stroke at Grant's right. Ewell, commanding Jackson's old corps, was to test the possibilities of seizing Wilderness Tavern ridge and cutting communications between the Federal right and their crossings over the Rapidan.

Although no details of the proposed operation are given, there is the hint that Longstreet's strategic reserve would move by the left to support Ewell in developing the critical phase of the operation and then participate in its final exploitation. If, however, a shift to the left for offensive operations against the Federal right appeared impracticable, Lee was determined to crush the Federal left, with Ewell inclining from the right, before Grant could complete his massive concentration. But whatever may have been the scope of Lee's proposed operation against the Federal right on Wilderness Tavern ridge, this program, as well as the one originally intended against the left, was frustrated by a pugnaciousness on the part of this new adversary that constantly impinged on the liberty of movement required by Lee to complete his dispositions. The persistence with which Hancock and Sedgwick pressed their assaults against the right and left wings of the Confederate army between 6 oclock and dark of the 5th won two positive advantages, despite the fact that these attacks, like their predecessors of that day, failed in the attainment of their avowed tactical objectives. Ewell was denied any opportunity of examining the possibilities of a thrust toward Wilderness Tavern ridge; Sedgwick's attack offered ample proof that, even if Grant had diverted powerful reserves toward the Confederate right, his own right was still sufficiently strong to sustain an offensive operation of such magnitude as to leave no doubt concerning its defensive capabilities. Hancock's operation against the Confederate right on the Plank Road ridge developed a pitch of destructive violence shortly before nightfall that Lee could not have foreseen at 6 p.m.

Lee appears to have held the optimistic view reflected in his instructions of 6 p.m. to Ewell and Longstreet until 7 o'clock, when he again communicated with Ewell. The II Corps Commander was informed that "we hold our own as yet." At the same time, Lee reiterates his intention of taking the offensive either by the right or the left. Ewell is informed that:

> . . . General Longstreet and General Anderson are expected up early and unless you see some means of operating against their right, the General wishes you to support our right. It is reported that the enemy is massing against General Hill, and

if an opportunity presents itself and you can get Wilderness Tavern ridge and cut the enemy off from the river, the General wishes it done. The attack on General Hill is still raging. Be ready to act as early as possible in the morning.[5]

Longstreet Ordered to Relieve Hill

As night settled over the battlefield, Lee faced a situation that was not foreseen at 7 o'clock. While Ewell had held his ground, he was unable to move, as Lee desired, against Wilderness Tavern ridge. In other words, the Confederate left was neutralized. On the right, Hill's brigades had been saved from imminent disaster only by the fall of darkness.

Meantime, detailed reports concerning the desperate state of affairs along A. P. Hill's front came back to army headquarters. Wilcox relates Lee's reaction to this intelligence:

> About nine o'clock General Wilcox, from a partial examination made under difficulties—thick woods and darkness of the night—but mainly from reports of his officers, learned that his line was very irregular and much broken and required to be rearranged. He repaired to General Lee's tent, intending to report conditions of his front, and to suggest that a skirmish line be left where the front then was, the troops be retired a short distance, and the line rectified . . . As General Wilcox entered the tent, General Lee remarked that he had made a complimentary report of the conduct of the two divisions on the Plank Road, and that he had received a note (holding it in his hand) from General Anderson, stating that he would bivouac at Verdiersville for the night; but, he continued, "he has been instructed to move forward; he and Longstreet will be up, and the two divisions that have been so actively engaged will be relieved before day." General Wilcox, hearing this, made no suggestions about the line, as he was to be relieved before day. The failure to rearrange his line and the delay in the arrival of the three rear divisions, was near proving fatal to the Confederates.[6]

Greatly perturbed, Wilcox returned to his division. A precarious situation, nevertheless, had gone from bad to worse. There was now no assurance that Longstreet would arrive on the field in time to relieve Hill's troops before dawn and permit them to reform and replenish their ammunition supply before closing into the interval at Chewning's plateau, or taking position in reserve, as occasion might require.[7] Lee, however, accepted the situation with an equanimity that is difficult to understand. So far as we know, no warning was given by army headquarters that the relief before day break was problematical and that the battle-wearied units along Hill's straggling line should be aroused and given an opportunity to defend themselves. The Confederate infantry slept on their arms, while Hancock and Wadsworth methodically prepared the powerful attacks that were intended to sweep the field at dawn.

Hill Attempts to Reform His Battered Front (Map 16)

Whatever the extent to which army headquarters may have been dominated by a belief that the situation would take care of itself, the III Corps commander was by no means quiescent. About midnight, A. P. Hill rode off toward Parker's Store, in the hope of getting definite information concerning Longstreet's column.[8] Calling at army headquarters for supplementary orders, Hill was again instructed to let his men sleep. Yet unmistakable evidence of the enemy's vast offensive preparations accumulated through the night. "We expected," says Colonel Palmer, III Corps chief of staff, "an attack in overwhelming numbers at the first blush of dawn." [9]

Either in violation of original orders, or in consequence of subsequent instructions, which could have been issued after Hill's belated visit at army headquarters, the III Corps commander began regrouping his brigades during the hours between midnight and dawn, in order to secure an effective defense or, perhaps, with a view to covering a quick withdrawal should the Federals attack in overwhelming force before Longstreet's arrival on the field. The line held by McGowan, Scales, and Thomas across the Plank Road at dark on May 5 was established as might be described in present-day parlance as a forward zone of defense or, to employ the language of 1864, the first echelon of a defense formation in depth. McGowan consolidated his front on the left of the Plank Road, forming the five South Carolina regiments from left to right in the order "Orr's Rifles—13th—1st—14th—12th."

Thomas' Brigade was withdrawn from the left of the line and and shifted to the south side of the road, going into line on the right of Scales' Brigade. McGowan's right and Scales' left joined at the Plank Road.[10] Colonel Stone, commanding Davis' Brigade, Heth's Division, brought up his four Mississippi regiments and the 55th North Carolina from reserve and formed on the line they had held with such conspicuous gallantry in the fighting of the 5th, until relieved at sundown by Thomas.

In recognition, perhaps, of the menace imposed by Wadsworth, General McGowan withdrew his left; the brigade line "struck the road at an acute angle, making a salient with Thomas [Scales?]." [11] Stone no doubt withdrew his line to conform with McGowan, reforming on the refused line, his right joining McGowan's left.[12]

After falling back from the extreme left at dark of the 5th to take a position in support to Scales, Lane's Brigade had bivouacked near the south side of the Plank Road. At dawn General Lane began forming his North Carolina regiment in line of battle to support Scales and Thomas, in his immediate front.[13]

Three of Wilcox's brigades, together with Davis (Stone commanding) of Heth's Division are thus identified in the forward line, Davis-McGowan-Scales-Thomas; the left wing, Davis-McGowan, being withdrawn at an angle to the Plank Road; the right wing, Scales-Thomas, striking the road perpendicularly. The remaining brigade of Wilcox's Division, Lane's, stood in reserve to the right wing.

During the night, Cooke's Brigade, Heth's Division, which had endured the full fury of Hancock's first drive along the Plank Road, was sent some distance to the rear. A new position was organized in a stubble field to the north, or left of the road. Contrary to orders, according to the historian of the 27th North Carolina, a strong entrenchment was thrown up.[14] Evidence concerning the positions taken by Kirkland and Walker, Heth's remaining two brigades, is of so vague a nature as to prohibit a definite statement. Reference to the sudden collapse of Kirkland's Brigade by reason of heavy pressure on the left would indicate that this unit formed on the north side of the Plank Road and, perhaps, on the left rear of the line Davis-McGowan-Scales-Thomas.[15] Since there is no evidence to identify any of Heth's troops on either side of the Plank Road during the 6th, it seems reasonable to suppose that Kirkland and Walker may have taken a position in line astride the Plank Road in rear of Lane and that Kirkland-Walker-Lane constituted the second element of a defense formation in depth. Wilcox's statement to the effect that Heth formed in his rear, together with the fact that none of Heth's brigades can be found on the right of the Plank Road, tends to strengthen the assumtion that Hill adopted an echelon formation with four brigades, Davis-McGowan-Scales-Thomas, on the right front, and three brigades, Kirkland-Walker-Lane, in the left rear, with Cooke's brigade in general reserve. This disposition, it might be observed, offered the typical solution for such a situation; it was employed by Ewell the day before on the Turnpike with conspicuous success; Jackson, with a similar threat to his right flank, used the defense *en echelon* with great effect at Fredericksburg during the battle of December 13, 1862.[16]

At 3:30 a.m., when Longstreet should have been up, if the relief was to be effected by dawn, Wilcox sent for pioneers "to come to the front with axes, spades, etc., to fell trees and construct works." It was daylight, however, before the work parties arrived. "The enemy," adds Wilcox, "was found to be too close to permit their use." [17]

Pegram's, Cutts', and McIntosh's Battalions of the III Corps Artillery moved up during the night from the reserve park near Parker's Store and stood in readiness to take position in the line, as circumstances might dictate. Elements of McIntosh's Battalion were placed to the left of Poague's gun position on relatively high ground to the north and east of Chewning's plateau and which looked across the stream beds running northward from the Plank Road ridge into Wilderness Run.[18] Either these elements, or gun detachments thrown forward from Poague's position, came into action at an early hour, developing an enfilade fire on the right of Wadsworth's advancing column.[19] The report of General Pendleton, Lee's chief of artillery, would indicate, however, that the majority of McIntosh's, Pegram's, and Cutt's batteries were held in reserve until Longstreet's arrival on the field.[20]

About the break of day A. P. Hill left III Corps headquarters in charge of Colonel Palmer and rode northward to examine the interval between his own left and Ewell's right. It is not stated whether this was done with a view to closing the gap with III Corps troops after their relief on the Plank Road by Longstreet's Corps, or for the purpose of verifying indications of hostile dispositions on his left. The presence of Confederate artillery on the right of Wadsworth's line of advance shortly after 5 a.m. may have had some connection with Hill's reconnaissance.

In contrast to the inactivity that prevailed for the greater part of the night along Hill's front, where the heaviest attack was destined to fall, preparations were pushed with great vigor and noisy clamor on Ewell's line. In consequence perhaps of Lee's directive as issued at 7 p.m. of May 5, or possibly in response to later instructions from army headquarters directing that a diversion be created on the left to distract Grant's attention from the right, Ewell had ordered an attack at 4:30 a.m. Gordon's Georgia Brigade had shifted over from the right of Rodes' Division to join Early and take position on the extreme left of the corps line, and extending the flank to Flat Run. Jones moved his Virginia regiments up from reserve and formed astride the Turnpike between Steuart, of Edward Johnson's Division, on his left, and Battle of Rodes' Division, on his right. These adjustments added the numerical equivalent of two and a half brigades to the II Corps sector between the Turnpike and Flat Run.

During the night Ramseur's Brigade, Rodes' Division, together with three regiments of Pegram's Brigade and three from Edward Johnson's Division—the approximate equivalent of two brigades—arrived on the field. It is not stated whether the detached regiments rejoined their units. Ramseur replaced Jones in general reserve.[21]

The shift of units to the left was accompanied by all the boisterousness and loud disorder of moving troops released from restraints of discipline—shouting, cheering, and the rumbling of heavy vehicles over occasional stretches of log roads. The tumult seems to have been purposeful, seeking to create an impression that the line was being heavily reinforced. If such was the design, it succeeded in increasing Federal apprehension as to the security of their right flank, which had been a matter of constant concern. At the same time, this very concern, together with the preparations that were being pushed for the attack of 5 a.m. put the Federals on the alert for the assault which Ewell intended to deliver half an hour earlier.[22]

There were considerable adjustments in artillery dispositions along the II Corps front during the early morning. Although reports of these movements are vague as to the time element, it would seem that some were made at, or even before, dawn, and in anticipation of the fighting of the 6th, while others were effected during the early course of the battle. Colonel Carter, in accordance with orders "early on the morning of the 6th . . . to concentrate as many guns as could be spared on our left, which was a good deal exposed," placed several pieces in position to support Gordon. "During the day," states General Long, chief of artillery, II Corps, "the enemy made an attack on Gordon's Brigade . . . Some of these guns were used with considerable effect in assisting to repel this attack." [23]

Longstreet and Anderson March to the Front

At 1 a.m., about the time Burnside's three white divisions were stirring in their bivouacs near Spotswood Tavern with early preparations for the march to the center of the battle-line, Longstreet's two divisions, Kershaw leading, with Alexander's artillery and train following in a well-closed column, set out from Richard's Shop toward Parker's Store.[24] Anderson's Division, with a greater distance to march than had either

Burnside or Longstreet, was probably on the march from New Verdiersville to the Store by midnight.[25]

Like the fight on the Plank Road during the late afternoon of the 5th, the battle as a whole had now resolved itself into a race of reserves. As such, it was a contest to try to the uttermost the iron nerve of Grant and the fortitude of Lee. Burnside, to quote Colonel Lyman again, "had a genius for slowness." Longstreet was also a deliberate marcher. Although Anderson, like Longstreet, was capable of being aroused to a furious pitch during the heat of battle, he was reputed to be an indolent man and a somewhat easy-going chief of division. Unfortunately for Grant, Burnside's talent for dawdling became more pronounced on the battlefield than when marching to the sound of the guns. It was even a greater misfortune that his corps was, for the greater part, composed of partially trained reserves and no match in action for the Confederate veterans against whom they were to be pitted.

At daybreak, when Burnside's formations should have been deploying across the interval, his advance was filing past Grant's headquarters camp on the Germanna Plank Road, while the rear of his close-packed column extended back some three miles toward Germanna Ford.

Shortly before dawn, as Hill had given up all hope of the promised relief and was making belated efforts to prepare some sort of a defense, Kershaw's advance came to a halt several miles from the battlefield. The wagon tracks which plainly marked the road through the woods spread out upon entering a clearing. Robinson, the guide, and for many years Sheriff of Orange County, was at a loss to find the way. Field, impatient of delay, doubled his column on Kershaw while Robinson explored the edge of the woods beyond. Just as Field's advance had closed up within a brigade's length of the head of Kershaw's column, the road was found and the two infantry divisions resumed the march in double column. In this formation they turned into the Plank Road at sunrise.

Marching on the Plank Road toward the dawn, Anderson's

Division reached Parker's Store a short time after the I Corps column had entered the road. The III Corps Division was obliged to rest on its arms while Kershaw and Field filed by. The I Corps artillery and train parked near the Store, permitting Anderson to close on Longstreet's infantry and push toward the crashing musketry which astonished even the veterans of Gettysburg.

If Lee could have so exerted his will as to have secured a greater celerity of movement on the part of Longstreet and Anderson after 5 p.m. of May 5, when he first realized the impossibility of closing the gap between Hill and Ewell, as well as the impracticability of permitting Longstreet to continue the flank movement against the Federal left by way of Shady Grove Church and Todd's Tavern, there is every reason to believe that the perilous crisis which brought the Army of Northern Virginia to the verge of destruction at 6 a.m. on the 6th, might have been averted.

Lee, however, followed his customary practice of permitting his corps commanders, or general officers in charge of strategic detachments, complete liberty of action within the requirements prescribed or indicated by the army commander. While this system of command obtained astonishing results during his offensive-defensive campaigns in Virginia against McClellan, Pope, Burnside, and Hooker, it did not meet the demands of offensive warfare during the campaigns of Antietam and Gettysburg. The practice became perilous when employed against the sound strategy and remorseless tactics of Ulysses S. Grant.

In the light of his subsequent experience with Grant, it is difficult to understand Lee's equanimity after he became aware of Hill's critical condition on the Plank Road, together with the fact that his efforts to hasten Longstreet's march to the front had not succeeded. Certainly it was no false compassion on Lee's part that the III Corps infantry should have been permitted to sleep undisturbed along the battlefront. In view, however, of Lee's previous experience with Meade and his predecessors in command of the Army of the Potomac, it is easy to see why he should not have been disturbed by the gravity of the situation. While there was no assurance that Longstreet would be up before daybreak, he would certainly be on the field at an early hour of the forenoon. This delay, to be sure, was regrettable; it denied many possibilities; but the Federals had rarely if ever evinced any acute sense of the value of time. It was therefore reasonable to suppose that he would be given ample time to put Longstreet into position and extricate Hill. Such no doubt were his thoughts when he dismissed the idea of sending Major McClellan back to Richard's Shop with a written order or when about midnight he repeated his instructions to Hill that his men should not be disturbed. Nor was Lee's reasoning without a large measure of justification. But for the fact that Meade and his corps commanders were overruled by Grant, the attack on Hill would not have been launched until 6:30 a.m., a half hour after the head of Longstreet's column arrived at the battlefront.

The very nature of the impending struggle would be deliberately distorted in any attempt to imply that Lee was sustained by a complacent belief that the final test of strength would give him a crowning victory. The quality of his strength was of a different order. If Grant evinced an implacable determination to bend circumstances to his will and fight the battle out to its inevitable issue, Lee exhibited a superb fortitude that neither disaster nor the shadow of defeat could shake. The determination of the one was objective; the fortitude of the other may best be described as subjective. It was an attribute of character that had permeated every unit of his army, transforming it from a host of miscellaneous regiments from remote provinces of the Old South into a finely tempered instrument of war, and endowing it with an offensive spirit that is scarcely without parallel in the annals of battle.

In contrast to the newly formed association between Grant and the Army of the Potomac, the vital bond between Lee and the Army of Northern Virginia was of a spiritual essence. Flaming in battle, it inspired achievements that rank with some of the most astonishing feats of arms during all time. His deliverance from utter defeat in the Wilderness is such a feat. Hannibal, the Carthaginian, inspired a similar loyalty among the Numidians, Gauls, and Iberians that constituted his army; Gustavus Adolphus, the royal Swede, infused just such a fervor in the Protestant soldiery he led against the Catholic forces of the Empire.

Neither patriotism, religious fanaticism, nor professional pride will explain these miracles of the battlefield. The answer, perhaps, may be found in that illusive but meaningful phrase—the personal equation. Whether Lee may have been inferior to Grant as a strategist, or infinitely superior as a tactician, he was endowed with those superlative qualities of leadership that survive defeat. Time has transformed the veneration of his veterans into one of those historic legends that defy analysis.

CHAPTER 19

GRANT ASSAILS LEE'S LINE

At 4:30 a.m. the Wilderness was awakened by the roar of Ewell's artillery. Early's infantry on the extreme left of the Confederate line swarmed out of their trenches and advanced in line of battle across the swampy ground toward Sedgwick's right front. Launched without warning and pressed with great vigor, the attack swept over Federal outposts, driving the skirmishers back on the main line of Neill's and Seymour's brigades.

Neill and Seymour Receive Ewell's Attack

With its offensive fury only fanned by slight resistance, the attack nevertheless was unable to exploit the advantages that might otherwise have attended so quick a thrust. Crouched for a forward movement at 5 a.m., the regiments of Seymour and Neill sprang into action. The fierce shock of attack and counterattack, with volleys flaming at point-blank range, swayed back and forth. Unable to hold the ground so rapidly won, the Confederate line of battle wavered, then fell back across the marsh. The full force of Seymour's and Neill's brigades were thrown into the counter-thrust. But if Ewell was unable to develop an overwhelming offensive, he was well prepared to offer a stout defense. According to Colonel Bidwell, commanding Neill's brigade, the pursuing Federals struck a solid line of breastworks. He reports that:

> . . . at the appointed hour we made a vigorous assault, but the enemy having during the night strengthened their position, combined with the natural obstacles in our front of a marsh covered with a heavy growth of thorn bushes, caused us to retire with a heavy loss to the line occupied during the night. About two hours later we were again ordered to ad-

319

vance with the whole line, but could not gain any ground, when an order came to entrench where we were.[1]

Sedgwick and Warren Counterattack

As Seymour and Neill struck back in counterattack, Wright pushed out, carrying the forward movement along the entire VI Corps front. His advance met bitter resistance.[2] Thrice the 1st Division brigades fought their way to the parapets of Edward Johnson's trenches, only to break before the blast of Confederate volleys. While Wright attacked, V Corps skirmishers covering Warren's assault column astride the Turnpike pressed up to the enemy's lines. Closing to the front, Griffin and Crawford awaited orders to storm the works. At 5:30 a.m., Warren notified Humphreys that all V Corps troops were disposed for the assault, excepting the two reserve brigades of Robinson. The firing at this time, he observed, would indicate that the attack had begun promptly at five o'clock. A disquieting note, however, was added: "The head of Burnside's column is just going on to the (Lacy) field, and in consequence of their not being in position, I have sent the heavy artillery, under Colonel Kitching, 2,400, to support General Wadsworth."[3]

The necessity of detaching a part of his reserve to offset the effects of Burnside's tardy advance and a consequent inability to lend his weight to the general attack, caused Warren to conduct his own holding operation against Ewell with greater caution. This deliberation quickly evoked an impatient suggestion from army headquarters urging that the V Corps commander throw his pickets and skirmishers well out to the front.[4]

Warren gave a ready response to the demand. By 6 a.m., Griffin's first and second lines of battle advanced along the north side of the Turnpike, crossing Sanders' field, and pressed up within close range of the Confederate line. Morris' brigade, Rickett's division, inclined left to support Bartlett.[5] South of the Turnpike Sweitzer, with Ayres' Regulars in support, struck across his old battleground. To the left, Crawford's two brigades, Fisher and McCandless, advanced rapidly through the woods south of Sanders' field and passed over the enemy's advanced positions. In expectation, perhaps, of a violent assault, the Confederate artillery ceased fire, to prepare their ammunition for salvos of grape* and canister. Warren brought up a number of guns to play on the enemy. At 6:25 a.m., he reported: " . . . Griffin has moved up to the enemy's position and driven him to his lines . . . We are driving them rapidly on the left and prisoners are coming in." [6]

Despite favorable progress, Warren advised Meade "not to make the final assault until the preparations are made." [7]

Want of preparation, it would seem, refers rather to Burnside's tardy movements than to his own advanced dispositions. In the dispatch just quoted, he calls to the attention of army headquarters that "General Burnside's ought soon to be in position to intercept the retreat of the enemy's right." [8]

Warren, with the acquiescence of army headquarters, had determined that the situation reported at 6:25 a.m. could not be materially improved without exorbitant cost in life. Certainly if the operation was originally intended as a holding attack, there was every reason to believe that it had succeeded in neutralizing Ewell's entire corps. Pressure on the right and right center, therefore, was all that could be expected or desired at this phase of the general offense.

Hancock had attacked on the left at 5 a.m. Wadsworth, according to the dispatch dated at 5:40, had made his connection with the right of Birney's assault column. The powerful attack was now driving the Confederates "handsomely" along the Plank Road. All prisoners examined at II Corps headquarters were A. P. Hill's corps indicating that Longstreet had not as yet made his presence felt. These advices were transmitted by Humphreys to Warren in an undated dispatch, arriving at V Corps Headquarters sometime between 6:20 and 6:40. [9] At 6:55, Warren reported to the Chief of Staff that ". . . Matters

---

* L. Van L. Naisawald, an authority on Civil War artillery, states that the U.S. Army stopped making grapeshot in 1859, as canister was more effective. The Confederates however, may have had some captured stocks of pre-War grapeshot.—Editor

are much as they have been for the last half hour. Our line does not apparently advance . . . No considerable firing going on on the right." [10]

Elation over Hancock's rapid progress, with its promise of complete destruction of Hill's defense force before Longstreet arrived on the field, seems to have distracted attention from two important elements in the development of Grant's offensive plan. One was the consideration that Burnside, after clearing the Chewning plateau, was to make dispositions to either swing left and fall on Longstreet's Corps, should that force attempt to relieve Hill on the Plank Road, or for the purpose of disputing possession of the plateau with Longstreet, should the veteran Confederate I Corps arrive at the front and attempt to fill the interval between Hill and Ewell. Examination of this phase of the program may best be made in connection with the narration of Burnside's operation. The second consideration relates to the pressure that Warren and Sedgwick were expected to exercise for the purpose of holding every element of Ewell's corps on its original front. Although anticipating a dramatic series of events on the Federal left, consideration of this phase may best be given here.

Developments on the V-VI Corps front soon revealed that the pressure put by Warren's and Sedgwick's attack columns on the Confederate left was not of sufficient intensity to prevent Ewell from keeping Ramseur's Brigade, his corps reserve, in hand. Looking from the Federal point of view, this development accompanied a disastrous reversal to Hancock's swift and apparently overpowering advance along the Plank Road. News came to Warren in a dispatch of 7:15 a.m. that Longstreet had come up on Hancock's left front and that Meade "considers it of the utmost importance that your attack should be pressed with the utmost vigor. Spare ammunition and use the bayonet." [11]

These instructions called for an exhibition of violence that had not heretofore been contemplated. Longstreet's timely arrival had anticipated Hancock's destruction of Hill's holding force. While this possibility had been foreseen, there had been no provision for the contingency that Burnside's mass of maneuver would not be in position to participate in the general offensive. Warren therefore must strike with all the energy he was capable of exerting. Considerations that the field supply of ammunition had been expended at such a rate as to cause some apprehension at army headquarters [12] did not modify the inexorable tone of Meade's demand for immediate and persistent action against Ewell. The emergency was such that Warren must substitute cold steel for fire action.

The evidence of regimental commanders in Griffin's division is unanimous on the point that no assault was delivered.[13] At 7:43, as we will learn in Chapter 20, there came a report from Warren's signal station, which commanded the view across Wilderness Run out over Chewning's plateau, that "The enemy are advancing a column of troops past the point occupied by General Crawford yesterday to the right." [14] This ominous news was transmitted at 8:15 to army headquarters:[15]

> Signal officer reports about a brigade of enemy at point where General Crawford was yesterday [Turner's (Chewning's) house]. They are entrenching. The following dispatch just received, dated 7:40: "Wadsworth has been slowly pushed back, but is contesting every inch of ground." [16]

Ewell Extends Across the Gap

While standing in corps reserve, Ramseur had been subject to call from either Edward Johnson or Rodes, as occasion might require. As Burnside's column debouched from the edge of the woods at the northeast edge of Jones' field, the movement, according to Ramseur, was construed as an attempt "to envelop General Rodes' right and cut off the Second Corps from the army." [17] Ramseur briefly explains his shift to the right across Burnside's line of advance:

> The distance from General Rodes to Lieut. Gen. A. P. Hill's left being about a mile, General Rodes ordered me to form on Brigadier-General Daniel's right and push back Burnside's advance. Moving at a double-quick, I arrived just in time to check a large flanking party of the enemy, and by strengthening and extending my skirmish line half a mile to the right of my line I turned the enemy's line . . . This advance on

our right enabled our right to connect with Lieutenant General Hill's left.[18]

While it is not possible to establish that the Confederate unit seen and reported at 7:43 a.m. by the V Corps signalmen was Ramseur's Brigade, there is large room for doubt that any other Confederate unit was available at this particular time for the maneuver described by Ramseur. At the same time it is not altogether improbable that an element of either Wilcox's or Heth's Divisions, which were breaking rapidly as Longstreet began his deployment shortly after 6 a.m., may have been hastily reformed and sent to occupy the high ground at Chewning's, and that Ramseur, who met Burnside (whom he describes as "a large flanking party of the enemy") advancing across the open part of Jones' field, extended his skirmish line, as he states, "half a mile to the right" and connected with an element of Heth's Division at Chewning's farm.[19] But wherever Ramseur may have rested his right flank, there is no question that he was drawn from Ewell's reserve and that he extended the II Corps line across Burnside's path of advance.

In contrast to Ewell's skillful utilization of his reserve, Warren failed to employ his own powerful reserve to advantage. Fearful that Burnside would be unable to support Wadsworth's flank attack, Warren sent Kitching's heavy artillery brigade to the Plank Road where, if anything, there were too many troops.[20] The obvious remedy to the tardiness of Burnside's appearance, it seems, should have been a violent thrust at Rodes' right front. Warren had strong reserves for such an effort; Ramseur alone was available to Ewell. But where Warren either maneuvered his reserve forces to no purpose, or kept them in idleness, Ramseur appeared at the vital point in the very nick of time.

Burnside Fumbles

Burnside's tardy appearance opposite the gap between Ewell and Hill is generally regarded as the dissipation of an opportunity that seldom comes in war to a general of tarnished reputation to rehabilitate his past fame and, by the simple expedients of rapid movement and tough fighting, to clinch a decisive victory for the army he had once commanded. But Burnside was neither quick nor tough. Here his dilatory movements in the Wilderness are on a par with his sluggish action at Antietam.

In expectation that the head of Burnside's column would pass the crossroads near Wilderness Tavern, Warren had detailed Major Roebling, his chief of staff, to meet the IX Corps commander at the edge of the Lacy field, where the woods road winding up the valley of the Wilderness Run departs from the Turnpike. Captain Cope, Warren's topographical engineer, who had accompanied Wadsworth's column to the Plank Road the previous afternoon, was also put at Burnside's disposal. Both officers rode out at early dawn across the field to await Burnside's column.

As the hour of attack approached and Burnside failed to appear, Warren sent Lieutenant Schaff, the young ordnance officer detailed by Meade from Army Headquarters as a supplementary aide on the V Corps staff to Major Roebling, with instructions that both he and Captain Cope should report without further delay at V Corps Headquarters. Schaff had orders to report to General Burnside and make himself available as guide.

Roebling and Cope galloped away. Schaff waited impatiently. A roar of musketry was heard in the south, indicating that Hancock's column had engaged the enemy. Then Potter, in the advance of Burnside's column, filed past Wilderness Tavern and turned into the pike. Burnside should have crossed the Lacy field at least an hour and half earlier in order to have timed his movement through the gap with the attack of Hancock and Wadsworth. The prediction made by Major Duane, Acting Chief of Engineers, U. S. Army, as Burnside rode away from the conference of corps commanders the night before had come true. "He won't be up," Duane had avowed. "He won't be up, I know him well." [21]

Schaff's account of his meeting with Burnside throws both

an interesting and informative light on this stage of the IX Corps operation. He recalls that:

> When he came, accompanied by a large staff, I rode up to him and told him my instructions. He was mounted on a bob-tailed horse and wore a drooping army hat, a large gold cord around it. Like a sphinx, he made no reply, halted and began to look with a most leaden countenance in the direction he was to go . . . After a while he started off calmly toward the Lacy house, not indicating that my services were needed—he probably was thinking of something that was of vastly more importance. I concluded that I wasn't wanted, and was about to go my own way, when I caught sight of Babcock of Grant's staff coming at great speed down the hill just the other side of the run. He had been out with Hancock, and as he approached, I called, "What's the news, Babcock?" Without halting he replied, "Hancock has driven them a mile and we are going to have a great victory!" [22]

Report of Burnside's laggard pace was borne to Hancock by Lieutenant Colonel Lyman who galloped southward with a string of mounted orderlies to establish a courier service between army and II Corps headquarters. Lyman reported to Hancock. The wing commander, according to Meade's aide was wreathed in smiles. [23]

"We are driving them beautifully, sir," cried the general. "Tell Meade we are driving them most beautifully. Birney has gone in and he is clearing them out be-au-ti-fully."

The force of Hancock's statement, observes Lyman, was apparent from the receding fire and the absence of Minié balls. Then Lyman turned to Hancock and said, "I am ordered to tell you, sir, that only one division of Burnside's is up but that he will go into action as soon as he can be put into position."

Hancock's face changed. "I knew it," he cried vehemently, "just what I expected. If he could attack *now* we would smash A. P. Hill to pieces." [24]

Hancock's high hopes were doomed to cruel disappointment. Potter's 2d Division, followed by Willcox's 3d, pushed on across the Lacy field and over the main stream of Wilderness Run into the pine thickets beyond. Stevenson's 1st Division fell out of the column and massed in reserve near the cross-roads at Wilderness Tavern. Continuing the march toward Chewning's plateau, Potter followed the woods road over high ground on the right of the west branch of Wilderness Run. The objective, according to General Burnside, was Parker's Store.[25]

As the column approached Jones' field, the 6th New Hampshire swept in skirmish order across the open ground, driving the Confederate skirmishers back on their supporting line. The 48th Pennsylvania was sent out as flank skirmishers on the right and left. Colonel Simon G. Griffin's brigade, in the advance of Potter's division, deployed across the road; Bliss' brigade formed on Griffin's left;[26] Hartranft's brigade, the leading unit of Wilcox's division, came up on Bliss' left, completing the three brigade front, Griffin-Bliss-Hartranft. "Looking southwest," according to Hartranft, the line apparently was formed on the west side of a small brook flowing southward into the branch.[27] Christ's brigade, closing the rear of the column, moved up and formed in reserve on the road. Seven companies of the 1st Michigan Sharpshooters were extended to the right to connect with the left of Warren's line.[28]

These dispositions were completed under sharp infantry and artillery fire from the heights beyond the edge of the woods, where elements of Cutts' artillery battalion and an unidentified force of Confederate infantry had hastily taken position to oppose Burnside's advance.[29] "The action had become quite brisk," reports General Potter, "and I was about preparing to charge the enemy, when I received an order to withdraw my command, move to the left, and attack on the right of General Hancock, near the Plank Road."[30]

This order was delivered in person by Colonel Comstock and, perhaps, verbally. General Hartranft states in connection with the deployment of the IX Corps line facing Chewning heights that his brigade came up on the left about 7 a.m., and that the order to move by the left was received sometime later. It is known, however, that army headquarters did not issue such an order before 8 a.m., for at that time Meade informed Hancock that two of Burnside's divisions had advanced nearly to Parker's Store and that they were ordered to attack across the II Corps front.[31] An hour later, Hancock received word that Colonel Comstock had gone out to General Burnside to point out to him where to attack the enemy on or near the Plank Road.[32]

This order definitely terminated the mission of the IX Corps divisions as Grant's strategic mass of maneuver. This decision was taken in consequence of ominous developments on the Plank Road, which now claim attention.

Birney and Wadsworth Attack

Promptly at 5 a.m. the double-shotted gun at II Corps headquarters roared Hancock's signal for the advance. The brigades of Ward and Hays went forward. Delayed in the completion of his formation by capture of Lieutenant Colonel Baldwin, brigade officer of outposts, McAllister was obliged to bring his command up on the line by obliquing to the right. No confusion, fortunately, attended here the same maneuver that had been so disastrous in the face of the enemy the afternoon before. With Brewster closing in his rear, McAllister connected with Hays' left. Closely connected from flank to flank, the two battle lines of the first wave moved out into the deep thickets toward Hill's front. Eustis, Wheaton, and Grant, with Brewster on the left, followed in two lines. The brigades of Carroll and Owens came in support. As the signal gun echoed through the woods, Wadsworth's four brigades moved down on the Confederate left. Baxter held the center, with Rice on the right, Cutler on the left, and Stone in reserve.

Abroad since early dawn in his endeavor to prepare a connected line, Wilcox heard the scattering fire of Federal skirmishers on his right "just as the rising sun appeared above the tree tops." The firing travelled swiftly across the Plank Road. Then came the sound of distant volleys on the left rear of the Confederate front. The roar swelled with alarming in-

tensity. Its volume, says Wilcox, "was of the heaviest kind
. . . . The fighting was severe as long as it lasted." [33]

Moving along the south side of the Plank Road, Ward's
brigade struck the front of Scales' Confederate Brigade. Ward's
right regiment, the 141st New York, drove the 13th North
Carolina from its hastily constructed breastworks and took the
regimental colors.[34] The assault at this point appears to have
fallen without warning. Captain R. S. Williams, Company I,
of the 13th, tells the story:

> General Scales and our Colonel Hyman were standing be-
> hind our company, when one of my sergeants called to me
> and said: "Look in front!" I looked, and the woods were blue
> with the enemy. I turned to the Colonel and General Scales
> to tell them. The enemy were coming closer behind us. I told
> them to look—we were almost surrounded. General Scales
> waved his sword above his head and called on the men to
> follow him. He dashed off at right angles to his brigade and
> took his brigade out by the right flank. I was wounded in the
> shoulder. I kept following our retreating, or stampeded, troops
> who circled back to the road, where we met Longstreet's corps
> coming in. Lee was standing there.[35]

The route of Scales' Brigade left McGowan, on the north
side of the road, in a dangerously exposed position. Owing
to the inclination of his front to the line of the Plank Road,
and the circumstance of Scales' collapse, the Federal onset had
much of the force of a flank attack. The South Carolina
Brigade, however, was warned in time to escape the full penalty of surprise.

Formed in a slight depression between the two hostile lines,
McGowan's skirmishers developed the enemy's advance and
withdrew slowly to the main line of battle. The Federal advance was reported as being cautious and orderly. The pressure, however, on McGowan's exposed right flank became
intolerable. Threatened by the rush of Federal troops through
Scales' broken front, the 12th South Carolina bent back its
line and retired. The movement continued right to left along
the brigade front, the 14th, 1st, 13th, and Orr's Rifles giving
way in turn, "There was no panic," asserts the brigade his-

torian. "The men fell back from deliberate conviction that it was impossible to hold the ground." [36]

Davis' Brigade, Heth's Division, on the left front of Mc-Gowan, was overwhelmed while attempting to join in line. The rifles of the 55th North Carolina were still stacked when the rout began.[37]

Isolated on the extreme right, Thomas' Brigade gave way before the roaring wave of attack, his scattered Georgia regiments falling back past the right flank of Lane's Brigade.

Lane was endeavoring to form his North Carolina regiments on a line perpendicular to the Plank Road when the storm burst against Scales and Thomas, on his immediate front. The brigadier gives a frank account of the rout:

> Just as I had succeeded in forming the 33d, 18th, and 37th, with one-half of 33d broken back parallel to the road, the enemy in large numbers pressed back Scales, and the troops [McGowan and Davis] to the left of the road being driven out in disorder, the enemy struck our left at the angle formed by the two wings of the 33d Regiment . . . Unable to stand the front and flank fire, we were forced back in disorder with the other troops . . .[38]

The collapse of Lane's line was so quick and complete that the 37th Regiment, according to Lieutenant O. W. Wiggins of Company E, "was carried back by other troops without firing a gun." [39]

Hit on the left flank by Wadsworth's powerful column, Kirkland's Brigade crumpled while attempting to form in line. "Our left flank," states Colonel W. J. Martin, commanding the 11th North Carolina, "rolled up as a sheet of paper would be rolled without power of resistance. If a single brigade had changed front to left, it might have stopped the rout."[40] Walker escaped capture by promptly abandoning his position. In the ardor of pursuit, Baxter and Cutler of Wadsworth's division swept across the Plank Road, blocking the right of Birney's assault column while brigade and regimental staffs frantically strove to remove the obstructing units.

Of the eight Confederate brigades engulfed in Birney's

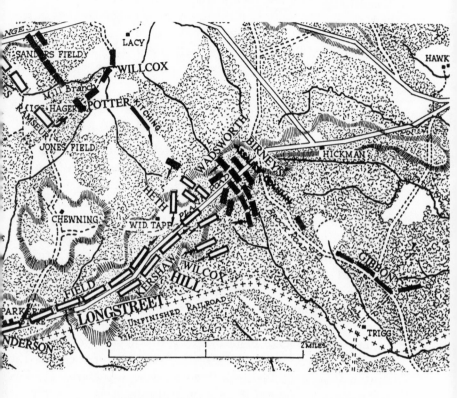

MAP 18. HILL'S DEFENSE COLLAPSES

Hancock's assault column under Birney swamps Hill's first and second
lines. Sweeping down from the north, Wadsworth overshoots his mark and
blocks the right of Birney's column. Birney's left pushes on, opening a gap
at the center. Reforming on the north side of the Plank Road, Wadsworth
advances in column of brigades. Getty, moving right to connect with
Wadsworth, runs into the three-brigade formation at Cooke's reserve position.
Unopposed, Birney's left toils forward. Fatigued and disordered by the swift
advance over difficult terrain, Birney's formation is ill-prepared to meet the
attack of Longstreet's fresh brigades.

For simplicity, Hill's brigades are not named on this map; but Wilcox's
brigades are falling back in column, McGowan being on the road and Lane,
Scales, and Thomas, in that order, south of the road. Heth's brigades are
north of the road; Kirkland is falling back in column, while Walker and
Davis rally briefly at Cooke's reserve position.

and Wadsworth's swift converging movement, Cooke's alone appears to have held with the desperate tenacity that had marked the conduct of all during the prolonged combat of the previous afternoon. But only Cooke, it must be realized, had been afforded the opportunity of entrenching his position. And Cooke had made these preparations in violation of orders.[41]

Hill's Defense Collapses

Securely entrenched at the edge of the stubble field to which he had withdrawn during the night, and supported by Williams' North Carolina Battery, Cooke's five North Carolina regiments braced themselves to face the oncoming torrent. Coming hastily in on the left, the brigades of Kirkland and Davis (Stone commanding) appear to have rallied and lent Cooke a measure of support in slowing the right of the Federal advance.[42] The 26th North Carolina, Kirkland's Brigade, reformed and charged straight at the enemy, enabling the brigade to get into line on the new front.[43] Stone's Mississippi regiments turned fiercely at bay. Cooke, Kirkland, and Stone met the onrush of Eustis and Wheaton, who had struggled bitterly against these same brigades during the previous afternoon. The combat was renewed with greater ferocity as the scattered units of Wilcox's Division now swept past Cooke's right flank, Scales and Thomas tearing their way through the dense thicket, Lane and McGowan streaming along the road.

Cooke opened fire, staggering the attackers with the first serious resistance they had encountered since pressing forward with the echo of Hancock's signal gun. The guns of Williams' Battery broke in on the roar of musketry with a thundering salvo.

Owing to the dense white clouds rising from the Federal line of battle and effectively screening his target from observation at the battery position, Captain Williams improvised a method that anticipated subsequent developments in the technique of indirect fire. In agreement with the artillerist, Captain Lawton of Company D, 48th North Carolina, crept forward to observe and report on Williams' practice. With an infantry captain performing virtually the role of a modern Forward Observation Officer, the North Carolina Battery found its target and hurled a torrent of explosive shells into the attacking brigades.

Though Cooke, with the support of Kirkland, Davis, and the guns of Williams' Battery, dealt a staggering blow to Birney's advance, he was unable to arrest or divert the powerful thrust. His flanks enveloped and his front assailed, Cooke reluctantly gave orders to abandon the position and fall back. Williams limbered up. Stone's three Mississippi regiments, the 2d, 11th, and 42d, continued firing as Kirkland and Cooke, with Williams' guns, withdrew toward Widow Tapp's farm.

The obstruction interposed by Wadsworth in overshooting his mark contributed largely to Getty's difficulty in moving on Cooke. Collapse of all resistance on the left gave Birney's first echelon a leftward pull. Getty, on the right of the second echelon, responded to the pull, crossing to the south side of the Plank Road. Then, as Wadsworth's errant brigades changed direction and obliqued to the north side of the Plank Road, a wide gap opened on Getty's right. Inclining back across the road, he struck Cooke's entrenched position. Although neither contestant identified his adversary in this encounter, two significant facts point to Getty's presence in the stubblefield. Getty alone suffered severely during the assault that swept Hill from the Plank Road ridge. Again, only Cooke and his supports offered stiff resistance.

In the meantime, Rice's brigade had become involved on the extreme right of Wadsworth's original line. While moving forward in the converging attack, a Confederate battery enfiladed the line from the right. Rice detailed the 56th Pennsylvania and 76th New York regiments under command of Colonel Hoffman, of the 56th, to capture the guns. The two regiments changed front to rear on the left companies and opened on a Confederate skirmish line that had taken position on the crest of a hill about 300 yards distant. The skirmishers promptly disappeared. Then, screened by the woods, Rice moved his force by the right, intending to come up on the line of the battery and take the guns with a quick bayonet charge. The maneuver, though skillfully conducted, fell short of its objective; Hoffman captured the battery pickets, only to find that the guns had been hooked in and taken 400 yards to the rear. They were soon put in action, and again opened with so effective a fire of spherical case that Hoffman was forced to withdraw from his advanced position.[44]

The incident on Rice's right retarded his progress toward the Plank Road, thus avoiding his involvement in the jam on Birney's right. In extricating the two V Corps brigades from the south side of the road, Cutler appears to have refaced his command before Baxter, who had probably gone a greater distance southward across Birney's front, could change direction. At any rate, Wadsworth finally succeeded in forming his division in column of brigades, Cutler leading, with Stone, Baxter, and Rice following, probably in the order named. In this formation he advanced along the north side of the road.

Encountering severe artillery fire, the lines, according to Cutler, "were, by order of General Wadsworth, closed in mass to avoid the artillery fire of the enemy."[45]

It cannot be stated with positive assurance that Getty advanced into the accurately directed fire of Williams' North Carolina battery. On the other hand, it would be difficult to account for the presence of Federal troops, other than Getty's, in the stubblefield facing Cooke, during the brief time-interval between the collapse of Hill's first line of defense and the brief delaying action fought by Cooke and his supports. Yet it is certain that the North Carolina battery found a target, wreathed with the white smoke of blazing volleys, and that Williams fired salvo after salvo, withdrawing his guns only when Cooke's regiments left their trenches.

Rout of Hill's Corps

Meantime following the line of least resistance, Birney's assault troops continued their inclination to the left, extending the front until it described a vast semicircle from Wadsworth's extreme right, which lay north of the Plank Road at the east edge of Widow Tapp's clearing, and reaching across the Plank Road around to a point almost due south of the right flank of Poague's artillery battalion, lining the fringe of trees at the west edge of Widow Tapp's clearing.

Scarcely an hour had passed since Hancock's signal gun had sent the 13 brigades of Birney and Wadsworth against the 8 of A. P. Hill. Back of the gun lines of Poague's Battalion, Lee, with A. P. Hill, who had returned from his reconnaissance over the Chewning plateau and, in all probability, had reported the tardy development of Federal operations in that quarter, now witnessed the collapse of the Confederate right. The din of musketry rolled westward like a storm-driven thunder cloud. The smoke of roaring volleys rose out of the woods and obscured the highest boughs near the edge of Widow Tapp's clearing. Small knots of Confederate infantry suddenly appeared at the forest fringe.

Poague's gunners sprang to life, preparing their ammunition to sweep the front with canister. The gun limbers stood by, ready at the signal to limber up and gallop to the rear. Lee sent Colonel Taylor with instructions to put the trains at Parker's Store in readiness for an instant retreat. Colonel Venable rode down the Plank Road to find Longstreet and hasten his troops to the front. General Wilcox rode up and reported that his troops were breaking and could not hold their ground unless given immediate support. Lee directed Wilcox to get the reinforcements from Longstreet.[46]

As the thundering volleys drew nearer, whole regiments rushed from the woods and ran across the open ground toward the guns. The Plank Road was choked with fugitives. Fragments of Lane's North Carolina regiments, who had saved the flank at dusk the day before, were intermingled with the remnants of Scales' Brigade. McGowan's South Carolinians, the very men who restored the center and held until dark, swept by in a disordered throng. Lee recognized the brigadier riding helplessly along in a rushing stream of infantry.

Beside himself with wrath and chagrin, Lee spurred into the press and confronted the brigade commander. "My God, General McGowan," he shouted, "is this fine brigade of yours fleeing like wild geese?" McGowan's angry retort was reassuring: "Sir, my men are not beaten; they want only a place to reform and fight." [47]

There can be no dobut that Lee's practiced eye had already noted a cohesive tendency in every scattered group to bunch together and restore a semblance of military formation. Truly, the III Corps infantry was not beaten. Demoralization that responds to the affrighted cry of *sauve qui peut* had not yet transformed the elements of Hill's shattered lines into a panic-stricken rabble. The men needed only direction and encouragement. This Lee and Hill, seconded by divisional staffs, togther with brigade and regimental officers, gave with consummate skill and energy.

Lee's Strong Language

Biographers have discreetly drawn a curtain over one aspect of the scene—the amazing vigor of Lee's vocabulary. By the same motive that has persistently sought to invest the character of Washington with every attribute of a priggish demi-god, this tacit conspiracy of silly myth makers has obscured the fact that Lee, who knew his troops, met the crisis with a tempestuous eloquence that was most suitable to the occasion and thoroughly appreciated by the rank and file. The reverberations of one of his tongue lashings is described by a file-closer of McGowan's Brigade, as that unit was rallied and reformed in rear of the artillery lines:

> General Lee and General Hill were here, evidently excited and chagrined. The former expressed himself rather roughly to us, especially us file-closers; but I am not sure but his anger implied a sort of compliment to our past performances. [48]

The same sort of myth making has been at work in obscuring the facts of Hill's hasty retreat from the Plank Road position. The stand made by Cooke's North Caroline Brigade, with the supporting elements of Davis, Kirkland, and the North Carolina Battery, offers a fair indication of the performance that the other brigades of Heth and Wilcox might have made had they not been overwhelmed in the midst of belated efforts to prepare their lines of defense. The chronicles of the numerous North Carolina regiments in this disastrous affair tell a consistent story; they agree with the historian of McGowan's South Carolina Brigade: all save Cooke were compelled to execute a rapid withdrawal to avert either annihilation or capture. No excuses are offered; there is no attempt to make a case for their own corps at the expense of Longstreet and the troops that arrived in time to save the day. Indeed, the candor of these soldier-historians is refreshing. Veterans with a just pride in the valor of their units, they find no difficulty, like veterans the world over, in testifying that they broke in the face of overwhelming odds and quit the field in some disorder that they might reform and fight again on better terms. Such candor, to be sure, is disconcerting to post-war politicians and propagandists of lost causes, who fail to grasp the significant facts of the case and must have a prolonged and desperate defense, while Longstreet leisurely marched to the sound of their despairing volleys.

The brigades of Heth and Wilcox need no apologists; they did achieve a miracle. Despite their crushing defeat and a retreat that many of the participants do not hesitate to describe as a "stampede," they retained their integrity as military organizations and reformed their ranks in an incredibly short period of time. Wilcox's brigades, who had taken the full shock of Birney's first echelon and who, therefore, were the first to crowd into the open ground of Widow Tapp's farm, were speedily reorganized and sent to the left, following the same road they had taken the previous afternoon toward Chewning's plateau. Heth's brigades, coming in on the heels of Wilcox's broken formations, made a quick response to orders placing them in support to Poague's artillery mass, with their left extending toward Wilcox. Without this remarkable recovery and the consequent ability to rapidly march into position across the interval, thereby affording support to Longstreet on his left—an advantage that A. P. Hill had been denied the afternoon before—it is difficult to see how the I Corps could have sustained the bitter contest that raged from 6:30 until 10 o'clock and finally wrested the initiative from Birney's massive column of attack.

CHAPTER 20

LONGSTREET STOPS HANCOCK

While Lee and Hill were directing the swift work of reorganization in rear of Poague's artillery lines, Wilcox, accompanied by an aide, cantered down the Plank Road toward Parker's Store. At no great distance from the guns he met Kershaw, riding with his old brigade at the head of Longstreet's column.

In accordance with the orders he had received from Lee, Wilcox instructed Kershaw to push forward with all possible haste and throw his division in line of battle to the right of the road. The deployment, he advised, must be effected with great speed, lest his own troops break and ruin the maneuver with their rush through Kershaw's half-formed lines. The aide was instructed to accompany General Kershaw and indicate the line of deployment. Wilcox then rode on to find Longstreet and direct him to Lee's headquarters.[1]

Kershaw and the aide galloped knee to knee up the road, past Poague's guns and on to a point some 400 yards in advance of his column, when a swarming mass of Confederate infantry broke from the woods and rushed back over the open ground toward Poague's guns.

Kershaw Attacks on the Right

Kershaw looked over the ground. A dense thicket stretched from the line on which he was expected to deploy to the battle front, where Wilcox was making his last stand. Small disordered groups of stragglers were tearing through the woods on both sides of the Plank Road. Their haste foretold the collapse of A. P. Hill's entire line. Kershaw realized that there was no time for an orderly relief of the hard pressed troops at the front. There remained only the possibility of rescuing

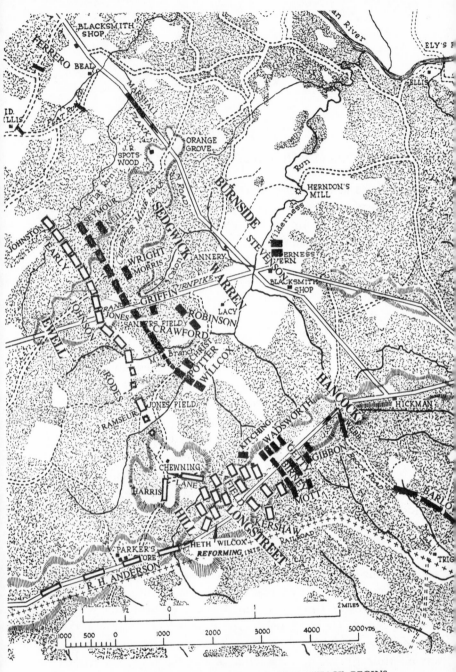

MAP 19. LONGSTREET'S COUNTERATTACK BEGINS

The situation at about 6:30 a.m., May 6. The V-VI Corps holding attack has failed to pin down Ewell. Ramseur, held in corps reserve after returning from his detached mission, now moves across Burnside's path of advance. Longstreet, passing through Hill's shattered units, is launching an assault which staggers Hancock's attack column, while Hill reforms his brigades. Anderson is moving up to reinforce Longstreet.

broken units by halting the enemy's pursuit. He galloped back toward the head of his column.

But recently entrusted with command of a division of infantry, Kershaw had yet to win his major general's spurs.

Meeting Colonel John W. Henagan, commanding his old brigade, at a point opposite Lee's battle headquarters and just in rear of Poague's gun position, Kershaw reined in and instructed the brigadier to file to the right and form in line of battle with his left resting on the Plank Road.[2]

After giving these orders, Kershaw turned again and went forward to direct the deployment. The approaching enemy caused a modification of his plan. In order to protect the front of the guns, he threw Colonel Franklin Gaillard's 2d North Carolina, the leading element of Henagan's column, on the north (left) side of the Plank Road. Henagan filed to the left, going the distance of a two-brigade front and leaving an interval between Colonel James D. Nance's 3d North Carolina, his left regiment, and the Plank Road. This space was to be filled by Benjamin Humphreys' Brigade, the second in Kershaw's divisional column. Following Humphreys, Bryan's Brigade would form on the right of the line.

As Henagan's regiments were moving to the left, retreating fragments of Heth's and Wilcox's brigades broke through the partially formed line of battle and retarded completion of the formation until the last disordered throng hastened to the rear. Only the superb troop leadership of Kershaw's regimental officers, and the steady confidence given by their men, averted a complete catastrophe. Without giving ground they coolly opened their ranks and permitted the fugitives to pass through. No doubt the agitation of the latter drew some caustic remarks from the I Corps men.[3]

Weary and disarrayed, the left echelon of Birney's assault column surged forward in a final effort to clinch the victory. The left of the crescent-like line swept Poague's batteries with long range musketry. The right charged toward the gap in Kershaw's line between Nance and Gaillard. Nance fell at the head of his regiment. Gaillard's right companies gave way. The center and left was thrown into a huddled mass. Gaillard fell while striving to rally his troops. Desperately wounded, Lieutenant Colonel Kennedy was carried to the rear. The command devolved upon Captain Wallace.

Undismayed, Kershaw threw Humphreys' Brigade into the gap. The field of fire no longer obstructed by fugitives from the infantry front, Poague's guns broke their long silence and poured volleys of grape and canister at the oncoming Federals. Humphreys and Henagan held while Bryan moved up on the right of the line. His deployment completed, Kershaw spurred to the front and, "riding like a centaur," led his division forward.[4]

Colonel William F. Perry, who commanded Law's Alabama brigade of Field's Division and later participated in a feat of similar gallantry on the north side of the Plank Road, pays a generous tribute to the chief of the rival division. "Kershaw," he wrote in later years, "reached the field and went into action. He had arrived like Desaix at Marengo, in one of those great crises which few men are called upon to meet twice in a lifetime." [5]

Lee Changes His Plan

After delivering Lee's instructions to Kershaw, General Wilcox went on to find Longstreet and conduct him to Lee's battle headquarters. Longstreet, accompanied by General E. P. Alexander, I Corps chief of artillery, reported to the army commander.[6]

A more explicit account of this historic battlefield conference would throw into clear relief the planning and execution of Longstreet's greatest tactical performance. His counterattack on this field unquestionably averted a crushing defeat of the Army of Northern Virginia and enabled Lee to prolong the war for another year.

The presence of Wilcox at the conference, together with the part he played in designating Kershaw's line of deployment, suggests that Lee originally intended to employ Wilcox's

Division in conjunction with a counter-offensive stroke which would be delivered by the I Corps. Details of the proposed operation are obscure. We know, however, that Kershaw was to deploy, as he did, on the right of the Plank Road, along a line some 400 yards in advance of Poague's artillery position. It is also known that Field had instructions to deploy his division on the right of the road some distance in rear of the gun positions. In short, the I Corps would form in column of divisions on the south side of the Plank Road.

The intended disposition of Hill's III Corps is largely conjectural. But if Longstreet's column formation on the right is assumed, the deployment of Hill's divisions—Wilcox, Heth, and Anderson—would be governed by two requirements: (1) the necessity of forming a column of divisions on the left corresponding to Longstreet's on the right; (2) the desirability of holding one division in reserve, to serve either as a force of maneuver or to reinforce the attack column. Acting in the former capacity, this division would fill the gap across the Chewning plateau. Wilcox presumably was to go into line on the left, his right connecting with Kershaw's left at the Plank Road. Either Heth's battered brigades or the fresh units of Anderson's Division would form the second element in the column of divisions on the left, the final decision depending on the speed with which Heth's troops could be reformed.

To anticipate events for the moment, Longstreet's two divisions deployed on both sides of the Plank Road, Kershaw on the right, Field on the left. Totaling 13 brigades, Hill's 3 divisions—Wilcox, Heth, and Anderson—constituted a reserve of sorts in rear of Poague's guns while the work of reforming broken units went swiftly forward. As soon as possible, the 8 brigades of Wilcox and Heth, with one from Anderson's Division, moved by the left to extend the Confederate front over the Chewning plateau. The right elements of this new line, together with the four remaining brigades of Anderson's Division, were available as supports to Longstreet's attack force on the Plank Road.[7]

The tentative plan presupposed two conditions that no longer obtained when Kershaw began his deployment. First, the divisions of Heth and Wilcox were stampeding to the rear instead of holding off the enemy in an orderly retirement. Again, Kershaw's and Field's divisions were marching on the Plank Road to their prospective fronts of deployment in a double column, the former on the right, the latter on the left. Unless Field halted until the road was cleared on his right, the difficulties of deploying both divisions simultaneously were such as to bring the whole plan into question. Yet the fact remains that G. T. Anderson's Brigade, the leading element in Field's column, did deploy on the right. Furthermore, Field received instructions to discontinue deployment on the line established by G. T. Anderson and, according to his own statement, was ordered to form on the left of the Plank Road "in the quickest order I could make." Field adds:

> Throwing the Texas brigade, which was second (in column), on the left of the road and in line perpendicular to it, Benning in rear of that, and Law in rear of that, the Texas brigade, led by its gallant General Gregg, dashed forward as soon as it was formed, without waiting for those in its rear to get ready.[8]

Field Attacks on the Left

The crisis on the north side of the Plank Road was as grave as the one met by Kershaw on the south side. Only the original formation of Birney's assault column and the circumstances of his advance against Hill's defense lines enabled Longstreet to recover the time he lost in the belated deployment on the left. Withheld by design in Birney's original formation, then delayed by confusion of the collision with Wadsworth's column, and again retarded by Cooke's resistance in the stubble field, the right elements of the second and third echelons of the Federal assault column emerged from the woods on the east side of Widow Tapp's clearing sometime after Kershaw had completed his deployment and moved against the left (first) echelon of Birney's attack formation.

Poague switched his fire to the front, blasting the new

target with a preparatory bombardment and screening the preparations of Field's brigades for the counter-stroke.[9]

Filing left, Gregg's Texans came into line immediately in rear of the flaming guns. As the formation was completed, Longstreet rode down the line, his horse at a walk. Addressing each company, he said: "Keep cool, men. We will straighten this out in a short time—keep cool."

"In the midst of the confusion," remarks Colonel W. H. Palmer, III Corps chief of staff, "his coolness and manner was inspiring." The staff officer adds:

> When the Texas Brigade had formed they were moved through the guns. General Lee rode on their flank. The tall Texan on the left lifted his hat and called to General Lee go back, and it was taken up by the others. General Lee lifted his hat to them and moved slowly to the rear. It did not strike me as remarkable at the time. The brigade was noted for steadiness and courage, and had been detached from him. It had been months since he had seen them. There was no heroic leading. He was glad to be with them; he was saluting them.[10]

The story of Gregg's charge is told by J. B. Polly, a veteran of the 5th Texas regiment. Advancing under fire some 400 yards, the Texans "crashed into the enemy's main line of battle." In the furious grapple, Gregg's 4th and 5th Regiments broke away and drove across the Plank Road, which ran diagonally athwart their path of advance. Supporting artillery fire swept the road on their right. The left staggered under a heavy enfilade of hostile musketry. Perceiving a strong force of Federal infantry pushing down the Plank Road toward his left, Gregg ordered an instant retreat, which was conducted in good order to a line about 200 yards in front of Poague's guns. Two-thirds of the brigade lay on the battlefield. A young lieutenant was the sole survivor of one company. For months he paraded alone to answer morning roll call for his company.[11]

Little is known about the charge of Benning's gallant Georgians. They reached their objective, struck fiercely and then, like Gregg's Texans, rolled back with an appalling toll of dead and wounded strewn along their path of advance and retreat.

Perry, marching in column on Benning's rear, closed toward the guns. Lee, followed by a large cavalcade, rode up as the brigade filed into line. Inquiring of the men as to their unit and learning that it was Law's old brigade, Lee replied, "God bless Alabama!"

A thundering cheer answered his heartfelt tribute. Of the many word pictures inspired by the martial splendor of Lee on the battlefield, the image impressed on Perry's mind during the turmoil of that hour and expressed in glowing words at a later day is one of surpassing beauty. Here the unconscious betrayal of a deep and abiding awe explains something of the force behind the astonishing feat of arms achieved by these Texas, Georgia, and Alabama regiments. Perry wrote:

> The central figure of that group . . . was General Lee. The conception of his appearance in my mind to this day is that of a grand equestrian statue of colossal proportions. His countenance, usually placid and benign, was blazing with martial ardor. The lamb in his nature had given place to the lion, and his spirit seemed transformed through everyone who looked upon him. It was impossible not to feel that every man that passed him was, for the time being, a hero.[12]

The Alabama regiments deployed from left to right in the order 15th-44th-48th-4th-47th. Perry's accurate description of the terrain over which he passed leaves no doubt as to the direction of attack. The open ground slopes gradually away from the Plank Road ridge for about 300 yards, then drops into a ravine. Narrow toward the ridge, this drainage opens out to the north. Gregg and Benning passed between the road and the head of the basin. The ravine with its swampy bottom lay athwart Perry's line of advance.

The Alabama brigade moved with increasing speed to the brow of the declivity. Here the center and left regiments found themselves opposed by dense masses of the enemy, some of whom had already crossed the swamp and were dressing their lines at 50 yards' range, some were in the act of crossing, while others were crowding down the moderately steep descent from

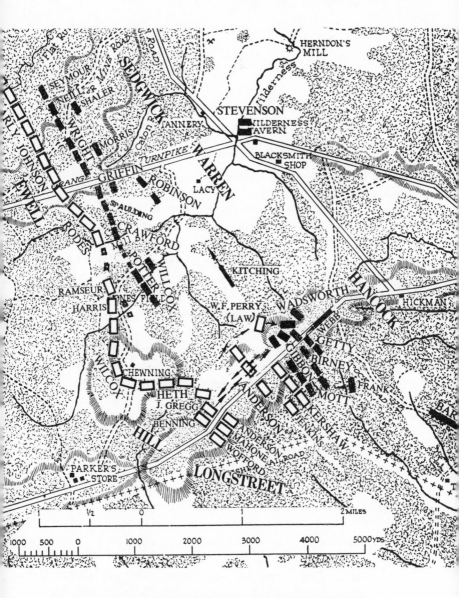

MAP 20. LONGSTREET SMEARS HANCOCK'S RIGHT FLANK

The situation about 7:45 a.m., May 6. There is a stalemate on the north flank, and Burnside is stalled in the center of the Federal line. Heth and Wilcox have sideslipped to the left to close the Confederate gap across the Chewning plateau. The important development is that Longstreet, in his counterattack along the Plank Road Ridge, is pressing back Hancock's brigades. The arrows show the attack and withdrawal of Gregg and Benning, followed by W. F. Perry's destructive flank charge against Wadsworth. Col W. F. Perry commands Law's brigade; on following maps, since there is a brigade commanded by E. A. Perry and another by Perrin, to minimize confusion W. F. Perry's command will be shown as "Law."

the far side. The Alabamians volleyed on the run and, shouting their bloodcurdling Rebel yell, dashed forward. The volley, the war whoop, and the impetuous charge astonished and unnerved the advancing Federals. Firing a ragged volley in return, they precipitously fell back into the ravine.

Perry Presses the Attack

As the Alabamians rushed down into the ravine they were raked by an enfilading fire from the left. A Federal force that had crossed the morass reached the forward edge and moved into a clump of trees at the farther limits of the open ground. There they were poised for a turning movement against Perry's left. Incited only to renewed efforts by greater peril, the Alabamians drove across the swamp and up the opposite slope.

Perry, meanwhile, ordered Colonel W. C. Oates, commanding the 15th Alabama, which he describes as the largest and one of the best regiments in his command, "to change direction in marching—that is to wheel his battalion to the left while advancing so as to face the woods—and attack furiously." [13]

Fearful of pressing the pursuit across the swamp while a hostile force threatened his left rear, Perry halted on the ascent to high ground beyond and galloped off the left toward the woods, where Oates was about to attack. He was just in time, he relates, "to witness the successful execution of one of the most brilliant movements I have ever seen on a battlefield."

Upon receiving Perry's order to change front and attack, Colonel Oates wheeled his regiment in an arc of 60 degrees and, crossing the open ground, charged into the woods. A few flaming volleys decided the issue. The Federals fell back, according to Perry, in the wildest confusion. Oates lost 1 man killed and 11 wounded in the encounter. [14]

In following the progress of Perry's Brigade over Widow Tapp's field and across the swampy bottom to the northeast, it should be realized that his five Alabama regiments held the extreme left of Longstreet's advancing line of battle. Bryan's Brigade of Kershaw's Division held the right. Henagan and Humphreys stood in the order mentioned on Bryan's left, extending the line to the Plank Road. According to the reliable first hand evidence from Confederate sources, Perry's brigade alone held the entire sector of Longstreet's line on the north side of the Plank Road.

Old Soldiers' Tales

Aside from the brief summary reports of Longstreet and Kershaw, only two brigade commanders, Perry and Bryan, contribute in the form of official reports first-hand information concerning the I Corps counterattack.[15] The withdrawal of Gregg and Benning left only four brigades in Longstreet's line. These four brigades, according to the available evidence, wrecked the advance of a Federal assault column consisting of four divisions totalling 11 brigades, with two in close reserve and two heavy artillery regiments of brigade strength. Admitting that both Field and Kershaw performed feats of arms almost beyond belief, credulity can hardly be stretched to the point of accepting a miracle. Some vital bits of evidence must be missing.

In relating the incidents of his deployment and advance on the right of the line, Bryan furnishes a clue. He states in his report of the operation that

> At one time some fears were entertained that the many stragglers to the rear would cause some confusion to my command, and that I should be unable to get them in good order to the front. These fears were soon removed, for both officers and men aided me in the endeavor to stop the tide of stragglers to the rear, whom they marched boldly to the front . . . At the command forward the gallant fellows sprang forward with a shout, driving back the enemy's first line without firing a gun. The second line of the enemy was behind a line of log breastworks, which checked for a moment our rapid advance, but after a few well-directed volleys the enemy broke from their entrenchments, the command pursuing to the distance of about a mile to a swamp, when the enemy being reinforced and my ammunition being reduced to only 5 rounds, I ordered the command to fall back to the enemy's

log breast-works, which I held till relieved by General Jenkins.[16]

General McGowan's retort to Lee that his retreating men only wanted a place to form applied to most of Hill's III Corps units. If Bryan rallied stragglers in full flight, the process of reforming the broken units in rear of Poague's artillery position must have proceeded with startling rapidity. If there was a miracle, it was performed here. Colonel Palmer contributes evidence on this point.

> When the Texans moved forward Longstreet had no time to form more troops in front; he halted and faced his men as they were marching in the road, and broke by brigades and moved *in echelon* to meet the turning movement of the enemy. It was a beautiful movement. The Texans, part of McGowan's, and much of Davis' Mississippi brigade under Colonel Stone and other troops of Heth and Wilcox, were holding all the ground around the guns, and to the right across the road; and General Longstreet's echelon movement caught the sweeping enemy and forced him back steadily and surely.[17]

The evidence furnished by Bryan and Palmer would indicate that some of Heth's and Wilcox's units were available as supports to Longstreet's line. Then Anderson's III Corps division, closing on the rear of the I Corps, offered a reserve of five fresh brigades. Upon arrival, Anderson was instructed by Lee to report to Longstreet for orders. Counting Gregg and Benning, who contributed materially in the first phase of the counterattack, Longstreet had with the 8 of his I Corps and the 5 of Anderson's Division a disposable force of 13 fresh brigades to pit against the 13 in Birney's moving assault force. Then, while Hancock held 5 brigades in reserve on the Plank Road, with the 2 of Stevenson's division in general reserve, Lee had the 8 of Wilcox and Heth to meet either Burnside's threatened attack on Longstreet's left, or the reinforcement of Birney by Hancock's reserve. Only in the event that Burnside's column and Hancock's reserve, with Stevenson's division added, should strike in concert, would Lee's position on the Plank Road ridge be seriously imperiled. But the concerted movement was never made. Instead, Birney was fought to a standstill. His massive formation badly disordered by the swift advance through dense thickets, with overlapping lines and units intermixed, he was unprepared to parry the savage blows dealt by Longstreet's fresh brigades.

An effort to supplement the dearth of first-hand evidence from regimental histories, memoirs, and impressionistic sketches involves the difficulty of reconciling different accounts of the same incident written years after the event and colored with the personal point of view—the coloration sometimes deepened by trends of postwar controversy. Palmer and Venable, for instance, give different versions of the celebrated "Lee to the Rear" episode.

Dr. Freeman prefers Venable's version on the grounds that Venable was with Lee throughout the morning. Yet Venable tells an unbelievable tale. One cannot imagine a sergeant of the Army of Northern Virginia, and a Texan at that, laying hands on Lee's bridle rein. It is still more difficult to imagine a score of private soldiers leaving the ranks of a brigade in motion toward the enemy to manhandle the army commander's horse.

Admittedly less colorful for purposes of myth-making, Palmer's version does more credit to the dignity of the army commander and the discipline of the Confederate infantry. Of all the versions, his is most consistent with military psychology.[18]

Field, who in 1899 wrote his account of the battle, is at odds with both himself and Palmer in stating that Gregg dashed forward without waiting for the others to form, that Benning followed at a few paces interval and that Perry, immediately in rear of Benning, suffered less than his predecessors, "the enemy's course having been somewhat checked." Despite his self-contradiction, Field describes an attack in column of brigades rather than one in echelon by brigades.

In brief, the series of shrewd blows delivered against Birney's massive assault column cannot be described in the detail that would give an accurate and instructive account of Longstreet's brilliant performance. Although the results are known, no two participants are in complete agreement as to how the astonishing culmination was achieved. No two accounts can be reconciled, one with the other, when narrating the same event. The stories told by these eyewitnesses describe for the most part isolated events, unrelated as to time and place in the general movement. Perry excepted, no one tells who hit whom. Their accounts may be compared to close-up views taken at random in a vast, raging tumult. While characteristic of the action, they fail when pieced together to offer a pictorial reproduction of the whole movement.

Perry's close-up view of events on the left is the only glimpse we have of that sector of Longstreet's line on the north side of the Plank Road. However incomplete, his account cannot be ignored.

Perry Smashes Wadsworth

We left Perry's five Alabama regiments as Colonel Oates charged into the woods and scattered the Federal force that threatened to turn the Confederate line. No one was more surprised than Oates himself over the victory he won at such slight cost. He discovered the cause after interviewing his prisoners.

They were from the 15th Regiment, New York Heavy Artillery, one of the two regiments constituting Colonel J. Howard Kitching's Heavy Artillery Brigade. These so-called heavy artillery units were in reality regiments of foot soldiers trained as infantry to man the breastworks connecting gun positions that girdled the national capital. Their ranks filled with men who has enlisted in a belief that their military service would be devoted to the defence of Washington, these two regiments had been incorporated in the Army of the Potomac and sent to the front. Inured to garrison routine, they were helpless in the face of Perry's veteran regiments.[19]

Having dispersed Kitching's brigade, Oates led his 15th Alabama back to the left of Perry's line. Here another crisis impended.

In crossing the morass, the 44th and 48th Alabama Regiments had inclined to the left; the 4th on the extreme right of the brigade line, and the 47th, holding its connection on the left of the 4th, advanced over the unbroken ground between the Plank Road and the upper end of the swamp. A wide gap opened between the right and left wings of the brigade. Opposite Perry's attenuated line stood Wadsworth, his command massed four ranks deep in column of brigades. Getty's right had crossed the Plank Road to connect Wadsworth's left.[20] The remaining elements of Getty's division, together with Hays' and de Trobriand's brigades of Birney's division and Mott's two brigades — McAllister and Brewster, milled in a confused mass opposite Kershaw's front.

The right wing of Perry's line reeled under a murderous enfilade from the south side of the Plank Road. The 44th and 48th, on the left of the gap, staggered before the pressure of Wadsworth's advance. Colonel John A. Jones commanding the 44th was seriously wounded. Major George W. Carey seized the regimental colors and ran to the front. Riding in from the left, Perry found the 44th on the verge of collapse, its right in the air, its left companies broken and fugitives running back to hide in the woods. While exhorting the men to stand fast, his horse, already bleeding from a serious wound, fell in exhaustion.[21]

The gap on the right of the 48th stood open, inviting an inrush from the center of Wadsworth's heavy column. Once started, the torrent must inevitably sweep Longstreet's thin line from its precarious mooring. It was one of those fluctuations in the uncertain ebb and flow of desperate combat when the tide of battle swings with the quick judgment and resolute action of troop leaders on the firing line.

After forming on the left of Perry's isolated wing, Colonel Oates discovered that his regiment overlapped the Federal line and that the regiments on his right were giving way under the fury of volleys that flashed from Wadsworth's front in quick rotation of fire by ranks. Impressed by the "regularity and effectiveness of the method," Oates wheeled the 15th to the right. Calmly dressing his line with the meticulous care of an exacting tactician, he gave directions for a deliberate and well-aimed volley. One blast, according to the colonel, "stopped the racket." [22] As Oates wheeled right, Perry succeeded in rallying his left wing regiments. Before the Federals recovered from the havoc of Oates' devastating volley, he advanced and struck with a ferocity that multiplied his numbers fourfold. Wadsworth's dense formation buckled in wild confusion, the front ranks rushing back, the rear ranks pressing forward. The three Alabama regiments closed in, striking relentlessly to incite the spread of demoralization. Wadsworth's brigades rolled back, a throng of disintegrating units.

General Cutler, commanding the Iron Brigade, tells in a few words the story from the Federal side. After disentanglement from confusion of the collision with the right echelon of Birney's column, Cutler relates that

> The division was then formed in four lines, the left resting on the plank road. These lines were, by order of General Wadsworth, closed in mass to avoid the artillery fire of the enemy. While in this position it was furiously attacked by infantry and artillery, driven back and badly scattered, a large portion of them taking the route over which they had marched the night before. This portion of the command was rallied and got together by me near Old Wilderness Tavern. That portion which retired on the plank road was rallied by General Wadsworth and Rice.[23]

End of the First Phase

The oversight of both Perry and Cutler in failing to mention the time at which this incident occurred is most unfortunate. A valuable contribution to our knowledge of the battle would be given were it possible to make a reliable estimate of the lapse of time between Longstreet's arrival on the field and the first serious dislocation on the right of Birney's front. It is assumed that Kershaw had already pushed his left back to the second line. However, a fairly satisfactory solution may be derived from the exchange of dispatches between Meade's and Hancock's headquarters, now connected by field telegraph.[24]

At 7:40 a.m. Captain E. B. Cope, an *aide de camp* on War-
ren's staff and assigned on the 6th to Wadsworth's division,
reported to V Corps headquarters that "Wadsworth had been
slowly pushed back but is contesting every inch of ground." [25]
While Cope's message was en route to Warren, Hancock at
8 a.m. received a message from Meade notifying him that
Wadsworth's division had been assigned to his command.[26]
Lieutenant Schaff, temporarily serving as an *aide de camp* to
Warren, left V Corps headquarters with the order instructing
Wadsworth to report to Hancock.

Riding southward, Schaff narrowly escaped capture by Confederate skirmishers in the woods about a mile southwest of
the Lacy house. Bearing sharply east he ran into swarms of
stragglers. Enquiry disclosed that they belonged to Cutler's
brigade and that Wadsworth's division had been driven back
with heavy loss. Thereupon the lieutenant wrote a brief dispatch, reporting the position of the enemy skirmish line. His
message was time-dated 8:30 a.m.[27]

Assuming that Cope's communication of 7:40 accurately
described an action in which Wadsworth was contesting every
inch of ground, the collapse must have occurred sometime
between 7:40 and 8:30 a.m., when Schaff met the swarm of
stragglers. It is not to be supposed that they were loitering in
the woods.

Continuing toward Wadsworth's front, Schaff soon fell in
with Cutler himself, leading back the remnants of his command. Schaff estimates the number at "seven or eight hundred,
or possibly twice that number, for they were scattered all
through the woods." He gives the following picture of the
unfortunate brigadier.

> He was rather an oldish, thin, earnest-looking, round-head
> sort of man, his stubby beard and hair turning gray. He was
> bleeding from a wound across his upper lip and looked
> ghastly and I have no doubt felt worse; for he was a gallant
> man . . . On my asking him where Wadsworth was, he said,
> I think he is dead," and one of his officers said, "Yes, we
> saw him fall." [28]

Schaff turned back to report at army headquarters. No credence, he relates, was given his report of Wadsworth's repulse. Not until General Cutler reported in person would army headquarters accept the bitter truth.

By 8:40 a.m., just ten minutes after Schaff's meeting with the stragglers, II Corps headquarters was aware of the disaster. Lieutenant Colonel Lyman wired Meade that "General Wadsworth has now only 2,000 fit for duty," and that Stevenson's division, IX Corps, which had been released at Hancock's request from general reserve, was moving out on the Plank Road toward the battle front. Lyman added: "Hancock has ordered an attack to be pressed at once, especially on the right and center. He thinks the enemy drawing off or massing elsewhere, perhaps on his left. There is a lull." [29]

The lull mentioned by Lyman marks the culmination at 8:40 a.m. of the first phase of Longstreet's counter-offensive action against Birney's assault force. Since Hancock first reported the presence of I Corps troops at 6:20 a.m., this phase had endured through a period of two hours and twenty minutes.

As Hancock suspected, Longstreet was massing for another movement. While the II Corps commander erred in his expectation that Longstreet would attack from his left rather than his right, he considered preparations for both contingencies. Meanwhile, he determined to anticipate the enemy's plans by reviving his frontal assault along the Plank Road ridge.

CHAPTER 21

HANCOCK TRIES TO REVIVE HIS ATTACK

The release of Stevenson's 1st Division, IX Corps, from general reserve to reinforce Hancock marks a turning point in the Battle of the Wilderness. This reorientation of effort coincides with the beginning of the second phase, on May 6, of the contest for domination of the Plank Road ridge. In relinquishing control of his only reserve division, the Supreme Commander recognized that the mission originally assigned Burnside's independent mass of maneuver had been relegated to a position of secondary importance to the one which Hancock's command would presently undertake on the Plank Road.

To recapitulate briefly, Birney had scattered the divisions of Heth and Wilcox between 5 and 6:20 a.m., only to recoil before the onset of fresh formations from Longstreet's I Corps. Reorganized and reinforced under Hancock's direction, Birney's column endeavored to complete the mission initiated at dawn. Longstreet, distrustful of winning a decision by frontal attack, fought furiously to maintain his front while he assembled a striking force of three brigades to be thrown across Birney's left rear.

Hancock Commands the Left Wing

The process by which Hancock's command authority was extended from the four divisions of his II Corps to the left wing of Grant's army group reflects those trends that gradually altered the course originally prescribed for development of the offensive program. During preparation for the grand assault, Meade assigned Getty's 2d Division, VI Corps (less Neill's brigade), to Hancock. At dawn on the 6th Hancock's command consisted of Birney's assault column and Gibbon's provisional

357

corps, holding the left of the reserve line on the Brock Road. Events on the Plank Road between 5 and 7 a.m. hastened the process of consolidating the command structure of all formations committed to this operation.

At 7 a.m. Meade notified Hancock that Stevenson's division would, if needed, be ordered to his support. The offer was hedged with reservations, Hancock being cautioned to "call for it . . . only in the last necessity."[1] Then an hour later Hancock received notice from army headquarters that Wadsworth had been instructed to report to him. When Hancock at 8:40 a.m. ordered the attack on the Plank Road to be resumed, he exercised direct command over 6 of the 11 divisions of the Army of the Potomac. With the reinforcement brought at this time by Stevenson, the left wing commander had 7 divisions, just half the number comprising Grant's army group.

This notable extension of Hancock's command prerogative, together with the release of Stevenson for service on the Plank Road, reveals the nature of the change that had taken place in Grant's original plan. Instead of a combination of movements over the Chewning plateau and down the Plank Road, culminating in irresistible pressure on the front and left rear of Lee's right wing, victory was to be sought by a power drive against the front, with Burnside lending limited support on the right of the main attack force under Birney. In other words, the extravagant expectations that General Burnside, commanding Grant's strategic mass of maneuver, and reinforced at a propitious moment by Stevenson's reserve division, would clinch the victory had now dwindled to a hope that the IX Corps commander might reappear on the stage in a subordinate tactical role—something like the one successfully supported by Wadsworth between 5 and 6 p.m.

Upon reporting at left wing headquarters, General Stevenson received instructions to throw Carruth's brigade forward on the Plank Road. Leasure's brigade went into corps reserve, replacing Webb (Gibbon's division)* who had moved out at about 7 a.m. to report to Birney.[2]

As Webb pushed forward on the north side of the Plank Road toward the battlefront, stragglers from Baxter's brigade, one of the four scattered during Wadsworth's overthrow, were drifting back toward left wing headquarters. Colonel Richard Coulter, commanding the unit, rode up with a few of his officers and, assisted by members of Hancock's staff, succeeded in rallying an aggregation of some 600 fugitives. Like McGowan's men, they needed only a place to stand. After refitting and receiving a supply of ammunition, the brigade was sent to Gibbon's sector, where false rumors and exaggerated apprehensions were creating a situation that virtually paralyzed Hancock's strenuous efforts to revive the frontal attack against Longstreet.[3]

In order to understand the paralysis that accompanied the augmentation of Hancock's striking power, it is necessary to review briefly the reaction at army and left wing headquarters to the reports of Longstreet's appearance on the battlefield and the impact of his first counteroffensive blows. In reality, the story of this phase of the battle amounts to scarcely more than a series of explanations as to why the sustained advance that characterized the first phase could not be repeated.

The intervention of troops from Longstreet's Corps did not come as a surprise to either Meade or Hancock. Grant's battle plan had invisaged three possibilities in the direction of Longstreet's approach—one towards the Federal left by the Catharpin and Brock Roads; another over the Chewning plateau; the third on the Plank Road. Burnside's course of action had been prescribed for each one of these three eventualities. The clever trip-wire operation that stalled him at the east edge of Jones' field, and kept his force of maneuver immobile during every

---

* The distinction between the brigades of Gibbon's 2nd Division, II Corps, and the elements comprising his provisional corps should be kept in mind. After Owens went forward, the provisional corps consisted of Barlow's four-brigade division. It was later reinforced by the brigades of Leasure, IX Corps, and Eustis, VI Corps.

critical stage of the swinging battle on the Plank Road, explains the concern at army and left wing headquarters. If Meade and Hancock were not surprised, they suffered grave discomforture.

Hancock reported through Colonel Lyman at 5:40 a.m. that Birney was "driving the enemy handsomely" and had joined with Wadsworth. Lyman added that there was no indication of Longstreet, but that "Hancock has a rifle-pit on the left to be ready for him, and scouts out." [4]

Forty minutes elapsed while Hancock waited eagerly for news from the front and, at the same time, listened anxiously for the sound of gunfire heralding Burnside's belated attack on the right. Then Lyman reported at 6:20 that Birney's left had encountered troops of Longstreet's Corps on the south side of the Plank Road. Ten minutes later ominous tidings went to Meade: "General Hancock request that Burnside go in as soon as possible. As General Birney reports, we about hold our own against Longstreet and many regiments are tired and shattered." [5]

Meade's reply came at 7 o'clock. Without reference to the plea for immediate relief by action on Burnside's part, Meade informed Hancock that he might, in case of last necessity, call for Stevenson's division. [6]

Replying immediately, the left wing commander did not plead a case of last necessity. He observed, however, that if he had more force he could use it, but that he did not know whether he could get it in time or not. His reluctance to call for Stevenson's division may be attributed to the fact that he was contemplating the employment of a larger force than the one conditionally promised by Meade and which could be thrown against Longstreet in less time than would be taken by Stevenson to get into action. [7]

Gibbon and Burnside Play Safe

After holding off Longstreet for nearly an hour, Hancock had sent Major W. G. Mitchell, *aide de camp,* to General Gibbon with an order to move Barlow's division against the enemy's right, and fight up toward the Plank Road. Major Mitchell delivered the message at 7:05 a.m., midway in the ten-minute interval between receipt of Meade's qualified offer of reinforcements and Hancock's reply that he could use more troops if they arrived in time.[8]

The caution that prompted General Gibbon in giving only a tardy and incomplete compliance with Hancock's direction invited the disaster that usually attends a policy of timidity, when one of bold aggression promises the only safe and profitable course of action. The enemy's dispositions were by no means clear to Hancock or, for that matter, to army headquarters. Meade, it will be recalled, had warned Hancock an hour before dawn that, according to report, Longstreet's I Corps, with the divisions of Kershaw, Field, and Pickett present, was on the Catharpin Road. R. H. Anderson's Division was approaching the battlefield from Verdiersville. Two of these four divisions had been identified by 6:20 a.m.

At 7:05, when Hancock ordered Gibbon to attack Longstreet's right on the Plank Road, army headquarters was obsessed by fears that the two unidentified divisions might swing in from the Catharpin Road on the Federal left. Directly responsible for this flank, Gibbon shared these fears. Yet Hancock's fighter instinct bade him take the chance. He had no faith in Burnside. As every general officer of both armies knew only too well, the possibilities of frontal attack in the Wilderness were extremely limited. Gibbon must clinch the victory that had eluded the feeble grasp of Burnside, the general with "A genius for slowness."

Timely intelligence concerning the enemy's dispositions and intentions offered the only rational solution to the problem of securing the Federal left. Thrown forward at dawn in sufficient strength to overcome Stuart's cavalry, Federal columns of horse riding out from Todd's Tavern and down the cutoff route from the Brock Road through Trigg's farm to the Catharpin Road could have secured this vital information. Adequately informed, army and left wing headquarters might have directed operations on the Plank Road with the knowledge that Pickett's Division was nowhere in the area of the battlefield and that Anderson's Division had followed Longstreet's column into action.

Only after two brigades of Sheridan's cavalry moved in consequence of an order issued at 8 a.m.—three hours after the dawn—to worry the flank of a phantom division supposed to be on the Brock Road, did Hancock have the information that established beyond doubt the validity of his order to send Gibbon forward at 7:05.[9] At the same time, it must be admitted that Hancock tolerated Gibbon's inaction instead of removing him from command and entrusting the maneuver to Brigadier General Francis C. Barlow, a fiery young chief of division who, though trained in the profession of law, shared Hancock's fighter instinct.

On his part, Gibbon never gave a satisfactory explanation of his hesitant conduct. He ignored repeated communications from left wing headquarters urging immediate action. He eventually sent Frank's 3d Brigade, Barlow's division, to feel toward the enemy's front. Frank was stumbling through the woods somewhere on Birney's left as Webb advanced on the right.[10]

The prospects of a second assault were none too hopeful. The first, owing largely to difficulties of the terrain and only incidentally to enemy resistance, had reached the verge of collapse when Longstreet's fresh formation struck their counterblows. Gibbon had refused, or had been unable for reasons never disclosed, to move into position and launch the same sort of flank attack that Longstreet delivered with devastating effect later in the forenoon. Burnside's action on the right was still a deferred hope.

General headquarters cannot be entirely dissociated from the apathy and incompetence that characterized Burnside's conduct throughout the day. At 8 a.m Hancock was assured that "two of Burnside's divisions have advanced nearly to Parker's Store and are ordered to attack to their left which will be your front. They ought to be engaged now, and will relieve you." [11]

This comforting news came forty minutes before issuance of the order for the renewal of Birney's attack. If true, it would greatly enhance the possibilities of the impending advance and go far toward absolving Burnside of blame for his failure to support Birney during the first phase of his drive. Yet the assurance sent through Meade was as far from reality as the advice given Warren the afternoon before that Hancock was up at the Plank Road and would attack immediately when, as a matter of fact, only the II Corps headquarters party had reached the designated point. Burnside's position on the east edge of Jones' field was approximately one-third of the distance between general headquarters and Parker's Store.

The term "nearly" may have been employed to indicate any point in the remaining two-thirds of the distance. If so, the loose manner of expression in this instance would seriously reflect on the competence of any staff from which such a message emanated. Hancock waited in vain for the attack which Grant and Meade momentarily expected.

An hour later Hancock received another optimistic message. Lieutenant Colonel Comstock, of Grant's staff, had, he learned, gone out to General Burnside "to point out to him where to attack the enemy on or near the Plank Road." The left wing commander, who was straining every effort to energize his own attack, also learned that army headquarters expected him to strike "at the same time with Burnside." [12]

Birney Moves on Longstreet

Even before issuance of the order for renewal of the frontal attack, Hancock had taken steps to rectify the disorder in Birney's column. As already stated, he sent Webb's brigade to join Getty's division, which had suffered severely while holding the interval between Wadsworth and the two brigades of Birney's 3d Division. Carruth's brigade moved forward under the personal direction of General Stevenson to reinforce Wadsworth's decimated command. Under authority of left wing headquarters, Wadsworth assumed command of all troops on the north side of the Plank Road. Getty's three brigades reformed along a line of abandoned earthworks—possibly those thrown up by Hill's troops just before dawn.[13]

The ultimate effects of Hancock's efforts to restore his offensive power amounted to the addition of three fresh brigades to the front line of Birney's assault column. These—Webb, Carruth, and Frank—were roughly equivalent to Grant, Eustis, and Wheaton, of Getty's division, which, according to the plan of attack, were to be placed in reserve.

While Hancock was compelled to strike without the aid of supporting movements on either flank, the internal organization of his assault column was far from satisfactory when the storm burst. As Webb's brigade went forward, the brigadier was instructed to connect with Getty's troops in position. It was evidently intended to form the three brigades of Gibbon's division—Owen, Carroll, and Webb—from left to right in the order mentioned across the interval held by Getty, while Carruth's IX Corps brigade reinforced Wadsworth on the right of the column, and Mott's division, which had not been as heavily engaged as Wadsworth, continued to hold the extreme left. Owens and Carroll (Gibbon's division), after inclining to the left front during the original advance and, passing the left of the Vermont Brigade, relieved the two brigades, Hays and Ward, of Birney's division. The greater part of these latter units seem to have remained in close support, detaching regiments to the right and left of the battle front as required.[14] No doubt it was Birney's intention to place the divisions, Mott-Gibbon-Wadsworth, in the advance from left to right, with Carruth replacing Wadsworth's losses and Frank, of Barlow's division, reinforcing Mott's left flank. After refitting and receiving a fresh supply of ammunition, Getty would form the main reserve of Birney's column.

Execution of the plan was both hazardous and difficult. Any regroupment of formations in the Wilderness became a dubious undertaking. Attempted in the presence of Longstreet's troops its chances of success were unpredictable.

No one seems to know just what happened. The confusion into which the right of the column was immediately plunged suggests that Longstreet struck first. Such at least, is to be inferred from the report of General Webb, who never succeeded in forming his brigade as originally ordered, and whose report is the only first-hand evidence concerning this phase of the battle. Webb relates that

> I received orders to . . . report to General Birney, which was promptly done. General Birney ordered my command to deploy on the right of the Plank Road, and move forward to join Brigadier General Getty, of the Sixth Corps. I deployed and advanced as ordered. I of course failed to find the line of General Getty, since I do not know that any of our troops ever had been where I was ordered. We met the enemy in force across the Plank Road and engaged him. This fight opened without the employment of a line of skirmishers on my part, since I had been distinctly ordered to relieve Brigadier-General Getty with my brigade by Major-General Birney in person. From this moment to the time when my line was destroyed by the forcing in of the troops on my left, I was totally unaware of any special object in disposing of my command, and I am still at a loss to determine whether or not it was my duty to attack and attempt to drive the enemy on the Plank Road or to hold my position in connection with a line taken up by the rest of the army. I tried to drive the enemy and failed to do so, and I believe because I struck him at a time when I had no reason to suppose that I would meet any but General Getty's command. The enemy, finding that my line was but a few hundred yards in length and entirely without support, forced me to change front to rear at a double-quick.[15]

The only possible explanation of this extraordinary adventure is that General Webb, expecting to find Getty's line much farther to the front, passed while advancing in column between Grant's right and Wheaton's left. Wadsworth was somewhere on the right front of Getty's position, reorganizing the remnants of his division. Carruth was pushing out from the Brock Crossing to reinforce Wadsworth.

Caught in an isolated position, Webb could only change front to rear and fight his way back. Fortunately Carruth came to his rescue. The time of this event, according to Lieutenant Colonel Lyman, was 9:30 a.m. Webb promptly changed front forward on the left and formed a new line which included his own regiments and those of Carruth. "No regiment in the line," states Webb, "had on its flanks regiments of its own corps." While preparing to advance, he discovered that General Stevenson was his senior in rank. Wadsworth promptly resolved the difficulty by incorporating the two intermixed brigades into his command and ordering them forward. But the prospects of victory, according to Webb, had vanished. His men had lost their dash. He adds: "They had no feeling of confidence and had had time to discover that the enemy's line was overlapping my right. The change of front had taken from them all confidence in the line now assumed."[16]

If uncertainty and confusion on the front line tended to destroy confidence of the troops in their officers, a series of distracting events at the left of the reserve line so imposed on Hancock's will as to impair his ability to distinguish between fact and fancy. Just 45 minutes before Carruth went to Webb's rescue, information came, as already related, from army headquarters that Sheridan had received instructions at 8 a.m. to make an attack with a division of cavalry on Longstreet's flank. This, no doubt, was reassuring. But measures taken for the security of the left gave no additional force to the frontal attack.

The objective of the cavalry movement was not Longstreet's line on the Plank Road; it was an unidentified division supposed to be approaching by way of the Catharpin Road, or on the cut-off route through Trigg's farm to the Brock Road. Yet this was the last word of encouragement to be received by the left wing commander for many anxious hours.

Fearful Phantoms and Fighting Skirmishers

At 9:10 a.m., while expectations still ran high in anticipation of favorable news from Birney, Major Mitchell rode into Hancock's headquarters with the alarming news that a Confederate force was advancing on the Brock Road.[17] As if to verify the report, a brisk crackle of musketry, with a deeper note of artillery, came from the direction of Trigg's farm. Then heavy rifle fire was heard down the Brock Road in the vicinity of Todd's Tavern, indicating that Sheridan was hotly engaged with Longstreet's infantry.

Hancock immediately sent the aide to Birney for reinforcements. Birney detached Eustis' brigade with orders to report to Gibbon. Meantime Brooke's brigade and a section of Arnold's Rhode Island Battery were shifted from Barlow's divisional line to reinforce Miles' brigade, at the extreme left in a return trench line which, making a right angle with the Brock Road, faced south.[18]

Upon going into position, Brooke threw up "slight breastworks and placed the artillery to cover the road." Eustis was held in support. At 9:40 Leasure's brigade, Stevenson's division, reported to Gibbon. These dispositions withdrew one brigade from Birney's assault column and diverted another that would otherwise have been available for the attack. Brooke, after preparing his position and sending a reconnaissance out on the Brock Road, dispelled the illusion that had caused the costly distraction. Finding no enemy, he reported to General Barlow and at 10 o'clock received instructions to return to his former position, leaving Miles' troops to hold the refused sector.[19]

According to Hancock's subsequent explanation, "the infantry reported as moving on the Brock Road proved afterward to be a body of several hundred convalescents who had marched from Chancellorsville and were now following the route of the Second Corps around by Todd's Tavern." [20] No doubt the morale of these weary convalescents must have been greatly improved by witnessing the consternation inspired by their presence.

Then another illusion vanished. Two brigades of Sheridan's cavalry under Custer were hotly engaged, not with a division of hostile infantry down by Todd's Tavern, but with Rosser's brigade, reinforced by a body of Confederate horse, who rode down on Custer's command in an open field opposite the Furnace-Brock Road intersection.

The alarming tumult at Trigg's was intended by enterprising Confederate cavalrymen as an annoyance to Federal troops who, by the nature of their disposition, were jumpy about their flank. A dismounted force of cavalry supported by a noisy horse battery skirmished toward the Federal works. Timed with the march of the II Corps convalescents on the Brock Road, and the rapid fire of Custer's cavalry carbines down toward Todd's Tavern, the harmless tumult at Trigg's, either by accident or design, had something of the effect that would have attended the smashing of a division in the line.

The pressure on Hancock's iron nerve was not restricted to the alarm of phantom columns rushing in on his left. His right, the very quarter from which Burnside's mass of maneuver was expected to break and roll like a thunderstorm across his front, now became a horizon to which he must look with apprehension.

At 9:30, while Wadsworth was reorganizing his front with the reinforcements brought by Webb and Stevenson, Hancock received word from Meade that Cutler, arriving with the remnants of his brigade at army headquarters, had reported the presence of "enemy's skirmishers within three-eighths of a mile of the crest to the right and front of General Warren's headquarters." The harassed left wing commander also learned that he was expected to "make immediate dispositions to check this movement of the enemy across and through General Warren's left." [21]

Whatever may have been Hancock's reflections in regard repeated promises of a relieving attack on his own right front he promptly made arrangements to meet the demands of army headquarters. Major Mitchell rode off with an order instructing Birney to send troops to his right to correct this matter and to fill up the gap left by Cutler's retirement. According to Mitchell who delivered the dispatch at 9:40 a.m., "General Birney at once sent two brigades for that purpose and said

that he would send more if required." [22] At the same time
Lyman pictured to Meade in one of his vividly phrased mes-
sages the multitude of aggravations that tossed the distracted
Hancock first one way then another. The volunteer aide wrote:

> Second Brigade (Leasure) of Stevenson's division, has gone
> to strengthen Gibbon's left. General Birney will detach from
> his right to drive back the enemy at the gap left by the brigade
> of Cutler. Artillery, if heard on our left, will be from Gibbon,
> whose skirmishers are now being pressed back.[23]

There is no information concerning the brigades designated
by Birney to fill the interval toward Warren's left. Major
Mitchell is authority for the statement that Birney at 10:25
reported through a staff officer to Hancock that he "had connected with Warren's left, thus filling gap made by Cutler's
falling back." [24]

The distraction of fighting phantoms on the left and aggravations incident to detaching forces on the right to appease fears excited at army headquarters by the appearance
of Confederate skirmishers near Warren's command post had
scarcely been allayed when Hancock was aroused by intima-
tions that Burnside intended to offer the support of aggressive
action on the right. In an undated dispatch the IX Corps commander stated that it was his desire to cooperate with an advance which, he understood, would be made by General
Owens. He added: "Please let me know what your intentions
are, that I may keep up the communication." [25] There is no
record of a reply from left wing headquarters.

A subsequent communication from army headquarters sheds
some light on the proposition broached by Burnside. At 10:10
a.m. Hancock received a note from army headquarters dispatched 20 minutes earlier. Upon reading the implication that
Meade was worried lest he delay his attack until Burnside
moved in to engage, Hancock's cup of bitterness overflowed.
He read the following:

> Your dispatch of 9:25 (not found) is received. The recall-
> ing of the dispatch to you was not intended to stop your
> simultaneous attack with Burnside, but to prevent your delay-
> ing your attack for Burnside. Your dispatch saying that you

were about attacking was received just after that about attacking simultaneously with Burnside was sent to you.[26]

Hancock and Longstreet Fight It Out

Whatever may have been the impulse to give vent to his feelings, and under sufficient provocation General Hancock could rise to astonishing heights of eloquence, he replied with expressions which were both restrained and hopeful.

> The enemy hold a line of earthworks on the Orange Road in my front. The skirmishers are pushing the enemy's thin line rapidly before it. The line they abandoned was a finished one, 300 yards behind the rough one from which we drove them yesterday.[27]

In describing this isolated incident in a ding-dong battle, Hancock may have construed the rapid withdrawal from Birney's front as an indication that Longstreet had reached the limit of his endurance and that his line was about to crumble. Yet the retrograde movement was characteristic of the fighting that had swayed back and forth since 8:40 a.m. and without decided advantage to either contestant.

The objectives of both sides are pertinent to the issue. In contrast to Hancock's purpose of seeking victory by the violence of a frontal attack, Longstreet looked elsewhere for his decision. He was not reduced to the extremity of holding off half of Grant's army group with four brigades, the most liberal estimate of the force at his disposal while maintaining his front. At the same time, he had to assemble the column which was to be thrown against Birney's left rear. Thus the odds against Longstreet in the front-to-front contest were approximately two to one. The question therefore arises: how did he manage to hold his own against this numerical superiority?

There is no ready answer. A tradition of victory and the superior troop leadership so often evinced by the Army of Northern Virginia in its combats with the Army of the Potomac offers only a partial explanation. The complete answer is to be found in the display of tactical genius by Longstreet, which more than redressed his disparity in numerical strength.

Unfortunately the evidence, while pointing to a plausible

theory, does not sustain the case before the court of history. Longstreet is our principal witness. His evidence is submitted 39 years after the event in his *Memoirs*. At the same time he offers the only possible explanation of what really happened. What was the nature of his tactical performance?

In throwing forward the divisions of Kershaw and Field, Longstreet realized, as did Grant in seeking to avoid battle in the Wilderness, that "full lines of battle could not be handled through the thick woods." He therefore ordered "the advance of the six brigades (of Kershaw and Field) in heavy skirmish lines, to be followed by stronger supporting lines."

Longstreet's description of the deployment is not as explicit as it might be. He does not state positively that these six units advanced entirely in skirmish order. Nor does he describe the composition of his strong supporting lines. Obviously the heavy skirmish line and the supporting lines could not have been furnished by the six brigades. Two—Gregg and Benning—were soon out of action.

Furthermore, the wide extent of deployment would argue that Longstreet's skirmish formation must have included a much larger proportion of the strength of its supporting units than was ordinarily prescribed in tactical manuals of the day. It therefore follows that he drew on seven available brigades for the units sent in support to the skirmish formation. These were G. T. Anderson's and Jenkins' Brigades, Field's division, and Wofford's Brigade of Kershaw's Division, together with the four of R. H. Anderson's Division.

We know that three of these seven units—G. T. Anderson, Wofford, and Mahone's Brigade of R. H. Anderson's Division —were selected for the turning movement. Owing to reasons that no one seems able to explain, Stone, commanding Davis' Mississippi Brigade, either managed to get his name on the preferred list or simply "crashed the party." These arrangements left four brigades for the support lines. It is known that Jenkins relieved Bryan on the left of Kershaw's sector and later returned to the Plank Road, where he stood in readiness

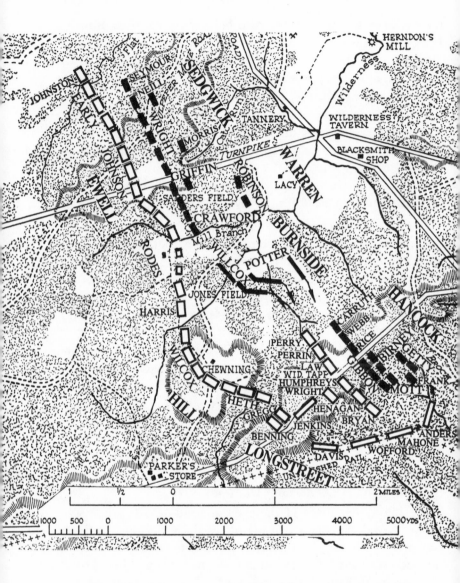

MAP 21. LONGSTREET STARTS AROUND THE FEDERAL
SOUTH FLANK

The stalemate on the north flank continues. Burnside, ordered to move by the left flank and attack Longstreet, has begun this movement. Longstreet, after assembling and enveloping force, is moving the brigades in column against Hancock's left and rear.

The remnants of Wadsworth's force, including the heavy artillery brigade under Kitching, have been withdrawn in reserve near the Lacy house, but have been omitted from this map.

to attack down the road as the flanking column swept across Birney's rear.

Finally, Longstreet's extended line of skirmishers was not restricted to the customary function of feeling out the enemy and then falling back on the main line of battle. Here is the crux of the whole question: it had a combat mission. The rolling fire of loosely formed skirmishers answered the intermittent volleys flashing from carefully dressed Federal lines of battle.

Compelled to fight under conditions that forbade any close control over full lines of battle, Longstreet adopted a tactical formation suitable to the situation. Briefly, he improvised an unconventional method of deployment—one approximating if not actually duplicating the extended order formation that some years later was designed to insure control of troops advancing in the face of intense fire delivered by breechloading rifles and cannon. Indeed, the transition was even then overdue, as the newer rifled musket gave increased rapidity of fire with greater range and accuracy.*

The Army of the Potomac was slower to perceive these trends. A gallant officer and widely esteemed as a tactician of superior ability, General Birney held rigidly to the classic order of battle. He paused repeatedly while regimental lines dressed on their colors in order to lend maximum effect to his crashing volleys, only to be thrown again into disarray as soon as he attempted to exploit a temporary advantage over Longstreet's elusive skirmishers.

Whether or not Longstreet tunes his account to the results he actually achieved, his brief narrative of the event vividly characterizes a clash between two tactical systems, one passing into obsolescence, the other looking to the future. He says:

---

* It cannot be claimed that Longstreet was alone in anticipating the extended order system. The western armies were given to unconventional practices in the use of skirmish lines. Sherman frequently employed the expedient by advancing half the strength of a regiment and holding the rest in support. The practice of strengthening the conventional skirmish line and giving it a combat mission really marks the transition from the double rank line of battle to the extended order formation. Cf. Wagner, Arthur, Col., U.S.A., *Organization and Tactics* (B. Westermann & Co., London and New York, 1895).

Hancock's lines, thinned by their push through the woods, and somewhat by the fire of the disordered divisions, weaker than my line of fresh and more lively skirmishers, were checked by our first rolling fire, and after a brisk fusilade were pushed back to their entrenched line, when the fight became steady and firm, occasionally swinging parts of my line back and compelling the reserves to move forward and recover it.[28]

Sometime after 10 o'clock Longstreet's rolling musketry died away. As though by mutual consent the volley firing of Birney's battle lines gradually ceased. An ominous quiet settled over the battlefield.[29]

On the right the holding attacks of Warren and Sedgwick, after failing to pin Ewell to his front, had expended their energy. At 9:30 a.m., just as Lyman reported that Colonel William F. Bartlett, commanding the 57th Massachusetts Infantry, Carruth's brigade, was putting his regiment in the line finally established by Webb, Meade instructed Warren to "suspend your operation on the right and send some force to prevent the enemy from pushing past your left, near your headquarters." Directing Hancock 15 minutes later to extend his right toward Warren's exposed flank, Meade stated in a postscript: "We have no troops to spare here." [30]

Admitting an attitude of caution bordering on timidity at army headquarters, it still seems unreasonable to conclude that Meade was unnerved by the appearance of a handful of venturesome skirmishers within sight of Warren's headquarters at the Lacy house. Meade was made of sterner stuff.

A complete file of the dispatches issued by army headquarters during this critical phase of the Wilderness battle, instead of the fragmentary collection published in the *Official Records,* would more fully disclose the considerations that really governed Meade's conduct. He now faced another one of those bewildering situations that had been contrived by Lee's astute generalship and that tended to renew the caution long shared by the high command of the Army of the Potomac and most eloquently expressed in the phrase "You don't know Bobby Lee."

Perhaps the detailed examination of Longstreet's counterattack had diverted attention from Lee's role as the presiding genius of the battlefield.

While adhering to his practice of delegating complete liberty of action to his corps commanders in making tactical dispositions they deemed most expedient, Lee reserved the power of decision in coordinating the total effort. He approved Longstreet's plan of containing Birney while assembling the flanking force. He ordered Hill to throw his reformed brigades across the Chewning plateau to fill the gap between Longstreet and Ewell. Rescued from disaster, Hill stood across the path that Burnside should have taken to victory. Whatever the nervousness Meade seems to have betrayed over far-ranging Confederate skirmishers, he fully appreciated the significance of a hostile artillery mass on the Chewning plateau.

An hour after directing Warren to suspend the holding attack, he amended the order. At 10:35 a.m. the army chief of staff notified Warren that

> The Major-General commanding directs that under existing circumstances your attack and that of General Sedgwick be suspended. You will at once throw up defensive works to enable you to hold your position with the fewest possible number of men, and report at once what number of men you will have disposable for an attack upon Hancock's right. General Sedgwick has the same instructions. You will confer with him respecting the line you are both to hold.[31]

The orders dispatched at 10:35 signify the breakdown of Grant's offensive program. His right was entrenching. His mass of maneuver, with a greatly restricted mission, was wandering in search of its target. Hancock's left wing had all but expended its offensive power. Sheridan was still at grips, according to report, with an infantry column of the I Confederate Corps at the extreme left of the line.

Yet Grant's decision to reinforce his left from the right did not constitute a conscious surrender of the initiative, no more so than did the reinforcement of Hancock by Wadsworth's four brigades the afternoon before. But in point of fact, his adversary seized the initiative before this second group of reinforcements could be assembled and shifted to the left. Lee was destined to exercise the initiative from noon to nightfall with no greater advantage than Grant had been able to secure between 10:30 a.m. on the 5th and the collapse of Birney's assault column just before noon on the following day.

Before considering the development of Lee's offensive, it becomes necessary to narrate the brief and partial participation of Sheridan's cavalry during the declining phase of the Federal offensive.

CHAPTER 22

SHERIDAN TAKES A HAND

It has been remarked in the foregoing that the most persistently misunderstood features of the Wilderness Campaign are the operations of Sheridan's and Stuart's cavalries. And of these operations the least understood is the brief so-called offensive action undertaken by a division of the Federal horse shortly after 8 a.m. of the 6th, in accordance with orders which Sheridan had received.

Strictly speaking, there was no offensive action, so far as any elements of Sheridan's mounted corps are concerned. After having taken position to cover the Furnace-Brock Road intersection and having established communication with Gregg's 2d Cavalry Division at Todd's Tavern, Brigadier General George A. Custer, commanding the 1st Brigade, 1st Division, received orders from his divisional headquarters which were intended to implement instructions previously issued at army headquarters directing Sheridan to make an attack with a division of cavalry on Longstreet's flank and rear by the Brock Road.[1]

These orders had been delivered to Sheridan at Chancellorsville by 8 o'clock, then transmitted to 1st Cavalry Division Headquarters at Aldrich and thence to Custer. Custer received them by courier about 8:30 a.m.[2]

Custer's interpretation of the orders, stated in his official report, is suggestive. While in position at the crossroads, he reports, "An order was received from the division commander directing me to take the First and Second Brigades and move out on the Brock pike for the purpose of harassing Longstreet's corps, which was reported to be moving on Hancock's left flank." [3] The original order had instructed Sheridan to make an attack on Longstreet's flank and rear by the Brock Road.

A moment's consideration of these two statements will make it clear without any great effort of reason that Custer could not very well have waited at the road intersection until the greater part of the Confederate infantry column filed by on the Brock Road and then have attacked this same column "on . . . flank and rear by the Brock road." Clearly, the infantry marked as Custer's objective must have been elsewhere.

Army headquarters was aware by 7 a.m. that Birney's advance had encountered troops of Longstreet's corps at 6:20. But there was nothing to indicate at that time any attempt on the part of Confederate troops in Birney's front to execute a turning movement against Hancock's left. And even if this had been the case, it is hardly reasonable to suppose that two cavalry brigades would have been sent on such a mission, when four infantry brigades were available. Then, in consideration of Meade's views with reference to the limitations of cavalry, he certainly would have been the last at army headquarters to sanction the employment of two mounted brigades in an attempt to attack and harass an infantry force deployed in a deep thicket. Furthermore, the Brock Road led nowhere near the flank and rear of that force.

If the nature of the orders precluded any possibility that Meade thought of striking either at the flank or rear of a Confederate infantry column on the Brock Road between the Catharine Furnace-Brock Road intersection and Hancock's left flank, or at the right rear of Longstreet's line of battle, then opposing Birney's assault column, where then was Custer's target?

Custer's Phantom Target

The answer seems obvious enough. It could have been nowhere other than the only other road leading in to Hancock's left flank and, at the same time, accessible to attack by way of the Brock Road. Custer therefore was expected to find his objective on the road running northeast from the Catharpin, past Whitehall Mill and Trigg's farm to the Brock Road. It will be recalled that Gibbon's defensive dispositions were made in view of the possibility of Longstreet's approach by this route and that the principal mass of the II Corps Artillery was so emplaced as to command this very avenue of approach. It will be borne in mind that Hancock when first instructed to prepare his attack for 4:30 a.m., was cautioned to keep a "sharp lookout" on his left. Later, he received explicit intelligence that Longstreet was moving along the Catharpin Road toward his left flank.[4] It was in recognition of this explicit information, rather than the first general warning, that Hancock made the formidable defensive dispositions elsewhere described.[5] But until all of Longstreet's elements were accounted for, the obsession of a flank attack hung as a lowering cloud over army headquarters. Humphreys, in his *Virginia Campaign*, explains this feeling:

> It must be remembered that according to our information, Pickett's division was with Longstreet, and only Field's and Kershaw's divisions had as yet been encountered; and that Anderson's division of Hill's corps had not then been felt by our troops, nor its presence known to them. These two divisions, with perhaps some of the brigades of the other divisions of Longstreet, might well be the force which, later, about 9 o'clock, threatened Hancock's left flank at Trigg's, though in point of fact, it turned out to be Confederate cavalry dismounted, with some artillery.[6]

When Custer received his directions to move out and harass Longstreet's column, his command, excepting a thin picket line of two companies and a small reserve, was concealed in the deep woods on the east side of the Brock Road.

His four Michigan regiments were formed, left to right, in the line 7th-5th-1st-6th, the troopers standing to horse. The band took post on the left rear of the 1st Michigan.[7]

Thrown out into the clearing, which extended some 600 or 700 yards along the west side of the Brock Road, with the sweep of the forest enclosing a field about 350 yards wide, Custer's pickets, under Captain Maxwell, were formed on an extended line, well up toward the trees. The supports took

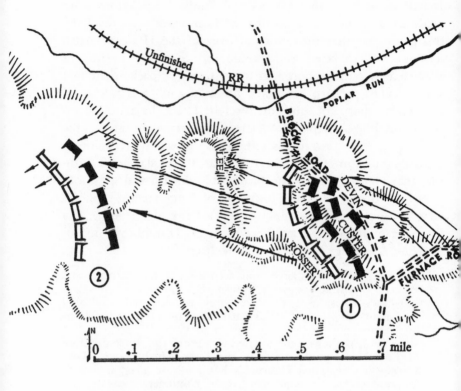

MAP 22. CUSTER'S FIGHT ON THE BROCK ROAD

Alerted at 8 a.m., May 6, to move out from his position at the intersection of the Furnace and Brock Roads, and to attack a column of
Confederate infantry supposed to be approaching from the left, Custer
faces a headlong onset from Rosser's Virginia cavalry.

1. Situation at about 9 a.m. After an indecisive mounted action,
Custer deploys his four Michigan regiments, dismounted, in a ravine
cutting diagonally across the open ground west of the Brock Road.
Reinforced by two of Fitz Lee's regiments, Rosser threatens Custer's
right. Custer in turn is reinforced by Devin's four regiments which
were on the Furnace Road.

2. Situation at about 9:45 a.m. Using his own brigade and part of
Devin's, and supported by 8 cannon in position on the high ground
to his rear, Custer attacks, turns Rosser's left, and drives him from
the field.

station in the rear toward the road. A deep ravine cut diagonally across the center of the field and ended at the high ground south of the road intersection.

Upon reading his instructions, Custer cantered out toward the picket line to confer with Captain Maxwell regarding the movement. The sharp crackle of rifle fire ran along the line of pickets; a rumble of galloping horses answered the loud fusilade. Riding furiously out of the forest came a large body of Confederate horse—the 35th Virginia Cavalry, Rosser's Brigade, and better known as "White's Comanches."

Realizing in a flash that only his pickets and their supports were visible to the enemy, Custer raced back to bring his main force into action.

An Enemy in the Flesh

At the first sound of fire, the main line regiments, troopers mounted and horses snorting and pawing in the excitement of movement after a tedious stand-to, pushed up to the near edge of the clearing along the road. Custer, swerving in a wide circle as he galloped down on the front of the 1st Michigan, ordered the band to strike up and, flashing his saber toward the advancing mass of Confederates, shouted his command: "Forward by divisions!" A trooper of the 1st describes the charge:

> As the band struck up the inspiring strains of "Yankee Doodle," the First Michigan broke by subdivisions from the right, the Sixth following in line, regimental front, and the two regiments charged with a yell through the thick underbrush out into the open ground just as the Confederate troopers emerged from the woods on the opposite side. Both commands kept on in full career, the First and Sixth inextricably intermingled until they reached the edge of the ravine, when stopped, the Confederates surprised by the sudden appearance and audacity of the Michigan men and their gallant leader; Custer well content with checking Rosser's vicious advance. Some of the foremost of either side kept on and crossed sabers in the middle of the ravine. Among these was Lieutenant Cortez P. Pendill, of the Sixth Michigan, who was severely wounded among the very foremost. One squadron of the Confederates, possibly a small regiment, charging in columns of fours, went past our right flank, and then,

like the French army that marched up a hill and then marched down again, turned and charged back without attempting to turn their head of column toward the place where Custer was standing at bay, with his Michiganders clustered thick about him. Pretty soon, the Confederates ran a battery into the field and opened up on us with shell. Every attempt to break Custer's line, however, ended in failure, the Spencer carbines proving too much of an obstacle to be overcome.[8]

Like so many cavalry fights of the Civil War, the harmless and indecisive clash of mounted action gave way to the less spectacular but bloodier business of fighting afoot. The fire power of Custer's magazine rifles quickly cleared the front of mounted Confederates. Dismounting, Rosser's men returned to the fray, attacking violently with the supporting fire of their horse battery, which broke out of the woods and swung into action with a roaring blast of canister.[9]

Reinforced by an element of Fitzhugh Lee's Cavalry Division, the dismounted attack was extended along the Federal right. The flank swayed, threatening to uncover Custer's communications by the Furnace Road.

Custer met the threat of envelopment by refusing his right regiment, the 6th, and sending the 5th from his center to extend the line of the 6th. The flank held precariously. The ravine, which had marred the splendor of Rosser's and Custer's mounted action now became a feature of great importance to the Federal defense. Running diagonally from left front to right rear, it furnished a ready-made work, with its face at a convenient angle for the refused flank.

While these dispositions were being completed, Custer's horse battery emerged from the tree-lined Furnace Road, its light guns bounding behind their galloping six-horse teams. Hastily instructed, the battery commander led his rumbling column to the crest of a slight elevation. Here the subsections swung forward into line, action front. The gun teams and gunners' mounts, after the manner of horse batteries in action, were formed in rear of the gun line. Each roaring gun flash caused a nervous jerk of horses' heads.

Devin Rides To The Rescue

Following the battery into action came Devin's four clattering regiments, the 4th, 6th, and 9th New York, and 17th Pennsylvania, with a section of horse artillery from Gregg's division. These two pieces joined Custer's guns on the hill, giving him an eight-gun battery. The Confederate artillery was promptly silenced, three of their guns being smashed by direct hits. The 17th Pennsylvania reinforced the right, the 6th New York went into close support to the right; the 4th was held in general reserve, while the 9th formed to cover the artillery.[10]

Devin had arrived in the nick of time. Custer's men had reached the limit of endurance. Quick to seize the momentary advantage that is usually created by the appearance of fresh troops on a swaying battlefield, Custer ordered an advance all along the line. Pivoting on the left, the 6th and 5th Michigan, with the 17th Pennsylvania on their right, pressed forward in dismounted order. Mounted, a squadron of the First Michigan led by Captain Maxwell charged to the front. Rosser and the forces that had come to his support gave way before the fierce onset and fell back into the woods, leaving their wounded strewn over the field.[11] Orders having been received not to pursue the enemy beyond this point, Custer established communications with the left of the II Corps and held his position until ordered later in the day to withdraw to the Furnace.[12]

An Abortive Offensive

In no sense of the word can Custer's action be regarded as an offensive movement. While making preliminary dispositions to move out by the Brock Road and harass Longstreet's column, his outposts had been rushed by White's "Comanches," of Rosser's Brigade. This Virginia regiment, the 35th, had crossed the Po early that morning in the advance of Rosser's Brigade. After entering the open pine country which stretched across the upper Po basin to the Brock Road ridge, White received orders "to ride over everything he came to . . . and . . . to drive them as far as he can." [13] While there is no evidence to suggest that Rosser's movement was part of a concerted scheme to penetrate Sheridan's cavalry cordon between Todd's Tavern and the left of the infantry line, and then dash up the Catharine Furnace Road toward the trains at Dowdall's Tavern, White's orders seem to have had a significant purpose. They indicate, at least, that the Federal cavalry was presumed by their opponents to be on the defensive and that a bold offensive stroke here and there might be productive of startling results. White no doubt was over-impetuous. His headlong charge at Custer's pickets necessarily involved Rosser's four Virginia regiments in a fierce and indecisive combat with the four Michigan regiments of Custer's brigade and Devin's reinforcing units.

Divided Honors

The honors appear to have been evenly divided. In the counter-charge of the 1st Michigan, Stagg's "Wolverines" smote White's "Comanches" with such fury as to visit on his Virginians the indignity of getting down and fighting it out on foot.

This action offers an intensely interesting commentary on relations between the Federal army commander and his chief of cavalry. It emphasizes the futility of trying to control, from army headquarters, the movements of a cavalry force far in the advance or out in an extended position on the flank.

Sheridan and Stuart Reach a Deadlock

Having dispersed, according to the requirements of army headquarters, his mounted formations on a wide front facing south and west to protect the trains, Sheridan was required to strip his reserve and assemble a force to move offensively against a phantom infantry column, which was thought at Meade's headquarters to be threatening the left of the army. Such procedure calls into question the competence of the officer responsible for the performance of a specific function— in this instance, Sheridan's ability to properly cover the approaches he had undertaken to watch.

It is not supposed, in this connection, that army headquarters should have refrained from transmitting to the chief of cavalry any intelligence concerning developments that had come to the army commander by means not available to his chief of cavalry. Ths question of adopting an adequate course of action to cope with any particular development should, nevertheless, be governed by local conditions on the cavalry front and give recognition to the bearing of detailed information, which is the business of the cavalry commander to discover. To specify the amount of force and the line of operations in a contingency that exists only on a basis of rumor, or resides in the fears that are induced by an obsession regarding a probable act of the enemy, denies the very purpose of effective command in the field through an intelligent delegation of responsibility.

Sheridan, to be sure, was completely out of accord with army headquarters. Against his better judgment and over his protest he had been required to limit the scope of the offensive activities he had originally wished to pursue, so as to provide properly for the protection of the trains. Now, without regard to the dispositions he had taken to fulfill this defensive function, he must provide an offensive force to meet a contingency founded on rumor. This so-called cavalry offensive was scotched by a local but violent attack of Confederate cavalry at its point of concentration on the line of defense.

Although authorized to attack if opportunity was offered, Sheridan's dispositions for defense of the trains precluded any possibility of serious offensive action. The Confederate cavalry conducted its operations in a manner that appears to have been most consistent with the situation. Deprived by disparity of numbers and firepower from any reasonable hope in successfully pursuing a large-scale offensive, the Confederate horse undertook to make the enemy's scheme of defense as costly and burdensome as possible. Rosser's lively foray held a large body of Federal cavalry—two brigades—on the Brock Road, covering the Brock-Furnace intersection and maintaining close contact with Gibbon in the infantry lines to the right and Gregg at

Todd's Tavern to the left. Hampton's brigades, meantime, continued their noisy demonstrations at Trigg's, paralyzing Gibbon into inaction and aggravating fears that pictured Longstreet's infantry on the march by every road leading to the Federal left. Fitzhugh Lee, the threat of whose force at Hamilton's Crossing had immobilized Sheridan's strongest division during the crucial hours of maneuver on the morning of the 5th, contained Gregg's division at Todd's Tavern, lending a hand to Rosser, on his left, and keeping an eye on Wilson at Piney Branch Church, to the right.

While contributing materially to the tactical program of the 6th, Fitzhugh Lee never lost sight of the primary strategic mission that fell to Lee's mounted force after the two main armies had established contact and completed their deployment. Describing in his official report of operations the position of his division "across the Spotsylvania (Brock) Road in close proximity to Todd's Tavern," Fitzhugh Lee adds: "I was so located as to retard any prolongation of Grant's left toward points on the Central Railroad." [14]

CHAPTER 23

LONGSTREET DEMOLISHES BIRNEY'S COLUMN

Neither Lee nor Longstreet was misled by the astonishing results attending the rapid series of shocks delivered by Kershaw's and Field's six attacking brigades on the head of Birney's massive formation. A veteran of forest warfare, Lee knew the limitations of frontal attack in the Wilderness region of northern Virginia. No doubt he was well aware that during the celebrated attack of May 2, 1863, on Hooker's right at Chancellorsville, Jackson's column of divisions had become so utterly disorganized in sweeping Howard's feeble and unready units from its path as to compel a halt before the Confederates had reached their final objective. Jackson, he knew, had received his fatal wound two hours later—about 9:15 p.m.—while attempting to revitalize the offensive.

The Miracle of the Wilderness

It is interesting to speculate on the results that might have been obtained by an attack of six seasoned Federal brigades sweeping headlong into Jackson's disordered lines, just as they came to the halt at 7:10 p.m. The effect would probably have been similar to that produced by Longstreet's six I Corps brigades on Birney's moving column. In fact, Birney had encountered more opposition from Hill's eight brigades on this occasion than had Jackson from the eight of Howard at Chancellorsville. For these reasons, there is nothing miraculous about the sudden arrest imposed by Longstreet upon the powerful offensive that was driving with every appearance of irresistible might against Lee's right flank astride the Plank Road during the second day of the Battle of the Wilderness. Already cracking under pressure of internal strain, this for-

midable mass must soon disintegrate into a harmless agglom-
eration of disorganized units, unless quickly relieved by the
long-expected attack of Burnside's troops from the right, or
by a movement of Gibbon's reserve—as Hancock had vainly
ordered—from the left. The real miracle of the Wilderness
was the fear and paralysis created by phantom columns of
Longstreet's Corps, rushing along every road from Richard's
Shop to the battlefront.

No one was better aware of the realities of this situation than
Longstreet himself. A tactician of consummate ability, with a
profound distrust of the doctrine of wholesale attack, or, as
more elegantly styled by its European proponents, *la offensive
a outrance,* Longstreet abhorred the practice—all too frequently
indulged during the War of American Secession—of staking
the decision of battle on brutal and violent frontal attacks,
unrelieved by a skillfully coordinated flanking maneuver.
These deep convictions brought him to the verge of mutiny
on the battlefield of Gettysburg. To him, Pickett's charge was
little short of a crime.[1] In Widow Tapp's field, however, Lee
and Longstreet were in complete and absolute agreement.
Temperamentally the bond was as close here, perhaps, as it
had ever been between Lee and Jackson. Longstreet had arrived in time to save the flank from destruction; the fate of
the battle was in his hands.

The attacks *en echelon* had been scarcely launched when
General M. L. Smith, Chief Engineer Officer, Army of Northern Virginia, reported to Longstreet for instructions. This
arrangement of course was made by the army commander;
Lee, in fact, was putting his chief engineer at the disposition
of the I Corps commander.

Plans to Hit Birney's Left

General Smith's assignment to the I Corps is subject to
many interpretations. It may be inferred that he brought from
army headquarters the suggestion for a movement by the right
and, after explaining the proposal to Longstreet, made himself available for the preliminary reconnaissance. On the other

hand it seems more logical to explain the assignment by reason of the fact that Longstreet was a stranger to the Wilderness, his corps having participated neither in the campaign of Chancellorsville nor in the Mine Run operation. Lee therefore took the very necessary precaution of providing the I Corps with a topographer who knew the region. At the same time, General Smith's rank would indicate that he was in the confidence of both Lee and Longstreet, and that the engineer officer, who is reputed to have been an able tactician himself, was in complete accord with the army and I Corps commanders as to the necessity of a movement by the right flank.[2] Whatever the degree of his responsibility in the matter, Smith set off through the woods south of the Plank Road toward the cut of an unfinished railroad, which ran in a general east and west direction, paralleling the Plank Road. Passing some distance below or south of Kershaw's right, the location line followed a flat curve to the south and then ran on a tangent which passed obliquely across the front of Gibbon's reserve position at the extreme left of Hancock's line.

Its broad right of way cleared through the forest and its bed levelled for the laying of ties and steel rails, this partially complete avenue of travel was available to either side for maneuver against the flank of the other. Just why this possibility had been overlooked by the Federals has never been explained. For 17 hours, that is from 2 p.m., May 5, when Hancock joined Getty at the Brock Crossing, until 7 a.m., May 6 when Gibbon failed to throw his entire force forward and support the left of Birney's attack, the long tangents shooting straight through the thickets at Lee's right flank seem to have had no significance to Hancock or Gibbon. Nor did they attract Barlow and the lesser officers of his division, whose units held the left of the Federal flank and looked eastward along the right of way. There is no authentic record to show that even a small party reconnoitered the route, or that it was picketed beyond the point of direct observation from Gibbon's main line of trenches. Yet Barlow was well aware of this avenue of approach, having moved twice across it during the Battle of Chancellorsville.

While Smith was away in the woods on his exploration, Longstreet's attention was engaged by a multitude of distractions. After the first shock of counterattack there was little to apprehend from Birney's mass for at least an hour or more. Once disordered, such massive columns could not be reorganized in a hurry. A heavy and aggressive skirmish formation with sufficient support to maintain a uniform pressure all along the line, would cover the Confederate front and give ample warning of a renewed offensive, whenever it came.

Hill Closes the Gap

The real danger lurked on the left flank. The interval toward Ewell was still open. Longstreet had been called over to the Plank Road on account of that same gap. The terrific punishment dealt by Birney's assault on the divisions of Heth and Wilcox had imposed another delay in establishing a Confederate line across the interval. But the broken III Corps brigades were being rapidly reorganized. The five brigades of R. H. Anderson's Division, an all-Southern contingent of reinforcements representing 21 regiments from Mississippi, Virginia, Georgia, Alabama, and Florida, closed up toward Widow Tapp's field. Anderson was assigned to Longstreet's command.[3] A. P. Hill, according to Colonel Palmer, his chief of staff, moved to the left into the interval "with the unengaged of Heth and Wilcox," meaning, no doubt, those of the reformed units that could be spared from the reserve line in rear of the artillery.[4] Upon reaching "a second large field (Chewning farm) screened from the field in which the guns (Poague's) were by a strip of woods," the menacing appearance of enemy skirmishers induced Hill to ask for a brigade of Anderson's Division.

Colonel Palmer rode back to army headquarters with the request. Addressing the plea to Lee, Palmer was referred to Longstreet. The III Corps chief of staff thus presented to the I Corps commander his request to borrow one of his own brigades. Longstreet, however, realized the peril. Just as Lee had been obliged to relinquish the wide-swinging flank movements on Grant's extreme left by reason of the open interval beyond Hill's left, so now Longstreet recognized that the restricted movement he hoped to develop against Birney's flank depended first of all upon Hill's ability to hold the interval into which he had just advanced. He replied to Palmer, asking which one he wanted. "The leading brigade," promptly answered the chief of staff.[5]

Harris' Brigade was detailed. Palmer led the detachment to Chewning's farm, where the situation was soon put to rights. Perry and Perrin, of Anderson's Division, were to reinforce Field. Mahone was put in reserve to Kershaw's line, taking position near G. T. Anderson's Brigade, Field's Division, on the right of the Plank Road.[6]

In the meantime the battle raged with unabated violence to the front. The steady roar of Longstreet's musketry mingled in ceaseless din with the intermittent crash of Birney's volleys. Fresh units relieved the first line brigades and, holding sturdily, covered the rapid reorganization taking place to the rear.

About 9 o'clock the dense Federal formation pressed forward in response to orders to renew the assault.[7]

Aside from an increased intensity of fire, it is doubtful if the Confederates were aware that their antagonists were striking in a last supreme effort to seize the victory that had eluded their grasp some three hours before. The six brigades that had snatched away the prize and had thrown the Federals back were still holding their ground. Now, with numbers no greater than Hill had had in the face of the Federal onset at dawn, these six I Corps brigades stood opposed to a second onset, more powerful in weight of numbers than the first, and equally determined to force the issue to victory. How they held during the crucial hour from 9 to 10 without drawing on the reserve that was being assembled for the flank operation is difficult to explain. Even the spectacular brilliance of their charge in echelon pales before this display of grim endurance, this astonishing power to retain the integrity of their organization up to the point of physical annihilation. Although giving ground, they stemmed the second torrent of attack and created the possibilities for an astonishing culmination of the fight so unauspiciously begun when Henagan and Gregg first went into action.

With an emotional calm and intellectual detachment amid thundering tumult that has perhaps never been surpassed on the battlefield unless by Ney, whose utter sang-froid inspired from Napoleon the sobriquet, "bravest of the brave," Longstreet matured his plans for the movement on Birney's left.

Movement of the Flanking Force

While awaiting the return of General Smith, Longstreet instructed Lieutenant Colonel G. Moxley Sorrel, his chief of staff, to assemble three brigades for the operation. Neither Longstreet nor Sorrel is clear in their accounts of the affair as to whether the units were designated by the I Corps commander, or selected by Sorrel acting on Longstreet's authority. At any rate the required units were available. The brigade of G. T. Anderson, who had originally held the advance of Field's divisional column, and had deployed to the right of the road before Gregg, Benning, and Perry were thrown to the left, was still in reserve on the right rear of the guns. Wofford, of Kershaw's Division, who had been left behind at Parker's Store as train guard, but subsequently called to the front by Kershaw, had temporarily taken position near G. T. Anderson. Mahone's Virginia Brigade, of R. H. Anderson's Division had, as already stated, been detached from the divisional column to a position on the south side of the road, near the guns and in reserve to Kershaw's battle line. Finally, the three Mississippi regiments of Davis' Brigade had fallen back after the last stubborn stand along Cooke's entrenched line, to the south side of the Plank Road. Here, Colonel Stone had reformed his Mississippians. Isolated from their division, they were ready to take a hand in any fight that was offered.

The brigades of G. T. Anderson, Wofford, and Mahone, of Field's, Kershaw's, and R. H. Anderson's Divisions, respectively, were designated for the attack force. With regard to

command of the force, Longstreet states that he directed Lieutenant-Colonel Sorrel to conduct the brigades of Generals
Mahone, G. T. Anderson, and Wofford beyond the enemy's
left and attack him on his left rear. He adds parenthetically:
"I have since heard that the brigade of General Davis formed
a part of this flanking force." [8] Mahone says in his official
report of the operation that "being the senior brigadier present, I was by Lieutenant-General Longstreet charged with the
immediate direction of this movement."[9]

Neither Mahone nor Sorrel mentions the presence of Stone's
Mississippians in the column. Having been reformed by their
gallant leader, Colonel Stone, and reluctant to play the idle
role of an orphan brigade, the belligerent Mississippians probably attached themselves to the first column they saw marching to the front. They did not rejoin their III Corps comrades
until 6 p.m., when they were withdrawn.

General Smith returned from his reconnaissance about 10
o'clock that morning and reported that the heavy woodland
concealed the route of the proposed flank march, and that
there was no force of the enemy in observation. The engineer
amplified this observation with a statement that "Hancock's
left on the Brock Road was in strong, well-guarded position,
but there was room along its front for our troops to march
near the unfinished railroad beyond view of that left on the
Brock Road." [10]

Smith's amplification unfolded new possibilities. He had
not only established the practicability of turning the left of
Birney's assault column, but had seen enough of the position
occupied by Gibbon's defensive flank to express an opinion
that the entire right wing of the Federal army might be
turned. The probable route of the turning force, as indicated
by General Smith, would, after reaching the bend of the railway, parallel the right of way. Then, swinging to the south
and east of Trigg's, it would strike the Brock Road between
Gibbon's return trenches and the intersection of the Catharine
Furnace Road.

Longstreet immediately requested General Smith to take

a small party and pass beyond the Brock Road and find a way for turning the extreme Union left on that road.[11] He then instructed Colonel Sorrel to conduct the force he had had assembled, by way of the unfinished railroad and up through the woods toward Birney's left rear.

As the flanking column pushed along the railway cut past Birney's flank and halted to form for attack the din of musketry that had thundered incessantly through the forest since dawn died away. A brief subsidence of violence, like the calm that comes with the shift of wind in a roaring typhoon, settled over the battlefield.

Rout of Birney's Assault Column

Union veterans sensed a new peril. On the Federal left, where quiet was most profound, Colonel McAllister, commanding the 1st Brigade, Mott's division, and holding the second line of battle, grew apprehensive of the calm. He reports that:

> All now became quiet, the pickets ceased firing, and my men laid down. I took an orderly with me and went through the picket-line to reconnoiter. By crawling along from tree to tree in front I discovered a ravine; parallel with it lay a number of very large trees; behind these trees and in a ravine were the enemy's pickets; a short distance in rear of the enemy's pickets was a railroad cut, and on the left across a ravine was an embankment; there was the position of the enemy. After taking a careful survey of it, I came back and sent an aide to report the fact to General Mott, commanding the division.[12]

McAllister's alarming discovery was too late to permit an effective change of front to left. While the aide was looking for General Mott, the Confederates moved from the railroad cut. Filtering through occasional rifts in the forest boughs, brilliant shafts of sunlight flashed on their bayonets and danced with fleeting shadows along the rushing rows of steel.

The column swept forward in line of brigades, Mahone holding the center, with Anderson on the right, Wofford on the left, and Stone probably in reserve. The interior formation of the brigades is not known. Frequent mention in Federal reports of "dense masses" pouring in on their left rear would indicate that each brigade was formed in considerable depth, possibly in column of regiments.[13]

Obsessed by dread of impending attack on their left, the Federals with vast elaboration had fortified a strategic highway. Yet they had neglected to adopt the routine precautions against tactical surprise on the flank of their assault column. This strange confusion of purpose in propitiating imaginary fears and overlooking real dangers invited all the disastrous consequences that usually attend a policy of appeasement. The courageous Hancock had attempted to arrest the fatal drift when he ordered Gibbon forward. But excessive caution overruled Gibbon's will to resolute and timely action. Hancock's bravest men were now called upon to pay the drastic penalty.[14]

After notifying his division commander of the presence of Confederate troops in the railway cut, McAllister appears to have made no disposition to meet an attack on his flank until he heard firing to the left and rear. "I soon discovered we were flanked," he relates. Strenuous efforts were then made to meet the peril. With Colonel Sewell's 5th New Jersey on the left, the second line regiments formed front to right on the right regiment, then, executing an about face and wheeling half-left by regiments, they came into line facing the enemy, the 5th New Jersey on the right of the new line.[15] The maneuver had just been completed when General Mott rode up. While the brigadier was explaining the situation, a violent attack struck the troops holding along his original front. Under a storm of musketry pouring in from front, flank, and rear, McAllister's huddled ranks gave way. His description of the rout of his own brigade characterizes the continuous process of disintegration as the Confederate attack, passing steadily from the front and moving with increased momentum on the flank and rear, rolled up Birney's brigades, one by one, from the left to the Plank Road.

> Here, my horse was mortally wounded by two or three rifleballs, but still able to move slowly. At this time my line broke in confusion and I could not rally them short of the breast works (on the Brock Road). Sick myself and unable to walk, I urged my wounded horse slowly along before the

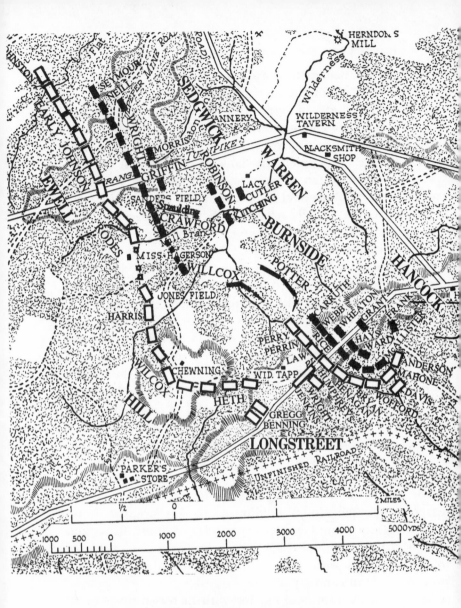

Map 23. CONTINUATION OF LONGSTREET'S ENVELOPMENT OF HANCOCK

The situation at about 11:45 a.m., May 6. The stalemate on the north flank is not changed. Burnside continues his snail-like movement toward Longstreet's left flank. Longstreet's assault is rolling up Hancock's left flank; it has struck McAllister, whose huddled ranks are giving way.

Off the map to the lower right are the following brigades comprising Gibbon's provisional corps: Baxter, Brooke, Leasure, Smyth, Eustis, and Miles. This force is pinned down by false reports of a phantom enemy corps approaching from the south.

enemy's advancing line and reached the breast-works in safety. There I changed horses and reformed my brigade. My staff was very active and soon had them formed, as ordered, behind the second line of breast-works, my right resting near General Ward's brigade, the interval being filled up by a few stragglers that were between the two brigades.[16]

Glimpses of the field here and there picture the swift disintegration and tend to confirm the supposition that each brigade in turn crumpled and fled as had McAllister's, and under the same inexorable pressure from front flank and rear. Time after time units changed front to rear and, according to report, would have stayed the onset had not troops on the original front given way. And these troops according to their version of the fighting, fell back in order to conform to the retirement of units who were supposed to cover their left. In a measure both interpretations are correct; neither could hold.[17]

Captain Cannon, commanding the 40th New York, who with 3d Maine covered the flank of Ward's brigade, states that after the entire line on his left had given way, "our front was then changed to the rear, temporarily checking their advance,[18] but, in consequence of the exposed condition of our left flank, . . . and the heavy fire received in rear from our own troops that had given way, we were compelled to fall back in order to escape being captured."[19] A veteran of the 141st New York, a sister regiment of Ward's brigade, declares that "without supports, without ammunition, with lines badly broken . . . the regiment was forced to retire with fixed bayonets."[20]

Lieutenant Colonel Weygant, who assumed command of the 124th New York (the "Orange Blossoms") upon the wounding of Colonel Cummings at 9 a.m., describes the Federal rout in the official history of his regiment. While "dubs" were falling back from the first line to boil coffee and prepare a belated breakfast, their places being taken by similar groups from a regiment of Carroll's brigade (Gibbon's division), in the second line, a terrific fire broke out on the left. The Confederates advanced six lines deep, doubled up Mott's command, and threw his units into such disorder that it became impossible to rally them. Continuing the story, Weygant relates that:

> The 124th changed front to the left, but I might as well have tried to stop the flight of a cannon ball by interposing the lid of a cracker box. Back pell-mell came the ever swelling crowd of fugitives, and the next moment the Sons of Orange were caught up as by a whirlwind, and broken to fragments; and the terrific tempest of disaster swept on down the Union Line, beating back brigade after brigade, and tearing to pieces regiment after regiment, until upward of 20,000 veterans were fleeing, every man for himself, through the disorganizing and already bloodstained woods, toward the Union rear . . . I now became thoroughly disheartened, and, abandoning all hopes of gathering my command south of the Rapidan, sheathed my sword, and moved back with the rabble.[21]

The pressure making for haste being somewhat relaxed by fatigue and the receding sound of musketry, the "Sons of Orange" finally responded to efforts of their officers to stand and fight. Some 50 men were rallied by Weygant and Corporal Edwards around a stand of colors. Just as the detachment was formed in closed ranks, General Birney and his staff approached. Weygant called his men to attention. As his saber swung to the salute, a shell burst under the General's horse. When the smoke rolled away, the numerous staff had vanished; Birney, striving desperately to control his bolting steed, disappeared into the woods. The colors, Weygant, his corporal, and the detachment went back without further pause to the Brock Road.

Perhaps the shock of the exploding shell, rather than the collapse of his attack column, or the one as an unnerving culmination to the other, offers an explanation of the violent and unreasonable censure published by Birney in a general order the day following, May 7, and stating:

> The Major-General commanding the division regrets that its famous reputation for bravery and good discipline should have been tarnished by the conduct of the skulks, cowards, and scoundrels, wearing officers' uniforms, who aided in the disgraceful stampede of yesterday morning after the division

had added to its reputation by its glorious conduct on the day before and that morning by its advance. Those regiments that disgraced themselves by the cowardly conduct of their officers will be noticed in the official report of this great battle of the rebellion without they show by their conduct of to-day their regret for their cowardice.—By command of Major-General Birney.[22]

Valiant Resistance on Birney's Right

After the reorganization that had been effected by Wadsworth, who assumed command of all troops north of the Plank Road, Rice's brigade, together with remnants of the V Corps that had constituted his original command, were placed in the first line, while the intermixed regiments of Webb's and Stevenson's commands held the second line of battle. This formation was probably completed before Birney's second attack had come to a standstill.

As Kershaw's line went forward to support the flanking movement, Field, who had been reinforced by the brigades of Perry and Perrin of Anderson's division, extended the attack on the north side of the Plank Road. Wadsworth accepted the challenge, striking back with such vigor that the left of the Confederate attack recoiled. The opposing lines stood face to face, gripped in the fury of a blazing fire fight.[23]

The very intensity with which Wadsworth's troops sustained the action only led to a swift collapse of their lines. Aware that the Federal left was tottering, Wadsworth galloped down the Plank Road to urge a holding attack by Webb's left regiments, which had been extended across the road. Failing to find Webb, who at that moment was engaged on the right of his line, Wadsworth ordered Lieutenant-Colonel Macy, commanding the 20th Massachusetts, to charge straight up the Plank Road into the face of the enemy's fire and hold as long as possible. He then sent instructions that Webb ascertain the cause of disorder on the left, and gather any four regiments he could find to support the holding attack.[24]

Colonel Macy, according to report, protested the useless sacrifice that obedience to the General's order would entail. Wadsworth wrathfully replied that if the colonel was reluctant to lead his regiment, he would set the example. Then, waving his sword, he galloped to the front.

Macy promptly ordered the charge; his men swept forward, cheering in defiance of the volley that smote their line. Among the first to fall was the colonel, who was sent to the rear with a shattered foot. The command devolved upon Major Abbot, who was described by both Hancock and Gibbon as one of the most promising young officers of the Army.[25]

Abbot led the 20th through a storm of musketry up to the enemy's front. As his line reeled under the blast of a volley fired at point blank range, the major fell, shot through the head. In the wild melee that followed, the men of the 20th recovered the prostrate body of their gallant young commander who was still breathing fitfully, and carried him to the rear.

In the midst of the close-range firing that broke the attack of the 20th Massachusetts, General Wadsworth lost control of his horse. Bolting, the infuriated beast dashed straight toward the Confederate lines. The general, probably with the assistance of Lieutenant Rogers, his *aide de camp,* succeeded in turning the horse back, but not in time to escape either death or captivity. Shot through the back of the head, General Wadsworth fell to the ground. Lieutenant Rogers, convinced that the general had been instantly killed, rode on to II Corps headquarters and (at 12:45 p.m.) reported the incident.[26]

Upon returning from the right and being informed of Wadsworth's instructions, Webb crossed the road just in time to witness the final collapse of the line on that side of the highway. "Seeing," he says in his report, "the impossibility of effecting anything, I returned to my command and found it in column on the road." [27]

In fact, only the fortuitous circumstance of the 19th Maine's return to the front after having replenished its supply of ammunition saved Webb's line from attack on the left rear. Seeing the collapse of Federal troops everywhere on the left of his column, Colonel Connor, the regimental commander, later brigadier general and Governor of Maine, promptly formed line to the left, with a view to covering the flank of Webb's brigade. In a letter addressed subsequently to the Assistant Adjutant General of the brigade, Colonel Connor relates this brief but important episode of the battle:

> The regiment was withdrawn in line as directed, and a supply of ammunition was found not more than a hundred or 150 yards to the rear. As soon as the cartridge boxes were replenished, firing was heard in the woods to our left and the sound grew nearer, indicating that our forces in that direction were giving way to the enemy. You were with my regiment at that time . . . my impression is that you had come to show me where the ammunition was placed . . . and I said to you that I would change my front forward on my left company in order to cover our people who were being driven back, and I suggested to you that you had better inform General Webb of the force apparently coming on, to flank his left, since his attention might be so occupied with his front that he would not notice it in time, and also of the action I proposed to take. You rode forward towards the position and I changed my front so that my line was just in rear of the Plank Road and parallel with it. In a few minutes the Vermont Brigade of the Sixth Corps broke from the woods into the road in a confused mass and streamed down the Plank Road toward the Brock Road. General L. A. Grant, the brigade commander, and other officers were striving to rally them but they were crowded together in such a huddle and the pursuing enemy was so close upon them that it was hardly possible for them to reform. It was on the Plank Road at the left of my regiment and just in front of it. The Vermonters came out of the woods just at that point. As soon as they were clear of my front, and the enemy were close at hand, I opened fire. I was soon after struck in the thigh by a shot coming from the right and fell by the side of the road. When I was down I saw General Webb just behind me and he asked if I was hit. I was then taken off the field in a blanket by some of my men.[28]

In the northward drive of the flanking column, the nature of the movement, as well as the difficult terrain over which it swept, necessarily imposed considerable modifications on the original formation. These can only be inferred. It is known that Mahone, who had originally formed in the center, held the left as the attack swept up to the Plank Road. Wofford's brigade was on right. Anderson had been slowed down by his impact with McAllister's line; Mahone, advancing swiftly on

his right, had forged ahead and, at the same time, had inclined
to the left in order to hit the rear of the enemy's line before
he could swing his reserve formations outward and interpose
a new front. Just how the movement of Anderson's Georgians
and Stone's (Davis') Mississippians conformed to these ten-
dencies is not known. It may be inferred, however, from the
indefinite descriptions in the various accounts of Confederate
officers, that the four flanking brigades approached the Plank
Road in some sort of line, Mahone on the left, Wofford on
the right, with Anderson and Stone either crowding up in the
center or forming a second line. Certainly these four units,
unless individually formed in great depth, could not have
deployed in line on the relatively narrow front between
Mahone's left and the Brock Road.

As Connor threw his 19th Maine across the flank of
Webb's line and covered its withdrawal, Brigadier General
Rice, commanding the 2d Brigade of Wadsworth's division,
made a similar disposition on the left of the first line. Succeeding to the command of the division upon Wadsworth's
fall, Rice assigned Colonel Hoffman to take over his brigade,
the 2d, 4th Division. Hoffman, pivoting on his left battalion,
wheeled the brigade into line facing the Plank Road. As the
right, moving on the outer circle of the swing, passed across
the front of Field's line it received a terrific enfilade of musketry. A Confederate battery that had taken position on a slight
rise in close support to Field's line also opened with a raking
storm of shell fire. The right of the new-formed line staggered
and broke. The left met a volley from Mahone's Brigade
which, dashing through the broken mass of Grant's Vermonters, emerged from the trees at the south side of the Plank
Road.[29]

Upon news of the collapse of Birney's left, Hancock endeavored to restore order and to reform his line of battle
along the Orange Plank Road from its extreme advance to its
junction with the Brock Road, by throwing back his left in
order to hold his advanced position along that road and on
its right.[30] The swift strokes by which the four flanking bri-

gades carried the work of demoralization along Birney's line thwarted any execution of Hancock's resolute design. A remark of Mahone in this connection seems quite to the point: "His long lines of dead and wounded which lay in wake of our swoop furnished evidence that he was not allowed time to change front, as well as the execution of our fire." [31]

Birney no doubt was endeavoring to carry out this plan when the incident of the bursting shell, as described by Lieutenant-Colonel Weygant, separated him from his staff.[32] Soon after this unhappy affair Birney reported at the II Corps Headquarters and stated that he "thought it advisable to withdraw the troops from the woods, where it was almost impossible to adjust our lines, and to reform them in the breastworks along the Brock Road on our original line of battle." [33] With a heavy heart, Hancock gave his approval.

The order to withdraw seems to have come as a belated recognition of a state of affairs that had already been accepted by the troops at the front. Field and Mahone were rapidly closing in on the remnant of Wadsworth's command. Anxious to speed the advance of the 12th Virginia, on the left of Mahone's line, Colonel Sorrel spurred forward to take the colors from the hands of the regimental color-bearer and carry them to the front. Recalling the incident in later years to a comrade, Sorrel relates that:

> He [Ben May] was doing all that man could do with his colors, but seemed to be somewhat embarrassed by the bushes, and I thought perhaps I might help to get them forward, mounted as I was. As you say, he positively refused to let them leave his own hands. I was filled with admiration for his splendid courage. I think it was on the 12th (during the Battle of Spotsylvania Court House, May 8-20, 1864) that poor May was shot, and I received from a member of the Twelfth Virginia an affectionate message that he sent me. As our troops reached the Plank Road a volley was given the enemy, who was trying to rally on the opposite side. Our rapid movements through the woods had disordered our line, as you correctly describe it. Leaving them for a moment, while recovering good order, I hastened to General Longstreet with a view to bringing up supports to follow up our splendid success. I met the General nearby, Jenkins' brigade im-

mediately behind him. He had heard the sound of our rifles and, with the quick instinct of the General that he was, was following us up with a strong and powerful support to pursue his victory.[34]

Longstreet, sitting astride his charger at the head of Jenkins' Brigade, calmly watched the final collapse of Wadsworth's shattered command. As Mahone's line pressed up to the road, a sudden blaze of dried leaves and twigs across the path of advance caused a hasty crowding to the right, while the 12th Virginia pushed straight across and struck the left of the Federal line. Supplementing the heavy pressure of Field's attack, this sharp blow demolished the last vestige of Federal resistance. Longstreet was now ready to launch the culminating phase of his offensive.

Just before Colonel Sorrel's personal report had given final confirmation of the success of the turning movement, General Smith had returned from his second reconnaissance. He affirmed the possibility of turning the left of Hancock's reserve position on the Brock Road. Longstreet, convinced not only of the practicability of the maneuver, but of Smith's ability as a tactician to execute the design, instructed the engineer officer to take the brigades of Mahone, Anderson, Davis, and Wofford, move them by inversion from their position facing the Plank Road and strike Hancock's left rear on the Brock Road. General Smith rode away to execute the order as Sorrel galloped up with his report of success.

In the proposed movement by inversion, Wofford, the right element of the initial alignment, would move by the left and rear and establish the left of the resulting formation. The other three elements, moving in succession from right to left, each advancing by the left and rear, would come up successively on the right of the line established by Wofford, Mahone, would complete the maneuver by forming on the extreme right. While Smith was swinging his units into position to attack by the flank, Longstreet proposed that Field and Kershaw should deliver a frontal assault on the Brock Road works. It was his apparent intention to move the storming troops in double column some distance down the road and then deploy his lines of assault right and left.

As Wofford's left stepped off, the troops designated "moved for the frontal assault," according to Longstreet, "down the Plank Road, Jenkins' Brigade by the road, Kershaw's Division alongside." [35] Longstreet, with his I Corps staff, Kershaw, Field, and Jenkins, with their respective divisional and brigade staffs, rode in advance—as brilliant a cavalcade, perhaps, as ever has preceded a column of American troops. Every face kindled with a look of stern elation that the sudden promise of victory brings, like the burst of sunlight on a storm-tossed sea, to features grown haggard in a continuous tumult of desperate strife.

After Longstreet had briefly discussed with his chiefs of divisions the dispositions of their troops for reopening battle, Jenkins pressed to the front to congratulate his corps commander on the recent success and express his belief in a decisive victory. He said: "I am happy; I have felt despair for the cause for some months, but am relieved, and feel assured that we will put the enemy back across the Rapidan before night."[36]

Like the answer of Fate itself, a volley blazed from the fringe of trees along the south side of the road. Its blast of Minié balls crashed through the clattering cavalcade. Jenkins fell, mortally wounded. Captain Doby, of Kershaw's staff, and his orderly, Bowman, were killed. Longstreet reeled in his saddle, struck by a ball that entered at the throat and passed through his right shoulder.

The 12th Virginia, having found itself isolated on the north side of the road, had faced about and started back across the highway to rejoin its brigade, when a unit of Mahone's line, mistaking the movement for a Federal counterattack, fired the fatal volley. Jenkin's column immediately faced right and prepared for action, thinking that the volley had come from Federals attacking from that quarter. The ready-witted Kershaw, whose coolness and resolution had contributed so much in turning the tide of Birney's attack, was first to perceive the situation. He wheeled his horse to quiet Jenkins' men, who, with levelled guns, were in the act of returning the volley. His clear voice carried like a trumpet down the line, calling: "F-r-i-e-n-d-s!" The rifles were grounded in silence; the men, fearing another volley, threw themselves prone.[37]

After recovering his seat, Longstreet attempted to ride on. The free flow of blood, however, quickly warned him of the serious nature of his wound and that he must relinquish the command. As he turned to ride back, members of his staff saw him sway. Leaping to the ground, they lifted the wounded general from his saddle and, carrying him to the roadside, propped his back against a tree. Word was sent to the rear, both to advise Lee of the mishap and to call up a stretcher detachment.

Field hastened to Longstreet's side. In answer to an anxious inquiry as to his condition, he replied that others would look after him, and directed Field, as the senior officer present, to take command. Blowing bloody foam from his lips as he talked, the stricken corps commander described the combination of front and flank attack he intended to deliver. The two lines marching by the right on the Plank Road toward the enemy, and the flanking brigades moving in the initiation of Smith's maneuver by inversion to the left, that is, in the opposite direction, presented a perplexing picture to anyone unaware of the scheme. Field, if Longstreet's version of the affair is accurate, grasped the combination and, leaving Longstreet, went to expedite the operation.

Lee Revises Longstreet's Plan

Longstreet was carried to the rear; Lee, apprehensive of the news, quickly appeared at the front. Viewing the confusion of overlapping lines and apparent aimlessness of movement, and doubtful of Field's ability to execute the complicated maneuver, he cancelled the operation and instructed Field to form his troops in parallel order.

Lee's disinclination to risk attack at once not only sacrificed the possibilities of a supporting movement against the enemy's left flank, but lost the inestimable advantage of immediate pursuit. It may never be known whether or not Lee, in his analysis of the whole situation, failed in striking a nice balance between the disorder of retreating Federals and the apparent confusion in which he found Longstreet's formations. It is not known whether he exaggerated this element of the situation and minimized the one more remote to his view, and thus made a fatal mistake of judgment—one that cost him his last chance of winning a decisive victory. History is a zealous guardian of her adopted heroes.

Longstreet himself harbored some doubt as to Lee's willingness to permit an execution of the operation he had planned. He writes these significant words: "With patience to wait ten minutes to see my flanking brigades stretched out on their march to retrieve my *aplomb,* we could have found a good battle against Hancock's strong left, while we broke over his confused front. Fearing another change, I hurried on to execute before it could be ordered." [38]

General Field, the one witness capable of presenting weighty evidence in this difference of opinion between Lee and Longstreet, leaves the whole matter in doubt by agreeing with both. He comments that:

> Could we have pushed forward at once, I believe Grant's army would have been routed, as all that part which I had attacked was on the run. But as the troops were now formed, my division and some others, probably, were perpendicular to the road and in line of battle, while all those which had acted as the turning force were in line parallel to the road, and the two were somewhat mixed up. No advance could be possibly made till the troops parallel to the road were placed perpendicular to it. Otherwise, as the enemy had fallen back down the road, our right flank would have been exposed to him. Besides, our two bodies being on the road at the same point, one perpendicular and the other about parallel to it, neither could move without interfering with the other. To rectify this alignment consumed some precious time—time, as we learned later, the enemy was employing in reforming his broken columns and throwing up a new line of work.[39]

Longstreet, the deliberate marcher, urged haste in the attack and feared any change of plan that might deny his divisions the well-earned opportunity of "breaking over" Hancock's confused front. Lee, believing that he had a sufficient margin of time in which to reform and deliver a more effective attack, determined to avoid the uncertain gains of a headlong pursuit. Since the pursuit was not pressed, no one can say that it would have struck with devastating effect. Nor is it certain that Smith's four brigades could have turned Gibbon's defense force out of its strongly fortified position, with the whole artillery of the II Corps, less a single battery in support.[40] The four brigades at Gibbon's disposal—Miles, Smyth, Frank, and Brooke, of Barlow's division—had not as yet been engaged. At the same time, if the mere threat of attack at 7 o'clock had held Gibbon in his lines, the appearance of four brigades in battle order would undoubtedly have pinned his entire force to their trenches. This was not the case when Lee attacked at a later hour and Brooke's brigade went from Gibbon's front to the threatened sector. Then Burnside's two divisions, Willcox and Potter, were hovering in the woods somewhere on the flank of Field's line. While their aimless wandering showed irresolution of purpose, this mass might, in the event of a repulse at the Brock Road, be transformed into a dangerous menace.

Yet a sudden rupture of Hancock's reserve line would be irreparable. Justification of the decision for an immediate attack could only be found in an extreme degree of demoralization to which the defending troops had been subjected. Here Longstreet's intuition seems to have been fundamentally sound. He had witnessed the break in Birney's lines. We have a glimpse of the rout, as seen from the Federal side, in one of the many inimitable word pictures of the battle which Lieutenant-Colonel Theodore Lyman has hastily sketched in his letters from the front. Not only does Lyman substantiate the truth of Weygant's more detailed and emotional account of the rout, but clearly infers that the shattered morale of the Federals could scarcely have withstood the fierce onset of a Confederate pursuit. While in the lines a few days later at Spotsylvania Court House, Lyman wrote:

At a little after eleven Mott's left gave way. The musketry now drew closer to us, stragglers began to come back, and in a little while, a crowd of men emerged from the thicket in full retreat. They were not running, nor pale, nor scared, nor had they thrown away their guns; but were just in the condition described by the Prince de Joinville, after Gaines' Mill. They had fought all they meant to fight for the present, and there was an end of it! If there is anything that will make your heart sink and take all the backbone out of you, it is to see men in this condition! I drew my sword and rode among them, trying to stop them at a little rifle-pit that ran along the road. I would get one squad to stop, but as I turned to another, the first would quietly walk off. There was a German color-bearer, a stupid, scared man (who gave him the colors, the Lord only knows!) who said, "Jeneral Stavenzon, he telled me for to carry ze colors up ze road." To which I replied I would run him through the body if he didn't plant them on the rifle-pit. And so he did, but I guess he didn't stick.[41]

Meantime, Longstreet was carried on a stretcher back down the Brock Road toward Widow Tapp's farm. His broad-brimmed hat had been placed over his face for protection against the noon-day sun. His massive shoulders and chest were bathed in blood. Within six hours after his arrival on the field he had rescued the Army of Northern Virginia from certain defeat and, turning the tide with swift and brilliant counter strokes, had prepared the offensive blow that Lee, for reasons that history will not disclose, failed to deal.

Chapter 24

LEE LAUNCHES LAST GRAND ASSAULT

When Longstreet was borne on his stretcher to the rear, the Battle of the Wilderness, as a contest of craft between the opposing army commanders, virtually came to an end. Grant, to be sure, was reluctant to recognize that his adversary had seized the initiative; he would not submit to Lee's lead without another attempt to resume the offensive. Lee, refusing to believe that his failure or inability to pursue Birney's broken brigades was vital to the issue, still entertained hopes of another Chancellorsville. He mounted with meticulous care an offensive aimed at the center of Hancock's line. While falling short of its objective, this blow anticipated Grant's effort to recreate his own offensive power, thus bringing the contending forces into a final stalemate.

Lee Holds the Initiative

Two minor operations bracketed Lee's assault on the Brock Road. One was a continuation by Burnside of his supporting movement on Hancock's right. Nearly two hours after Birney's column had collapsed, Burnside developed an abortive attack on Field's right, but scarcely distracted attention from preparations for the drive at Hancock's center. The other was a belated attack on Federal right during the eerie twilight hour in the Wilderness. It fell as one of those complete and paradoxical surprises which break with the terrifying realization of a dreaded peril that has ceased to be a momentary threat. Launched with great ardor by Brigadier-General J. B. Gordon, and given a somewhat indifferent support by Early, his skeptical division commander, this operation, after rolling up Sedgwick's two right brigades, collapsed in disorder before the stiffening resistance of local reserves. Because of panic induced by its initial success, together with the fact that it hastened the withdrawal of the Federal right across the basin of Caton Run to a line covering the Germanna Plank-Orange Turnpike intersection at Wilderness Tavern, a measure which Meade had contemplated soon after the holding attack against Ewell had been suspended, Gordon's flank movement has been celebrated beyond the actual significance of the operation.

Burnside Stopped on Field's Right

Reports of the disaster that Longstreet's counter-stroke from the Tapp field had inflicted on Wadsworth's column between 7:30 and 8 a.m. did not reach army headquarters until nearly 9 o'clock. Knowledge of this event, therefore, came about the same time as the notice that Hancock would launch his second offensive at 8:40.[1] The sudden realization that Wadsworth would be unable to support Hancock's right with the strength that had been originally anticipated led to the decision to divert Burnside from his thrust in the direction of Parker's Store. Instead, he was to throw his force against the left of the Confederates opposing Birney's attack column on the Plank Road.[2] To this end, Colonel Comstock left army headquarters about 9 a.m. The staff officer reported to Burnside in Jones' field and explained the change of plan.[3]

Burnside led Potter's division by the left rear, Hartranft's brigade, Wilcox's division, following in support. Christ's brigade was left in its reserve position to picket the Parker's Store road.[4]

At 10 a.m., just about the time General Smith returned from his first reconnaissance and reported the practicability of a flanking movement by way of the unfinished railroad, Colonel Comstock advised Grant that Burnside had gained one and one-half miles to his left to connect with Wadsworth, "and now moves at once toward Hancock's firing with Potter's division, supported by a brigade (Hartranft)." Comstock added: "I should think Hancock's firing is a mile away." [5]

Of the many mysteries of the Wilderness, the misadventures of Burnside while traversing that two miles of woodland is one of the deepest and most inexplicable. It appears that Burnside opened communication with Hancock and suggested a desire to time his attack with the advance of Owen's brigade, and that Hancock keep in touch with him.[6]

The distance traversed by Sorrel's four flanking brigades—about two miles—between 10 o'clock, when the maneuver began, and noon, when they drove up to the Plank Road, was scarcely less than the distance from Jones' field to the left of Field's line on the Plank Road. Yet it took Burnside approximately five hours—from 9 a.m. to 2 p.m.—to cover this distance and to develop his attack on the Confederate flank. Never had he given a more striking demonstration of his genius for slowness.

Comstock's message was read at general headquarters at 10:50 a.m. An hour passed with no sound of volley fire that was anxiously awaited as Burnside's announcement that he had thrown his brigades at Longstreet's left rear. Always appreciating the value of time, and nowhere more than on the battlefield, Grant became apprehensive that Lee would again profit by Burnside's inexcusable squandering of this precious element. At 11:45 he sent a peremptory order through Brigadier General Rawlins, his Adjutant General, to the IX Corps commander requiring that he attack at once.

Grant's apprehension was well-founded. Mahone with his hard-hitting colleagues was already on Birney's left rear. News of their devastating blows was soon to reach general headquarters. Without knowledge as yet of the impending disaster, Rawlins instructed Burnside to:

> Push in with all vigor so as to drive the enemy from General Hancock's front, and get in on the Orange and Fredericksburg plank road at the earliest possible moment. Hancock has been expecting you for the last three hours, and has been making his attack and dispositions with a view to your assistance . . . By command of Lieutenant-General Grant.[7]

The Clash

Little is known concerning the essential features of the action. Colonel Perry, commanding Law's Alabama Brigade,

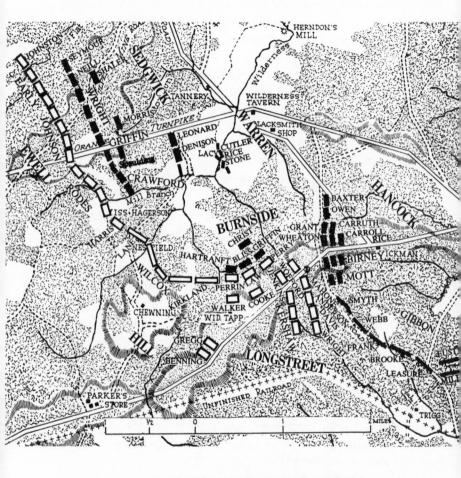

MAP 24. BURNSIDE'S BELATED ATTACK

The situation at about 1 p.m., May 6. Burnside's attack initially struck Law's brigade, commanded by Col. W. F. Perry. The latter was surprised and driven back, but the situation was restored for the Confederates by the arrival of E. A. Perry and Perrin on this line, as shown. These veteran brigades were too much for Burnside's raw troops, who withdrew and began to entrench. Sedgwick and Warren are also entrenching, in order to release troops to reinforce Hancock. But Hancock is also throwing up breastworks, and does not feel able to launch another assault. Gibbon's provisional corps has come up on Hancock's left.

Lee is assembling another attack force for the purpose of striking the Federal works along the Brock Road.

and still holding the left of Field's line, indicates that he encountered considerable trouble from Burnside's advance, which probably struck his left sometime before 2 o'clock. The attack, according to Perry, came as a complete surprise, compelling him to throw back his flank and give considerable ground before E. Perry's Florida brigade and Perrin's Alabama brigade of Anderson's Division came to the rescue. The ten Alabama regiments of Perry's and Perrin's commands, together with the three of the Florida Brigade, quickly forced back Burnside's advance and threw up a light entrenchment.[8] Burnside ordered up Potter's two brigades—Bliss' and Griffin's—composed of 12 regiments representing Maine, Massachusetts, New Hampshire, Vermont, Rhode Island, Pennsylvania, and New York, and sent them against the Confederate line.

Recruits for the most part, and experiencing their baptism of fire, the IX Corps troops rushed gallantly into the volleys of the veteran regiments from Florida and Alabama. The first line reached the Confederate works, recoiled and fell back. The second line advanced, while Hartranft, with four Michigan regiments (the 2d, 8th, 17th, and 27th) the 109th New York, and 51st Pennsylvania, struck fiercely on the right, carrying the works and driving the defenders out. Hartranft's quick feat, however, was speedily undone. Potter's line collapsed; Hartranft's raw troops were thrown into disorder by a savage counterattack and driven back in panic. Lacking sufficient strength to maintain the action, Burnside prudently withdrew across swampy ground and, without molestation by the enemy, entrenched.[9]

The grand maneuver that was to have restored the fame of Ambrose E. Burnside by clinching a brilliant victory for the army he had once commanded, ended only in this brief exchange of musketry. Intent on other business, neither Lee nor Hancock gave serious heed to the echo of his volleys.

Lieutenant Colonel Lyman was impressed with the bitter irony of this situation when at 1:15 p.m. he galloped back from army headquarters to the Brock Crossing. He had carried a full report of the collapse on the Plank Road to Meade.

Returning, he found Hancock alone, in rear of the Brock Road. The aide was asked to sit down under the trees. Hancock "was very tired indeed," relates Lyman. "All his staff were away to set in order the troops." At 2 p.m. Burnside "made a short attack with loud musketry." Lyman ventured to urge Hancock to try to attack also. The corps commander shook his head regretfully, saying that "it would be to hazard too much." [10]

Warren Ordered to Reinforce Hancock

The work of organizing the Federal defense along the Brock Road was feverishly pushed as Lee reformed for the attack. Meade's decision of 10:35 a.m. was to definitely suspend offensive operation on the right and, after entrenching the lines, hold all but a minimum defense force as a general reserve available, if required, to reinforce Hancock's left. This was one of the precautions taken by army headquarters on May 6 that really anticipated an actual danger. This decision, it will be noted, was made about the time that Sorrel's flanking column was filing down the cut of the unfinished railroad. [11]

Warren took immediate steps to release a large part of his command. At 11 a.m. he informed Humphreys that he had ordered up his entrenching tools and that the regular engineer officers would direct construction of the field works. He estimated that the fortification of his front would make available a total of 7,700 comparatively fresh troops, consisting of "two brigades of Pennsylvania Reserves (Crawford), say about 2,200; two brigades of General Robinson, 2,000; two brigades of General Griffin, 2,000; engineer troops, 1,500." The remainder, Wadsworth's division, and the heavy artillery brigades, would hold the entrenched line. Warren also assured the chief of staff that he would go at once in person and consult with General Sedgwick. [12]

These precautionary measures undoubtedly facilitated a quick dispatch of reinforcements to Hancock, when his entire forward line collapsed. News of this disaster reached Warren at noon. [13] Immediate reaction at army headquarters to the crisis was somewhat different than the attitude expressed in its dispatch of 10:35 a.m. might have led Warren to believe. The alternative of advancing Warren's left, as a measure of relief to Hancock, was actually considered. After stating the fact of Hancock's retirement, Meade added: "It may perhaps be necessary either to make an advance from your left, or send troops to him from your command. Have some in readiness." [14]

A gap of an hour and a half in the correspondence between army and V Corps headquarters relating to the development of operations precludes serious speculation as to the reasons why the alternative of weakening the right to reinforce the left was finally adopted. Was there serious apprehension at army headquarters that the degree of demoralization in Hancock's ranks was such as to offset the advantages of superior numbers and a strong defensive position, and this to an extent that only the reinforcement of fresh troops would insure a successful defense? Or did army headquarters follow its all too frequent practice of adopting the most pessimistic view and then determining to appease its fears?

There are reasons for believing that this is the case. Evidence hidden by the gap in correspondence between V Corps and army headquarters is partially supplied by that between Meade and Sheridan. In justifying at 11:40 a.m. his disinclination to press the advantage won by Custer at the Brock-Furnace Road intersection, Sheridan stated that "I think it best not to follow up any advantage gained, as the cavalry is now very far out from this place (Chancellorsville) and I do not wish to give them any chance of getting at our trains." [15]

Sheridan Withdrawn From Todd's Tavern

Replying to Sheridan at 1 p.m., Humphreys informed the chief of cavalry that Hancock had been heavily pressed, his left turned; and added: "The Major-General commanding thinks that you had better draw in your cavalry so as to secure the protection of the trains. The order requiring an escort for the wagons tonight has been rescinded." [16]

In view of the fact that Sheridan had held with apparent

ease the outer line connecting on the left of the infantry and covering Todd's Tavern and Piney Branch Church, the order to withdraw to an inner line around Chancellorsville appears to have been actuated by a fear that Hancock's front was in a precarious state. The disposition proposed to Sheridan amounts to a withdrawal of the left, corresponding to the subsequent refusal of the right. One relinquished command of the strategic Brock Road toward Spotsylvania Court House, Grant's main line of operation through the Wilderness; the other abandoned his line of communications by way of Germanna Ford and jeopardized the alternate line over Ely's Ford.

The beginning of a movement of the great trains from Chancellorsville toward Ely's Ford, as an additional measure of precaution, points clearly to grave doubts concerning Hancock's ability to hold the Brock Road front. At 2:35 p.m., Sheridan warned army headquarters that:

> The trains are now moving to Ely's Ford. The trains of the Second Corps would not move without an escort, so I have sent 1,300 dismounted men to Ely's Ford with it. I have sent a regiment to scour the country to United States Ford and watch the roads. United States Ford is not in a passable condition for cavalry or infantry without much labor; it is also quite deep. The enemy's cavalry again attacked me and were repulsed and driven, leaving their dead and wounded on the field. They are now working toward my left, and I have made new dispositions in accordance with orders received from the major-general commanding.[17]

Hancock Hastens Defensive Preparations

At 2 p.m., one brigade, Robinson's division, and two regiments of heavy artillery of Marshall's provisional brigade, IX Corps, reported to Hancock. At 1:30 V Corps headquarters received an order to "send the other brigade of Robinson's to report to General Hancock immediately." [18]

These accessions gave Hancock a force of 18 brigades, representing divisions from every corps of the army group and comprising approximately half the strength of Grant's entire command.

Fearful of the storm brewing in the depth of the woods, Hancock's officers worked steadily through the early afternoon to regroup their scattered commands. Stray detachments were directed back and forth to the sectors allotted their respective units. Some were commandeered by anxious colonels who had lost the better part of their regiments. Staff officers went to the rear to hasten carts and pack mules, tied in tandem, and bearing small arms ammunition to the front. Fierce vociferations accentuated the turmoil, as mule tandems indulged their stubborn propensity to wrap themselves around a tree—and stay wrapped—belaboring blows and violent derogations notwithstanding.

By 2 o'clock, according to Lieutenant Colonel Lyman, Hancock had a continuous line but not organized enough to advance, and that "he has troops enough to hold, if he can hold at all." This discouraging picture was momentarily relieved by reports that Burnside was attacking heavily, that "all the enemy seem to have gone to fight Burnside," and that "There is no enemy in Hancock's front south of the Orange Plank Road." [19]

The formation of Hancock's defense is only vaguely known. The II Corps divisions were apparently in the line, left to right Barlow-Gibbon-Mott-Birney. Getty took his old position on Birney's right. Leasure's IX Corps brigade, after having swept the front of the works from left to right, took position on the right, probably connecting his left with Getty's right. Robinson states that his two brigades formed "on the right of the Second Corps," meaning, no doubt, that he went into position on the extreme right of Hancock's line. Colonel Morrison, commanding the heavy artillery regiments from Marshall's provisional brigade, was directed "to take position on left of the Orange Plank Road, about 200 paces in rear of our line of battle." [20]

News of these conflicting circumstances seems to have made a profound impression at army headquarters. The bogey of a crushing attack on Hancock's left had vanished; Hancock had his forces in hand, and Burnside at last had come into action.

After having abandoned the idea of relieving the crippled left by advancing the right and sending, instead, reinforcements directly from the right to the left, it now appears that Burnside's attack promised results equivalent to those that had been associated with an advance of the right. If Burnside could be supported by the right, and at least hold his own, he would tend to neutralize the effect of an early attack in force on Hancock. If, however, Lee did not take the offensive against the Federal left within a relatively short time, the initiative must pass to Hancock by virtue of his greater numbers and the favorable position of Burnside's mass. Upon receipt just before 2:15 p.m. of a dispatch from Burnside, Meade instructed Hancock as follows:[21]

> I have been expecting to hear from Lyman as to the morale of your command. Should Burnside not require any assistance and the enemy leave you undisturbed, I would let the men rest till 6 p.m., at which time a vigorous attack made by you, in conjunction with Burnside, will, I think, overthrow the enemy. I wish this done."

Upon receipt, at 3 p.m., Hancock immediately replied to this message:

> The present partially disorganized condition of this command renders it extremely difficult to obtain a sufficiently reliable body to make a really powerful attack. I will, however, do my best and make an attack at that hour in conjunction with General Burnside. What development of the attack do you desire? Will you indicate a front?[22]

An hour later, 4 p.m., Hancock reported to Seth Williams, Meade's assistant adjutant general, that the woods on his left front had, by accident or design of the enemy, been set afire and that it would be impossible to attack in that direction. There was no connection on his right, as yet, with Burnside. At the same time he promised to "assist Burnside in case he attacks, in some shape, at 6 o'clock, anywhere." [23]

These communications clearly indicate that the apprehension at army headquarters of a crushing counter-offensive against the Federal left, which took an uneasy turn at 9:30 a.m., when reports of Wadsworth's first repulse were verified.

The feeling at Meade's headquarters bordered on panic at noon, when the first news of Hancock's disaster came to hand, but gradually was mollified between 2 and 3 in the afternoon. The flow of reinforcements from right to left stopped. Of the 7,700 effectives Warren had earmarked as disposable, only 2,000 were actually sent to Hancock.

The situation now was not unlike that of the period between 7 and 8 a.m., when the coordinated offensive of the four corps elements of the Federal army group was abandoned in favor of a main drive along the Plank Road, supported by Burnside on the right, and a single division of cavalry on the left. In the present situation, however, the entire cavalry corps was relegated to a strictly defensive role, having fallen back by Meade's order from the outer defensive line through Todd's Tavern and Piney Branch Church to one resting on the Catharine Furnace and Aldrich.[24]

There is one vital distinction, however, to be noted in the two situations. During the forenoon Hancock fought desperately to retain the initiative that had been seriously challenged by Longstreet; now he was obliged to wait and take it, providing that the opportunity came by default from Lee. While Lee actually avoided a default, and thereby frustrated the Federal plan of again assuming the offensive, he so far presumed on the time margin that the circumstances of battle had allowed him in mounting his offensive that the Confederate attack was necessarily doomed to failure.

There is convincing evidence that both army and II Corps headquarters had little apprehension of attack after 3 p.m. Expectation of such a development would have enjoined some distribution of the 10 light batteries of quick-firing Napoleons along the extensive front. Of the 30 available pieces of this type, only the six of Dow's 6th Maine Battery were so disposed to take part in the action. Lieutenant Colonel Lyman's evidence on this point seems conclusive. He relates that:

> In our front all was quiet; and I got permission to go back to the 2d Corps hospital and look up the body of Major Abbot. Two miles back, in an open farm surrounded by

woods, they had pitched the hospital tents. I will not trouble you with what I saw there, as I passed among the dead and dying. Abbot lay on a stretcher, quietly breathing his last—his eyes were fixed and the ashen color of death was on his face. Nearby lay his colonel, Macy, shot in the foot. I raised Macy (Colonel of the 20th Massachusetts, wounded in the same action with Abbot) and helped him to the side of Abbot, and we stood there till he died. It was a pitiful spectacle, but a common one that day. I left in haste, after arranging for sending the remains home, for the sudden sound of heavy firing told of some new attack. The Rebels (unquenchable fellows they are!) seeing that Burnside had halted, once more swung round and charged furiously on Hancock to his very rifle-pits. I rode at once to General Meade, to ask that Burnside might attack also. This he did, without further orders and with excellent effect. When I got back to the crossroad, I was told the enemy had broken through on the plank road and cut us in two . . . [25]

Lee's Plan

One of the many perplexing phases of our knowledge of the Battle of the Wilderness or, for that matter, of the history of the Army of Northern Virginia, is that which pertains to Lee's frontal assault on the Brock Road position. Of the six celebrated offensive thrusts delivered by Lee—those of Gaines' Mill, Malvern Hill, Groveton, the 3d of May at Chancellorsville, Pickett's charge on Cemetery Ridge, and the assault of May 6 in the Wilderness—the drive at Hancock's center is least known; it is seldom considered as one of the six of Lee's great tactical offensives. With Malvern Hill and Cemetery Ridge, it goes down in military history as one of his three tactical failures.

We have practically no definite knowledge concerning the plan, formation, and development of this operation. So far as may be judged by the pressure brought to bear on Hancock's front, it seems that Lee intended to rupture the center of the entrenched line. It is probable that the attacking force consisted of 13 brigades—three of Heth, four of Field, four of Kershaw, and Stone's ubiquitous Mississippians.[26] It is reasonably certain that the two Alabama brigades of Perry and Perrin and Edward A. Perry's Florida brigade, with, possibly, one of Hill's, were holding Burnside, while Wilcox's Division and Wright's Brigade of R. H. Anderson's Division were formed on the new front extending from Tapp's field across the Chewning plateau to Ewell's right.[27] One, perhaps two, of Wilcox's brigades may have been included in the attack force, making a possible total of 15 brigades.[28]

The development of the operation is a matter of conjecture. Hancock's front from his left center to a point some distance north of the Plank Road appears to have been felt by a rolling fire. Jenkins' Brigade, commanded by Bratton, was held in reserve, ready, it seems, to drive at any soft spot found along the center of the Federal line.[29]

Lee's Last Grand Assault

At 4:15 p.m. the Confederate assault brigades swarmed from the woods and advanced to the outer edge of the abatis, or felled trees with trimmed and sharpened bows pointed to the front. There they met a steady fire from the breastworks.

If the assault had been launched in the hope that a determined rush of bayonets would incite panic among a still disorganized defense, the Confederates had reason to quickly amend the view. As their musketry blazed from a point some distance to the north of the Plank Road and swept down across the fronts of Getty, Birney, and Mott, to the edge of the smoke cloud that hovered over the burning woods, the fire poured back in reply across the barrier was steady, accurate, and heavy in volume. Every Confederate effort to storm across the zone of slashings only ended in a slackening of their musketry and an appalling increase of casualties. The affair was developing into one of those indecisive fire fights from which the assailants could not withdraw without conceding defeat, when the elements abruptly intervened in their behalf.

The forest fire that had been smoldering in front of Barlow's line slowly spread across Mott's front and now, suddenly fanned by the rising afternoon breeze, swept in rolling billows of smoke across the slashings to Mott's first line of works. The logs caught fire; the defenders backed steadily away, holding their

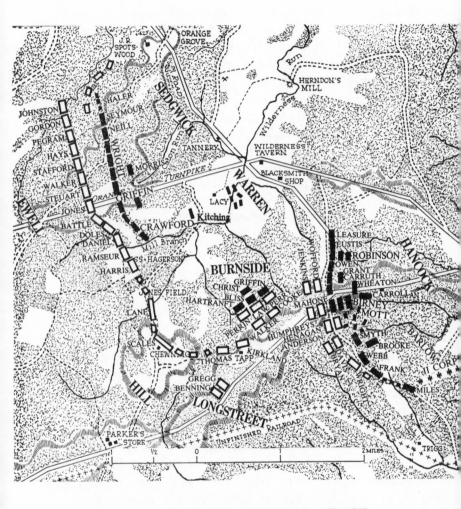

MAP 25. LEE'S LAST GRAND ASSAULT

The situation at about 4:30 p.m., May 6. Lee's frontal assault is striking Hancock's center. A forest fire raging on the Federal south flank produces a smoke screen which covers the right of the Confederate attack formation. G. T. Anderson's brigade has broken into Mott's sector.

On the north flank, Confederate skirmishers are feeling for the flank of the Federal defensive position.

The 84 guns of the Federal II Corps Artillery are shown, symbolically, in position in extension of Gibbon's flank.

alignment in a desperate effort to sustain the defense of their burning rampart. Then through the blinding smoke and flame poured a torrent of flashing bayonets. The fierce, pulse-stirring Rebel yell rang above the thundering tumult. G. T. Anderson's brigade dashed into the breach.

Mott's first line wavered, then gave way in wild disorder. As men of the division that had broken twice in battle during the last 24 hours turned their backs to a third peril, fear spread like the flames that had leapt across the abatis. Many supporting troops quit their works in panic. A portion of Birney's front was carried away in the flight. The battle flags fluttering above the Confederate charging line marked the forward rush.[30]

The Federal stampede swept back through the woods toward Chancellorsville. Madness engendered by flight was communicated to a section of the army trains. Terrified drivers climbed to their seats. Teams were lashed into rapid motion. Soon the road to Ely's Ford was crowded with rumbling wagons.

Hancock Breaks Lee's Assault

The morale of a well-disciplined army, like that of a great nation, cannot be destroyed by a single blow or by the temporary collapse of a single element. On the right of the breach Getty's three brigades—Grant, Wheaton, and Eustis—with Hays' brigade of Birney's division, stood firm. Birney, still commanding the troops that had been assigned to his attack column, ordered Carroll to restore the line with his brigade. Gibbon detached Brooke's brigade, Barlow's division, from the left with instructions to reinforce Birney.

While these reinforcements hastened to the scene, Captain Dow, commanding Battery F, 6th Maine Light Artillery, checked the Confederate storm troops with rapid blasts of double-shotted canister. With three discharges a minute, each fire hurling 284 canister pellets, or 852 a minute, these smoothbore Napoleons served in the tactical role of heavy machine guns in defensive fighting. Considering the density of their target, there can be no doubt that each of Dow's Napoleons proved as deadly as any modern machine gun. Indeed, it was a gunner's harvest. The two-gun section under Lieutenant Rogers at the crossing was wheeled out on the Plank Road in front of the infantry parapets and crossed its fire with that of the two sections under Dow's immediate command.[31]

As the thundering guns sent their blasts of canister, round after round, into the crowded Confederate ranks, shooting down five stands of colors only to see them reappear, the flames crept to Dow's log emplacements and set them afire. Unhindered, the discharges continued without pause in their terrible regularity. Then behind the smoking log works came a rapid series of powder explosions.

Recruit gunners employed in carrying ammunition to the guns failed to detach the powder charges from extra canister at the limbers. Strewn carelessly about the gun positions, these powder-packed cartridges lay dangerously close to the crackling logs. A fallen ember rolled against one of the cartridges. Lurid columns of yellow flame capped by curling puffs of white smoke rose in rear of the four-gun battery. Five cannoneers were prostrated with hideous burns but the guns fired on, unmindful of the roaring inferno.

Dow's bursts of canister could not have held for long against the inrush through the breach in the line. The Confederates were pressing their advantage. Their men were aroused to the highest pitch of battle ardor; one desperate thrust and victory was theirs. They were ready for the sacrifice. Only a counter-rush of cold steel could deny their imperious purpose.

Carroll's Counterattack Restores the Broken Line

Jogging at "double-quick step" in a well closed column, Carroll's brigade moved across the interval. At hoarsely shouted commands, the column swung into line. A row of bayonets glistened beneath the battleflags of nine regiments. There were two from New York (the 10th and 108th), two from Ohio (the 4th and 8th), with the 1st Delaware, 12th New Jersey, 14th Connecticut, 14th Indiana, and the 7th West Virginia—a truly representative Federal brigade. The thunderous shout of the Northerners was answered by a shrill Rebel yell. Dow's guns ceased their fire. The opposing lines met with a clash of steel. Contending battle flags swayed back and forth over the melee. A Confederate color went down, then another; the others moved to the rear. With a deafening cheer the pursuing Federals swept out over the ashes of Mott's abatis to the edge of the woods. Here a halt was called. The Confederates disappeared, their musketry dying away in the heart of the woods.

The victorious Federal regiments were led back to the ruins of Mott's old front line and ordered to restore the works. Brooke's brigade moved in on Carroll's right. Many of the men of Mott's division, who had been rallied by their officers during the fight, returned and joined the steadfast units of the second and third lines. New stacks of canister were piled behind Dow's smoking guns.

The last great charge that Lee was ever to launch with an expectation of destroying the Army of the Potomac had recoiled in defeat. The question raised at noon and deferred in favor of attack during the mid-afternoon had been answered by Dow's canister and Carroll's cold steel. Hopes of another Chancellorsville had vanished forever.

While the desperate combat raged around Mott's broken front, army headquarters experienced a difficult half hour. After having galloped directly from the II Corps field hospital to inform Meade of the Confederate assault and suggest that Burnside be ordered to make a diversion by attacking toward the Plank Road, Lyman hastened back to the Brock Crossing. He found that the road to Hancock's headquarters was blocked at the intersection and that General Stevenson, who had returned from Burnside's front and was directing Leasure's brigade, had no orders to reinforce Hancock. At 5:15 p.m. Lyman informed Meade of the circumstance. A few minutes later one of Birney's aides delivered a dispatch at army headquarters reporting that the enemy had broken through Mott's division at the Plank Road and had separated two of Hancock's divisions from the rest.[32] Humphreys at 5:30 p.m. instructed Warren to: "Send what men you can spare to General Hancock's assistance. The enemy has broken through his line, and communication between the two parts is cut off. Get Sedgwick's two brigades to supply the place of yours."[33] Then at 5:30 he directed Lyman: "Tell General Stevenson, from General Meade, to report at once to General Hancock and if he cannot find him to report to General Birney with his troops." Referring to the report brought in by Birney's aide, Humphreys added: "You did not mention it. What are the facts?" [34]

Lyman immediately endorsed this dispatch with this reassuring news: "The line is completely restored. General Stevenson has his order and is in position." [35]

Meantime Hancock was preparing a summary report of the attack that had produced such startling repercussions both at Chancellorsville and at army headquarters. Dispatched at 5:25 p.m., Hancock's report stated that

> At 4:15 p.m., the enemy made a very determined assault upon my lines, covering a great part of the front. The attack was strongest from the left up to the Plank Road. The enemy was finally and completely repulsed at 5 o'clock. The ammunition being almost exhausted, and the hour for Burnside's attack not having arrived, I did not advance, but threw skirmishers out in pursuit. I wish now to know whether to make the assault you mentioned. I find some slight prospect of attacking farther up the Brock Road, but it may be only skirmishers, but still I do not like to leave my position to make an advance with this uncertainty. The enemy's attack was continuous along my line and exceedingly vigorous. Toward the close one brigade of the enemy (Anderson's brigade) took my first line of rifle-pits from a portion of the Excelsior Brigade, but it was finally retaken by Colonel Carroll. The attack and the repulse was of the handsomest kind. Please send me your orders.[36]

Lyman's reassuring endorsement and Hancock's summary report were in Meade's hands by 5:45 p.m., when the chief of staff instructed Warren to recall the troops just sent to Hancock. Humphreys explained that these troops "have been halted by the Major General commanding upon hearing from General Hancock that his line was not broken, though the outer rifle-pit was taken from the Excelsior Brigade; but immediately retaken by Carroll." [37]

Doubtful that he had made himself entirely clear in his report of 5:25 regarding the proposed offensive operation, Hancock hastily elaborated his views, stating at 5:30 that his wagons had been sent a considerable distance to the rear on account of the enemy's assault that morning and were now too far back to deliver a fresh supply of ammunition. His best troops, he pointed out, were those whose ammunition was most depleted. Furthermore, the enemy appeared to be somewhat active on his right, where there was a degree of disorder among his own troops that required correction. "Therefore," he urged, "my opinion is adverse, but I wait your order." [38]

The reasoning of the left wing commander convinced army headquarters that the advance would be inadvisable. Hancock's message was acknowledged at 5:45 p.m. by army headquarters with the statement: "The Major-General commanding directs that you do not attack today. Remain as you are for the present." [39] As an afterthought and perhaps with some implication of censure, Meade instructed Hancock to send for his ammunition wagons and have them close up with his corps.[40]

Commanding Wills in Deadlock

In an undated dispatch, but undoubtedly sent at the same time if not earlier, Grant advised Burnside that:

> General Hancock has been severely engaged for some time, the enemy having forced his line in one place, but being immediately repulsed. In consequence of this, orders have been sent Hancock suspending the order to attack at 6 p.m. In your movements for the balance of the day, or until you receive further orders, hold your own and be governed entirely by circumstances. Should the enemy attack Hancock, give such aid as you can. After dark, and all is quiet, put your men in a good position for defense and for holding our line, and give your men all the rest they can get.[41]

Grant here clearly relinquished the offensive he had seized at 7:34 a.m. of the 5th and had pursued with implacable determination throughout that day, intensifying his attacks until dark and then, continuing the offensive on the 6th, held resolutely to his purpose until the repeated counter-blows of

Longstreet and Lee had brought the battle to a stalemate. Where Grant had refused, on the night of the 5th, to sanction the additional repose asked for his men by Meade, he now instructed Burnside to withdraw from the enemy's front and give his men all the rest they could get.

Lee at the same time had failed to out-maneuver his adversary in the Wilderness and deal the punishment he had inflicted the year before on Hooker. Now these two powerful wills stood in temporary deadlock.

Chapter 25

DARKNESS STAYS GORDON'S ATTACK

The Battle of the Wilderness was not destined to end with the complete appearance of the deadlock it had actually assumed when Grant instructed Burnside to withdraw from the enemy's front and permit his men to rest. Gordon's spectacular feat on the left of Ewell's line came as a sort of anti-climax to Lee's tremendous attack on the Plank Road. But, like the fighting on the right, this daring stroke missed its aim and despite appearances of a blow that all but staggered the Army of the Potomac, it only served to tighten the deadlock that really set in when Lee determined, either through faulty judgment, or by reason of a sound analysis of the situation, to stay the pursuit of Birney's routed columns.

Gordon Plans to Hit Sedgwick's Right

The story of Gordon's adventure is obscure, though his own narrative leaves little to doubt.[1] After the collapse of Seymour's attack on Early's front during the forenoon, the enterprising Gordon reconnoitered to his left front and discovered the right of Sedgwick's line. It appeared that the Confederate line overlapped the Federals and that a thick belt of woods extended some 400 yards northward from Seymour's flank to an open field on the right bank of Flat Run. According to Gordon's report of his observations, the whole Federal right wing was apparently occupied with repeated assaults on the front of Edward Johnson's Division, who held the sector between Early's Division and the Turnpike. Elated by this discovery, Gordon then sent scouting parties to the rear of the enemy's line. After penetrating a distance of two or more miles his scouts returned and reported that no supports could be found, and that the only precautionary measure taken by the enemy was the posting of vedettes.[2]

All the requirements for a flank attack appeared to be present. An ideal *place des armes* to which the attackers could march under perfect concealment and form at right angles to the enemy's line, was within striking distance of their target. The enemy was preoccupied with heavy fighting on the other flank. Provision for the security of his right was inadequate. Gordon hastened to division headquarters. Upon learning that General Early had gone to the north side of Flat Run to confer with Brigadier General R. D. Johnston, whose brigade had just marched in from Hanover Junction and was taking position at the extreme left of the Confederate line, Gordon reported the situation to General Ewell, recommending that he be permitted to attack with his own brigade, properly supported.[3]

The corps commander appears to have been favorably impressed by the proposal. He was reluctant, however, to act without first consulting General Early, Gordon's division commander.[4]

Early Reluctant to Attack

The matter was referred to Early upon his return from the left of the line. The division commander was emphatic in his opposition to the proposed operation, pointing to "the danger and risk of making the attack under the circumstances, as a column was threatening our left flank and Burnside's corps was in rear of the enemy's flank on which the attack was suggested." He added, according to his own version of the affair, that the "impolicy of the proposal was obvious." "Failure," he insisted, "would involve disaster not only to the corps, if the enemy showed enterprise, but to the entire army."[5]

Early's objections are entitled to consideration, not altogether because he opposed his brigadier's suggestion and gives a deprecatory version of the whole affair, but on account of the fact that he had just returned from the extreme left flank, where there were indications of threatening activity on the part of the enemy. Early had good reason to apprehend an enemy movement down the Flat Run Road, which ran from Beal's farm on the Germanna Plank Road, along the divide between Russell Run and Flat Run to Robertson's Tavern where his trains were parked. In summarizing his objections, he emphasized that there was no reserve to call upon.

The reference in Gordon's report of intense fighting on the front of Edward Johnson would imply that General Early was on the extreme left of the Confederate line while Ferrero's 4th Division of the IX Corps was, between 7 and 9 a.m., relieving Marshall's provisional brigade of the IX Corps. This unit, it will be recalled, had taken over from Wilcox's Division, IX Corps, the picketing of roads leading westward past the Confederate left toward Jacob's Mill and Robertson's Tavern.[6]

An appreciation of Early's point of view tends to substantiate the force of his objection. A turning movement in the direction of Robertson's Tavern constituted a threat with which Ewell would find great difficulty in dealing. Aware of this danger, Early had no means of judging that the presence of both Ferrero's division and Marshall's provisional brigade—a total force consisting of seven infantry and two strong heavy artillery regiments, together with four cavalry regiments and two batteries of light artillery—was not an offensive disposition. Exhausted after their forced march from Hanover Junction, R. D. Johnston's four North Carolina regiments could scarcely have appeared to Early as capable of holding the wide sector between Flat Run and Germanna Ford against the large forces that appeared to be gathering on the Jacob's Mill and Flat Run roads.[7] Furthermore, Early was not in a position to verify the fact that the greater portion of Burnside's corps had moved from the Federal right toward the center. The consideration that Marshall's pickets seemed to be receiving large reinforcements, including cavalry and artillery, would tend to convince one in Early's position that Burnside, or a considerable portion of his command, was still in reserve to the Federal right and that vigorous action was contemplated there.

Within certain limits, Early's estimate of the general situation was fairly accurate. A portion of Burnside's corps—Stevenson's division—was in reserve. Held until about 8 a.m. at Wilderness Tavern, Stevenson would have been available for the very purpose mentioned by Early—the smashing of an unsupported attack on the Federal right flank and countering with a heavy movement around the Confederate left, which was without reserves and could hardly have withstood a renewed assault of VI Corps troops along its front, combined with a turning movement by IX Corps reserves and supported by the large forces known to be in front of R. D. Johnston's Brigade, on the extreme Confederate left.

In view of the general situation up until 8 a.m., Early's objections to the proposal for an attack on Seymour's right seem to have been well taken. Ewell concurred in the division commander's opinion. At the same time, an unsupported flank offered an invitation that few general officers of the Army of Northern Virginia could resist; Ewell determined to investigate the matter for himself.[8]

General Ewell received Gordon's report of his reconnaissance about 9 a.m.[9] His concurrence with Early, then, must have been between 9 and 10 o'clock. The rapidity of developments during this hour tended to remove most of the objections that Early had urged. At 9:30 Warren had received orders to suspend operations on the right and extend his left to prevent Confederate forces who had, according to report, followed Cutler's retreat and were threatening to turn the right of Grant's right wing. The general reserve under Stevenson had moved to the left, while Marshall's provisional brigade had crossed Flat Run to form a local reserve to Sedgwick at Spotswood's farm, near the Germanna Plank-Culpeper Mine Road intersection.[10] There were no indications of an aggressive attitude on the part of those Federal troops picketing the sector between Flat Run and the Rapidan.[11] Thus the shift of local and general reserves from the right toward the left, and the actual suspension of hostilities along the Federal right, tended to create a new situation in which Seymour's exposed flank became more inviting to attack than when originally proposed by Gordon. In reference to the difference of opinion between the brigadier and his division commander Ewell remarks: "This necessitated a personal examination which was made as soon as other duties permitted, but in consequence of this delay and other unavoidable causes the movement was not begun until nearly sunset." [12]

Early on his part does not admit being overruled by the corps commander and forced to participate in an operation that his better judgment condemned as dangerous and courting counter-measures of a disastrous nature. He claims that after removal of his principal objection, the threat from Burnside, he suggested the adoption of Gordon's proposal. Upon Early's endorsement of the scheme, Ewell ordered the movement. Early then planned the details of the operation.

Lee Approves Gordon's Plan

In his *Recollections,* Gordon offers still another version of the affair. Both Ewell and Early were overruled, according to Gordon, by Lee. The army commander, Gordon states, rode over to the left after his repulse on the Brock Road to inquire at Ewell's headquarters why the II Corps had not given greater cooperation during the day's fighting. Present at the time, Gordon spoke up in support of his scheme. Lee listened in frozen silence and then, disregarding the presence of Gordon's two senior officers, gave the brigadier personal directions to launch the attack.[13]

Gordon's version is open to serious question. In the first place, his testimony controverts both Early and Ewell, whose versions are in substantial agreement, and are positively opposed to Gordon on this last point. In the second place, Lee was not in the habit of ignoring the opinions of his corps commanders, even when in opposition to his own views. It may certainly be expected that Lee would have preserved the same punctilious attitude toward Ewell that Ewell himself had maintained toward Early.

Regardless of circumstances attending the conception and development of the scheme, it was determined about sunset to venture the attack. Gordon advanced from his trenches and formed in battle order in the open field opposite the flank of the Federal line. Without apparent molestation from Federal pickets on his front and, seemingly, without even knowledge of the movement on their part, R. D. Johnston crossed to the south side of Flat Run and placed his four North Carolina units in support to Gordon's six Georgia regiments. Johnston was assigned to the attack column with orders to follow Gordon and obey his orders. Early detailed Major Daniel, his Assistant Adjutant General, with a courier, to maintain communication with Gordon's moving column and enable Early to time the supporting attacks of his brigades in succession down the line, according to the progress of the flanking column. Early moved Pegram's Brigade into position to await Major Daniel's signal to begin the supporting movement.[14]

Given the sovereign advantage of surprise, the movement should, theoretically, have been progressive, both as to its ability to incite an increasing degree of disorganization and panic, and to increase the weight of its own striking power, as one brigade after another pivoted in and added its bayonets to the accumulating attack. The mechanics of Longstreet's flank movement had successfully operated on this principle. Unfortunately for Gordon's sanguine hopes there were practical limitations to such a movement.

In order to appreciate these limitations as well as the circumstances which gave the venture of the bold and enterprising young brigadier a degree of success that won the frank but somewhat grudging admiration of both his reluctant seniors, it is necessary to examine the state of affairs on the Federal right. Here indeed matters had come to a pass that seems difficult to understand.

Contraction of Sedgwick's Line

The V and VI Corps had been definitely assigned a passive role at 10:35 a.m., when both corps commanders were instructed to suspend their attacks, throw up defensive works, and report the number of effectives that might be released for an attack on Hancock's right.[15] Warren, as already stated, estimated that the entrenchment of his front and the adoption of purely defensive tactics would enable him to release an estimated force of 7,700.[16]

Sedgwick was less optimistic. Replying, he stated that:

> It (throwing up works) will be commenced at once. I am afraid that as soon as the work is commenced they will annoy us with shells and delay the work. They have four batteries in front of my line. It is my opinion to hold this line securely; not a regiment should be withdrawn. General Wright is strongly of that opinion. If absolutely necessary I can send Russell's brigade (Wright's Division) which has suffered least.[17]

The work of entrenching was rapidly pushed under the supervision of Captain Michler, the Army Engineer Officer, and his party of pioneers. Entrenching tools were passed from left to right. As the afternoon shadows lengthened and the eerie twilight crept into the deep forest, Seymour's brigade received the tools. Men stacked their rifles and set to work, with a skirmish line out to give warning of attack. Sedgwick then reported that his breastworks were nearly up, "except in some places where the men cannot work without drawing too much fire." Among these places was the front taken over by Shaler's brigade, who moved from a position in support to Seymour during the forenoon and extended the Federal line leftward. Sedgwick also expressed an opinion at this time that he might dispense with Morris' and Upton's brigades, but did not think "that it would be safe to reduce more." [18]

All the disposable troops of Warren and Sedgwick, which may now be estimated at approximately 10,000 (Warren's original 7,700 less 2,000 of Robinson sent to Hancock, plus 4,000 of Morris and 1,000 of Upton), were under requisition for the left. Here more than half the effective forces of the army group were now concentrated. Four divisions supported by 48 guns were strongly entrenched on that wing. But little attention was given to the extreme right of the line. Without artillery, without supports, and having only partially completed field works, this flank lay exposed in a manner that even the optimistic Gordon had not fully perceived.

On the covering flank beyond Flat Run, Ferrero's units had so completely lost contact with the Confederates that R. D. Johnston, when required on the south side of the Run, was able to slip away unobserved. Then heavy losses incurred by VI Corps brigades during their costly attacks on Ewell's front had caused a considerable contraction of the line to the left.[19] This necessarily drew in the right flank of Seymour's brigade from high ground in the woods, where it had been seen by Gordon during his morning reconnaissance, some distance southward and down into the bottom of the ravine of a brook flowing north and east toward Flat Run.[20]

In order to counteract the difficulty of holding a line that was dangerously overlapped by the enemy's front and continuously subjected to an enfilade fire of infantry and artillery, Brigadier General Alexander Shaler was ordered early in the forenoon to report to Seymour with his small brigade of three regiments—the 65th, 67th, and 122d New York.[21] General Shaler records in his personal diary that:

> I was ordered to form in 2d line in echelon in rear of his (Seymour's) right flank. The changes in the line to the left of this point made it necessary to occupy at once a part of the front line, and at Genl. Seymour's command I was obliged to relieve all the skirmishers on the flank and in front of the right battalion. This disposition left me but one regiment in the second line, and in a few minutes a regiment was called for to report to Genl. Neill, who occupied a position to the left of the road upon which we entered the field. This regiment, the 67th N. Y., was badly cut up, losing about 90 men out of 320. In a few hours it reported back to me, but not until we had moved forward and attacked the enemy's entrenchments. This operation cost many good officers and men and resulted in no earthly good. It shortened our lines so much that the 67th also had to (be) put in the front line, and the most extraordinary fact was seen that an army of 100,000 men had its right flank in the air with a single line of battle without entrenchments. I lost no time in informing Genl. Seymour that I would not be held responsible for any disaster that might befall the troops at this point, calling on him for at least 4,000 or 5,000 more men to properly defend that point.[22]

Shaler's plea for reinforcements fell on deaf ears. If Seymour made any representation to army headquarters concerning the difficult plight on his right, there is no record of the case. He himself was powerless to send the required reinforcements. His own report would indicate that with the best of will he could have done nothing on his own authority to rectify the perilous situation. He states: "The two brigades were now virtually in a single line, the One Hundred and Thirty-eighth (138th) New Pennsylvania and One Hundred and Tenth (110th) Ohio being alone held in the second line as supports." [23]

In truth the situation, as General Shaler indicates in his diary, called for a disposition similar to that on left, where Gibbon was given the authority of a provisional corps commander, with a force that was more than adequate for his needs. On the right flank, to the contrary, there was no general officer of sufficient rank and authority in command to impose his views on army headquarters. Ferrero with his covering force was directed by Grant to report to Sedgwick for orders; Shaler was put under command of Seymour, who had neither the force nor, it would seem, the ability to cope with the situation. Ten thousand disposable troops were massed at the center of the V and VI Corps line, standing in virtual idleness while army and general headquarters determined whether or not they should be sent to the left. Half that force—the number demanded by Shaler—would have secured the right. In this connection he remarks:

> This condition of affairs would in my judgment have been excusable to a degree had it been impossible to make other dispositions. But such was not the case. Within half a mile to our left were troops arranged in three lines of battle, and the corps had in it at least five general officers of distinguished ability, either one of whom would, with a reasonable force, have certainly averted the disaster which befell the troops at this point.[24]

As the sun sank behind the trees, Seymour's regiments had all but completed their breastworks. The left of his line met Neill's trenches at a wagon track which cut in a northeasterly direction through the trees toward the Culpeper Mine Road.

Crossing the trenchline at an angle, this crude road ran near the crest of the slope which drops down into the ravine where Seymour's right joined Shaler's left.[25] A short return trench, about 30 feet in length, on the right of Seymour's brigade line, ran along the brook flowing northeastward into Flat Run. The rank and file were still at work with pick and shovel, their arms stacked. The pickets were well out to the front. Their erratic fire betrayed the strain that recruit soldiers inevitably suffer when exposed over-long to wary and continuous sniping from hostile sharpshooters. Every puff of smoke, every stir of the branch of a tree excited ragged bursts of musketry. In this state of mind, hovering phantoms could no longer be distinguished from a charging line of battle.[26]

Shaler's three regiments extended the front in "a single attenuated line, where a strong, well supported one should have been" across the ravine and up to the crest of the prominence, where Seymour's right had originally rested.[27]

Gordon Attacks

About 6 p.m. Gordon's column of attack moved silently out from the field where his two brigades had formed. A swift advance of perhaps 200 yards into the woods brought the covering skirmishers in contact with Shaler's slender line of flankers. A brief exchange of fire sent them running back toward their supporting line of battle. Then the Rebel yell echoed through the forest. Gordon's Alabamians swept down on the flank; Johnston's North Carolinians swung around to the rear. Pegram's five Virginia regiments struck diagonally across the front, and, dispersing Seymour's picket, rushed with a roaring volley into his line. Men dropped their entrenching tools; some scrambled toward the rifle stacks; others ran to the rear, empty-handed.[28]

Shaler best describes the rout:

> The enemy moved against us in front, on the flank and in the rear, completely enveloping us in fire. The density of the woods prevented us from discovering their preparatory movements, and therefore the attack was something of a surprise. The attack in front would have been easily repulsed. But no

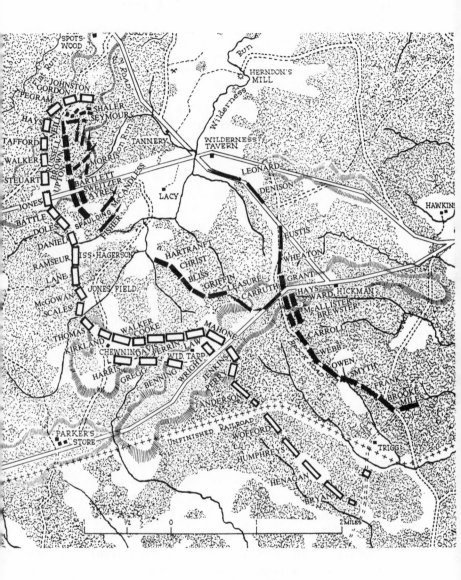

MAP 26. GORDON'S ATTACK

The situation at about 7:30 p.m., May 6. Gordon, supported by Pegram and Johnston, smashes Seymour and Shaler. VI Corps local reserves stop this attack. Crawford's division moves north to reinforce the Federal flank.

Lee now abandons his assault and commences to entrench along his front. On the Federal side, Burnside is also entrenching and connecting with Hancock's Brock Road line. The broken units of Wadsworth's division near the Lacy house have been omitted from this map.

troops in the world could stand an attack on their sides, and
they fell back in disorder. The enemy took advantage of the
discomfort of these eight regiments (Shaler's and Seymour's)
and seriously interrupted the composure of all those on the
line extending to the road upon which we extended.[29]

As the two right brigades gave way, the second line of Neill's
brigade changed front to rear and formed along the wagon
track which, skirting the crest along the south side of the
ravine, looked down along Seymour's trenches into the scene of
wild disorder below. Brigadier General Bidwell commanding
the brigade, and others who witnessed the rout, maintain that
Seymour's line was the first to break, leaving Shaler's three
regiments no alternative but immediate flight.[30]

The remnants of both brigades fled up the slope toward the
line Bidwell had thrown across the path of Gordon's assault.
Both Shaler and Seymour made desperate efforts to rally their
men and extend the line to the right, while Early's supporting
attack stormed against the front of Neill's brigade. This brigade
held the refused front, which momentarily stayed the torrent.
The remnants of Shaler's New York regiments formed on the
right rear. Seymour succeeded in rallying many of his men
and placing them in Bidwell's line. While riding out to intercept fugitives running by to the right, both brigadiers fell into
the hands of Gordon's pursuing Alabamians.

The defense that Shaler and Seymour had helped to build
stood fast. Gordon's right, colliding with the line, recoiled.
The 31st Georgia fell back in disorder; its commander, Colonel Clement Evans, rode back and informed General Early
of the repulse. Early ordered Pegram's Brigade, then maneuvering for position, to attack, Evans guiding the advance.[31]

The supporting attack, if Early's account is accurate, completely missed its target. Instead of swinging left on Neill's
front and striking in conjunction with Gordon on the refused
line, Colonel Hoffman, commanding Pegram's brigade, inclined in the falling dusk too far to the right, crossed the Culpeper Mine (Spotswood) Road, and struck at the front of one
of the brigades of Wright's division. Colonel Terrill's 13th

Virginia regiment, according to Early, "occupied part of the line when Hoffman ordered the brigade to retire on account of darkness and the confusion produced by the difficulties of the advance." [32]

While the supporting attack as described by Early miscarried, a confused battle raged in the gathering dark on the right rear of Neill's Brigade. The left of Gordon's Brigade and R. D. Johnston's North Carolinians, according to the confused accounts of subsequent fighting in various Federal reports, must have passed around to the right of the defensive barrier erected on Neill's exposed flank and then, instead of cutting in by their own right toward the rear of Wright's entrenchments, drove on to the left. Deprived of the progressive supporting attack which might have pried Wright's brigades out of their entrenched fronts, the ardent Confederates pursued in diminished force their leftward drive.

While devoid of military objectives, the rapid advance was productive of dangerous moral effects. A far-ranging detachment shot across the Germanna Plank Road and captured a group of Northern newspaper correspondents in full flight toward the Rapidan. [33] The stories released after a brief detention by these panic-stricken newsmen, were not calculated to enhance the prestige of the Army of the Potomac. An affrighted VI Corps staff officer fled to army headquarters and reported that General Sedgwick had been killed and the VI Corps routed. Stragglers drifting in to the crossroads at Wilderness Tavern gave credence to the tale.

Grant Stops a Panic

The elements of wholesale panic were present. One false step by the High Command and Lee would be given the victory he had despaired of winning. Grant, quietly studying the hysteria of the VI Corps officer, calmly removed the cigar from his mouth and said, "I don't believe it." Meade, his temper roused to an imperious pitch, ordered the officer under arrest for spreading false rumors. [34]

Confronted with an actual peril, instead of the shadow of

fear, army headquarters acted with great resolution and promptitude. Forgetting the left flank, measures were immediately taken to divert disposable reserves to the right.

The two VI Corps brigades that has been earmarked for movement to the left were now called upon to help restore the right. Captain Halsted of the VI Corps staff carried orders to Morris that he reinforce the broken flank with three regiments. Lieutenant Colonel Duffy, acting divisional inspector-general, called on Upton for two of his regiments. Warren in response to orders sent Crawford's division.

Under command of Brigadier General Morris, the 10th Vermont, 14th New Jersey, and 106th New York—fresh regiments with full ranks—moved off toward the sound of scattering fire on the right rear. The direction of advance diverged slightly from the line of Wright's entrenched front; Morris, while failing to join his left on the right of the temporary formation established across Neill's refused formation, was prevented by masses of retreating Federals from bringing his own right up on a front across the enemy's course of attack. He therefore determined, according to his report of the operation, to change front "so as to face the right, in order to injure the enemy as much as possible with my fire as he advanced."[35]

While completing this disposition, he sent an aide in search of General Sedgwick, to report his position and ask for further instructions. Morris' request brought Sedgwick with a large part of his staff galloping to the scene. The line was quickly established. Whether or not a connection on the left with Neill's refused flank was effected, the fact is not clearly stated. The subsequent maneuver of Upton on the right of Morris' line would indicate that these defensive requirements were satisfactorily fulfilled.

When notified of the break on the right and required to furnish two regiments from his brigade, Upton detailed the 121st New York and 95th Pennsylvania. Lieutenant Colonel Duffy led this force into the fray. With the intention of following the detachment as soon as possible, Upton sent for his horse and made arrangements for assigning his front line regiments to Colonel Penrose, commanding the 2d Brigade of his division.

Upton to the Rescue

It becomes difficult to relate the reports of Upton and Morris, as separate accounts of a series of movements that culminated in the establishment of a connected line. It appears that Upton's two regiments bore away to the right, diverging from the direction taken by Morris, and ran into hostile fire on his left. "The dense undergrowth," relates Upton, "necessarily lengthened out the column, and at the same time masses of men breaking through their ranks threw both regiments into unavoidable confusion."[36]

The flood of fugitives, to say nothing of the Confederate musketry impelling its course, swept diagonally from left front to right rear across the path of Duffy's advance. Under these circumstances, there was no alternative but to rally the straggling column on a secure defensive position. Duffy promptly threw the remaining elements of his force into a set of rifle pits that had been built to cover General Sedgwick's field headquarters.[37] Here a brief stand was made. Failing, however, to break the force of persistent attacks, Duffy's men quit the position and fell back through the woods.

Upton in the meantime had secured his horse and started after his detachment. Riding forward, he met stragglers in increasing numbers from Duffy's column. These he reformed and advanced with a view to reinforcing Duffy in the rifle pits.

"At every step," Upton reports, "officers and men who were falling back stated that there were no Union troops in front or on the right, from which latter direction bullets were then coming." In this difficult situation he discovered Morris' line which had been thrown back, according to Upton, to meet the attack. Upton promptly formed on the right of Morris and threw out two companies of the 95th Pennsylvania as skirmishers.[38]

As Upton consolidated his position darkness settled over the battlefield. The hostile fire died down. Denied the support essential to success by failure of Early's brigades to participate in the movement—as had Kershaw's and then Field's in the operation against the Federal left—Gordon broke off the attack and returned to his trenches.

Whether indicative of a want of harmony and consequent lack of precision in execution, or reflecting merely an honest difference of opinion, the conflicting claims of Early and Gordon suggest much interesting speculation. In his official report Gordon insists that only darkness and failure of a supporting attack on the Federal front withheld a victory of decisive proportions. He claims that:

> The rout was complete. Large numbers left their arms at the works or threw them away, with knapsacks, haversacks, etc., in their flight. The enemy's killed, according to the count kept by the officer commanding pioneer corps, amounted to nearly 400, among them one brigade commander. Several hundred prisoners were captured, among these two brigade commanders—General Seymour and Shaler. Besides these, many hundreds were passed to the rear and made their escape in the darkness.
>
> I must be permitted in this connection to express the opinion that had the movement been made at an earlier hour and properly supported, each brigade being brought into action as its front was cleared, it would have resulted in a decided disaster to the whole right wing of General Grant's army, if not in its entire disorganization. The loss in my brigade amounted to about 50.[39]

Either in justification of his original opposition to the venture, or, conceivably by reason of his failure to execute the culminative movement by brigades down the line, General Early contends that only darkness averted a grave disaster to the Confederate left. He writes in his *Autobiography* that:

> Notwithstanding partial confusion, Gordon threw the Federal flank into great confusion. The advance of Pegram's Brigade and demonstration of (R. D.) Johnson in the rear, where it encountered part of the enemy's force and captured some prisoners, contributed materially to the results . . . .
> It was fortunate, however, that darkness came to close the affair, as the enemy, if he had been able to discover the disorder on our side, might have brought up fresh troops and availed himself of our condition. As it was, doubtless, the lateness of the hour caused him to be surprised, and the ap-

proaching darkness increased the confusion in his ranks, as he could not see the strength of the attacking force, and probably imagined it to be much more formidable than it really was. All of the brigades engaged in the attack were drawn back and formed on a new line in front of the old one, and obliquely to it.[40]

Comments

It is impossible, of course, to reconcile a conflict of personal opinions in a situation where the principals offer differing views to explain their want of success in a common enterprise, one censuring the other for an excess of zeal, while the reputedly overzealous party replies that his colleagues were unduly conservative and seemed reluctant from beginning to end to furnish the degree of cooperation and support that would have secured a sweeping victory.

It must be remembered that Gordon, after being raised to rank of major general at Spotsylvania, relieved Early in command of the Second Corps upon the latter's failure to realize Lee's expectations during his detached mission in the Shenandoah Valley and while the main force of the army lay entrenched at Petersburg. An embittered man, Early no doubt found little satisfaction in Gordon's brilliant subsequent career as commander of Jackson's old corps, winning laurels before the Army of Northern Virginia was ultimately compelled to lay down its arms at Appomattox. Yet Early had good reason to reflect that none of Gordon's achievements could compare with his own brilliant coup at Spotsylvania Court House when, temporarily commanding A. P. Hill's three divisions—Heth, Wilcox, and Mahone—he saved Lee's army from the converging movement of Hancock and Burnside, holding off one and striking at the other in a combination of beautifully balanced movements across the base of Lee's triangular formation. Here, indeed, he had good reason to reflect was a feat of arms that would have enhanced even the renown of Stonewall Jackson.

While these speculations may offer reasons for a tendency on Early's part to deprecate the extent of Gordon's flank movement in the Wilderness, and question the soundness of the operation, they offer little help in an analysis of facts of the situation. Early, it is obvious, contends that the unexpected disorder attending the first shock of Gordon's attack magnified its actual effect, and that the fall of darkness prevented the enemy from realizing this fictitious element of the situation. Gordon, on the other hand, regards the temporary disorder produced by the first impact of his own column as only a forecast of wholesale panic that a resolute development of the attack would have incited.

Perhaps the most significant aspect of the question is the silence of Ewell, the corps commander, on the point at issue between division and brigade commander. Had he played a role in this affair similar to that of Longstreet in the flank movement on the Confederate right, the results, if Gordon's view of the situation is sound, would have been as spectacular as those achieved by Longstreet. But the fact that Ewell did not act in such a manner would indicate that, while conceding certain limited possibilities in the movement as proposed by Gordon, he never went so far as to regard it other than a minor operation on the left of his line, and one that should be left to the judgment of the left division commander. In other words, Ewell, by his silence, commits himself on the side of Early.

One aspect of the problem remains unanswered. Did both Ewell and Early fail to grasp an opportunity that Gordon alone perceived? The answer to this question depends largely on the evidence submitted by Gordon himself. It seems doubtful that generals of the attested skill, prescience, and energy of Ewell and Early would have overlooked such an opportunity.[41]

In the midst of the turmoil on the Federal right, it is not difficult to understand that Gordon could have been as easily misled by the havoc he wrought, as were many of the Federals who quit the field in panic. General Shaler's description of the situation at the moment of his capture seems pertinent here. The general writes in his diary:

> By extraordinary efforts on the part of Sedgwick and other officers, the panic was stopped at the road (at the right flank of Neill's brigade) and a line formed to advance against the

enemy. I had contributed my efforts, and galloping to the right to collect what scattering men might have taken to the road to the rear, and to see to the more perfect organization of that part of the line, found myself in an instant surrounded by a dozen or more butternuts each having his gun pointed in the direction of my innocent carcass—a summons to surrender and dismount was answered precisely as a good soldier would obey any lawful order of his superior. To my extreme disgust and mortification I found myself a prisoner of war and captured by a dozen or more straggling vagabonds, who with half the number of my fellows, I could have driven from the woods and captured with ease. My sword was jerked from me by a nasty nosed ruffian, but in a moment after when the danger of my situation was over, an officer stepped from behind a tree and received it. My horse, my splendid stallion, was to share my fate. By a circuitous route I was taken to the rear and turned over to Capt. Page, inspector of Gordon's brigade of Georgia troops who treated me kindly, especially after I had given him my gold belt, which according to the value placed upon their money was worth 330 dollars. For this act of forced kindness I was permitted to ride 2½ miles on an old nag which could be sold in N. Y. for 20 shillings. Here at Locust Grove, I met Genl. Seymour who was captured a few minutes before. We were very kindly treated by Col. Seward, Insp. Gen. of Ewell's Corps and furnished with a comfortable bed and breakfast.[42]

Shaler's account implies that Gordon's column had become badly disordered by the time it struck the line refused along the woods road at the right of Neill's brigade. This observation substantiates Early's comment as to the rapid disintegration of Gordon's attack column.

If these two independent estimates of the situation are to be regarded as reliable, it would appear that the force of Gordon's attack was spent by the time he had rolled up the thin and ill-prepared fronts of Shaler and Seymour and that it recoiled against the first solid line faced in the direction of the attack. Under these conditions, a supporting attack on the entrenched front of the Federal line between Neill's right and the turn-pike could have made little impression.

The panic that spread toward army headquarters appears to have been incited by R. D. Johnston's movement across the right rear of the Federal line. Swinging out instead of turning in toward the rear of the Federal trenches, Johnston apparently hastened the steps of scattered fugitives and then collided with Morris' and Upton's detachments. That the excitement at army headquarters was superficial and quickly dispelled is indicated by General Humphreys, who records in his *Virginia Campaign* that:

> Soon after this flank attack began, staff officers of the Sixth Corps rode in to General Meade's Headquarters and informed me (General Meade was at General Grant's headquarters nearby) that in endeavoring to carry a dispatch to the right of their line they found that it had just been broke and rolled up; that the enemy occupied the position, and that part of them were advancing down the Germanna Plank road on our right and rear, following the fugitives from Shaler's and Seymour's brigades; and they added that probbly both Sedgwick and Wright were captured. I at once made dispositions to meet this with the Provost Guard and some troops that General Warren had sent me (Crawford's Division) and the reserve artillery nearby, and then sent notice of the affair to General Meade, who at once came over with General Grant. Soon the staff officers whom I had sent up the Germanna road to rally the fugitives returned, reporting there was no enemy on it; reports from a brigade of Warren's corps sent in the same direction confirmed their report, and then information was received from General Sedgwick and General Wright showing the actual condition of the corps.
>
> I have mentioned these details because exaggerated statements concerning this affair, which quickly spread through the army, gave rise, I think, to unfounded rumors.[43]

The burden of Humphrey's testimony here is that, although considerable panic was spread by the first shock of Gordon's attack, the defense had been stabilized before the Confederates could exploit the situation by pressing a relentless pursuit. Neither Gordon nor Early had sufficient force in hand to develop the movement beyond its initial phase of success. If ever intended as a major offensive operation, the planning was quite as faulty as that for the corresponding defense dispositions of the Federals.

Meade Refuses His Right

The danger, as well as the poor economy of attempting to hold a front that had long since been deprived of its offensive possibilities, led to a belated decision to refuse the entire right.

Pivoting at the point of junction of Warren's reserve trenches with the Turnpike, a line was traced northeastward along the watershed between the upper course of Caton Run and Wilderness Run. Cutting across the lower course of Caton Run at the southward bend of the stream, the line continued over the Germanna Plank Road and along high ground, looking northwestward into a south flowing branch of the run and terminating at a slight elevation some 2,500 yards from its pivot on the Turnpike. Shortening the advanced line by more than 2,000 yards, and interposing the densely wooded ravine of Caton Run between Ewell's front and the sector extending diagonally across from the pivot on the Turnpike to the crossing of Germanna Plank Road, the new front was undoubtedly the strongest natural position along the entire line.

After the trace had been marked out, V and VI Corps troops were withdrawn from the trenches paralleling the Turnpike, where the defenders had endured a ceaseless enfilade from Confederate batteries and from those facing Ewell's front north of the Turnpike, where troops had suffered a continuous bombardment without support from their own guns. Pickets were left to cover the movement.

By dawn the new lines were manned, VI Corps troops taking over the extreme right of the front and joining the V Corps flank some distance north of the road. A pall of smoke lay over the battlefield; forest fires smoldered on every sector of the front.

During the course of the day, Burnside connected his right with the left of the V Corps and entrenched his entire front. He established contact on the left with Hancock's right. All detached troops joined their respective corps. Entrenched along its entire front, Grant's army group was formed from right to left in the order, VI Corps-V Corps-IX Corps-II Corps, with Sheridan's cavalry on the left rear.

Lee completed the entrenchment of his front, carrying the system of field works from Ewell's right in two parallel lines over Chewning's plateau to the Plank Road and thence by a single line across the unfinished railroad. Ewell advanced his

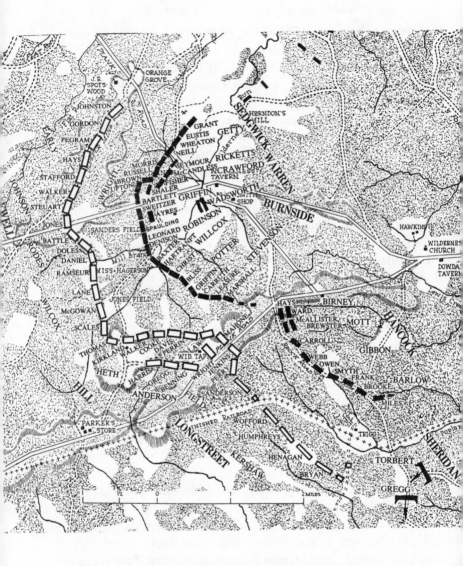

MAP 27. THE MORNING OF MAY 7

By morning of May 7 most brigades have rejoined their divisions, and the corps are again sorted out. Meade has refused his north flank, and both sides are continuing to entrench. Sheridan's cavalry has been relieved of its mission of guarding the trains, being replaced by Ferrero's division. Sheridan withdrew his cavalry, somewhat, after Hancock's reverse on the 6th, but later reoccupied his line covering the Federal south flank. Sheridan is now moving Torbert and Gregg to Todds Tavern, and Wilson (off the map) is at Piney Branch Church. Only light skirmishing occurs on this day. The battle is over.

line north of the Turnpike to high ground looking across the ravine of Caton Run, entrenching this sector and enclosing both Federal and Confederate trench lines that had been thrown up during the 5th and 6th. Lee's three corps were formed in the order, II-III-I, from left to right, with the cavalry on the extreme right facing Sheridan.

Aside from the secure right flank, the Federal line was far from satisfactory. Warren complained that the high ground toward Parker's Store commanded his entire front. "We are not strong here," he insisted, "commensurate with the importance of the position, and if the whole army lies quiet and they concentrate upon us, we may be driven out."[44]

The advantage of closing the interval across Chewning's plateau, which Grant had denied Lee on the 5th, was now apparent to Warren. Then Burnside's line was too long for the number of holding troops. Then, finally, the chronic fear concerning Hancock's left was revived by discovery of the overlapping Confederate line. The II Corps Commander was apprehensive on this score, causing considerable delay in the return of units to their various corps.

These difficulties, no doubt, would have prevented the renewal of hostilities in the Wilderness had not Grant already taken the decision to move by the left and seek battle on more favorable ground.[45]

CHAPTER 26
GRANT AND LEE

Recall of Gordon's attack column and refusal of the Federal right across the Germanna Plank Road signified that the Army of Northern Virginia had spent its offensive power and that the Federal army group, though driven to cover, was still a formidable antagonist.

Both armies had maneuvered on May 5th for favorable positions from which to launch offensive action. In the fighting attending these efforts Grant on the whole retained the upper hand, preserving the initiative he had seized when he abandoned his turning movement against the Confederate right rear and struck in succession at Lee's elements as they arrived on the line of deployment. In pressing these attacks Grant prevented Lee from closing the gap in his front across the Chewning plateau and thus denied the Confederate commander the conditions he sought in developing his offensive plan of action. Clearly the first day's battle was a partial victory for Grant.

The early dawn of May 6 looked upon a Confederate army in dire straits. Wearied by beating off two violent attacks on the 5th, Ewell, holding the left, now faced an enemy counting twice the number of bayonets he could call into action. If grave on the left, the situation on Lee's right was one of stark desperation. Saved from annihilation only by the fall of darkness on the 5th, the shattered elements of A. P. Hill's III Corps could offer but feeble resistance to the massive Federal columns poised for the attack at dawn. Longstreet's Corps, in line of march to the front, was overdue.

In the action of May 6 Grant attempted to exercise to the full the initiative he had seized and maintained on the 5th. During the initial phase of the onset at dawn, two of his three offensive elements failed to deliver their attacks with a violence and rapidity that assured the culminating fury of concerted action. Sedgwick and Warren together were unable to prevent Ewell from releasing the troops that delayed Burnside's advance through the gap in Lee's line.

Burnside, instead of timing his advance across Hill's left rear with Hancock's successful drive along the Plank Road ridge, or striking later at Longstreet's left in concert with the renewal of Hancock's offensive effort, procrastinated in a manner that confirmed beyond all doubt the aptness of the sobriquet he had earned as the Sluggard of Antietam. Deprived of the advantage that should have resulted from Warren's and Sedgwick's holding attacks, together with the quickening effects of Burnside's expected blow, Hancock's assault column not only failed to destroy the broken units of Hill's holding force, but was unable to foil Longstreet's counter-stroke.

While Longstreet's swift riposte restored the stricken Confederate right and transferred the initiative to Lee, the Confederate commander was unable to exploit the advantage suddenly thrust into his hands. Either overestimating the disorder and consequent immobility of his troops at the culmination of Longstreet's flank movement, or underestimating the degree of demoralization among Hancock's routed units and therefore failing to balance nicely the hazardous prospects of immediate pursuit against future possibilities of a well-ordered advance on a reorganized line of defense, Lee postponed the assault and permitted the fleeting promise of victory to elude his grasp. Continuation of the counteroffensive died out in two indecisive attacks. One, recoiling from the center of Hancock's entrenched line, at least secured the advantage of averting a renewal of the Federal offensive against Lee's right, as planned for 6 p.m.; the other, after compelling Grant to draw back his right wing, served only to tighten the deadlock that in reality set in when Longstreet was borne on his litter to the rear.

In the last act of this thundering drama, Lee delivered the final thrust; Grant executed the final retrograde movement— an obvious change of theme from the one initiated by Grant on the morning of the 5th when he took the offensive and attempted to destroy Lee before he could complete his concentration. With the Federal right sharply refused, Lee was in a position to deny Grant the use of his communications by way of the Germanna Plank Road to Brandy Station, on the Orange and Alexandria Railroad. In the withdrawal of Sheridan's cavalry on the left, Grant had temporarily relinquished command of the crossroads at Todd's Tavern and consequent freedom of movement by the Brock Road toward open ground beyond the Wilderness. Lee, moreover, had occupied and fortified the Chewning plateau, a circumstance that gravely threatened the center of the Federal line and made a continuation of offensive operations in the Wilderness more hazardous than those already attempted.

There can be no doubt that Lee, in a limited tactical sense, had the advantage. The test of victory, however, hinged on his ability to prevent any action that Grant might take in removing the disabilities incurred by reason of the tactical reverse he had suffered on the 6th. In other words, was Lee in a position to compel his adversary either to fight the battle to its finish in the Wilderness or to retreat across the river line, as Hooker had done the year before.

But Lee did neither. He made no effort to occupy the Germanna Plank Road between Grant's refused right and the Rapidan. Nor did he attempt to strengthen his hold on Todd's Tavern against the superior cavalry force that Sheridan could throw against that point.

At 6:30 a.m. on the morning of the 7th Grant transmitted a directive to Meade, instructing the army commander to "make all preparations during the day for a night march, to take position at Spotsylvania Court House." Meade promptly ordered Brig. Gen. Edward Ferrero, commanding the Negro division of the IX Corps, to proceed to Chancellorsville and Dowdall's Tavern and, after posting a brigade at each point, "to report to . . . Major General Sheridan for further orders." At the same time Meade apprised the cavalry commander that:

You are already authorized to make such offensive dispositions against the enemy as consistent with the security of the trains. A division of colored troops having been ordered to assist you in the protection of the trains, you are again authorized to detach any portion of your command for offensive operations, cutting the enemy's communications &c.

Released from the onerous duty of watching the wagon parks, Sheridan clattered with all his suppressed ardor across the Furnace-Brock Road intersection and down to Todd's Tavern, where he met and scattered the Confederate cavalry. Extending his left to Piney Branch Church, he reoccupied the cavalry line he had established on the night of May 5.

Aside from local resistance offered by his cavalry, Lee made no attempt to dispute Sheridan's offensive action. Nor did he extend his left across the Germanna Plank Road. That is, Lee was unable or unwilling to exploit for strategic purposes the transient tactical gains that the refusal of his adversary's flanks appeared to have conferred on him. Without molestation from Lee, Grant restored liberty of movement to the left.

This reasoning encounters the objection that Sheridan's cavalry operations of May 7 should be regarded as the opening phase of the Battle of Spotsylvania Court House, an operation of even greater violence than the one waged in the Wilderness and, indeed, which was forced on Grant by the need of redeeming his repulse in the forest battle. Then, in keeping with this tactical quibble, it may be argued that since Grant's supply line by way of Germanna Ford and Brandy Station appears to have been threatened, he had no alternative other than abandonment of his battle front in the Wilderness and adoption of a new line of operations which could be supported by waterborne communications through Chesapeake Bay into the estuary of the Rappahannock. Thus his withdrawal from Lee's battle front, together with the shift of communications, should be regarded as a retreat, as Lee did during the night of May 7 and the early morning hours of the 8th. Some Confederate writers still retain this belief, despite the fact that Grant "retreated" in the direction of **Richmond**.

Such reasoning is refuted by the fact that the Orange and Alexandria Railroad lost its importance to Grant as a supply line after the crossing of the Rapidan. Before quitting the north bank he had taken the necessary precautions to abandon this line by sending back the rolling stock to Manassas Junction. With this purpose in mind, he carried sufficient supplies in the Great Trains—his moving base—to subsist his army group until his "floating reserve" could be moved through the Bay to one of the many suitable depots—Fredericksburg, Belle Plain, or Port Royal—in the estuary of the Rappahannock; White House Landing at the head of the York estuary; or City Point in the mouth of the James River.

A broader view of the problem should take into consideration the fact that Lee's army was Grant's objective and that the vast preparations made for continuous movement across the northern and eastern approaches to Richmond were directed to a single purpose—destruction of the Army of Northern Virginia. It therefore seems reasonable to regard the movement from the Rapidan to the entrenchments girding Richmond and Petersburg as a sustained conflict, its storm center sweeping from May 5 to June 18 in a vast semi-circle around the Confederate Capital and really constituting a single battle in the modern sense of the term. In this light, it should be most logically designated as the Battle of Virginia.

It is, therefore, the first violent phase of this 44-day battle with which we are concerned—the movement of the contending armies from their winter cantonments into the Wilderness and the fighting that raged during the 5th and 6th of May in the dreary woodland. To what extent then did either Grant or Lee contribute to their respective aims in seeking this test of strength or, to couch the question in other words, to what degree did one or the other suffer retardation of his preconceived strategic purpose?

A positive answer is obscured by the fact that the 44-day battle, like the meeting engagement in the Wilderness, ended in a tactical draw. Just as the Army of Northern Virginia repelled Grant's offensive thrust on the morning of May 6, so this same army stood firm in the Petersburg works during the assault of June 15-18. Lee had frustrated Grant's determination to destroy the Army of Northern Virginia; Grant had succeeded in driving Lee from the Rapidan-Rappahannock line. The cost, however, had been exorbitant. The appalling loss of life had strengthened a large body of opinion in the North, which openly advocated a negotiated peace with the Confederacy. Early in the Presidential campaign of 1864 Lincoln despaired of reelection. The tide of defeatist sentiment was reversed, not by military events on the Richmond-Petersburg front, but by the fall of Atlanta, together with Sheridan's spectacular triumph over Early at Cedar Creek and the psychological lift given by Farragut's personal heroism in the Battle of Mobile Bay.

The valor of a great sea fighter did much to mollify resentment over the sickening slaughter of the masses. Lashed to the foremast of his flagship to avert the consternation should he fall to the deck below, the doughty admiral surveyed the scene of battle from a vantage point similar to the one now enjoyed by a fleet commander in his conning tower, but without the protection of encasing steel. Steaming straight over the minefield that had taken one ship from the line, Farragut roared through his speaking trumpet the order that sent a thrill through the nation: "Damn the torpedoes. Full speed ahead!"

Lincoln's reelection meant predominance of the war party and the inevitable doom of the Confederacy. Lee's masterly conduct of tactical operations during the 44-day battle of attrition would have given a strategic decision in the politico-military sphere had not the achievements of Sherman, Sheridan, and Farragut reversed the tide of defeatism in the North. After the November election there remained but one despairing hope for the Confederacy—a junction of the two principal field armies, with the expectation that Lee's genius might achieve the miracle of defeating Sherman and Grant in detail. But here the decision was primarily a political one; the Government of the Confederacy was unequal to such an ordeal. Lee overstayed his time in Virginia.

There remains another aspect of the Wilderness battle that requires attention. This concerns the interpretation or estimates of the situation which both commanders formulated in their minds at the dawn of May 7, when the first summary reports of their corps and division commanders had been appraised. Regardless of the final outcome of the campaign, it is important to understand just how these two adversaries reacted on the morrow of battle in the light of their understanding of the issue of events.

Grant, we know, withdrew from his battle line in the Wilderness because the position became untenable after Lee's occupation of the Chewning plateau. But it is difficult to regard this movement as a retreat, any more than his withdrawal from the front of Lee's position on the North Anna River can be so regarded. In this instance he moved by his left flank, and again toward Richmond, rather than risk the hazards of a frontal attack.

Lee's inability to prevent these flanking movements indicate a failure on his part to realize the strategic purpose he expressed to President Davis on April 15: "If I am obliged to retire from this line (the Rapidan-Rappahannock River line) either by a movement of the enemy or want of supplies, great injury would befall us." Lee, in short, fought in the Wilderness for the same reason that had determined his decision to fight at Fredericksburg in December 1862 and at Chancellorsville in May 1863, namely to hold the river line as the military frontier of Virginia.

Further exploration of the problem becomes involved in controversial aspects of the movement on Spotsylvania Court House. If, as Dr. Douglas S. Freeman argues in his interpretation of this battle, Lee divined Grant's advance by the left on Spotsylvania Court House and interposed his I Corps across Warren's advance on the Brock Road, it logically follows that, given Lee's preconceived strategic aim, he was compelled to abandon the line of the Rapidan-Rappahannock in order to cope with Grant's unimpaired freedom of movement toward Richmond. If, on the other hand, Lee sent the I Corps to occupy the road junction at Spotsylvania Court House on the assumption that indications of movement during the 7th behind the Federal lines pointed to a retirement down the Rapidan to Fredericksburg—and that in such an eventuality he was determined to follow the Federal retreat—then it seems reasonable to assume that Lee moved from the Wilderness with a view to fighting another battle for preservation of the river line. So much is implied in his dispatch to the Confederate Secretary of War early on May 8. It is important to note that Lee speaks of being in motion on Grant's right, meaning of course that the Federals were in retreat. He could not have followed on the left rear without incurring the danger of putting a hostile force between his own army and Richmond. His dispatch to the Secretary reads: "The enemy has abandoned his position and is moving toward Fredericksburg. This army is in motion on his right flank, and our advance is at Spotsylvania Court House."

Taking the literal interpretation, it would appear that Lee did not regard his two-day battle with Grant as a defeat in any sense of the word. On the contrary, he made the mistake of thinking that he had defeated his adversary. With this faulty premise in mind, he was misled by Sheridan's cavalry offensive of May 7, construing it as an operation to cover a quick withdrawal to Fredericksburg.

Assuming that Grant was actually in retreat toward Fredricksburg, Lee instructed Anderson, commanding Longstreet's Corps, to withdraw from the front and, after resting his troops, to proceed to Spotsylvania Court House on the morning of the 8th. Unable to find suitable camping space in the burning forest, Anderson sought and obtained permission to march during the night. He was forming his command in column as Warren's V Corps started down the Brock Road. Then Sheridan's unaccountable lapse in neglecting to issue orders for operations of his divisional units in covering the infantry advance, as indicated by Meade at 3 p.m., contributed to the circumstances that enabled Lee to avert the full consequences of his mistake. As the head of the V Corps column approached

Todd's Tavern at midnight, Warren found his road blocked by the bivouacs of Merritt's and Tobert's cavalry divisions. The time lost in routing out the sleeping troopers and clearing hostile cavalry from the Brock Road enabled Anderson to reach the Court House and entrench while Warren was still in column of march. As indicated in his dispatch to the Confederate Secretary of War, Lee was unaware of any race to Spotsylvania Court House until he learned that Anderson had won the course.

Any final conclusions regarding the results of the fighting of May 5 and 6 in the Wilderness thus involves a careful survey of the 13-day operation around Spotsylvania Court House, the successive phases of which are, in many respects, as closely related to fight of May 6 as is this action to the encounter engagement of the 5th in the Wilderness. It is, in fact, difficult to single out and assign an aspect of decisive importance to any particular engagement in the vast swing around Richmond. The decisive aspect was the accumulative effect of the movement—not any one of the hammer blows with which Grant pounded Lee on the anvil of Richmond, while Sherman's devouring host swept through the granary of the deep South.

Yet the Battle of the Wilderness has a meaning unique in military history. The encounter ended with the armies facing one another across the wreckage wrought by the first trial of strength between Robert E. Lee, dreaded opponent of the Army of the Potomac, and Ulysses S. Grant, hero of the war in the West. Both armies paid a staggering price in fighting to a tactical impasse. Grant counted 17,666 casualties, representing 14 per cent of his effective strength. Unknown, Lee's losses are thought to be in same ratio to his total force. This estimate gives approximately 8,700 in killed, wounded, and missing.

With all the later condemnation of Grant's exorbitant wastage of manpower in execution of his so-called "bludgeon tactics," these losses were less than those sustained by the Army of the Potomac in its two preceding encounters with

Lee at Chancellorsville and Gettysburg. Then, while the wastage of life proceeded at an appalling rate at Spotsylvania Court House, Cold Harbor, and during the first general assault on the lines at Petersburg, it must be taken into consideration that the actual hours of fighting during the frightful march from the Rapidan to the lines of Petersburg far exceeds those of any similar period of time during the American Civil War and, indeed, anticipates the furious tempo of contemporary warfare.

Grant was undoubtedly inferior to Lee in the art of directing an army on the battlefield, and lacked the Virginian's fine sensibilities in appreciating the human element behind roaring musketry and thundering artillery. He was also less successful in exacting the utmost of effort from his lieutenants and the rank and file without impairing their morale. Nevertheless Grant possessed to a greater degree the clear-sighted vision of the grand strategist, foreseeing prospective lines of operations with respect to disposable forces and means of movement, and sensing those points at which a tactical triumph, if correctly timed, would be attended with strategic consequences of far-reaching importance. Moreover, his strategic insight was propelled by an undaunted optimism and an implacable will that seems brutal in the vast application of its power.

This optimism and quality of will were characteristics that none of the generals who led the Army of the Potomac exhibited in battle against Lee. Yet, Burnside excepted, all were soldiers of equal if not superior tactical ability in comparison to Grant. A similar comparison stands between Grant as generalissimo and the three former generals in chief of the Army. These were leaders of exceptional merit—Scott, the superb but aging field marshal, McClellan, the creator and most beloved of the commanders of the Army of the Potomac, and Halleck, despite a multitude of petty faults that disqualified him from command in the field, an able military administrator and justly entitled to much credit as an organizer of victory in the West.

These men grappled with the problems of applying anti-
quated maxims and archaic forms of staff organization to a
revolutionary situation in waging war. The traditions and
experience of the young republic were ill-adapted to the task
of transforming its potentials into striking power on the field
of battle. The growing National Army was naively regarded
as a new and alluring field for the extension of political
patronage; the procurement and supply of the forces became
a lucrative supplement to the time-honored pork barrel; strategic programs took the guise of political platforms, with
violent adherents contending for a particular plank, and advancing the interests of a favorite general.

Yet out of this chaos came a scheme of grand strategy, growing like a medieval cathedral under the hands of unknown
craftsmen. Grant, the master artisan, grasped the unity of the
plan. Lincoln, the supreme architect, completed and adorned
the facade, as it were, inspiring in such utterances as his Gettysburg Address and Second Inaugural a profound sense of dedication to the task of preserving the Federal Union. To this
force of public opinion he harnessed a supreme military command, lacking, it is true, a general headquarters or a War
Department general staff, but far superior to any instrument
of high command evolved by the Confederacy.

Without Lincoln's statemanship, Grant's strategic insight
and implacable will would have been wasted, as had the talents
of many promising soldiers during the formative period of the
war. Although Grant himself had fallen into disfavor after
Donelson, again after Shiloh and, following his great triumph
at Vicksburg, had lapsed into a virtual state of retirement,
Lincoln perceived his salient characteristic. In reply to de-
tractors he said: "I cannot spare him. He fights."

Early the morning of May 7, 1864, Grant justified this faith
in his directive instructing Meade to advance on Spotsylvania
Court House. In the terse phrases of the military document
that he penned, Grant translated to the soldiers of his command the meaning of Lincoln's Gettysburg address.

As Warren's V Corps, the leading element in the advance

on Spotsylvania Court House, filed in rear of the II Corps line, Hancock's infantrymen waited tensely behind their battered breastworks. Would the column turn eastward on the Orange Plank Road, thereby announcing a retreat, or continue southward on the Brock Road toward another battleground beyond the Wilderness? When the head of the dark column went straight on past the intersection, prolonged cheers echoing through the burning forest aroused a blaze of musketry from Confederate pickets in warning of an impending attack. Thus did the rank and file of the Army of the Potomac dedicate themselves to the cause for which so many of their comrades had given their "last full measure of devotion."

APPENDIX A—TABLES OF ORGANIZATION

THE UNION ARMY
Lieutenant General Ulysses S. Grant
Escort: B, F and K, 5th U. S. Cav., Capt. Julius W. Mason.
ARMY OF THE POTOMAC, Maj. Gen. George G. Meade.
Provost Guard, Brig. Gen. Marsena R. Patrick: C and D, 1st Mass. Cav., Capt. Edward A. Flint; 80th N. Y. Inf. (20th Militia), Col. Theodore B. Gates; 3d Pa. Cav., Maj. James W. Walsh; 68th Pa. Inf., Lieut. Col. Robert E. Winslow; 114th Pa. Inf., Col. Charles H. T. Collis.
*Volunteer Engineer Brigade,** Brig. Gen. Henry W. Benham: 15th N. Y. Engineers, Maj. William A Ketchum; 50th N. Y. Engineers, Lieut. Col. Ira Spaulding. *Battalion U. S. Engineers,* Capt. George H. Mendell. *Guards and Orderlies*: Oneida (N. Y.) Cav., Capt. Daniel P. Mann.
SECOND ARMY CORPS, Maj. Gen. Winfield S. Hancock.
Escort: M, 1st Vt. Cav., Capt. John H. Hazelton.
FIRST DIVISION, Brig. Gen. Francis C. Barlow.
First Brigade, Col. Nelson A. Miles: 26th Mich., Maj. Lemuel Saviers; 61st N. Y., Lieut. Col. K. O. Broady; 81st Pa., Col. H. Boyd McKeen; 140th Pa., Col. John Fraser; 183d Pa., Col. George P. McLean. *Second Brigade,* Col. Thomas A. Smyth: 28th Mass., Lieut. Col. Geo. W. Cartright; 63d N. Y., Maj. Thomas Touhy; 69th N. Y., Capt. Richard Moroney; 88th N. Y., Capt. Denis F. Burke; 116th Pa., Lieut. Col. Richard C. Dale. *Third Brigade,* Col. Paul Frank: 39th N. Y., Col. Augustus Funk; 52d N. Y. (detachment 7th N. Y. attached), Maj. Henry M. Karples; 57th N. Y., Lieut. Col. Alford B. Chapman; 111th N. Y., Capt. Aaron P. Seeley; 125th N. Y., Lieut. Col. Aaron B. Myer; 126th N. Y., Capt. Winfield Scott. *Fourth Brigade,* Col. John R. Brooke: 2d Del., Col. William P. Bailey; 64th N. Y., Maj. Leman W. Bradley; 66th N. Y., Lieut. Col. John S. Hammell; 53d Pa., Lieut. Col. Richards McMichael; 145th Pa., Col. Hiram L. Brown; 148th Pa., Col. James A. Beaver.
SECOND DIVISION, Brig. Gen. John Gibbon.
Provost Guard: 2d Co. Minn. Sharp-shooters, Capt. Mahlon Black.
First Brigade, Brig. Gen. Alex. S. Webb: 19th Me., Col. Selden Connor; 1st Co. Andrew (Mass.) Sharpshooters, Lieut. Samuel G. Gilbreth; 15th Mass., Maj. I. Harris Hooper; 19th Mass., Maj. Edmund Rice; 20th Mass., Maj. Henry L. Abbott; 7th Mich., Maj. Sylvanus W. Curtis; 42d N. Y., Maj. Patrick J. Downing; 59th N. Y., Capt. William McFadden; 82d N. Y. (2d Militia), Col. Henry W. Hudson. *Second Brigade,* Brig. Gen. Joshua T. Owen: 152d N. Y., Lieut. Col. George W. Thompson; 69th Pa., Maj. William Davis; 71st Pa., Lieut. Col. Charles Kochersperger; 72d Pa., Col. De Witt C. Baxter; 106th Pa., Capt. Robert H. Ford. *Third Brigade,* Col. Samuel S. Carroll: 14th Conn., Col. Theodore G. Ellis; 1st Del., Lieut. Col. Daniel Woodall; 14th Ind., Col. John Coons; 12th N. J., Lieut. Col. Thomas H. Davis; 10th N. Y. (Battalion),

---

* With the exception of eleven companies of the 50th N. Y. under Lieut. Col. Spaulding, this command, with its commander, was at the Engineer Depot, Wash., D. C.

Capt. George M. Dewey; 108th N. Y., Col. Charles J. Powers; 4th Ohio, Lieut. Col. Leonard W. Carpenter; 8th Ohio, Lieut. Col. Franklin Sawyer; 7th W. Va., Lieut. Col. J. H. Lockwood.

THIRD DIVISION, Maj. Gen. David B. Birney.

First Brigade, Brig. Gen. J. H. H. Ward: 20th Ind., Col. W. C. L. Taylor; 3d Me., Col. Moses B. Lakeman; 40th N. Y., Col. Thomas W. Egan; 86th N. Y., Lieut. Col. Jacob H. Lansing; 124th N. Y., Col. Francis M. Cummins; 99th Pa., Lieut. Col. Edwin R. Biles; 110th Pa., Lieut. Col. Isaac Rogers; 141st Pa., Lieut. Col. Guy H. Watkins; 2d U. S. Sharp-Shooters, Lieut. Col. Homer R. Stoughton. *Second Brigade*, Brig. Gen. Alexander Hays: 4th Me., Col. Elijah Walker; 17th Me., Col. George W. West; 3d Mich., Col. Byron R. Pierce; 5th Mich., Lieut. Col. John Pulford; 93d N. Y., Maj. Samuel McConihe; 57th Pa., Col. Peter Sides; 63d Pa., Lieut. Col. John A. Danks; 105th Pa., Col. Calvin A. Craig; 1st U. S. Sharp-shooters, Maj. Charles P. Mattocks.

FOURTH DIVISION, Brig. Gen. Gershom Mott.

First Brigade, Col. Robert McAllister: 1st Mass., Col. N. B. McLauglen; 16th Mass., Lieut. Col. Waldo Merriam; 5th N. J., Col. William J. Sewell; 6th N. J. Lieut. Col. Stephen R. Gilkyson; 7th N. J., Maj. Frederick Cooper; 8th N. J., Col. John Ramsey; 11th N. J. Lieut. Col. John Schoonover; 26th Pa., Maj. Sameul G. Moffett; 115th Pa., Maj. William A. Reilly. *Second Brigade*, Col. William R. Brewster: 11th Mass., Col. William Blaisdell; 70th N. Y., Capt. William H. Hugo; 71st N. Y., Lieut. Col. Thomas Rafferty; 72d N. Y., Lieut. Col. John Leonard; 73d N. Y., Lieut. Col. Michael W. Burns, 74th N. Y., Lieut. Col. Thomas Holt; 120th N. Y., Capt. Abram L. Lockwood; 84th Pa., Lieut. Col. Milton Opp.

ARTILLERY BRIGADE, Col. John C. Tidball: 6th Me., Capt. Edwin B. Dow; 10th Mass., Capt. J. Henry Sleeper; 1st N. H., Capt. Fred. M. Edgell; G, 1st N. Y., Capt. Nelson Ames; 4th N. Y. Heavy (Third Battalion), Lieut. Col. Thomas R. Allcock; F, 1st Pa., Capt. R. Bruce Ricketts; A, 1st R. I., Capt. William A. Arnold; B, 1st R. I., Capt. T. Fred Brown; K, 4th U. S., Lieut. John W. Roder; C and I, 5th U. S., Lieut. James Gilliss.

FIFTH ARMY CORPS, Maj. Gen. Gouverneur K. Warren.

Provost Guard: 12th N. Y., Battalion, Maj. Henry W. Rider.

FIRST DIVISION, Brig. Gen. Charles Griffin.

First Brigade, Brig. Gen. Romeyn B. Ayres: 140th N. Y., Col. George Ryan; 146th N. Y., Col. David T. Jenkins; 91st Pa., Lieut. Col. Joseph H. Sinex; 155th Pa., Lieut. Col. Alfred L. Pearson; B, C, F, H, I, and K, 2d U. S., Capt. James W. Long; B, C, D, E, F, and G, 1st Battalion 11th U. S. Capt. Francis M. Cooley; A, B, C, D, and G, 1st Battalion, and A, C, D, F, and H, 2d Battalion 12th U. S., Maj. Luther B. Bruen; 1st Battalion 14th U. S., Capt. E. McK. Hudson; A, C, D, G, and H, 1st Battalion, and A, B, and C, 2d Battalion 17th U. S. Capt. James F. Grimes. *Second Brigade*, Col. Jacob B. Sweitzer: 9th Mass., Col. Patrick R. Guiney; 22d Mass. (2d Co. Mass. S. S. Attached), Col. William S. Tilton; 32d Mass., Col. George L. Prescott; 4th Mich., Lieut. Col. George W. Lumbard; 62d Pa., Lieut. Col. James C. Hull. *Third Brigade*, Brig. Gen. Joseph J. Bartlett: 20th Me., Maj. Ellis Spear; 18th Mass., Col. Joseph Hayes; 1st Mich., Lieut. Col. William A. Throop; 16th Mich., Maj. Robert T. Elliott; 44th N. Y., Lieut. Col. Freeman Conner; 83d Pa., Col. O. S. Woodward; 118th Pa., Col. James Gwyn.

SECOND DIVISION, Brig. Gen. John C. Robinson.

First Brigade, Col. Samuel H. Leonard: 16th Me., Col. Charles W. Tilden; 13th Mass., Capt. Charles H. Hovey; 39th Mass., Col. Phineas S. Davis; 104th N. Y., Col. Gilbert G. Prey. *Second Brigade*, Brig. Gen. Henry Baxter: 12th

Mass., Col. James L. Bates; 83d N. Y. (9th Militia), Col. Joseph A. Moesch; 97th N. Y., Col. Charles Wheelock; 11th Pa., Col. Richard Coulter; 88th Pa., Capt. George B. Rhoads; 90th Pa., Col. Peter Lyle. *Third Brigade,* Col. Andrew W. Denison: 1st Md., Maj. Benj. H. Schley; 4th Md., Col. Richard N. Bowerman; 7th Md., Col. Charles E. Phelps; 8th Md., Lieut. Col. John G. Johannes. THIRD DIVISION (Pennsylvania Reserves), Brig. Gen. Samuel W. Crawford. *First Brigade,* Col. William McCandless: 1st Pa., Col. William C. Talley; 2d Pa., Lieut. Col. Patrick McDonough; 6th Pa., Col. Wellington H. Ent; 7th Pa., Maj. LeGrand B. Speece; 11th Pa., Col. Samuel M. Jackson; 13th Pa. (1st Rifles), Maj. W. R. Hartshorn. *Third Brigade,* Col. Joseph W. Fisher: 5th Pa., Lieut. Col. George Dare; 8th Pa., Col. Silas M. Baily; 10th Pa., Lieut. Col. Ira Ayer, Jr.; 12th Pa., Lieut. Col. Richard Gustin.
FOURTH DIVISION, Brig. Gen. James S. Wadsworth.
First Brigade, Brig. Gen. Lysander Cutler: 7th Ind., Col. Ira G. Grover; 19th Ind., Col. Samuel J. Williams; 24th Mich., Col. Henry A. Morrow; 1st N. Y. Battalion Sharp-shooters, Capt. Volney J. Shipman; 2d Wis., Lieut. Col. John Mansfield; 6th Wis., Col. Edward S. Bragg; 7th Wis., Col. William W. Robinson. *Second Brigade,* Brig. Gen. James C. Rice: 76th N. Y., Lieut. Col. John E. Cook: 84th N. Y. (14th Militia), Col. Edward B. Fowler; 95th N. Y., Col. Edward Pye; 147th N. Y., Col. Francis C. Miller; 56th Pa., Col. J. Wm. Hofmann. *Third Brigade,* Col. Roy Stone: 121st Pa., Capt. Samuel T. Lloyd; 142d Pa., Maj. Horatio N. Warren; 143d Pa., Col. Edmund L. Dana; 149th Pa., Lieut. Col. John Irvin; 150th Pa., Capt. George W. Jones.
ARTILLERY BRIGADE, Col. Charles S. Wainwright: 3d Mass., Capt. Augustus P. Martin; 5th Mass., Capt. Charles A. Phillips; D, 1st N. Y., Capt. George B. Winslow; E and L, 1st N. Y., Lieut. George Breck; H, 1st N. Y. Capt. Charles E. Mink; 2d Battalion 4th N. Y. Heavy, Maj. William Arthur; B, 1st Pa., Capt. James H. Cooper; B, 4th U. S., Lieut. James Stewart; D, 5th U. S., Lieut. B. F. Rittenhouse.
SIXTH ARMY CORPS, Maj. Gen. John Sedgwick.
Escort: A, 8th Pa. Cav., Capt. Charles E. Fellows.
FIRST DIVISION, Brig. Gen. Horatio G. Wright.
First Brigade, Col. Henry W. Brown: 1st N. J. Lieut. Col. William Henry, Jr.; 2d N. J., Lieut. Col. Charles Wiebecke; 3d N. J., Capt. Samuel T. Du Bois; 4th N. J., Lieut. Col. Charles Ewing; 101st N. J., Col. Henry O. Ryerson; 15th N. J., Col. William H. Penrose. *Second Brigade,* Col. Emory Upton: 5th Me., Col. Clark S. Edwards; 121st N. Y., Lieut. Col. Egbert Olcott; 95th Pa., Lieut. Col. Edward Carroll; 96th Pa., Lieut. Col. William H. Lessig. *Third Brigade,* Brig. Gen. David A. Russell: 6th Me., Maj. George Fuller; 49th Pa., Col. Thomas M. Hulings; 119th Pa., Maj. Henry P. Truefitt, Jr.; 5th Wis., Lieut. Col. Theodore B. Catlin. *Fourth Brigade,* Brig. Gen. Alexander Shaler: 65th N. Y., Col. Joseph E. Hamblin; 67th N. Y., Col. Nelson Cross; 122d N. Y., Lieut. Col. Augustus W. Dwight; 82d Pa. (detachment).
SECOND DIVISION, Brig. Gen. George W. Getty.
First Brigade, Brig. Gen. Frank Wheaton: 62d N. Y., Col. David J. Nevin; 93d Pa., Lieut. Col. John S. Long; 98th Pa., Col. John F. Ballier; 102d Pa., Col. John W. Patterson; 139th Pa., Lieut. Col. William H. Moody. *Second Brigade,* Col. Lewis A. Grant: 2d Vt., Col. Newton Stone; 3d Vt., Col. Thomas O. Seaver; 4th Vt., Col. George P. Foster; 5th Vt., Lieut. Col. John R. Lewis; 6th Vt., Col. Elisha L. Barney. *Third Brigade,* Brig. Gen. Thomas H. Neill: 7th Me., Col. Edwin C. Mason; 43d N. Y., Lieut. Col. John Wilson; 49th N. Y., Col. Daniel D. Bidwell; 77th N. Y., Maj. Nathan S. Babcock; 61st Pa., Col. George F. Smith. *Fourth Brigade,* Brig. Gen. Henry L. Eustis: 7th

Mass., Col. Thomas D. Johns; 10th Mass., Lieut. Col. Joseph B. Parsons; 37th Mass., Col. Oliver Edwards; 2d R. I., Lieut. Col. S. B. M. Read.
THIRD DIVISION, Brig. Gen. James B. Ricketts.
  First Brigade, Brig. Gen. William H. Morris: 14th N. J., Lieut. Col. Caldwell K. Hall; 106th N. Y., Lieut. Col. Charles Townsend; 151st N. Y., Lieut. Col. Thomas M. Fay; 87th Pa., Col. John W. Schall; 10th Vt., Lieut. Col. William W. Henry. *Second Brigade,* Brig. Gen. Truman Seymour: 6th Md., Col. John W. Horn; 110th Ohio, Col. J. Warren Keifer; 122d Ohio, Col. William H. Ball; 126th Ohio, Col. Benj. F. Smith; 67th Pa. (detachment), Capt. George W. Guss; 138th Pa., Col. Matthew R. McClennan.
  ARTILLERY BRIGADE, Col. Charles H. Tompkins: 4th Me., Lieut. Melville C. Kimball; 1st Mass., Capt. William H. McCartney; 1st N. Y., Capt. Andrew Cowan; 3d N. Y., Capt. William A. Harn; 4th N. Y. Heavy (First Battalion), Maj. Thomas D. Sears; C, 1st R. I., Capt. Richard Waterman; E, 1st R. I., Capt. William B. Rhodes; G, 1st R. I., Capt. George W. Adams; M, 5th U. S., Capt. James McKnight.
  NINTH ARMY CORPS,* Major General Ambrose E. Burnside.
  Provost Guard: 8th U. S., Capt. Milton Cogswell.
FIRST DIVISION, Brig. Gen. Thomas G. Stevenson.
  First Brigade, Col. Sumner Carruth: 35th Mass., Maj. Nathaniel Wales; 56th Mass., Col. Charles E. Griswold; 57th Mass., Col. William F. Bartlett; 59th Mass. Col. J. Parker Gould; 4th U. S., Capt. Charles H. Brightly; 10th U. S. Maj. Samuel B. Hayman. *Second Brigade,* Col. Daniel Leasure: 3d Md., Col. Joseph M. Sudsburg; 21st Mass., Lieut. Col. George P. Hawkes; 100th Pa., Lieut. Col. Matthew M. Dawson. *Artillery:* 2d Me., Capt. Albert F. Thomas; 14th Mass., Capt. J. W. B. Wright.
SECOND DIVISION, Brig. Gen. Robert B. Potter.
  First Brigade, Col. Zenas R. Bliss: 36th Mass., Maj. William F. Draper; 58th Mass., Lieut. Col. John C. Whiton; 51st N. Y., Col. Charles W. Le Gendre; 45th Pa., Col. John I. Curtin; 48th Pa., Lieut. Col. Henry Pleasants; 7th R. I., Capt. Theodore Winn. *Second Brigade,* Col. Simon G. Griffin: 31st Me., Lieut. Col. Thomas Hight; 32d Me., Maj. Arthur Deering; 6th N. H., Lieut. Col. Henry H. Pearson; 9th N. H., Lieut. Col. John W. Babbitt; 11th N. H., Col. Walter Harriman; 17th Vt., Lieut. Col. Charles Cummings. *Artillery:* 11th Mass., Capt. Edward J. Jones; 19th N. Y., Capt. Edward W. Rogers.
THIRD DIVISION, Brig. Gen. Orlando B. Willcox.
  First Brigade, Col. John F. Hartranft: 2d Mich., Col. William Humphrey; 8th Mich., Col. Frank Graves; 17th Mich., Col. Constan Luce; 27th Mich. (1st and 2d Co's Mich. Sharp-shooters attached), Maj. Samuel Moody; 109th N. Y., Col. Benjamin F. Tracy; 51st Pa., Lieut. Col. Edwin Schall. *Second Brigade,* Col. Benjamin C. Christ: 1st Mich. Sharp-shooters, Col. Charles V. De Land; 20th Mich., Lieut. Col. Byron M. Cutcheon; 79th N. Y., Col. David Morrison; 60th Ohio (9th and 10th Co's Ohio Sharp-shooters attached), Lieut. Col. James N. McElroy; 50th Pa., Lieut. Col. Edward Overton, Jr. *Artillery:* 7th Me., Capt. Adelbert B. Twitchell; 34th N. Y., Capt. Jacob Roemer.
FOURTH DIVISION,† Brig. Gen. Edward Ferrero.
  First Brigade, Col. Joshua K. Sigfried: 27th U. S., Lieut. Col. Charles J. Wright; 30th U. S., Col. Delavan Bates; 39th U. S., Col. Ozora P. Stearns; 43d U. S., Lieut. Col. H. Seymour Hall. *Second Brigade,* Col. Henry G. Thomas:

---

  * This corps participated in the Wilderness and Spotsylvania campaigns, under the direct orders of Lieut. Gen. U. S. Grant, until May 24th, 1864, when it was assigned to the Army of the Potomac.
  † All the infantry were colored troops.

30th Conn. (detachment), Capt. Charles Robinson; 19th U. S., Lieut. Col. Joseph Perkins; 23d U. S. Lieut. Col. Cleveland J. Campbell. *Artillery:* D. Pa., Capt. George W. Durell; 3d Vt., Capt. Romeo H. Start.

CAVALRY: 3d N. J., Col. Andrew J. Morrison; 22d N. Y., Col. Samuel J. Crooks; 2d Ohio, Lieut. Col. George A. Purington; 13th Pa., Maj. Michael Kerwin.

RESERVE ARTILLERY, Capt. John Edwards, Jr.: 27th N. Y., Capt. John B. Eaton; D, 1st R. I., Capt. William W. Buckley; H, 1st R. I., Capt. Crawford Allen, Jr., E, 2d U. S., Lieut. James S. Dudley; G, 3d U. S., Lieut. Edmund Pendleton; L and M, 3d U. S., Lieut. Erskine Gittings.

PROVISIONAL BRIGADE, Col. Elisha G. Marshall: 24th N. Y. Cav. (dismounted), Col. William C. Raulston; 14th N. Y. Heavy Art'y, Lieut. Col. Clarence H. Corning; 2d Pa. Prov. Heavy Art'y, Col. Thomas Wilhelm.

CAVALRY CORPS, Maj. Gen. Phillip H. Sheridan.

Escort: 6th U. S., Capt. Ira W. Claflin.

FIRST DIVISION, Brig. Gen. A. T. A. Torbert.

First Brigade, Brig. Gen. George A. Custer: 1st Mich., Lieut. Col. Peter Stagg; 5th Mich., Col. Russell A. Alger; 6th Mich., Maj. James H. Kidd; 7th Mich., Maj. Henry W. Granger. *Second Brigade,* Col. Thomas C. Devin: 4th N. Y. (guarding trains), Lieut. Col. William R. Parnell; 6th N. Y., Lieut. Col. William H. Crocker; 9th N. Y., Col. William Sackett; 17th Pa., Lieut. Col. James Q. Anderson. Reserve Brigade, Brig. Gen. Wesley Merritt: 19th N. Y. (1st Dragoons), Col. Alfred Gibbs; 6th Pa., Maj. James Starr; 1st U. S. Capt. Nelson B. Sweitzer; 2d U. S., Capt. T. F. Rodenbough; 5th U. S., Capt. Abraham K. Arnold.

SECOND DIVISION, Brig. Gen. David McM. Gregg.

First Brigade, Brig. Gen. Henry E. Davies, Jr.: 1st Mass., Maj. Lucius M. Sargent; 1st N. J., Lieut. Col. John W. Kester; 6th Ohio, Col. William Stedman; 1st Pa., Col. John P. Taylor. *Second Brigade,* Col. J. Irvin Gregg: 1st Me., Col. Charles H. Smith; 10th N. Y., Maj. M. Henry Avery; 2d Pa., Lieut. Col. Joseph P. Brinton; 4th Pa., Lieut. Col. George H. Covode; 8th Pa., Lieut. Col. Samuel Wilson; 16th Pa., Lieut. Col. John K. Robinson.

THIRD DIVISION, Brig. Gen. James H. Wilson.

Escort: 8th Ill. (detachment), Lieut. William W. Long. *First Brigade,* Col. Timothy M. Bryan, Jr., Col. John B. McIntosh: 1st Conn., Maj. Erastus Blakeslee; 2d N. Y., Col. Otto Harhaus; 5th N. Y., Lieut. Col. John Hammond; 18th Pa., Lieut. Col. William P. Brinton. *Second Brigade,* Col. George H. Chapman: 3d Ind., Maj. William Patton; 8th N. Y., Lieut. Col. William H. Benjamin; 1st Vt., Lieut. Col. Addison W. Preston.

ARTILLERY, Brig. Gen. Henry J. Hunt.

Artillery Reserve, Col. Henry S. Burton.

First Brigade, Col. J. Howard Kitching: 6th N. Y. Heavy, Lieut. Col. Edmund R. Travis; 15th N. Y. Heavy, Col. Louis Schirmer. *Second Brigade,* Maj. John A. Tompkins: 5th Me., Capt. Greenleaf T. Stevens; 1st N. J., Capt. William Hexamer; 2d N. J., Capt. A. Judson Clark; 5th N. Y., Capt. Elijah D. Taft; 12th N. Y., Capt. George F. McKnight; B, 1st N. Y., Capt. Albert S. Sheldon. *Third Brigade,* Maj. Robert H. Fitzhugh: 9th Mass., Capt. John Bigelow; 15th N. Y., Capt. Patrick Hart; C, 1st N. Y., Lieut. William H. Phillips; 11th N. Y., Capt. John E. Burton; H, 1st Ohio, Lieut. William A. Ewing; E, 5th U. S., Lieut. John R. Brinckle.

HORSE ARTILLERY.

First Brigade,* Capt. James M. Robertson: 6th N. Y., Capt. Joseph W.

---

* Detached with Cavalry Corps.

Martin; B and L, 2d U. S., Lieut. Edward Heaton; D, 2d U. S., Lieut. Edward B. Williston; M, 2d U. S., Lieut. A. C. M. Pennington; A, 4th U. S., Lieut. Rufus King, Jr., C and E, 4th U. S., Lieut. Charles L. Fitzhugh. *Second Brigade,* Capt. Dunbar R. Ransom: E and G, 1st U. S., Lieut. Frank S. French; H and I, Capt. Alanson M. Randol; K, 1st U. S., Lieut. John Egan; A, 2d U. S., Lieut. Robert Clark; G, 2d U. S., Lieut. William N. Dennison; C, F and K, 3d U. S., Lieut. James R. Kelly.

The effective strength of the Union army in the Wilderness is estimated at 118,000 of all arms.

The losses of this army were as follows:

Battle	Killed	Wounded	Captured or Missing	Total
The Wilderness	2,246	12,037	3,383	17,666

THE CONFEDERATE ARMY

ARMY OF NORTHERN VIRGINIA

GENERAL ROBERT E. LEE

I ARMY CORPS, Lieut. Gen. James Longstreet.

KERSHAW'S DIVISION, Brig. Gen. Joseph B. Kershaw.

Kershaw's Brigade, Col. John W. Henagan: 2d S. C., Lieut. Col. F. Gaillard; 3d S. C., Col. James D. Nance; 7th S. C., Capt. James Mitchell; 8th S. C., Lieut. Col. E. T. Stackhouse; 15th S. C., Col. John B. Davis; 3d S. C. Battalion, Capt. B. M. Whitener. *Humphrey's Brigade,* Brig. Gen. Benjamin G. Humphreys: 13th Miss., Maj. G. L. Donald; 17th Miss.; 18th Miss., Capt. W. H. Lewis; 21st Miss., Col. D. N. Moody. *Wofford's Brigade,* Brig. Gen. William T. Wofford: 16th Ga.; 18th Ga.; 24th Ga.; Cobb's Ga. Legion; Phillips Ga. Legion; 3d G. Battallion Sharp-shooters. *Bryan's Brigade,* Brig. Gen. Goode Bryan: 10th Ga., Col. Willis C. Holt; 50th Ga., Col. P. McGlashan; 51st Ga., Col. E. Ball; 53d Ga., Col. James P. Simms.

FIELD'S DIVISION, Maj. Gen. Charles W. Field.

Jenkins' Brigade, Brig. Gen. Micah Jenkins: 1st S. C., Col. James R. Hagood; 2d S. C. (Rifles), Col. R. E. Bowen; 5th S. C., Col. A. Coward; 6th S. C., Col. John Bratton; Palmetto (S. C.) Sharp-shooters, Col. Joseph Walker. *Anderson's Brigade,* Brig. Gen. George T. Anderson: 7th Ga.; 8th Ga.; 9th Ga.; 11th Ga.; 59th Ga., Lieut. Col. B. H. Gee. *Law's Brigade,* Brig. Gen. E. McIver Law: 4th Ala., Col. P. D. Bowles; 15th Ala.; 44th Ala., Col. W. F. Perry; 47th Ala.; 48th Ala., Lieut. Col. W. M. Hardwick. *Gregg's Brigade,* Brig. Gen. John Gregg: 3d Ark., Col. Van H. Manning; 1st Tex.; 4th Tex., Col. J. P. Bane; 5th Tex., Lieut. Col. K. Bryan; *Benning's Brigade,* Brig. Gen. Henry L. Benning: 2d Ga.; 15th Ga., Col. D. M. DuBose; 17th Ga., 20th Ga.

ARTILLERY, Brig. Gen. E. Porter Alexander.

Huger's Battalion, Lieut. Col. Frank Huger: Fickling's (Va.) Btry.; Moody's (La.) Btry.; Parker's (Va.) Btry.; J. D. Smith's (Va.) Btry.; Taylor's (Va.) Btry.; Woolfolk's (Va.) Btry. *Haskell's Battalion,* Maj. John C. Haskell: Flanner's (N. C.) Btry.; Garden's (S. C.) Btry.; Lamkin's (Va.) Btry.; Ramsay's (N. C.) Btry Cabell's Battalion, Col. Henry C. Cabell: Callaway's (Ga.) Btry.; Carlton's (Ga.) Btry.; McCarth's (Va.) Btry.; Manly's (N. C.) Btry.

II ARMY CORPS, Lieut. Gen. Richard S. Ewell.

EARLY'S DIVISION, Maj. Gen. Jubal A. Early.

Hay's Brigade, Brig. Gen. Harry T. Hays: 5th La., Lieut. Col. Bruce Menger; 6th La., Maj. William H. Manning; 7th La., Maj. J. M. Wilson; 8th La., 9th La. *Pegram's Brigade,* Brig. Gen. John Pegram: 13th Va., Col. James B. Terrill; 31st Va., Col. John S. Hoffman; 49th Va., Col. J. C. Gibson; 52d Va.; 58th Va. *Gordon's Brigade,* Brig. Gen. John B. Gordon: 13th Ga., 26th Ga., Col. E. N. Atkinson; 31st Ga., Col. C. A. Evans; 38th Ga., 60th Ga., Lieut. Col. Thomas J. Berry; 61st Ga.

JOHNSON'S DIVISION, Maj. Gen. Edward Johnson.

Stonwall Brigade, Brig. Gen. James A. Walker: 2d Va., Capt. C. H. Stewart; 4th Va., Col. William Terry; 5th Va., 27th Va., Lieut. Col. Charles L. Haynes; 33d Va. *Steuart's Brigade,* Brig. Gen. George H. Steuart: 1st N. C., Col. H. A. Brown; 3d N. C., Col. S. D. Thruston; 10th Va.; 23d Va.; 37th Va. *Jones' Brigade,* Brig. Gen. John M. Jones: 21st Va.; 25th Va., Col. J. C. Higginbotham; 42d Va.; 44th Va.; 48th Va.; 50th Va. *Stafford's Brigade,* Brig. Gen. Leroy A. Stafford: 1st La.; 2d La., Col. J. M. Williams; 10th La.; 14th La.; 15th La.

RODES' DIVISION, Maj. Gen. Robert E. Rodes.

Daniel's Brigade, Brig. Gen. Junius Daniel: 32d N. C.; 43d N. C.; 45th N. C.; 53d N. C.; 2d N. C. Btry. *Ramseur's Brigade,* Brig. Gen. Stephen D. Ramseur: 2d N. C., Col. W. R. Cox; 4th N. C., Col. Bryan Grimes; 14th N. C., Col. R. T. Bennett; 30th N. C., Col. F. M. Parker. *Doles' Brigade,* Brig. Gen. George Doles: 4th Ga.; 12th Ga., Col. Edward Willis; 44th Ga., Col. W. H. Peebles. *Battle's Brigade,* Brig. Gen. Cullen A. Battle: 3d Ala., Col. Charles Forsyth; 5th Ala.; 6th Ala.; 12th Ala.; 26th Ala. *Johnston's Brigade,* Brig. Gen. Robert D. Johnston: 5th N. C., Col. T. M. Garrett; 12th N. C., Col. H. E. Collman; 20th N. C., Col. Thomas F. Toon; 23d N. C.

ARTILLERY, Brig. Gen. Armistead L. Long.

*Hardaway's Battalion,** Lieut. Col. R. A. Hardaway: Dance's (Va.) Btry.; Graham's (Va.) Btry.; C. B. Griffin's (Va.) Btry.; Jones' (Va.) Btry.; B. H. Smith's (Va.) Btry. *Nelson's Battalion,** Lieut. Col. William Nelson: Kirkpatrick's (Va.) Btry.; Massie's (Va.) Btry.; Milledge's (Ga.) Btry. *Braxton's Battalion,** Lieut. Col. Carter M. Braxton: Carpenter's (Va.) Btry.; Cooper's (Va.) Btry.; Hardwicke's (Va.) Btry. *Cutshaw's Battalion,†* Maj. W. E. Cutshaw: Carrington's (Va.) Btry.; A. W. Garber's (Va.) Btry.; Tanner's (Va.) Btry. *Page's Battalion,†* Maj. R. C. M. Page: W. P. Carter's (Va.) Btry.; Fry's (Va.) Btry.; Page's (Va.) Btry.; Reese's (Ala.) Btry.

III ARMY CORPS, Lieut. Gen. Ambrose P. Hill.

ANDERSON'S DIVISION, Maj. Gen. Richard H. Anderson.

Perrin's Brigade, Brig. Gen. Abner Perrin: 8th Ala.; 9th Ala.; 10th Ala.; 11th Ala.; 14th Ala. *Mahone's Brigade,* Brig. Gen. William Mahone: 6th Va., Lieut. Col. H. W. Williamson; 12th Va., Col. D. A. Weisiger; 16th Va., Lieut. Col. R. O. Whitehead; 41st Va., 61st Va., Col. V. D. Groner. *Harris' Brigade* Brig. Gen. Nathaniel H. Harris: 12th Miss.; 16th Miss., Col. S. E. Baker; 19th Miss., Col. T. J. Hardin; 48th Miss. *Wright's Brigade,* Brig. Gen. Ambrose R. Wright: 3d Ga.; 22d Ga.; 48th Ga.; 2d Ga. Bn., Maj. Q. J. Moffett. *Perry's Brigade,* Brig. Gen. E. A. Perry: 2d Fla.; 5th Fla.; 8th Fla.

HETH'S DIVISION, Maj. Gen. Henry Heth.

Davis' Brigade, Brig. Gen. Joseph R. Davis: 2d Miss.; 11th Miss.; 42d Miss.; 55th N. C. *Cooke's Brigade,* Brig. Gen. John R. Cooke: 15th N. C.; 27th N. C.; 46th N. C.; 48th N. C. *Kirkland's Brigade,* Brig. Gen. William W. Kirkland: 11th N. C.; 26th N. C.; 44th N. C.; 47th N. C.; 52d N. C. *Walker's Brigade,* Brig. Gen. Henry H. Walker: 40th Va.; 47th Va., Col. R.

---

* Under the direction of Colonel J. T. Brown.
† Under the direction of Colonel Thomas H. Carter.

M. Mayo; 55th Va., Col. W. S. Christian; 22d Va., Bn. *Archer's Brigade,* Brig. Gen. James J. Archer: 13th Ala.; 1st Tenn. (Prov. Army), Maj. F. G. Buchanan; 7th Tenn., Lieut. Col. S. G. Shepard; 14th Tenn., Col. William McComb.

WILCOX'S DIVISION, Maj. Gen. Cadmus M. Wilcox.

Lane's Brigade, Brig. Gen. James H. Lane: 7th N. C., Lieut. Col. W. Lee Davidson; 18th N. C., Col. John D. Barry; 28th N. C.; 33d N. C., Lieut. Col. R. V. Cowan; 37th N. C., Col. William M. Barbour. *Scale's Brigade,* Brig. Gen. Alfred M. Scales: 13th N. C., Col. J. H. Hyman; 16th N. C., Col. W. A. Stowe; 22d N. C.; 34th N. C., Col. W. L. J. Lowrance; 38th N. C., Lieut. Col. John Ashford. *McGowan's Brigade,* Brig. Gen. Samuel McGowan: 1st S. C. (Prov. Army), Lieut, Col W. P. Shooter; 12th S. C., Col. John L. Miller; 13th S. C., Col. B. T. Brockman; 14th S. C., Col. Joseph N. Brown; 1st S. C. (Orr's) Rifles, Lieut. Col. G. McD. Miller. *Thomas' Brigade,* Brig. Gen. Edward L. Thomas: 14th Ga.; 35th Ga.; 45th Ga.; 49th Ga., Lieut. Col. J. T. Jordan.

ARTILLERY, Col. R. Lindsay Walker.

Poague's Battalion, Lieut. Col. William T. Poague; Richards' (Miss.) Btry.; Utterback's (Va.) Btry.; Williams' (N. C.) Btry.; Wyatt's (Va.) Btry. *McIntosh's Battalion,* Lieut. Col. D. G. McIntosh: Clutter's (Va.) Btry.; Donald's (Va.) Btry.; Hurt's (Ala.) Btry.; Price's (Va.) Btry. *Pegram's Battalion,* Lieut. Col. W. J. Pegram: Brander's (Va.) Btry.; Cayce's (Va.) Btry. Ellett's (Va.) Btry.; Marye's (Va.) Btry.; Zimmerman's (S. C.), Btry. *Cutt's Battalion,* Col. A. S. Cutts: Patterson's (Ga.) Btry.; Ross' (Ga.) Btry.; Wingfield's (Ga.) Btry. *Richardson's Battalion,* Lieut. Col. Charles Richardson: Grandy's (Va.) Btry.; Landry's (La.) Btry.; Moore's (Va.) Btry.; Penick's (Va.) Btry.

CAVALRY CORPS, Maj. Gen. James E. B. Stuart.

HAMPTON'S DIVISION, Maj. Gen. Wade Hampton.

Young's Brigade, Brig. Gen. P. M. B. Young: 7th Ga., Col. W. P. White; Cobb's (Ga.) Legion, Col. G. J. Wright; Phillips (Ga.) Legion; 20th Ga. Bn., Lieut. Col. John M. Millen; Jeff Davis (Miss.) Legion. *Rosser's Brigade,* Brig. Gen. Thomas L. Rosser: 7th Va., Col. R. H. Dulany; 11th Va.; 12th Va., Lieut. Col. Thomas B. Massie; 35th Va. Battalion. *Butler's Brigade,* Brig Gen. M. C. Butler: 4th S. C., Col. B. H. Rutledge; 5th S. C., Col. John Dunovant; 6th S. C., Col. Hugh K. Aiken.

FITZ. LEE'S DIVISION, Maj. Gen. Fitzhugh Lee.

Lomax's Brigade, Brig. Gen. Lunsford L. Lomax: 5th Va., Col. Henry C. Pate; 6th Va.; 15 Va. *Wickham's Brigade,* Brig. Gen. Williams C. Wickham: 1st Va.; 2d Va., Col. Thomas T. Munford; 3d Va., Col. Thomas H. Owen; 4th Va.

W. H. F. LEE'S DIVISION, Maj. Gen. W. H. F. Lee.

Chambliss' Brigade, Brig. Gen. John R. Chambliss, Jr.; 9th Va.; 10th Va.; 13th Va. *Gordon's Brigade,* Brig. Gen. James B. Gordon: 1st N. C.; 2d N. C., Col. C. M. Andrews: 5th N. C., Col. S. B. Evans.

HORSE ARTILLERY, Maj. R. P. Chew.

Breathed's Battalion, Maj. James Breathed: Hart's (S. C.) Btry.; Johnston's (Va.) Btry.; McGregor's (Va.) Btry.; Shoemaker's (Va.) Btry.; Thompson's (Va.) Btry.

Lee's effective force at the commencement of the campaign was not less than 61,000, and Beauregard's command about Richmond and Petersburg, including the troops sent from North Carolina and South Carolina up to May 15th, approximated 30,000.

The losses of these armies are only partially reported. In the Wilderness Ewell's corps lost 1250 killed and wounded; McGowan's brigade (Wilcox's division), 481 killed, wounded, and missing; Lane's brigade (Wilcox's division), 272 killed and wounded, and 143 missing; Kershaw's brigade (under Henagan), 57 killed, 239 wounded, and 26 missing; Bryan's brigade (Kershaw's division), 31 killed and 102 wounded; Mahone's brigade, 20 killed, 126 wounded, and 7 missing; Gordon's brigade, 50 killed, wounded, and missing.

APPENDIX B—BIBLIOGRAPHY

NOTES

CHAPTER I

1. An attempt to document every statement in this generalized account of the rise to fame of Ulysses S. Grant and Robert E. Lee would amount to an affectation of scholarship. The incidents mentioned are, for the most part, authenticated facts of history. Arrangement of these facts in their chronological order is revealing, and suggests many of the interpretations put upon them in this sketch. For the reader who may be interested in the background from which the adversaries of the Wilderness emerged, the following books are suggested. In view of the stated purpose, the list of titles offered here necessarily excludes many works of outstanding scholarship. Complete titles, with author identification, place, and date of publication will be found in the Reading List.

   Two excellent one-volume treatments of the Civil War are useful: Woods and Edmonds, *A History of the Civil War in the United States* and Henry, *The Story of the Confederacy*. *Battles and Leaders of the Civil War* is recommended as a collection of papers, many of which were written by the foremost leaders on both sides, and present the war in the light of those who fought its great battles.

   On the Federal side are several suitable works, including the *Personal Memoirs of U. S. Grant*. The following may be added: (1) Porter, *Campaigning with Grant* (2) Conger, *The Rise of U. S. Grant* (3) Fuller, *The Generalship of U. S. Grant* (4) Fuller, *Grant and Lee, A study in Personality and Generalship*.

   For comparable books on Lee's side, we have the memoirs of a few of his distinguished subordinates, together with biographical studies and other works written largely from the Confederate point of view. This list includes. Alexander, *Military Memoirs of a Confederate* (Chas. Scribner's Sons New York, 1907). Gordon, *Reminiscences of the Civil War*. (3) Longstreet, *From Manassas to Appomattox*. (4) Maurice, *Robert E. Lee the Soldier*. While serving the purpose of a general treatment of the war, Dr. Freeman's four-volume study *R. E. Lee, A Military Biography* presents an invaluable character analysis of the great Confederate soldier. A comparable biography of Grant is yet to be written.

2. 36 WR 527, 547, 571, 573, 584. In this and all following notes referring to *The War of the Rebellion: A Compilation of the Official Records of the Union and Confederate Armies* (Government Printing Office, Washington, 1881-1902), the citations are to the serial numbers of the volumes rather than by referring to Series, Volumes, and Parts. Thus 37 WR 527 means Serial No. 37, p. 527.

3. Grant to Halleck, 7 Dec. 1863, 56 WR 313.

4. Halleck to Grant, 8 Jan. 1864, 60 WR 40 ff.

5. Grant to Halleck, 19 Jan. 64, 60 WR 395.

6. Hq. Armies of the United States, Orders No. 1, 17 Mar. 64, 59 WR 83.

7. Badeau, Adam, *Military History of Ulysses S. Grant* (D. Appleton & Co., New York, 1881) II, Appendix to Chapter 5. Grant's military secretary, Badeau, cites a computation entitled "Aggregate Available National Force Present for Duty, May 1, 1864" as his authority for the Federal total (662,345). He derives his total for Confederate strength (302,442) from "A Statement of Rebel Forces Taken From the Returns in Rebel Archives Office Nearest in Date to May 1, 1864." *Ibid.*

Although subject to considerable correction, these figures are important for the reason that they entered into the planning by both sides for the campaign of 1864. However, Livermore's corrected figures are given for the following: Army of the Potomac and the IX Corps (101,895), The Army of Northern Virginia (61,025), Sherman's Army (110,123), Johnston's Army of Tennessee (59,469). Livermore, Thos. L., *Numbers and Losses in the Civil War in America* (Civil War Centennial Series, Indiana University Press, Bloomington, 1957) pp. 110-11, 119. The strengths of Grant's two supporting columns, Butler's Army of the James (33,000) and Sigel's Valley force (23,000), are taken from estimates appearing in Grant's military correspondence, while that of the proposed Mobile assault force (30,000) is similarly established. Strength of the Richmond Defense Force, after reinforcement by Beauregard (30,000) is derived from correspondence between Lee and Davis. Returns of Breckenridge's Valley army (7,731) appear in 60 WR 1334. In summary, Grant had 157,895 troops for his converging movement on Richmond, while the Confederate high command had 98,756 for defense of its capital. Sherman mustered 110,123 against Johnston's 59,756 in the advance on Atlanta.

As a matter of historic interest Badeau's figures for the totals of Federal and Confederate strength fall far short of the actual numbers. Livermore puts the Federal total at 860,737 on January 1, 1864 and 959,460 on January 1, 1865, with an average of 910,098 for the year 1864. Comparable Confederate figures, according to Livermore, are 481,160 on January 1, 1864 and 445,203 on January 1, 1865, with an average of 463,181 for the intervening year. Livermore, *op. cit.* p. 47.

8. The best single statement of Grant's plan for the Grand Campaign is found in his directive of April 4, 1864 to Sherman. Grant to Sherman, 4 Apr. 64, 59 WR 245.

9. Lee to Davis, 15 Apr. 64, 60 WR 1282, 1284, 1290.

CHAPTER 2

1. War Department, Adjutant General's Office, Orders No. 98, 1864. The Orders state in part "The headquarters of the Army will be in Washington and also with Lieutenant-General Grant in the field. Maj. Gen. H. W. Halleck is assigned to duty in Washington, as Chief of Staff of the Army, under direction of the Secretary of War and the Lieutenant-General commanding."

2. Goerliz, Walter, *History of the German General Staff*, Brian Battershaw trans. (Frederick A. Praeger, Inc., New York, 1954) pp. 75-77; Stackpole, Edward J., *Chancellorsville Lee's Greatest Battle* (The Stackpole Co., Harrisburg, 1958), p. 33. Hereinafter cited as Stackpole, *Chancellorsville*.

3. Major Benjamin F. Fisher, Chief Signal Officer, Rpt of Opns, 21 July 64, 67 WR 281-84.

4. Stackpole, *Chancellorsville, pp.* 34-35.

5. Grant to Banks, 31 Mar. 1864, 61 WR 11.
6. Grant to Meade, 9 Apr. 1864, 60 WR 828.
7. Grant to Meade, 12 Apr. 1864, 60 WR 889.
8. The account of Meade's logistical preparations on his report to Grant. See Meade to Grant, 17 Apr. 1864, 60 WR 889.
9. The best discussion of the problems weighed in determining the direction of advance in presented by Maj. Gen. Andrew A. Humphreys, Chief of Staff, A. of P., in his work *The Virginia Campaign of '64 and '65* (Charles Scribner's Sons, New York, 1883) pp. 9-11. Hereinafter cited as Humphreys, *Va. Campaign.*
10. Diary and personal papers of Lt. Col. Cyrus B. Comstock, confidential *aide de camp* to Grant (Div. of Mss., Library of Congress) contain correspondence between the Provost Marshal's Dept. and Humphreys bearing on information disclosed by Confederate deserters and refugees relative to Longstreet's movement toward Gordonsville and rumors of reinforcements from Beauregard's command.
11. Grant to Halleck, 60 WR 278; Porter to Navy Dept., 27 Apr 1864, 60 WR 278.
12. Porter, Horace, *Campaigning With Grant* (The Century Co., New York, 1897).
13. Grant to Halleck, 27 Apr. 1864, 60 WR 992, 997; Halleck to Grant, 28 Apr. 1864, 60 WR 1003; Grant to Halleck, 60 WR 1017.
14. Humphreys, *Va. Campaign*, p. 12.
15. *Ibid.*, p. 11.
16. Hq. A. of P., Orders, May 2, 1864, 68 WR 331.
17. Grant to Burnside, 2 May, 68 WR 337; Same to Same, 1:15 p.m., 4 May 1864, 68 WR 380.
18. Hq. A. of P., Orders, May 4, 1864, 68 WR 371.
19. Sheridan to Humphreys, 4 May, 68 WR 389.

CHAPTER 3

1. Lee to Davis, 3 Dec. 1864, 56 WR 779; 60 WR 1144.
2. Lee to Davis, 30 Mar. 1864, 60 WR 1244.
3. Lee to Breckenridge, 11 Apr. 1864, 60 WR 1272.
4. Lee to Davis, 15 Apr. 1864, 60 WR 1282.
5. Lee to Bragg, 16 Apr. 1864, 60 WR 1285.
6. Lee to Davis, 18 Apr. 1864, 60 WR 1290-91.
7. *Ibid.*
8. Lee to Davis, 19 Apr. 1864, 60 WR 1326.
9. Wilcox, Cadmus, M., "Grant and Lee in the Wilderness," *Annals of the War Written by Leading Participants North and South*, p. 488. Hereinafter cited as *Annals.*
10. Lee to Davis, 28 Apr. 1864, 60 WR 1321.
11. Alexander, E. P., *Military Memoirs of a Confederate*. Chas. Scribner's Sons, N. Y., 1907 pp. 193-94.
12. Ewell, Rpt of Opns, 67 WR 1070; Hotchkiss, Jed, "The Wilderness Campaign Against Grant," *Confederate Military History*. 13 Vols. (Confederate Publishing Co., Atlanta, 1899) III, 431. Hereinafter cited as Wilderness, *CMH.*
13. Ewell, Rpt of Opns, 67 WR 1070.
14. Wilcox, Cadmus M. "Wilderness," *Annals*, 488,

CHAPTER 4

1. Grant, Rpt of Opns, 67 WR 18; Wilson, Rpt of Opns, 67 WR 875; Warren, Hq Journal, 67 WR 539; Robinson, Rpt of Opns, 67 WR 361.
2. Hancock, Rpt of Opns, 67 WR 318.
3. Wilson, Rpt of Opns, 67 WR 871-72.
4. Warren, Journal, 67 WR 539.
5. Taylor to Fisher, signal, 9:30 a.m., 4 May, 68 WR 372.
6. Cowles to Ewell, 4 May, 68 WR 888.
7. Wilson, Rpt of Opns, 4 May 67 WR 875-76; Throop, Rpt of Opns, 67 WR 580. According to Col. William A. Throop, the 1st Michigan Infantry, 3d Brigade, Griffin's division reached the junction of the Germanna Plank Road and the stone road (Orange CH and Fredericksburg Pike) at about 1 p.m. *Ibid.* Wilson, 67 WR 876.
8. Wilson, *op. cit.*, 876-77.
9. Gregg, Rpt of Opns, 67 WR 852; Humphreys, *Va. Campaign,* 19.
10. Hancock to Meade, 4 May, 68 WR 374.
11. Reports vary from 1 to 2 miles as to the distance of Griffin's advance out the Turnpike. Cf. Throop, Rpt of Opns, 67 WR 579, and Knox, *ibid,* 586.
12. Schaff, Morris, *The Battle of the Wilderness* (Houghton, Mifflin Co., New York and Boston, 1910), 96; hereinafter cited as Schaff, *Wilderness;* Porter, *Grant,* 97; Warren to Humphreys, 3:05 p.m., 4 May, 67 WR 378.
13. Getty, Rpt of Opns, 67 WR 676; Wright, *op. cit.*, 665; Cannon, *op. cit.*, 747; Humphreys, *Va. Campaign,* 19.
14. Hancock to Williams, 1:40 p.m., 4 May, 68 WR 375; Brooke, 407.
15. Sheridan, Rpt of Opns, 67 WR 787; Ramseur, Rpt of Opns, 1081. Ramseur states, "On the 5th I discovered by a reconnaissance as far as Culpeper Court House, that the main body of the enemy had crossed to the south side of the river."
16. Humphreys, *Va. Campaign,* 20.
17. *Ibid.*
18. Porter, *Grant,* 41; Schaff, *Wilderness,* 85.
19. *Ibid.,* 86.
20. Porter, *op. cit.,* 43 ff.
21. Grant, Ulysses S., *Personal Memoirs,* 2 Vols. (C. L. Webster & Co., 1885-86), II, 191.
22. Taylor to Fisher, 11 a.m. and 3 p.m., 68 WR 372.
23. Grant to Burnside, 1:15 p.m., 68 WR 380.
24. Grant to Burnside, 68 WR 337; Grant to Meade, 67, 352; Dent, Gen. Hq., to Burnside, 352; Burnside Rpt of Opns, 67 WR 905; Itinerary of the 1st Division, Ninth Corps, 916; Potter, Rpt of Opns, 2d Division, 927; Willcox, Rpt of Opns, 942; Humphreys, *Va. Campaign,* 2021.
25. Humphreys, *op. cit.,* 21.
26. *Ibid.*
27. Humphreys to Hancock, 68 WR 375.
28. Forsyth to Gregg, 68 WR 389.
29. Wilson to Forsyth, 68 WR 390.
30. *Ibid.*
31. Signal, Taylor to Fisher, 67 WR 372.
32. Humphreys, *Va. Campaign,* 12.
33. 68 WR 371.
34. Stackpole, *Chancellorsville,* 22-23.
35. Sheridan, 67 WR 348.
36. Sheridan to Humphreys, 67 WR 428.

37. Comstock, Cyrus B., Personal Diary, in Comstock Papers, Div. of Mss., Library of Congress.
38. Schaff, *Wilderness*, 111.

CHAPTER 5

1. Longstreet, James. *From Manassas to Appomattox: Memoirs of the Civil War in America.* J. B. Lippincott, N. Y. and Phila., 1903, p. 556. Hereinafter cited as Longstreet, *Memoirs.*
2. Sorrel to Field, 68 WR 947.
3. Lee, Fitzhugh, *Manuscript Report,* Confederate Museum, Richmond. It seems probable that Fitzhugh Lee's reports on May 4th were telegraphed via Hanover Junction-Gordonsville-Orange Court House to Lee's Headquarters.
4. Taylor to Ewell, 68 WR 948.
5. Styles, Robert, *Four Years Under Marse Robert,* 245.
6. Stuart to Lee, 11:15 p.m., May 4, 1864, 108 WR 887-888.
7. Long, A. L. *Lee,* 327.

CHAPTER 6

1. Wilson, Rpt of Opns, *ibid.,* 887.
2. Wilson, Rpt of Opns, *ibid.* 877; Pennington, Rpt of Opns, *ibid.,* 903.
3. Wilson, Rpt of Opns, *ibid.,* 877; Chapman, *ibid.,* 897.
4. McDonald, William N., *A History of the Laurel Brigade, Originally the Ashby Cavalry of the Army of Northern Virginia and Chew's Battery,* 226 ff. (Hereinafter cited as *Laurel Brig.*)
5. Wilson, Rpt of Opns, 67 WR 897.
6. Pennington, Rpt of Opns, *ibid.,* 903.
7. Wilson, Rpt of Opns, *ibid.,* 877; Chapman, *ibid.,* 897.
8. Wilson, Rpt of Opns, 67 WR 877.
9. Sheridan, Rpt of Opns, *ibid.,* 787.
10. Warren to Humphreys, 68 WR 225 ff., 413.
11. *Circular,* Headquarters V Corps, 4 May, 68 WR 378-379.
12. Warren to Getty, *ibid.,* 421.
13. Schaff, Morris, *Wilderness,* 123; Swan, William W., "The Battle of the Wilderness," *Massachusetts Military Historical Society* Papers, IV, 127. (Hereinafter cited as *M.M.H.S.P.*)
14. Locke to Jenkins, *ibid.,* 415.
15. Schaff, Morris, *Wilderness,* 126.
16. Warren to Humphreys, 68 WR 413.
17. Throop, W. A., Rpt of Opns, 67 WR 540.
18. White, W. B., Rpt of Opns, *ibid.,* 575.
19. Humphreys, A. A., *Va. Campaign,* 23.
20. Humphreys to Hancock, 68 WR 406.
21. Crawford to Locke, *ibid.,* 418; Locke to Humphreys (First indorsement), *ibid.,* 418.
22. Meade to Grant, *ibid.,* 403.
23. White, Mass., Rpt of Opns, 57 WR 575.
24. Meade to Grant, 68 WR 404.

CHAPTER 7

1. The center of distribution of Hancock's forces was some eight miles from that of Warren's. After receiving orders at 11:40 a.m. (see Humphreys

to Hancock, 68 WR 407) to concentrate at the Brock-Plank Road intersection. Hancock did not complete his concentration until sometime after 5 p.m. At 4:05 p.m., Hancock had not as yet completed preparations to attack with two divisions (Cf. Hancock to Humphreys, 4:05 p.m., 5 May, 68 WR 410).

2. Crawford to Locke, 68 WR 418; *Supra*, 181.
3. Wadsworth to (Griffin ?), 68 WR 420.
4. Getty, Rpt of Opns, 67 WR 676. "The division moved at 7 a.m. on the 5th to Old Wilderness Tavern."
5. Robinson Rpt of Opns, *ibid.*, 593.
6. White, *ibid.*, 575; Throop *ibid.*, 580.
7. Upton, 67 WR 665.
8. Hancock to Humphreys, 68 WR 407.
9. Meade to Grant, 68 WR 403. Cf. Humphreys, A. A., *Va. Campaign;* Hyde, Thomas Worcester, *Following the Greek Cross; or, Memoirs of the Sixth Army Corps,* 183, (Hereinafter cited as *VI Corps*) Hyde carried a message from Meade to Grant, meeting the Lieutenant General while riding from Germanna to the front.
10. Grant to Meade, 68 WR 403.
11. *Ibid.*, 403.
12. Atkinson, C. F., *Grant's Campaigns of 1864 and 1865,* pp. 136-37. Hugh Rees, Ltd., London, 1908.
13. Meade, Rpt of Opns, 67 WR 189.
14. Jenkins, Commanding Outposts, to Locke (Indorsement), Locke to Jenkins, 68 WR 415.
15. Griffin to Bartlett (Indorsement), Locke to Griffin, *ibid.*, 416; White, Rpt of Opns, 67 WR 575.
16. Stonewall Jackson's infantry mustered 35,695 ("effective total"). This figure is derived by subtracting the "effective total," 7,638, of Early's Division, from 33,333, the "effective total" of the II Corps infantry, 40 WR 696.
17. Wadsworth to (Griffin ?), 68 WR 420.
18. Locke to Griffin, *ibid.*, 68, 416; White, Rpt of Opns, *ibid.*, 67, 575.
19. Dalton, Assistant Adjutant General, First Division, VI Corps, Rpt of Opns, 67 WR 660; Upton, Rpt of Opns, *ibid.*, 665.
20. Locke to Griffin, 8 a.m., 68 WR 416.
21. Schaff, Morris, *Wilderness,* 129.
22. *Ibid.*, 129, 130.
23. Schaff, Morris. *Wilderness.*
24. Locke to Humphreys (Indorsement), Crawford to Locke, 68 WR 418.
25. Meade to (Grant ?) (Second Endorsement), Crawford to Locke.
26. Meade to Grant, 9 a.m., 68 WR 404.
27. Schaff, Morris, *Wilderness,* 130.
28. Roebling to Warren, 68 WR 418.
29. Sypher, Josiah Rhinehart, *History of the Pennsylvania Reserve Corps: A Complete Record of the Organization, and of the Different Companies, Regiments, and Brigades,* 510. (Hereinafter cited as *Pa. Res. Corps.*)
30. Roebling, according to Schaff, Morris, *Wilderness,* 131-132.
31. Beaudrye, Louis Napoleon, *Historic Records of the Fifth New York Cavalry, First Ira Harris Guard,* 122. (Hereinafter cited as *5th N. Y. Cav.*); Palmer, Wm. H., *Some Reminiscences,* 28. (Hereinafter cited as "Letter to Royal," *Reminiscences.*)
32. Beaudrye, Louis Napoleon, *5th N. Y. Cav.*, 122.

33. Sypher, J. H., *Pa. Res. Corps*, 510.
34. Wilcox, Maj. Gen. Cadmus M., "Grant and Lee in the Wilderness," *Annals of the War Written by Leading Participants, North and South,* 489. (Hereinafter cited as "Wilderness," *Annals*); Clark, Walter, ed., *Histories of the Several Regiments and Battalions from North Carolina in the Great War, 1861-1865. Written by Members of the Respective Commands,* III, 94. (Hereinafter cited as *North Carolina Regiments*).
35. The first dispatch sent by Crawford from Chewning's farm was an hour in transit.
36. Major B. F. Fisher, Chief Signal Officer, Army of the Potomac, 67 WR 283. In the battle of the Wilderness communication by flag signals was established between the headquarters of General Warren at the Lacy house and those of General Crawford near Parker's Store. This communication was very opportune, as the enemy, moving against this advanced position, allowed but limited time to the officer commanding in which to receive instructions.
37. Wadsworth to (Griffin ?), 68 WR 420.
38. Roebling to Warren, *ibid.,* 418.

CHAPTER 8

1. Humphreys, A. A., *Va. Campaign,* 24.
2. Schaff, Morris, *Wilderness,* 135. ". . . he came to the front with all speed: it was then about nine o'clock."
3. Grant to Meade, 68 WR 403.
4. Grant to Burnside, *ibid.,* 423-424.
5. Meade to Grant, *ibid.,* 404. Meade calls Grant's attention in this dispatch to the conflicts of orders, his own and Grant's, given Ricketts.
6. Comstock to Burnside, *ibid.,* 424.
7. Humphreys, A. A., *Va. Campaign,* 24; *Supra,* 94.
8. Locke to Robinson, 68 WR 417; Robinson, Rpt of Opns, 67 WR 593; Graham, Rpt of Opns, *ibid.,* 601.
9. Upton, Rpt of Opns, 67 WR 665.
10. Crawford to Locke, 68 WR 418.
11. Humphreys, A. A., *Va. Campaign,* 21; *Personal Diary of Cyrus B. Comstock,* etc., 5 May 1864. *Supra,* 139 et seq.
12. Locke to Wadsworth, 10:30 a.m., 68 WR 420; Humphreys, A. A., *Va. Campaign* 25; Humphreys to Hancock (received 11:45 a.m.), 68 WR 407; Getty, Rpt of Opns, 67 WR 676.
13. Cf. Getty, 67 WR 676, stating that he was ordered to move at noon toward the Brock Crossing, and Humphreys, A. A., *Va. Campaign,* 25, stating that the orders for both Getty and Hancock to move to the Brock Crossing.
14. Humphreys, A. A., *Va. Campaign,* 25.
15. Humphreys to Warren, 11 a.m., 68 WR 413.
16. Humphreys to Hancock, 68 WR 407.
17. Getty Rpt of Opns, 67 WR 676; *Supra,* 215, note 111.
18. Bidwell, Rpt of Opns, *ibid.,* 719.
19. Upton, Rpt of Opns, *ibid.,* 665.
20. Meade to Grant, 68 WR 404.
21. Swan, William W., *Massachusetts Military Historical Society Papers* (M.M.H.S.P.) II, 129.
22. Swan, William W., *ibid.,* 129.
23. Tilton, W. S., Col. Rpt of Opns, 67 WR 559-60.

24. Swan, William W., "Wilderness," 2 *M.M.H.S.P.*, 130.
25. Crawford to Locke, 68 WR 418.
26. Warren to Crawford, *ibid.*, 418.
27. Crawford to Locke, *ibid.*, 419.
28. Warren to Crawford, *ibid.*, 419.
29. Crawford to Locke, *ibid.*, 420.
30. Humphreys to Hancock, *ibid.*, 407.
31. Stevens, Hazard, "The Sixth Corps in the Wilderness," 4 *M.M.H.S.P.*, 190.
32. *Ibid.*, 190.

CHAPTER 9

1. Styles, Robert, *Four Years Under Marse Robert*, 245.
2. Ewell, Rpt of Opns, 67 WR 1070; Pendleton, Rpt of Opns, *ibid.*, 1038; Long, Rpt of Opns, *ibid.*, 1084.
3. Wilcox, C. M., "Wilderness," *Annals*, 489; *North Carolina Regiments*, I, 172 (2d N.C.).
4. Pendleton, Rpt of Opns, 37 WR 1039.
5. McDonald, W. M., *Laurel Brig.*
6. Longstreet, Rpt of Opns, 67 WR 1054; Field, C. W., "Campaign of 1864 and 1865. Narrative of Major General C. W. Field," in *Southern Historical Society Papers*, XIV, 543. (Hereinafter cited as "Campaign, 1864," *S.H.S.P.*).
7. *North Carolina Regiments*, II, 288 (5th N. C.), 336 (12th N.C.).
8. Cf. Freeman, D. S., *R. E. Lee*, II, 277.
9. Palmer, William H., "Letter to Royal," *Reminiscences*, 28-29.
10. The first brush, according to Beaudrye, chaplain and historian of the 5th New York Cavalry, occurred about two miles west of Parker's Store. *Supra*, 198.
11. Beaudrye, L. N., *5th N. Y. Cav.*
12. McIntosh, J. B., commanding 1st Brigade, 3d Cavalry Division, Rpt of Opns, 67 WR 885; Pendleton, Rpt of Opns, *ibid.*, 1039.
13. Ewell, Rpt of Opns, 57 WR 1070.
14. Wilcox, C. M., "Wilderness," *Annals*, 489; *North Carolina Regiments*, II, 446, III, 303.
15. Ewell, Rpt of Opns, 57 WR 1070; Long, Rpt of Opns, *ibid.*, 1084-1085.
16. Wilcox, C. M., "Wilderness," Annals, 489; *North Carolina Regiments*, III, (48th N.C.) 248, (55th N.C.) 303.
17. Humphreys, A. A., *Va. Campaign*, 29; Wilcox, C. M., "Wilderness," *Annals*, 492.
18. Pendleton, Rpt of Opns, 67 WR 1039.
19. MS. Report of Fitzhugh Lee, Confederate Museum, Richmond, 3.
20. Wilcox, C. M., "Wilderness," *Annals*, 492; Caldwell, J. F. J., *The History of a Brigade of South Carolinians known as "Gregg's" and subsequently as McGowan's Brigade*," 127 (hereinafter cited as *McGowan's Brig.*).
21. McGowan's Brigade, bringing up the rear of Wilcox's Division, reached Wilderness Run (west branch) just north of Chewning's farm about 4 p.m.
22. Palmer, William H., "Letter to Royal," *Reminiscences*, 28; Pendleton, Rpt of Opns, 58 WR 1039.
23. The fighting around Chancellorsville, 1-6 May 1863, evinced little adaptability on the part of the Army of the Potomac to cope with its opponent in forest fighting.

CHAPTER 10

1. Robinson, Rpt of Opns, 67 WR 593. Graham, Rpt of Opns, *ibid.*, 601. Bowerman, *ibid.*, 603. If, as stated by Col. White (*ibid.*, 575), Griffin's

and Wadsworth's division were connected between 8 and 9 a.m., there was no room between them for the Maryland brigade.

2. Cowdry, Rpt of Opns, 67 WR 614, Anderson, *ibid.*, 614-15.
3. Walsh, Rpt of Opns, 67 WR 616. Daws, R. R., *Service With the Sixth Wisconsin Volunteers* (Marietta, Ohio, 1890), 247.
4. Cutler, Rpt of Opns, 67 WR 610.
5. Tilton, Rpt of Opns, 67 WR 559.
6. As related in chapter 11, Rice pushed across the front of Daniels' Brigade, on the extreme right of Ewell's right echelon.
7. 67 WR 227 and 559.
8. 67 WR 555 and 557. Brainard, Mary Genevieve Green, comp., *Campaigns of the 146th Regiment, New York Volunteers, also known as Halleck's Infantry and the 5th Oneida and Garrard's Tigers* (G. P. Putnam's Sons, New York and London), 187 ff. Hereinafter cited as Brainard, *146th N. Y.*
9. This figure represents the average brigade strength in Warren's V Corps and is determined from the following

$$\frac{24{,}436 \times .93}{11} = 2039$$

In the above, 24,436 is the infantry strength, V Corps, as reported present for duty on 3 April 1864, 60 WR 1036. Following Livermore, 93 percent is taken to determine actual combat strength. The number of brigades is the denominator. Using the reported infantry strength of Ewell's Corps as reported on 30 April 1864, 60 WR 1297, we have

$$\frac{20{,}710 \times .93}{12} = 1435$$

10. 67 WR 197-98.
11. *Ibid.*, Atkinson, *Grant*, 162.
12. 67 WR 1070. Thurston, Col. S. D., 3d N. C. Infantry, "Steuart's Brigade in the Wilderness," SHSP IX, 146-154; cf. "The Third North Carolina," *North Carolina Regiments*, I, 199.
13. 67 WR 1040, 1085.
14. Lyman, *Meade's Headquarters*, 59, 67 WR 557, 586, 573. Swan, W. W., "The Battle of the Wilderness," *M.M.H.S.P.*, 130 ff. The staff officers had difficulty in carrying the orders to regimental commanders and I feel certain that some regiments went forward merely because they saw others leave the woods. *Ibid.*, 130.
15. Schaff, *Wilderness*, 160. Powell, W. H., *The Fifth Army Corps. A Record of Operations During the Civil War in the U. S., 1861-65* (G. P. Putnam's Sons, London, 1896), 608. Hereinafter cited as *Powell, V Corps.*
    Cf. Sweet, company commander, 146th N. Y., quoted by Brainard, op. cit., 191.
16. 67 WR 640. Brainard, *op. cit.*, 191.
17. Brainard, *op. cit.*, 185. Powell, *op. cit.*, 609.
18. *Ibid*
19. *Ibid.*
20. Powell, *op. cit.*, 609-10.
21. *Ibid*, 610. Tilton, Rpt of Opns, 67 WR 559; Cunningham, *ibid.*, 569.
22. Thurston, *Steuart's Brigade*, 148. *The North Carolina Brigades, I*, The 1st N. C., 150, 199. Quoted by Brainard, 192.
23. Waldron, *War Memoir*.
24. Sweet, quoted, by Brainard, 191 ff.

25. 67 WR 580.
26. 67 WR 573, 575, 586, 589, 590, 560, 567, 569.
27. Citations given in the preceding note carry the story of Bartlett's temporary breakthrough, his repulse, and retirement.
28. *Ibid.*
29. Smith, L. J., comp., *Antietam to Appomattox with the 118th Pa. Vols. Corn Exchange Regiment* (L. J. Smith, Philadelphia, 1892), 400. Hereinafter cited as Smith, *118th Pa.*
30. Regimental Association, comp., *Under the Maltese Cross, Campaigns of the 155th Pa. Regiment* (Philadelphia, 1910), 563-64. Hereinafter cited as Reg. Assn., *155th Pa.*
31. Lyman, *Meade's Headquarters*, 90.

CHAPTER 11

1. Curtis O. O., *History of the Twenty-Fourth Michigan of the Iron Brigade* (Winn and Hammond, Detroit, 1891), 230-31. Hereinafter cited as Curtis, *24th Mich.* See also Rpt of Opns, 67 WR 617.
2. "Report of colors captured from the enemy by the Fifth Corps, from 4 May to 4 November 1864," 67 WR 545.
3. Rpt of Opns, 67 WR 593, *ibid.*, 601.
4. Rpt of Opns, 67 WR 623. Humphrey's *Va. Campaign*, 26-27.
5. Gordon, John Brown, *Reminiscences of the Civil War* (Charles Scribner's Sons, New York; Martin & Hoyt Co., 1904), 238. Hereinafter cited as Gordon, *Reminiscences.*
6. 67 WR 1076-77.
7. The author paced the route that Gordon would have followed had he actually enveloped Rice's left flank. Walking as close to the average rate of 2½ miles an hour as the obstacles of the terrain permitted—a faster pace than six regiments in deployed order could have maintained—it took just short of two hours to go from Gordon's reserve position to a point beyond Daniels' right, where Gordon would have had room to clear the Confederate line and hit Rice's left rear.
8. Smith, Abraham P. *History of the Seventy-Sixth New York Volunteers* (Cortland, New York, 1867), 284 ff. 67 WR 623.
9. *Ibid.*
10. 67 WR 610-11. (2) *ibid.*, 617.
11. 67 WR 604.
12. See Chapter 9.
13. 67 WR 623. Clark, Walter (ed.) *Histories of the Several Regiments and Battalions from North Carolina in the Great War 1861-1865. Written by Members of the Respective Commands.* 5 Vols. (Published for the State by E. M. Uzzell, Printer & Binder, Raleigh, 1901), III, 45th N. C., 422. Hereinafter cited as *N. C. Regiments.* 67 WR 640-41.
14. Losses given here are from Sypher, Josiah Rhinehart, *History of the Pennsylvania Reserve Corps: A Complete Record of the Organization, and the Different Companies, Regiments, and Brigades* (Elias Burr & Co., 1865), 294. Hereinafter cited as Sypher, *Pa. Reserve Corps.* Cf. Thomas, O. R. *History of the Bucktails. Kane Rifle Regiment of the Pennsylvania Reserve Corps.*, 294. Hereinafter cited as Kane, *Bucktails.*
15. Brainard, 146th N. Y., 192. Thurston, *Steuart's Brigade*, 184. *N. C. Regiments*, I, 1st N. C., 150, 199.
16. Brainard, *146th N. Y.*, 193.

17. *Ibid.*, 195.
18. *Ibid.*
19. *N. C. Regiments*, I, 1st N. C., 150.
20. *Ibid.* 67 WR 640.
21. *N. C. Regiments*, I, 1st N. C., 150. Thurston, *Steuart's Brigade*, 149.
22. *Ibid,* 150.
23. *Ibid.*
24. *Ibid.* 67 WR 640.
25. *Ibid.* Thurston, *Steuart's Brigade.*
26. 67 WR 55960, 593.
27. Rpt of Opns, 67 WR 603.
28. Rpt of Opns, 67 WR 611, 623. 68 WR 409.
29. 67 WR 593, 596.
30. Return of Casualties in the Union forces, Battle of the Wilderness, 5-7 May 1864, 67 WR 123, 125.
31. 67 WR 640-41.
32. 67 WR 1070, 1076. Thurston, *Steuart's Brigade*, 149.
33. The order of brigades in Ewell's original line remained unchanged, excepting for the withdrawal of Jones. In forming the new line, the right echelon advanced to the line of the left echelon with Gordon on the extreme right and Early's Division, less Gordon, holding the left toward Flat Run.
34. 67 WR 1041-41, 1084-85.
35. Lyman, *Meade's Headquarters*, 90.
36. *Ibid.*, 91. The author admits a slight embellishment of Lyman's account. Lyman abruptly concludes with Meade's remark: "and it's only his way of talking." While a reasonable presumption, there is no documentary evidence that Grant lit a fresh cigar. But since no disciplinary action was taken against Griffin, we may safely conclude that the impression he made was for the moment over-powering and that his exit was an unceremonious as his entrance. Griffin would have been at home in the army of Henry V.

CHAPTER 12

1. Humphreys to Warren, 12:45 p.m., 5 May 1864, 68 WR 414.
2. Hancock to Williams, 11:40 a.m., 5 May 1864, 68 WR 407.
3. Humphreys to Hancock, 1:30 p.m., 5 May 1864, 68 WR 409.
4. Humphreys to Warren, 2:15 p.m., 5 May 1864, 68 WR 414.
5. Humphreys to Hancock, 2:15 p.m., 5 May 1864, 68 WR 414.
6. Hancock, Rpt of Opns, 67 WR.
7. Hancock to Humphreys, 2:40 p.m., 5 May 1864, 68 WR 409-10.
8. Hancock to Humphreys, 3:15 p.m., 5 May 1864, 68 WR 410.
9. Humphreys to Hancock, 68 WR 410.
10. Humphreys to Warren, (rec'd. 4 p.m.), 5 May 1864, 68 WR 414.

CHAPTER 13

1. Humphreys to Hancock, 3:15 p.m., 68 WR 410. Lyman, Theodore, *Letters*, 91.
2. *Ibid.*, 91
3. Getty, Rpt of Opns, 67 WR 676. Wheaton, *ibid.*, 681. L. A. Grant, *ibid.*, 696.

4. Hutchinson, Nelson V. *History of the Seventh Volunteer Infantry in the Rebellion of the Southern States Against Constitutional Authority, 1861-1865*, 175-76 (Hereinafter cited as Hutchinson, *7th Mass.*); Roe, Alfred S., *The Tenth Regiment, Massachusetts Volunteer Infantry, 1861-1864*, p. 272; Woodbury, Augustus, *The Second Rhode Regiment*, 337-38.

5. Getty, *ibid.*, 677. Tidball, Chief of Artillery, II Corps, *ibid.*, 507.

6. Hancock, *ibid.*, 319.

7. Humphreys to Hancock, 12 m., 68 WR 404; Humphreys to Hancock, 1:30 p.m., *ibid.*, 409; Humphreys to Hancock, 2:15 p.m., *ibid.*, 409; 3 p.m., 410.

8. Wilcox, C. M., "Wilderness," *Annals*, 492; *North Carolina Regiments* (15th N. C.), I, 744; (27th N. C.) II, 446; (46th N. C.) III, 75; (48th N. C.), III, 118; III, 303; Humphreys, A. A., *Va. Campaign*, 29

9. *North Carolina Regiments* (11th N. C.), I, 594; (26th N. C.), II, 382-383; (44th N. C.), III, 27; (47th N. C.,), III, 111.

10. *North Carolina Regiments* (44th N. C.), 27; (52d N. C.), III, 245.

11. These figures are based on the average of 2,000 to the brigade and averaged with the number of regiments per brigade. The Vermont regiments were generally maintained at a greater average strength than other state regiments. Cook's Brigade mustered 1,800 effectives. *North Carolina Regiments*, IV, 507. Wilcox estimates the strength of Hill's two divisions (Wilcox and Heth) at 13,000. Wilcox, C. M., "Wilderness," *Annals*, 493.

12 *Supra*, 188-89.

13. Getty, Rpt of Opns, 67 WR 677; Wheaton, *ibid.*, 681; Grant, *ibid.*, 696; Parsons, *10th Mass.*, 27.

14. Lt. Col. Parsons' "Narrative," quoted by Hutchinson, *7th Mass.*, 175-76.

15. Wheaton, Rpt of Opns, 67 WR 682.

16. *Ibid.*, 682.

17. McLaughlin, *ibid.*, 691.

18. Grant, L. A., *ibid.*, 696-697.

19. *Ibid.*, 697; Leaver, Col. T. O., 3d Vt., *ibid.*, 709; Pingree, Col. S. M., 4th Vt., *ibid.*, 710; Hamilton, Capt. E. A., 5th Vt., *ibid.*, 714.

20. Hancock to Humphreys, 4:05 p.m., 68 WR 410.

21. DeTrobriand, Brig. Gen. Regis, commander, 1st Brig. (Ward), Rpt of Opns, 67 WR 467.

22. Grant, *ibid.*, 697; Cf. Cannon, Capt. M. M., 40th N. Y., *ibid.*, 473; Tyler, Lt. Col. C. W., 141st Pa., *ibid.*, 477; Craft, David C., Chaplain, 141st Pa., *History of the One Hundred Forty-First Pennsylvania Volunteers, 1862-1865*, 178 (hereinafter cited as *141st Pa. Inf.*).

23. Tyler, 67 WR 447; Cannon, *ibid.*, 473.

24. Grant, *ibid.*, 697.

25. *Supra*, 207-208.

26. Wilson, Capt. Jno., 1st U. S. Sharp-shooters, Rpt of Opns, 67 WR 485. Maj. Charles P. Mattock commanded the Sharpshooter detachment.

27. Neeper, Lt. Col. W. B., 57th Pa., Rpt of Opns, *ibid.*, 483.

28. Wheaton, 67 WR 334, 682; Carroll, *ibid.*, 446.

29. Martin, James M., comp., *History of the Fifty-Seventh Regiment, Pennsylvania Veteran Volunteer Infantry*, 107; hereinafter cited as *57th Pa. Inf.*. 63d Pennsylvania, Hays, Gilbert Adams, comp., *Under the Red Patch; Story of the Sixty-Third Regiment Pennsylvania Volunteers, 1861-1864*, Pittsburgh, 1908, 232. Hays' losses in killed, wounded and missing were

1,390; Grant's Vermont brigade lost 1,269; Ayres' brigade, Griffin's division, suffered 936 casualties; Ward's brigade, 851; *57th Pa. Inf.*, 107.

30. McAllister, Col. R., 1st Brig., 67 WR 487; Schoonover, Lt. Col. Jno., 11th N. J., *ibid.*, 493.
31. Godfrey, Capt. T. C., 5th N. J., *ibid.*, 496; Thompson, Capt. T. C., 7th N. J., *ibid.*, 498; McAllister, *ibid.*, 487; Schoonover, Lt. Col. Jno., 11th N. J., *ibid.*, 492; Darling, Charles B., *Historical Sketch of the First Regiment Infantry, Massachusetts Volunteer Militia*, 459 (hereinafter cited as *1st Mass. Inf.*).
32. McAllister, 67 WR 847.
33. *Ibid.*, 487.
34. Schoonover, *ibid.*, 492-493,
35. Thompson, *ibid.*, 498.
36. McAllister, *ibid.*, 487-488.
37. Cudworth, W. H., Chaplain, 1st Mass., *History of the First Massachusetts Infantry*, Boston, Walker Fuller, Co., 1886, 459.
38. Burns, Col. M. W., 73d N. Y., Rpt of Opns, 67 WR 503; Thompson, *ibid.*, 498-499.
39. McAllister, *ibid.*, 488.
40. Weygant, C. H., *124 N. Y. Inf.*, 287.
41. Lyman, Theodore, *Letters*, 92.
42. *Ibid.*, 92.
43. *Ibid.*, 92; Gibbon, Rpt of Opns, 67 WR 429.
44. Carroll, *ibid.*, 446; Webb, *ibid.*, 437; Gibbon, *ibid.*, 430: "As Owen's brigade arrived upon the ground it was posted on Webb's right." Carroll, *ibid.*, 446: "By his (Birney's) command I advanced in the wood on the right of the Plank Road."
45. 68 WR 411.
46. *North Carolina Regiments* (11th N. C.), I, 594.

1. Wilcox, C. M., "Wilderness," *Annals*, 492; Caldwell, J. F. C., *McGowan's Brig.*, 127.
2. *Ibid.*, 127, 492.
3. *Ibid.*, 493.
4. Locke to Humphreys, 5:45 p. m., 68 WR 414.
5. As reported by Wilcox from Chewning's farm, Wilcox, C. M., "Wilderness," *Annals*, 492.
6. Tompkins, Chief of Artillery, VI Corps, Rpt of Opns, Daily Memoranda of Artillery Brigades, 5 May 67 WR 753.
7. Robinson, Rpt of Opns, *ibid.*, 593.
8. Marshal, *aide-de-camp* to Ewell, 68 WR 952.
9. Porter, Horace, *Grant;* Schaff, Morris, *Wilderness*, 190; Pearson, H. G., *Wadsworth*, 268.
10. Robinson, 67 WR 593.
11. Hofmann, Rpt of Opns, *ibid.*, 623, states that the movement began at 6 p.m. Cope, Capt. E., *aide-de-camp*, 68 WR 421, informed Warren at 6:20 p.m.: "Wadsworth has been driving the enemy. They have opened batteries with canister on him."
12. *North Carolina Regiments*, I, 594.

13. Carroll, Rpt of Opns, 67 WR 446; Goddard, H. P., *14th Conn. Inf.*, 237; Kelper, William, *4th Ohio Inf.*, 164; Sawyer, F. A., *8th Ohio Inf.*

14. Hancock, Rpt of Opns, 67 WR 320; Barnes, Charles H., *History of the Philadelphia Brigade, Sixty-Sixth, Seventy-First, Seventy-Second, and One Hundred and Sixth Pennsylvania. Voluteers*, 217; Joseph R. C., *History of the One Hundred and Sixth Regiment, Pennsylvania Volunteers, 2d Brigade, 2d Division, 2d Corps*, 1861-1865.

15. *Supra*, 208, 215.

16. Hancock, Rpt of Opns, 67 WR 320.

17. *North Carolina Regiments*, I, 594.

18. Lyman, Theodore, *Letters*, 92. Carroll led his troops in action the next day.

19. Ricketts, Capt. R. B., Battery F, 1st Pa., Rpt of Opns, 67 WR 531.

20. *North Carolina Regiments*, III, 27.

21. Webb, Rpt of Opns, 67 WR 437; Bruce, George Anson, *The Twentieth Regiment of Massachusetts, Volunteer Infantry*, 1861-1865, 350 (hereinafter cited as *20th Mass. Inf.*).

22. Cudworth, *1st Mass.*, 460.

23. Miles, Rpt of Opns, 67 WR 370; Brooke, *ibid.*, 407.

24. Fleming, Capt. James, 28th Mass., *ibid.*; "This regiment being the only one in the Second Brigade (Smyth) who were armed with rifles (magazine), it was constantly acting as skirmishers, while the brigade was at work throwing up their intrenchments of logs and earth."

25. Brooke, Brig. Gen., 4th Brig., 1st Div., Rpt of Opns, 67 WR 407.

26. Hancock to Humphreys, 68 WR 411.

27. Caldwell, J. F. C., *McGowan's Brig.*, 127.

28. Wilcox, C. M., "Wilderness," *Annals*, 492; *North Carolina Regiments* (13th N. C.), I, 676; *ibid.*, (34th N. C.), 588.

29. Caldwell, J. F. C., *McGowan's Brig.*, 128.

30. Wilcox, C. M., "Wilderness," *Annals*, 129.

31. Caldwell, J. F. C., *McGowan's Brig.*, 129-30.

32. Ricketts, Capt. R. B., Battery F, 1st Pa., Rpt of Opns, 67 WR 531.

33. Caldwell, J. F. C., McGowan's Brig., 130. Cf. *North Carolina Regiments* (13th N. C.), 588.

34. *North Carolina Regiments* (13th N. C.), 676.

35. *Ibid.* (55th N. C.), III, 303. A short account of Co. G., Lamar (Rifles), 11th Miss., gives a hint of the prowess of this redoubtable brigade—one of the best of the Army of Northern Virginia. Buford, Thomas P., *Lamar Rifles*, A History of Company G, Eleventh Mississippi Regiment C. S. A., Roanoke, Va., Stone Printing Co. (no date).

36. Brooke, Rpt of Opns, 67 WR 407.

37. *Supra*, 222.

38. *North Carolina Regiments* (33d N. C.), II, 569; *ibid.* (28th N. C.), II, 479; Lane, J. H., "Report," 9 *S.H.S.P.*, 125.

39. *North Carolina Regiments* (55th N. C.), III, 303.

40. Palmer, W. H., "Letter to Royal," *Reminiscences*, 29; Lane, J. H., "Report," *S.H.S.P.*, 125; Cf. *North Carolina Regiments*, (37th N. C.), II, 665.

41. Lane, J. H., "Report." *S.H.S.P.*, 125.

42. *North Carolina Regiments*, II, 665.

43. Lane, J. H., "Report," *S.H.S.P.*, 125.

44. It must also be realized that the mass of Federal operation reports of the battle of the Wilderness were not written until October 1864, over four

months after the battle, with four major operations intervening. *Orders,* No. 265, which called for reports of operations from the Rapidan to the James, were issued on 1 October 1864, 67 WR 391.

45. Seymour to Meade, 68 WR 411.
46. *Supra,* 360-61.
47. 68 WR 411.
48. *Ibid.,* 411.
49. *Supra,* 234.
50. Lane, J. H., "Report," 9 *S.H.S.P.,* 126.
51. Brooke, Rpt of Opns, 67 WR 407.
52. The regulation pace of infantry in column of route is three miles per hour.
53. Brooke, 67 WR 407.
54. Lane, J. H., "Report," *S.H.S.P.,* 126.
55. *Ibid.,* 126; Brooke, 67 WR 407: "It was by this time quite dark, and very difficult to pass through the dense thicket of hte wilderness."
56. Palmer, W. H., "Letter to Royal," *Reminiscences,* 30; *North Carolina Regiments* (28th N. C.), II, 479.
57. Marshall to Ewell, 68 WR 953.
58. Cope to Warren, 5 May 1864, 6:20 p.m., 68 WR 421.
59. Cowdrey, Capt. E. H., Asst. Adj. Gen., Div., Rpt of Opns, 67 WR 614; Pearson states that Stone was drunk. *Pearson, Wadsworth,* 270.
60. Hofmann, Rpt of Opns, 67 WR 323; Cutler, *ibid.,* 611; Cowdrey, *ibid.,* 615.

Chapter 15

1. There is no statement as to a strategic objective in the repeated attacks against Ewell's left.
2. Dalton, Asst. Adj. Gen., Div., Rpt of Opns, 67 WR 659; Upton, 2d Brig., Rpt of Opns, *ibid.,* 665; Birdwell, 3d Brig., Rpt of Opns, *ibid.,* 719; Edwards, 1st Brig., Rpt of Opns, *ibid.,* 672.
3. Tompkins, commanding Artillery VI Corps, 67 WR 753.
4. The author checked this time and distance. Cf. Barnes, Charles H., *History of the Philadelphia Brigade, Sixty-Sixth, Seventy-First, Seventy-Second, and One Hundred and Sixth Pennsylvania Volunteers,* 113 (hereinafter cited as *Philadelphia Brig.*).
5. Ewell, Rpt of Opns, 67 WR 1070.
6. Brewer, E. T., *History of the Sixty-First Pennsylvania Volunteer Infantry,* Pittsburgh, 1911, 183.
7. Michler, Rpt of Opns, *ibid.,* 296; *supra,* 124.
8. Grant's silence here, as at 4 p.m., implies approval of Warren's inaction.
9. Humphreys to Warren, 68 WR 414.
10. Upton, Rept of Opns, 67 WR 605; Cf. Best, Isaac O., *History of the 121st New York State Infantry,* 117 (hereinafter cited as *121st New York Inf.*).
11. Hufty, Capt. B., 4th N. J., *ibid.,* 663. Cf. Barnes, C. H., *Philadelphia Brig.,* 113.
12. Bidwell, commanding Neill's Brig., 67 WR 719; Bidwell, Frederick David, *History of the Forty-Ninth New York Volunteers,* 43, 44 (hereinafter cited as *49th N. Y. Inf.*).
13. *Supra,* 187 et seq.
14. Humphreys to Hancock, 1:30 p.m., 68 WR 409; *ibid.,* Humphreys to Hancock, 2:15 p.m., 409.
15. Haines, Alanson Austin, *History of the Fifteenth Regiment Volunteers,* 141 (hereinafter cited as *15th N. J. Inf.*); Thurston, *Steuart's Brigade,* 148.

16. Upton, Rpt of Opns, 67 WR 665, 666.
17. Hyde, T., *VI Corps*, 184; Haines, A. A., *15th N. J. Inf.*, 141.
18. *Ibid.*, 142.
19. Barnes, C. H., *Philadelphia Brig.*, 113; Lee to Confederate Secretary of War, 68 WR 921. Cf. Journal of Major Monier, 10th La., *Military Record of Louisiana*, 44.
20. Early, J. A., *Autobiographical Sketch*, 346.
21. Edwards, Col. O. O., 3d Brig., Rpt of Opns, 67 WR 672; Anderson, J. S., "Through the Wilderness With Grant," *Report of the Proceedings of the Fifth Wisconsin Volunteer Infantry. Sixteenth Annual Reunion, 22-28 May 1908*, 8-9.
22. *Ibid.*, 9; Early, J. A., *Autobiographical Sketch*, 346. Early states that most of the 25th Virginia were captured.
23. Bidwell, Rpt of Opns, 67 WR 719.
24. *Supra*, 319.
25. Tompkins, Chief of Artillery, VI Corps, Rpt of Opns, 67 WR 753; Long, Chief of Artillery, II Corps (Confederate), Rpt of Opns, *ibid.*, 1085; Barnes, C. H., *Philadelphia Brig.*, 115; Haines, A. A., *15th N. J. Inf.*, 143.
26. Long, 67 WR 1085; Bidwell, *ibid.*, 719; Bidwell, F. D., *49th N. Y. Inf.*, 44.
27. Hyde, T., *VI Corps*, 185.
28. Stevens, George Thomas, *Three Years in the Sixth Corps*, 310-311 (hereinafter cited as *VI Corps*).
29. Humphreys to Officer Commanding V Corps, 2:15 p.m., 68 WR 414; Comstock to Burnside, 3 p.m., *ibid.*, 424.
30. Humphreys to Hancock, 3:15 p.m., *ibid.*, 410.
31. Humphreys to Warren, 4 p.m., *ibid.*, 414.
32. *Supra*, 248-49.
33. Seymour, Rpt of Opns, 67 WR 728.
34. Early, J. A., *Autobiographical Sketch*, 346.
35. *Supra*, 205, 120, 131-32, 187.
36. Seymour, Rpt of Opns, 67 WR 728; Morris, Rpt of Opns, *ibid.*, 722; Keifer, Col. J. W., 110th Ohio, *ibid.*, 730.
37. Lyman to Meade, 5:05 p.m., 68 WR 410-411.
38. Humphreys to commanding officer, V Corps, 6 p.m., 68 WR 415.
39. Hofmann, Rpt of Opns, 67 WR 823; Cope to Warren, 6:20 p.m.
40. Humphreys, A. A., *Va. Campaign*, 3; Footnote 1, 13.
41. Seymour, Rpt of Opns, 67 WR 728; Keifer, *ibid.*, 730.
42. Early, J. A., *Autobiographical Sketch*, 346.
43. Keifer, Rpt of Opns, 67 WR 731.
44. Bidwell, 67 WR 719; Bidwell, F. D., *49th N. Y. Inf.*, 55.
45. Brewer, A. T., *History of the Sixty-First Regiment Pennsylvania Volunteers*, Philadelphia, 1911, 81, 82.
46. Uuton, 67 WR 665; Barnes, C. H., *Philadelphia Brig.*, 115; Haines, A. A., *15th N. J. Inf.*, 141 ff.
47. Morris, 67 WR 722.
48. Wainwright, *ibid.*, 640; Humphreys, A. A., *Va. Campaign*, 33.
49. *North Carolina Regiments* (18th N. C.), II, 24.
50. Schaff, Morris, *Wilderness*, 30.
51. Infra, 279-80.

CHAPTER 16

1. Cowles, Maj. W. H. H., 1st N. C., to Stuart, Chief of Cavalry, 109 WR 681. Wilson, J. H. *Under the Old Flag*, I, 374. Wilson states that while serving as Chief of the Cavalry Bureau he induced the Chief of Ordnance to con-

tract for all Spencer carbines that could be turned out. Upon assignment to the 3d Cavalry Division, Wilson made requisition for 5,000, or enough to supply the entire division. But 3 months elapsed before deliveries were completed. *Ibid.*

2. Sheridan to Humphreys, 4 May, 68 WR 389.

3. Wilson, 67 WR 876.

4. Cowles, Maj. W. H. H., 1st N. C. Cav., to Stuart, Chief of Cavalry, 109 WR 888; Cowles to Ewell, 68 WR 952.

5. Schaff, Morris, *Wilderness*, 93. Wilson does not mention this incident in his report.

6. Orders, 4 May, 68 WR 371; *supra*, 140-141, quoted in full.

7. Wilcox, C. M., *"Wilderness,"* Annals, 489.

8. *Supra*, 92 et seq.

9. Itinerary, 1st Me., 67 WR 864; Merrill, Samuel H., *The Campaigns of the First Maine and First District of Columbia Cavalry*, Portland, Pailey and Noyes, 1866, 190.

10. Comstock Mss. Diary, 6 May 1864. "Sheridan moved with Gregg's and Torbert's cav' divisions toward Hamilton's Crossing. The movement was to protect the trains."

11. Wilson, Rpt of Opns, 67 WR 877; *supra*, 172.

12. Sheridan to Humphreys, 12 a.m., 68 WR 427. Quoted below, 411.

13. Sheridan's dispatch of noon to Humphreys is dated "Hdqrs. Cavalry Corps. . . . *Camp near Piney Branch Church*, Va. . . ." *ibid.*, 427.

14. This dispatch does not appear in *Official Records*.

15. 68 WR 427.

16. Forsyth to Gregg, 1:10 p.m., *ibid.*, 429.

17. Gregg to Forsyth, *ibid.*, 2:45 p.m.

18. Wilson, Rpt of Opns, 67 WR 877.

19. Gregg, Rpt of Opns, *ibid.*, 852; Kester, Col. J. W., 1st N. J. Cav., *ibid.*, 860.

20. Kester, *ibid.*, 860.

21. Crowninshield, Benjamin William, *A History of the First Regiment of Massachusetts Cavalry*, 205 (hereinafter cited as *1st Mass. Cav.*).

22. Rpt. of Opns., 67 WR 860; Crowinshield, B. W., *1st Mass. Cav.*, 205.

23. Sheridan, Rpt of Opns, 67 WR 788; Longstreet, in Longstreet, James, *Memoirs*, 556. Longstreet states that a cavalry fight took place near Richard's Shop just before his arrival there at 5 p.m., 5 May.

24. *Supra*, 267. A Confederate horse artillery gunner supports this view. Neese, George M., *Three Years is the Confederate Horse Artillery*, New York and Washington, The Neale Publishing Company, 260-261.

25. Wilson, Rpt of Opns, 67 WR 877.

26. Custer states that he "encamped about one mile beyond (Chancellorsville) on the Fredericksburg Plank road." 67 WR 815.

27. Merritt, Rpt of Opns, *ibid.*, 811; Devin, *ibid.*, 833. Wilson, Rpt of Opns, *ibid.*, 877; Chapman, *ibid.*, 897.

28. Williams to Sheridan, 6 p.m., 68 WR 428.

29. Sheridan to Williams, 11:10 p.m., *ibid.*, 428.

30. Meade to Grant, 10:30 p.m., *ibid.*, 405.

31. Grant to Meade, *ibid.*, 405.

CHAPTER 17

1. 68 WR 481, 483-484. Normal workings of Grant's staff organization are best illustrated in execution of Grant's decision to advance by the left to Spotsylvania Court House. The decision took form in his directive of

6:30 a.m., 7 May, to Meade. Meade's orders were issued at 3 p.m. to his corps commanders.

2. Porter, Horace, *Grant*, 53-54.

3. Comstock to Burnside, 68 WR 425. Stevenson did not make the move as ordered; no explanation is given. Possibly failure on Wilson's part to attack at 6 p.m. caused the order affecting Stevenson's division to be cancelled.

4. 68 WR 424; *Supra*, 191.

5. *Supra*, 279. Dispatch quoted in full. Cf. 68 WR 428.

6. 68 WR 428; *Supra*, 287. Dispatch quoted in full. The references are to dispositions intended to relieve the train guards mentioned in Sheridan's reply.

7. Sheridan to Williams, 68 WR 428.

8. Circular, 5 May 8 p.m., *ibid.*, 406.

9. Meade to Hancock, *ibid.*, 412.

10. Comstock to Burnside, *ibid.*, 425.

11. Williams to Hunt, *ibid.*, 406.

12. Meade to Hancock, *ibid.*, 412.

13. Meade to Warren, *ibid.*, 415.

14. Orders, 5 May, *ibid.*, 421.

15. Meade to Grant, *ibid.*, 404-405.

16. Cf. Schaff, Morris, *Wilderness*, 225.

17. The time given here is, possibly, somewhat late. Meade drafted the request to Grant at 10:30 p.m. Since Meade's headquarters camp was located eastward across the Germanna Plank Road from Grant's camp. Roebling, after conferring with Warren following the break-up of the conference, probably went across and continued discussion of the question with Lieutenant Colonel Comstock. Cf. *ibid.*, 210, 213, 230. Grant's reply to Meade's request for postponement of the attack bears no time-date. 68 WR 405.

18. Roebling, *Journal*, quoted by Schaff, Morris, *Wilderness*, 230. The reliability of Col. Roebling's *Journal* is attested by General A. A. Humphreys in the Preface (VI) to his *Va. Campaign*.

19. Warren's headquarters at the Lacy House would not have been more than a ten minute hand canter from Grant's camp.

20. Warren to Wadsworth, 68 WR 458.

21. Warren to Crawford, *ibid.*, 445.

22. Warren to Griffin, *ibid.*, 447.

23. Sheridan, Rpt of Opns, 67 WR 788.

24. Hancock, Rpt of Opns, *ibid.*, 321; Gibbon, *ibid.*, 430. For formation of Birney's assault column, see following: Regis de Trobriand, Rpt of Opns, *ibid.*, 469; Neeker, Lt. Col. 57th Pa., Rpt of Opns, *ibid.*, 483; Tyler, Lt. Col. C. W., 141st Pa., Rpt of Opns, *ibid.*, 477; McAllister, Rpt of Opns, *ibid.*, 488; Getty, Rpt of Opns, *ibid.*, 677; Wheaton, Rpt of Opns, *ibid.*, 682; Grant, Rpt of Opns, *ibid.*, 698; Carroll, Rpt of Opns, *ibid.*, 446.

25. Corodrey, Capt. F. H., Ass't Adj., 4th Div., Rpt of Opns, *ibid.*, 615; Cutler, *ibid.*, 611; Hofmann, *ibid.*, 623; Walsh, Maj. C. M., 7th Ind., *ibid.*, 617.

26. Warren to Griffin, 68 WR 455-456.

27. Warren to Crawford, *ibid.*, 457.

28. Tilton, Col. W. S., 22d Mass., Rpt of Opns, *ibid.*, 560; Burt, Maj. M. W., 22d Mass., Rpt of Opns, *ibid.*, 567; Cunningham, Maj. J. A., 22d Mass., Rpt of Opns, ibid., 567.

29. Itinerary, First Brigade, First Division, V, *ibid.*, 554; Lentz, Maj. J. D., Rpt of Opns, *ibid.*, 555; Pearson, Col. A. L., 155th Pa., Rpt of Opns, *ibid.*, 557.
30. Spaulding, Col. Ira, 50th N. Y. Engineers, Rpt of Opns, *ibid.*, 307.
31. Hunt, Brig. Gen. H. J., Chief of Artillery, "Extracts from Journal of," *ibid.*, 290.
32. Warren to Humphreys, 68 WR 449.
33. Crawford to Locke, 68 WR 457.
34. It is difficult from regimental reports, many of which are missing, to determine the number of regiments originally designated to the train guard and those returned to the line.
35. Morris, Rpt of Opns, 67 WR 722.
36. Dalton, Maj. H. R., Assistant Adjutant General, 1st Division, VI, Rpt of Opns, *ibid.*, 660.
37. Rawlins to Ferrero, 68 WR 464.
38. Richmond to Ferrero, *ibid.*, 463.
39. Estimated in numbers of divisions. Roughly, the Federal division averaged 5,200 bayonets, the Confederate 5,500. *Supra*, 75.
40. Comstock to Burnside, 68 WR 425; Warren to Wadsworth, *ibid.*, 458.
41. Atkinson, C. F., *Grant's Campaigns*, 165.
42. Grant, U. S., *Memoirs*, II, 195-196.
43. Atkinson, C. F., *Grant's Campaigns*, 166 et seq.
44. The dispositions required to fulfill his primary mission—protection of the trains—necessarily precluded all but minor and local offensive action. See *Infra*, 551.
45. *Supra*, 280.

CHAPTER 18

1. Cf. Freeman, D. S., *Lee*, III, 281-282.
2. Longstreet, James, *Memoirs*, 556.
3. H. B. McClellan Mss., cited by Freeman, D. S., *Lee*, III, 284.
4. Palmer, William H., "Letter to Royal," *Reminiscences*, 29.
5. Marshall to Ewell, 68 WR 953.
6. Wilcox, C. M., "Wilderness," *Annals*, 495.
7. Venable, C. S., "Lee to the Rear," *S.H.S.P.*, XIV, 108. Venable states that Lee intended to employ Hill, after being relieved by Longstreet, either on the right or left.
8. Palmer, William H., "Letter to Royal," *Reminiscences*, 30.
9. *Ibid.*, 31; Wilcox, C. M., "Wilderness," *Annals*, 495.
10. Caldwell, J. F. C., *McGowan's Brig.*, 131; *North Carolina Regiments*, III (55th N. C.), 303, Buford, T. P., *Lamar's Rifles*, 60.
11. Caldwell, J. F. C., *McGowan's Brig.*, 132.
12. Adjutant C. M. Cooke, in his account of the 55th N. C., Davis' (Stone's) Brigade (*North Carolina Regiments*, 303), mentions troops on his left, but does not specify organizations. He does not mention those on his right. Buford, in *Lamar Rifles*, 60, states that Wilcox's four brigades were on his left—that Stone "occupied the right of General Heth's Division." Buford undoubtedly means that Wilcox was on his right.
13. Lane, J. H., "Report," 9 *S.H.S.P.*, 126; *North Carolina Regiments*, II (33d N. C. P., 569.
14. *Ibid.*, II (27th N. C.), 446; *ibid.*, I (15th N. C.), 744.
15. *Ibid.*, II (11th N. C.), 595. "Our left flank and the unformed line

rolled up as a sheet of paper would be rolled without effective power of resistance."

16. Redway, George William, *Fredericksburg, A Study in War.*

17. Wilcox, C. M., "Wilderness," *Annals,* 495.

18. Pendleton, Rpt of Opns, 67 WR 1040.

19. Hofmann, Col. J. William, 56th Pa., Wadsworth's division, Rpt of Opns, *ibid.,* p. 623. Describing the advance at dawn on A. P. Hill's left flank, Hofmann reports: "The enemy now succeeded in bringing a battery to bear, enfilading us from the right flank."

20. Pendleton, Rpt of Opns, *ibid.,* 1040.

21. Ramseur, Rpt of Opns, 67 WR 1081. Ramseur is one day ahead of the calendar in the dates of his reports. He made the reconnaissance toward Culpeper Court House on 5 May, not 6 May, as stated, etc.

22. Cf. Ball, Col. William H., 122d Ohio, VI, Rpt of Opns, *ibid.,* 745. "Through the night the rebels were actively engaged in cutting timber, strengthening their works and moving to the right. Brigadier General Seymour who took command of the brigade that morning, was repeatedly notified during the night and early morning of the 6th of the movements of the enemy." Also, McClennan, Col. M. R., 136th Pa., VI, Rpt of Opns, *ibid.,* 751. "In the meantime (night of 5-6 May) the enemy could be heard chopping trees and fortifying in our front and beyond and opposite our right flank. I personally reported this fact to General Seymour and recommended him to take measures to prevent a flank attack."

23. Long, Rpt of Opns, *ibid.,* 1085.

24. Burnside, Rpt of Opns, *ibid.,* 906; Potter, *ibid.,* 927; Longstreet, *ibid.,* 1054; Kershaw, *ibid.,* 1061; Field, C. W., "Campaign, 1864," *S.H.S.P.* 453.

25. Anderson, R. H., in Walker, Cornelius Irvine, *The Life of Lieutenant General Richard Heron Anderson of the Confederate States Army,* 273 (hereinafter cited as *R. H. Anderson*).

CHAPTER 19

1. Bidwell, Rpt of Opns, 67 WR 719.

2. Ms. Diary, Comstock, 6 May, ". . . enemy (probably) attacked Wright at 4:50 a.m. Heavy fighting on Wright's and Warriors fronts. Wright charged enemy's defenses three times but failed to carry them."

3. Warren, "Journal," 67 WR 540; Warren to Humphreys, 68 WR 449.

4. Humphreys to Commanding Officer, V Corps, *ibid.,* 449.

5. Morris, Rpt of Opns, 67 WR 722-723.

6. Warren to Humphreys, 68 WR 450.

7. Warren to Humphreys, *ibid.,* 449.

8. Warren to Humphreys, *ibid.,* 450.

9. Humphreys to Warren, *ibid.,* 450.

10. Platt to Humphreys, *ibid.,* 450.

11. Humphreys to Commanding Officer, V Corps, *ibid.,* 450.

12. S. Williams, Circular, 7 a.m., 68 WR 439.

13. 67 WR 555-592.

14. Castle, Signal Officer, to Locke, 68 WR 450.

15. The signal message was received at V Corps Headquarters at 7:43 a.m. An orderly, according to F. T. Locke, Assistant Adjutant General, V Corps, pushed after Warren with the message, without showing it to any of the staff officers on duty at V Headquarters. It was not transmitted to Army Headquarters until 8:15 a.m., half an hour after delivery at V Corps.

16. Platt to Humphreys, *ibid.*, 451.
17. Ramseur, Rpt of Opns, 67 WR 1081.
18. *Ibid.*, 1081.
19. *Ibid.*, 1081.
20. Warren to Humphreys, 68 WR 449.
21. Schaff, Morris, *Wilderness*, 225-226. Schaff describes Burnside's departure from the council of corps commanders, 5 May, as follows: "At the close of his interview with Meade and the other corps commanders gathered there, he said, as he rose—he had a very grand and oracular air—"Well, then, my troops shall break camp by half past two!" and with shoulders thrown back and measured step disappeared in the darkness.
22. *Ibid.*, 231-232.
23. Lyman, Theodore, *Letters*, 94.
24. *Ibid.*, 94.
25. Burnside, Rpt of Opns, 67 WR 906.
26. Potter, Rpt of Opns, *ibid.*, 67, 928; Cutcheon, Col. B. M., 20th Mich., Rpt of Opns, *ibid.*, 67, 966; Cutcheon, Col. Byron M., *The Story of the Twentieth Michigan Infantry, July 15, 1862, to May 30, 1865*, Lansing, Mich., 1904. (Hereinafter cited as *20th Mich.*)
27. Wilcox, Rpt of Opns, 67 WR 942; Hartranft, *ibid.*, 948.
28. Humphrey, Col. William, 2d Mich., Rpt of Opns, *ibid.*, 953; Luce, Col. 17th Mich., Rpt of Opns, *ibid.*, 957; De Land, Col. C. V., 1st Mich. Sharpshooters, Rpt of Opns, *ibid.*, 972.
29. Probably Ramseur's Brigade, *supra*, 323-24.
30. Potter, 67 WR 928.
31. Meade to Hancock, 68 WR 441.
32. Humphreys to Hancock, *ibid.*, 442.
33. Wilcox, C. M., "Wilderness," *Annals*, 496.
34. Tyler, Lieutenant Col. C. W., 141st N. Y., Rpt of Opns, 67 WR 477.
35. *North Carolina Regiments* (13th N. C.), I, 675.
36. Caldwell, J. F. C., *McGowan's Brig.*, 133.
37. *North Carolina Regiments* (55th N. C.), III, 303.
38. Lane, J. H., "Report," 9 *S.H.S.P.*, 126.
39. *North Carolina Regiments* (37th N. C.), II, 665.
40. *Ibid.*, (11th N. C.), I, 595.
41. *Ibid.* (27th N. C.), II, 446; (15th N. C.), I, 744.
42. There is very little evidence to support this. The controversy between Wilcox and Marshall concerning operations of III Corps, 6 May, gives emphasis to the general feeling that Wilcox's brigades quit the field before Heth's. If the withdrawal of the North Carolina regiments of Kirkland's Brigade was characteristic of the division, it would appear that both Wilcox and Heth crumpled rapidly under the impact of the Federal blow, but that some of Heth's formations probably rallied on Cooke's reserve line, giving some color to the belief that Heth was last to quit the field. Cf. Wilcox, Cadmus M., "Four Years with General Lee," A Review by General C. M. Wilcox, in *Southern Historical Society Papers*, VI, 71-77.
43. North Carolina Regiments (26th N. C., Kirkland's Brigade) II, 382-383.
44. Hofmann, Rpt of Opns, 67 WR 623.
45. Cutler, Rpt of Opns, *ibid.*, 611.
46. Wilcox, C. M., "Wilderness," *Annals*, 496.
47. Alexander, E. P., *Civil War*, 503.
48. Caldwell, J. F. C., McGowan's Brigade, 133.

CHAPTER 20

1. Wilcox, C. M., "Wilderness," *Annals,* 496.
2. Rpt of Opns, 67 WR 1061.
3. *Ibid.*
4. Rpt of Opns, 67 WR 1040, 1061.
5. Perry, Wm. F., "Reminiscences of the Campaign of 1864 in Virginia," *Southern Historical Society Papers,* VII, 543-44. Hereinafter cited as Perry, 7 *S.H.S.P.*
6. Wilcox, "Wilderness," *Annals,* p. 496; Alexander, E. P., *Military Memoirs of a Confederate,* Chas. Scribner's Sons, N. Y., 1907, p. 503; Longstreet, *Memoirs,* p. 560.
7. Wilcox, "Wilderness," *Annals,* p. 496-97.
8. Field, C. W., "Campaign of 1864 and 1865." Narrative of Major General C. W. Field, *Southern Historical Society Papers,* XIV, p. 543-44. Hereinafter cited as Field, 14 *S.H.S.P.*
9. Rpt of Opns, 67 WR 1040.
10. Palmer, W. H., "Letter to Royal," W. C. *Some Reminiscences,* p. 32. Hereinafter cited as *Royal.*
11. Polly, J. B., *Hood's Texas Brigade,* pp. 232-33; Field, 14 *S.H.S.P.* 544.
12. Perry, 7 *S.H.S.P.* 52.
13. *Ibid.,* p. 53.
14. *Ibid.*
15. General Perry describes his account in 7 *S.H.S.P.* as a reproduction of his Rpt of Opns, the official copy of which was lost at Appomattox. Judging by the average length of such reports, the general's effort appears to be an expansion rather than a reproduction of the original. Nor does his brigade suffer in the process of expansion. The accounts of Wilcox in *Annals* and Field in 14 *S.H.S.P.* have something of the value that Perry assigns to his post-dated report. It should be emphasized here that the so-called official reports, Federal and Confederate, covering the Wilderness-Cold Harbor phase of the 1864 campaign in Virginia were written several months later, during the trench stalemate of Petersburg. Marred by faults characteristic of reminiscent writings, their inclusion in the *Official Records* does not endow them with the attributes of infallibility. The point cannot be too strongly urged that the only body of absolute primary source evidence relating to the Wilderness battle is that furnished by dispatches written during the course of the fighting. The rest is circumstantial and should be treated as such.
16. Rpt of Opns, 67 WR 1063.
17. Palmer, in *Royal,* p. 32.
18. Cf. Freeman, *Lee* III, p. 288, footnote No. 5. Freeman is not entirely satisfied, admitting that singular difficulties are encountered in establishing the sequence of events, largely because those who recorded Lee's meeting with the Texans did so long after the incident. Meantime, the imagination of old soldiers had been at work, blending fact with fancy.
19. Perry, 7 *S.H.S.P.* 53-54.
20. Rpt of Opns, 67 WR 677, 682.
21. Perry, 7 *S.H.S.P.,* 54-55.
22. *Ibid.;* Oates, Wm. C., *The War Between The Union and The Confederacy and its Lost Opportunities, With a History of The 15th Alabama Regiment and the Forty-eight Battles in which it was Engaged.* The Neal Publishing Co., (New York, 1905).

23. Rpt of Opns, 67 WR 611, 615.
24. Maj. B. F. Fisher, Chief Signal Officer, does not mention such a connection. However, time markings on various messages transmitted from army to II Corps Headquarters indicate that they were only 10 minutes in transit.
25. Disp., 68 WR 451.
26. Disp., 68 WR 440, 441.
27. (1) Schaff, "Wilderness," p. 235. (2) Disp., 68 WR 420. Schaff comments in his book that due to an editorial error this dispatch is listed under date 5 May.
28. Schaff, "Wilderness," p. 236.
29. Disp., 68 WR 442.

CHAPTER 21

1. Disp., 68 WR 440.
2. (1) Disp., 68 WR 442. (2) Rpt, 67 WR 322, 437, 906.
3. Rpt of Opns, 67 WR 596.
4. Disp., 68 WR 439.
5. Disp., 68 WR 440.
6. Disp., 68 WR 440.
7. Disp., 68 WR 440-41.
8. Rpt, 68 WR 321, 351.
9. Disp., 68 WR 442.
10. Rpt of Opns, 67 WR 321.
11. Disp., 68 WR 441.
12. Disp., 68 WR 442.
13. Rpt, 67 WR 321, 351.
14. (1) Rpt of Opns, 67 WR 321, 438, 473-74, 469, 483. (2) Craft, David, *History of the One Hundred Forty-First Regiment, Pennsylvania Volunteers, 1862-1865*, 180.
15. Rpt of Opns, 67 WR 437-38.
16. Rpt of Opns, 67 WR 438.
17. Rpt of Opns, 67 WR 532.
18. Rpt of Opns, 67 WR 322, 353, 407.
19. Rpt of Opns, 67 WR 407-408.
20. Rpt of Opns, 67 WR 322.
21. Disp., 68 WR 442, 451.
22. Rpt of Opns, 67 WR 353.
23. Disp., 68 WR 443.
24. Rpt of Opns, 67 WR 353.
25. Disp., 68 WR 443.
26. Disp., 68 WR 443.
27. Disp., 68 WR 443.
28. Longstreet, *Memoirs*, p. 561.
29. Rpt of Opns, 67 WR 489.
30. Disp., 68 WR 442, 451.
31. Disp., 68 WR 451.

CHAPTER 22

1. *Supra*, 361-62.
2. Rpt. of Opns., 67 WR 816; Disp. 68 WR 466.
3. Custer, Rpt of Opns, 67 WR 816.
4. *Supra*, 288; Rpt 67 WR 320-21; Hancock, Rpt of Opns, *ibid.*, 320-321.

5. *Supra*, 293-94.
6. Humphreys, A. A., *Va. Campaign*, 41.
7. Custer, Rpt of Opns, 67 WR 816; Stagg, Col. P., 1st Mich., Rpt of Opns, *ibid.*, 826; Alger, Col. R. A., 5th Mich., *ibid.*, 827; Kidd, J. H., *Personal Recollections of a Cavalryman, With Custer's Michigan Cavalry Brigade*, 265-266. (Hereinafter cited as *Custer's Mich. Cav. Brig.*)
8. *Custer's Mich. Cav. Brig.*, 268.
9. *Ibid.*, 268; Custer, 67 WR 816.
10. *Ibid.*, 816; Kidd, *Custer's Mich. Cav. Brig.*, 268-269; Devins, Rpt of Opns, 67 WR 833; McDonald, W. M., *Laurel Brig.*, 235. From McDonald's account, it would appear that Rosser brought only one gun into action. The piece, under command of Lt. Carter, was detached from Thompson's Battery.
11. Kidd, J. H., *Custer's Mich. Cav. Brig.*, 270. Custer, 67 WR 816; McDonald, W. M., *Laurel Brig.*, 236-237. McDonald describes the scene as follows: "The care of the dead and dying, and the plunging of the wounded and frightened horses, created unavoidable confusion. Under the circumstances, it seemed impossible to form column. Stuart was there, riding among the men and officers, and calling them to be steady. The ordeal was a terrible one for the cavalry, and though apparently deaf to orders amidst the thunder of bursting shells, yet most of the men stood firm."
12. Custer, *ibid.*, 816.
13. McDonald, W. M., *Laurel Brig.*, 234. McDonald states that "White's Battalion had been christened by Rosser 'The Comanches' on account of the wild and reckless dash with which they usually bore down on the enemy." *Ibid.* 228.
14. Fitzhugh Lee, Mss. Report, 4.

CHAPTER 23

1. This is not offered as an opinion on the Lee-Longstreet controversy relating to Gettysburg. Nor is it suggested that Longstreet was a strategist of extraordinary brilliance. Eckenrode and Conrad have made a suggestive case that he displayed no particular promise, as did Stonewall Jackson, in his independent commands. See Eckenrode, Hamilton James, and Conrad, Bryan, *James Longstreet, Lee's War Horse* (hereinafter cited as *War Horse*.). Yet given a tactical situation contrived by Lee's leadership, such as Fredericksburg or Second Manassas, it would be difficult indeed to find a finer master of the art of handling troops on the field of battle than Longstreet. The Wilderness situation was one made to order, as it were, for his peculiar genius. It is needless to point out that had he arrived later than he did, Lee would have suffered a decisive defeat. Had he arrived in time to have deployed in the conventional line of divisions, as he originally intended to do, and have struck Birney's assault column before its initial impetus had been expended, it is questionable if the Confederate counter-attack would have attained the degree of success that Longstreet's echelon formation actually achieved. The latter formation, combined with the undoubtedly superior troop leadership of the Confederate forces, was best adapted to the conditions of forest warfare. These circumstances, together with the inspiration of Lee's presence on the field, all conspired to achieve what would appear to the uncritical glance as a miraculous feat of arms.
2. Longstreet, James, *Memoirs*, 563.

3. Anderson, R. H., letter written 14 May 1879, quoted by Walker, Cornelius Irvine, *The Life of Lieutenant General Richard Heron Anderson of the Confederate States Army,* 159. (Hereinafter cited as *R. H. Anderson.*)

4. *Ibid.,* 159; Palmer, William H., "Letter to Royal," *Reminiscences,* 33-34.

5. *Ibid.,* 34.

6. Walker, Cornelius I., *R. H. Anderson,* 159.

7. Hancock, Rpt of Opns, 67 WR 322. "At 8:30 a.m., Birney's, Stevenson's, Mott's, and Wadsworth's divisions again advanced along the Orange Plank road with Webb's, Carroll's, and Owen's brigades and became furiously engaged with the enemy." Lyman to Meade, 8:40 a.m., 68 WR 442: ". . . General Hancock has ordered the attack to be at once pressed."

8. Longstreet, Rpt of Opns, 67 WR 1055.

9. Mahone, *ibid.,* 1090.

10. Longstreet, James, *Memoirs,* 561.

11. *Ibid.,* 561.

12. McAllister, Rpt of Opns, 67 WR 489.

13. Mahone, *ibid.,* 1091.

14. Humphreys, A. A., *Va. Campaign,* 45, Footnote.

15. McAllister, Rpt of Opns, 67 WR 489.

16. *Ibid.,* 489.

17. Humphreys, A. A., *Va. Campaign,* 43-44. Cf. Davis, Lt. Col., 69th Pa., 67 WR 444; Broatch, Capt. J. C., 14th Conn., *ibid.,* 453; Ellis, Col. T. G., 14th Conn., 455; Spaulding, Capt. Joe, 19th Me., *ibid.,* 440.

18. Cannon, Capt. M. M., 40th N. Y., 474.

19. *Ibid.,* 474.

20. Craft, D., *141st Pa. Inf.,* 181.

21. Weygant, C. H., *124th N. Y. Inf.,* 293-294.

22. "General Orders No. 29," 67 WR 468.

23. Hofmann, Col. J. W., 56th Pa., Rpt of Opns, 67 WR 624; Cowdrey, Asst. Adj. Gen. 4th Div., *ibid.,* 615.

24. Webb, Rpt of Opns, *ibid.,* 438; Pearson, Henry Greenleaf, *James S. Wadsworth of Genesee. Brevet Major General of United States Volunteers,* 281, (hereinafter cited as *Wadsworth*); Bruce, George Anson, *The Twentieth Regiment of Massachusetts Volunteer Infantry, 1861-1865,* 353, (hereinafter cited as *20th Mass. Inf.*)

25. *Ibid.,* 353; Hancock, Rpt of Opns, 67 WR 326.

26. Pearson, H. G., *Wadsworth,* 283-284; Bruce, G. A., *20th Mass. Inf.,* 353; Hofmann Rpt of Opns, 67 WR 624. None of these accounts agree. Cf. Longstreet, James, *Memoirs,* 563.

27. Webb, Rpt of Opns, 67 WR 438.

28. O'Connor to Barnes, quoted by Smith, J. D., *The History of the 19th Maine Regiment of Maine Volunteer Infantry,* 142-43.

29. Longstreet, James, *Memoirs,* 563; Hofmann, 67 WR 624.

30. Hancock, Rpt of Opns, *ibid.,* 323.

31. Mahone, Rpt of Opns, *ibid.,* 1091.

32. *Supra,* 398.

33. Hancock, Rpt of Opns, 67 WR 323.

34. Sorrel to Turner, 29 January 1892, Appendix, Sorrel, M. G., *Recollections,* 299-302.

35. Longstreet, James, *Memoirs,* 563.

36. *Ibid.,* 563.

37. *Ibid.,* 564; Kershaw Rpt of Opns, 67 WR 1062; Sorrel, M. G., *Recollections,* 302.

38. Longstreet, James, *Memoirs,* 564-565.
39. Field, C. W., "Campaign, 1864," 14 *S.H.S.P.,* 545. If Field means that the confusion of the lines and columns made an advance physically impossible, however desirable such a movement may have been, it is not logical to say that he is in agreement with both Lee and Longstreet. If, however, he attempted to execute Longstreet's plan, as Longstreet himself contends, it would appear that Lee cancelled the operation, either through belief in the impracticability of the plan itself or distrust of Field's ability to execute the plan. Field's account of the operations of 6 May are so ambiguous that his omission of the mention of Longstreet's plan can hardly be construed as a denial of the existence of the plan.
40. Tidball, Col. J. C., Commanding Artillery Brigade, Rpt of Opns, 67 WR 507-508; Hunt, Brig. Gen. J. H., Chief of Artillery, *ibid.,* 284, 290.
41. Lyman, Theodore, "Letters," 95-96.

CHAPTER 24

1. Cf. Platt to Humphreys, 9:05 a.m., 68 WR 451, and Lyman to Meade, 8:40 a.m., *ibid.,* 442.
2. The author is aware of no evidence to support this view, other than the fact that Burnside's line of operation was redirected at this time.
3. Humphreys to Hancock (received 9:15 a.m.), *ibid.,* 442.
4. Burnside, Rpt of Opns, 67 WR 906; Potter, *ibid.,* 928; Wilcox, *ibid.,* 952; Hartranft, *ibid.,* 948.
5. Comstock to Grant (received 10:50 a.m., *ibid.,* 460.
6. Burnside to Hancock, *ibid.,* 442.
7. Rawlins to Burnside, *ibid.,* 461.
8. Perry, W. F., "Campaign in Va.," 7 *S.H.S.P.,* 59-60.
9. Potter, Rpt of Opns, 67 WR 928; Hartranft, *ibid.,* 940. Harris' Brigade, Anderson's Division, was sent at 3 p.m. from reserve to reinforce Perry and Perrin. Anderson, R. H., in Walker, C. I., *R. H. Anderson.*
10. Lyman, Theodore, "Letters," 96. Footnote.
11. Humphreys to Warren, 10:35 a.m., 68 WR 451-452.
12. Warren to Humphreys, *ibid.,* 452.
13. Meade to Warren, 12 a.m., *ibid.,* 452.
14. Meade to Warren, 12:45 p.m., *ibid.,* 452.
15. Sheridan to Humphreys, *ibid.,* 466.
16. Humphreys to Sheridan, *ibid.,* 467.
17. Sheridan to Humphreys, *ibid.,* 467.
18. Humphreys to Commanding Officer, Fifth Corps, *ibid.,* 453.
19. Lyman to Meade, 68 WR 444.
20. Mitchell, *Addenda,* (copy of daily memoranda), Hancock's Rpt of Opns, 67 WR 353.
21. Meade to Hancock, *ibid.,* 444-445.
22. Hancock to Meade, *ibid.,* 445.
23. Hancock to Williams, *ibid.,* 445.
24. Humphreys to Sheridan, 1 p.m., *ibid.,* 467; Forsyth to Gregg.
25. Lyman, Theodore, "Letters," 97.
26. The evidence here is vague. This estimate is scarcely more than a guess. Kershaw implies that only one of his brigades, Wofford's was engaged. Kershaw, *ibid.,* 1062. The Operation Report of Col. James R. Hagood, 1st S. C. Inf., *ibid.,* 1068, would indicate that Henegan's (Kershaw's old) brigade participated in the attack.

27. It is reasonable to suppose that Lee should have thrown in every available brigade. Perry, W. F., *Va. Campaign*, 7 *S.H.S.P.*, 601.
28. This is unlikely, there being no positive evidence to this effect. It is taken for granted, however, that Stone's Mississippians got into the fight.
29. This is inferred from Colonel Hagood's Rpt of Opns, 67 WR 1068. Cf. Hyde, T., *VI Corps*, 47, footnote.
30. Hancock, Rpt of Opns, 67 WR 324; McAllister, *ibid.*, 489-490; Humphrey's A. A., *Va. Campaign*, 47-48.
31. Dow, Rpt of Opns, *ibid.*, 514.
32. Lyman to Meade, 68 WR 445.
33. Humphreys to Commanding Officer, Fifth Corps, *ibid.*, 454.
34. Humphreys to Lyman, *ibid.*, 446.
35. *Ibid.*, 446.
36. Hancock to Meade, *ibid.*, 445-446.
37. Humphreys to Warren, *ibid.*, 454.
38. Hancock to Meade, *ibid.*, 446.
39. Humphreys to Hancock, *ibid.*, 447.
40. *Ibid.*, 6 p.m., 447.
41. Grant to Burnside, *ibid.*, 462.

CHAPTER 25

1. Gordon, John Brown, *Reminiscences of the Civil War*, 243-261, (hereinafter cited as Gordon, *Reminiscences*.)
2. Gordon, Rpt of Opns, 67 WR 1077.
3. *Ibid.*, 1077; Ewell, Rpt of Opns, *ibid.*, 1071.
4. *Ibid.*, 1071; Early, J. A., *Autobiographical Sketch*, 348.
5. *Ibid.*, 348.
6. *Supra*, 297; Rawlins to Ferrero, 8 a.m., 68 WR 464.
7. *North Carolina Regiments* (5th N. C.), I, 288; *Ibid.*, (12th N. C., 640.)
8. Ewell, Rpt of Opns, 67 WR 1071; Early, J. A., *Autobiographical Sketch*, 348.
9. Rpt. of Opns, 67 WR 1071.
10. Humphreys to Warren, 68 WR 451; Humphreys to Platt, *ibid.*, 451.
11. Lyman to Meade, *ibid.*, 442; Michler to Ferrero, *ibid.*, 464.
12. Ewell, Rpt of Opns, 67 WR 1071.
13. Gordon, J. B., *Reminiscences*, 258.
14. Early, J. A., *Autobiographical Sketch*, 349.
15. Humphreys to Warren, 68 WR 452.
16. Warren to Humphreys, 11 a.m., *ibid.*, 452.
17. Sedgwick to Humphreys, 11:30 a.m., *ibid.*, 459-460.
18. *Personal Diary of Brig. Gen. Alexander Shaler*, 6 May 1864; Sedgwick to Humphreys, 68 WR 460.
19. Seymour, Rpt of Opns, 67 WR 729.
20. *Personal Diary of Brig. Gen. Alexander Shaler*, 6 May 1864; Shaler, Alexander, *Shaler's Brig.* Existing remains of Seymour's breastworks on the Wilderness battlefield show the return line at the right of the line in the ravine. See Master Plan. Fredericksburg and Spotsylvania National Military Park.
21. Dalton, Asst. Adj. Gen. Div., Rpt of Opns, 67 WR 660; *Personal Diary of Brig. Gen. Alexander Shaler*, 6 May 1864.
22. *Ibid.*, 6 May 1864.
23. *Ibid.*, 6 May 1864.
24. *Ibid.*, 6 May 1864.
25. *Ibid.*, 6 May 1864.

26. Haines, A. A., *15th N. J. Inf.,* p 148.
27. *Personal Diary of Brig. Gen. Alexander Shaler,* 6 May 1864.
28. *Ibid.,* 6 May 1864; Haines, A. A., *15th N. J. Inf.,* Gordon, Rpt of Opns, 67 WR 1077.
29. *Personal Diary of Brig. Gen. Alexander Shaler,* 6 May 1864.
30. Bidwell, Rpt of Opns, 57 WR 719; Haines, A. A., *15th N. J. Inf.,* p. 149.
31. Gordon, Rpt of Opns, 67 WR 1077; Early, J. A., *Autobiographical Sketch,* 349.
32. *Ibid.,* 349.
33. Lyman, Theodore, *Letters.* 96.
34. Accounts of the scene at army headquarters vary. Cf. Porter, Horace, *Grant,* 68 ff.; Schaff, Morris, *Wilderness,* 318 ff. *Infra.,* 634.
35. Morris, Rept. of Opns, 67 WR 723.
36. Upton, Rpt of Opns, *ibid.,* 666-667.
37. *Ibid.,* 666.
38. *Ibid.,* 666.
39. Gordon, Rpt of Opns, *ibid.,* 1077.
40. Early, J. A., *Autobiographical Sketch,* 349.
41. Schaff, Morris, *Wilderness,* 319-320.
42. *Personal Diary of Brig. Gen. Alexander Shaler,* 6 May 1864.
43. Humphreys, A. A., *Va. Campaign,* 50 footnote No. 2.
44. Warren to Humphreys, 7:40 a.m., 6 May 1864, 68 WR 499.
45. Grant to Meade, 6:30 a.m., 7 May 1864, *ibid,* 481.

Sources

A. *Unpublished Official Documents*

Adjutant General, Army of the Potomac, *Tri-Monthly Return of the Army of the Potomac, Maj. Gen. George G. Meade, U. S. Army, Commanding, for April 30, 1864,* War Department Archives, The National Archives, Washington, D. C.

Adjutant General, IX Corps, *Return of the Ninth Army Corps, Maj. Gen. Ambrose E. Burnside, U. S. Army, Commanding,* War Department Archives, The National Archives, Washington, D. C.

Adjutant General, Army of Northern Virginia, *Field Return of the Army of Northern Virginia, General Robert E. Lee. C. S. Army, Commanding, April 20, 1864; Headquarters Orange Court House, Va.,* War Department Archives, The National Archives, Washington, D. C.

Harke, George H., Col. and Deputy Provost Marshal Gen., comp., *Organization of the Army of Northern Virginia* [Endorsement]: "Organization of the Army of Northern Virginia, From the records of the Bureau of Information, Prov. Mar. Genl's Department, Headquarters, Army of the Potomac, April 13, 1864."

Cyrus B. Comstock Papers, Division of Manuscripts, Library of Congress, Washington, D. C.

B. *Unpublished Private Documents*

Papers of Lieut. Col. Cyrus B. Comstock, U. S. A., Confidential *Aide-de-camp* to Lieut. Gen. U. S. Grant, Commanding U. S. Armies. Division of Manuscripts, Library of Congress, Washington, D. C.

Personal Diary of Lieut. Col. Cyrus B. Comstock, October 16, 1863-December 7, 1870. Division of Manuscripts, Library of Congress, Washington, D. C.

Personal Diary of Gen. Alexander Shaler, U. S. A., Armory of 7th Regiment, N. Y. N. G., New York. Accessible by permission of officer commanding.

Gorgas, Josiah, Chief of Ordnance, C. S. A., *Notes on Ordnance Department of the Confederate States*. National War College Library, Washington, D. C.

Waldron, C. S., V Corps, Army of the Potomac, *War Memoir*, Transcript copy, Library of Fredericksburg and Spotsylvania County Battlefields Memorial National Military Park.

C. *Public Documents*

U. S. War Department, *The War of the Rebellion: A Compilation of the Official Records of the Union and Confederate Armies*. 128 vols. The Government Printing Office, Washington, D. C., 1881-1902.

U. S. Surgeon General's Office, *The Medical and Surgical History of the War of the Rebellion (1861-1864)*, The Government Printing Office, Washington, D. C.

U. S. War Department, *Rifle and Infantry Tactics: For the Exercise and Manoeuvres of Troops When Acting as Light Infantry or Riflemen. Prepared Under Direction of the War Department by Lieutenant Colonel W. J. Hardee*, Philadelphia, J. B. Lippincott, 1855.

Clark, Walter, ed., *Histories of the Several Regiments and Battalions from North Carolina in the Great War 1861-1865. Written by Members of the Respective Commands*. 5 vols. Published by the State, Raleigh, E. M. Uzzell, Printer and Binder, 1901.

Military Record of Louisana, Bartlett Napier, ed., New Orleans, L. Graham & Co., 1875.

The Military Annals of Tennessee, John Berrien Lindsley, ed., Nashville, 1886.

D. *Works, Autobiographical Writings, and Papers of Participants*

Battles and Leaders of the Civil War. 4 vols. Johnson, R. U., and Buel, C. C., ed., New York, The Century Co. 1884-1888.

Confederate Military History, A Library of Confederate States History, in Twelve Volumes, Written by Distinguished Men of the South, and Edited by Clement A. Evans of Georgia, Atlanta, Ga., Confederate Publishing Company, 1899.

Massachuetts Military Historical Society, T. F. Dwight, ed., *Papers of the Military Historical Society of Massachusetts*, Vol. 5, Boston, Cadet Armory, 1895-1918.

Papers of the Southern Historical Society, Richmond, Va.

Alexander, Edward Porter, Brig. Gen. C. S. A., *Military Memiors of a Confederate*. Charles Scribner's Sons, New York, 1907.

Allen, Stanton P., *Down in Dixie; Life in a Cavalry Regiment in the War Days, from the Wilderness to Appomattox*. Boston, D. Lothrop Company, 1892.

Badeau, Adam, Brig. Gen., U. S. A., Military Secretary to U. S. Grant, *Military History of Ulysses S. Grant*, 3 vols. D. Appleton and Company, New York, 1881.

Baquet, Camille, *History of the First Brigade, New Jersey Volunteers, from 1861 to 1865*. Published by the State of New Jersey, 1910, Trenton, N. J., MacCrellish & Quigley, State Printers, 1910.

Barnes, Charles H., *History of the Philadelphia Brigade, Sixty-Sixth, Seventy-First, Seventy-Second and One Hundred and Sixth Pennsylvania Volunteers*, Philadelphia, J. B. Lippincott & Co., 1876.

Beach, William Harrison, *The First New York Cavalry from April 19, 1861, to July 7, 1865.* New York, The Lincoln Cavalry Association, 1902.

Brewer, A. T., *History of the Sixty-First Regiment Pennsylvania Volunteers* (Philadelphia, 1911).

Cudworth, W. H., *History of the First Massachusetts Infantry.* Fuller Co., Boston, 1886.

Beaudrye, Louis Napoleon, *Historic Records of the Fifth New York Cavalry, First Ira Harris Guard,* 2d ed. Albany, N. Y., S. R. Gray, 1865.

Best, Issac O., *History of the 121st New York State Infantry,* Chicago, Ill., J. H. Smith, 1921.

Bidwell, Frederick David, *History of the Forty-Ninth New York Volunteers,* Albany, J. B. Lyon Company, Printers, 1916.

Brainard, Mary Genevive Green, comp., *Campaigns of the One Hundred and Forty-Sixth Regiment, New York State Volunteers, Also Known as Halleck's Infantry, the Fifth Oneida, and Garrard's Tigers,* New York and London, G. P. Putnam's Sons.

Bruce, George Anson, *The Twentieth Regiment of Massachusetts, Volunteer Infantry, 1861-1865.* Boston and New York, Houghton, Mifflin and Company. 1906.

Caldwell, J. F. J., *The History of a Brigade of South Carolinians known as "Gregg's" and Subsequently as McGowan's Brigade,* Philadelphia, King and Baird, Printers, 1866.

Caster, John O., *Four Years in the Stonewall Brigade,* Guthrie, Okla., State Capital Printing Co., 1893.

Chamberlin, Thomas, *History of the One Hundred and Fiftieth Regiment, Pennsylvania Volunteers, Second Regiment, Bucktail Brigade,* Philadelphia, J. B. Lippincott, 1895.

Cheney, Newell, *History of the Ninth New York Volunteer Cavalry, War of 1861-1865,* Poland Center, N. Y., Martin Merz & Son, 1901.

Cook, Benjamin F., *History of the Twelfth Massachusetts Volunteers (Webster Regiments),* Boston Twelfth (Webster) Regiment Association, 1882.

Cowtan, Charles W., *Services of the Tenth New York Volunteers (National Zouaves) in War of the Rebellion,* New York, C. H. Ludwig, 1882.

Craft, David, *History of the One Hundred Forty-First Regiment, Pennsylvania Volunteers, 1862-1865,* Towanda, Pa., Reporter-Journal Printing Company, 1885.

Crowinshield, Benjamin William, *A History of the First Regiment of Massachusetts Cavalry.* Boston and New York, Houghton, Mifflin and Co., 1891.

Curtis, Orson O., *History of the Twenty-fourth Michigan of the Iron Brigade,* Detroit, Mich., Winn and Hammond, 1891.

Darling, Charles B., comp., *Historical Sketch of the First Regiment Infantry, Massachusetts Volunteer Militia.* Boston, 1890.

Dickert, D., *History of Kershaw's Brigade, With Complete Roll of Companies, Biographical Sketches, Incidents, Anecdotes, Etc.,* Newberry, S. C., Elbert H. Aull Co., 1899.

Early, Jubal Anderson, Lieut. Gen., C. S. A., *Autobiographical Sketch and Narrative of the War Between the States.* Philadelphia and London, J. B. Lippincott, 1912.

Field, C. W., Maj. Gen., C. S. A., "Campaign of 1864 and 1865. Narrative of Major-General C. W. Field," in *Southern Historical Society Papers,* XIV, 542-563.

Floyd, Frederick Clark, *History of the Fortieth (Mozart) New York Volunteers, which was composed of Four Companies from New York, Four Companies from Massachusetts, and Two Companies from Pennsylvania.* Boston, F. H. Gilson Company, 1909.

Gibbon, John [Brig. Gen., U. S. A.], *Personal Recollections of the Civil War,* New York, London, G. P. Putnam's Sons, 1928.

Gilbert, Frederick, *The Story of a Regiment, Being a Record of the Military Services of the Fifty-Seventh New York Volunteer Infantry in the War of the Rebellion,* 1861-1865, Chicago, F. Veteran Association, 1895.

Goddard, Henry Perkins, *14th C. V. Regimental Reminiscences of the War of the Rebellion by Henry P. Goddard, Late Captain Fourteenth Regiment, Connecticut Volunteers.* Middleton, Conn., C. W. Church, Printer, 1877.

Gordon, John Brown, Lieut. Gen., C. S. A., *Reminiscences of the Civil War.* New York, Charles Scribner Sons; Atlanta, Martin & Hoyt Co., 1904.

Grant, Ulysses Simpson, *Personal Memoirs of U. S. Grant,* 2 vols., New York, C. L. Webster & Co., 1885-1886.

Haines, Alanson Austin, *History of the Fifteenth Regiment Volunteers.* New York, Jenkins & Thomas, Printers, 1883.

Hall, Hillman Allyn, *History of the Sixth New York Cavalry (Second Ira Harris Guard) Second Brigade, First Division-Cavalry Corps, Army of the Potomac.* Worcester, Mass., The Blanchard Press, 1908.

Hall, Isaac, *History of the Ninety-Seventh Regiment Volunteers ("Conkling Rifles") in the War for the Union.* Utica, Press of L. C. Childs & Sons, 1890.

Harris, Nathaniel H., Brig. Gen., C. S. A., "Report of General Harris Concerning an Incident at the Battle of the Wilderness," in *Southern Historical Society Papers,* VII, 131.

Haynes, Edwin Mortimer, *A History of the Tenth Regiment, Vermont Volunteers,* 2d ed., Rutland, The Tuttle Company, 1894.

Hays, Gilbert Adams, *Under the Red Patch; Story of the Sixty-Third Regiment, Pennsylvania Volunteers, 1861-1864.* Pittsburgh, Pa., Sixty-third Pennsylvania Volunteers Regimental Associations, 1908.

Hood, John Bell, *Advance and Retreat. Personal Experiences in the United States and Confederate States Armies.* New Orleans. Published for the Hood Orphan Memorial Fund, 1880.

Hotchkiss, Jed., Maj. and Topographical Officer, II Corps, Army of Northern Virginia, "The Wilderness Campaign Against Grant," *Confederate Military History,* III, 431-444. Maj. and Topographical Officer, II Corps, Army of Northern Virginia, "Virginia in 1861—Geological Characteristics," *Confederate Military History,* III, 3-31.

Humphreys, Andrew Atkinson, Chief of Staff, Army of the Potomac, *The Virginia Campaign of '64 and '65. The Army of the Potomac and the Army of the James.* Charles Scribner's Sons, New York, 1883.

Hutchison, Nelson V., *History of the Seventh Volunteer Infantry in the War of the Rebellion Against Constitutional Authority,* 1861-1865. Tenton, Mass., 1890.

Hyde, Thomas Worcester, *Following the Greek Cross: or, Memoirs of the Sixth Army Corps.* Boston and New York, Houghton, Mifflin and Company, 1894.

Johnston, Joseph Eggleston, *Narrative of Military Operations, Directed During the Late War Between the States,* by Joseph E. Johnston, General, C. S. A. New York, D. Appleton & Co., 1874.

Keifer, Joseph Warren (Brevet Maj. Gen., U. S. A., ex-speaker of the House of Representatives), *Slavery and Four Years of War. A Political History of Slavery in the United States, Together with a Narrative of the Campaigns and Battles of the Civil War in which the Author Took Part: 1861-1865.* G. P. Putnam's Sons, New York and Londan, 1900.

Kepler, William, *History of the Three Months and Three Years of Service from April 16, 1861, to June 22d, 1864, of the Fourth Regiment, Ohio Volunteer Infantry in the War for the Union.* Cleveland, Leader Printing Company, 1886.

Kidd, J. H., Lieut. Col., 6th Michigan Cavalry, *Personal Recollections of a Cavalryman, With Custer's Michigan Cavalry Brigade.* Iomid, Michigan, Sentinel Printing Company, 1908.

Kirk, Hyland C., *Heavy Guns and Light. A History of the 4th New York Heavy Artillery.* New York, C. T. Dillingham, 1889.

Lane, J. H., General, C. S. A., "Battle of the Wilderness—Report of General Lane," in *Southern Historical Society Papers*, 124-129.

Law, E. M., Maj. Gen., C. S. A., "From the Wilderness to Cold Harbor," *Battles and Leaders of the Civil War*, IV, 118-144, New York, 1888.

Lewis, Osceola, *History of the One Hundred and Thirty-Eighth Regiment, Pennsylvania Volunteer Infantry.* Morristown, Pa., Wills, Tredell, & Jenkins, 1866.

Longstreet, James, Lieut. Gen., C. S. A., *From Manassas to Appomattox; Memoirs of the Civil War in America*, 2d ed. Philadelphia, J. B. Lippincott, 1903.

Lyman, Theodore (Volunteer *Aide-de-camp* to Meade), *Meade's Headquarters, 1863-1865; Letters of Colonel Theodore Lyman from the Wilderness to Appomattox*, George R. Aggasiz, ed. Boston, The Atlantic Monthly Press, 1922.

Marbaker, Thomas D., *History of the Eleventh New Jersey Volunteers, from its Organization to Appomattox; to which is added Experiences of Prison Life and Sketches of Individual Members.* Trenton, McCrellish & Quigley, Printers, 1898.

Martin, James M., comp., *History of the Fifty-Seventh Regiment, Pennsylvania Veteran Volunteer Infantry.* Meadville, Pa., McCoy & Calvin Printers, 19—?

McClellan, H. B., Maj., Chief of Staff, Cavalry Corps, Army of Northern Virginia, *The Life and Campaigns of Major-General J. E. B. Stuart, Commander of the Cavalry of the Army of Northern Virginia.* Boston and New York, Houghton, Mifflin & Company; Richmond, Va., J. W. Randolph and English, 1885.

McDonald, William N., *A History of the Laurel Brigade, Originally the Ashby Cavalry of the Army of Northern Virginia and Chew's Battery*, Bushrod C. Washington, ed. Baltimore, The Sun Job Printing Office, 1907.

Monier—, Maj., 10th Louisiani Regiment, Army of Northern Virginia, "Journal of Major Monier," *Military Annals of Louisiana*, New Orleans.

Nash, Eugene Arus, *A History of the Forty-Fourth Regiment, New York Volunteer Infantry, in the Civil War.* Chicago, R. R. & Sons Company, 1911.

Neese, G. N., *Three Years in the Confederate Horse Artillery.* Neale Pub. Co., New York and Washington.

Oates, William C., *The War Between the Union and the Confederacy and Its Lost Opportunities, with a History of the 15th Alabama Regiment and the Forty-eight Battles in which it was Engaged.* New York and Washington, The Neale Publishing Company, 1905.

Owen, William Miller, *In Camp and Battle with the Washington Artillery of New Orleans.* Boston, Ticknon & Co., 1885.

Palmer, Wm. H., Col. and Chief of Staff, III Corps, Army of Northern Virginia, to Royall, William Lawrence, May 11, 1908, *Some Reminiscences*. New York and Washington, The Neale Publishing Company, pp. 28-32.

Parker, John Lord, *Henry Wilson's Regiment; History of the Twenty-Second Massachusetts Infantry, the Second Company Sharpshooters, and the Third Light Battery*. Boston. Published by the Regimental Association, Press of Rand Avery Co., 1887.

Perry, William F., Brig. Gen., "Reminiscences of the Campaign of 1864 in Virginia," in Southern Historical Society Papers, VII, 50-63.

Polly, J. B., *Hood's Texas Brigade*. New York and Washington. The Neale Publishing Company, 1910.

Porter, Horace *(Aide-de-camp* to U. S. Grant), *Campaigning With Grant*. New York, The Century Company, 1897.

Powell, William Henry, *The Fifth Army Corps (Army of the Potomac), A Record of Operations During the Civil War in the United States of America, 1861-1865*. London, G. P. Putnam's Sons, 1896.

Preston, Noble D., *History of the Tenth Regiment of Cavalry, New York State Volunteers, August, 1861, to August, 1865*. New York, D. Appleton & Company, 1892.

Regimental History Committee, comp., *History of the Third Pennsylvania Cavalry, Sixtieth Regiment, Pennsylvania Volunteers, in the American Civil War, 1861-1865*. Philadelphia, Franklin Company, 1905.

Regimental Association Committee, comp., *History of the Thirty-Sixth Regiment, Massachusetts Volunteers, 1862-1865*. By a Committee of the Regiment. Boston, Rockwell and Churchill, 1884.

Regimental Association, comp., *Under the Maltese Cross, Antietam to Appomattox. The Loyal Uprising in Western Pennsylvania, 1861-1865; Campaigns 155th Pennsylvania Regiment, Narrated by the Rank and File*. Pittsburgh, Pa., The 155th Regimental Association.

Sawyer, Franklin, *A Military History of the 8th Regiment, Ohio Volunteer Infantry—Its Battles, Marches, and Army Movements*, George A. Groot, ed. Cleveland, O., Fairbanks & Co., Printers, 1881.

Schaff, Morris, Ordnance Officer, Army of the Potomac, *The Battle of the Wilderness*. Boston and New York, Houghton, Mifflin Company, 1910.

Shaler, Alexander, *Shaler's Brigade. Survivors of the Sixth Corps. Reunion and Monument Dedication at Gettysburg, June 12th, 13th, and 14th, 1888*. Philadelphia. Published by order of the Brigade Association, 1888.

Sheridan, Philip Henry, *Personal Memoirs of P. H. Sheridan, General, United States Army*. New York, C. L. Webster & Company, 1888.

Sherman, William Tecumseh, *Memoirs of General William T. Sherman*. New York, D. Appleton & Company, 1886.

Small, Abner Ralph, *The Sixteenth Maine Regiment in the War of the Rebellion, 1861-1865*. Portland, Me., Published for the Regimental Association, by B. Thurston & Company, 1886.

Smith, J. D., *The History of the Nineteenth Maine Regiment of Volunteer Infantry, 1862-65*. Introduction by Bvt. Maj. Gen. A. S. Webb. Minneapolis, 1909.

Smith, J. L., comp., *Antietam to Appomattox with 118th Pennsylvania Volunteers, Corn Exchange Regiment*. Philadelphia, J. L. Smith, 1892.

Sorrel, Moxley G., Brig. Gen., C. S. A., *Recollections of a Confederate Staff Officer*. New York and Washington, The Neale Publishing Company, 1905.

Stevens, George Thomas, *Three Years in the Sixth Corps*. Albany, S. R. Gray, 1866.

Stevens, Hazard, Brig. Gen., U. S. A., "The Sixth Corps in the Wilderness," *Massachusetts Military Historical Society Papers*, IV, 177-203, 1887.

Stewart, Robert Laird, *History of the One Hundred and Fortieth Regiment, Pennsylvania Volunteers.* Philadelphia, Printed by the Franklin Bindery, 1912.

Swan, William W., Bvt. Lieut. Col., "The Battle of the Wilderness," *Massachusetts Military Historical Society Papers,* IV, 119-163, 1880.

Sypher, Josiah Rhinehart, *History of the Pennsylvania Reserve Corps: A Complete Record of the Organization, and of the Different Companies, Regiments, and Brigades.* Lancaster, Pa., Elias Barr & Co., 1865.

Thomas, Henry W., *History of the Doles-Cook Brigade, Army of Northern Virginia, C. S. A.* Atlanta, Ga., The Franklin Printing and Publishing Company, 1903.

Van Santwood, Cornelius, *The One Hundred and Twentieth Regiment, New York Volunteers.* Rondout, N. Y., Press of the Kingston Freeman, 1894.

Venable, C. S., Col., C. S. A., "The Campaign of the Wilderness to Petersburg," *Southern Historical Society Papers,* XIV, 525-526.

Walcott, Charles Folsom, *History of the Twenty-First Regiment, Massachusetts Volunteers, in the War for the Preservation of the Union, 1861-1865.* Boston, Houghton, Mifflin & Company, 1882.

Walker, Francis Amasa, *History of the Second Corps in the Army of the Potomac.* New York. C. Scribner's Sons, 1886.

Wallace, William, Col., 2d S. C., C. S. A., "Operations of Second South Carolina Regiment in Campaigns of 1864 and 1865," in *Southern Historical Society Papers,* VII, 128-131.

Ward, Joseph Rieply Chandler, *History of the One Hundred and Sixth Regiment, Pennsylvania Volunteers, 2d Brigade, 2d Division, 2d Corps, 1861-1865.* Philadelphia, Grant, Faires & Rodgers, 1883.

Webb, Alexander S., "Through the Wilderness," *Battles and Leaders of the Civil War,* New York, 1888, III, 152-169.

Weygant, Charles H., *History of the One Hundred Twenty-Fourth Regiment, N. Y. S. V.,* Newburgh, N. Y., Journal Printing House, 1877.

Whittemore, Henry, *History of the Seventy-first Regiment, N. G. S. N. Y., Including the History of the Veterans Association, With Biographical Sketches of Members.* New York, W. McDonald & Company, 1886.

Wilcox, Cadmus M., Maj. Gen., C. S. A., "Four Years with General Lee," A Review by General C. M. Wilcox. [Recently published by Colonel Taylor] In *Southern Historical Society Papers,* VI, 71-77. Maj. Gen., C. S. A., "Grant and Lee in the Wilderness," *Annals of the War Written by Leading Participants North and South.* Philadelphia, The Times Publishing Company, 1879, 488-494.

Wilson, James Harison, Maj. Gen., U. S. A., *Under the Old Flag; Recollections of Military Operations in the War for the Union; The Spanish War; the Boxer Rebellion, etc.,* 2 vols. New York and London, D. Appleton and Company, MCMXII. Maj. Gen., U. S. A., *The Life of John A. Rawlins.* New York, The Neale Publishing Company, 1916.

Wilson, Mrs. Arabella M., comp., *Disaster, Struggle, Triumph. The Adventures of 1000 "Boys in Blue," from August, 1862, to June, 1865.* Prepared by the Historical Committee of the Regiment. Albany, Argus Co., Printers, 1870.

Wise, Jennings Cropper, *The Long Arm of Lee; or the History of the Artillery of the Army of Northern Virginia; with a Brief Account of the Confederate Bureau of Ordnance.* Lynchburg, Va., J. P. Bell Company, Inc., 1915

Worshaw, John H., *One of Jackson's Foot Cavalry; His Experiences and What He Saw During the War 1861-1865.* New York, The Neale Publishing Company, 1912.

APPENDIX   511

E. *Secondary Material*

Atkinson, C. F., Imperial General Staff, *Grant's Campaigns of 1864 and 1865. The Wilderness and Cold Harbor.* (May 3-June 3, 1864). London, Rees, Ltd., 1908.

Battine, Cecil W., Capt. Royal Army, *The Crisis of the Confederacy: A History of Gettysburg and the Wilderness.* London and New York, Longmans, Green and Company, 1905.

Conger, Col. Arthur L., *The Rise of U. S. Grant.* New York: The Century Company, 1931.

Fieberger, Col. Gustave J., *Campaigns of the American Civil War.* West Point, N. Y., United States Military Academy Printing Office, 1914.

Freeman, Douglas Southall, *R. E. Lee. A Biography.* New York and London: Charles Scribner's Sons, 1935. (4 vols.)

Fuller, J. F. C. Maj. Gen., Royal Army, *The Generalship of Ulysses S. Grant.* New York, Dodd, Meade & Company, 1929.

.... *Grant and Lee, A Study in Personality and Generalship.* London, Eyre and Spottiswoode, 1933.

Henry, Robert Self, *The Story of the Confederacy.* Indianapolis, Bobbs-Merrill Company, 1931.

Humphreys, Henry H., *Andrew Atkinson Humphreys. A Biography.* Philadelphia, The John C. Winston Company, 1924.

Lee, Maj. Gen. Fitzhugh, C. S. A., *General Lee.* New York, Appleton and Company, 1894.

Long, Armistead L., Military Secretary to Gen. Lee, *Memoirs of Robert E. Lee; His Military and Personal History.* New York, Philadelphia, and Washington: J. M. Stoddardt & Company, 1886.

Maurice, Maj. Gen. Sir Frederick B., British Army, *Robert E. Lee, the Soldier.* Boston and New York, Houghton, Mifflin Company, 1925.

Meade, George, Capt., *The Life and Letters of George Gordon Meade.* 2 vols. George Gordon Meade, ed. New York, Charles Scribner's Sons, 1913.

Pearson, Henry G., *James S. Wadsworth of Genesee, Brevet Major General of United States Volunteers.* New York, Charles Scribner's Sons, 1913.

Redway, Maj. George W., Royal Army, *Fredericksburg, A Study in War.* London, S. Sonnenschain & Co.; New York, The McMillan Company, 1906.

Styles, Robert, Maj., C. S. A., *Four Years Under Marse Robert.* New York and Washington, The Neale Publishing Company, 1903.

Taylor, Walter H., *Four Years with General Lee; Being a Summary of the More Important Events Touching the Career of General Robert E. Lee.* New York, D. Appleton and Company, 1877.

Wagner, Arthur, *Organization and Tactics.* London and New York, B. Westermann and Co., 1895.

Walker, Cornelius I., *The Life of Lieutenant General Richard Heron Anderson of the Confederate States Army.* Charleston, S. C., Art Publishing Company, 1917.

White, Henry Alexander, *Robert E. Lee and the Southern Confederacy, 1807-1870.* New York, G. P. Putnam's Sons, 1902.

INDEX

Note: Place names have not been indexed. Practically all such names will be found on Maps 1-5.

A

Abbot, Maj. Henry L., 20th Mass., 400, 421-22

Alabama troops, 162, 167, 175, 176, 241, 242, 346, 348, 354, 390, 415, 440ff.

Ammunition, Federal estimate of needs, 24-5

Anderson, Brig. Gen. Geo. T., C.S.A. (Brig.), 344, 371, 391-95, 402, 404, 425, 428

Anderson, Maj. Gen. Richard H., C.S.A. (Div.), 74, 85, 87, 140, 146, 219, 240-41, 258, 298, 308, 314, 316, 343, 361-62, 371, 390, 462

Andersonville Prison, 160

Another fight on Catharpin Road, 271

Archer, Brig. Gen. Jas. J., C.S.A., 218

Army of the Cumberland, 10

Army of the James, 16

Army of the Mississippi, 41

Army of Northern Virginia (see also Lee, R. E.), Lee given command, 6; mentioned, 14, 15, 17, 41, 44, 162

Army of the Potomac (see also Meade, Grant), 5, 6, 11, 15, 16, 22, 23, 35, 39, 43, 46

Army of the Tennessee, 11

Artillery, amounts required, 25; Grant's preponderance, 17

Artillery Reserve, Federal, 36, 37, 64

Artillery, types, 154

Ayres, Romeyn B., Brig. Gen. (Brig.), 98, 133, 153, 154, 156, 157, 159, 161, 162, 165, 168, 176, 245, 296, 320

Ayres strikes Ewell's left center, 157

B

Babcock, Col. Orville E., ADC to Grant, 56

Baker, Capt, 115

Baldwin, Lt. Col. Clark B., 11th N.J., 328

Banks, Maj. Gen. Nathaniel P., 12, 16, 18, 23, 28, 29

Barlow, Brig. Gen. Francis C. (Div.), 51, 107, 186, 187, 201, 226, 232, 233, 236, 237, 253, 257, 293, 298, 360, 362, 389, 408, 419, 423, 425

Barbour, Col. William M., 37th N.C., 234, 238

Barry, Col. John D., 18th N.C., 235

Bartlett, Brig. Gen. Jos. J. (Brig.), 97, 111, 133, 134, 153, 155, 157, 161, 162, 165-68, 171, 172, 175, 176, 296. 320, 374

Bartlett ruptures Ewell's center, 161

Battle, Brig. Gen. Cullen A., C.S.A. (Brig.), 144, 156, 162, 164, 167, 171, 172, 178, 313

Battle scenes, 250

Baxter, Brig. Gen. Henry (Brig.), 154, 176, 177, 191, 221, 222, 241, 242, 295, 328, 333, 334, 359

Beauregard, Gen. Pierre G. T., C.S.A., 6, 17, 28, 41

Beaver, Col. Jas. A., 148th Pa., 237

Belo, Col., 55th N.C., 232

Benning, Brig. Gen. Henry L., C.S.A. (Brig.), 344, 371, 392

Bent, Capt. Luther S., 18th Mass., 99

Bernard, Geo., 182

Bidwell, Col. Daniel D., 49th N.Y. (Brig.), 130, 319, 442

Birney, Maj. Gen. David B. (Div.), 106, 107, 186-89, 192, 199, 207, 208, 213, 215, 257, 270, 293, 294, 321, 330, 334, 335, 338, 341, 344, 350, 351, 353, 356-370, 373, 374, 378, 388-98, 402-05, 408, 411, 412, 419, 423, 425, 426, 431

512

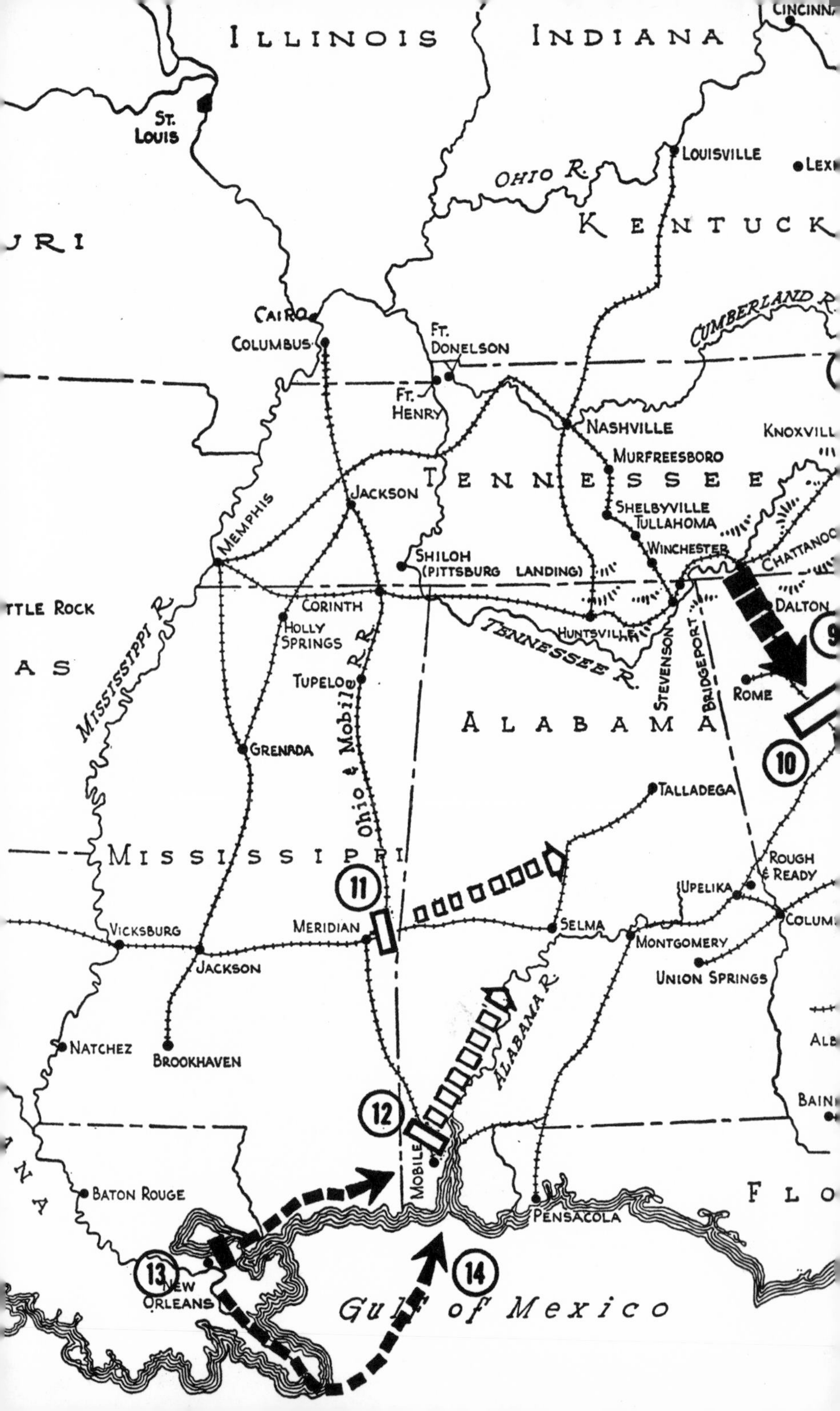
ILLINOIS
INDIANA
CINCINN
ST. LOUIS
LOUISVILLE
LEX
OHIO R.
KENTUCK
URI
CAIRO
COLUMBUS
FT. DONELSON
FT. HENRY
CUMBERLAND R.
NASHVILLE
KNOXVILL
MURFREESBORO
TENNESSEE
JACKSON
MEMPHIS
SHELBYVILLE
TULLAHOMA
WINCHESTER
CHATTANOO
SHILOH (PITTSBURG LANDING)
TTLE ROCK
CORINTH
DALTON
MISSISSIPPI R.
HOLLY SPRINGS
HUNTSVILLE
TENNESSEE R.
STEVENSON
BRIDGEPORT
AS
TUPELO
Ohio & Mobile R.R.
ROME
ALABAMA
GRENADA
10
TALLADEGA
MISSISSIPPI
ROUGH & READY
11
UPELIKA
VICKSBURG
MERIDIAN
SELMA
COLUM
MONTGOMERY
JACKSON
UNION SPRINGS
ALABAMA R.
NATCHEZ
BROOKHAVEN
ALB
BAIN
12
MOBILE
BATON ROUGE
PENSACOLA
FLO
13
NEW ORLEANS
14
Gulf of Mexico